THE ROUGH GUIDE TO

Alaska

There are more than two hundred Rough Guide titles covering destinations from
Alaska to Zimbabwe and subjects from Acoustic Guitar to Travel Health

Forthcoming travel guides include
Devon & Cornwall • Ibiza • Iceland
Malta • Tenerife • Vancouver

Forthcoming reference guides include
Cuban Music • Hip-Hop • Personal Computers
Pregnancy & Birth • Trumpet & Trombone

Rough Guides Online
www.roughguides.com

ROUGH GUIDE CREDITS

Text editor: Mary Beth Maioli
Series editor: Mark Ellingham
Editorial: Martin Dunford, Jonathan Buckley, Jo Mead, Kate Berens, Amanda Tomlin, Ann-Marie Shaw, Paul Gray, Helena Smith, Judith Bamber, Orla Duane, Olivia Eccleshall, Ruth Blackmore, Geoff Howard, Claire Saunders, Gavin Thomas, Alexander Mark Rogers, Polly Thomas, Joe Staines, Lisa Nellis, Andrew Tomičić, Richard Lim, Duncan Clark, Peter Buckley, Sam Thorne, Lucy Ratcliffe, Clifton Wilkinson, David Glen (UK); Andrew Rosenberg, Stephen Timblin, Yuki Takagaki (US)
Production: Susanne Hillen, Andy Hilliard, Link Hall, Helen Ostick, Julia Bovis, Michelle Draycott,

Katie Pringle, Robert Evers, Mike Hancock, Robert McKinlay, Zoë Nobes
Cartography: Melissa Baker, Maxine Repath, Ed Wright, Katie Lloyd-Jones
Picture research: Louise Boulton, Sharon Martins
Online: Kelly Cross, Anja Mutić-Blessing, Jennifer Gold, Audra Epstein (US)
Finance: John Fisher, Gary Singh, Edward Downey, Mark Hall, Tim Bill
Marketing & Publicity: Richard Trillo, Niki Smith, David Wearn, Chloë Roberts, Birgit Hartmann (UK); Simon Carloss, David Wechsler, Kathleen Rushforth (US)
Administration: Tania Hummel, Demelza Dallow, Julie Sanderson

ACKNOWLEDGEMENTS

The author would like to give special thanks to the staff of tourist offices all over the state, who have been unstintingly generous with their time, and to the operators of tour companies, hotels, hostels, museums, transport companies, and the good people of Alaska who have gone out of their way to help make sure this book is as accurate as possible. Enormous thanks and respect to the Rough Guide crew in London and New York, particularly Martin Dunford for suggesting I was the right man for the job, Andrew Rosenberg for deft use of the red pen in the early stages on through later drafts, and Mary Beth Maioli for picking up the reins and guiding me through to the very end.
In Alaska I'd particularly like to thank: Alison Caputo at Auk Nu Tours, Buckwheat Donahue at Skagway CVB, Cindy Rolands in Skagway, Jeff Johnson at Alaska Railroad, Jerre Wroble at Mat-Su CVB, Karen Petersen on Prince of Wales Island, Ken Morris at Anchorage

CVB, Leslie Seamon in Nome, Linda Mickle at AMHS, Lori Robinson at APLIC in Fairbanks, Margy Johnson in Cordova, Michelle Blackwell in Sitka, Pam Foreman in Kodiak, Pam Orr at Fairbanks CVB, Patti Mackey in Ketchikan, Rebecca Mix at Cape Fox Corporation, Toby Pyle and HI-AYH, Vicki Malone at CIRI, Vicki Rood at the Wrangell–St Elias National Park's Slana Ranger Station for invaluable assistance, and Victoria Lord at the Totem Heritage Center in Ketchikan.
The editor would like to thank Gerrard Kennedy and Rich McHugh for great Basics work, Melissa Baker, Katie Lloyd-Jones, Ed Wright and Maxine Repath for fantastic map design, Sharon Martins for dedicated picture research, Michelle Draycott and Rob McKinlay for smooth production, Russell Walton for terrifyingly swift proofreading, and especially Andrew Rosenberg and Martin Dunford for loads of advice, support and help when the going got tough.

PUBLISHING INFORMATION

This first edition published March 2001 by
   Rough Guides Ltd, 62–70 Shorts Gardens,
   London WC2H 9AH.
Distributed by the Penguin Group:
Penguin Books Ltd, 27 Wrights Lane, London W8 5TZ
Penguin Putnam, Inc. 375 Hudson Street, NY 10014,
   USA
Penguin Books Australia Ltd, 487 Maroondah Highway,
   PO Box 257, Ringwood, Victoria 3134, Australia
Penguin Books Canada Ltd, 10 Alcorn Avenue, Toronto,
   Ontario, Canada M4V 1E4
Penguin Books (NZ) Ltd, 182–190 Wairau Road,
   Auckland 10, New Zealand
Typeset in Linotron Univers and Century Old Style to an
   original design by Andrew Oliver.
Printed in England by Clays Ltd, St Ives PLC
Illustrations in Part One and Part Three by Edward Briant.

Illustrations on p.1 & p.487 by Mike Hancock
© Paul Whitfield 2001
No part of this book may be reproduced in any form
   without permission from the publisher except for the
   quotation of brief passages in reviews.
544pp – Includes index
A catalogue record for this book is available from the
   British Library
ISBN 1-85828-688-3

The publishers and authors have done their best to
ensure the accuracy and currency of all the information
in *The Rough Guide to Alaska*, however, they can
accept no responsibility for any loss, injury, or
inconvenience sustained by any traveller as a result of
information or advice contained in the guide.

THE ROUGH GUIDE TO

Alaska

written and researched by

Paul Whitfield

ROUGH GUIDES

We set out to do something different when the first Rough Guide was published in 1982. Mark Ellingham, just out of university, was traveling in Greece. He brought along the popular guides of the day, but found they were all lacking in some way. They were either strong on ruins and museums but went on for pages without mentioning a beach or taverna. Or they were so conscious of the need to save money that they lost sight of Greece's cultural and historical significance. Also, none of the books told him anything about Greece's contemporary life – its politics, its culture, its people, and how they lived.

So with no job in prospect, Mark decided to write his own guidebook, one which aimed to provide practical information that was second to none, detailing the best beaches and the hottest clubs and restaurants, while also giving hard-hitting accounts of every sight, both famous and obscure, and providing up-to-the-minute information on contemporary culture. It was a guide that encouraged independent travelers to find the best of Greece, and was a great success, getting shortlisted for the Thomas Cook travel guide award,

and encouraging Mark, along with three friends, to expand the series.

The Rough Guide list grew rapidly and the letters flooded in, indicating a much broader readership than had been anticipated, but one which uniformly appreciated the Rough Guide mix of practical detail and humor, irreverence and enthusiasm. Things haven't changed. The same four friends who began the series are still the caretakers of the Rough Guide mission today: to provide the most reliable, up-to-date and entertaining information to independent-minded travelers of all ages, on all budgets.

We now publish more than 200 titles and have offices in London and New York. The travel guides are written and researched by a dedicated team of more than 100 authors, based in Britain, Europe, the USA and Australia. We have also created a unique series of phrasebooks to accompany the travel series, along with an acclaimed series of music guides, and a best-selling pocket guide to the Internet and World Wide Web. We also publish comprehensive travel information on our Web site:

www.roughguides.com

HELP US UPDATE

We've gone to a lot of effort to ensure that the first edition of *The Rough Guide to Alaska* is accurate and up-to-date. However, things change – places get "discovered", opening hours are notoriously fickle, restaurants and rooms raise prices or lower standards. If you feel we've got it wrong or left something out, we'd like to know, and if you can remember the address, the price, the time, the phone number, so much the better.

We'll credit all contributions, and send a copy of the next edition (or any other **Rough Guide** if you prefer) for the best letters. Please mark letters: "Rough Guide Alaska Update" and send to:
Rough Guides, 62–70 Shorts Gardens, London WC2H 9AH, or Rough Guides, 4th Floor, 345 Hudson St, New York, NY 10014.
Or send email to: mail@roughguides.co.uk
Online updates about this book can be found on Rough Guides' Web site at www.roughguides.com

Not so long ago **Paul Whitfield** thought that Fairbanks was a town of igloos, Anchorage was snow-bound year round, and that the Alaska Pipeline was something ridden by the state's dedicated surfers. All that changed about three years ago during the initial research stages of this book, and though Paul has never lived in Alaska year-round, he feels he has spent almost enough time in Alaska to qualify for the Permanent Fund Dividend.

In the little free time he's had in recent years he has updated his Rough Guides to Wales and New Zealand, worked on updates to California and Mexico, and occasionally returned to his home in New Zealand where he tries to fit in whitewater kayaking and rock climbing.

CONTENTS

Introduction x

PART ONE BASICS 1

Getting there from Britain 3
Getting there from Ireland 6
Getting there from North America 7
Getting there from Australia and New Zealand 12
Visas and red tape 14
Working in Alaska 17
Insurance, health, and personal safety 19
Costs, money, and banks 22

Telephones, email, and mail 25
Information, maps, and Web sites 27
Getting around 30
Accommodation 44
Food and drink 48
Outdoor activities 52
Nightlife, festivals, and public holidays 60
Directory for overseas travelers 62

PART TWO THE GUIDE 65

• CHAPTER 1: SOUTHEAST ALASKA 67–180

Ketchikan and around 69
Wrangell and around 96
Petersburg and around 105
Sitka and around 113
Minor Ports 126

Juneau 128
Around Juneau 145
Haines and around 154
Skagway and around 162

• CHAPTER 2: ANCHORAGE 181–215

Arrival, information, and city transport 184
Accommodation 188
The City 193
Midtown and the coastal trail 198

Eating 205
Drinking and entertainment 208
Shopping 210
Listings 212

• CHAPTER 3: SOUTHCENTRAL ALASKA 216–288

Girdwood and Alyeska Resort 220
Portage Glacier 223
Whittier 225
Valdez and around 229
Cordova and around 241

Northeastern Kenai Peninsula 249
Seward and the Kenai Fjords National Park 251
Western Kenai Peninsula 262
Homer and around 271

• CHAPTER 4: SOUTHWEST ALASKA 289–322

Kodiak Island and the archipelago 291
Lake Clark National Park 301
Katmai National Park and McNeil River 303

The Alaska Peninsula and the Aleutian
    Islands 309
The Pribilof Islands 320

• CHAPTER 5: THE INTERIOR 323–410

The Mat-Su Valley 326
Talkeetna 341
Denali State Park 347
Denali National Park 351
North of Denali 370

The Glenn Highway to Glenallen 373
The Wrangell–St Elias National Park 376
Paxson, Delta Junction, and the Denali
    Highway 387
Tok, the Fortymile, and the Taylor Highway 398

• CHAPTER 6: FAIRBANKS AND THE ARCTIC NORTH 411–486

Arrival, information, and city transport 415
Accommodation 416
The City and environs 421
Outdoor activities 433
Eating 435
Drinking and entertainment 437
Listings 438
Chena Hot Springs and around 441

Circle Hot Springs and around 444
Manley Hot Springs and around 448
The Dalton Highway to Prudhoe Bay 451
Gates of the Arctic National Park 460
Arctic National Wildlife Refuge 463
Nome and around 465
Barrow 480

PART THREE CONTEXTS 488

A brief history 489
Chronology 498
Alaskan landscapes: terrain, flora, and fauna 499

Books 504
Glossary of Alaskan terms 508

Index 511

LIST OF MAPS

Alaska	x–xi
Chapter divisions map	65
Southeast Alaska	68
Ketchikan	70
Southwestern Revillagigedo Island	82
Southern Inside Passage	92–93
Wrangell	97
Petersburg and around	105
Petersburg	108
Sitka	114
Sitka and around	120
Greater Juneau	130–131
Downtown Juneau	135
Mendenhall Valley and the airport	138
Northern Inside Passage	146
Glacier Bay National Park	149
Gustavus	151
Haines	154
Skagway	163
Around Skagway and the Chilkoot Trail	169
Anchorage	181
Anchorage	185
Downtown Anchorage	189
Midtown Anchorage	199
Southcentral Alaska	217
Girdwood	222
Whittier	226
Valdez	230
Cordova and the Copper River Delta	242
Seward	252–253
Western Kenai Peninsula	263
Ninilchik	270
Homer	273
Homer Spit	276
Kachemak Bay	280
Seldovia	285
Southwest Alaska	290
Kodiak Island	292
Kodiak and around	294
Katmai National Park and Brooks Camp	304
Unalaska and Dutch Harbor	314
The Interior	324–325
Mat-Su Valley	328–329
Palmer	330
Wasilla	334
Talkeetna	342
Denali National Park	352
Denali Entrance area	356
Nenana	371
McCarthy Road	378–379
Delta Junction	391
Denali Highway	394–395
Eagle	405
Fairbanks and the Arctic North	412
Downtown Fairbanks	417
Fairbanks	422–423
Chena Hot Springs Road	442
Steese Highway	444–445
Dalton Highway: North	452
Dalton Highway: South	453
Nome	466–467
Around Nome	473
Kotzebue	476
Barrow	481

MAP SYMBOLS

▪▪▪▪	International borders	⚔	Campsite	⛳	Golf course
▪ ▪ ▪▪	State borders	◉	Hotel	⊠	Gate
▪▪▪	Chapter division boundary	▣	Restaurant/pub	Ⓗ	Hospital
═◯═	State/province highway	♠	Ranger Station	ⓘ	Tourist office
═══	Road	♦	Customs	⊠	Post office
───	Unpaved road/track	⋏⋏	Mountains	▪	Building
▭▭▭	Steps	▲	Peak	♁	Church (regional maps)
-----	Footpath	⚲	Viewpoint	⊞	Church (town maps)
━●━	Railway	⛲	Gardens	⊞	Cemetery
★	Bus stop	⇟	Waterfall	▨	Park
✈	Airport	⚶	Spring	▨	National park
✗	Airfield	⌒	Cave	▨	Forest
▩	Petrol station	⟋⟍	Volcano	⋯	Glacier
── ──	Ferry route	♟	Fort	⋯	Beach
════	Waterway	∴	Ruins	▨	Mud flats
♦	Point of interest	🏛	Monument	⁊⁊	Lava flow
▬	Shelter	♦	Museum	⚶	Marsh
⌂	Cabin	⛷	Ski area		

INTRODUCTION

Hardly anywhere in the world conjures up sharper images than **Alaska**; the name itself – a derivation of *Alayeska*, an Athapascan word meaning "great land of the west" – fires the imagination of many a traveler. Few who see this land of gargantuan icefields, sweeping tundra, glacially excavated valleys, lush rainforests, deep fjords and active volcanoes leave disappointed. **Wildlife** may be under threat in places elsewhere, but here it is abundant, with Kodiak bears reaching heights of eleven feet, moose stopping traffic in downtown Anchorage, wolves howling throughout the night, bald eagles soaring above the trees and rivers solid with fifty-plus-pound salmon.

Alaska's sheer size alone is hard to comprehend – its vast expanse covers an area more than double that of Texas (or six times the size of Britain), and its coastline is longer than the rest of the US combined. All but three of the nation's twenty highest peaks are found within its boundaries, along with the two largest National Parks, the two most extensive National Forests, and more active glaciers than in the rest of the inhabited world put together.

Not all the terrain is hospitable, though; a mere 620,000 people live in this huge state, of which forty percent live in Anchorage. Altogether, only a twentieth of one percent of the land area is developed, the rest remaining almost entirely untouched. In many ways it mirrors the American West of the nineteenth century, not surprising for a place often referred to as the **"Last Frontier"**: an endless space in which to stake a claim and set up anew without interference. Or at least that's how many Alaskans would like it to be. Throughout the twentieth century tens of thousands were lured by the promise of wealth, first by gold and then by fishing, logging, and, most recently, oil.

Alaska is the kind of place folks become obsessive about, and these obsessions fall into two camps. The majority love it, but treat it as a boundless treasure trove that is so far from Washington DC anything is fair play. This state of grace has largely gone, but the myth persists and many Alaskans believe in their right to do whatever they want, and bitterly resent anyone who suggests they do otherwise.

A minority came to Alaska for its pristine qualities and want to keep it that way. With growing pressure from these green-minded activists and the federal government, **environmental issues** have increasingly made front-page news. Current controversies include the practice of clear-cutting in the national forests, the prospect of oil exploration in the Arctic National Wildlife Refuge, over-fishing, and wolf culling which, according to animal-rights groups, is primarily to ensure that there are more caribou for hunters. Most famously, there's been the unholy mess created by the *Exxon Valdez* oil tanker in 1989, though there is now little visible evidence.

Largely marginalized from mainstream society are Alaska's **Native people**, who number around 86,000. Most choose to live in remote communities – known as "Native villages" – where services are often limited and earning a living can be entirely dependent on the number of salmon running that year. Very few live in the larger towns, and those that do often live in conditions that are harsh at best. Natives have largely been left behind by the state's periodic boom times, though a large land settlement in the 1970s paved the way for relatively wealthy Native corporations to provide much-needed income for their people.

Also deserving of some redress is the famed **gender imbalance**, though in

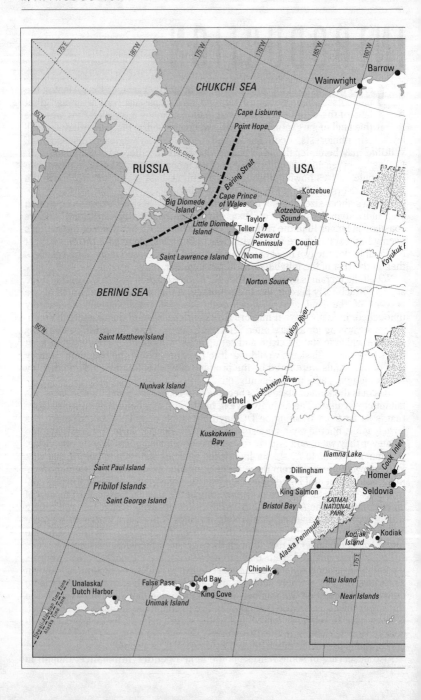

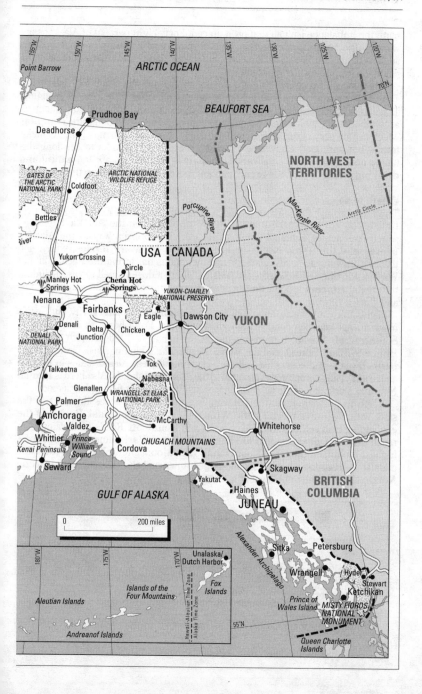

truth the imbalance isn't all that pronounced. Forty-eight percent of Alaskans are women (the lowest percentage in any US state), and it is only in small pockets such as oil communities and small fishing towns, that the excesses of male-dominated environments are apparent.

One thing that is no myth here is Alaska's deserved reputation for high prices; still, experiencing Alaska on a low **budget** is possible with a bit of planning. Traveling outside the peak summer season (see opposite) will save you money on accommodation, which can be quite expensive. The exceptions are **camping**, which can be very cheap or free, and the thirty or so **hostels**, mostly in the major towns, but sprinkled elsewhere throughout the state. Thanks to the long distances and high-priced rental cars, **transport** is far from cheap; and **eating and drinking** are, at best, about twenty percent more expensive than in the Lower 48.

Where to go

Traveling around the state demands a spirit of adventure, as well as patience. Unless you are flying, there are only two **approaches**: the **Alaska Highway**, which cuts across British Columbia and the Yukon on its way to the Alaskan Interior and the Arctic North; and the **Marine Highway ferries**, which slip through the elegiac fjords, glaciers, and mountains bordering the Pacific linking Washington State with **Southeast Alaska**, where a dozen small towns, including the capital **Juneau**, are starting points for salmon fishing, whale-watching trips, and glacier viewing.

Flights from out of state almost all land in **Anchorage**, the largest city, and just as much an Alaskan experience as the great outdoors. From here, it's easy to get to **Southcentral Alaska**, comprising the glacier-bound and wildlife rich waters of **Prince William Sound**, and the **Kenai Peninsula**, a kind of Alaska in miniature. Further west – and connected only by ferry – **Southwest Alaska** takes in **Kodiak** and a host of tiny communities en route to the **Aleutian Islands**. Also here is **Katmai National Park**, one of the best places to watch brown bears fishing for salmon.

North from Anchorage, the **Interior** is the most road accessible part of the state with highways reaching the **Wrangell–St Elias National Park** and the enchanting twin settlements of **McCarthy** and **Kennicott**. Roads (and trains) also reach offbeat **Talkeetna**, and the **Denali National Park**, home to the nation's highest mountain, the 20,000-foot **Denali** (aka Mount McKinley). The train line ends at **Fairbanks**, Alaska's second-largest town and the gateway to the **Arctic North**, site of some unbelievably remote villages.

TOP ALASKA ATTRACTIONS	
Anchorage	p.180
Arctic North	p.450
Aurora borealis viewing in Fairbanks	p.426
Denali National Park	p.351
Glacier Bay National Park	p.148
Hiking and fishing around Homer	p.279
Kodiak Island	p.291
Prince William Sound	p.224
Sitka	p.113
Wrangell–St Elias National Park	p.376

When to go

Alaska has a very short tourist season. For guaranteed long daylight hours and the greatest likelihood of fairly warm weather you'll need to travel in the **peak season** from Memorial Day weekend (the last in May) until Labor Day weekend (the first in September). During this time, climates in Southeast Alaska, Anchorage, and the Kenai Peninsula are mild (45–65°F) and much more rain (in some towns 180-plus inches per year) falls than snow. Remarkably, the Interior in summer often gets as hot as 80°F.

Everyone else has the same idea, so at this time hotel availability is at its tightest and prices go up accordingly. Being there with everyone else does have its advantages though, since some of the smaller adventure trips require a minimum number of customers before they go. If you want to avoid the crowds but still find most tourism businesses operating, try the last two weeks in May and first two in September – Alaska's **shoulder seasons**. The weather at this time can be just as warm as midsummer, and you've got the added bonus of watching trees transform themselves from bare to full foliage in a matter of days, or experience the boreal forest in its autumnal plumage.

There is some regional variation, but in general anyone here before mid-May or after mid-September will find their options limited: there will be few glacier and whale-watching cruises, kayaking operations will have locked away their paddles, Denali shuttle buses will have stopped running, flightseeing trips will be grounded, and even whole towns (admittedly tiny ones like Chicken and McCarthy) will have shut up shop for the winter.

The moderating effects of the ocean (and the more southerly latitude) mean that the season in **Southeast Alaska** is a little longer, with a few of the cruise-ship companies extending their seasons from early May to late September. In **Anchorage**, **Southcentral Alaska**, the **Interior**, and much of **Southwest Alaska** the mid-May to mid-September rule holds true, though in Anchorage, for example, the first serious snowfall probably won't come until mid-October, making this a good place to finish a late-season trip. In **Fairbanks and the Arctic North** your movements at the ends of the season may be more limited, particularly in the coastal towns of Nome, Kotzebue, and Barrow, where the sea ice may remain frozen until mid-June or later. It is often late May before the roads on the Seward Peninsula near Nome are plowed so if you are planning on exploring up here, go later.

Hikers should avoid May and early June unless they like high-stepping through snow on the trail; late August and September are generally a much better bet.

Visitors traveling to Alaska in September, particularly around Fairbanks, have a good chance of seeing the **aurora borealis**, but keen watchers need to come in **winter**. Even the tourist promoters admit that for most visitors November, December, and January are just too cold and dark to enjoy. March and the first week in April are generally best for winter activities – from aurora watching to dog mushing – with a thick layer of snow on the ground, lengthening days, and temperatures that are just about bearable. The rest of April, early May and October are neither really winter nor summer and good for nothing: the snow isn't thick enough for winter pursuits, too thick for summer activities.

What to take

It is important to be prepared for the physical demands of a trip to Alaska, and your level of comfort will largely be affected by **what you wear**. Dress in multiple thin **layers** rather than a couple of thick ones: it is warmer and gives you the freedom to strip a couple off when they're not needed. Visitors restricting themselves to the summer season (or even May and Sept in the southern parts of the state) and staying out of the mountains will get by quite happily with normal clothing plus perhaps a fleece jacket, a waterproof and windproof coat, warm hat, gloves, and a strong and comfortable pair of shoes. If you are heading to the north, especially before the end of May or after the end of August, you should consider thermal underwear and an extra warm layer. Winter visitors to Southeast Alaska need take no extra precautions, but if you're visiting the Interior or Arctic, then serious winter gear is prescribed – including down jackets, insulating pants, and good, warm footwear. The most suitable gear is widely available in Alaska, so bring the warmest stuff you've got, and buy once you arrive. Special considerations for **campers** are discussed on p.55. Don't bother bringing anything particularly formal. Only in the very fanciest of Alaska's restaurants would a jacket and tie seem appropriate, and even there you'll manage without.

Besides clothing, you'll want to bring a camera and binoculars, and rather more mundanely, bug spray; the **mosquito** is referred to as the "Alaska State bird," and only a repellent with 100 percent DEET keeps them off.

DAYTIME TEMPERATURES (°C) AND AVERAGE MONTHLY RAINFALL (MM)

RAINFALL (mm)

	Jan	Feb	Mar	April	May	June	July	Aug	Sept	Oct	Nov	Dec	Tot
Anchorage	20	18	15	10	13	18	41	66	66	56	25	23	371
Atka (Aleutians)	163	119	127	125	122	99	135	137	180	188	211	155	1761
Barrow	5	3	3	3	3	8	23	20	13	13	8	5	107
Fairbanks	23	13	18	8	15	33	48	53	33	20	18	15	297
Juneau	90	95	84	81	84	69	105	123	156	183	123	117	1310

TEMPERATURES (average daily maximums; °C)

	Jan	Feb	Mar	April	May	June	July	Aug	Sept	Oct	Nov	Dec	Avg
Anchorage	-7	-3	1	7	12	17	18	18	14	6	-1	-7	6
Atka (Aleutians)	3	3	3	6	7	11	13	14	14	8	5	3	8
Barrow	-23	-24	-2	-14	-4	4	8	7	1	-6	-14	-20	-7
Fairbanks	-19	-12	5	6	15	22	22	19	12	2	-11	-17	4
Juneau	-3	1	3	8.5	12	17	18	17	12	8.5	4	0	8

TEMPERATURES (average daily minimums; °C)

	Jan	Feb	Mar	April	May	June	July	Aug	Sept	Oct	Nov	Dec	Avg
Anchorage	-15	-13	-11	-3	2	7	9	8	4	-2	-9	-14	-3
Atka (Aleutians)	-1	-2	-2	0	2	4	7	8	6	3	1	-2	2
Barrow	-30	-32	-30	-22	-11	-2	1	1	-3	-11	-21	-27	-16
Fairbanks	-29	-23	-20	-8	2	8	9	7	1	-8	-21	-27	-9
Juneau	-9	-6	-4	-0.5	3	8	9	8	7	2	-2	-6	1

THE
BASICS

GETTING THERE FROM BRITAIN

Throughout the 1970s and 1980s Anchorage was a major refuelling stop for transpolar flights between Europe and Asia, but with the advent of long-haul jets it has become something of a backwater. For the international flights that do make it to Alaska, Anchorage International Airport is the primary port of call. There are currently no direct flights from Britain or Ireland (or the rest of Europe for that matter) to Alaska, with all flights requiring at least one change of plane in the US, and sometimes as many as two or three. The main hub for flights to Alaska in the US is Seattle, and lesser so Minneapolis with every flight from Britain or Ireland stopping at one or the other.

FARES AND AIRLINES

The tourist season for Alaska is very much mid-May to mid-September with **peak season** from June 1 to August 30. There is little outside of this time due to the harsh conditions although some brave the cold to catch the aurora borealis, Iditarod or winter ice-carving festivals. Flights can certainly become cheaper during the **off-season** (Sept through May), but there are also myriad weather-related conditions that you should be wary of. Airports are often forced to shut down due to harsh conditions, some for long and aggravating periods of time.

Almost all flights to Alaska leave from Heathrow apart from Delta's flight out of Manchester and Northwest's out of Gatwick. Alaska's main airport is **Anchorage International**, into which virtually all international flights arrive. Delta, Northwest, and Alaskan Airlines, however, fly onto Fairbanks from Seattle and Alaskan Airlines also has nonstop flights from Seattle to Ketchikan, Juneau, and Sitka (see p.8).

Airlines' APEX (see below) **fares** cost around £450/500 in low season rising up to £650/700 in high season (inclusive of airport tax). It is also worth noting Alaska Airlines' "**Best of the West**" **airpass** (see box, p.32) which, if you make your own travel arrangements to Seattle or Los Angeles, will give you the freedom to travel up to and around Alaska in your own time and can offer major savings.

Britain remains one of the best places in Europe to obtain flight **bargains**, though fares vary widely according to season, availability, and the current level of inter-airline competition. Shop around carefully for the best offers by checking the travel ads in the weekend papers, on the holiday pages of ITV's *Teletext* and, in London, scouring *Time Out* and the *Evening Standard*. Giveaway magazines aimed at young travelers, like *TNT*, are also useful resources.

Standby deals (open-dated tickets which you pay for and then decide later when you want to fly – if there's room on the plane) are few and far between, and don't give great savings: in general you're better off with an **Apex** ticket. The conditions on these are pretty standard whomever you fly with – seats must be purchased seven days or more in advance, and you must stay for at least one Saturday night; tickets are normally valid for up to six months. Airlines also do less expensive **Super-Apex** tickets, which fall into two categories: a fourteen-day advance purchase (about £100 cheaper) ticket that requires stays of between one week and eight months, and a 21-day (£150 cheaper) ticket covering stays of one to four weeks. Such tickets are usually nonrefundable or changeable.

Booking your ticket through the airlines isn't necessarily the cheapest option. It is always worth checking out what **flight agents** have on offer (see box p.4), especially if you are able to take advantage of their last-minute deals. The Internet also comes in handy as a useful resource for finding special deals; check out, *www .deckchair.co.uk*, *www.cheapflights.co.uk* or *www.lastminute.co.uk*.

FLIGHTS TO ALASKA FROM BRITAIN

British Airways (☎0845/722 2111, www.britishairways.com). Daily direct flights from Heathrow to Seattle, with an onward connection from Seattle to Anchorage on Alaska Airlines.

Delta Air Lines (☎0800/414767, www.delta-air.com). Daily direct flights from Heathrow to Anchorage with connections in Cincinnati and Seattle. Several flights weekly from Manchester to Anchorage with a connection in Atlanta, Salt Lake City or Cincinnati, and another change in Seattle. Connections also available in Seattle for Fairbanks.

KLM/Northwest (☎0870/507 4074, www.klm.co.uk). Flights from Heathrow to Amsterdam with a change in Minneapolis or Seattle, and onward connections to Anchorage. Northwest flies out of Gatwick via Minneapolis and onto Anchorage. Connections in Seattle for flights to Fairbanks.

SAS Scandinavian Airlines (☎0870/608 8886, www.scandinavianairlines.net). Daily flights from Heathrow to Seattle with a stopover in Copenhagen, and an onward connection to Anchorage on Alaska or Delta Air Lines.

United Airlines (☎0845/844 4777, www.ual.com). Daily flights from Heathrow to Seattle with a stopover in either Washington DC or Chicago, and an onward connection from Seattle to Anchorage.

FLIGHT AGENTS IN THE UK

Dial-a-Flight (☎0870/333 4488, www.dialaflight.com). Telephone sales of scheduled flights, with a Web site useful for tracking down bargains.

Flightline (☎01702/715151, www.flightline.co.uk). Another telephone-based outfit offering online searches for cheap charter and scheduled flights.

North-South Travel, Moulsham Mill Centre, Parkway, Chelmsford, Essex CM2 7PX (☎01245/608291, www.northsouthtravel.co.uk). Friendly, competitive travel agency, offering discount fares worldwide – profits are used to support projects in the developing world, especially the promotion of sustainable tourism.

STA Travel, 86 Old Brompton Rd, London SW7 3LH, branches nationwide (London call center ☎020/7361 6145, other enquiries ☎020/7361 6150; Northern call center ☎0161/830471, www.statravel.co.uk). Worldwide specialists in low-cost flights and tours for students and under-26s, though other customers welcome.

Travel Cuts, 295a Regent St, London W1R 7YA (☎020/7255 1944); 229 Great Portland St, W1N 5HD (☎020/7436 0459); 44 Queensway, London NW2 3RS (☎020/7792 3770). Established in Canada in 1974, Travel Cuts specialize in budget, student, and youth travel and round-the-world tickets.

usit CAMPUS, (national call center ☎0870/240 1010, www.usitcampus.co.uk) 52 Grosvenor Gardens, London SW1W 0AG. Student/youth travel (under 26) specialists, with 51 branches, including in YHA shops and on university campuses all over Britain.

If you are **under 26 or a student** be sure to look into the student specialist flight agents such as STA or usit CAMPUS as they have a large range of special offers on.

Although **courier** flights are sometimes an option for travelers really looking for a deal, there are no courier flights to Alaska available.

TOURS AND PACKAGES

Alaska is a destination where a little planning goes a long way, and sometimes it can be best to let someone else help with that. With a **wide range of options** on offer and some great-value package deals, it is worth looking into **tours and package** options before you set out, especially if there is a certain place or activity you are keen on experiencing. Your choices mostly fall into three main categories: accommodation packages, fly-drive deals, and guided tours. You can also choose to combine all three. One lure of the package deal is its value. By signing up with a group, the costs are often much lower than if you attempted the trip on your own. The only drawback to tours and packages is the loss of freedom and flexibility of travel.

ACCOMMODATION PACKAGES

Accommodation packages include flights and a hotel in the city you choose to stay. Although

SPECIALIST HOLIDAY OPERATORS

All Canada Travel & Holidays, Sunway House, Raglan Rd, Lowestoft, Suffolk NR32 2LW (☎01502/585825, *www.all-canada.com*). Specialists in customized travel who also offer a wide range of escorted Alaskan tours during peak season. Tour options include the two-day "Beauty and Bears of Kodiak" for £627 and the 23-day "Legends of Alaska" tour incorporating all of Alaska and some of British Columbia for £1867 (prices do not include international flights but do include internal flights, accommodation, and meals). They can also arrange fly-drive holidays.

AmeriCan Adventures, 64 Mount Pleasant Ave, Tunbridge Wells, Kent TN1 1QY (☎01892/512700, *www.americanadventures.co.uk*). Well organized and flexible adventure-camping specialists. Currently offering four tours of Alaska including the "Denali Adventure Tour," a seven-day tour with three days spent at Denali National Park (£434), and the "Yukon to Alaska" tour, a 25-day trip starting at £1085 that includes a three-day cruise (includes transport, accommodation and entrance to national parks but not international flights).

Contiki Services, Wells House, 15 Elmfield Rd, Bromley, Kent BR1 1LS (☎020/8290 6777, *www.contiki.com*). Reputable company offering coach tours of Alaska from May to Aug with a nine-day coach tour starting at £535 including accommodation but not flights.

Exodus Travels, 9 Weir Rd, London SW12 0LT (☎020/8675 5550, *www.exodus.co.uk*). Outdoor specialists offering two trips to Alaska: the "Adventure Tour," a sixteen-day camping trip for a maximum of twelve people; and the "Walking Tour," six full days trekking and three half-day treks. There are no optional add-on trips available. Both trips cost £1900 including flights.

Flydrive USA, PO Box 45, Bexhill-on-Sea, East Sussex TN40 1PY (☎01424/224400, *www.fly-driveusa.co.uk*). Travel specialists who offer some of the best fly-drive deals around, including a flight to Anchorage or Fairbanks for £709 (not including airport tax) with car rental starting at £203 per week.

Go Fishing Worldwide, 2 Oxford House, 24 Oxford Rd North, London W4 4DH (☎020/8742 1556, *www.go-fishing-worldwide.com*). Specializing in freshwater fishing trips to either Bristol Bay or the Kenai Peninsula from June to Sept. Prices start at £3035 for a week including flights, lodge rental, and meals. Also on offer are bear-watching trips starting at £710 for two days in Brook Falls; can arrange fly-drive holidays.

Jet Set Canada, 52 George St, Manchester M1 4HF (☎0870/707 0444, *www.jetset.com*). Specialists who arrange flights, accommodation, car rental, and coach tours in Alaska as well as specialized tours. Tour options include "Legends of Alaska," a 23-day coach tour for £2259/2545 (shoulder/peak) available from May to Aug and the "Yukon and Alaska Highlights Tour," a sixteen-day coach tour for £1999/2323 available from May to Sept. In each case prices are all-inclusive including international flights.

Limosa Holidays, Suffield House, 9 St Saviourgate, York YO18 8NL (☎01263/578143). Outdoor specialists offering a ten-day (£3065) or 20-day (£5240) bird-watching trip to Alaska. Prices include all flights, meals, permits, guide, and accommodation.

North America Travel Service, Kennedy Building, 48 Victoria Rd, Leeds LS11 5AK (☎0113/246 1466, *www.northamericatravelservice.com*). Customized tour specialists who also arrange fly-drive deals: a fifteen-day tour, including international flights, hotel accommodation, and a four-wheel-drive rental car is offered for £2100. They cannot organize any add-on tours for you though.

Ramblers Holidays Ltd, Box 43, Welwyn Garden City, Herts AL8 6PQ (☎01707/331133, *www.ramblersholidays.co.uk*). Tour operators offering a sixteen-day walking holiday from mid-July to mid-Aug, which includes Denali National Park and hiking along glaciers and mountain trails for £2121 including all flights and accommodation.

you can often do things cheaper independently, you won't be able to do the same things cheaper – in fact, the equivalent room booked separately will normally be a lot more expensive – and you can leave the organizational hassles to someone else. Drawbacks include the loss of flexibility and the fact that you'll probably have to stay in hotels in the mid-range to expensive bracket, even though less expensive accommodation is almost always available.

FLY-DRIVE DEALS

Fly-drive deals incorporate a cut-price car rental in the cost of your plane ticket and if you are planning to do a lot of driving then it is definitely worth looking into these options. The drawback is that the plane ticket you purchase may not be the cheapest option. Fly-drive deals are often tied in with accommodation packages giving the traveler a route around Alaska with no worries about booking a hotel each night.

Note that British citizens can drive in the US with a British driver's license, but there can be problems renting a car if you are under 25 years of age.

TOURS

The **guided tour** option is the most popular of all. It is possible to pick up one of the many on offer while you are out there (there are examples in every chapter) or to book yourself on one from home (see box overleaf for examples). Many of the tours in Alaska err on the adventurous side with camping and communal meals commonplace. With these types of trips you need to bring your own sleeping bag and contribute to a daily food kitty. Some of the tours will allow you to pick up on optional daily activities while others will have a more structured approach with your days activities already arranged.

GETTING THERE FROM IRELAND

There are no nonstop flights from Ireland to Alaska; in fact, you will have to make at least two plane changes before you get there. All but one service will require a flight to Heathrow first with an additional change in a US gateway city before reaching Anchorage.

The only exception is Delta Air Lines, who operate direct service from Dublin to New York then on to Salt Lake City, Utah, and finally Anchorage (this service does not require you to spend a night in a stopover city) for around IR£678 plus airport tax. You could also fly from Belfast, Dublin, or Shannon to Heathrow – Ryanair often has flights to London from Ireland as low as IR£50 – and then on to Seattle (see box p.4 for British carriers) where you can pick up an American carrier to Anchorage, Fairbanks (Delta and Alaskan), or make use of Alaska Airways' "Best of the West" airpass (see box p.32 for details). British Airways fly to Seattle for IR£601(low season)/IR£966(high season).

It is of course advised to check out the prices that flight agents offer (see box opposite) as they

AIRLINES

Aer Lingus, (Dublin ☎01/705 3333, Limerick ☎061/474239; Belfast; ☎0845/973 7747, *www.aerlingus.ie*). Daily flights from Dublin, Cork, and Shannon to Heathrow. Can arrange onward flight to Seattle with BA.

British Airways (in the Republic c/o Aer Lingus ☎1-800/626747, Belfast ☎0845/722 2111, *www.britishairways.com*). Daily flights from Belfast, Dublin, and Shannon to Heathrow and from Heathrow on to Seattle.

British Midland (Belfast ☎0870/607 0555, Dublin ☎01/283 8833, *www.britishmidland.com*). Daily flights from Belfast and Dublin to Heathrow.

Delta (☎1800/768080, *www.delta-air.com*). Daily flights to New York from Dublin en route to Salt Lake City, and on to Anchorage.

Ryanair (☎01/609 7800, *www.ryanair.ie*). Daily flights from Dublin, Cork, Knock, and Kerry to London Stansted.

TRAVEL AND FLIGHT AGENTS

American Holidays, 38–39 Pearse St, Dublin 2 (☎01/679 8800, www.american-holidays.com). General package agent offering a few tours of Alaska such as the "Yukon Gold and Alaskan Wonders" coach tour; an eleven-day trip for IR£2605 with flights and accommodation included.

Aran Travel, Granary Hall, 58 Dominick St, Galway (☎091/562595, www.granary-suites.ie). Worldwide flight agent with occasional deals to Alaska.

Fahey Travel, 3 Bridge St, Galway (☎091/563055). Flight agent, good last-minute bargains.

Joe Walsh Tours, 8-11 Lower Baggot St, Dublin 2 (☎01/676 3953); 117 St Patrick St, Cork (☎021/277959); 69 Upper O'Connell St, Dublin 1 (☎01/872 2555, www.joewalshtours.ie). Offers package deals to Alaska and has some tours available.

Trailfinders, 4/5 Dawson St, Dublin 2 (☎01/677 7888, www.trailfinders.com). Flight agent.

usitNOW, O'Connell Bridge, 19–21 Aston Quay, Dublin 2 (☎01/602 1600, www.usitnow.com); Fountain Centre, Belfast BT1 6ET (☎028 9032 4073); 66 Oliver Plunkett St, Cork (☎021/270900); 4 Shipquay Place, Derry (☎028/7137 1888). Ireland's main student and youth travel specialists.

often cut airline prices by buying seats in bulk and also may be able to offer cheap accommodation packages.

If you are under 26 it is well worth checking what student and youth travel specialist usitNOW has on offer.

GETTING THERE FROM NORTH AMERICA

Traveling to Alaska can be just as much of an adventure as being there. Driving up the Alaska Highway through Canada, and cruising the Marine Highway through the islands and channels of the Inside Passage are both excellent ways to approach Alaska, and with enough time and a sense of adventure it is great to combine both in one big loop. Air travel is obviously the fastest way to go, and not only leaves time for other holiday activities, but often turns out to be the cheapest way to reach Anchorage and the Interior.

BY AIR

Unless you live in the Pacific Northwest, you'll almost certainly find that the cheapest way to get to Alaska is to fly, and even from Seattle or Vancouver getting to Anchorage or Fairbanks is cheaper by air. Almost all the major American carriers fly to Alaska, primarily servicing Anchorage (and to a lesser degree Fairbanks) from where Alaska Airlines and smaller carriers fan out to the rest of the state, often by propeller-driven "bush planes." The vast majority of flights reach Alaska via **Seattle**, which also acts as a hub for direct access to the Southeast towns of Ketchikan, Juneau, and Sitka with Alaska Airlines.

With ongoing price wars between the major carriers, it's always worth checking the Sunday newspapers for limited **special offers**, and if you are under 26, look for deals with student travel agents such as STA Travel or Council Travel (see box, overleaf): Seattle to Anchorage round-trip for under $300 is a good deal. In the absence of special deals, the cheapest fares are with **APEX**

(Advanced Purchase Excursion Fare) tickets, which have to be purchased between 7 and 21 days ahead of your departure date and require a Saturday night stay-over. Typically, the further in advance you buy, the cheaper the ticket will be, though the rules will be more restrictive. Prices vary, but those we've quoted below are for round-trip tickets throughout most of the summer when you're likely to be going to Alaska; winter fares can be a little lower but not by a great deal. Flights to **Anchorage** are available from $330 from Seattle, $420 from Los Angeles, $600 from Chicago, $760 from Minneapolis and $850 from New York. From Canada, prices range between Can$920 from Toronto and Can$430 from Vancouver.

Many flights continue on from Anchorage to **Fairbanks**, often for only a slightly higher price, so you may want to make that your first stop and work south from there: typical round-trip fares are $440 from Seattle, $488 from LA, $875 from Minneapolis, $937 from New York, Can$678 from Vancouver and Can$970 from Toronto.

BY CAR

The most adventurous way to approach Alaska is by road along the **Alaska Highway** (aka the ALCAN Highway), two lanes of blacktop that stretch through remote, forested, and frequently mountainous scenery from Dawson Creek, on the BC/Alberta border, 1422 miles north to Delta Junction in Alaska. As daunting as that may sound, over a hundred thousand people in cars and RVs make the pilgrimage each summer braving limited and sporadic services, sometimes difficult weather, and a lot of frost heaves where repeated freezing causes the road to warp dramatically. Though constant road repairs through the summer can make the conditions unpleasant, it is not a particularly difficult drive, and if you put your foot down it can be done in four or five days, though it is much more enjoyable to spread it over ten days, stopping to look at the scenery and relaxing in campgrounds along the way. The Alaska Hwy and the sights and towns along the way to Alaska are covered in detail in *The Rough Guide to the Pacific Northwest* and *The Rough Guide to Canada*.

The highway remains **open all year**, with gas, food, and lodging every twenty to fifty miles in summer, though by early September places start closing down, frequently leaving hundred-mile gaps between services. Consequently you'll want to be certain your vehicle can take the punishment, though many people make the journey with no more problems than you might expect driving over two thousand miles of two-lane highway. When planning your travels, consider the **size of vehicle**: a couple of people, camping gear, spares, and a stack of food can soon overload a small car, something which will soon become apparent on rough and rocky roads. Then again, something huge and gas-guzzling will soon drain your wallet at those expensive Canadian pumps. Make sure you have a jack and wheel brace suitable for installing your **spare tire**, preferably not one of the narrow space-saver variety which don't perform well in adverse conditions. Protection from bugs, dust, and rocks is important, so you'll need new windscreen wipers and plenty of washer detergent, and may want to fit headlight covers and even mats to protect the underside of the fuel tank. Assorted spares – air filter, headlamp, hoses, and oil – and the tools to fit them are a good idea if you've got the mechanical knowledge, and even if you don't it is wise to carry the parts as local mechanics may not be able to get supplies quickly (and may charge the earth).

For general advice and help with route planning, contact the **American Automobile Association** (AAA; ☎ 1-800/222-4357 for roadside help; local numbers are in the *Yellow Pages*, *www.aaa.com*) which has offices in most US cities, or the **Canadian Automobile Association** (CAA; ☎1-800/267-8713; *www.caa .ca*).To find out about the latest **road conditions**, contact the State of Alaska Department of Transportation (☎907/456-7623), and for

information about the Yukon section surf *www.gov.yk.ca/depts/cts/highways/report.html*.

American citizens planning to drive their own cars into Canada should be certain to carry proper owner registration and proof of insurance coverage. The Canadian Non-Resident Inter-Provincial Motor Vehicle Liability Insurance Card, available from any US insurance company, is accepted as evidence of financial responsibility in Canada. See "Getting Around" for car-rental agencies.

RENTALS, DRIVEAWAYS, AND SHIPPING YOUR RIG

Most people who drive to Alaska take their own vehicle. Very few **rental** companies allow one-way drop-offs, and those that do charge astronomical prices. If you really want to drive up there and back and see something of Alaska you'll need a month and will probably pay $60 a day for a compact, more like $110 for a 4x4.

With fortuitous timing, luck and a degree of flexibility you may be able to get a **driveaway**, thereby avoiding trashing your own rig on the road to Alaska. Look in the *Yellow Pages* under "Auto-transporters & Driveaway Companies," or companies such as A Ace Automobile Transport (☎1-800/422-4142, *www.weshipcars.com*) and *www.carhauliersinc.com*. Typically there's no charge, but you'll be required to cover 300–400 miles a day and must pay for gas used. The same sort of deal applies with rental companies, who sometimes need cars and RVs delivered to Alaska at the beginning of the summer (especially in May), and back south in September and October; call around if you're interested.

Drivers who don't want to do the long haul in both directions can have their vehicle shipped between Anchorage and Seattle in about five days with Totem Ocean Trailer Express, PO Box 24908, Seattle, WA 98124 (in Seattle ☎1-800/426-0074, in Alaska ☎1-800/234-8683, *www.totemocean.com*). In summer, northbound rates are about double the southbound rates, which are around $750 for any passenger car or small truck, and $1000–1300 for a camper or smallish RV, then per-foot rates for RVs.

THE ALASKA HIGHWAY BY BUS

Traveling by bus is the least appealing way to reach Alaska. There is none of the expedition feel of driving yourself, and you won't save much time or money over using the AMHS ferries. In fact, if you just want to get to Anchorage or Fairbanks then it is cheaper to fly; but then you miss out on the scenery.

TOUR OPERATORS

Adventures Abroad ☎1-800/665-3998;
www.adventures-abroad.com. Adventure specialists based in Vancouver.

Alaska Discovery ☎1-800/586-1911,
www.akdiscovery.com. Experienced Alaska tour
provider. They offer everything. Kayaking, hiking,
bear watching, whales, everything.

Alaskan Extreme Travel ☎1-888 404-7060,
www.alaskanextreme.com. A full-service travel
agency specializing in adventure travel in Alaska.
Providing airline, car, hotel, train, and other specialized reservations around the world.

Backroads (☎1-800/462-2848,
www.backroads.com). Cycling, hiking, and multi-
sport tours. Mid-June–Sept.

Explore Tours ☎1-800-523-7405,
www.exploretours.com. A thorough,
well organized tour agent serving all of
Alaska.

Mountain Travel-Sobek (in US, ☎1-800/227-
2384, *www.mtsobek.com*). Adventure tours to
Alaska.

Travel Alaska ☎1-888-522-5556,
www.travelalaska.net. The largest online reservation system for all travel arrangements in
Alaska, Yukon & British Columbia.

There is **no direct bus service** to Alaska. If
you are **starting in Seattle**, Greyhound (☎1-
800/231-2222) run frequent buses (every 1 to
2hr) on the three-hour trip to Pacific Central
Station, 1150 Station St, Vancouver where you
can transfer to Greyhound Canada (☎1-800/661-
8747) for their service to Whitehorse, Yukon
(mid-June to mid-Sept daily except Sat, mid Sept
to mid-June Mon, Wed and Fri at 7.30am). It
takes a grueling 45 hours to reach Whitehorse
with three-hour breaks in Prince George and
Dawson Creek. The **fare** from Seattle to
Whitehorse can be as low as US$138, and often
works out cheaper than buying a ticket to
Vancouver (US$22) then buying another ticket to
Whitehorse. From Vancouver there is a walk-on
fare of Can$300, though it is only Can$175 if
booked seven days in advance, and Can$149 if
reserved 14 days ahead.

From Whitehorse there are several summertime services into Alaska: Alaska Overland run
daily to Skagway (☎867/667-7896; 3hr; $30);
Alaska Direct (☎1-800/770-6652) run all-day (as
opposed to all-night) services to Anchorage (16hr;
$165) and Fairbanks (13hr; $140) three days a
week (Sun, Wed, and Fri); and Alaskon Express
(☎1-800/478-6388) run to Skagway (daily; 2hr;
$45), Anchorage (Sun, Tues, and Thurs; $200); and
Fairbanks (Sun, Tues, and Thurs; $170), the latter
two both overnight trips stopping at Beaver
Creek, Yukon, where you have to find your own
accommodation.

A completely different approach is to join the
slightly countercultural **Green Tortoise** (☎1-

800/867-8647 or 415/956-7500; *www.greentor-
toise.com)*, who run one of their converted sleep-
er buses up to Alaska, with one thirty-day trip
(starting early July; $1500 + $250 for food kitty)
starting in San Francisco and heading northbound
to Anchorage from where you fly back to Seattle
(included); and a second trip (starting mid-Aug)
doing the same thing in reverse. The tours run to
Prince Rupert, ferry to Ketchikan, Juneau, and
Haines then drive to Fairbanks, Denali (for 5 days),
Anchorage, and Seward.

BY TRAIN

There is **no direct rail connection** to Alaska
from the rest of North America though rail can be
combined with sea travel to reach the 49th state,
most easily done by catching Amtrak to
Bellingham, WA, then taking the AMHS ferries
(see below). In **Canada**, **Via Rail** (in Canada ☎1-
800/561-7860, in the US ☎1-800/561-3949,
www.viarail.ca) run right across Canada and
serve Prince Rupert which is on the AMHS ferry
system. Trains run from Jasper (on the trans-
Canada route) three days a week (currently Wed,
Fri, and Sun) and a seven-day advance purchase
will cost around Can$120, though you have to
spend a night in Prince George along the way. In
summer you should try to reserve a couple of
months in advance, especially if you want the luxury of a sleeping compartment.

BY SEA

Most towns in coastal Alaska are connected by
the **Alaska Marine Highway System** (AMHS),

state-funded vehicular ferries discussed in detail (along with prices) in "Getting around" (p.33). If you travel by ferry, always **reserve** as far in advance as you can.

The ferries serve two ports outside Alaska, the most convenient for US visitors being **Bellingham**, in Washington State 87 miles north of Seattle. A once-weekly service departs Friday at 6pm and skips all Canadian ports making straight for the southernmost Alaskan port of Ketchikan (after 40hr), and on to Wrangell (50hr), Petersburg (54hr), Juneau (64hr), Haines (70hr), and Skagway (71hr). Booking as early as April isn't unreasonable, particularly if you are taking a vehicle, and cabins on this route book out within four hours of going on sale, usually early in the previous December. To get to the Bellingham ferry dock, drivers should take exit 250 (the Fairhaven Parkway) off I-5, just south of downtown Bellingham and follow signs for the Fairhaven Transportation Center. Plan to arrive two hours before departure time. There are frequent buses and trains to Bellingham from Seattle and further afield, both well integrated with the ferry schedule and both dropping you close to the ferry terminal.

One way of cutting costs on the journey to Alaska (particularly if you are taking a vehicle on the ferries) is to make your way to **Prince Rupert** in British Columbia and link up with Alaska's AMHS ferries there (typically 6 weekly; see p.35 for details of fares). The initial Bellingham to Prince Rupert section of the ferry journey is the least interesting, so traveling overland to Prince Rupert may save you both time and money without losing much in the way of scenic grandeur. Prince Rupert can be reached by car, train (see opposite), and by Greyhound Canada who, in summer, run one or two buses a day on the twelve-hour run from Vancouver (Can$175, 14-day advance purchase Can$149).

By combining a couple of ferry systems it is also possible – though less convenient – to reach Alaska by sea directly from **Seattle**. Various possibilities exist, but the simplest sequence involves catching the vehicular Victoria Clipper (in summer 4 daily; 3hr; $60 one-way for foot passengers; ☎206/448-5000 or 1-800/888-2535, *www.victoriaclipper.com*) from Pier 69 in downtown Seattle to Victoria on Vancouver Island. Once in Victoria, catch a Laidlaw Coach Lines bus (daily at 5.40am and every second day at 11.45am; Can$84) to Port Hardy at the northern tip of the island. From Port Hardy, BC Ferries (☎250/386-3431 or 1-888/223-3779 in BC, fax 250/381-5452, *www.bcferries.com*) operate a morning departure (7.30am; Can$109, small car Can$218, twenty percent savings outside peak season) every other day in summer taking around seventeen hours to reach Prince Rupert, then returning the next day to Port Hardy. You'll need to spend the night in Port Hardy.

PACKAGE TOURS

Many operators run **all-inclusive packages** that combine plane tickets and hotel accommodation with activities like whale-watching, kayaking, hiking, or camping. Even if the "package" aspect isn't necessarily your thing, these deals can work out to be more convenient and sometimes more economical than arranging the same trip yourself, providing you don't mind losing a little flexibility. This is especially the case in Alaska, where tour operators often have access to remote areas unknown to most visitors. With such a vast range of packages available, it's impossible to give a complete picture – but the list provided (see box opposite) should get you on your way.

THE ALASKA PASS

Those planning on traveling to the heartland of Alaska, either by road or sea may find considerable savings by purchasing the AlaskaPass. Most of the major long-haul ferry, rail, and bus companies in Alaska, British Columbia, and the Yukon honor the pass so you can travel from Bellingham, Victoria or Vancouver up the Inside Passage or through British Columbia and the Yukon.

There are two types of passes: one is valid for a number of consecutive days of travel (15 days for $699, 22 days for $799, and 30 days for $949); the other is the AlaskaPass Flexible, which covers a number of days over a longer period (8 days in 12 for $499, and 12 days in 21 for $729). Kids (3 to 11) travel for half price.

Buy your pass from AlaskaPass Inc, PO Box 35, Vashon, WA 98070 (☎1-800/248-7598, *www.alaskapass.com*). Your pass includes a booklet of timetables, discount coupons and carrier contact addresses.

GETTING THERE FROM AUSTRALIA AND NEW ZEALAND

There are no direct flights from Australia or New Zealand to Alaska, all routes require at least one change of plane. The most popular route is across the Pacific to LA or San Francisco, then a connecting flight to Anchorage, or a trans-Pacific flight to Seattle followed by a flight or ferry ride to one of the Southeast Alaskan towns. Savings can be made by skipping the Lower 48 entirely and flying to Anchorage via Asia, though there are far fewer flights and you may have to spend a night, or the best part of a day, in the airline's home city. Fares don't vary greatly with season, though you may find they jump up by $200 or so over June and July.

We've quoted fares below that can often be undercut by short term specials and discounts offered through airline Web sites and travel agents, which generally offer the best deals and have the latest information on limited special offers, such as free stopovers and fly-drive-accommodation

AIRLINES

Air New Zealand (Auckland ☎09/357 3000; Australia ☎13 2476; *www.airnewzealand.com*). Daily flights to LA from major cities in Australia and New Zealand, via transfers in Auckland, or several times a week via either Auckland and Honolulu/Papeete, or Auckland, Fiji/Tonga, and Honolulu.

Air Pacific (Australia ☎1800/230 150; New Zealand ☎09/379 2404; *www.airpacific.com*). Daily flights from Auckland and Sydney, and three weekly from Melbourne and Brisbane to Nadi (Fiji) from where there are daily connections to LA. Fiji stopover not usually required.

Canada 3000 (Auckland ☎09/308 3370; Sydney ☎02/9567 9631; *www.canada3000.com*). Budget charter operator flying to Vancouver twice weekly from Auckland, Sydney, and Brisbane, from early Nov to early April.

Cathay Pacific (Australia ☎13 1747; New Zealand ☎09/379 0861; *www.cathaypacific.com*). Daily to LA from major cities in Australia and New Zealand via a transfer or stopover in Hong Kong.

China Airlines (Auckland ☎09/308 3364; Sydney ☎02/9244 2124; *www.china-airlines .com*). Three weekly flights from Auckland via Sydney to Taipei (Taiwan), then daily to LA. Low rates, but a 12hr lay-over in Taipei.

JAL Japan Airlines (Sydney ☎02/9272 1100; Auckland ☎09/379 9906; *www.jal.co.jp/english*). Several flights a week to LA from Sydney, Brisbane, Cairns and Auckland with an overnight stopover in either Tokyo or Osaka included in the fare.

Korean Air (Auckland ☎09/307 3687; Brisbane ☎07/3226 6000; Christchurch ☎03/365 5147; Melbourne ☎03/9920 3853; Sydney ☎02/9262 6000; *www.koreanair.com*). Several flights per week from Auckland, Brisbane, and Sydney to Seoul, with connections to Anchorage as well as LA and San Francisco.

Qantas (Australia ☎13 1313; New Zealand ☎ 0800/808 767 or 09/357 8900; *www.qantas.com.au*). Daily to LA from major Australian cities, through Sydney or Auckland then nonstop across the Pacific.

Singapore Airlines (Australia ☎13 1011; New Zealand ☎09/379 3209; *www.singaporeair.com*). Daily to LA from major Australian cities and Auckland, all via Singapore.

United Airlines (Australia ☎13 1777; New Zealand ☎0800/508648 or 09/379 3800; *www.ual.com*). Daily to LA and San Francisco from Sydney, Melbourne, and Auckland, then daily connections right through to Anchorage.

packages. Flight Centre and STA (which offer fare reductions for ISIC card holders and under 26s) generally offer the lowest fares. Seat availability on most international flights out of Australia and New Zealand is limited, so it's best to book several weeks ahead.

Currently the only flights from Australasia to Alaska that don't go through the Lower 48 are those **via Asia** with Korean Air who charge as little as Aus$1645 (NZ$1925) for a flight to Seoul with connections (after a twelve-hour layover) direct to Anchorage.

The way most people travel from Australia and New Zealand to Alaska is via the Lower 48, particularly **through LA**, which is typically reached on a twelve- to fourteen-hour nonstop flight, although some allow stopovers in Honolulu and a number of the South Pacific Islands. Almost all major US airlines have code-share flights from LA to Anchorage (United fly direct), but the best deal is usually the Alaska Airlines **"Best of the West" airpass** (see box, p.32), which effectively allows you to buy a round-trip ticket from LA to Anchorage for US$300.

Travelling **from Australia**, fares to LA and San Francisco from eastern cities cost the same, while from Perth they're about Aus$600–800 more. There are daily nonstop flights from Sydney to LA and San Francisco on United Airlines and to LA on Qantas for around Aus$2100. Going to LA via Asia generally works out more expensive with the more established airlines (like Singapore Airlines), but China Airlines only charge Aus$1705 for a round-trip from Sydney to LA via Taipei.

From **New Zealand**, most flights are out of **Auckland** (add about NZ$200–250 for Christchurch and Wellington departures) with the best deals on Air Pacific via Fiji (around NZ$1850), and the American Airlines/Qantas direct flight (NZ$1950), though the direct flights with United (NZ$2139) and Air New Zealand (NZ$2189) aren't that far behind. If you don't mind your journey taking a lot longer, you can save some money by going to LA via Taipei (Taiwan) with China Airlines, who charge as little as NZ$1550, though you'll have to spend at least half a day between flights in Taipei.

AUSTRALIAN DISCOUNT AND SPECIALIST AGENTS

Adventure Specialists, 69 Liverpool St, Sydney (☎02/9261 2927). A good selection of adventure treks and tours.

Adventure World, 73 Walker St, Sydney (☎02/9956 7766); Level 4, 197 St Georges Terrace, Perth (☎08/9226 4524); *www .adventureworld.co.nz*. Individual and small-group trips with small-boat cruises and packages combining Southeast, train trips, and kayaking and wilderness experiences.

Australian Travel & Information Centre, Level 8, 350 Kent St, Sydney (☎02/9262 4755 or 1800/227 268, fax 9290 1905). Mainly geared towards travel around Australia but budget fares are frequently available.

Flight Centre, 1 MacQuarie Place, Sydney (☎02/9241 2422); 19 Bourke St, Melbourne (☎03/9650 2899); plus dozens of branches nationwide; *www.flightcentre.com*. Call ☎1300/362 665 to speak to a consultant, or ☎13 1600 to find your closest branch. Near ubiquitous High Street agency frequently offering some of the lowest fares around.

Harvey World Travel. Franchised organization with agencies all over Australia. The nearest can be found with a local call ☎13 2757.

STA Travel, Shop 6, 127–139 Macleay St, Kings Cross, Sydney (☎02/9368 1111, fax 9368 1609); 273 Little Collins St, Melbourne (☎03/9654 8722, fax 9654 8919); plus other offices in Cairns, state capitals, and major universities (nearest branch ☎13 1776, fastfare telesales ☎1300/360 960); *www.statravel.com.au*. Major player in student, youth, and budget travel.

Sydney International Travel Centre, Level 8, 75 King St, Sydney (☎02/9299 8000 or 1800/251 911, fax 9475 1255, *www.sydneytravel.com.au*). Individually tailored holidays, flights, bus and rail tours.

Trailfinders, 91 Elizabeth St, Brisbane (☎07/3229 0887); 3 Hides Corner, Lake St, Cairns (☎07/4041 1199); 372 Lonsdale St, Melbourne (☎03/9600 3022); 976 Hay St, Perth (☎08/9226 1222); and 8 Spring St, Sydney (☎02/9247 7666); *www .trailfinders.com/australia*. Australian outposts of British specialists offering tailor-made trips. Knowledgeable staff skilled at turning up odd itineraries and good prices.

Travel.com.au, 76 Clarence St, Sydney, (☎02/9249 5444 or 1800/000 447, *www.travel .com.au*). Youth-oriented center with an efficient travel agency offering good fares, a travel bookshop, and Internet café.

NEW ZEALAND DISCOUNT AND SPECIALIST AGENTS

Adventure World, 101 Great South Rd, Auckland (☎09/524 5118, fax 520 6629, *www.adventureworld.co.nz*). Individual and small-group trips with small-boat cruises and packages combining Southeast, train trips, and kayaking and wilderness experiences.

Budget Travel (*www.budgettravel.co.nz*). Major countrywide flight discounter. Calling ☎0800 /808 040 takes you straight to your nearest agency.

Harvey World Travel. Franchised organization with agencies all over New Zealand.

Flight Centre Countrywide travel agent associated with its Australian counterparts and with numerous branches. Calling ☎0800/354 448 takes you to your nearest agency, or visit National Bank Towers, cnr Queen St and Darby St, Auckland (☎09/309 6171); Shop 1M, National Mutual Arcade, 418 Colombo St, Christchurch (☎03/379 6396); 50–52 Willis St, Wellington (☎04/472 8101); *www.flightcentre.com*.

STA Travel, 10 High St, Auckland (☎09/309 0458); 130 Cuba St, Wellington (☎04/385 0561); 90 Cashel St, Christchurch (☎03/379 9098); plus other offices in Dunedin, Hamilton, Palmerston North, and universities; *www.statravel.com.au*. Major player in student, youth, and budget travel. National freephone ☎0800/874 7737.

usit BEYOND, nr Shortland St Jean Batten Place, Auckland (☎09/379 4224); South British Building, Level 4, 326 Lambton Quay, Wellington (☎04/473 1348) and offices in Hamilton, Palmerston North, and Christchurch; *www.usitbeyond.co.nz*. Youth-oriented travel agency, formerly YHA travel, and your first stop for ISIC student cards. Nationwide freephone ☎0800/359 8748.

If you are thinking of heading up to Alaska **in winter** for some aurora viewing, dog sledding or extreme snowboarding then the cheapest fares are likely to be with Canada 3000 who can get you to Vancouver from Auckland, Brisbane, or Sydney for as little as Aus$1100 (NZ$1200) round-trip, though rates rise by about fifty percent around Christmas and New Year. From Vancouver you'll probably have to get to Seattle and fly to Anchorage or Fairbanks from there. Drawbacks are packed planes, inconvenient routes, and flights are limited to winter visits to Alaska, but they do offer rock-bottom rates.

If you prefer to have all the arrangements made for you before you leave, then **specialist agents** (see boxes, overleaf and above) can help you plan your trip, though there are few pre-packaged tours that include airfares from Australia and New Zealand.

VISAS AND RED TAPE

US and Canadian citizens do not require passports to enter Alaska, but must carry some form of identification such as birth certificate or naturalization papers: trying to cross the border with a driver's license or social security card is likely to see you turned back. Others must have a valid passport and required visas. Overland travelers shouldn't expect the rules to be relaxed by the Canadian border guards just because you need to pass through their country to get to Alaska, and it is worth keeping in mind that Canadian customs officials may also ask you to prove you have sufficient funds for the journey. Waving a credit card should see you through, but a wad of travelers' checks helps.

VISAS

In recent years there has been a **Visa Waiver Pilot Program** under which citizens of 28 countries – Andorra, Argentina, Australia, Austria, Belgium, Brunei, Denmark, Finland, France, Germany, Iceland, Ireland, Italy, Japan, Liechtenstein, Luxembourg, Monaco, Netherlands, New Zealand, Norway, Portugal, San Marino, Slovenia, Spain, Sweden, Switzerland, the United Kingdom, and Uruguay – need only a full passport and a **visa waiver form** to enter the United States for a period of less than ninety days. As we go to press, the scheme has been extended to February 2001, and may well continue in a similar vein once Congress enacts suitable legislation. Under the scheme, those arriving by air or sea need to show an onward or return ticket (at land borders this is not necessary) and must compete a visa waiver form provided either by your travel agency or by the airline (usually on the plane).

If you intend to work, study, or stay in the country for more than ninety days you must apply for a visa in advance. You should also apply for a visa in advance if you are a convicted felon, have a communicable disease – HIV/AIDS or TB in particular – or admit to being a communist or fascist.

Citizens of countries not covered by the Visa Waiver Program or people who don't fulfill the scheme's requirements need a **non-immigrant visa**. Forms are available from your nearest embassy or consulate (see box, overleaf), and can be downloaded from *http://travel.state.gov /visa_services.html*. You'll need a passport valid until after your return date (an extra six months is no longer required for residents of most countries: check when you apply), a passport photo, and will be charged the equivalent of US$45. Expect it to take up to three weeks, though it could be substantially quicker.

Anyone approaching Alaska through Canada (either overland or on BC Ferries) will need to complete **Canadian formalities**. British citizens, as well as citizens of the European Union (EU), Norway, and most Commonwealth countries (including Australia and New Zealand) only need a valid passport. US citizens will probably find they can get away with just a drivers license, though the authorities have every right to demand a birth certificate or naturalization papers, and you should definitely carry them. If you are traveling on the Alaska Marine Highway System from Bellingham, WA, your first stop will be in Ketchikan, Alaska, so although you will be traveling through Canadian waters, for immigration purposes you are not considered to be entering Canada. **Motorists** driving through Canada will be asked to show some proof of vehicle ownership and liability insurance cover.

IMMIGRATION CONTROL

The standard immigration regulations apply to all visitors, whether or not they are using the Visa Waiver Program. During the flight, you'll be handed an immigration form (and a customs declaration; see below), which must be given up at immigration control once you land. The form requires details of where you are staying on your first night (if you don't know, write "touring") and the date you intend to leave the US. You probably won't be asked unless you look disreputable in the eyes of the official on duty, but you should be able to prove that you have enough money to support yourself while in the US – $300–400 a week is usually considered sufficient – as anyone revealing the slightest intention of working while in the country is likely to be refused admission. You may also experience difficulties if you admit to being HIV positive or having AIDS or TB. Part of the immigration form will be attached to your passport, where it must stay until you leave, when an immigration or airline official will detach it.

CUSTOMS

If you are flying to Alaska via another US airport you will have to retrieve your bags and pass through customs at your first point of entry. Customs officers will relieve you of your customs declaration and check whether you are carrying any fresh foods. You'll be asked if you've visited a farm in the last month: if you have, you may well have your shoes (and possibly any camping gear) taken away for inspection. Unless you subsequently leave the US you will not need to complete customs or immigration procedures on arrival in Alaska.

The **duty-free allowance** is 200 cigarettes or 50 cigars (*not* Cuban), $100 worth of gifts (which may include up to 100 more cigars) and, if you are over 21, 34 ounces (1 liter) of spirits. Foodstuffs (particularly fresh fruit and vegetables, meats, and seeds) can be brought in but need to be declared and inspected. It is prohibited to carry into the country any articles from North Korea, Iran, Iraq, Libya, or Cuba, obscene publications, drug paraphernalia, lottery tickets, chocolate liqueurs, or pre-Columbian artifacts. Anyone caught carrying drugs into the country will not only face prosecution, but be entered into the records as an undesirable and probably denied entry for all time. There is no limit to the amount of **cash** you can bring into the US, but amounts over $10,000 must be declared.

Exports are also restricted, particularly antiquities and anything made from endangered species (for more on this, see the box on p.212). **Hunters and anglers** wanting to take home their trophies or just a freezer shelf full of salmon, halibut, or moose steaks will usually find your guides can make the necessary arrangements.

US EMBASSIES AND CONSULATES

In countries where there is consular representation in several cities, the embassy has been listed first.

Australia
Moonah Place, Yarralumla, Canberra, ACT 2600 (☎02/6214 5600, fax 6214 5970, *www.usis-australia.gov/embassy*).
553 St Kilda Rd, Melbourne, VIC 3004 (☎03/9625 5900, fax 9525 0769, *www.usis-australia.gov /melbourne*).
59th floor, MLC Centre, 19–29 Martin Place, Sydney, NSW 2000 (☎02/9373 9200, fax 9221 0573, *www.usconsydney.org*).
13th floor, 16 St George's Terrace, Perth, WA 6000 (☎08/9231 9400, fax 9231 9444, *www.usis-australia.gov/perth*).

Canada
490 Sussex Drive, Ottawa, ON K1N 1G8 (☎613/238-5335, fax 688-3082, *www.usembassycanada.gov*).
615 Macleod Trail SE, Calgary, AB T2G 4T8 (☎403/266-8962, fax 264-6630).
Suite 910, Cogswell Tower, 2000 Barrington St, Halifax, NS B3J 3K1 (☎902/429-2485, fax 423-6861).
PO Box 65, Postal Station Desjardins, Montréal, PQ H5B 1G1 (☎514/398-9695, fax 398-0973).
2 Place Terrasse Dufferin, CP 939, Québec City, PQ, G1R 4T9 (☎418/692-2095).
360 University Ave, Toronto, ON M5G 1S4 (☎416/595-1700, fax 595-0051).
1095 W Pender St, Vancouver, BC V6E 2M6 (☎604/685-4311, fax 685-5285).

Denmark
Dag Hammerskjöld Allé 24, 2100 Copenhagen (☎35 55 31 44, fax 35 43 02 23, *www.usembassy.dk*).

Ireland
42 Elgin Rd, Ballsbridge, Dublin (☎01/668 8777, fax 668 9946, *www.usembassy.ie*).

Netherlands
Museumplein 19, 1071 DJ Amsterdam (☎020/575 5309, fax 575 5310, *www.usemb.nl/consul.htm*).
Lange Voorhout 102, 2514 EJ, Den Hague (☎070/310 9209, fax 361 4688 *www.usemb.nl*).

New Zealand
29 Fitzherbert Terrace, Thorndon, Wellington (☎04/472 2068, fax 471 2380, *www.usembassy.state.gov/wellington*).
3rd floor, Citibank Center, 23 Customs St East, Auckland (☎09/303 2724, fax 366 0870, *www.homepages.ihug.co.nz/~amcongen*).

Norway
Drammensveien 18, 0244 Oslo (☎22/44 85 50, fax 44 33 63, *www.usa.no*).

South Africa
877 Pretorius St, Arcadia 0083, Pretoria (☎12/342 1048, fax 342 2244, *www.usembassy.state.gov/posts/sf1*).
7th floor, Monte Carlo Bldg, Heerengracht, Foreshore, Cape Town (☎21/421 4280, fax 425 3014).
2901 Durban Bay Bldg, 333 Smith St, Durban 4000 (☎31/304 4737, fax 301 0265).
1 River St, Killarney, Johannesburg (☎11/644 8000, fax 646 6916).

Sweden
Dag Hammarskjölds Väg 31, SE-115 89 Stockholm (☎08/783 53 00, fax 661 19 64, *www.usis.usemb.se*).

UK
5 Upper Grosvenor St, London W1A 2JB (☎020/7499 9000, premium-rated visa hotline ☎0906/150 0590, *www.usembassy.org.uk*).
3 Regent Terrace, Edinburgh EH7 5BW (☎0131/556 8315, fax 557 6023).
Queen's House, 14 Queen St, Belfast BT1 6EQ (☎028/9032 8239, fax 9024 8482).

EXTENSIONS AND LEAVING

The date stamped on your passport is the latest you're legally allowed to stay. Leaving a few days later may not matter, especially if you're heading home, but more than a week or so can result in a protracted, rather unpleasant interrogation from officials, which may cause you to miss your flight and be denied entry to the US in the future. Your American hosts and/or employers could also face legal proceedings.

To get an **extension** before your time is up, apply at the nearest **US Immigration and Naturalization Service** (INS) office; the address will be under the Federal Government Offices listings at the front of the phone book. They will automatically assume that you're working illegally and it's up to you to convince them otherwise. Do this by providing evidence of ample finances, and, if you can, bring along an upstanding American citizen to vouch for you. You'll also have to explain why you didn't plan for the extra time initially. If you have arrived via the Visa Waiver Program (or whatever replaces it) you may not be able to extend your stay, and if you suspect you may want to stay beyond the maximum ninety days it is usually better to obtain a suitable visa before leaving home.

STAYING ON

Anyone planning an extended legal stay in Alaska should apply for a special **working visa** at any American Embassy *before* setting off. Different types of visas are issued, depending on your skills and length of stay, but unless you've got relatives (parents or children over 21) or a prospective employer to sponsor you, your chances are slim at best.

Illegal work is not as easy to find as it used to be, now that the government has introduced fines as high as $10,000 for companies caught employing anyone without a **social security number** (which effectively proves you're part of the legal workforce). Even in the traditionally more casual establishments like restaurants and bars, things have really tightened up, and if you do find work it's likely to be of the less visible, poorly paid kind – dishwasher rather than waiter (for more on this topic see "Working in Alaska" below). Making up a social security number, or borrowing one from somebody else, is of course completely illegal, as are **marriages of convenience**; usually inconvenient for all concerned and with a lower success rate than is claimed.

WORKING IN ALASKA

Stories of astonishing wages in Alaska still hang wilting on the travelers grapevine, but the reality is that you are unlikely to earn a bundle. Some people do get rich quick, though more frequently they spend the summer up here working hard in unpleasant conditions and going home with little more than what they came with, having spent their meagre earnings quickly. Nonetheless, it is one way of spending time in Alaska without blowing your savings, and you may end up with an experience you'll cherish for a lifetime.

Most high-earning legends stem from the late 1970s construction of the Alaska Pipeline, or from good fishing seasons when fishermen returned with a share of the profits that amounted to a small fortune. Such hauls are rare these days, and your chance of getting a good slice of the action is slim. Alaskan unemployment is some of the highest in the US, and there are plenty of experienced old-hands around who will always get first pick over first-timers with no proven track record.

This kind of hierarchy can work in your favor if you are prepared to work more than one season up here; those who make it through the summer are almost guaranteed work the following year, often in a better position with a greater earning potential. You can also improve your chances of getting something worthwhile by **planning ahead**. Most employers want their new employees to work the full season from May to sometime in September, and they recruit between December of the previous year and February. You can get work by just turning up and asking around in May, but many positions will already be taken and you'll be hoping to fill in for no-shows and early sackings.

Securing a position in advance also opens up the possibility that your employer may pay for, or subsidize, your travel to Alaska, though this is more usual if you've worked for that employer before. More frequently you'll get free or cheap accommodation, and maybe meals, especially if you are working away from town.

No matter where you hope to work, be sure to **ask questions** about rates of pay, work and living conditions, expected duties, hours of work, potential overtime, tips, taxes, location of the work, time off, and anything else you can think of to get the lay of the land; and get as much of it as you can down in writing. You always hear of unscrupulous employers exploiting their hired help, demanding they work long hours for limited pay, then extracting all manner of deductions from the wage packet for transportation, lodging, laundry, or whatever.

US citizens have no legal difficulties working in Alaska, but if you are **not a US citizen** you will need a work visa to legally work in the United States. These can be obtained from the US embassy before you leave home (see box, p.16), though in practice, it is almost impossible to get one for the sort of seasonal work typically on offer in Alaska. Most visas go to foreigners working in summer camps in the Lower 48, and to those sponsored by an employer, who needs to prove that there is no US citizen available to take the job. Some people choose to work illegally, though with employers facing stiff fines if caught they are often reluctant to involve themselves, and if caught you may find yourself fined, deported, and unwelcome in the future. If you are still keen, the best bets are usually with the smaller restaurants and tourism operators who are prepared to pay cash-in-hand.

JOBS

The major considerations are the type of job you're after and the location; there's not much

point landing a job on a fish processing ship in the Bering Sea if you are interested in exploring Alaska in your free time.

Many of the jobs on offer are in coastal regions, particularly in **salmon canneries** and other fish processing plants which hire staff, usually offering around $6–8 an hour for standing beside a noisy and wet canning line gutting or filleting fish. If you can hack the arduous and boring work, it is possible to earn a packet doing long shifts with plenty of overtime, and keeping living costs down by bringing a tent or staying in cannery-owned bunkhouses. The season in each place is often short and the catch uncertain, so you'll need to be flexible enough to cope with early lay-offs and may have to move towns several times during the summer. You can sometimes land jobs by turning up at canneries early in the morning – Ketchikan, Petersburg, Pelican, Cordova, Kodiak are all worth trying – but it is far better to contact companies well in advance. Many of the companies are based in Seattle so consult the Seattle *Yellow Pages* (or surf the Net) and phone, preferably in January or February, though there may be fill-in places as late as May and June.

Working offshore on **fish processing ships** is more of a lottery. In a good season rewards can be higher than for onshore workers (around $14 an hour), but it is dirty, miserable, and dangerous work with no relief from the pitching seas; boats often stay at sea for weeks at a time.

On the whole, there's more fun and profit working with the **tourism industry**, often in the most beautiful parts of Alaska where tourists like to be. Jobs might include driving buses (either between towns or on city tours), hotel reception, expediting, tour narrator, or hotel work. Rates around $6 an hour are normal in jobs where tips are common, more like $7–11 an hour where no tips are likely. If you've got specialist skills you might even get a position as a rafting guide or leading mountain-bike trips, though these are seldom offered to first-time Alaska workers. The biggest operators are Gray Line of Alaska, 300 Elliott Ave W, Seattle, WA 98119 (☎206/277-5581, *www.graylinealaska.com*), and Princess Tours, who have a Summer Jobs Hotline (☎206/727-3199 ext 65050), and a downloadable application form on their Web site *www.princessalaskalodges.com*. You might want to try smaller companies we've listed throughout the *Guide*, or approach the bigger hotels directly.

There is also the possibility of working for the **federal government** through one of their land management agencies – the National Park Service *(www.nps.gov/personnel)*, the Forest Service *(www.fs.fed.us)*, the Fish and Wildlife Service or the Bureau of Land Management *(www.ak.blm.gov)*. You can log on to each organization's Web site but eventually they all lead to the Federal Government's Office of Personnel Management site *(www.usajobs.opm.gov)* which handles most positions.

For a wide listing of jobs available throughout the state surf to the Department of Labor's Alaska Jobs Bank at *www.labor.state.ak.us/esjobs/jobs*.

VOLUNTEER WORK

For those not legally allowed to work in the US, the only chance of working for the Federal Government is as a **volunteer**, and even US citizens might want to take this approach as it is much easier to land a volunteer position than a paid job. Though you will probably get free accommodation and food, and may even have some of your transport costs taken care of, you won't get paid. In return for this poor remuneration you may get to work in fabulous places learning valuable skills working alongside professionals conducting wildlife surveys, or helping restore salmon breeding areas. Then again you may end up doing fairly dull work such as cleaning up campgrounds, or find yourself working in rugged conditions doing something physically demanding; always make sure what you are letting yourself in for. The Web sites of the federal agencies listed above will take you to information on their volunteer programs, the most active being that run by the Forest Service.

INSURANCE, HEALTH, AND PERSONAL SAFETY

Alaska is a fairly safe place to visit. There is some physical danger from the sheer hostility of the environment, but nothing you can't learn to handle (or avoid altogether). In recent times there have been some fatal sightseeing accidents, and road conditions can pose a challenge, but on balance the risks are few. Things do go wrong, and when they do it is very comforting to know you are well covered with a good insurance policy.

INSURANCE

A typical travel insurance policy usually provides cover for the loss of baggage, tickets, and – up to a certain limit – cash or checks, as well as cancellation or curtailment of your journey. Most of them exclude so-called dangerous sports unless an extra premium is paid: in Alaska this can mean any mountain activities, white-water rafting, skiing, and possibly even backcountry hiking. Read the small print and benefits tables of prospective policies carefully; coverage can vary wildly for roughly similar premiums. Many policies can be chopped and changed to exclude coverage you don't need – for example, sickness and accident benefits can often be excluded or included at will. If you do take medical coverage, ascertain whether benefits will be paid as treatment proceeds or only after a return home, and whether there is a 24-hour medical emergency number. When securing baggage cover, make sure that the per-article limit – typically under £500 or equivalent – will cover your most valuable possession. If you need to make a claim, you should keep receipts for medicines and medical treatment, and in the event you have anything stolen, you must obtain an official statement from the police. Bank and credit cards often have certain levels of medical or other insurance included and you may automatically get travel insurance if you use a major credit card to pay for your trip, particularly gold cards.

Most travel agents and tour operators in the **UK** are likely to require some sort of insurance when you book a package holiday, though according to UK law they can't make you buy their own (other than a £1 premium for "schedule airline failure"). If you have a good all-risks home insurance policy it *may* cover your possessions against loss or theft even when overseas. Many private medical schemes, such as BUPA or PPP, also offer coverage plans for abroad, including baggage loss, cancellation or curtailment and cash replacement as well as sickness or accident.

Americans and **Canadians** should also check that they're not already covered, although Canadian provincial health plans should provide coverage for medical mishaps in the US.

CRIME AND THE LAW

Alaska has recently earned itself a reputation for **violent crime**, with three times the level of sexual violence than any other state, and a higher rate of homicides in Anchorage than the national average for a city of the same size. Still, much of this takes place behind closed doors or in places you are not going to visit, so as a visitor you are unlikely to be affected. You are more liable to be a victim of **theft**, though instances of bag snatching and personal assault are rare. Avoid carrying around and flaunting huge wads of cash, stash your valuables in the hotel safe (if there is one), and keep a photocopy of the important pages of your passport along with a record of the travelers' checks you haven't spent. Because of an increase in **theft from vehicles** at trailheads, especially those close to town, you should avoid leaving valuables in your car or truck. In practice, this is difficult to do, but at least store stuff out of sight.

Assuming you don't fall victim to any of this, you'll probably spend your entire time in Alaska without coming into contact with any of Alaska's various law enforcement agencies. Perhaps the easiest way to attract their attention is to fail to buy the appropriate hunting or **fishing license** or to infringe the bag-limit rules in some way. It is a complex business with rules that vary throughout the state, so always be sure to know what you are allowed to take. **Drugs** are, of course, totally illegal, though the Alaskan legal system has had a varied relationship with **marijuana**. It was illegal for years before being decriminalized in 1975 when a court declared that the State's constitutional right to privacy allowed people to smoke and possess, but not transport or sell, small quantities for personal use. For all practical purposes it was legal until a referendum in 1990 reversed the decision and marijuana was again made illegal.

PREJUDICES

More than almost anywhere else, Alaska seems to celebrate individuality, and those forging a different path than the mainstream may find that their individualism is unexpectedly celebrated. Nonetheless, prejudice exists and, especially in the more rural areas, it's best to keep a low profile. Harassment will seldom be more than a little verbal abuse, but overtly homosexual behavior, for example, is liable to elicit a more vigorous response. **Gay** men and women will find support groups and even a small **scene** in Anchorage, Fairbanks, and Juneau (we've listed contacts throughout the book) but very little elsewhere.

Women should feel generally safe in Alaska. You'll certainly encounter attitudes that may seem decades out of date, but perhaps no more so than anywhere. Alaska's famed paucity of women is more myth than reality these days, but there are still a lot of men living lonely lives in the bush, fishing at sea for weeks on end, or working on male-dominated oilfields, and women sitting in a bar are unlikely to avoid their attentions for long. Still, small-town familiarity combined with long hours of summertime daylight, mean that personal safety is likely to be less of an issue than at home, though it's best to always exercise the usual precautions.

Racism in Alaska is probably less prevalent than in large parts of the Lower 48, and what exists is likely to be directed at Native Alaskans. The vast majority of non-Natives are white, but with large military bases throughout Alaska black servicemen are a common enough sight to add some level of diversity. In the end, no matter what your race, you'll soon be recognized as a money-spending tourist, and whatever inherent prejudice there may be will soon evaporate.

HEALTH AND WELL-BEING

Travelers from Europe and Australasia do not require **inoculations** or special health certification to enter the US. Once in Alaska, if you have a serious **accident**, emergency medical services (dial ☎911) will get to you quickly and charge you later. Should you need to see a **doctor**, lists can be found in the *Yellow Pages* under "Clinics" or "Physicians and Surgeons," and there'll be a basic consultation fee of $50–100, payable in advance. Medication isn't cheap either – keep all your receipts for later claims on your insurance policy. Many **minor ailments** can be remedied using the fabulous array of potions available in **drugstores**. Foreign visitors should bear in mind that many pills available over the counter at home need a prescription in the US – most codeine-based painkillers, for example. Local brand names can be confusing; ask for advice at the **pharmacy** in any drugstore.

Tap **water** is perfectly drinkable in Alaska, and many rural campsites have potable water from hand pumps, but if you are drinking water from rivers or lakes it should be boiled, filtered or chemically treated (see p.55 for more).

At some time you'll probably find yourself on a ferry or day-cruise and will be glad that most travel in protected waters. Nonetheless those prone to **motion sickness** can improve their chances of feeling good by remaining close to the center of the ship, getting plenty of fresh air and avoiding reading or stuffy places. As a precaution, use one of the motion sickness patches or pills available over the counter at drugstores.

COLD, RAIN, WIND, AND SUN

You are not likely to come down with any unpleasant diseases in Alaska, but dealing with the physical demands of the environment will be a day-to-day concern. **Hypothermia** can also be a problem at any time in Alaska, but during the main May to September summer season, **cold temperatures** are likely to be less of a problem than you might expect. Still, you'll need to bring two or three warm layers (wool, polypropylene, and synthetic fleece are good materials; cotton is not), a hat, and some gloves, and always be prepared: a vehicle breakdown on a remote road in September could quickly turn into a nightmare if you are underdressed. Hypothermia isn't just about temperature, and protection from the **rain** may well be more of an issue, especially in Southeast Alaska where you are bound to encounter a downpour at some point. **Wind** too can be a problem in coastal areas (and on whale-watching cruises and the like), so a good waterproof and windproof coat is pretty much essential along with decent shoes and warm socks.

The sun also shines in Alaska, and with potentially twenty hours of sunshine a day through much of the summer **sunburn** is a real risk. Despite the low angle of the sun you should still slap on some sunscreen during the day, especially near snow and water where the reflection can catch you unawares; don't forget to cover the underside of your chin and nose. A peaked hat or baseball cap is a good idea, and be sure to wear glacier goggles or very dark sunglasses if spending time on or around glaciers.

BUGS, BEARS, AND OTHER NASTIES

In Alaska you don't need to worry about snakes, spiders or poison oak, but bears and particularly mosquitoes can be troublesome. The size and number of **mosquitoes** is legendary, and with good reason, though you also have to contend with **no-see-ums** (very small bitey things) and **white socks** (small black flies with white feet). They are seldom all around at the same time, but each has its few weeks of infamy in the summer so always carry some bug dope of maximum potency. Anything with a high levels of DEET is very effective, but also very nasty, so to reduce reliance on this wear long-sleeved shirts buttoned up to the neck, tuck your pants into your socks and use citronella candles if you are sitting outside in the evening. Broad-brimmed hats with nets covering your face are only really necessary in extreme circumstances, usually on remote rafting, canoeing, and fishing trips.

Bears can be found all over Alaska – town centers excepted – though it is only brown (grizzly) and black bears that are widespread; polar bears are rarely seen apart from in Arctic towns such as Barrow and Kotzebue, and summer sightings are rare. Despite the number of grizzly stories you might hear, the risk of a bear attack is extremely low and with a small amount of knowledge and some common sense there is no need to let fear get the better of you. We've covered bear encounters in more detail in the box on p.54, but generally you just need to remember that bears don't like surprises and as long as you make noise whenever you are walking in forests

or through scrub they are likely to move away before you know they are there. Some people advocate carrying a small bell, but talking, singing, or just clapping your hands is usually enough.

Alaska is full of smaller mammals, most of which won't bother you, though there is always a slim possibility you might get bitten, in which case you should definitely seek immediate medical treatment, and consider a series of **rabies** shots if you have any suspicion that the animal may be infected.

If you are a fan of shellfish, you need to be aware of **paralytic shellfish poisoning** (PSP), which attacks a handful of people each year and occasionally results in death. Shellfish sold commercially are routinely tested and are safe for consumption, but if you have collected your own, particularly from unmonitored beaches where there may be no warning signs, seek medical help if you sense tingling or numbness in the lips and tongue, and loss of muscle coordination, dizziness, weakness, or drowsiness.

COSTS, MONEY, AND BANKS

Alaska's astronomical prices have legendary status. The cost of transporting goods from the rest of the US has always made a big impact, but the reputation stems more from the pipeline construction years of the mid-1970s when bulging pay packets pushed prices to the stratosphere. There's

no doubt that Alaska remains one of the most expensive states to visit, but in recent years prices have moderated to the point where Anchorage doesn't seem much more costly than any American city of similar size. Outlay really increases when you try to get out into the bush. Flights are always expensive and sometimes that is the only way to get to remote villages or to the headwaters of a pristine river for a float trip. Things should only improve, though, with increased infrastructure and tourism.

Alaska is a US state and you'll be using US currency; its proximity to Canada does not mean that Canadian dollars will be accepted – and if they are, the exchange rate won't be in your favor. **US currency** comes in **bills** of $1, $5, $10, $20, $50, and $100 plus various rarely seen larger denominations. Confusingly they are all the same size and the same green color. The most commonly used bills are progressively being replaced by modern variants equipped with all manner of counterfeit-busting trickery, but the treasury passed up a big opportunity and has continued with the single-dimension green banknote for all denominations. Check each bill carefully and expect bartenders and shopkeepers to state the value of the bill you just gave them. The dollar is made up of 100 cents with **coins** of 1 cent (known as a penny), 5 cents (a nickel), 10 cents (a dime), 25 cents (a quarter), and a new gold-tinted dollar coin that's still struggling to gain acceptance. For phones, vending machines, and buses it always pays to keep a stack of change handy, especially quarters.

COSTS

There's no hiding from the fact that you are going to spend a fair bit of money on your travels here. If you are used to Lower 48 prices you can safely assume that in the bigger towns you'll be paying 10–30 percent more for groceries and meals, and in remote communities anything up to double the usual cost. There is also a general trend for the towns of Southeast Alaska (which are closer to the supply entrepot of Seattle) to be marginally cheaper than elsewhere.

The **minimum expenditure** if you are camping, hitching or cycling, preparing most of your own food and keeping a tight rein on tours and activities would be in the region of $30 a day, rising to $40–60 if you stay in hostels, use buses, trains, and ferries and indulge in the odd meal out. Couples staying in the cheaper motels, eating at unpretentious restaurants and not skimping on the main attractions and activities are looking at around $70–90 each per day; and if you rent a car for at least some of your stay, sleep in comfortable B&Bs and eat well, you should reckon on at least $120 a day. All these figures can be ramped up dramatically if you start flying out to remote communities or staying at wilderness lodges, though this can be offset by abstemious days hiking when you'll spend nothing.

Accommodation can be frighteningly expensive and is likely to be your biggest single expense, though off-season rates, especially in winter, can be half the summer rate; even May and September can offer savings. Camping in wilderness areas is often free, but if you want water and an outhouse expect to pay $6–10 per site; full-facility RV parks charge $18–25. Hostels vary from $7 to $25 per person (typically around $17), and some have a simple double room for two for as little as $45. You might occasionally find the odd roadhouse with poky rooms for $60, but generally there's a big step up from hostels to motels and B&Bs, both of which seldom cost less than $80. Resorts and hotels start around $120 in high season and go up from there. Remember that many communities add a **hotel tax** (usually 5–8 percent) to their quoted price.

As for **food**, the high price of groceries means you'll still need $15–20 a day for a basic life-support diet; anything perishable and imported – fruit, vegetables, and dairy products particularly – will be astronomically priced. Eating in restaurants is likely to set you back at the very least $30 a day, more so if you choose to splurge on dinner, and a considerable amount more if you add in a few drinks and a bit of socializing.

Given Alaska's size it should come as no surprise that **traveling costs** quickly mount up. A tour of Anchorage, the Kenai Peninsula, Denali, and Fairbanks can be done cheaply on buses and the train, but the public transport network is skeletal and at some stage you'll probably want to **rent a car**. For a compact car expect to pay $40–60 a day – perhaps more if your own vehicle insurance doesn't cover you – but this could be a good investment as it enables you to stay in cheaper out-of-town motels, or perhaps pull off the road and camp for nothing.

There's more good news. With few exceptions (mostly in Southeast), there is **no sales tax** on goods and services, so what you see is what you pay. **Tipping** is expected in restaurants, bars, and taxis, and a guide or tour host will welcome a similar appreciation; leave around fifteen percent of the bill.

Kids get in to most things free if they're under five, likely around half-price of an adult fare under the ages of twelve to, say, fifteen. There is often a small **discount** of around ten percent for military, seniors, and sometimes (though not often) students. Take some **student ID** if you've got one but it isn't worth making an effort to obtain one if you haven't. The **Hostelling International** membership card (see p.45) can also reap a few discounts.

EXCHANGE RATES

International exchange rates seem to fluctuate more every year, but as we go to press one US dollar trades for Aus$1.9, Can$1.5, €1.2, £0.70, and NZ$2.5.

CREDIT CARDS, TRAVELERS' CHECKS, AND BANKS

If you don't already have a **credit card** you should seriously think about getting one before traveling to Alaska; it'll make your life a lot easier when renting a car, bike, or whatever, as they won't feel obliged to extract a huge deposit. Even checking into a hotel you may be asked for an imprint to establish your creditworthiness. Besides, paying by plastic is accepted almost everywhere and 24hr **ATMs** are now so common (even in tiny, remote communities) that you can always get a **cash advance** when you need it. Visa and MasterCard (known elsewhere as Access), and to a lesser extent American Express, Diners Club and Discover are all widely accepted. You should also carry a **cash machine card** that works on either Cirrus or Plus, international systems widely established in Alaska that enable you to obtain money from your home account.

It is always worth checking with your home bank, but accessing your own account or obtaining a credit-card cash advance can often work out cheaper than buying travelers' checks. Nonetheless, **US dollar travelers' checks** are still the safest way to carry money for both American and foreign visitors. They offer the security of being replaced if stolen, and can be used as cash in restaurants and shops; just hand over the signed check and you'll get your change in cash. Don't be put off by "no checks" signs in the window: that only refers to personal checks. With the exception of Canadian currency, **exchanging foreign travelers' checks and bills** is almost impossible; currently even Juneau and Fairbanks don't have any foreign exchange facilities and there are only a couple of places in Anchorage.

Bearing in mind all the above, you'll probably have little cause to visit the inside of **banks**, which are generally open Monday to Friday from 10am to 4.30pm.

EMERGENCY CASH

If things go horribly wrong, or you unexpectedly decide to do that ten-day float trip down some Arctic river and suddenly need $3000, the best way to get money sent out is to get in touch with your bank at home and have them **wire money** to the nearest bank. Depending on how much you're prepared to pay for a fast buck, this takes anything from a few minutes to a week and prices vary depending on where you are sending from, how much and even whether you do it via the

STOLEN TRAVELERS' CHECKS AND CREDIT CARDS, AND WESTERN UNION OFFICES

Keep a record of the numbers of your **travelers' checks** separately from the actual checks; if you lose them, ring the issuing company on the toll-free number below. They'll ask you for the check numbers, the place you bought them, when and how you lost them and whether it's been reported to the police. All being well, you should get the missing checks reissued within a couple of days – and perhaps an emergency advance to tide you over.

EMERGENCY NUMBERS

American Express (TCs) ☎1-800/221-7282; (credit cards) ☎1-800/528-4800
Citicorp ☎1-800/645-6556
Diners Club ☎1-800/234-6377

MasterCard (Access) ☎1-800/307-7309
Thomas Cook ☎1-800/223-7373
Visa ☎1-800/227-6811

WESTERN UNION OFFICES
www.westernunion.com

Australia ☎1-800/649 565
Canada ☎1-800/361-1872
Ireland ☎1-800/395395

New Zealand ☎0800/270 000
UK ☎0800/833833
USA ☎1-800/325-6000

Web site or by phone. Thomas Cook and American Express both operate such services, but generally the most convenient is Western Union (see box, opposite), with near-instantaneous transfers to a local agent (maybe a post office, bank, car-rental agency or even a kiosk in a supermarket) and the facility for the sender to phone the transfer through using their credit card.

TELEPHONES, EMAIL, AND MAIL

In most parts of Alaska you're not going to have any trouble keeping in touch. Even remote villages have efficient telephone communications and daily mail deliveries. Internet access is everywhere, even tiny communities having wired public libraries.

TELEPHONES

It is almost always cheaper to call from a private phone, but in most cases you'll find yourself having to use **public telephones** (mostly run by AT&T Alascom). These almost always work and are plentiful but are seldom sited on street corners; in most parts of Alaska winter conditions dictate that phones are sited in shopping malls, convenience stores, and even in the entrance to fast-food outlets. They take 5¢, 10¢, and 25¢ coins and charge either 25¢ or 35¢ for a **local call** of unlimited duration. Since the whole of Alaska has the same ☎**907 area code** (with the sole exception of Hyder in the very Southeast corner, area code ☎604), this is no indication of what constitutes a long-distance call. As a guide, anywhere in the town you're in and its immediate surroundings will be a local call (just dial the

number) and anywhere outside that will be non-local or **long distance** (dial ☎1-907 and the number): a disembodied voice will come on the line telling you how much to pay for the call. **Call rates** for non-local and long-distance calls are much lower at weekends and between 6pm and 8am. Calls from motel and **hotel rooms** are usually much more expensive, though local calls are usually free.

Many government agencies, car-rental firms and just about everyone with something to sell have **toll-free numbers**, which always have the prefix ☎1-800, ☎1-877, or ☎1-888). Within the US you can dial such numbers free of charge, though some numbers only operate within Alaska: it isn't apparent until you try. Numbers with the prefix ☎1-900 are premium-rated lines, generally quite expensive and frequently salacious. You'll also come across companies using the mnemonic device of including letters in their number. The letters are on the buttons, thus for example, ☎1-800/BLUE CAB becomes ☎1-800/2583 222.

Occasionally you'll need to talk to folk who can only be contacted on **mobile phones**, which have numbers indistinguishable from land lines, but cost more to dial.

PHONE AND CHARGE CARDS

If you are making a lot of long-distance calls it almost always works out much cheaper if you buy a **phone card**, usually available in denominations of $5, $10, $20, and $50 from convenience stores, supermarkets, post offices, and motel front desks. Unlike the rest of the world, the US has eschewed installing separate machines that read magnetic-strip cards and instead you buy a "card" with a number printed on it. This effectively gives you an account with the issuing company. Simply dial the ☎1-800 number on the card and you'll be prompted to punch in your account number followed by the phone number you are after. A card normally gives you a fixed number of minutes of talk time irrespective of where in the US and Canada you call, or what time of day. Rates are now as low as 5¢ a minute (or even lower), though there is sometimes a connection fee (around 50¢) charged per call, and all cards have an additional 50¢ charge for using a pay phone.

EMAIL

The cheapest and often the most convenient way to keep in touch is with **email**. If you are patient it is usually possible to get free Internet access at the local library, but high demand and a booking system means you often have to wait hours (or even days) to get on. For more immediate needs there is almost always a shop (or café) nearby offering Internet access, and in some cases it won't cost you more than the price of your coffee. More often you'll have to pay around $2.50 for fifteen minutes, though some places impose a half-hour minimum ($5–6). Fear of viruses makes many a place ban the use of your own disks, though for those traveling with laptops, they often have dataports allowing you to plug in directly. Commercial photocopying and printing shops such as Kinko's are also a good bet, the high prices justified by fast machines hooked up to top-quality printers and scanners. Most mid- to upper-end hotels and motels now also have dataports in all rooms.

By far the easiest way to collect and send email on the road is to sign up with one of the dozen-or-so advertisement-funded **free email accounts**. All the major search engines will take you straight to one – *www.hotmail.com*, *www.yahoo.com*, *www.rocketmail.com* and more: just go to their Web page, fill in the form and you're done. Emails are kept indefinitely, but you are typically limited to a total of 2Mb of disk space (discourage friends from sending you clever, space-guzzling attachments) and if you fail to use the account for around three months (depending on the service supplier) you'll be closed down.

MAIL

With the sophistication of the US phone network and the ease of sending emails you may want to bypass the US Postal Service altogether. Compared to the mail in Britain and Australasia it is both slow and careless though things tend to turn up eventually. Alaskan **post offices** are usually open Monday to Friday from 9am to 5pm, and Saturday from 9am to noon. **Stamps** can also be bought from automatic vending machines, the lobbies of larger hotels, and many retail outlets and newsstands. Blue **mail boxes** stand on city street corners but are less common in rural areas.

Ordinary **mail** costs 33¢ for a letter (weighing not more than one ounce) sent within the US; postcards are 20¢. The international rate for letters weighing up to half an ounce (a single sheet) is 48¢ to Canada, 40¢ to Mexico, and 60¢ elsewhere. Postcards are 45¢, 40¢, and 55¢ respectively, and aerogrammes to all destinations are 50¢.

Letters can be sent c/o **General Delivery** (what's known elsewhere as **poste restante**) to the main post office in each town and must be addressed using AK, for the state of Alaska, followed by the five-digit **zip code**: we've included zip codes of larger towns in "Listings" at the end of that section. Mail will usually be held for thirty days before being returned to sender – so make sure there is a return address on the envelope. If you are receiving mail at someone else's address, it should include "c/o" and the regular occupant's name, otherwise it is likely to be returned. This is especially true in small towns where the postie is likely to know people by name. Mail will also be held at hotels if labeled "Guest Mail, Hold for Arrival" along with a collection date.

INFORMATION, MAPS AND WEB SITES

Alaska does relatively little to promote itself at a statewide level, preferring to let individual businesses and local tourism organizations conduct their own promotions. Nonetheless, for advance information a good starting point is the Alaska State Division of Tourism (see box, below) who publish the annual *North! to Alaska* booklet (*www.north-to-alaska.com*), which is mostly glossy tourism promotion material on Alaska and the Yukon, though it does contain the current AMHS ferry timetable, and important contact numbers. Of course, the Internet is a great source for up-to-date information and we've listed some of the most useful (and fun) Web sites to help you get started.

You can also obtain the hefty and useful *Official State of Alaska Vacation Planner* by either calling the Alaska Tourism Marketing Council or visiting their Web site (see box, below), though if you live outside the US you'll have to pay $10 (US dollar check, money order, or credit card).

VISITOR CENTERS

Once in Alaska you'll soon be weighed down with leaflets and brochures, most easily available

USEFUL ADDRESSES FOR ADVANCE INFORMATION

Alaska Department of Fish and Game, PO Box 25526, Juneau, AK 99802-5526 (☎465-4100, *www.state.ak.us/local/akpages/FISH.GAME*). Manage hunting and fishing throughout the state.

Alaska Marine Highway System, PO Box 25535, Juneau, AK 99802-5535 (☎465-3941 or 1-800/642-0066 in US, fax 277-4829, *www.dot.state.ak.us/amhshome*).

Alaska Native Tourism Council, 1577 C St, Suite 304, Anchorage, AK 99501 ☎274-5400, fax 263-9971)

Alaska Public Lands Information Centers The Web site for all four locations is *www.nps.gov.aplic/center*. Anchorage: 605 W 4th Ave, #105, AK 99501-5162 (☎271-2737, fax 265-2323); Fairbanks: 250 Cushman St, #1a, AK 99701-4640 (☎456-0527, fax 456-0514); Ketchikan: Southeast Alaska Discovery Center, 50 Main St, AK 99901 (☎228-6220, fax 228-6234); Tok: PO Box 359, AK 99780-0359 (☎883-5667, fax 883-5668).

Alaska State Division of Tourism, Dept VP, PO Box 110801, Juneau, AK 99811-0801 (☎465-2010, fax 465-2287, *www.dced.state.ak.us/tourism*).

Alaska Tourism Marketing Council, Dept. 117, PO Box 196710, Anchorage, AK 99519-6710 (☎1-800/327-9372, fax 276-1042, *www.travelalaska.com*).

Alaska Wilderness Recreation and Tourism Association, 2207 Spenard Rd, Suite 201, Anchorage, Alaska 99503 (☎258-3171, fax 258-3851, *www.awrta.org*).

MAP OUTLETS

UK

Cardiff Blackwell's, 13–17 Royal Arcade, CF1 2PR (☎029/2039 5036).

Glasgow John Smith and Sons, 57–61 St Vincent St, G2 5TB (☎0141/221 7472).

London Daunt Books, 83 Marylebone High St, W1 (☎020/7224 2295), and 193 Haverstock Hill, NW3 4QL (☎020/7794 4006); National Map Centre, 22–24 Caxton St, SW1 (☎020/7222 2466, *www.mapsworld.com*); Stanfords, 12–14 Long Acre, WC2E 9LH (☎020/7836 1321); 52 Grosvenor Gardens, SW1W 0AG (☎020/7730 1314); and within the British Airways offices at 156 Regent St, W1R 5TA (☎020/7434 4744); The Travel Bookshop, 13–15 Blenheim Crescent, W11 2EE (☎020/7229 5260).

IRELAND

Belfast Waterstone's, Queens Building, 8 Royal Ave, BT1 1DA (☎028/9024 7355).

Dublin Easons Bookshop, 80 Middle Abbey St, Dublin 1 (☎01/873 3811); Fred Hanna's Bookshop, 27–29 Nassau St, Dublin 2 (☎01/677 1255); Hodges Figgis Bookshop, 56–58 Dawson St, Dublin 2 (☎01/677 4754).

NORTH AMERICA

Rand McNally (☎1-800/333-0136 ext 2111, *www.randmcnallystore.com*) have 29 locations throughout North America. Call or check out their Web site for the nearest location or online orders.

Chicago Rand McNally, 444 N Michigan Ave, IL 60611 (☎312/321-1751); The Savvy Traveller, 310 S Michigan Ave, IL 60604 (☎312/913-9800, *www.thesavvytraveller.com*).

Los Angeles Rand McNally, Century City Shopping Center, 10250 Santa Monica Blvd, CA 90067 (☎310/556-2202).

Montréal Ulysses Travel Books, 4176 St-Denis, (☎514/843-9882, fax 843-9448, *guiduly@ulysses.ca*).

New York BritRail's British Travel Bookshop, 551 5th Ave (☎212/490-6688); The Complete Traveler Bookstore, 199 Madison Ave at 35th St, NY 10016 (☎212/685-9007); Rand McNally (*www.randmcnallystore.com*), 150 E 52nd St, NY 10022 (☎212/758-7488); Traveler's Choice Bookstore, 2 Wooster St, NY 10013 (☎212/941-1535).

San Francisco The Complete Traveler Bookstore, 3207 Fillmore St, CA 92123 (☎415/923-1511 or 1-800/950-3514, *www.completetraveler.com*); Phileas Fogg's Books & Maps, 87 Stanford Shopping Center, Palo Alto, CA 94304 (☎1-800/233-FOGG in California; ☎1-800/533-FOGG elsewhere in US); Rand McNally, 595 Market St, CA 94105 (☎415/777-3131); Sierra Club Bookstore, 85 2nd St, CA 94105 (☎415/977-5600).

Seattle Elliot Bay Book Company, 101 S Main St, WA 98104 (☎206/624-6600); Wide World Books and Maps, 4411 Wallingford Ave N (☎206/634-3453 or 1-888/534-3453, *www.travelbook-sandmaps.com*).

Toronto Open Air Books and Maps, 25 Toronto St, ON M5C 2R1 (☎416/363-0719).

Vancouver International Travel Books and Maps, 552 Seymour St, BC V6B 3J5 (☎604/687-3320).

Washington DC Rand McNally, 7101 Democracy Blvd, Bethesda, MD 20817 (☎301/365-6277).

AUSTRALIA

Adelaide The Map Shop, 6–10 Peel St (☎08/8231 2033, fax 8231 2373, *www.mapshop.net.au*).

Brisbane Worldwide Maps and Guides, 187 George St (☎07/3221 4330, fax 3211 3684, *enterprise.powerup.com.au/~wwmaps*).

Melbourne Map Land, 372 Little Bourke St (☎03/9670 4383, fax 9670 7779, *mapland @lexicon.net.au*); Melbourne Map Centre, 738–740 Waverley Rd, Chadstone, and PO Box 55, Holmesglen, VIC, 3148 (☎03/9569 5472, fax 9569 8000; *www.melbmap.com.au*).

Perth Perth Map Centre, First Floor, Shaft Lane, 884 Hay St (☎09/8322 5733, fax 9322 5733, *www.q-net.net.au/~perthmap*).

Sydney Dymocks, 350 George St, (☎02/9223 5974, fax 9232 3061); Travel Bookshop, 6 Bridge St (☎02/9241-3554, fax 9241 3159, *www.blueskies.com.au/travelbook*).

through visitor centers (the term we've used throughout the book), which also go by such names as visitor information center, Chamber of Commerce, and Conventions and Visitors Bureau (CVB). At best they're well-stocked places laden with bumf on just about everything in the state and staffed by enthusiastic and knowledgeable personnel, but can be just a small office with a handful of leaflets, or even a simple rack of advertising in the corner of the village store. Hours are equally varied, with some opening whenever they've got a volunteer available, but most staying open daily in summer from 9am or 10am through to 5pm or later. In general they don't make bookings for tours or accommodation, but will often have a phone you can use.

In small towns the visitor center is likely to be your first contact for information about local hikes and cabins, though occasionally there is a separate visitor center run by the US Forest Service. National Parks also have visitor centers, but by far the best sources of information about the outdoors are the four inter-agency **Alaska Public Lands Information Centers** (APLIC) – in Anchorage, Fairbanks, Tok, and Ketchikan (see box, p.27, for contact information) – run jointly by the authorities responsible for National Parks, State Parks, National Forests, National Wildlife Refuges, and the Bureau of Lands Management (BLM). They will provide just about everything you need to plan hiking, camping, canoeing, fishing, or wildlife viewing trips.

MAPS

Specialist travel booksellers (see box, opposite) should have general maps of Alaska. Once there you'll find that gas stations sell tolerably useful

---

USEFUL WEB SITES

TRAVEL AND TOURISM SITES

Alaska Internet Travel Guide *www.alaskaone .com/travel/alaska.htm*. Numerous helpful listings for Alaska travel sites.

Alaska Highway *www.alcanseek.com/alcan .htm*. Good for checking up-to-date conditions along the Alaska Highway.

Alaska Marine Highway System ferries *www.dot.state.ak.us/external/amhs/home.html*. Alaska Marine Highway System homepage for downloadable ferry schedules, reservations,

fares, and the lowdown on vessels and ports.

Alaska Railroad *www.akrr.com*. Alaska railroad timetables and reservations.

Division of Tourism *www.dced.state.ak.us /tourism*. Official state tourism site and a good starting point for access to National and State parks, CVB addresses, a calendar of events, local weather and online Alaska road map.

OUTDOOR SITES

Gorp *www.gorp.com*. General outdoor activities site that's great for adventure trip listings and has wide Alaska coverage.

Mountain Biking *www.dirtworld.com/trails /traillist_alaska.htm*. Brief listing of around a dozen bike trails in Alaska.

National Parks *www.nps.gov/parklists/ak.html*. Access page for all Alaska's national parks, preserves and monuments.

US Fish and Wildlife *www.r7.fws.gov*. The US Fish and Wildlife service, the first stop for information on National Wildlife Refuges, bird populations and general wildlife management.

GENERAL SITES

Alaskan.com *www.alaskan.com*. Commercial site with extensive Alaskan links.

Anchorage Daily News *www.adn.com*. Alaska's biggest and most influential newspaper.

Museums List *www.educ.state.ak.us/lam /museum/weblist.html*. Links to Alaskan museums, cultural centers, and historic sites with good Web sites.

Northern Alaska Environment Center *www .northern.org*. Grassroots organization campaigning for the preservation of the Arctic National Wildlife Refuge and boreal forests. Extensive links to like-minded sites.

Northern Lights *www.pfrr.alaska.edu/~pfrr /aurora*. Aurora videos, forecasts, and much more.

and cheap state maps, the best of which is the one by Rand McNally ($3), which at an inch to 75 miles gives only a broad sweep but does have handy enlargements of most of the areas where you are likely to spend time. Map enthusiasts won't be able to resist the weighty and unwieldy *DeLorme Alaska Atlas and Gazetteer* ($20) which covers most of the state at an inch to five miles, marks all hikes, huts, peaks, landing strips, and comes complete with contour lines and GPS grids. There's little worthwhile in between these two extremes though there are regional maps, perhaps the most useful being the *Southeast Alaska Inside Passage Recreation Guide* ($7), which includes a town plan of each community.

If you are planning to do some serious hiking you'll need a topographic map. These are sold by visitor centers in popular hiking areas such as Denali National Park, at the Alaska Public Lands

Information Centers, and by mail order through Earth Science Information Center, US Geological Survey, 507 National Center, Reston, VA 20192 (☎1-888/275-8747, fax 303/202-4693, *www.ask .usgs.gov*. An order form can be downloaded from their Web site and, on top of the price of the maps you can expect to pay $5 handling ($25 for international orders).

USEFUL WEB SITES

The remote nature of Alaska encouraged the people of the last frontier to adopt the Internet early and wholeheartedly, a trend that has continued. Increasingly, almost everything you're going to need to know will be available on the Net, though finding just what you want can still be time consuming. We've included **Web addresses** throughout the guide, and brought together a few more interesting sites of general interest in the box overleaf.

MEDIA

The standard of media coverage in Alaska is much as you'd expect of the United States but on a smaller scale. There are fewer TV and radio stations than in the Lower 48, though some towns have such poor reception that almost everyone has cable, with the usual fifty-plus channels. Mostly it is the usual stuff you'll find all over the US, with inserts for local news, weather, and current affairs, but other locally-produced shows are rare. In villages you may come across the Rural Alaska Communications Service which serves almost 250 rural communities with commercial content from Anchorage stations, material from the Alaska Public Broadcasting Service (PBS), and some local or regional programming.

Radio varies greatly throughout the state with only the serious, publicly-funded Alaska Public Radio Network (various AM frequencies) having wide coverage; much of its content is straight from **National Public Radio**.The bigger towns have a selection of niche stations (alternative rock, classic rock, Seventies, country, etc), but smaller places might have just one, and it is on these that you should listen out for "bushlines," a kind of radio bulletin board for people who don't have phones. The whole town, and particularly

those in cabins out in the bush, will listen to the messages, usually prosaic instructions for someone to meet somewhere, or sending thanks for the side of moose delivered Tuesday. Between towns there may be nothing at all: get a rental with a cassette player for those long hauls.

The widest circulation morning **newspaper** is the *Anchorage Daily News*, which provides Alaska's most comprehensive coverage of local and world events. It is pretty much the de facto state newspaper, much to the chagrin of a good portion of the state's residents, not just because they resent Anchorage's dominance, but because of its left-leaning, liberal politics (at least by Alaskan standards). Some years back it absorbed the city's afternoon paper, the *Anchorage Times* and as a sop to its former readers and "in the interests of preserving a diversity of viewpoints in the community," the *Anchorage Daily News* prints the "Voice of the Times," a daily half-page of right-wing Libertarian views. The *Fairbanks Daily News-Miner* and *Juneau Empire* are the two others with a large regional following, the former covering much of the Interior and the North, the latter found all over Southeast. None are likely to win you over with outstanding standards of journalism, but they're quite adequate, and the weekend magazine sections offer interesting insights into aspects of the state you may not otherwise come across. In addition, each sizeable town produces its own local interest rag – the *Arctic Sounder*, the *Tundra Drums*, the *Nome Nugget*, and a dozen more around the state – though the content often fails to live up to the promise of the title. Supermarket magazine stands in the bigger towns might stock the major dailies from the Lower 48 but most likely you'll be reduced to *Time* and *Newsweek* for wider coverage.

Alaska-specific **magazines** are rare, though you might look for the monthly *Alaska*, which tries for a wide coverage of outdoor issues but fails to disguise its hunting and fishing heritage. Those looking to spend a lot more time in Alaska should seek out *Alaska Men USA* (www.alaskamen-online.com), a matchmaking magazine which claims to feature "interesting and exciting men whose individualism, spirit and vitality make them unique among men of the world."

GETTING AROUND

During a stay in Alaska, it is not unusual to ride ferries, buses and trains, drive a rental car, cycle, fly out to bush communities, and hike. Come in winter and you may well ski, ride a snow machine, and drive a dog team. In any case, getting around is liable to take up a fair bit of your time and money, but don't treat it as a hardship – often the journey is as enjoyable as the destination. The scenery is wonderful whether viewed from a bus headed up towards the Arctic Ocean, on the train headed for Denali, chugging through the Inside Passage on a ferry, or stopped beside the road gazing across the tundra. Better still, wildlife is often less disturbed by people encased in their metal cocoon and with the extra height you have for peering over trees this can constitute some of your best animal spotting.

All the mountain ranges, glaciers, and vast stretches of boggy wilderness put up significant barriers to ground transportation – only surmounted by taking to the air or water. Consequently Alaskans **fly** more than anyone else in the nation, and you should follow suit to reach remote villages or even just to do some flightseeing. Indeed, much of Alaska is inaccessible to road traffic, but the Kenai Peninsula, the Interior, and the region around Fairbanks all have a fair **highway** network that you could spend weeks exploring, though a couple of sections are best viewed from wonderfully scenic **train** lines. For many, the highlight is making full use of the **ferry system**, which links over thirty ports, mostly in the Southeast "panhandle," but also around Prince William Sound, the Kenai Peninsula, and west beyond Kodiak Island to the Aleutian Islands. Thoroughly relaxing, they leisurely thread their way through unbelievably narrow channels and across deep sounds where whales and dolphins make regular appearances.

If you stick to the roads and ferry routes, **transportation costs** aren't especially high, and considering the distances involved, ferries and buses are quite cheap. You can see a lot of what the state has to offer this way, but start flying out to remote bush communities and you'll soon start racking up the bills. **Savings** can be made on transport by investing in an **AlaskaPass** (see box, p.11, for full details) which combines ferries, the Alaska Railroad, and assorted bus systems throughout Alaska, British Columbia, and the Yukon; and Alaska Airlines' **airpass** (see box, overleaf), the latter only available to foreign visitors.

DOMESTIC FLIGHTS

Alaskans make more than twice the number of commercial flights as the US average and the statistics for small planes are astounding. Roughly one in every sixty Alaskans is a certified pilot and almost all of them own their own plane. That is something like sixteen times the number of planes per capita as the rest of the United States.

Clearly, flying is the quickest way to get around – and sometimes the only way – especially as surface travel is hampered by long distances, impassable mountain ranges and inconveniently sited bodies of water. Short **scheduled flights** can save you a lot of time, and sometimes money. If you need to get from Juneau to Anchorage you can wait for the monthly ferry to Valdez, continue by ferry to Whittier then catch the train (taking two days in all), or fly more cheaply in ninety minutes. Likewise it takes a day by bus from Valdez to Anchorage, and yet you can fly in fifty minutes for much the same price. Services between the larger towns are mostly run by the state carrier Alaska Airlines, though in some areas flights are contracted out to partner airlines such as Reeve and PenAir. If any of these fly to your destination, this will almost certainly be the cheapest way to go, especially if you are an overseas visitor and have pre-bought an Alaska Airlines **airpass** (see box, below), which offers in-state flights for $99 each way – a big saving on longer routes. Otherwise, it is difficult to pin down exact **fares**, which vary enormously depending on demand – even within a few minutes – and how far in advance you can reserve. In general the most expensive fares are those bought less than seven days in advance. By buying a **round-trip ticket** over a week ahead you can expect to save around twenty percent; a fourteen-day advance purchase will save perhaps thirty percent and a ticket bought 21 days ahead will cut almost forty percent from the walk-up rate. Between the largest cities – Anchorage, Fairbanks, Juneau, and Seattle – there are sometimes "three-day fares" that can be bought up to

three days before flying but usually require you to take the red-eye flight in the middle of the night. These can work out cheaper than 21-day advance-purchase tickets. **One-way tickets** are generally half the round-trip fare, though there is a more limited range of deals: a 21-day advance-purchase ticket, saves some thirty percent over the walk-in fare. Deals are also to be found on the Alaska Airlines Web site.

As an example, a round-trip from Anchorage to Fairbanks could range from $120 if bought well in advance, up to $380 for a walk-up. Other routes tend to vary less: Anchorage–Juneau round-trip costs $280–380, and Juneau–Ketchikan $180–270.

Smaller companies operate scheduled services from Anchorage and Fairbanks to the larger remote communities carrying mail, newspapers and essential supplies. These places rely so heavily on air deliveries that you may well find yourself on a 737 almost entirely given over to freight with only two dozen seats left for passengers.

BUSH PLANES

Scheduled flights are fine for getting around, but you cannot truly appreciate Alaska without spending at least some time in those workhorses of Alaskan aviation, the **bush planes** – typically small Cessnas, Beavers, and Piper Navajos. It sometimes seems that there isn't a place in the state that they won't land, and hair-raising stories of pioneering touchdowns on postage-stamp lakes and crevasse-riddled glaciers are legion. Talk of narrow escapes from horrendous crashes gets similarly lurid coverage, but that shouldn't deter you: **bush pilots** fly twice as much as the US average and probably negotiate more tricky maneuvers in a week than pilots elsewhere do in

---

ALASKA AIRLINES' "BEST OF THE WEST" AIRPASS

Big savings can be made on internal and out of state flights with Alaska Airlines provided you're not a US citizen (or are a US citizen but currently reside in some other country) and are starting your travels outside the US. Their "Best of the West" **airpass** requires you to buy between two and ten coupons (called sectors), each valid for one one-way Alaska Airlines flight. Flights beginning and ending within the state are classed as Silver Sectors (US$99), which for short flights is no saving, but you'll cut costs enormously on trips to places such as Barrow, Nome, and Dutch Harbor. Flights such as one from Anchorage to

Ketchikan which stops twice but retains the same code number can still be bought for just one $99 coupon.

Flights beginning or ending outside the state (say Seattle or LA) are Gold Sectors ($149), and two of these can often work out cheaper than a round-trip ticket from LA to Anchorage.

The airpass (which cannot be bought in the US) does not have to be bought in conjunction with any international flights, but all coupons must be used within 60 days of using your first one, and all flights must be taken within 120 days of arrival in the US.

MAIN SCHEDULED AIRLINES IN ALASKA

Alaska Airlines (☎1-800/252-7522, *www .alaskaair.com*). The main intrastate and international airline with flights to all major towns in Alaska and frequent out-of-state flights to Seattle, San Francisco, Los Angeles, Chicago, Detroit, Puerto Vallarta (Mexico), and more; and strong links with the Pacific Northwest's Horizon Air.

ERA Aviation ☎1-800/866-8394, *www.eraaviation.com*. Alaska Airlines partner with flights from Anchorage to Bethel, Cordova, Homer, Iliamna, Kodiak, Valdez, and Whitehorse, Yukon.

Horizon Air ☎1-800/547-9308, *www.horizonair .com*. Essentially a branch of Alaska Airlines operating throughout the Pacific Northwest.

Reeve Aleutian ☎1-800/544-2248, *www .reeveair.com*. Alaska Airlines' partner with flights from Anchorage to the Pribilof Islands, Dutch Harbor, Cold Bay, Sand Point, and the Russian Far East.

PenAir ☎1-800/448-4226 or 243-2323, *www .penair.com*. Works in partnership with Alaska Airlines covering the Southwest and Aleutians with flights from Anchorage to Dutch Harbor, King Salmon, Dillingham, the Pribilof Islands, Unalakleet, and others.

---

a lifetime of flying. Besides, most are very good at distracting you with endless tales of derring-do on the Last Frontier.

Many fly on regular schedules using the larger towns as hubs for services to tiny villages. Services are run to a less rigid but still frequent timetable, and **fares** tend to be more stable than on the intercity routes. You'll also come across dedicated mail flights that briefly visit three or four communities and often have a few seats for passengers. Take the whole tour, or just use one leg to reach a particular village.

Apart from regular services, **chartered bush planes** are the only way to get to some of the real gems of the great Alaskan outdoors. Nowhere is too tough. They come equipped with floats for lake and river landings, skis for snow and glaciers, ordinary wheels for gravel airstrips and bulbous tundra tires for rough field and gravel bar touchdowns. Even international airports are designed to cope with all types: the tarmac runway flanked by a gravel strip and a float pond.

Arranging a flight is usually no problem. Reserving in advance is always a good idea, but in summer pilots work long hours and can usually tack an extra flight onto the end of their schedule to get you out to your river bar. The price is usually for the plane and pilot, with little or no extra cost for additional passengers. Consequently it is a good idea to join up with others to make up a full load. If you are going somewhere popular, the bush plane company may well do this for you, but the more exotic the destination, the more you'll have to organize this yourself. Remember that unless they have found a return fare, you are

paying for the plane until it gets back to base, though when flying into USFS cabins – which are often continuously booked throughout the summer – you can almost always share the cost with the previous occupants flying out. A five-seater bush plane will typically cost around $300 an hour.

There are a number of **precautions** to consider when arranging **pick-ups**. Firstly make sure your can get to the designated spot. Hiking across tundra is slow going and apparently benign rivers can turn out to be impassable. There is always the possibility of getting stranded with supplies running low, but it is more likely your pilot will return to the designated spot later on (or the next day) and maybe even initiate a search, all of which will cost you money. Make sure you have a clear **contingency plan** understood by all parties. Weather can make it impossible for your pilot to pick you up at the arranged time, and it is comforting to know when subsequent attempts will be made. With this in mind, make sure you don't have any pressing engagements (like international flights) immediately after bush trips.

Pilots know their patch very well and will only arrange to pick you up somewhere they know they can land but it always pays to check. Spring break-up (mid-April to late May) severely limits water landings in the interior, and around the coast you should consider the **tides** to ensure the pilot can get close in to the shore.

FERRIES

If you are heading north through Southeast Alaska, you'll almost certainly be making extensive use of the **Alaska Marine Highway**

System (AMHS; see box, p.37, for addresses), also known as the state ferry or even the "blue canoe." This state-run network of nine vehicular passenger ferries provides the principal means of transport between 34 ports in Southeast and Southcentral Alaska. Our chapter maps (p.68, p.217, and p.290) show the routes and ports of call made by ferries, which are each named after an Alaskan glacier, in line with some arcane state law. You'll soon get to recognize them by the routes they ply – the *Bartlett* around Prince William Sound, the *Malaspina* between Haines, Juneau, and Skagway, and so on. In general, the ferry system is highly integrated with daily departures from major ports and perhaps one or two a week in each direction from smaller places. The main problem is that the ferry system comes in two separate sections: the Southeast, which extends from Bellingham in Washington state to Haines and Skagway; and Southcentral/Southwest, which covers Prince William Sound, the Kenai Peninsula, Kodiak Island, and the Aleutian chain. One ferry does make **"inter-tie" trips** between Juneau and Valdez but only once a month in each direction in June, July, August, and September. If you don't catch these you'll have to fly or go by road through Canada to make the link.

Ferries tend to be in port for only a short time (1–3hr) and many of the Southeast ferry docks are inconveniently sited several miles from the heart of town making it difficult (if not impossible) to get a feel for the place without making **stopovers**. These should be planned in advance: you need to buy a series of journeys between your chosen ports of call rather than buying, say, Bellingham to Juneau and expect to stop off where you feel like. If you have bought such a ticket and decide to make extra stopovers then alterations can be made for a fee, which varies according to the changes. This will also affect your reservations, an important consideration in the busy summer months.

Facilities on board depend a little on the ferry in question, but all carry vehicles and passengers, have coin-operated lockers, and have somewhere you can lay down a sleeping roll. All except the *LeConte*, *Aurora*, and *Bartlett* have cabins (or state rooms, as they are grandiosely called), mostly with private bathrooms. If you can't afford a cabin on the longer journeys, obtaining a good place to sleep becomes critical, to the point that in Bellingham it can be a mad dash for the top-deck **solarium** and observation lounge, widely regarded

as prime spots for their fresh air, good views and nighttime peace. Some people even erect their tent on the upper deck, making sure to secure it firmly against the stiff breeze when under way.

Lounges have reclining seats you can sleep in; pillows and blankets can be rented for a modest fee on most sailings; and all except the *Bartlett* (which runs between Whittier, Valdez, and Cordova) have hot showers (either free or coin-operated). In addition there are usually free education programs run by interpreters from the Tongass National Forest, as well as films and Alaska videos.

Meals are available in the ship's buffet-style restaurant, and if not gourmet affairs, they are pretty good and reasonably priced by Alaskan standards. The larger boats also have a bar. You are welcome to lug aboard your own supplies to prepare snacks (they even provide free hot water – good for tea, coffee, and packet soups) but use of backpacking stoves is strictly prohibited.

TIMETABLES, RESERVATIONS, AND FARES

When it comes to planning your travels it is imperative to get hold of up-to-date **timetables**, which change each year in line with predicted tidal variations. The *North! To Alaska* brochure (see "Information and Maps," p.27) contains the summer schedule (valid May–Sept; usually available from Dec), and you can order a dedicated timetable directly from AMHS, and consult and download a schedule from their Web site.

During the summer months, especially June and July, vehicle space and cabins can be fully booked, though foot passengers can usually get on. If you are traveling at this time it is wise to make **reservations** as far in advance as possible. AMHS's toll-free number can be used for reservations from the Lower 48 but it is often difficult to get through so you are better off mailing or faxing your requirements. The Web site has a reservation form you can print out; or simply list the relevant details: the journeys required, number, names, and ages (if under 12) of those in the party, width, height, and overall length of any vehicles, a mailing address and phone number, alternate travel dates, and the date you plan to leave home. If full, ask to be put on a waitlist. Cabin waitlists exist for trips north from Bellingham, Juneau to Valdez, and west to the Aleutians; vehicles can only be waitlisted on the latter two. **Payment** is expected soon after your booking is confirmed and can be made using a

FERRY RATES

	Bellingham	Prince Rupert	Ketchikan	Metlakatla	Hollis	Wrangell	Petersburg	Sitka	Juneau	Haines	Skagway	Valdez
Ketchikan	164	38										
Metlakatla	168	42	14									
Hollis	178	52	20	22								
Wrangell	180	56	24	28	24							
Petersburg	192	68	38	42	38	18						
Sitka	208	86	54	58	54	38	26					
Juneau	222	104	74	78	74	56	44	26				90
Haines	222	122	92	96	92	74	62	44	24			
Skagway	252	130	98	102	98	82	70	50	32	17		
Tenakee	226	104	74	78	74	56	32	22	22	38	46	

FERRY RATES							
	Unalaska	Kodiak	Seldovia	Homer	Seward	Whittier	Valdez
Kodiak	202						
Seldovia	246	52					
Homer	242	48	18				
Seward	250	54	100	96			
Whittier	316	120	166	162			
Valdez	292	98	142	138	58	58	
Cordova	292	98	142	138	58	58	30

major credit card, a certified or cashier's check, or a money order in US dollars.

In practice, foot passengers can often wend their way through the Southeast without making any reservations by putting themselves on **standby**, and pay for their ticket at the terminal. Once in the Southeast you will find that mechanical breakdowns, tides, logistics, and occasionally industrial action can play havoc with the schedule. It always pays to **double-check departure times** with the nearest office to your port of call.

Up-to-date **fares** are available from the AMHS Web site (see box, opposite), the total fee being arrived at by adding together the various components – passenger fares, cabins, vehicles, etc. Typical one-way passenger fares are: Ketchikan–Juneau ($74); Juneau–Skagway ($32); Valdez–Cordova ($30); Valdez–Whittier ($58); and Homer–Kodiak ($48). **Round-trip** fares are double the single journey fare; **kids'** fares (2–11 inclusive) are around sixty percent of the adult fare; and under two's travel free. **State rooms** start with a two-berth cabin (roughly the adult fare) and range up to a large four-berth affair (1.4–1.6 times the adult fare). A small **car** (up to fifteen feet long) will cost 2.2 times the adult fare, something up to 21 feet will be 3.3 times, a **motorbike** costs 1.3 times, and a **bicycle** or **kayak** travels for one-fifth of the adult fare.

For details of ferry connections from Bellingham, WA, and through British Columbia, see "Getting there from North America," p.10.

TRAINS

Mention that you are traveling on the **Alaska Railroad** and Alaskans will usually mumble something about never having gotten around to riding it, largely because **train travel** in Alaska is something of a luxury unless you're one of the few hundred people who live in the bush close to tracks and rely on the train for your access to town. Nonetheless, it is a luxury cherished by the state's summer visitors who make up the vast majority of the passengers, paying around twice the comparable bus fare.

There is just one passenger line, a 470-mile run from the ice-free port of Seward to Fairbanks in the heart of the Interior, traversing two major mountain ranges, almost looping around on itself, spanning deep chasms, and crossing mile after mile of spruce forests threaded by braided rivers and beaver-dammed streams. With steep mountain passes, discontinuous permafrost, ice floes during spring break-up, and the sheer remoteness of it all, construction difficulties seemed insurmountable, but by 1923 President Warren Harding was able to visit Alaska in time to drive the **golden spike** near Nenana.

Services along the line are both infrequent and slow, pretty much precluding their use as practical transport, but the stately pace and matchless scenery make the **Alaska Railroad** the most pleasurable way to get to the few places it does reach.

With so much of Alaska's tourist industry tied in to the major cruise and package companies it comes as no surprise to find that most trains are

AMHS FERRY CONTACT NUMBERS

When planning and reserving your ferry travel contact the Alaska Marine Highway System, 1591 Glacier Ave, Juneau, AK 99801-1427 (☎907/465-3941 or 1-800/642-0066, fax 907/277-4829), or consult their Web site *www.state.ak.us/ferry*, which has schedule and fare information along with details of how to make reservations. Locally, call the numbers listed below:

Anchorage	☎272-4482	Kodiak	☎486-3800
Angoon	☎788-3653	Petersburg	☎772-3855
Bellingham, WA	☎360/676-8445	Prince Rupert, BC	☎250/627-1744
Cordova	☎424-7333	Seldovia	☎234-7868
Haines	☎766-2113	Seward	☎224-5485
Hollis	☎826-3432	Sitka	☎747-3300
Homer	☎235-8449	Skagway	☎983-2229
Juneau	☎465-3941	Tok	☎883-5667
Kake	☎785-3804	Valdez	☎835-4436
Ketchikan	☎225-6181	Wrangell	☎874-3711

largely made up of luxurious, dedicated Princess and Holland America carriages. Independent travelers will find themselves getting jounced along in less salubrious cars; still very spacious, air-conditioned, and comfortable, but with high-back seats set so low you find yourself standing up to get a good view of the scenery. Of course, you can amble along to the upper-deck **observation car**, or hang out in the **dining car**, which sells good food at only slightly inflated prices. Get there before the lunchtime rush, wait it out until much later, or bring your own tucker. The journey is accompanied by a running commentary complemented by a free route map.

Tickets can be bought in advance from Alaska Railroad Corporation Passenger Services, PO Box 107500, Anchorage, AK 99510-7500 (☎265-2494 or 1-800/544-0552, fax 265-2323, *www.akrr.com*), but seats are not allocated until just before you travel; arrive at the station half an hour early.

Alaska's only other train service is the **White Pass & Yukon Railroad**, an almost exclusively tourist-oriented service which climbs the mountains behind Skagway following a route used by Klondike gold-seekers. It is covered in detail on p.170.

ANCHORAGE TO DENALI AND FAIRBANKS

North of Anchorage the train gradually shakes off the city and the towns of the Mat-Su Valley as it threads through spruce forests, which occasionally draw back to reveal grand vistas of the Alaska Range and Denali. Passengers are always spotting wildlife, and you'll probably see bears, moose, eagles, or at least the evidence of industrious beavers. North of Talkeetna, Denali appears increasingly monstrous, and as you climb towards the Alaska Range the trees thin out providing ever longer views. You see almost nothing of Denali National Park itself from the train, but since almost everyone gets off here that's of little consequence.

Between Anchorage and Fairbanks the main train is the **Denali Star** (daily from mid-May to mid-Sept) which departs Anchorage at 8.15am, stopping at Wasilla (9.45am), Talkeetna (11.25am), and Denali Park (3.45pm), and arriving in Fairbanks at 8.15pm. In the opposite direction the daily service leaves Fairbanks at 8.15am and calls at Denali Park (noon), Talkeetna (4.40pm), Wasilla (6.20pm), and Anchorage (8.15pm). In addition there is the **Local "Flag Stop" Service** (early May to late Sept Thurs–Sun only), which only runs from Talkeetna 55 miles north to Hurricane and back. Designed around the needs of bush dwellers who pull up in their canoes or off-road buggies next to the track and hang out a white sheet to get the train to stop, this is claimed to be the only such service left in the US. It mostly runs through pretty swampy country and so is of little use to hikers, though anglers benefit, and you could just go for the ride to get a taste of bush life. **In winter**, there is the combined **Aurora** service (late Sept to early May), a flag-stop train – usually just two carriages and a luggage car with a very limited buffet service – run from Anchorage to Fairbanks on Saturday, returning to Anchorage on the Sunday; there are no weekday trains.

All **fares** are one-way and depend on whether you travel during the peak season (early June to early Sept) or the value season (mid-May to early June and the second and third weeks in Sept). From Anchorage to Fairbanks the fares are $175 peak, $140 value and there are section fares: Anchorage–Talkeetna ($75, $60); Anchorage–Denali ($125, $100); Talkeetna–Denali ($70, $56); Talkeetna–Fairbanks ($100, $80); and Denali–Fairbanks ($50, $40). Bikes, canoes, and kayaks can be carried on the train at a cost of $20 per trip. If these prices seem too steep and the bus is beckoning, consider making the run from Talkeetna to Denali, the most spectacular section.

ANCHORAGE TO SEWARD

From Anchorage, the line heads south past the wildlife viewing area of Potter Marsh and along Turnagain Arm to Portage Junction, from where the Whittier Spur runs through a couple of tunnels to Whittier. The main line then continues up the Placer River valley into the Kenai Mountains, all plunging gorges overhung by massive glaciers – the Spencer, Bartlett, and Trail glaciers all come within a few hundred yards of the track – before following the broad Resurrection Valley to Seward.

The **Coastal Classic** (mid-May to mid-Sept daily) runs south from Anchorage leaving at 6.45am and arriving in Seward at 11.05am. The return service leaves Seward at 6pm arriving back in Anchorage at 10.25pm giving day-trippers almost seven hours in Seward; the one-way **fare** is $55 (round-trip $90), and bikes cost $5.

A separate service, the **Glacier Discovery** (mid-May to mid-Sept daily), leaves Anchorage at 10am for Whittier arriving at 12.30am. The return service leaves Whittier at 6.45pm and gets into Anchorage at 9.45pm. The fare is $45 one-way, but just $55 round-trip. There are no services south of Anchorage in winter.

BUSES

There are **no winter buses**, but from early May to mid-September all the blacktop roads in Southcentral and Interior Alaska have scheduled **bus services**. In most cases there are only one or two buses a day in each direction, making bus travel possible but not very flexible. The main exception is the 360-mile run from Anchorage past

---

LONG-HAUL BUS COMPANIES AND THEIR ROUTES

Alaska Backpacker Shuttle (☎1-800/266-8625 or 344-8775, fax 522-7382, *www.alaska.com /~backpack*). Daily service between *Anchorage HI* hostel (departures at 8am) to Talkeetna Junction, Denali, Nenana, and Fairbanks visitor center (departures at 9am), plus one day from Anchorage (8am) to Seward (11am) and back.

Alaska Direct Bus Lines (☎1-800/770-6652 or 277-6652, *www.tokalaska.com/directbus.shtml*). One service (three days a week) from Anchorage to Whitehorse via Palmer, Glenallen, and Tok, and another between Fairbanks and Whitehorse (also three times weekly) via Delta Junction and Tok.

Alaskon Express (☎1-800/544-2206, *www .graylinealaska.com*). Large buses run by Gray Line with services from Anchorage to Denali, Seward, Tok, Valdez, and through the Yukon to Skagway. There's a service from Fairbanks to Tok but no connection between Fairbanks and Denali.

Homer Stage Line (Anchorage ☎563-0800, Homer ☎235-2252, Soldotna ☎262-4584). One run from Homer to Anchorage in the morning and back again that afternoon; operates Mon–Sat in high summer, 2–3 days a week in spring and fall

and once a week in winter. Another runs at least 3 days a week (currently Mon, Wed & Fri) from Homer to Seward and back.

Park Connection (☎245-0200, *www.alaska-tour .com*). A daily run in each direction between Seward, Anchorage, Talkeetna township, and Denali; ideal if you want to bypass Anchorage.

Parks Highway Express (☎1-888/600-6001, *www.alaskashuttle.com*). Fairbanks-based service with daily runs between Fairbanks and Anchorage. There are also three runs a week between Fairbanks and Valdez (southbound on Wed, Fri & Sun; northbound on Mon, Thurs & Sat), and a thrice-weekly service between Fairbanks and Dawson City via Tok and Chicken (Wed, Fri & Sun eastbound; Mon, Thurs & Sat westbound).

Seward Bus Line (Seward ☎224-3608, Anchorage ☎563-0800). One daily run from Seward to Anchorage, returning the same afternoon.

Talkeetna Shuttle Service (☎733-1725 or 1-888/288-6008). Once or twice daily during the mid-April to mid-June mountaineering season from Anchorage airport to Talkeetna via the *Anchorage HI* hostel.

the entrance to Denali National Park to Fairbanks, which is plied by several buses each day. In the past, companies have been notoriously short-lived, but there seems to have been increasing stability in recent years. Nonetheless, if you plan to travel by bus it pays to pick up the relevant timetables from visitor centers when you reach Alaska. Detailed coverage of routes, frequency, and journey times is given in "**travel details**" at the end of each chapter, and we've given an outline of the major companies' operations in the box (opposite). Bus stops (usually visitor centers, major hotels, and hostels) are noted in town accounts.

The **biggest player** is Gray Line's Alaskon Express, which operates full-size buses on a daily basis along most of their routes. The exception is the service that links Skagway in the Southeast to the Interior via Whitehorse in the Yukon, which runs three times a week with buses spending the night at Beaver Creek, Yukon. Typical Alaskon **fares** are: Skagway–Tok ($167), Tok–Anchorage ($111), Tok–Fairbanks ($72), Valdez–Anchorage ($70), and Anchorage–Seward ($40).

Almost all other companies run faster and slightly cheaper minibuses, but seldom along the same routes as Alaskon. Along the Anchorage–Denali–Fairbanks route competition keeps fares low with all companies more or less in line with one another. Nonetheless it is worth shopping around as there are bargains to be had, and some companies' timetables work better than others. **Expect to pay** $60–70 between Anchorage and Fairbanks, $30 from Fairbanks to Denali, $40–45 from Anchorage to Denali, $65 from Fairbanks to Valdez, $112 from Fairbanks to Dawson City, Yukon, $30–35 from Anchorage to Seward, and $45 from Anchorage to Homer. **Round-trip** rates are usually twice the one-way fare though there are sometimes small savings to be made.

DRIVING

If you are prepared to make the epic journey up the Alaska Highway, or can afford a rental vehicle, **driving** is the best way to explore Southcentral, the Interior and parts of the North. You can get to places well beyond the reach of public transport, set your own timetable, and access points of interest in the larger towns much more easily. Anchorage and Fairbanks in particular have grown up since the invention of the car and are shaped around the assumption that everyone has one. With the exception of Denali, national and state parks are very poorly served by

public transport. What's more, two or more people traveling together and renting a car can save a fair bit of money by staying in cheaper but less central accommodation, or camping out pretty much anywhere.

Road conditions (call ☎456-7623 or consult the Web site at *www.dot.state.ak.us/external /central/mno/rdrpt_c.html*; pre-recorded travel hotline ☎1-800/478-7675) vary enormously, from four-lane freeways in Anchorage and Fairbanks to remote gravel roads with a hundred miles between settlements. Come in summer, stick to the paved highways, and you'll encounter no more difficulty than driving at home: stray onto dirt roads and you need to slow down and take some precautions. **Snow** is possible in any month of the year, especially on a couple of high passes, and winter really starts showing its face by the end of September. If in doubt, don't travel. If you must, then take it slow and be sure you have survival gear in case of an accident or breakdown. In winter, many of the gravel highways are impassable, but the asphalt roads are kept open year-round.

Though distances are great, **gas** is still relatively cheap. It is about the same as in the Lower 48, and way cheaper than in Europe. Basic unleaded (fine for most rental vehicles) is currently around $1.80 a US gallon (which is equivalent to 3.8 liters) in Anchorage and Fairbanks, $2 further out, and over $2.50 in remote spots. At most gas stations you can use your credit card to pay at the pump, even if it is unattended.

RENTING A CAR

Renting a car in Alaska is not cheap, but for two or more people traveling together it can work out to be good value, particularly if you rent in Anchorage where competition keeps rates down. That said, you can rent a car in almost any small town; sometimes handy if you are normally using public transport but need to get somewhere otherwise inaccessible – the hot springs around Fairbanks for example.

Through most of the summer it is important to **reserve well in advance** (see box, p.41, for contact numbers). Arrive in June without a reservation and you'll be lucky to find anything, and even if you find a vehicle most agencies charge more for walk-ins. Plan to drop off your rental where you picked it up: even the major rental agencies charge high **relocation fees** amounting to around $150 between Anchorage and Fairbanks, and more like $300 between Anchorage and either Haines or Skagway. Some companies don't allow you to go into **Canada**, or charge a fee, so make sure you are clear on this point when you make your reservation. Note that **Canadians** are not allowed to drive a US rental car into Canada.

The other major consideration is whether you will want to drive on **gravel roads**. Most agencies refuse to insure or provide logistical back-up once you stray from the paved highways, and yet seeing many of Alaska's finest features requires travel along just such roads. If this is the case, you won't be able to drive to McCarthy in the Wrangell-St Elias National Park, Chicken and Eagle along the Taylor HWY, Manley Hot Springs near Fairbanks, or along the Steese and Denali highways.

There are a number of ways round this, and the best is to rent from Affordable Rentals (listed in our Anchorage and Fairbanks accounts), who rent almost-new cars at affordable prices and allow them to be used (and insured) on all roads except the Dalton Hwy north of the Yukon River and the Top of the World HWY from Chicken to Dawson City in the Canadian Yukon. A second alternative is to rent from whomever and ignore their rules. This is a common enough practice, but remember that even if you have insurance independent of the rental agency, the fact that you are breaking the rental agreement by driving off the paved highways is likely to invalidate your insurance. Consider too that no one is going to organize a mechanic for you, so if you get in trouble you may have to stump up for large towing bills. The last option is to **rent a 4x4**, most of which can be insured for gravel roads. The downside here is that you'll be paying at least twice the daily rate of an ordinary compact (say $100–120 a day).

Car-rental agencies fall into two main groups. The **majors** – Avis, Budget, Hertz, National, and Dollar – all rent new compacts for around $45–55 a day in summer with unlimited mileage. **Local companies** are usually about $5–10 a day cheaper in return for slightly (sometimes substantially) older vehicles and a poorer back-up network. We've listed the best of these at the end of major town accounts and you'll find more in the local *Yellow Pages*. Many companies offer **weekly rates**, though in peak season the savings are small.

Insurance can raise your car rental fees considerably. If you have your own vehicle insurance at home it is worth checking if it provides any coverage for rentals (either with or without some extension fee): there are no hard and fast rules, but most US policies will cover you in Alaska. When paying by credit card (especially gold cards)

DRIVING TIPS FOR NON-US CITIZENS

In most cases, a **driver's license** from your home country is valid in the United States: check with a national motoring organization if you have any doubt. Road rules are similar to those in the UK or Australasia except that you drive on the right; if you've just come off a long flight, consider waiting a day or so before driving. **Seatbelts** are now compulsory for front-seat passengers. In urban areas the **speed limit** is usually 35–45mph; on the open road 55mph is common and sections of the George Parks Hwy from Anchorage to Fairbanks, and the Seward Hwy south of Anchorage, allow you to belt along at 65mph. If the **police** flag you down, don't get out of the car or start searching for your license; simply sit with your hands on the wheel; when questioned, be polite and don't attempt to make jokes. Of course, **driving while intoxicated** (DWI) is a very serious offense, and if you are carrying any alcohol it should be kept unopened in the trunk.

A couple of things that may be new to you: At junctions you can **turn right on a red light** provided there is no traffic coming from the left; otherwise red means stop. Stopping is also compulsory, in **both** directions, when you come upon a **school bus** with its lights flashing, disgorging passengers. Driving with **headlights on** during daytime is only required along the Seward Hwy (south from Anchorage to Seward), but reflections off water and long shadows cast by the eternal low sun make vehicles less visible, and many people now light up as a matter of course once out of town.

Foreign drivers who are members of motoring organizations may find they can get reciprocal membership at the **American Automobile Association** (AAA; main AK office: 1100 E Northern Lights Blvd, Anchorage; ☎278-4222 or 1-888/391 4222, *www.aaa.com*), which offers maps and guides to international affiliate members who present their valid membership card.

it is also worth checking if this provides any cover. Quite likely you will find yourself faced with a **Collision Damage Waiver** (CDW, sometimes called Liability Damage Waiver), a form of insurance that's well worth considering as it covers you for damage to the vehicle you are driving. It may cost you $12–15 a day but otherwise you are liable for every scratch to the car – even those that aren't your fault. Often CDW comes with several levels of cover, the cheaper ones leaving you liable for, say, the first $1000–2000 of any claim, while the more expensive policies cover you for everything. Always make sure you understand the fine print.

RENTING AN RV

In summer, Alaskan roads and campgrounds are thick with **RVs** (recreational vehicles or motorhomes). Most have been driven up the Alaska Hwy or transported by ferry up the Inside Passage, but many more are rented in Alaska (principally Anchorage) from one of around a dozen agencies. Deciding to rent an RV isn't something to be undertaken lightly: summer rental rates (based on a minimum one-week rental period) start at around $130 a day for a model that's comfortable for two – and on top of that you may have mileage charges, insurance, and a lot of gas (some RVs achieve under ten miles per gallon). Unless you've lugged half your kitchen with you then there may also be a fee for a "housekeeping" kit of pans, plates, bedding, and towels.

All this is offset by the reduction in accommodation costs. Instead of $70–100 a night in a motel you can get away with $18–25 a night for a full hookup in a campground, or nothing at all parked by the side of the road. Some RV-rental companies even offer a free pass for camping in state parks and selected commercial campgrounds around Alaska.

Motorhomes come in several sizes, some lumbering behemoths that are the curse of everyone else on the road, others relatively nimble though

---

RV RENTALS

Almost the following RV rental companies are based in Anchorage, and all offer airport transfers.

ABC Motorhome & Car Rentals, 3875 W International Airport Rd (☎279-2000 or 1-800/421-7456, fax 243-6363, *www.abcmotorhomes.com*). Large company renting late-model RVs with everything included except your gas. Rates start at $160 a day for an upscale camper with shower and toilet and range to $180 for a compact, $200 for a standard and $220 for an intermediate model.

Alaska Motorhome Rentals (☎1-800/254-9929, *www.alaskarv.com*). Smaller company offering compact models for $150, intermediate RVs for $170, and one-way Skagway drop-offs.

Alaska Panorama RV Rentals, 712 W Potter Drive (☎562-1401 or 1-800/478-1401, fax 561-8762, *www.alaskan.com/alaskapanorama*). Family-run RV-rental business with compacts for $140 a day, standards at $155, intermediate models costing $165–175, and large motorhomes for $200 a day.

Alaska Truck & Camper, 502 W Northern Lights Blvd (☎562-0897 or 1-877/562-0897, fax 561-

1437, *www.alaskan.com/alaskacamper*). Company specializing in camper-style motorhomes, with one model ($100 a day) that's only just big enough for two to sleep and cook in, plus large models ($130–145). They offer plenty of free miles even during peak season, and have a one-off fee ($95) for providing a housekeeping kit.

Alexander's RV Rental, 212 E 51st Ave (☎563-5115 or 1-888/660-5115, *www.anc-biz.com/alexandersrv*). Smallish company offering new motorhomes with good shoulder-season discounts. Standard models from $130, intermediate $150, and huge 34-foot beasts for $170 a day. All these are charged at an additional 17¢ a mile.

Great Alaskan Holidays, 3901 W International Airport Rd (☎248-7777 or 1/888/225-2752, fax 248-7878, *www.akholidays.com*). Major player offering rigs with all the extras included. Rates can be unlimited mileage (compact $165, large $185) or charges at 17¢ a mile ($135/$160).

---

obviously less spacious. Generally the smallest offered is the **camperhome** (roughly $130–160), essentially an eighteen-foot flat-deck truck with a camper strapped onto the back. These sleep two reasonably comfortably (and perhaps one child) and have a toilet and cooking stove but not much room to move. A **compact** ($140–180) measures around 21 feet and sleeps two adults and two kids in some comfort. The **standard** 23-foot models ($150–200) are more spacious again with a higher level of fittings and appliances. Two (or even three) couples traveling together might prefer a 26-foot **intermediate** ($180–200) or 30-foot **large** ($200–220) model. The **prices** quoted above are for summer **high season**; rates drop by twenty to thirty percent in May and September, and are reduced a little further in winter, but you'll pay around ten percent more if your rental is for less than a week. AAA and AARP members (American Association of Retired People, *www.aarp.org*) typically get five percent discount.

Some companies (see box, above, for company listings) charge premium all-in rates, while others cut corners on their basic rates, but add assorted extra charges: it is always worth asking. You might find you get fifty or a hundred **free miles** (especially during shoulder season) but most likely you'll pay 15–20¢ a mile. **Insurance** is often included,

but there may be a $1500 deductible on accidents; a collision damage waiver ($12–15 a day) will reduce this to a couple of hundred dollars or less. A housekeeping kit might be a few dollars a day or just a $100 flat fee; TVs, deck chairs, fishing rods, and bike racks may be included or extra; and 24hr roadside assistance may be included.

As with cars, you'll need to make **reservations** early, but once you've got your RV you've usually got access to most highways, including trips into Canada. **One-way rentals** are not usually worthwhile, though some companies will let you pick up or drop off a vehicle in Skagway for a $400 fee, or Seattle for $750. If you are headed north in May and early June it is worth calling around (try ABC to start with) for a delivery run, driving a new RV from the Lower 48 at around seventy percent of the normal rate. The **minimum age** for driver varies from 21 to 25.

If you are bringing your own RV to Alaska but don't want to drive both ways, consider shipping your rig (see "Getting there from the USA and Canada," p.9).

CYCLING

Traveling around Alaska by **bicycle** can be wonderful with plenty of time to savor the stunning scenery, long summer days, and relatively cool temperatures. It can also be a major slog, but this largely depends on where you go and how ambitious your plans. The Southeast is especially well suited for **touring** since you can take your bicycle on the **ferries** and then more easily explore the few miles of road around each port of call. You have to be a bit more dedicated to cycle in the Interior where distances between points of interest are great and (once you get off the main highways) the surfaces can be rough. Where public transport exists, you can usually take your bike on the **bus** (around $5–10 per trip) or **train** ($20 per journey), which makes parts of Alaska very accessible for **mountain biking** as you don't need to pedal every mile just to get to the good trails. With so many gravel roads, fat-tired mountain bikes are the machines of choice. You may never go off-road, but you'll appreciate good suspension and a forgiving geometry on **prime dirt routes** like the Denali Hwy, the Denali Park Road (certain days in May and Sept only), the Steese and Elliott highways around Fairbanks, the Taylor Hwy up to Eagle on the Yukon River, and the McCarthy Road in the Wrangell-St Elias National Park. The Dalton Hwy to Prudhoe Bay is another, though lengthy and esoteric possibility; and in the Southeast, Prince of Wales Island is excellent.

If you are sticking entirely to **paved roads** you'll do better either on a touring bike or with narrower tires fitted to your ATB. Of the paved road routes, the Kenai Peninsula is probably the most rewarding with wonderful scenery, challenging terrain and relatively short distances between towns. For something longer, try the route from Anchorage to Valdez (with a possible side trip to McCarthy) followed by a ferry to Whittier, Seward, or Homer and some time on the Kenai. The George Parks Hwy from Anchorage to Fairbanks is perhaps the busiest and least appealing of the main routes, though you can skip sections by riding a bus or train.

Bikes can be rented in larger towns ($20–30 a day) but for touring it is better to **bring your own bike**. Most international airlines will carry bicycles either free or for a small charge. Some companies will only ask you to remove the pedals, deflate the tires, lower the saddle and turn the handlebars ninety degrees; while others will demand you break it down to fit into a cardboard bike delivery box (usually available free from your friendly local bike dealer): ask before you fly. Before you plan numerous flights around Alaska with your bike it is worth considering that Alaska Airlines is not bike friendly, insisting on the box approach and charging US$50 for each day you fly.

To be fully prepared you should be kitted out for **rain** in the coastal areas, **cold** in the Interior and **bugs** whenever you stop. **Spare parts** are thin on the ground outside Anchorage and Fairbanks so be sure to carry anything you might reasonably need – tubes, cables, spokes, etc. One thing you probably won't need if you are here in the middle of summer is lights; it barely ever gets dark.

For more detailed information consult the *Alaska Bicycle Touring Guide* and *Mountain Bike Alaska*.

HITCHING

Among hitchhikers, Alaska enjoys a reputation for relative safety that seems completely out of step with the scaremongering in the rest of the US. **Don't hitch** remains the official advice, but with Alaska's skeletal public transport network many choose to do so anyway, if only to get back to your car at the end of a long hike. While Alaskan drivers are generally well disposed to picking up hitchers, there aren't many of them, and along gravel roads (where hitching is more common) you could wait hours without seeing anyone. In high summer, though, prospects are decidedly more rosy.

Sadly, Alaska has its share of unpleasant individuals, so always travel in pairs (no guarantee of avoiding trouble but safer than going solo). **Women**, especially, should trust their instincts: it is better to refuse a lift than regret it later, there will always be another vehicle at some point. Always ask the driver where they are going rather than telling them where you are headed, and keep your gear with you so you can make a quick getaway if it becomes necessary. Remember too that even the most helpful driver may drop you in the middle of nowhere with the weather deteriorating. You should really be fully equipped for a night out by the roadside, or make sure you can be dropped somewhere you can seek food and shelter.

Finding a good **hitching spot** is usually just a matter of walking towards the edge of town and using your common sense: pick a spot where you can be clearly seen and drivers can stop safely. Making a destination sign can be a good idea, but with so few roads it is usually pretty obvious where you are going.

ACCOMMODATION

At best, accommodation in Alaska is warm, welcoming, and often comes with a superb view, and maybe even a moose or bear strolling past your bedroom window. Unfortunately it is usually expensive for what you get and, especially in July and August, high demand allows hotels to ratchet the rates up even higher. If money is tight, the cost can be offset to some degree by nights spent in one of the increasing number of hostels or one of the US Forest Service cabins. Camping, too, is a big money saver, and nowhere near as cold as you might expect, especially in the middle of summer when you've got close to 24-hour daylight.

ROADHOUSES, HOTELS, AND MOTELS

The backbone of Alaska's accommodation was traditionally made up of **roadhouses**; all-in-one hotel, bar, restaurant, and stable establishments which cropped up a day's hike (or sled ride) apart along the trails. Most have gone the way of the miners and mail carriers who frequented them, but a few still fly the flag in rural areas typically offering warped floors, shaky beds, thin walls, a bathroom down the hall, and bags of character. Several have been taken over by proprietors who really care about the tradition and go to some lengths to provide good hearty food and a convivial lounge centered on a wood-burning stove. After camping and hostels, these are often the cheapest places to stay at around $50–70 per room.

As communities consolidated in the fledgling territory the roadhouses were replaced by **hotels**. A few originals exist in the larger towns, but the market is dominated by faceless corporate chains aimed squarely at businesspeople and package tourists. Standards are as high as you would expect but the prices are higher, at least in the peak summer months when you won't get a room in a top-line hotel in Anchorage for under $250. Off-season, and especially at weekends, such places are almost empty and prices drop dramatically: haggle a bit and you might find yourself with a tremendous bargain.

Almost invariably though you are better off in a **motel**. These tend to string out along approach roads into urban areas, but since most towns are pretty small this isn't much of an inconvenience. A few belong to nationwide chains, while most are independently run places, though standards vary little. All offer private bathrooms, cable TV and phone (often with free

ACCOMMODATION PRICE CODES

Accommodation listed in this book has been price coded using the symbols below. The rates quoted represent the **cheapest available** double or twin **room** (single rooms generally cost only 10–20 percent less) in high season. Fees for **tent sites** and cabins are quoted and are for the site or cabin unless otherwise stated. Most towns in Alaska impose some kind of local or bed tax, usually between 4 and 11 percent. We've included these taxes in our calculation of the price codes, but it is worth remembering that locally quoted prices will be exclusive of these taxes.

In **winter**, you can generally expect prices to drop by one (or possibly two) price codes except for hostels and campgrounds which don't vary.

① up to $50	④ $80–100	⑦ $160–200
② $50–65	⑤ $100–130	⑧ $200–250
③ $65–80	⑥ $130–160	⑨ $250 and over

local calls, the more upmarket places with phone jacks for Internet connection) for $70–100 a room. A coffee pot and in-room microwave are common, and many motels have at least some rooms with a kitchenette. Pay a little more and everything will be newer, larger, and possibly have a jacuzzi tub, but if you've got this sort of money then there is usually somewhere nicer to stay.

B&BS

The **bed and breakfast** (B&B) phenomenon arrived relatively recently here, but has quickly established a foothold. All over the state home-owners are throwing open a couple of rooms to guests throughout the summer, while others are following the Californian tradition and fashioning their places as boutique inns with every imaginable luxury. Some, recognizing a desire for privacy, offer a separate entrance so you don't feel like you're invading the family home.

If a tent or a hostel bunk is not for you then B&Bs may be the best bet, usually cheaper than a hotel or motel and with a high degree of personal attention. The host may well be your best introduction to the region, either helping plan your travels or just learning more about the state and its strange ways. What's more, there's always a substantial breakfast that may well keep you going past lunchtime. Summer room **rates** start around $80 (with genuinely swanky places charging perhaps $120–150) and there is sometimes a small supplement for stays of only one night, though rarely. In winter, many places close, but those that stay open might drop their rates to around $50 a night.

As ever, it is usually advisable to **book a few days ahead** (weeks if you want one particular B&B), though if you'd rather remain flexible you can get help from visitor centers which often call around the local area on the day and know what's available.

Throughout the *Guide* we've selected some of the best B&Bs in a range of prices, but in most places there are dozens of others, and if you are planning ahead it is worth spending some time browsing some of the B&B Web sites, usually with links to the homepages of each establishment and a provision for making reservations. Good starting points are *www.bbonline.com/ak*, *www.bedandbreakfast.com/USA/Alaska* and *www.bestinns.net/stateindex/ak*.

HOSTELS

For a roof over your head at minimal cost, **hostels** are your only viable option. With dorm beds starting at as little as $7 ($15–18 is more normal) and some establishments offering basic double rooms for $40–50 you can't go wrong. The trouble is, hostels are thin on the ground: Anchorage and Fairbanks are reasonably well supplied, and several smaller places have a hostel but in many regions you can go for hundreds of miles without finding one.

Basically Alaskan hostels come in two flavors. The only established network is the nationwide and internationally affiliated **HI-AYH hostels** (the prefix is shortened to HI in listings) currently with seven hostels around the state — Anchorage, Juneau, Ketchikan, Ninilchik (on the Kenai Peninsula), Sheep Mountain (near Palmer), Sitka, and Tok. Most are very simple and each has its own distinct character and rules. Most Alaskan hostels are still closed during the day (usually 9am to 5pm), maintain a curfew (typically 11pm), have separate men's and women's dorms and expect you to do a small morning chore. You'll usually be allowed to use your own sleeping bag, though a few places insist on a **sheets**, which can be rented at the hostel. No Alaskan hostels currently offer meals, but all provide **cooking facilities**: alcohol, smoking, and, of course, drugs are banned.

Nonmembers can stay at hotels by paying $3 per night over the normal rate, but you can often save money by becoming a member. US residents can get **membership** (free to those 17 and under, $25 for adults and $15 for those 55 and over) at any hostel, through their Web site, or by faxing the national office (there's a downloadable form on the Web site). International visitors should join in their home country (see box, overleaf).

Particularly if you are traveling in the high season it pays to **reserve ahead** directly with the hostel concerned. The credit-card reservation service in place at some other US hostels is not currently used in Alaska, and remember that many hostels are small operations so you'll probably have to pay in cash. The *Hostelling Passport to North America* handbook, published each May, lists more than 200 hostels and is free to members and overnight guests at HI-AYH hostels or direct from the national office.

The number of **independent hostels** is increasing by the year, as people start turning part

YOUTH HOSTEL INFORMATION

HI-AYH have a toll-free reservations system (☎1-800/909-4776) for several dozen hostels within the US, though none of the hostels in Alaska currently have this facility.

Australia 10 Mallett St, Camperdown, NSW 12450 (☎02/9565 1699, fax 9565 1325, *www.yha.org.au*).

Canada 205 Catherine St, Suite 400, Ottawa, ON K2P 1C3 (☎613/237-7884, fax 237-7868, *www .hostellingintl.ca*).

England and Wales Trevelyan House, 8 St Stephen's Hill, St Albans, Herts AL1 2DY (☎01727/ 855215, fax 844126, *www.yha.org.uk*); London shop and information office: 14 Southampton St, London WC2 7HY (☎020/7836 8541).

Ireland 61 Mountjoy St, Dublin 7 (☎01/830 4555, fax 830 5808, *www.irelandyha.org*).

New Zealand PO Box 436, 193 Cashel St, 3rd Floor Union House, Christchurch 1 (☎03/379 9970, fax 365 4476, *www.yha.org.nz*).

Northern Ireland 22 Donegall Rd, Belfast BT12 5JN (☎028/9031 5435, fax 439 699, *info@hini .org.uk*).

Scotland 7 Glebe Crescent, Stirling, FK8 2JA (☎01786/891400, fax 891333, *www.syha.org.uk*).

USA 733 15th St NW, Suite 840, Washington, DC 20005 (☎202/783-6161, fax 783-6171, *www .hiayh.org*).

of their homes into dormitory accommodation. The very short tourist season all but rules out dedicated hostels, so their character and quality is more dependent on the owner (it can go either way), and the restrictions are often looser with similarly varied effects; but in general the standard is high. They're mostly run along the same lines as HI places though sleeping bags are more likely to be acceptable, some places provide sheets as a matter of course, and others are closely associated with local tour and activity companies who often offer discounts to guests. No membership is required at independent hostels, just front up (reserving by phoning ahead at busy times) and sign in.

CAMPGROUNDS

It is quite possible to see most of Alaska without ever going near a campground, but spending nights out of doors is so much part of the Alaskan experience that it seems unsporting to spend every night in comfort. Even if you normally stick to more rigid forms of shelter it is worth bringing a tent; it is the only way you can begin to feel in tune with all that wilderness, and besides, the high price of everything else might just force your hand.

All you need to know for **backcountry camping** – including tent selection – is covered in our Outdoor Activities section (see p.52), but even if you're not about to go trudging off across the tundra you can still spend time in some wonderful campgrounds strung along the highway system. At its most basic, camping involves wandering off

the roadside and setting up camp: no one is likely to bother you if you stay just one night. In practice, this isn't as easy as it sounds, with much of the accessible landscape being unsuitable; either too heavily wooded, or too boggy. You'll occasionally come across free campgrounds with a pit toilet and nearby river water (which needs to be treated), but most campgrounds cost between $6 and $12 per site and comprise a spacious area divided into campsites often separated by trees, picnic tables, fire rings, a hand pump for drawing water, and an outhouse. This isn't usually the traditional wooden shack over a hole, but a concrete structure cleverly designed to minimize odors. You'll soon get used to them; you'll have to.

A few campgrounds have peaceful **walk-in sites** where you must leave your vehicle a few yards away, but most have car parking next to the site. Through the three months of summer many of the more popular places have a campground host who will come round and check you've paid your fees, though sometimes you just drop the money in an "iron ranger," a metal post with a slot in it. The fee is usually per site, typically allowing up to two vehicles and as many as ten or a dozen people, but sometimes (and we've indicated where throughout the book) the price is per vehicle.

The more spacious campgrounds have sites capacious enough to cope with all but the largest **RVs** offering so-called "dry parking," just a place to park with water and toilets accessible nearby. From there you step up to private campgrounds with proper shower and toilet blocks and varying degrees of connectedness: electrical hookup, then piped water, and finally full hookup with waste-water pipe and even cable TV and a modem jack. Tenters will normally pay around $15 in such places, with full hookup going for around $25.

CABINS

A tent undoubtedly gives you maximum flexibility in the wilderness, but sometimes you can save lugging the thing around by staying in **public-use cabins**. They're not intended to be used for a sequence of overnight stops, but are typically treated as a short-term base, with users flying or boating in, then exploring the area on foot or by canoe with an arrangement to be picked up several days later: a true wilderness experience without much struggle.

Several land-management authorities operate cabins, but by far the most numerous belong to the **US Forest Service** (USFS) which maintains over 200 throughout the Southeastern panhandle (the Tongass NF) and Southcentral Alaska (the Chugach NF). Usually they're in scenic or remote spots, sometimes beside a trail, but frequently only accessible by float plane or boat. Ketchikan, Petersburg, Sitka, Juneau, Cordova, and Seward are the closest access points to the majority of cabins, several of which are listed in the text. A full rundown of cabins, their features, access, and availability can be

---

RESERVING CAMPSITES AND CABINS ON PUBLIC LAND

With so many authorities managing public lands in Alaska, booking cabins and campsites can be a confusing business. To simplify the task, we've listed the main players below. All agencies that manage cabins on public lands throughout the state can be accessed from the APLIC Web site at *www.nps.gov/aplic/cabins*.

CAMPSITES

Bureau of Land Management All campgrounds on BLM land are first-come, first-served, there is no booking system.

Denali National Park see "Reserving in Advance" box on p.357.

National Forests There are a handful of campgrounds in the Chugach and Tongass national forests which can be booked through NRRS (see cabins information below).

State Parks and **State Recreation Areas** There is no reservation system for campgrounds in state parks, all are first-come, first-served.

CABINS

Bureau of Land Management The BLM's ten public cabins ($25 per night at weekends, $20 during the week) in the White Mountains north of Fairbanks can be booked up to 30 days in advance by phone (☎472-2251 or 1-800/437-7021) and credit cards are accepted. Alternatively write, or turn up in person at BLM Public Room, 1150 University Ave, Fairbanks, AK 99709-3844. Stays are limited to three consecutive nights and information about the cabins can be found at the White Mountains Web site at *aurora.ak.blm.gov/WhiteMtns*.

National Forests Chugach and Tongass. Around 200 cabins ($25–45 a night, mostly $35 in summer, $25 in the off-season) can be booked using a credit card up to 180 days in advance through the National Recreation Reservation Service (NRRS) by phone on ☎1-877/444-6777 or 518/885-3639 (daily: April–Aug 8am–midnight, Sept–March 10am–7pm EST) and on the Internet at *www.ReserveUSA.com*. The Web site also has some details about the cabins.

State Parks and **State Recreation Areas** Around forty recreational cabins all over the state, sleeping three to eight people and charged at $25–65 a night (mostly $35) plus a $5 reservation fee. Their Web site *www.dnr.state.ak.us/parks/parks.htm* has stacks of information on location, facilities, cost, and even availability, though you can't make reservations. There are no phone reservations either, so to make a booking (up to 180 days in advance) go in person or write to one of the Department of Natural Resources offices such as DNL, 550 W 7th Ave, Suite 1260, Anchorage, AK 99501-3557 (☎269-8400). Booking forms can be printed out from the Web site, payment should be by money order made out to "State of Alaska," and there's a maximum stay of between three and seven days.

...ne Internet (see box, overleaf) or through ...ous USFS ranger district offices which ...listed in the text for each town.

Cabins ($25–45 per night) tend to be clean but fairly primitive, typically sleeping four to six on wooden bunks and coming equipped with a wood-burning stove for heating. There'll be an outhouse, water nearby that needs treating, and possibly a canoe or rowboat. You need to bring everything you'd need for camping except a tent. The cabins are very popular with Alaskans and many are in great demand during hunting and fishing seasons. Nonetheless, with some flexibility and a willingness to visit the less popular areas you can usually find something pretty amazing, especially midweek.

WILDERNESS LODGES

Throughout this book you'll often read of incomprehensibly large pieces of wilderness without so much as a managed trail. It is all true except for tiny pockets around wilderness lodges. There are dozens of them out there, built on the dream of a charmed life in the wilderness. The great majority cater to the rod and gun set, who hunt and fish in remote and uncharted areas but stay in beautifully sited lodges or in cabins around a central lodge where gourmet meals and wines are served. Access is usually by float plane and you might typically expect to stay 3–7 days, often on a package with everything thrown in, including fishing guides and daily flights to remote rivers.

Of course, all of this comes at a price, which can be anywhere from $200 to $800 per person per day, with many places offering three-day packages in the $1200–2500 range, and seven-day packages for around twice that. We've listed a few in the appropriate sections of the *Guide*, but if you are especially interested in this kind of experience then get on the Internet and look at sites such as *www.theoutpostmall.com/alaska .htm* and *www.alaskafishing.com*, which have links to dozens of such places.

A few lodges wear the ecotourism badge, though many of these turn out to be fishing lodges by another name. For guidance here, seek out the assistance of the Alaska Wilderness Recreation and Tourism Association, 2207 Spenard Rd, Suite 201, Anchorage, AK 99503 (☎258-3171, fax 258-3851, *www.awrta.org*).

FOOD AND DRINK

Salmon, halibut, and king crab, lightly cooked, simply dressed, and served within hours of being hauled from cold Alaskan waters is a culinary highlight worth traveling for. Catch it yourself and the pleasure is doubled. After that, things go downhill pretty rapidly and in many parts of Alaska it seems like there is only one menu endlessly recycled with the prices getting higher the further away you get from the transport lines. You'd better like burgers, sandwiches, and clam chowder.

There is no hiding it, food in Alaska is expensive. The growing season is short but intense, and despite the high latitude people do manage to grow **huge vegetables**. The trouble is, few can grow things reliably enough to suit the wholesalers, so most of what you (and the restaurants) buy comes direct from Seattle either by barge up the Inside Passage, or by air freight. This adds to **costs**, that are already inflated because of high wages. Additionally, the range is often limited; most Alaskan communities are small – even large dots on the map might only represent a thousand people – and can't support establishments that cater to anything other than the mainstream demands. Still, for short visits the selection is varied enough, and at its best the quality can be outstanding.

ALASKAN SPECIALTIES

Alaska doesn't really have a distinctive cooking style, but its cuisine stands apart in its use of local ingredients. The treat is tucking into an abundance of **fresh seafood** plucked from the waters around the coast or hauled out of the super-rich rivers inland. Mention Alaska and thoughts quickly turn to **salmon**. The five species of Pacific salmon (see p.503 in Contexts for further discussion of these species) have been canned around the Alaskan coast in vast quantities for over a century and shipped all around the world. As salmon stocks have declined, so has the number of canneries, though a few still exist at remote locations. Most salmon is now vacuum packed for export or frozen ready for delivery to restaurants, the main exception being the **Copper River Kings**, the early season catch (at the beginning of June) being whisked off to Seattle restaurants where they're on a plate within hours of being caught. The better restaurants around the state serve salmon fresh, usually simply prepared, perhaps grilled over alder. It is listed on the menu along with the species – typically **king (chinook), red (sockeye), or silver (coho)** – and sometimes the river where the fish was caught. Freezing robs the fish of some of its delicacy, but if you are sticking to cheaper places and diners, that's what you're likely to get, often stuffed in a burger or even as salmon balls, batter-dipped and deep fried.

Of equal importance on every Alaskan menu is **halibut**, a white-meat flat fish that grows to enormous proportions (over 400 pounds is possible), though it is meat from the 30–50 pound specimens (known as "chicken halibut" for its tender flesh) that ends up on dinner plates, typically as a char-grilled fillet or wedged into a burger. Either way, the delicate flesh is superb. You'll also find more exotic fruits of the sea such as clams, most commonly in a chowder, and crab, sometimes king or, more likely, Dungeness.

Most Alaskans spend at least some of the year dining on their **hunting** acquisitions, principally moose, caribou, and, to a much lesser degree, bear. Though largely absent from restaurant menus, you may taste them at a private barbecue, and can often try caribou stew or moose steak at a salmon bake (see overleaf), or one of the tourist-oriented dinner shows, where the gold-rush stage entertainment is accompanied by tasty morsels designed to mimic the pioneer diet.

Gold prospectors and early trappers aimed to lighten their hard and tasteless bread by using a **sourdough culture**, a yeasty concoction passed from one generation to the next. There are people in the state who claim their sourdough is a distant relative of one that some ancestor carried over the Chilkoot Pass or Valdez Glacier. Sourdough bread remains popular and can be wonderful dunked into a steaming pot of clam chowder. Almost any diner will give you the option of sourdough bread for your sandwich, and will also have sourdough pancakes served up for breakfast. One local delicacy to look out for in May is the fiddlehead, the still-unopened head of a fern that is used in salads and even as a pizza topping in some of the more adventurous restaurants.

You are more likely to hear about **Eskimo delicacies** than taste them. Unlike most Alaskans, Natives are permitted a subsistence harvest of sea mammals such as seals and whales. If you are in one of the northern coastal towns such as Barrow and Kotzebue during the spring and fall hunting season you may be around for a kill. Once it has been butchered, the whale is brought in from the sea ice and some of the blubber, or muktuk, is distributed in the community, and sometimes to visitors. Seal oil was once a staple in the north, and still gets used in Native villages, sometimes for Eskimo ice cream (akutug), a confection in which it is combined with caribou or reindeer fat, sugar, and water, fluffed up into a sorbet and served in a sea of ice and berries – something of an acquired taste.

RESTAURANTS

The staple of the Alaskan culinary scene is the **diner**. Found everywhere, this is where you'll come for **breakfast** ($4–8), the most filling and often the best value meal of the day. The staple is eggs cooked any way you like – scrambled, sunny-side-up, over easy, etc – perhaps with hash browns and bacon, or worked into an omelette with onions, mushrooms, cheese, bell pepper, or sliced sausage. Pancakes are another favorite; either the full stack of three or a "short stack" of two, ample for most appetites. Have them either with maple syrup, or order sourdough or blueberry variations. More upmarket joints may also offer French toast, eggs Benedict or huevos rancheros and all of this comes washed down with as much weak **filter coffee** as you can stomach.

Breakfast is sometimes available all day, but often stops at 11am when the **lunch** menu takes over. Staples here are soups – usually clam chowder plus one other – sandwiches and burgers, in a variety of guises. **Sandwiches** are often served with a packet of chips (not fries), though of course fries are always available. Most diners offer a soup and sandwich combo ($7–9) or the more manageable soup and half sandwich ($5–7). Other favorites include BLTs, tuna melts, and the French dip – a chunk of toasted French bread with meat *au jus*.

In larger towns, diners often close around 4pm or 5pm, but in small communities the diner is the social center and stays open much later serving plates of steak, salmon, and halibut ($16–25), usually with potatoes and vegetables. The entrée (American for the main course) is typically preceded by salad topped by a choice of dressings; blue cheese, Italian, ranch, and thousand island being the most common. If you see something described as a **dinner**, you'll get soup as well as the entrée. There will probably also be Caesar salad ($8–10), pasta dishes ($12–17), and pizza ($10–16) with a huge variety of toppings. **Dessert** is typically fruit pie ($3) sometimes homemade with a fabulous range of fillings – cherry, blueberry, chocolate, lemon meringue – served either on its own or á la mode (with ice cream; $4). The only significant difference between a diner and an Alaskan restaurant is that the latter are licensed, though sometimes just for sales of beer and wine (about $4 a glass and up).

Meals are usually delivered in such huge portions that desserts seem superfluous. If you like a bit of variety it can be frustrating, but at least everyone is happy to "box up" what you leave for later.

Relief from diner boredom can be found at a **salmon bake**, sometimes just a restaurant with a menu heavy with salmon and halibut dishes, but more likely an outdoor venue, or well-ventilated but bug-proof enclosure, where they dish up an all-you-can-eat salmon and halibut feast which extends to ribs, caribou stew, baked potatoes, and a salad bar, usually for $15–20. These are most common in the tourist haunts of Southeast, though Anchorage, Fairbanks and a few other places get in on the act.

Relatively small numbers of **ethnic restaurants** are scattered around the state, many of them very authentic and run by native Mexicans, Chinese, Thai, and Vietnamese. In smaller towns they may well feel compelled to augment their menu with burgers, pizza, and pasta dishes, and sometimes lose their focus entirely. Chinese and some Thai places can be especially good value with heaped plates for $8–10, and all-you-can-eat lunchtime buffets for much the same price.

Fast-food culture is now fairly well established in Alaska, and towns of any size all have at least one of the major chains represented; Anchorage and Fairbanks have most of the familiar names.

If you just want to cut down on red meat, the Alaskan diet is ideal, but **vegetarians** are less well catered for. Still, diner breakfasts are varied, meat-free pizza is almost always available and you can survive for ages on salads and pasta dishes. **Vegans** will find things much harder and may want to spend at least some of their time self-catering.

SELF-CATERING

The lure of money-sucking whale-watching trips and flightseeing around Denali may fuel your desire to **economize** on food expenses. If you are camping, driving an RV, staying in hostels, or seeking out motels with kitchens, you can cut costs (and avoid an overly fatty or meat-laden diet) by cooking your own meals. You might even gather your own ingredients; it is easy enough to **catch your own fish** (salmon and halibut are the prize species), or even gather a bucket of razor clams. Berries – salmonberries, blueberries, wild strawberries, high- and low-bush cranberries – are also good from midsummer to fall and, if you know what you are looking for, there are mushrooms and fiddlehead ferns to be found.

For the less adventurous there are always **supermarkets** – Carr's, Safeway, and IGA are the major names. Every town has one (often at the expense of older grocery stores); in smaller towns just selling groceries, but often acting as the video rental outlet, Western Union counter and liquor store. Larger places may also have an extensive deli, in-shop bakery, fresh-fish counter and useful buy-as-much-as-you-need bulk food bins; while in remote communities, the supermarket may have fast-food outlets and sell everything from Carhartts clothing to snow machines. Near popular hiking areas you may also find **freeze-dried meals**, though you can often prepare something tastier for less money.

Prices depend mostly on location. In Anchorage, non-perishable items are only ten or twenty percent more expensive than in the Lower 48, though stuff like **milk, fresh vegetables**, and **fruit** might be fifty percent more, or even twice what you'd expect. Stores in main towns on the highway system and the larger ports of the Southeast will charge a little more, again with perishable products the worst affected. Visit places such as Dutch Harbor, Kotzebue, and Barrow and you'll find prices get seriously inflated: $4 for a half-gallon of milk isn't unheard of and the range of fresh vegetables may be seriously depleted. Lastly, don't expect grocery store seafood to come cheaply. It may be plentiful, but local wages are high and the prices correspondingly so.

DRINKING

Nights spent chatting in historic roadhouses or spit-and-sawdust wayside bars are likely to be some of the most enjoyable (though poorly remembered) times you'll have in Alaska. At their best, such places are dimly lit convivial places where the owner feels compelled to string up as many moose racks, stuffed salmon, ancient snow shoes, and fly-fishing rods as possible. As often as not you'll find a line of beards in baseball caps deep in conversation which is usually limited to hunting and fishing. In the towns it is a bit more cosmopolitan with Anchorage even boasting a couple of sleek and fashionable cocktail bars, and a slew of excellent microbreweries. But on the whole consumption prevails over style, and something to look out for is the bell all too prominently displayed above the bar in some establishments. Ring it and you're signaling your intention to buy a drink for everyone in the bar.

Sadly, Alaska has one of the highest rates of alcoholism in the US, a figure boosted by frighteningly high rates among Alaskan Natives. In an attempt to combat this problem, **many rural communities ban all alcohol sales** (see box, p.404), and in some cases forbid the transportation of any booze to that town. Elsewhere, the **drinking age is 21**, and anyone who could conceivably be thought to be under age (however remotely) may be asked to produce **picture ID** on entry to a bar. Ordinances also prevent supermarkets selling alcohol, though there is almost always a liquor store next door (or even part of the supermarket with a separate checkout system). **Bar hours** are more lenient and vary depending on who is in that night; only the most inveterate late-night drinker will have trouble finding a bar to lean on. It is a different story in public places where drinking is generally

proscribed. Sipping a glass of wine or beer in a park or on a beach isn't allowed, and America's puritanical attitudes to alcohol prevail even at outdoor festivals where drinkers will find themselves imprisoned in a kind of corral, and certainly not strolling about beer in hand.

American beers fall into two camps: wonderful and tasteless. You may be familiar with the latter, which are found throughout Alaska: light, fizzy brands such as Budweiser, Miller, Michelob, and Rainier costing around $3–4 a pint. The alternative is a fabulous range of microbrewed beers, some arriving in bottles from California and the Pacific Northwest while others are more local concoctions: Juneau's Alaskan Brewing Co is the major regional brewer, and their golden, medium-weight Amber Ale is an excellent starting point. Look out too for the beers from the Fairbanks' Silver Gulch Brewing and Bottling Co (claimed as the world's northernmost brewery) which even has the Anchorage beer cognoscenti taking notice.

Increasingly **Alaskan brewers** are setting up shop in their home towns brewing their own beer and selling it through **brewpubs**, where you'll find handcrafted beers such as crisp pilsners, wheat beers, and stouts on tap, at prices only marginally above those of the national brews (say $4–5 a pint). Anchorage is especially well catered for in this regard, though anywhere with the population to support it will have somewhere with some stainless-steel tanks in the corner. Most bars also stock a fair range of **foreign brews**, particularly European and Canadian beers, and Mexican beers such as Corona, Dos Equis, and the excellent Bohemia.

Beer is usually sold by the glass or pint (four-fifths the size of a British pint), though in all but the most pretentions places, a group can save money by buying a "pitcher" for around $10. Margaritas and daiquiris come by the pitcher too, though at higher prices.

No one has yet managed to successfully grow commercial quantities of grapes in Alaska, so there is no indigenous **wine industry**. Wine drinking is largely confined to restaurants where menus are dominated by Californian varietals at fairly high prices. **Cocktails** are always popular, though if you are expecting the half-price happy hour drinks common in the Lower 48 you'll be disappointed: Alaskan law forbids drink specials, though there is occasionally free food.

Many bars also have some form of **entertainment**, particularly at weekends. Typically this will involve a band in the corner cranking out blues, rock or country tunes with the emphasis on getting everyone up dancing. A **cover charge** is rare though you might be asked for a couple of dollars for the better-known local acts.

COFFEE AND TEA

An increasing social alternative to drinking dens is the **coffee shop** (look for any joint with "Java" in the title). With its longstanding economic and cultural ties to the Pacific Northwest it should come as no surprise that coffee culture is almost as highly developed here as it is in Seattle. The terms **espresso**, **cappuccino**, **and latte** have nearly become meaningless in themselves requiring half a dozen qualifiers before you'll get served anything: size, strength, regular or decaf, type of milk, amount of froth, additional syrup flavors, to go or stay, etc. It can all seem baffling at first, but most baristas are happy to explain, and the coffee is almost always excellent (though proper cups are rare; styrofoam is the norm). The good stuff can also be found in bookshop cafés, drive-in kiosks beside city streets, and in cybercafés where the purchase of a coffee (or any of the snacks and specialty teas on offer) may get you half an hour's free surfing.

Diner **coffee** is filtered, almost tasteless and keeps coming as long as you sit there. For those who don't like it black there is usually a basket of whiteners on the table ranging from non-dairy powders to half-and-half, and thick liquid halfway between milk and cream.

Restaurants also serve **tea**, though visitors from countries where tea drinking is more a religion than a way of quenching thirst will undoubtedly find what's on offer an insipid brew and may be induced to head straight for a coffee shop selling specialist teas, or try one of the herbal infusions also widely available. No matter what you go for it is likely to be inelegantly served by dropping a teabag into a mug of hot water: fish it out when it has reached the required strength.

Corporate America is well and truly entrenched in Alaska and you'll find all your favorite brands of **soft drink**, though the choice diminishes rapidly as you move away from the bigger towns.

OUTDOOR ACTIVITIES

Alaska has more outdoors than just about anywhere else, and a large portion of your time in Alaska is likely to be spent in it. This might be something as gentle as whale-watching in Prince William Sound or wandering along a paved path to the face of a glacier, but could equally involve ten-day rafting trips in the Arctic or hiking the Chilkoot Trail.

With such a vast expanse of territory and a limited transportation infrastructure, access to the wilderness can be an issue, especially if you haven't the money for frequent bush-plane flights or water taxis to remote bays. If you're going out into the bush it is important to try not to do too much but to decide on a couple of areas you most want to visit and concentrate your energies (and resources) on those.

Much of the outdoors is classed as public land, managed by state and federal authorities. Though there are **charges** for camping, access is usually free, with the exception of Denali National Park and Exit Glacier near Seward (both $5 for 7 days) which are run by the National Park Service. They offer the Golden Eagle Passport ($50 for one year from date of purchase) which gives free entry into almost all national parks, preserves, monuments, historic sites, and wildlife refuges in the United States, though this will only be a saving if Alaska forms part of a wider US exploration. US citizens and permanent residents who are 62 or older are eligible for a Golden Age Passport ($10) which is valid for life and also gives free entry to federal areas and a fifty percent reduction on camping fees.

WILDLIFE WATCHING

The single most popular outdoor activity in Alaska is looking for **wildlife**. In many cases it is barely an outdoor activity at all, frequently taking place through the windows of cars, trains, buses, and cruise ships.

Almost everyone who comes to Alaska wants to see whales, bald eagles, grizzly bears, black bears, caribou, and moose, and hopefully more elusive animals such as Dall sheep, mountain goats, wolves, and even polar bears. As long as you spend some time in the Interior and along the coast you should at least see the back and tail flukes of whales, or the rear of a bear as it scuffles away into the undergrowth. It may not be as spectacular as you've seen on TV or in magazines, but with the right mental approach even that feels like a privilege, and sometimes animals come surprisingly close. Undoubtedly the best investment you can make is in a pair of **binoculars**; boats running whale-watching trips and the like will supply several sets, but these may need to be shared around, so having your own is a boon. A pocket-sized 7x20 pair is perfect for most people; larger models are more unwieldy for casual use and higher magnifications can make it both difficult to find your subject and hard to keep the image steady when you do. Buy the best you can afford; quality makes a big difference.

If you are on a bus through Denali National Park or a cruise boat in Prince William Sound, someone will spot something, the driver/captain will stop or slow down and everyone will take photos and video footage until the animal gets bored, or spooked, and moves away. On foot, your approach is more important and your biggest assets will be **patience** and the ability to keep quiet and blend in with your environment. A little prior knowledge about an animal's habits (and the shape of their tracks and scat) should help you choose the right area for viewing, then you can stay in one place and let them come to you. Provided you are not upwind of them, animals may approach very close without even knowing you're there. When approaching an animal, don't try to get too close, and watch for signs that the

animal is getting edgy about your activities. Mammals tend to raise their head and look toward you with ears alert; get closer and they'll either run or get aggressive. Birds will keep their eye on you, cry out or even pretend to have a broken wing when they feel threatened. In either case, back off before they flee, and if birds do fly (especially if they are on a nest) be sure to move on straight away.

Wildlife photography is a specialist undertaking, and people return from Alaska disappointed with their albums filled with shots of brown smudges they claim are bears, and photos of wide open seas where whales were moments previously. If you've any aspiration of returning with quality images, you'll need a camera capable of taking lenses with focal lengths of at least 200mm (preferably 300mm or even 500mm), a tripod (or at least a monopod), and fast film (400ASA minimum) to capture animals in the low light of dawn and dusk when they tend to come out.

For recommended field guides see "Books" on p.504.

HIKING

Hiking in Alaska is no walk in the park, but it is the easiest and least expensive way of getting out into the wilderness. For many it is the main justification for the expense of getting to Alaska, and with good reason. There are few places on earth where it is so easy to get to places where you can walk for days without seeing a soul, and fewer still with such wonderful wildlife. The range of hikes varies enormously from short strolls along a hard-packed trail to see a glacier, to multiday fly-in epics. Many people come to Alaska and stick to the former, and even if you think you are in this category it is worth trying something slightly harder. You may find yourself captivated by stunning vistas of snowcapped mountains, dense dripping forests or vast stretches of tundra rolling away to the horizon.

Most of your hiking is likely to be along formed trails, but in theory you can stop almost anywhere – take a compass and set off for days across ranges of hills and fording rivers. However, the reality can be considerably different. In Southeast, dense forest restricts your passage, and in the boggy terrain of the Interior and North it is all too obvious why Native Alaskans and early pioneers traveled in winter when the rivers were frozen and skis, snow

BACKCOUNTRY DANGERS AND CONSIDERATIONS

For a discussion of keeping warm and dry, and avoiding mosquitoes and other annoyances, read our more general "Health, and well-being" section (p.21); what follows covers dangers specific to backcountry hikers and campers.

BEARS

Alaska's brown (grizzly) and black **bears** don't think of us as food and are seldom a problem, though they're inquisitive animals and in some cases have learned that humans often have snacks stashed away in tents. They don't like surprises, so **avoid bear encounters** by making plenty of noise either by whistling, clapping, singing or strapping a **bear bell** onto your pack. In open country try to walk with the wind at your back – a bear's sense of smell is better than its sight or hearing. **If you see a bear** and it hasn't seen you, move away, keeping downwind if possible; and never get between a mother and a cub. If the bear has seen you, **don't run** – as this tells the bear that you are worth chasing – but stand still, gently waving your arms while talking firmly but calmly and avoiding any aggressive behavior such as staring at the bear. If you look slightly away and move slowly backwards the bear will probably move off, but if it follows, hold your ground. Very rarely they will charge; if they do it is usually a bluff and if you stand firm (or as firm as you can manage) the bear will probably veer away at the last moment. If a bear gets so close it can touch you, fall to the ground, curl up with hands behind your neck and play dead until you are sure the bear has gone. If a black bear (which doesn't have a shoulder hump; see p.500 for more on bear identification) continues to attack, fight back.

Don't **camp** beside salmon streams or near paths worn by bears, usually identifiable by their tracks and scat. Learn to recognize droppings, which are always large but vary in content: grass in spring, animal hair and bones any time, and berries in fall. As they say up here "A Fed Bear is a Dead Bear" and you should do everything you can to prevent bears getting the idea that humans equal free food. Where they've been provided, use bear poles to hang your food or lockers to store it. Otherwise hang your food fifteen feet up a tree (carry rope). Any **smelly items** such as sun screen, toothpaste, and mosquito repellant should stay with the food, and you can probably do without soap and deodorant for a couple of days.

In open areas with no substantial trees, follow the **triangle principle** in which your tent, cooking spot and food storage area are at the points of an equal-sided triangle with sides at least a hundred yards (preferably 200yds) long. Your tent should be the most upwind of the three spots so a bear which does seek out your kitchen or pantry won't go past your tent to get to it. Choose **low-odor food** (not tuna, sardines, or bacon) and keep it stored in airtight containers or Zip-loc style bags. In areas with high bear concentrations you should use a **bear-resistant food canister** (BRFC), a hard plastic cylinder which holds enough food for about four days. These can be bought for around $75 from sports and outdoor stores or rented locally for $4 a day. Take all your **garbage** with you.

Many Alaskans carry a **gun** for bear protection, though unless you have specifically come to hunt, you probably won't have a gun and can survive just as well with the kind of good bushcraft described above. A compromise is to carry a handheld can of **pepper spray** or mace, which can be effective though you need to be careful not to use it directly upwind of yourself, and the range is only around six yards (rather closer than you really want to be). A can costs around $40, has a limited shelf life, and won't be allowed on scheduled flights, so you may feel that you can manage without.

shoes, and dog teams could be put to good use. Off-trail hiking can be an arduous task, watching every step to avoid bog-filled holes, high-stepping onto spongy mounds and then wrestling with low willow and blueberry; for more on hiking in tundra see the Denali practicalities on p.368).

With a short summer **hiking season**, picking your time can have the biggest impact on your wilderness enjoyment. Except for the odd lowland walk, don't even think about hiking in May. Large sections of the trails will still be covered in snow, and similar conditions persists well into June in some areas – strong waterproof boots and gaiters are essential at this time. By July most hikes will be free of snow and starting to dry out, but bugs can be at their worst. Generally the best time for hiking is late summer (mid-Aug to Sept) when days are still long, the ground is as dry as it is going to get, and nights

In Arctic Alaska you are no longer at the top of the food chain. **Polar bears** have been known to stalk humans over several miles, so in their territory you want to be in a very strong vehicle or equipped with a powerful rifle and the ability to shoot straight under pressure. Fortunately, unexpected encounters are rare, and polar bears only really come onshore in the very far north – Kotzebue, Barrow, and Prudhoe Bay for example – when the pack ice is solid, anywhere from October through to May.

RIVER CROSSINGS

When hiking away from formed trails you may well find yourself needing to cross a river, something which causes more hiker deaths each year than bear attacks. Most rivers in Alaska are **glacial rivers** which are very cold, contain silt which makes it hard to pick your route across, and exhibit rising water levels as the sun increases meltwater late in the day – early morning is the best time to cross and you should plan your trip accordingly. If in doubt, wait a few hours (or overnight) and try again, or go back. Pick the widest section of river you can find (it is likely to be the shallowest) and shuffle across facing the opposite shore keeping your feet apart to provide a secure brace. Groups should link up to form a line parallel to the current with the strongest person upstream; lone hikers should find a stout stick to use as a "third leg" which allows you to always keep two points of contact. If you do get swept off your feet, don't panic, rid yourself of your pack (some recommend wearing the pack loosely with the waist belt unbuckled) then float on your back with your feet pointing downstream and swim across the current to the bank. Don't put you feet down; ankles can get trapped.

HYPOTHERMIA

Hikers are usually aware of the possibility of hypothermia, though most cases occur under relatively benign conditions (say 30–50°F) when

people are least prepared. Always dress in layers: synthetic materials – polypropylene and fleeces – are best as they are warm, lightweight, and dry quickly. Avoid cotton (including jeans) as it provides little warmth, and none when wet. A windproof and waterproof layer (preferably breathable) is also essential, and you should beware of wet clothing – change after a river crossing and keep your wet gear to use for the next one. It is also a good idea to keep feeding yourself warm food and drinks, so a portable stove is quite important.

If anyone in your party exhibits symptoms of lethargy, irrational behavior, muscle cramps, and even taking off clothing claiming they are hot then you should treat them for hypothermia. Keep them out of wind and rain, ensure they are wearing dry clothing, and feed them high-energy foods and hot drinks. A sleeping bag and human warmth are the next stage. In extreme conditions send for medical assistance.

WATER PURIFICATION

Water from a spigot or pump in a campground should always be safe to drink, but any gathered from streams and lakes (no matter how clean it looks or how remote the area) should always be purified to kill the parasites which cause giardia. Many people carry a **water filter**, which must be rated down to five microns. Though convenient, filters are just one more thing to carry, and easily clog up in the silt-laden glacial waters; you should let any silty water settle overnight before filtering. **Iodine** tablets and solutions are just as effective if properly used and weigh next to nothing, though with very cold water you may need to leave it for twenty minutes before drinking. The iodine also leaves a slight taste which can be ameliorated by adding a small amount of powdered fruit drink which also gives you extra energy from the sugar. Be sure to add the powder after the iodine has done its job. **Boiling** water for at least five minutes also works but is inconvenient when hiking.

aren't that cold. In the North you might even see the aurora at this time.

Most land in Alaska (and almost all the territory covered by hikes in this book) is **public land**, owned either by the federal or state government and managed through a confusing array of bodies – national parks, national forests, state parks, and reserves of various kinds. With the exception of complex rules in Denali, and a booking system for the Chilkoot Trail, there is **no reservation system** for trails in Alaska, though restrictions exist for campsites and cabins (see "Accommodation," p.47).

No matter where you are going, you should always leave a reasonably detailed **trip plan** with someone responsible, and be sure to check in when you return. Besides a few short walks close to town, most of the hikes in this book will be more of a wilderness experience than you are used to. Conditions could be harsh, you may not see anybody for days, cell phones will be out of range, and nobody is going to come and help until after you are due back, which may be a couple of days away. Since you will need to be entirely self-sufficient, we've given a few helpful pointers below, but they are no substitute for discussing your plans with local park and forest service rangers, making sure your map-reading skills are well honed, and using a good deal of common sense.

EQUIPMENT

Some parts of Alaska have backcountry cabins, but most are not sited on hiking trails and can often only realistically be reached by float plane. Consequently, to spend any time hiking in the backcountry you'll need to bring a fair amount of equipment. If you live outside the US it is worth considering buying gear once you arrive. Anchorage has a good stock of outdoor stores selling **competitively priced gear** (particularly American manufactured goods), and charging no sales tax.

Put some thought into your choice of **tent**. A freestanding dome-style tent (or some variation on that theme) avoids trying to drive pegs into rocky Alaskan campgrounds, or trying to make them stay put in boggy tundra and the loose gravel of river bars. Something rated for **three seasons** is a minimum requirement since high winds and driving rain strike at any time of the year: a four-season model is better still. Remember that it can snow in any month in Denali, and tents injudiciously pitched in river valleys are frequently blown inside out throughout the summer. If you want to get any sleep at all, make sure it is also completely **mosquito proof** with an ample expanse of fine-mesh netting.

Campfires are not permitted in many areas, and the few huts and shelters you'll come across have only a heating stove unsuitable for cooking, so you'll need to carry a **cooking stove** and fuel. Something burning the efficient, widely available, and cheap **white gas** (aka Coleman Fuel; around $4 a gallon) is the best bet. Canisters for propane and butane stoves are only sporadically available (EPIgas is unavailable), and it is worth noting that owners of Trangia stoves will have difficulty obtaining methylated spirits (denatured alcohol in US parlance). It can be found at REI in Anchorage and in some hardware stores but costs roughly three times the price of Coleman Fuel and you'll go through it quicker; a serious consideration if you're spending a few nights in the backcountry.

A further issue is that airlines will not carry fuel (or even a bottle smelling of fuel) on scheduled flights. If you a charter a bush plane, some provisions will be made for flying fuel in, but if you are on a scheduled service to a bush town you want to be sure you can buy fuel when you get there: the best bet is to carry a stove which will burn standard unleaded gasoline (petrol). MSR make several compact, quality models which burn both Coleman Fuel and unleaded gasoline without modification.

You'll also want to bring along some form of insulated **sleeping mat**, a warm **sleeping bag**, some reliable method of **purifying water** (see box, overleaf), a detailed **map**, **compass**, **insect repellent** and an insect-proof **head net** (not stylish but you won't care). Extras might include **waterproof matches** and a lighter, a **first aid kit**, a signaling device such as a **whistle**, light or flare, and strong **plastic bags** for keeping clothes and sleeping bag dry.

MINIMUM IMPACT HIKING AND CAMPING

Wherever you go you should always practice **minimum impact** hiking and camping, but nowhere more so than in Alaska. Like all Arctic and sub-Arctic regions, the Alaskan landscape is very fragile and a small amount of damage can take a long time to recover: tundra plants grow so slowly that vehicle tracks can take decades to disappear and ten-foot-high trees only a few inches in diameter might be a hundred years old.

How you go about minimizing your impact depends on where you are hiking. On well-formed trails you'll probably be following familiar rules: stick to the trail, walk in single file, don't cut switchbacks, and only camp at designated sites where others have camped. When hiking in Denali or anywhere away from managed trails you do the exact opposite, the idea being that in trackless areas you should do what you can to avoid creating tracks. We've discussed this in more detail in our Denali account (p.366), but essentially you walk in small groups fanned out across the landscape each finding your own route, then camp where there is no evidence of previous campers, being sure to move on every day or so. Ensure you leave nothing behind, avoid lighting fires, and where possible camp on **river bars** where the evidence is washed away in spring floods. The breeze on river bars often keeps the bugs down as well, but you need to be prepared to move if rains cause the river to rise. Some people even carry light comfortable shoes to minimize the impact around the campsite.

Maintaining your personal hygiene can adversely affect the fragile environment. Bury **human waste**, and ashes from your burnt toilet paper, in a shallow hole at least a hundred feet away from a watercourse. If you bury it too deep, the permanently cold ground won't support decomposition. **Soap** should be used sparingly if at all; even biodegradable soaps take a long time to decompose up here and hikers downstream may be using the river for drinking water. Pots can be cleaned with river sand and hot water, and any sudsy water you do create should be discarded well away from streams and standing water.

RAFTING, CANOEING, AND KAYAKING.

Most people shy away from immersing themselves in Alaskan waters, but that doesn't rule out **rafting**, **kayaking**, and **canoeing**. Except for on commercial white-water rafting trips, visitors seldom get very wet, the emphasis mostly being on gentle appreciation of the surroundings, and maybe a bit of fishing. People do go kayaking on the inland rivers, but by far the majority of people kayaking in Alaska restrict themselves to coastal regions where you can paddle among whales in sight of huge tidewater glaciers.

RAFTING

Rafting trips in Alaska fall into two broad categories: float trips, usually on gentle water where you'll spend your time admiring the scenery and spotting wildlife; and white-water trips, where the focus is on getting wet, though the scenery is usually spectacular as well.

In a few places along the highway system, and even in Southeast, you'll find short **float trips** only a couple of hours long, perhaps finishing off with a barbecue beside the river, but many more are specialist multiday affairs through genuinely remote wilderness areas such as in the Gates of the Arctic National Park, the Noatak National Preserve, or Arctic National Wildlife Refuge. Some are even up to two weeks long and may make up your entire vacation, in other words your options are wide open.

White-water rafting trips exist mostly in a few road-accessible areas in the Interior and on the Kenai Peninsula. If you have been white-water rafting outside the US you may be used to small rafts entirely controlled by paddle-wielding

customers. Here, larger rafts are the norm, with the guide maneuvering the raft using oars, leaving the customers pretty much as passengers. On wilder trips, customers are armed with paddles though the guide still has ultimate control. Pure paddle rafting is a rarity here, and while this is undoubtedly a very safe way of running rafting trips, it does take the edge off the excitement of pulling together as a team to get through the rapids. The main rivers for short trips are Six-Mile Creek near Hope, the Matanuska River near Chickaloon, and the Nenana River by Denali National Park. There are also multiday trips, usually combining white-water rafting, wildlife viewing, and a complete wilderness experience: the pick of these are the Talkeetna River near Talkeetna and the Alsek and Tatshenshini rivers which are rafted from Haines.

If you can get a group together and have some backcountry experience you might want to **rent a raft** then charter a plane to fly you into the headwaters of some remote river and float down to some prearranged meeting point. Multiday trips usually involve a lot of drifting and occasional stretches of white water, which you can often **portage**, by carrying the raft around the worst of the rapids. It can be a heavy and tiring job, so it is good to learn how to **line** your vessel, allowing the raft to follow the river while you walk the bank holding on by a rope.

Companies running such trips are listed in the relevant sections of the *Guide*, and there's a good listing of Alaska river-rafting guides at *http://alaskan.com/outdoors/rafting.htm*.

CANOEING AND RIVER KAYAKING

Alaska has over a hundred **rivers** suitable for **canoeing and kayaking**, ranging in difficulty from flat water to some of the wildest water anywhere (see box, overleaf, for river grading). Some are road accessible, but there are often long distances between put-in and take-out, and access can still be difficult since car-rental agencies don't like renters putting racks on their cars and often don't allow driving on gravel roads. Consequently keen river paddlers are better off driving up from the Lower 48 or Canada and bringing their own gear. Rental kayaks and canoes are available but most companies have strict rules as to what rivers you put them in.

Some of Alaska's finest inland paddling is on **lakes**, particularly several sequences of lakes and easy rivers that can be combined into

RIVER GRADING

Both rivers and rapids are **graded according to the six-level system** below. The river class is dictated by the most demanding rapid. This lends itself to some creative thinking, since a river hyped as Class V might be almost entirely Class III with one Class V rapid. For those looking for an adventure, the expression to look out for when browsing brochures is "Continuous Class IV." Float trips, where the emphasis is more on the scenery and wilderness experience, tend to be on Class I and II rivers.

I Fast water and a few small waves.

II Choppier wave patterns and easily avoided rocks increase the dunking potential for inexperienced kayakers, though it is no problem in a raft.

III Bigger but still easily-ridden waves make this class bouncy and fun, though there may be more technical sections. Good proving ground for first-time rafters.

IV Huge, bouncier, and less predictable waves churned up by rocks midstream demand much

greater boat control and teamwork. This makes for excellent fun but dramatically increases the chance of a swim.

V Serious stuff with chaotic standing waves, churning narrow channels and huge holes ready to swallow you up. Best avoided by first-time rafters but thrilling for the experienced.

VI Dicing with death. Grade V taken to new heights; commercially unraftable and only shot by the most experienced of paddlers.

overnight or week-long trips. Much of the best lake paddling is not accessible by road, requiring bush flights to the access points. Rigid shell canoes and kayaks don't lend themselves to easy transport and those pilots who do fly them in – usually strapped to the floats of a floatplane – will often insist on a separate passenger-free flight for the boats, thereby adding to the overall cost of the trip. To get around this, many people opt for a **folding kayak** (sometimes known as a Klepper, in recognition of one of the most common brand names), typically a slot-together aluminum frame with an outer coating of plasticized canvas. These can be surprisingly rigid and hold enough gear for a two-week trip or longer. Rentals are sometimes available, but if you are doing an extended trip it often works out better to buy one and make sure it is comfortable and equipped to your specifications.

No matter where you are going, you'll need to do a little **advance planning**, best done by reading the river guidebooks listed in "Books" (p.504) and contacting one of the Public Lands Information Centers (see p.27), where you can also obtain their free *Planning a River Trip in Alaska* leaflet. You must also keep in mind the potential **dangers**, and remember that you'll need to be totally self-reliant; it may be days before anyone comes looking for you. Most Alaskan rivers are fed by snow melt and are incredibly **cold** and you should never underestimate how quickly a dunking can turn into a serious situation. To reduce the chances of a

swim you should lower your estimate of your abilities by one class, so if you normally paddle Class III, then you shouldn't be looking at anything harder than Class II in Alaska. There's no substitute for getting sound advance information about the river, but you should also **scout ahead**, even if you think you can cope with upcoming obstacles. Remember that damaging a boat or losing a paddle can mean a very long, arduous, and possibly life-threatening walk out. In addition, rapids aren't the only problem; rivers often meander through forested river valleys cutting away at the outside banks until trees along the bank fall in creating perhaps the biggest threat of all, **sweepers** (aka strainers) which drag their branches in the water and are deadly if you get washed into them [you don't get washed around them like you would a rock but get sucked under into a impenetrable tangle of branches]. If anything they are more common on easier class rivers posing a particular challenge to the inexperienced. Always steer well clear. Where there are log-jams or harder rapids than you are prepared to tackle you'll have to portage around the obstacle, or line your boat through (see "Rafting", overleaf, for explanations of both terms).

SEA KAYAKING

For most visitors the majority of Alaska's stupendously scenic coastline – longer than that of the rest of the US put together – remains inaccessible. You can ride the ferries and take a wildlife viewing cruise, but to see everything at your own pace the solution is **sea kayaking** (sometimes known here as blue-water paddling). Huge expanses of water sheltered from ocean swells by protective islands make Alaska a perfect sea-kayaking destination, and enthusiasts turn up with their own gear to spend weeks paddling along the coast, particularly around Misty Fiords National Park, Sitka, Glacier Bay, Prince William Sound, Resurrection Bay, Kachemak Bay, and Kodiak Island. For **beginners**, it needn't be as daunting as it might at first sound, and every summer hundreds of people with no paddling experience join guided trips ranging from a few hours to several days.

At their most basic, commercial trips might depart the harbor of a Southeast port and paddle around the wharves and along the nearby coastline, but it is only a small step up to transport a kayak to the face of some nearby glacier and paddle around. Longer trips may extend to several days, camping out each night and spending the next day moving on to the next campsite: kind of like hiking without a pack.

If you already have some experience you may want to **go it alone** either with your own equipment or gear rented locally: a double kayak always works out much cheaper than two singles and you can move quicker. You'll need to show the rental agency some evidence of your abilities, and should also have a solid knowledge of **winds and tides**, both of which can be treacherous even during the main mid-May to August paddling season. Be prepared for all eventualities no matter how benign the conditions when you set out, and always carry a couple of days' extra food and fuel in case you are delayed.

For kayak camping trips you'll need to put everything in small waterproof bags that will fit in the kayak; if you get wet and cold the last thing you need is a sodden sleeping bag. Always file a **trip plan** with friends or the agency managing the area, try to stick to it whenever possible, and let them know when you get back. Lastly, if you've arranged for a boat or plane to pick you up at a particular time, be sure to have a contingency plan in case something turns against you.

FISHING

In some circles Alaska is synonymous with **fishing**, and many people base their whole vacation around the pursuit of the fighting **salmon** and **trout** (see Contexts on p.502 for discussion of fish species) in the rivers of Southcentral and the Interior. Although there are a lot of fish out there, there can also be a lot of people lining the more accessible rivers so keen anglers should try to increase their chances by hiring **fishing guides** (costing perhaps $100–150 for half a day) or staying in isolated **fishing lodges**, where the remote locations have kept the fish-per-angler quotient high. You can still catch fish without going the big-money route simply by fishing in rivers you pass on your travels, or when you are out hiking or on backcountry trips. If you've got a lightweight rod at home, bring it along, or purchase one of the compact models that you can keep in your day-pack. Your chances of catching trophy-size fish are slim, but if you are just after something for your evening meal then a quiet hour or two by the riverside could hardly be better spent.

Even visitors who would never consider lugging fishing tackle around the state find themselves on **halibut fishing** trips, hoping to land a fifty-pound fish that will keep them in filets for the rest of their trip. Some end up landing a monster four or five times that size and have to give most of it away.

The **regulations** about where and when you can fish, your bag limit, and so forth are complex and for the latest information you should consult the Alaska Department of Fish and Game, PO Box 25526, Juneau, AK 99802-5526 (☎465-4100) who have a very informative Web site at *www.state.ak.us/local/akpages/fish.game*), which has all the rules, links to handy publications, and the latest fishing news and feature stories. The most important thing to know is that before you start fishing you'll need to get an Alaska State sport **fishing license** for non-residents which costs $10 for one day, $20 for three days, $30 for a week, $50 for two weeks, and $100 for a year. If you are going after king salmon you'll additionally need a king salmon tag ($10 a day, $20 for three days, $50 two weeks, and $100 for a year). Licenses are available from some 1200 shops and agencies around the state so there will always be one somewhere close by.

NIGHTLIFE, FESTIVALS, AND PUBLIC HOLIDAYS

Few places are as seasonal as Alaska, and most of the businesses you are likely to come into contact with are well attuned to making money while tourists are around. Consequently you'll find shops, cruises, tour offices, and restaurants have long opening hours every day of the summer, the only exceptions being public holidays - Memorial Day, Independence Day, and Labor Day - when some businesses may close. Museums are mostly open 10am–5pm throughout the week, with visitor centers usually staying open a little longer.

During the winter months most tourist-related businesses shut down altogether or operate vastly reduced hours; you should always call ahead to check opening hours and off-season schedules.

HOLIDAYS AND FESTIVALS

Many of the festivals listed below are covered in more detail in the relevant section of the *Guide*; **public holidays** are in bold.

JANUARY

New Year's Day (January 1).

Martin Luther King Day (Jan 15).

Russian Orthodox Christmas (Jan 7). Solemn services held in Kodiak, Sitka, and elsewhere.

FEBRUARY

Yukon Quest International Sled Dog Race (second week). Starts or finishes in Fairbanks.

Ice Climbing Festival near Valdez (middle week). Competitive ice climbing in Keystone Canyon.

Iceworm Festival in Cordova (middle weekend). Giant model iceworm paraded through the streets and general carousing.

President's Day (third Mon).

Fur Rendezvous in Anchorage (second to third weekend). Ten-day citywide "Fur Rondy," packed with uniquely Alaskan activities and events.

MARCH

Ice Carving Competition in Anchorage (first week).

World Ice Art Championships in Fairbanks (first two weeks). Major competition with larger-than-life sculptures.

Nenana Ice Classic Tripod raising (first weekend).

Iditarod Trail Sled Dog Race from Anchorage to Nome (for 12 days from first Sat).

Miners & Mushers Ball in Nome (second Sat). A black-tie ball coinciding with the Iditarod.

Bering Sea Ice Golf Classic in Nome (third Sat).Fund-raising 6-hole golf on ice.

Seward's Day (last Mon). Commemorates the signing (on March 30, 1867) of the treaty by which the United States bought Alaska from Russia.

Pillar Mountain Golf Classic (last weekend, or first in April). One-hole par 70 cross-country golf.

APRIL

Good Friday and **Easter Monday** (late March or early April).

World Extreme Skiing Championships near Valdez (first week). Has a parallel snowboarding event. *www.wesc.com*.

Alaska Folk Festival in Juneau (second week). ☎754-3316, *www.juneau.com/aff*.

Garnet Festival in Wrangell (third week).

MAY

Shorebird and Wooden Boat festivals in Homer (first weekend).

Copper River Delta Shorebird Festival in Cordova (first weekend). Serious bird-watching and associated events.

Little Norway Festival in Petersburg (third full weekend).

Memorial Day (last Mon). Signals the beginning of the summer season.

Polar Bear Swim in Nome (Memorial Day).

Kodiak Crab Festival (last weekend).

JUNE

Blues on the Green in Anchorage (first or second Sat). Alaska's premier blues festival, *www.sourdough.com*.

Colony Days in Palmer (second Fri).

NIGHTLIFE

With those **long Alaskan evenings** the tourist day doesn't need to stop at 6pm, and strolling along a Southeast boardwalk after dinner, or along a sub-Arctic beach at midnight with the sun still in the sky can be one of the trip's highlights. In small towns and anywhere off the beaten path the sun may be your only evening entertainment, though there will always be a local bar or movie theater around. If you are lucky you might find a **band** playing, though your chances are greater in the bigger towns where a few well-known names

have a loyal following. The music is seldom edgy, and is more likely to be a solid rock or blues band churning out reliable danceable tunes. You may also come across acoustic sets by Alaska's coterie of singer-songwriters. Out-of-state bands occasionally make it up here to play big venues in Anchorage and Fairbanks, and perhaps one of the summer festivals (see box, below).

In some of the most popular destinations you'll find events laid on especially for tourists. In areas with significant Native populations – particularly in coastal areas – groups perform **traditional dance** usually in full costume and often in a

---

Sitka Summer Music Festival (first three weeks). ☎747-6774, *www.sitkamusicfestival.org.*

Summer Solstice Celebrations in Fairbanks (weekend nearest to June 21). Fun run, midnight basketball, etc.

Midnight Sun Festival in Nome (weekend nearest to June 21).

Nalukataq in Barrow (mid- to late June). Celebration of the end of the spring whale hunt.

Edward Albee Theatre Conference (last week). ☎834-1612, *www.uaa.alaska.edu/pwscc.*

JULY

Independence Day (July 4). Street fair and fireworks in just about every town in the state.

Mount Marathon Race in Seward (July 4).

Forest Faire in Girdwood (around Independence Day). ☎783-2931.

Moose Dropping Festival in Talkeetna (second weekend).

World Eskimo-Indian Olympics in Fairbanks (second week).

Golden Days in Fairbanks (second two weeks).

Kodiak Bear Country Music Festival in Kodiak (middle weekend).

Hunter Creek Bluegrass Festival near Palmer (last weekend). Info on ☎338-3743.

Anderson-Clear Bluegrass Country Music Festival, Mile 283 Parks Hwy (last weekend).

AUGUST

Talkeetna Bluegrass Festival at Mile 102 Parks Hwy (first weekend). ☎696-1668.

Tanana Valley State Fair in Fairbanks (second week). ☎452-3750, *www.tananavalleyfair.org.*

Blueberry Arts Festival in Ketchikan (second week). ☎225-2211.

Alaska State Fair in Palmer (late Aug to early Sept). Ten days over two weekends.

SEPTEMBER

Labor Day (first Mon). Signals the end of the summer season.

Rubber Duck Race in Nome (Labor Day). Sub-Arctic pooh-sticks. ☎443-5549.

Bathtub Race in Nome (Labor Day). A wheeled bathtub push.

Blueberry Festival in Seldovia (weekend nearest Labor Day).

Equinox Marathon in Fairbanks (nearest Sat to Sept 21). *www.fairnet.org/rcn/rcn.html.*

Potato Festival in Willow (last Sat). Largest potato sculpture competition. ☎495-6457.

OCTOBER

Oktoberfest in Kodiak (first Sat). German music and food. ☎486-5557.

Columbus Day (second Mon).

Alaska Day (Oct 18). Anniversary of the formal transfer of the Territory from Russia and the raising of the US flag at Sitka in 1867.

Alaska Day Festival in Sitka (Oct 18).

NOVEMBER

Veteran's Day (Nov 11).

Thanksgiving (last Thurs).

DECEMBER

Talkeetna Winterfest in Trapper Creek (last three weeks). ☎733-2330.

Bachelor Society Ball and Wilderness Woman Contest in Talkeetna (second week).

Christmas Day (Dec 25).

replica of a traditional house. In the Interior and parts of Southeast it is the gold-mining heritage that holds sway, and mock-up saloons are host to

music hall shows, typically with performers in c.1900 costume and sometimes staying in character while waiting tables.

DIRECTORY FOR OVERSEAS TRAVELERS

ADDRESSES AND MILEPOSTS Larger Alaskan towns follow the straightforward grid system used elsewhere in the country whereby the Anchorage address 3901 Old Seward Hwy will be at the intersection of Old Seward Hwy and 39th St. In rural areas, every Alaskan highway – Alaska, Richardson, Glenn, George Parks, Taylor, and so on – is demarcated by mileposts marking the distance from the town regarded as the beginning of that highway. Addresses along that highway are simply given as the milepost reading to the nearest tenth of a mile.

CIGARETTES AND SMOKING The legal age for smoking in Alaska is 19. Vendors are required to keep them out of reach and not on display. Cigarettes and cigars are widely considered antisocial and, as in many other states, most public areas ban smoking and restaurants must provide a non-smoking section.

DEPARTURE TAX There is no Alaska-specific departure tax. US departure tax is included in the price of your air ticket.

ELECTRICITY Alaska uses the same power supply as the rest of the US: 110 volts at 60Hz. North Americans can use appliances with no

modification; pretty much everyone else will need a plug adapter and some form of transformer.

FLOORS In the US, what would be the ground floor in Britain is the first floor, the first floor the second floor and so on.

LAUNDRIES AND SHOWERS Many rural Alaskans live in cabins without running hot water and laundromats almost always have showers to cater to them and campers. Showers cost around $3 plus 50¢ for a towel.

MEASUREMENTS AND SIZES The US has yet to go metric, so measurements are in inches, feet, yards, and miles; weight in ounces, pounds, and tons. American pints and gallons are four-fifths of Imperial ones. Clothing sizes are always two figures less than they would be in Britain – a British woman's size 12 is a US size 10 – while British shoe sizes are half a size below American ones for women, and one size below for men.

PHOTOGRAPHY AND FILM Photography in Alaska has special demands requiring a lens as wide as 28mm to really capture the magnificent scenery, but something as long as 300mm (and consequently a tripod) if you don't want to have to explain that the distant brown smudge is a bear. Most point-and-shoot cameras will not return decent wildlife shots. Remember too that the best time for seeing animals is at the end of the day when light levels are low and shadows are long. Low light levels increase the need for faster films, usually 400ASA or better. Film and camera equipment is widely available in the larger towns, though in the more remote areas you'll be limited to the most popular film types. Prices are tolerable, though you may want to stock up before leaving home.

SHOES To avoid traipsing mud everywhere many Alaskans (B&B hosts included) ask you to remove your outdoor footwear.

SOUVENIRS Craft items bearing the Silver Hand logo are supposed to be authentic Native Alaskan handiwork; those marked with a polar bear symbol claim to be non-Native but Alaskan-made goods. For more on Native craft purchases, see the box on p.212.

TAXES There is no state sales tax, but some communities (particularly in Southeast) impose their own sales tax (typically 2–5 percent) and many cities charge an additional bed tax of 2–6 percent.

TIME ZONE Alaska Standard Time is observed throughout the whole state (except for a few far western Aleutian Islands not covered in this book) and **daylight saving** is observed from the first Sunday in April to last Sunday in October. In summer, when it is midday in Anchorage it is 1pm in Vancouver, 1pm in Seattle, 4pm in New York, 9pm in London, 6am in Sydney, and 8am in Wellington.

TIPPING You should always tip the waiting staff in a bar or restaurant at least fifteen percent, though something less will do if you are sitting at the bar. Failing to tip or under-tipping causes a lot of embarrassment and nasty looks, and a short pay packet for the waiter/waitress at the end of the week. That said, don't fret excessively if you've only got a dollar when you should really be tipping $1.50. No one is going to run you out of the restaurant, though it pays to keep a few small bills handy. A similar percentage should be added to taxi fares, and rounded up to the nearest 50¢ or dollar. A hotel porter should get roughly $1 for each bag carried to your room. When paying by credit card you are expected to add the tip to the total bill before filling in the total and signing.

VIDEO Like the rest of North America, Alaska uses the NTSC TV and video standard which is incompatible with the PAL system used in most of the rest of the world. If you buy a video, make sure it is in the right format or be prepared for an expensive conversion (though modern VCRs are often configured to play both formats).

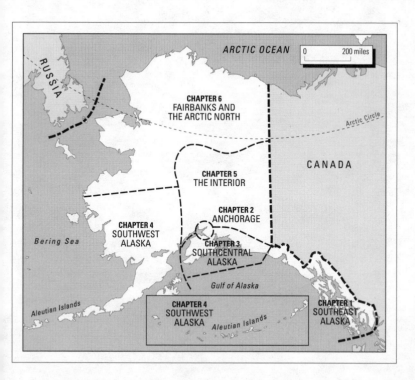

CHAPTER ONE

SOUTHEAST ALASKA

V isitors arriving in **SOUTHEAST ALASKA** have a treat in store, a landscape writ on a grand scale, stretching four hundred miles along the coast. This is the Alaskan Panhandle, flanked by impenetrable snow-capped coastal mountains and incised by hairline fjords which create an interlocking archipelago of densely forested islands. Along its length runs the continuous thread of calm waterways known as the Inside Passage. So narrow are some of the glacier carved channels that on larger boats you feel you could reach out and touch the steeply shelving rocks. Sheltered beaches are rare, and out of necessity, towns are crammed onto whatever flat land can be found, often spilling out over the sea on a network of boardwalks: shops, streets, and even whole salmon canneries are perched along the waterside, linked by picturesque spruce poles.

Like much of Alaska, Southeast is defined by its weather, though here the moderator is rain rather than cold. With a **maritime climate** and a latitude similar to Scotland, Southeast seldom gets really cold in the winter, and summer highs are tempered by incessant low cloud and heavy rainfall, which can top 200 inches a year in places; it is quite feasible to visit Southeast at any time, even for late-season events like the Alaska Day at Sitka. The mountains still get covered with snow though, and this lingers well into summer, making late summer and fall the best times for hiking.

The dripping leaves, sodden mosses, and wispy mist seem to suit ravens and **bald eagles** which are everywhere, and it comes as no surprise that they became the prime crest symbols of the native **Tlingit** (*Cling-AT*) people. They, along with the Haida and Tsimshian, have left an enduring legacy: **totem poles**, typically found clustered around replicas of the clan houses in which they once lived. Their original village sites were located to exploit the abundance of plunderable sealife: as they say here, "when the tide's out, dinner's in." The early Russian fur traders and American gold seekers didn't disrupt the social fabric too much, but with the arrival of the missionaries, the Tlingit abandoned their villages in favor of the schools and churches in white towns which sprang up around gold mines, forts, canneries, and fishing ports. Suddenly the motto changed to "we eat what we can, and can what we can't."

The importance of canneries gradually declined with the rise of **logging**. Almost the entirety of Southeast falls within the immense **Tongass National**

ACCOMMODATION PRICE CODES

All accommodation prices in this book have been coded using the symbols below. Note that prices are for the least expensive double rooms in each establishment. For a full explanation see p.44 in Basics.

① up to $50	④ $80–100	⑦ $160–200
② $50–65	⑤ $100–130	⑧ $200–250
③ $65–80	⑥ $130–160	⑨ $250 and over

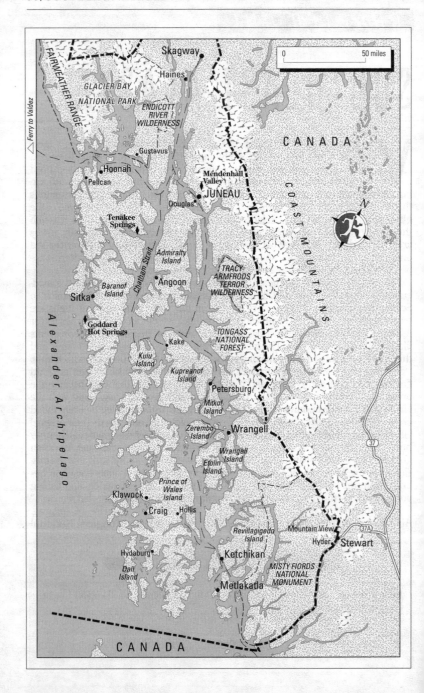

FERRY FARES

The price of AMHS ferry journeys is given in the chart in "Basics," p.35.

Forest, and for decades cutting rights ensured the profitability of pulp and saw mills, and guaranteed extensive clear cutting of old-growth spruce and hemlock forests. In the last decade, logging has rapidly declined. Some concede that the market has changed, but the families of most unemployed loggers and mill workers blame the shifting political climate fostered by the Clinton administration, that appears to favor conservation over jobs.

With mills closing or downsizing, small communities feel under siege and are turning to tourism as their savior. They hope to tap into the rich vein of the **cruise-ship industry**, which conditions almost every element of tourist life in Southeast. When a boat ties up (and most towns have at least one per day, sometimes four or five) it feels as if the circus is in town. Tour buses line the dock, helicopters and planes (perhaps three of each) buzz the skies, and the gift shops and restaurants brace themselves for the onslaught of visitors who bring much needed cash, but swamp towns like Ketchikan, Juneau, and Skagway.

Yet, even in the most popular ports of call, a little imagination and judicious timing can leave you in pristine environments without a soul in sight. The **totem parks** of Ketchikan may be busy, but nearby **Prince of Wales Island** also has totem parks that are off the tourist circuit. **Kayaking** is a superb way of seeking a little solitude, and the glacial granite masterpiece of **Misty Fiords National Monument** is a prime destination, also accessible on a day-trip. Up the coast the **garnet sellers** and beachside **petroglyphs** of **Wrangell** can both be visited on a short stopover, though the totem parks and some fine hikes take a little longer. The constricting **Wrangell Narrows** are just wide enough for ferries to reach the lively Norwegian fishing town of **Petersburg**, a base for the **LeConte Glacier**, the southernmost location of dozens of glaciers that regularly calve into the waters of the Inside Passage. The jewel in Southeast's crown is **Sitka** where Native and **Russian culture** come together in beautiful surroundings. The state capital, **Juneau**, puts up a good fight for your attention with a cosmopolitan edge, a fascinating gold mining history, and unparalleled access to the marvelous **Glacier Bay National Park**. From here, Lynn Canal runs north to two towns: **Haines**, with its unusual wintertime congregation of bald eagles and low-key charms; and the gold rush town of **Skagway**, the start of both the **White Pass and Yukon Route railway**, and the challenging **Chilkoot Trail**.

Ketchikan and around

KETCHIKAN, almost seven hundred miles north of Seattle, likes to bill itself as Alaska's "first city," the initial Alaskan port of call for northbound AMHS ferries and cruise ships. With over fifteen thousand people this ranks as Alaska's fourth largest city, and yet on arrival you are struck not so much by the town itself but by its insignificance after the miles of dense forest you've just sailed past or flown over. You'll be equally amazed by the disappearance of the downtown area behind a white wall of cruise ships. In summer, five thousand tourists flood downtown Ketchikan each day, possibly souring your opinion of this otherwise likeable community, and affecting almost every activity you take part in.

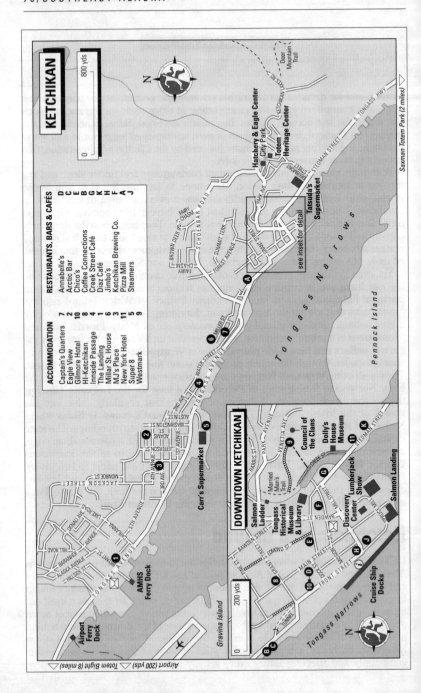

KETCHIKAN

0 — 800 yds

N

ACCOMMODATION

Captain's Quarters	7
Eagle View	2
Gilmore Hotel	10
HI-Ketchikan	8
Innside Passage	4
The Landing	1
Millar St. House	6
MJ's Place	3
New York Hotel	11
Super 8	5
Westmark	9

RESTAURANTS, BARS & CAFÉS

Annabelle's	D
Arctic Bar	C
Chico's	E
Coffee Connections	B
Creek Street Café	G
Diaz Café	K
Jimbo's	I
Ketchikan Brewing Co.	H
Pizza Mill	A
Steamers	J

Hatchery & Eagle Center
City Park
Totem Heritage Center

Tatsuda's Supermarket

Tongass Narrows

Pennock Island

Saxman Totem Park (2 miles)

Deer Mountain Trail

Carr's Supermarket

AMHS Ferry Dock

Airport Ferry Dock

Gravina Island

Airport (8 miles) Totem Bight Totem flight (200 yds)

DOWNTOWN KETCHIKAN

0 — 200 yds

N

Salmon Ladder
Tongass Historical Museum & Library
Married Man's Trail
Council of the Clans
Dolly's House Museum

Discovery Center
Lumberjack Show

Salmon Landing

Cruise Ship Docks

Tongass Narrows

Shoehorned onto the edge of **Revillagigedo Island** (pronounced Ruh-vee-uh-hih-HAY-do, but usually just referred to as "Revilla"), Ketchikan is – like most Southeast towns – squeezed tightly between forested hills and the plunging depths of the Inside Passage, in this case the waters of Tongass Narrows. Land is in such demand, that precipitous hillsides have been put to residential use, the houses linked by long staircases that are significant enough to have street names. Some lack vehicular access, while others drive home on streets that are really just wide boardwalks. Climb up to the wooden Warren, G, and Harding streets – jointly named for the 29th president who visited in 1923 – from where it is apparent just how much of the waterfront is on stilts. The other side of Ketchikan is the historic downtown core, now overdeveloped with flashy diamond and fur shops cheek-by-jowl with tacky souvenir emporia.

Nonetheless, this is one of the Southeast's more interesting towns. Nowhere else can you get such a broad sweep of Southeast Native culture, starting with one of the world's finest collections of authentic nineteenth-century totem poles in the **Totem Heritage Center**. A few miles along Ketchikan's limited road system, the **Totem Bight State Historic Park** and **Saxman Totem Park** both exhibit fine replicas in a more natural, outdoor setting; the latter also running a carving center where you can watch new totem poles being carved. There's also the celebrated boardwalks of **Creek Street**, now somewhat sanitized from their red-light

---

GLACIERS FOR BEGINNERS

The existence of a glacier is always a balancing act between competing forces: the snowfall at the **névé**, high in the mountains, battles with the rapid melting at the **terminal** lower down the valley, the victor determining whether the glacier will **advance** or **retreat**. Snowfall dozens of feet thick gradually compacts to form clear **blue ice** which accumulates to the point when it starts to flow downhill under its own weight. Friction against the valley walls slows the sides while ice in the center charges headlong down the valley giving the characteristic scalloped effect on the surface. Where a riverbed steepens it forms a rapid: under similar conditions glaciers break up into an **ice fall**, full of towering blocks of ice known as **seracs**, separated by **crevasses**.

Visitors expecting visions of pristine whiteness might be disappointed with some Interior glaciers where, at least in the lower regions, the surface is mottled with rock debris which has fallen off the valley walls. Some of the Alaska Range glaciers are so long and slow moving that whole forests can grow on the glacier's surface. When a glacier retreats, the rock carried down on the surface and under the glacier gets deposited as **terminal moraine**.

Of course this isn't true all over the state. In much of Southeast and Southcentral Alaska the snowfall is so great that glaciers are still a thick tongue of ice when they reach the sea. These **tidewater glaciers** are perhaps the most spectacular of all, with a face sometimes three miles wide, rising three hundred feet above the water and hundreds more below sea level. As the glacier creeps forward the buoyancy of the sea water becomes insufficient to support the enormous weight of ice and chunks are **calved off**, littering the bay with bobbing white hunks. Anything rising more than fifteen feet above the water is classed as a fully fledged **iceberg**, but smaller pieces are known as **bergy bits**, those between three and seven feet high are **growlers**, and anything less is just **brash ice**. Another term you'll hear bandied around on ferries and glacier cruises is a **shooter** which breaks off from the underside of the glacier and bobs up to the surface.

past but still a good place to stroll while checking out the craft and book shops, and the salmon in the waters below.

To escape the pressures of mass tourism make use of some of Ketchikan's **hiking trails**, though bear in mind Ketchikan is a strong contender to be the nation's **wettest town**; annual precipitation averages over 160 inches (and has topped 200 inches).

You might only want to spend a day or two in Ketchikan itself, and may soon tire of the downtown bustle when the cruise ships are in, but there is no shortage of intriguing destinations a short flight or ferry trip from the city. Flightseeing and boat charter companies are eager to take you into the granite wonderland of **Misty Fiords National Monument**, a trip that can be extended by staying in Forest Service cabins, or camping out beside your kayak.

A less committing approach to the grandeur of Southeast Alaska might be to spend a few days on **Prince of Wales Island**, where a rental vehicle or mountain bike opens up over a thousand miles of gravel roads, dozens of salmon streams, deserted bays, and lots of peace and quiet. Time it right and you can spend a couple of hours inside one of Alaska's largest **limestone caves**, and any time is good for visiting some impressive stands of 1930s **totem poles**.

Although many Alaskan Natives live in remote villages largely populated by their own people, the only Native reservation in the state is Annette Island, now the site of the Tsimshian community of **Metlakatla**, a place best visited on a cultural tour.

If it is **bears** you want to see, you've got a fair chance of spotting one just driving around Prince of Wales Island, but there is more structured viewing at Anan Creek (covered under out Wrangell account on p.102, but accessible from Ketchikan), and at **Hyder**, a tiny piece of Alaska that feels a lot more like Canada.

Arrival and information

AMHS **ferries** (☎225-6182, recorded information ☎225-6181) pull in almost daily in summer at the dock two miles north of downtown on N Tongass Hwy; city buses (see below) stop outside. Ketchikan's **airport** (with frequent Alaska Airlines flights from Seattle and Juneau, and occasional links to the smaller Southeast towns; ☎225-6800) is on Gravina Island, separated from the town by the two-hundred-yard channel of Tongass Narrows. A vehicular **shuttle ferry** (every 15min to 9.30pm; $2.50 round-trip, vehicles $5 each way) plies the gap and drops you two miles north of downtown (close to the AMHS ferry terminal) where you can catch a bus (see below) into town. Alternatively, hop aboard the frequent Airport Shuttle (daily 6am–7pm; $15; ☎225-5429) right outside the airport terminal, for a combined ferry ride and drive into town.

Stacks of leaflets and information on the town are available at the **visitor center**, 131 Front St (May–Sept daily 7am–5pm and extended when cruise ships stay later; Oct–April Mon–Fri 8am–5pm; ☎225-6166 or 1-800/770-3300, fax 225-4250, *www.visit-ketchikan.com*). For anything related to the outdoors, you're better off at the **Southeast Alaska Discovery Center**, 50 Main St (May–Sept daily 8am–5pm; Oct–April Tues–Sat 8.30am–4.30pm; ☎228-6220, fax 228-6234, *www.fs.fed.us/r10/ketchikan*), a multiagency facility (the same as APLIC in Anchorage, Fairbanks, and Tok), which is free if you are just going in for information or to the bookstore. You'll be directed downstairs to the comfortable confines of the trip-planning room where staff will help you plan camping, hiking, and kayaking trips, point you to the best cabins, and generally assist with maps and as many leaflets as you can carry. The Discovery Center is also pitched as a tourist attraction in its own right (see "Downtown" account, p.75).

Getting around and tours

Getting around the downtown area is very easy on foot, though to get to the ferry terminal and airport (and perhaps to your accommodation) you might need the **bus** services provided by The Bus (Mon–Sat 5.15am–9.45pm every 30min, Sun 8.45am–3.45pm every hour; $1.50). This makes an hour-long loop from the airport ferry dock, past the AMHS ferry dock, into town and the suburb of Bear Valley, then back through town and out towards the airport. This is satisfactory if you plan ahead, but for more impulsive moves you'll want a **taxi**: Sourdough (☎225-5544) and Yellow Cab (☎225-6800) are both fine.

Two of Ketchikan's main attractions, the totem parks, are beyond walking distance for most people, so you may want to **rent a car**, easily done from Alaska Rent-a-Car (☎225-22332 or 1-800/662-0007), Avis (☎225-4515), or Payless (☎225-6004 or 1-800/729-5377): rates are around $50 a day. If you are feeling energetic, **rent a bicycle** from Southeast Exposure, 515 Water St (☎225-8829), who do bike rentals for $12 for half a day, $22 a day.

Ketchikan has at least a dozen land-based **tours**, most of them independent of the cruise ship companies but so heavily promoted on board that cruise ship passengers usually vastly outnumber independent travelers. If you're interested you'll also find them assiduously promoted in the visitor center. For something a little different look out for the Native-run Alaska Native Personal Tours (2.5hr; $25; ☎247-6962), full of stories and anecdotes; the enthusiastic Classic Tours (☎225-3091) in a restored 1955 Chevy, visiting Saxman (2hr; $50), or additionally, a forest and looking at an eagle's nest (3hr; $65); or the more mainstream Alaska Sourdough Tours (3hr; $30; ☎225-4081 or 1-888/801-7596), which takes you around town and to the two major totem pole sites at Saxman and Totem Bight.

Accommodation

Ketchikan's modest range of accommodation sets the pattern for what you'll find all the way up the coast; downtown hotels and B&Bs, a couple of motels, a hostel or two and some wooded campgrounds out of town. There are few genuinely luxurious places, but in general standards are high and prices tolerable. Most of the hotels are downtown with B&Bs scattered along the road system.

The closest **campgrounds** to town are in the attractive Ward Lake Recreation Area, five miles northwest of the ferry terminal. Though these accept RVs, there are no hookups, and motorhome drivers wanting power and cable TV will have to stay fourteen miles north of downtown.

You should book directly with the establishments as far in advance as you can manage in summer, but if you're in real difficulty contact the visitor center, or Ketchikan Reservation Service (☎ & fax 247-5337 or 1-800/987-5337, *www.ketchikan-lodging.com*), who can arrange accommodation.

There are also dozens of Forest Service **cabins** around Ketchikan, some of which we've listed in the boxes on pp.83 and 84. If you're geared up for camping, then you've everything you need for staying in a cabin, but those less well equipped can rent everything they need from Alaska Wilderness Outfitting, 3857 Fairview Ave (☎225-7335, fax 225-8886, *www.visit.ktn.net/aae*), including a complete cooking kit for $20 a day.

Hotels, motels, and B&Bs

Captain's Quarters B&B, 325 Lund St (☎225-4912, *www.ptialaska.net/~captbnb*). Three spacious rooms separate from the owner's house, all with queen beds and cable TV, and one with a kitchen, in a nautically themed hillside house with some great views over the town. Continental breakfast included. ④.

Gilmore Hotel, 326 Front St (☎225-9423). Despite recent remodeling this 1927 establishment retains the tenor of an old-style hotel, with a range of rooms from poky doubles without a view (④), to larger waterview rooms (top end of ④) and much more spacious double queens with a tub in the bathroom (⑤). ④/⑤.

Innside Passage B&B, 114 Elliot St (☎ & fax 247-3700, *www.innsidepassagebedandbreakfast .com*). Two rooms and one apartment roughly midway between the ferries and downtown, with good views across the Narrows and a hearty breakfast. The apartment (④), which sleeps up to four, usually has a three-day minimum but call to inquire about availability; the rooms share a jacuzzi-equipped bathroom. ③.

The Landing, 3434 Tongass Ave (☎225-5166 or 1-800/428-8304, fax 225-6900, *landing@ktn .net*). Comfortable but unexciting Best Western hotel two miles north of downtown, right opposite the AMHS ferry terminal and within walking distance of the airport ferry. There's cable TV, a fitness center, a restaurant and bar on site, and a courtesy van into town. ⑥.

Millar Street House, 1430 Millar St (☎225-1258 or 1-800/287-1607, *bbkayak@ktn.net*). Low-cost B&B in a house perched on a hill just outside downtown and owned by the folk who run Southeast Sea Kayaks. Two simple rooms, but welcoming and you join the family for breakfast. ④.

MJ's Place, 2724 3rd Ave (☎225-2592, *www.alaskanow.com*). An apartment with two rooms, let separately but sharing bathroom, a large kitchen, and a lounge area where a light breakfast (with great muffins) is served. There's also a garden, deck, and hammock to relax in whenever the sun shines. It is just over a mile from downtown, but is two-minutes' walk from the bus line and about ten-minutes' walk from the AMHS ferry dock. ④.

New York Hotel, 207 Stedman St (☎225-0246, fax 225-1803, *www.thenewyorkhotel.com*). Older hotel that's particularly good value now that it has been refurbished in tasteful fashion with black-and-white-tiled bathrooms, and an antique vanity or armoire in each room. Most are quite small, but some have great harbor views, and a light breakfast is included. ③.

Super 8 Motel, 2151 Sea Level Drive (☎225-9088, & 1-800/800-8000, *www.super8.com*). The cheapest motel in town, fairly uninspiring but decent enough with all the facilities you'd expect. Suites ⑥, rooms ⑤.

Westmark Cape Fox Lodge, 800 Venetia Way (☎225-8001 or 1-800/544-0970, fax 225-8286, *www.westmarkhotels.com*). The grandest hotel in town and one of the best in this statewide chain, located on a hill above the town with international standard rooms, many with water views glimpsed through the spruce and hemlocks. Suites ⑧, rooms ⑦.

Hostels and campgrounds

Clover Pass Resort, Mile 14 N Tongass Hwy (☎247-2234 or 1-800/410-2234). The only site around Ketchikan with hookups; no tent sites. $25.

Eagle View Backpackers Hostel, 2305 5th Ave (☎225-5461, *seaeagle@ktn.net*). Suburban house shared with the owner and with great views of the Narrows, converted for use as a hostel. There's one double, a male dorm with four bunks, a women's room with two beds, a mattress and its own bathroom, and everyone is charged $25 which includes bed linen, towel and use of the kitchen, barbecue, and sauna. No lockout or curfew. Dale also runs kayak and sightseeing trips, and won't let you get bored even on the wettest days. Follow Jefferson off Tongass Hwy then turn right onto 5th. Closed Nov–March except by reservation. ①.

HI-Ketchikan, 400 Main St at Grant St (☎225-3319). Very basic and rigidly managed hostel in the United Methodist Church with simple dorm beds for $10 (nonmembers $13), reasonable kitchen and often some free baked goods in the evening. Bring a sleeping bag and expect a daytime lockout (9am–6pm), an 11pm curfew, and a chore requirement. For advance bookings send a money order for the first night's fee (and a SAE if you want confirmation) to PO Box 8515, Ketchikan, AK 99901. June–Aug only. ①.

Settlers Cove State Recreation Site, Mile 18.2 N Tongass Hwy (no phone). First-come, first-served campground and picnic area overlooking Clover Passage that is probably the nicest and least crowded (and most inconveniently sited) around Ketchikan. No hookups, but there's a beach and a short trail to a waterfall. $8.

Ward Lake Recreation Area (☎1-877/444-6677). Three Forest Service campgrounds in the temperate rainforest with easy access to scenic lakes and gentle trails. They are all located on (or just off) Revilla Rd, which cuts inland six miles north of Ketchikan. Ward Lake Rd leads off Revilla Rd at Mile 1.4 and runs to the first two campgrounds: *Signal Creek* (May to late Sept), with lots for small RVs, and the simpler *Three Cs* (April–Sept). Go 2.3 miles along Revilla Rd to get to *Last Chance* (late May to mid-Sept), amid old growth forest with designated RV lots. All cost $10.

The town and totem parks

Ketchikan's popularity as a tourist destination is due in part to its concentrated collection of sites around a central core **of historic streets**, notably **Creek Street**, now cleaned up from its seedy red-light past. It's an appealing spot for a stroll along the boardwalks, stopping to peek into one of the galleries or gaze over the bridge to watch the salmon make their way to the **Deer Mountain Tribal Hatchery**. Perhaps Ketchikan's most compelling claim to greatness is its unmatched expression of Southeast Native culture through the superb **Totem Heritage Center**, assorted totem poles all around town, and the two totem parks just outside town: the **Totem Bight State Historic Park** of replica poles and clan house, and the **Saxman Totem Park** at the Native village of Saxman.

Downtown

If Ketchikan is your introduction to Alaska, your first stop should be the **Southeast Alaska Discovery Center**, 50 Main St (May–Sept daily 8am–5pm; Oct–April Tues–Sat 8.30am–4.30pm; May–Sept $4, Oct–April free), a striking cedar-framed building with absorbing displays of the region's natural ecosystems, resources, and Native culture. Those who have already spent time in the state may find it a little simplistic, even promotional. It can be all too obvious that the Forest Service has provided much of the funding here; you might wonder why they've bothered replicating a temperate rainforest when there is seventeen million acres of it right outside the door. It also operates as an outdoor information center (see "Arrival and information", p.72).

For local flavor visit the small and well laid-out **Tongass Historical Museum**, 629 Dock St (mid-May to Sept daily 8am–5pm; Oct to mid-May Wed–Fri 1–5pm, Sat & Sun 1–4pm; $2), which is full of fascinating old photos of the town and its happenings, mining paraphernalia, and a great corner filled with Native artifacts: a carved bowl from the 1880s and large, carved **bentwood boxes**, watertight storage vessels, the sides of which are formed from a single piece of wood that was shaped by steaming and bending. There are also old "coppers" – essentially large sheets of copper that, in the early years of trade with Europeans, gave their owners great status and were accordingly the ultimate item to give away at potlatches (see box on p.76).

The bulk of Ketchikan's packaged heritage lies along **Creek Street**, a ricketylooking boardwalk perched high above the tidal waters of Ketchikan Creek. This was Ketchikan's **red-light district** from 1903 until 1954 when the brothels were closed down. Its notoriety was enhanced during Prohibition when boats laden with

TOTEM POLES

Despite the teachings of early missionaries, **totem poles** – the enduring image of the Alaskan and whole Pacific Northwest, coast – were never intended as objects of worship or religious veneration, but stood as cultural symbols recording the lineage, legends, history, and lore of a people; silent storytellers in a land with no written language. Equally, they were visual statements of a clan's wealth, the cost of employing highly esteemed carvers added greatly to the commissioner's prestige. The raising of a pole was always accompanied by a **potlatch**, a kind of feast where the clan could raise their prestige further by giving away a vast portion of their property. (In contrast to modern day values, your status was determined by how much you gave away rather than how much you accumulated in Tlingit culture.)

Totem poles exist from Puget Sound in Washington State right through the Alaskan Panhandle, exactly the range of the western red cedar, which is the preferred timber for its easy-to-work straight grain and unusual rotting characteristics. It decomposes from the inside out, thus lasting longer in the eternally damp climate though still only sixty to seventy years.

Every element in the preparation of a pole – selecting and felling the tree, the carving, the painting, and finally the raising – was marked by ceremony, culminating with singing, dancing, and drumming of the final potlatch given by the patron's clan. The assembled throng would be put to work digging a six-foot hole then raising the pole by means of a scaffold and ropes. Simultaneously the head of the clan would recite the history represented to publicly validate their right to use the crests and associated songs and dances. Once erected the poles were not changed or repaired but allowed to decay until they finally fell over and rotted into the undergrowth.

The raising of totem poles reached its **"golden age"** in the latter half of the nineteenth century, peaking around 1860. The combination of increased fur-trade wealth and a thriving culture unleashed a great burst of creativity, enhanced by access to abundant iron for carving, and newly available artificial pigments. Hundreds of poles sprouted up along the coast, and photos of the era show whole forests of poles clustered around traditional clan houses.

This era ended with the arrival of missionaries who discouraged pole raising, built schools and churches, and encouraged the Natives to abandon many of the old traditions. Meanwhile, late nineteenth-century tourists were fascinated with totem poles as an art form, and many poles were relocated to sites closer to the steamer routes, breaking the tradition of leaving poles in situ. From around 1875 onwards, private and museum collectors began removing them from abandoned villages. With the exception of the replicas described below there were very few poles carved between the late 1880s and the 1970s.

A brief resurgence of interest came in the late 1930s when the **Civilian Conservation Corps** (CCC) undertook an unemployment relief program to salvage poles and employ skilled carvers to create replicas. Honoring tradition, handmade tools as close as possible in design to pre-European models were utilized, and color matching, where necessary, was done by combining natural pigments with chewed, dry salmon eggs.

The skills retained by older carvers were passed on to a younger generation of artisans who still carve poles, often replicating older designs. Without these efforts the tradition of raising totem poles may not have survived into the twenty-first century, and yet there are still factions who believe the CCC project wrongly broke the tradition of leaving poles to rot where they stood, free from the well-meaning preserve and protective instincts of whites. The replica totems have survived well, and can be seen in totem parks on Prince of Wales Island, Saxman and Totem Bight in Ketchikan, Shakes Island in Wrangell, and in Sitka. In most cases the originals were discarded.

The real renaissance in totem pole carving didn't come until after the **Pole Survey and Retrieval Project**, which in the late 1960s set out to collect the last remaining original poles from abandoned villages. Only 44 were found. These formed the basis of Ketchikan's Totem Heritage Center collection and encouraged the development of a modern carving tradition both here and at the Carving Center at nearby Saxman. Reproductions and adherence to traditional forms and color schemes remains strong but, fostered by a renewed sense of cultural identity and tribal pride, brighter paints and modern elements have been increasingly incorporated. Today, replica and original poles are still raised in the traditional manner, but steel tools have replaced those of stone, bone, and sinew.

POLE TYPES

Totem poles fall into five main categories. Perhaps the best known, and the style seen reproduced all over the place, are **heraldic poles**, also known as crest poles or story poles for the complex series of designs showing the matrilineal genealogy and aspects of the history of the clan or family who commissioned it. Some of the same elements – particularly the family histories – are incorporated into **house posts**, which support the roof beams in clan houses, and the entrance poles designed into Haida clan houses.

Mortuary poles were designed to honor the dead and are usually topped with the crest symbol of that person. Many originally had a recess in the back where the ashes could be placed, but missionaries strongly discouraged cremation and this practice died away, the mortuary pole being replaced by the **memorial pole**. These often only had a couple of crest figures in a simple design, and were usually placed adjacent to the village or around the house of the deceased.

Finally there are **shame poles** or ridicule poles, the least common type but usually prominently placed where they could poke the most fun. They were generally erected to discredit someone who had failed to clear a debt, behaved dishonorably or broken their word, and would be cut down when amends were made.

Another feature to look out for are **watchmen** crouched on top of some Haida totems to protect the inhabitants with their supernatural powers. Their high status is often marked by a **potlatch hat**, which is otherwise reserved for memorial poles, with the number of rings around the hat denoting the number of potlatches the person threw.

INTERPRETATION

Totem poles often come without any explanation of their meaning, partly because the story associated with the pole belongs to that clan. Nonetheless, something can be gleaned from the design elements, which are based on interlinking ovoids – rounded rectangles – depicting anything from a whole head or torso down to even teeth. Typically ovoids exist within ovoids building a pattern one within another, interlinked by incomplete ovoids distorted to create U- and S-shapes which tie the whole together. All this encourages a high degree of stylization which can make detecting which creatures are represented difficult at first, though it gets easier with a few clues. First, animals always have ears on top, while humans have theirs on the side. The most common representations are of Eagle and Raven, which are easily confused, though the Eagle always has a hooked beak-tip. Bear and Wolf both have a rounder shape to their mouths, the latter sporting sharper teeth and a more slender snout. Whales crop up fairly often, particularly Killer Whale with his straight dorsal fin, sometimes created by adding a plank to the totem pole rather than carving it into the main body of the pole. Beaver always has two prominent front teeth and usually a flat, cross-hatched tail.

illicit liquor were floated up at high tide, the contraband being fed up through trap doors in the floors of the houses. Today the former houses of ill-repute have been smartened up, painted in bright colors and mostly set up as gift shops, though there are a few higher-quality galleries and an excellent bookshop (see "Listings", p.86). The main destination for those fancying a glimpse of the old days is **Dolly's House**, 24 Creek St (open when cruise ships are in from 10am–6pm; $4), once the home and workplace of Dolly Arthur, the town's most famous prostitute, and now a small museum with original decor and stuffed with saucy memorabilia. Ignoring the fact that Dolly only ceased her trade here half a century back, they've gone for the Victorian look, and "ladies" dressed in puffy gold rush dresses will usher you in for a tour and headful of anecdotes from Dolly's intriguing life.

A short **inclined tramway** ($2) climbs the bluff behind Creek Street to the lobby of the *Westmark Cape Fox Lodge* (see pp.74 and 83), which has a small display of quality Native crafts and commands a great view of the town and Tongass Narrows. In front of the hotel stands the "Council of the Clans" ring of short **totem poles** commissioned by the Cape Fox Native Corporation which owns the hotel. From here, Venetia Avenue leads down to Park Avenue and City Park.

An alternative route to City Park is known as the **Married Man's Trail** for the secretive escape route it provides from Creek Street. It follows a narrow boardwalk upstream past some small rapids and beside a **fish ladder** where you might occasionally see salmon fighting the current. This brings you to Park Avenue which runs inland to **City Park**, a small but attractive area of grass, small streams and a riot of summer blooms. Tall cages on the west side of the park mark the **Deer Mountain Tribal Hatchery and Eagle Center** (May to Sept daily 8.30am–4.30pm; $7, combo ticket with Totem Heritage Center $10), where a couple of injured bald eagles are kept to educate the public about these majestic birds. You may be more interested in the hatchery, concrete tanks with fish at different stages in their development. Either follow the guided tour or make your own way around learning about the king and coho salmon that find their way up Ketchikan Creek to breed here. Outside, a footbridge over Ketchikan Creek leads to the Totem Heritage Center (see below).

For something a little less serious, return to the waterfront behind the Discovery Center where you'll find the **Great Alaskan Lumberjack Show** (usually three shows daily, call for times ☎225-9050; $29), a ninety-minute extravaganza coaxed along by an MC whipping the audience into a lighthearted frenzy of US–Canadian rivalry as "frontier woodsmen" are put through their paces chopping and sawing wood, log rolling, tree felling, and speed climbing with spiked shoes. It has the tenor of a circus sideshow and, when it opened in 2000, put a few noses out of joint. The local pulp mill had only recently closed, and unemployed loggers – they don't even call themselves lumberjacks around here – were understandably put out by the tourist industry appearing to cash in on a dying industry.

TOTEM HERITAGE CENTER

The wonderful **Totem Heritage Center**, 601 Deermount St (mid-May to Sept daily 8am–5pm; Oct to mid-May Mon–Fri 1–5pm; $4, combo ticket with hatchery $10), was set up in 1976 to preserve and exhibit the largest collection of **original totem poles** in the US; 33 in all. Most of the poles you'll see around town and elsewhere in Southeast are replicas (see box, p.76), many of them based on the poles, house posts, and fragments gathered here. For much of the twentieth century it had been recognized that unless something was done the nation's rapidly dwindling stock of original nineteenth-century totem poles would rot away and be lost forever. So, in 1967, Totem Pole Survey and Retrieval Project was set up to collect the remaining poles from abandoned Tlingit and Haida villages within fifty miles of Ketchikan. Of the hundreds noted and photographed previously by explorers and early steamship tourists, only 44 remained, ten of which were unsalvageable.

Before entering, pause a moment to see how modern themes and techniques have been incorporated into the vibrantly painted "Honoring Those Who Give" pole, raised in 1999 to recognize those who helped fund the center. It was created by renowned carver **Nathan Jackson**, whose first pole "Raven-Frog Woman," carved in 1978, stands nearby. There's yet more of his work at Totem Bight State Park and in public places all over town.

Inside the center you are confronted with five magnificent poles from the "golden age" of totem-pole carving – two memorial, one heraldic, one potlatch, and one mortuary – all over a century old and some as much as 160 years old. Greatly weathered and often missing parts of various appendages, they are mostly free of any coloring, though under the beaver's chin on the Haida potlatch pole you can still see a hint of green, made from copper oxide mixed with crushed salmon eggs. For all their crumbling fragility, they still retain a menacing power, something robbed from the remaining poles and house posts that are too delicate to display upright. Almost a dozen such poles occupy an adjacent room, many of them broken and laid down in cradles, but still impressive. Panels around the walls have photos of how the poles appeared in their original locations, and explain almost all you ever wanted to know about this art form. Museum staff are on hand to fill in the gaps and conduct ad hoc tours.

The poles provide inspiration for the off-season **Native Arts Studies Program**, a series of non-residential courses covering anything from cedar bark weaving and introductory carving to more advanced techniques such as bentwood box manufacture and drum making. Courses run from mid-September to April, and run from $55 for a two-day workshop, to $100–150 for one- and two-week courses.

North of town

Following the Tongass Hwy north of the AMHS and airport-ferry docks, Ketchikan begins to thin out. The road hugs the coast to Ward Cove, an unsightly industrial wasteland occupied until 1997 by the Ketchikan Pulp Mill, and now the site of a much smaller saw mill and veneer plant. A road heads inland from here to the **Ward Lake Recreation Area**, the wooded site of picnic areas, three campgrounds, and several of the local hikes (see box, p.83).

On past the **float houses** (literally houses floating on pontoons) at anchor in Mud Bight you reach the **Totem Bight State Historic Park** (unrestricted access), a replica Native village breathtakingly set on a forested strip of coast overlooking the Narrows, ten miles north of town. Here, fourteen of the finest replica totem poles and a re-created tribal house look majestically out over the water making this about the best place to easily get a sense of what a Tlingit village looked like a hundred or more years back. The site was originally a summer fish camp and it is unlikely that it was even permanently settled, but in the late 1930s the CCC (see box, p.76) decided to reconstruct an entire Native village here. Lack of money and manpower during World War II stunted initial ambition, but the result still includes a very fine **clan house**. The front is strikingly painted in a raven design flanked by squat figures wearing potlatch hats, and centered on the large "Raven

Stealing the Sun" entrance pole. Once, the hole in this entrance pole would have been the sole way to get into the house, an important security feature. Inside, up to fifty people could live, with separate family areas on the raised platforms around the central fire pit, and belongings stored underneath the planks.

Eleven of the **totem poles** are clustered in a couple of semi-circles beside the clan house, almost all of them executed in the late 1930s, though a couple have had to be replicated again, this third generation were done in the 1990s, mostly by Nathan Jackson. There's a great variety: Tlingit and Haida – despite this being a traditionally Tlingit area – mortuary poles, grave markers, heraldic poles, and the lovely "Sea Monster" pole, topped by a human figure representing the village watchman.

On arrival, call at the Alaska Natural History Association **bookstore**, which stocks an excellent leaflet ($1 donation requested) explaining what the poles depict, and has an original section of a pole wedged into one corner.

The Tongass Hwy continues for another eight miles past Knudson Cove marina to **Settlers Cove** campground on the shores of Clover Passage.

South of town

Just under three miles along S Tongass Hwy from downtown Ketchikan, the Tlingit village of **SAXMAN** centers on the **Saxman Totem Park** (unrestricted access), which encompasses the world's largest collection of replica totem poles, a replica clan house, and an active carving center. Most people visit on a tour (see below) but it is possible to wander round the poles by yourself, armed with a walking tour map ($1) available from the Village Store on S Tongass Hwy. From there, stroll up the approach avenue of a dozen Tlingit poles to reach the main arc of poles. Look out for the famous Abraham Lincoln pole surmounted by an image of Honest Abe who has been carved with stunted legs, apparently because the only image the carvers had of him was in a photo which cut him off at the knees. There's also a shame pole to William Seward who visited Alaska in 1867 during its transfer from Russian ownership and attended four potlatches without ever throwing one in return, a dishonorable omission which earned him the distinctive red ears, nose, and lips on his pole.

Unless you are on a tour, you won't get to see inside the cedar-scented **Beaver Clan House** where the **Cape Fox Dancers** put on a diverting performance during which you'll learn a little Tlingit, and can join in one of the dances alongside the troupe made up of adults, kids, and even babes in arms, many wearing superb blankets and robes.

Possibly the most interesting bit of all is the nearby **Carving Center**, where highly respected Haida and Tlingit craftsmen (Nathan Jackson among them) can be seen at work on large poles, commissioned by institutions and individuals from all over the US. The carvers are usually happy to chat as they work on poles which proceed at a rate of around one foot per week. Don't set your hopes on possessing one anytime soon; they cost tens of thousands of dollars depending on size of pole, intricacy of design, and reputation of carver, and they're backordered for over a year.

Strictly, the Carving Center is only open to those on the Saxman Native Village **Tour** (May–Sept daily; 2hr; $30) run by the local Native corporation's Cape Fox Tours (☎225-4846, *www.capefoxtours.com*), which also includes transport from town, a short video, interpretation of the poles and a visit to the Beaver Clan House. If you don't need transport from town you can join the Saxman Native Village Tour by buying a ticket ($30) in the Village Store, a gift shop run by the

Saxman Native Arts Cooperative. Other Ketchikan tours also stop at Saxman, but miss out on the video (no great loss), the clan house, and the dancers.

Cape Fox Tours also run the Historic Ketchikan Tour (2hr; $20), which stops only briefly at Saxman before continuing to the disused and otherwise inaccessible **George Inlet Cannery**, standing majestically on poles over the tide at the end of S Tongass Hwy, thirteen miles from Ketchikan. Proximity to Ketchikan has saved the old Libby, McNeill, and Libby cannery, built here on George Inlet in 1913 and operated until 1958. It previously processed salmon caught using fish traps, but with statehood, fish traps were banned and the cannery was forced to close its doors. The site has never been completely abandoned – commercial fishermen still use the lockers here – and it has now been set up for tours which start with an excellent video covering a potted history of commercial salmon fishing. Material on the lifecycles of salmon and halibut are followed by operating fishing boat winches, a mock-up of a worker's shack on a fish trap, and a good deal of role playing. Unfortunately, most of the canning line has been removed, but there's enough left to evoke something of the old days.

Eating, drinking, and entertainment

Though cosmopolitan by Alaskan standards, Ketchikan is still a small town, so its attempts at sophistication are limited, though not entirely unsuccessful. It fares reasonably well with a range of good and inexpensive choices. It also supports most of the major fast food franchises, and a couple of **supermarkets**: Tatsuda's, 633 Steadman St (daily 7am–11pm), which has a deli and Chinese takeout is fairly central and reasonably large; for something bigger try Carr's at the Plaza Mall about a mile north of downtown.

Ketchikan drains in the late afternoon. The cruise passengers all shuffle back to their floating hotels, which almost imperceptibly slip away, leaving the town peaceful, but somehow robbed of its lifeblood. Still, there's plenty of hard **drinking** to be done, but steer clear of the *First City Saloon* on Water Street, a favorite with commercial fishers and cannery workers eager to forget the sight and smell of raw fish. If you want to sample some of the local brew, call in during the day at the **Ketchikan Brewing Co**, 607 Mission St (*www.ketchbrew.com*) for a few samples of their product, or visit *Creek Street Café*, where it is on tap.

Other than eating and drinking, there isn't a great deal to do in the evening, though you could try the Coliseum Twin Theatre, corner of Mission and Main streets, which shows first-run **movies**.

Annabelle's Keg & Chowder House, 326 Front St (☎225-6009). Venerable restaurant done in grand style with dark paneling, pressed tin ceilings, and formal dining chairs in the non-smoking section, and a more relaxed atmosphere in the bar. The sourdough pancake breakfasts and famed clam chowder lunches and moderately prices; dinner gets more spendy, ranging up to the tequila prawns with firecracker rice ($24) and the brandy peppercorn filet mignon ($28).

Arctic Bar, 509 Water St. Basic, dark, boozing bar with a great view over the water once the cruise ships have left.

Chico's, 435 Dock St (☎225-2833). Bargain authentic Mexican food and pizza with dinners starting at $9, or just grab a $5 burrito to eat in or take out.

Coffee Connections, 521 Water St (☎247-0521). A relaxed waterside spot for espresso and snacks with a few sunny seats and a deck that's ideal for browsing newspapers and magazines. If the view is often blocked by cruise ships (as it often is) get your coffee to go and sit in the adjacent Harborview Park.

Creek Street Café, 127 Stedman St (☎247-2233). Good burgers, sandwiches, and soups café with views across Ketchikan Creek to Creek St. Save room for something from the extensive range of chilled desserts.

Diaz Café, 335 Stedman St (☎225-2257). Some of the finest inexpensive food in town with widely acclaimed burgers and fries propping up a menu specializing in Chinese and tasty Filipino dishes: fried rice for $8, chow mein and chicken adobo all for around $12. Closed Mon.

Jimbo's Café, 307 Mill St (☎225-8499). Despite its location right where the cruise ships disgorge their charges, this is very much a locals diner where you can earwig gossip at the counter or grab the window seat and watch the world go by. Very reasonable rates for breakfasts, burgers, and sundaes. Open 24hr in summer.

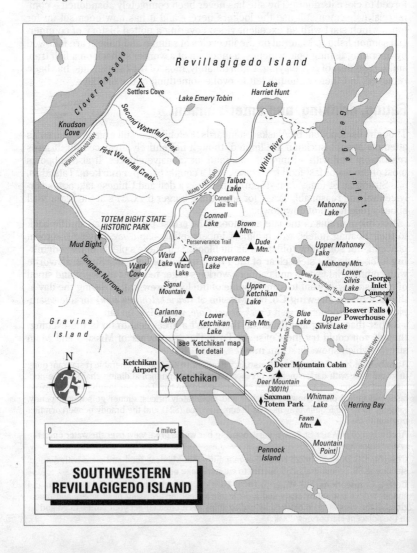

SOUTHWESTERN
REVILLAGIGEDO ISLAND

HIKES AROUND KETCHIKAN

Extremely high rainfall and what can sometimes seem like near constant cloud and drizzle may put some people off hiking around Ketchikan, but if you strike it lucky, or are feeling especially hardy, it can be very rewarding. The two low-level trails listed below (Connell Lake and Ward Lake) can be tackled in any season, though snow cover on Deer Mountain Trail limits access to the alpine sections: late June to September is the best time. Only Deer Mountain is readily accessible from town, though you could easily hitch to Ward Cove and hike inland from there. All hikes are marked on the "Around Ketchikan" map. The Discovery Center and visitor center both have free detailed leaflets on all these hikes.

Connell Lake Trail (4.5 miles round-trip; 2–3hr; 100ft ascent). Easy trail mostly beside Connell Lake and running to Talbot Lake with good birding, excellent berries in summer and fall, and fishing access to both lakes. The trail starts on Connell Lake Rd which spurs off Revilla Rd just past the entrance to *Last Chance* campground.

Deer Mountain Trail (9 miles one-way; 2 days; 3350ft ascent). Easily accessible trail that makes a perfect escape from the daytime crowds for a couple of hours, switchbacking up across the face of Deer Mountain through old growth sitka spruce, hemlock, and red cedar. It takes an hour or so to reach a wooded viewpoint (1500 feet) with a wonderful view over the city, Pennock, Gravina, Annette, and Prince of Wales islands; and close to three hours to reach the 3000-foot alpine summit of Deer Mountain. Deer Mountain Trail can be extended as an overnight one-way trek to the Beaver Falls Powerhouse on George Inlet either camping beside Blue Lake, or staying in the four-bunk Forest Service **cabin** on the upper flank of Deer Mountain. This must be reserved in advance if you want to stay ($25; ☎1-877/444-6777). This alpine section of the hike is exposed to bad weather and is steep in places, remaining high for several hours before a final steep descent past Silvia Lakes. The trail starts near a trailer park half a mile along Deermount St near the junction of Fair St (see "Ketchikan" map) and finishes fourteen miles out along S Tongass Hwy. There is very little traffic out this way, so it is best to arrange a ride back to town before you start, or do the whole thing in reverse and finish in town.

Perseverance Trail (4.5 miles round-trip; 2–3hr; 450ft ascent). An easy but enjoyable (partly boardwalk) trail up to Perseverance Lake through temperate rainforest and muskeg. It starts at 1.5 miles along Ward Lake Rd, inland from Ward Cove.

Ward Lake Nature Trail (1.3-mile loop; 1hr; negligible ascent). Gentle stroll past panels on the region's flora and fauna. The trailhead is seven miles along N Tongass Hwy to Ward Cove then a mile inland along Ward Lake Rd.

Pizza Mill, 808 Water St (☎225-6646). Ketchikan's oldest pizza joint and still a great low-key place for gourmet pizzas (known here as Yuppie Pies; from $10 for a 12-inch), subs, burgers ($6–8), burritos ($6–7), salads, and draft beer. No credit cards.

Steamers, 76 Front St, above Dockside Trading (☎225-1600). Large, spacious, and bustling restaurant opposite the cruise-ship dock with great views and occasional live music. The food's good too – try the $26 hazelnut halibut with Frangelico cream sauce.

Westmark Cape Fox Lodge, 800 Venetia Way (☎225-8001). Fairly upmarket dining in the town's best hotel with great views over town. Prices are manageable for lunch of burgers ($9–10), steamer clams and sourdough bread ($13, or excellent halibut and chips; $11). Dinner is more formal and dishes range from a chicken fettuccini ($18) to scallops, shrimp, and lobster ($24).

KAYAKING AROUND REVILLAGIGEDO ISLAND AND MISTY FIORDS NATIONAL MONUMENT

Wherever you are in Southeast Alaska, the range of places you can go paddling is only limited by your imagination and your budget. Dozens of possibilities present themselves, but from Ketchikan the most common destinations are relatively short paddles close to town, and trips into Misty Fiords National Monument, which can take on the feeling of an expedition without requiring really long periods away from civilization.

The simplest approach is to hook up with one of the **two kayaking companies** in Ketchikan: Southeast Exposure, 515 Water St (☎225-8829, fax 225-8849, *www.southeastexposure.com*); and Southeast Sea Kayaks, 430 Millar St (☎225-1258 or 1-800/287-1607, *www.ktn.net/seakayaks*). Both offer almost identical trips: Southeast Exposure are more tightly linked-in with the cruise ships, the larger numbers being reflected in lower prices; while Southeast Sea Kayaks tend to charge a little more in return for more personal treatment and no minimum numbers.

For a taster, try a paddle around the **Ketchikan waterfront** (2.5hr; $50–70), though for something a little more rural you're better off visiting the **Tatoosh Islands** (4hr; $82–100) involving a van ride to Knudson Cove marina, an inflatable trip out to the Tatoosh Islands and a couple of hours of paddling. Both companies offer customizable extended day-trips ($80–100) close to Ketchikan, and guided multiday trips to **Misty Fiords National Monument** (4–6 days; $700–1000) with access by tour boat and nights spent camping beside the fjord.

GOING IT ALONE

The two guided kayaking companies rent kayaks at similar rates and will drop you along the road system for a small fee: Southeast Exposure rent double fiberglass sea kayaks ($50 a day), fiberglass singles ($40), and plastic singles ($30). You don't need much prior experience to be let loose around the Ketchikan waterfront, but for longer journeys you'll have to be a moderately competent paddler and have some knowledge of tides and backcountry camping. Don't be put off though, the generally sheltered waters in these parts (see below for suggested trips) can be tackled by people of quite modest ability. Wherever you go, get the latest information (maps, tide tables, etc) either from the rental company or from the Discovery Center, and be sure you leave an itinerary of your likely movements.

George Inlet (1–2 days). Pretty coves, loads of small islands and the old George Inlet cannery add to this 1–2-day trip to the south and west of Ketchikan. Either paddle from downtown or get a ride out to the Hole-in-the-Wall marina (7.5 miles south on Tongass Hwy).

Listings

Arts and crafts Ketchikan prides itself on its nationwide reputation for indigenous and non-Native crafts. Locally renowned artists display their work, but some of the most striking material is that produced by Alaska Natives, which here reach their highest expression. Wandering around town you'll see a lot of cheap stuff, but the more discerning galleries are full of good stuff, much of it correspondingly expensive. Check out the Native-owned Carver at the Creek, 28 Creek St (☎225-3018), where Norman Jackson can be seen executing fine carving amid work by other Native craftspeople – lovely Tlingit blankets ($2000–4000), wooden masks from around $800, cedarbark hats, silverwork, and fine prints, some excellent ones for under $100.

Gravina Island Circumnavigation (3–4 days). Sixty miles of rocky shoreline with abundant wildlife, all easily accessible from Ketchikan. Note that one ten-mile section offers almost no protection from the weather.

Moser Bay (1 day). Just four miles from the northern end of Tongass Hwy there's the trailhead for Wolf Lake Trail which runs through 2.5 miles of forest and muskeg to the poorly maintained three-sided shelter (first-come, first-served; free).

Naha Bay (2–4 days). A wonderful opportunity to get a real wilderness feel without straying too far from Ketchikan. There's great scenery, plenty of wildlife, and excellent salmon and trout fishing along the Naha River. It can also work out pretty cheap since you can camp out every night and start your paddle right from town. Alternatively, save time and get a ride out to Knudson Cove marina (14.5 miles north of town) or even to the end of N Tongass Hwy (18 miles north). Aside from the pleasures of gentle paddling, you can hike the Wolf Lake Trail from Moser Bay (see above) and the 5.4-mile Naha River National Recreation Trail, which leads from Naha Bay past Jordan Lake to Heckman Lake. Both lakes have Forest Service cabins ($35). You don't need to paddle into the nearby Roosevelt Lagoon to access the trail, but be warned that racing tides make its entrance very dangerous and if you do want to paddle there, use the old tramway to transport your kayak.

Tatoosh Islands (1–4 days). Easily accessible islands just north of Ketchikan with beautiful beaches, seal haul-outs, and plenty of opportunity for camping and exploring.

MISTY FIORDS

The most ambitious kayaking destination is **Misty Fiords National Monument**, for which Southeast Sea Kayaks sell a superb trip-planning kit ($16) complete with topographic maps. It can be reached directly from Ketchikan, though it is at least two days paddle each way and requires open water kayaking skills. Most paddlers get a ride with Alaska Cruises (see "Misty Fiords" section, p.87) who charge $175–200 for combined drop-off and pick-up, depending on location. Once there, the scope is enormous with some people happily spending three or four weeks in the monument.

The main northern arm of Behm Canal is a little exposed for most paddlers, who aim for narrow corners such as Rudyerd Bay, Punchbowl Cove, and Walker Cove, typically camping or finding their way to some of the Forest Service cabins (which must be booked in advance; $35) and shelters (first-come, first-served; free) marked on our "Southern Inside Passage" map. Possibilities include: Alava Bay Cabin; following the mile-long trail at the back of Punchbowl Bay up the face of a solidified lava flow to Punchbowl Lake and the three-sided Punchbowl Lake Shelter; hiking a mile from Rudyerd Bay to Nooya Lake Shelter; hiking the 2.3-mile Winstanley Lake Trail to Winstanley Lake Shelter; Winstanley Island Cabin; Manzanita Bay Shelter; and Manzanita Lake Cabin, reached by the 3.5-mile Manzanita Lake Trail from near the shelter.

Also check out Soho Coho, 5 Creek St (☎225-5954, *www.trollart.com*), which is particularly good for prints, paintings, and original work by local artists; and Eagle Spirit Gallery, 310 Mission St (☎225-6626), with quality merchandise including bentwood boxes. For more information, pick up the free *Ketchikan Arts Guide* available all over town.

Banks Several downtown, all with ATMs, including First Bank, 331 Dock St.

Boat charters There are dozens of boat charter operators keen to take you out fishing, sightseeing in Misty Fiords National Monument, or who will drop you off at some remote cabin. Get a group of four or five together and this can work out to be a flexible and cost effective alternative to the cruise boats: Northern Lights Charters (☎247-8488 or 1-888/550-8488) are particularly good and have a booth at the visitor center.

Bookshop Parnassus Books, upstairs at 5 Creek St (☎225-7690), is easily the best bookstore in town with a matchless selection of Alaskana, alternative topics, as well as more mainstream titles.

Car rental Alaska Car Rental, 2828 Tongass Ave (☎225-5000 or 1-800/662-0007, fax 225-5041) offer the lowest rates and have a desk at the airport (☎225-2232). Avis (☎225-4515) and Payless (☎225-6004) are also at the airport.

Flightseeing and air charter companies Pacific Airways (☎225-3500 or 1-877/360-3500, *www.flypacificairways.com*) operate scheduled flights to Metlakatla, and Prince of Wales Island, and operate good value flightseeing trips to Misty Fiords; Promech Air, 1515 Tongass Ave (☎225-3845 or 1-800/860-3845, fax 225-3422, *www.promechair.com*), also fly float planes to Misty Fiords, Metlakatla, and various points on the coast of Prince of Wales Island. For some relatively cheap flightseeing, join one of their mail flights (daily 7am) which might visit two or more places around Prince of Wales Island usually for around $60 (though it could be up to $130 for the longer runs); Taquan Air, 1007 Water St (☎225-8800 or 1-800/770-8800), have scheduled departures for Hyder and Prince of Wales Island, as well as flightseeing trips to Misty Fiords ($160), around the local area ($70–110), and to Anan Creek Bear Observatory (3hr; $300).

Internet access Soapy's Internet Station upstairs in the Salmon Landing Mall, and on Front St by the tunnel (open when ships are in town; ☎247-9191), has fast machines operated by cards that cost $3 for 15min, $5 for 50min and $10 for 100min. Cyber by the Sea, upstairs inside Salmon Landing (Mon–Sat 9am–6pm, Sun 10am–4pm; ☎247-6904), has Macs and PCs and charges $6 for half an hour. The library (see below) has free use for members. Membership is available for a $5 fee plus a $20 deposit refundable when you leave town – worthwhile for stays of a few days.

Laundry and showers The Mat, 989 Steadman (daily 6am–11pm; ☎225-0628) is half a mile south of downtown.

Left luggage The Home Office, Plaza Mall (Mon–Sat 9am–8pm, Sun noon–5pm; ☎225-7587) have three sizes of lockers ($3–5 a day). It is roughly a mile from both the downtown area and the AMHS ferry dock.

Library Ketchikan Public Library, 629 Dock St (Mon–Wed 10am–8pm, Thurs–Sat 10am–6pm, Sun 1–5pm; ☎225-3331).

Medical assistance Ketchikan Medical Clinic, 3612 Tongass Ave, near the AMHS ferry dock (Mon–Fri 7.30am–5.30pm; ☎225-5144).

Pharmacy Downtown Drugstore, 300 Front St (☎225-3144).

Post Office The main post office, 3609 Tongass Ave (☎225-9601) is a few yards north of the AMHS ferry dock, and there's a more convenient suboffice at the corner of Main St and Mission St (Mon–Sat 9am–5.30pm). The **General Delivery** ZIP Code is 99901.

Taxes City sales tax is 5.5 percent. Hotel rooms incur a whopping 11.5 percent tax which is included in our price codes.

Misty Fiords National Monument

The essential excursion from Ketchikan is a visit to the Connecticut-sized **MISTY FIORDS NATIONAL MONUMENT**, an awe-inspiring tranche of narrow fjords flanked by **sheer 3000ft glacially scoured granite walls** strung by gossamer waterfalls and surrounded by dense rainforest. Located between twenty and sixty miles east of Ketchikan, Misty Fiords drapes partly over the eastern side of Revillagigedo Island but is primarily defined by the mountainous terrain between two fjords, the 117-mile Behm Canal and the 72-mile hairline thread of Portland Canal, which marks the US–Canada border.

At its most atmospheric when wreathed in low-lying cloud, Misty (as it is often known) was created by presidential proclamation in 1978, and remains almost entirely undeveloped. No roads lead here. There aren't even any airstrips, so access is by cruise boat, float plane, or kayak. As with so many vast areas of wilderness, most people visit roughly the same area, though it is quite possible to get air-charter companies to fly you anywhere you want. Day-cruises and scheduled flightseeing trips tend to concentrate on the area around **Rudyerd Bay**, off Behm Canal some twenty minutes by plane or fifty sea miles from Ketchikan. Here the cliffs plunge as far below the surface as they soar above it, notably in **Punchbowl Cove**, widely regarded as the highlight of the monument and an obligatory stop on every boat trip. Along the way you pass the volcanic plug of **New Eddystone Rock**, a 237-foot pillar of rock rising from the middle of Behm Canal, which Captain Vancouver, exploring here in 1793, obviously thought was reminiscent of the lighthouse-topped namesake off the southern English coast. The trees around its base are almost swamped at high tide, but there is just enough room for kayakers to pitch a tent, provided the waves aren't too high.

Wildlife spotting opportunities are plentiful, with seals, porpoises, and orca in the fjords and bears, deer, mountain goats, and more on land, all watched over by bald eagles.

Cruises, flights, and cabins

The most convenient way to see something of Misty Fiords is with Alaska Cruises (☎225-6044 or 1-800/225-1905, fax 225-8636, *www.goldbelttours.com*) who run six-hour **cruises** ($145) and four-hour **cruise and flight packages** ($198). Trips are geared around the combo packages, so if you can afford the extra cash, go for the cruise/fly option (preferably in that order), not only to take in the excellent airborne views, but to avoid the identical itinerary and commentary on the return journey.

If time is limited you can **fly both ways**; several flightseeing companies (see opposite) have good deals. These same companies will also fly you and your supplies in to one of the fourteen **rustic cabins** rented out by the Forest Service ($25–45, mostly $35; ☎1-877/444-6777), two of which are beside salt water, the remaining twelve are on freshwater lakes, often linked to the fjord by a short trail. Alternatively you can kayak here (see box, p.84) and gain access to some cabins that way.

Metlakatla

If you arrive by float plane at the small Native village of **METLAKATLA**, twelve miles southeast of Ketchikan, you'll set foot at the very spot where Anglican missionary **William Duncan** landed back in 1887 along with 823 followers, all Tsimshian Natives. They were on the run both from British Columbia, where Tsimshian land claims weren't respected, and from the more threatening Canadian bishops of the Church Missionary Society (CMS) who had fallen out with Duncan. Fortunately he had friends in high places in New York – Henry Wellcome and Thomas Edison to name two – who pulled strings for him in Washington and coaxed the US government to grant the community Annette Island, site of a largely abandoned Tlingit settlement and now the **only Native American reservation** in Alaska.

Under the leadership of Father Duncan, Alaska's only Tsimshian settlement became one of the most successful CMS missions; a model of religious, social, and economic independence that became a template for similar communities elsewhere. Duncan had already spent thirty years working with the Tsimshian in BC, and continued his efforts to get rid of intertribal slavery while keeping the church in control of secular as well as religious activities. He also became something of a patriarch, allegedly siring dozens of children to Native women.

The group's landing point proved highly suitable, with a waterfall (close to the modern ferry dock) that could be harnessed for power and water, a sloping beach which made an ideal site for a cannery, and enough timber to start a sawmill, build frame houses and the church. What is known as the **Duncan Memorial Church**, on 4th Avenue, is a replica of the original that burned down in 1948 and is guarded by Duncan's grave. Although Duncan is well remembered, his religion has failed to flower, and none of Metlakatla's nine churches are now Anglican.

There's more to be seen in the single-story wooden-frame **Duncan Cottage Museum**, Jail Street, close to the small boat harbor (open when the occasional small cruise ship is in or by appointment on ☎886-8687; $2), in the house where Duncan lived from 1894 until his death in 1914. It contains plenty of photos and material on the life and times of Duncan and the people of Metlakatla along with the Bible Duncan brought with him from England, a very early Edison phonograph, a prominent portrait of Queen Victoria, and Duncan's bedroom complete with his personal effects and a couple of large safes. There's also discussion of World War II when Annette Island became an important military base.

Once you've seen the museum, there's not a great deal to do. Entry to the tribal longhouse and Native dancing are only for those on the Metlakatla Native Village Tour (see below), and an hour or two is enough to wander the waterfront with its cannery, the recently closed sawmill, and the only **fish traps** left in the state. With time on your hands, stroll half a mile out along Western Avenue until you reach Pioneer Park, a small nub of land threaded by rough boardwalks with great sea views. Alternatively, hike a mile and a half out along Airport Road to the sandstone outcrop of **Yellow Hill**, which affords a great view over the town and Prince of Wales Island. **Cyclists** have the run of the island's fairly extensive road system, giving access to more hiking along the **Purple Lake Trail**, four miles south of town, and to the appropriately named **Sand Dollar Beach**.

Practicalities

It will only take most visitors a few hours to see all they want to of Metlakatla, so AMHS **ferry** passengers will want to visit on Saturday when the *Aurora* makes two round-trips from Ketchikan. The first boat departs Ketchikan at 6.15am (only staying in port for thirty minutes) and the second leaves Metlakatla at 8.45pm giving over twelve hours in town. There are several other ferry sailings each week, but all combinations require overnight stays. The ferry arrives a mile from town and you may well get offered a lift.

Unfortunately, most of the town's sights are closed on Saturday, so you may find it more convenient to arrive by float plane with Promech Air (☎225-3845 in Ketchikan, ☎886-3845 in Metlakatla) who fly several times daily charging $27 each way (almost twice as much as the ferry), or Pacific Airways (☎1-877/360-3500, in Craig ☎826-5400, in Ketchikan ☎225-3500, *www.flypacificairways.com*), who are a dollar cheaper. Bearing these factors in mind, many find it more convenient to visit on the four-hour Metlakatla Native Village Tour (May–Sept Wed & Fri; $40; reservations essential ☎1-877/886-8687, fax 886-7997, *www.tours.metlakatla.net*), which includes a salmon bake, tribal dance in full regalia, and a tour of the town's fish processing facility; flights are extra. The dance presentation alone (same days) costs $10.

If you do decide to stay the best **accommodation** is either *Uncle Fred's Café and Inn*, on Western Avenue, across the street from the new boat harbor (☎886-5007; *unclefred@att.net*; ②), which has motel-style rooms with private entrances, or the *Metlakatla Hotel and Suites* (☎886-3456, *methot5@metlakatla.net*; ③), which has slightly larger rooms but is otherwise a second-choice option. There are no formal campgrounds and **camping** isn't encouraged, though if you walk far enough out of town you can pitch a tent pretty much anywhere for a night or two: try along Western Road beyond the cemetery. In the unlikely event you want to stay on the island more than four days, you'll need to see the secretary of the tribal council in the municipal building in Milton Street; no appointment is necessary.

Uncle Fred's is the best **place to eat**, with quality home-style cooked meals and gourmet pizza, though the prices are high and you might just want to grab a burger, donut, or espresso at the Laesk Mini-Mart on Milton Street, which is your best bet for **groceries**. Note that this is a dry community, so **no alcohol** is allowed.

Prince of Wales Island

Prince of Wales Island is Alaska's second largest (after Kodiak), over 135 miles long and threaded by more miles of road than the rest of Southeast put together – over 1500 in total. Though many are dead-end logging roads, they provide unparalleled access to this mountainous landscape shaped by ancient glaciers and subsequently flooded to create a deeply indented coastline pocked by small bays and rocky coves. **Wildlife** is abundant, and everywhere you go there are streams thick with salmon – indeed, the **fishing is legendary**, and many of the island's visitors are here to haul in prize specimens while staying in the exclusive fishing lodges that line the coast.

The spruce and hemlock forests that cloaked the steep island's hillsides for millennia have, in recent decades, become the most savagely logged area of the Tongass National Forest. Forestry has downsized drastically in recent years, but scars left by clear-cuts can appear unsightly for a number of years after cutting. Still, the forest seems to recover quickly and without trees crowding in on all sides the long views are excellent. What's more the logging legacy makes this a wonderful place to explore by 4WD or mountain bike (or even just an ordinary saloon).

With the exception of the limestone **caves** in the north of the island and several excellent collections of recarved totem poles, there are few sights, but POW (as it is often known) is a great place to unwind for a few days. It's not the sort of place that rewards a quick visit – you really need time to explore and slip into the pace of the place; perhaps resting up in one of twenty Forest Service cabins, many with lake access and good fishing, or spending a few days paddling one of the canoe routes, or just strolling the driftwood-strewn beaches. The island is also a big hunting destination – in late April and May **bear hunters** hog the roads and rental cars can be hard to get.

Traditionally, Prince of Wales Island was Tlingit territory, but around three hundred years ago – and a hundred years before European contact – **Haida** from Canada's Queen Charlotte Islands got a toehold and gradually occupied much of the island. They continued to trade with their kin on the Nass River in what is now British Columbia, and during the fur-trade years amassed great wealth. At this time, the potlatch reached its peak and totem-pole raising was at its height, a tradition remembered in the **totem parks** at Hydaburg, Klawock and, most notably, Kasaan.

By the late nineteenth century, Presbyterian missionaries and fishing interests were well entrenched here, the former suppressing Native traditions, with the latter bringing disease and altering the economic dynamic. Haida numbers dropped from an estimated 10,000 to around 800 as canneries were set up around the coast. The importance of these gradually gave way to logging, which for the second half of the twentieth century was the mainstay of the local economy. Mills have closed in the last five years leading to high unemployment in some areas. The Clinton administration is not well liked around here, and "environmentalist" is a dirty word.

Planning, arrival, and getting around

Before you head out to Prince of Wales Island, visit the trip-planning room in the Discovery Center in Ketchikan for detailed information on the campgrounds, canoe routes, hikes, and the twenty-odd Forest Service cabins. They also stock the worthwhile *Prince of Wales Island Forest Service Road Guide* ($4.50), and may also have copies of the comprehensive *Explore Prince of Wales Island* brochure, otherwise available from the visitor center in Craig (see p.94).

Prince of Wales islanders hope that by the summer of 2002 there'll be a new twice-daily ferry between Ketchikan and Hollis. Currently the cheapest way to get to Prince of Wales Island is by the near-daily AMHS **ferry** from Ketchikan which drops you (usually around 9pm) in Hollis, where there's nothing more than a booking office and public phone.

HIKING AND CANOEING ON PRINCE OF WALES ISLAND

Though there are a couple of well-known short trails, Prince of Wales Island isn't especially noted for its hiking, and serious outdoors fans might be better off considering the two excellent canoe routes, best tackled from May to September. The coastline lends itself superbly to **kayaking** – anything from a day or two to a several-week circumnavigation – and while no formal routes have been mapped out (though there are plans), you can get some good ideas, along with full details of the hikes and paddles described below, from the Discovery Center in Ketchikan.

One Duck Trail (2.5 miles round-trip; 2hr; 1200ft ascent). Moderately steep but rewarding hike with magnificent views from the small shelter and open muskeg at the top. Starts on Hydaburg Rd, two miles south of the Hollis-Craig Hwy.

Soda Lake Trail (5 miles round-trip; 3hr; negligible ascent). Fairly easy walking across muskeg and through forest ending at Soda Lake and some bubbling mineral springs with good bird and wildlife spotting. Starts on Hydaburg Rd, twelve miles south of the Hollis-Craig Hwy.

Honker Divide Canoe Route (3–4 days; 30 miles; 150ft elevation gain). A rugged and strenuous route formerly used by early trappers and requiring good canoeing and backcountry camping skills. Long sections may need lining unless there has been recent rain, waterfalls and rapids need to be portaged, and there will be sweepers to avoid. It is a rewarding experience though, and the Honker Lake cabin (only accessible through this route) may be available for the first or second nights.

Sarkar Lake Canoe Route (6–8 hours; 15-mile loop; negligible ascent). Easy route through a roadless area linking half a dozen lakes by means of stream and short boardwalk portages, often spread over 2–3 days. Good fishing and wildlife viewing. There's a Forest Service cabin beside Sarkar Lake, two miles from the put-in.

Since there is **no public transport** on the island, you really need to either bring a **bicycle** or prearrange for a **rental car** to meet you at the ferry. Klawock-based Wilderness Rent-a-Car (☎755-2691 or 1-800/949-2205, *wildernesscarrental @go.com*) offer vehicles from $59 a day (though most are $80–90; book early) plus 30¢ a mile after the first hundred, and charge an extra $50 for the convenience of being able to pick up and drop off the car at the ferry. Alaska Rentals (☎826-2966, fax 826-2932, *www.alaskarentals.com*, *info@alaskarentals.com*) offer older Suburbans and Broncos for $50 a day plus 30¢ a mile ($75 a day unlimited mileage) and also do the $50 drop-off deal. For stays of three days or more it may work out cheaper to rent something in Ketchikan and bring it over on the ferry (around $50 each way for a small car).

If you only want to visit the main town of Craig, you could perhaps hitch, or go by Sea Otter **taxis** (☎755-2362 or 1-800/642-0066), who will run you from Hollis to Craig for around $25 if booked in advance.

An alternative approach is to take a scheduled float plane flight from Ketchikan with Pacific Airways (☎1-877/360-3500 or in Craig ☎826-5400, in Ketchikan ☎225-3500, *www.flypacificairways.com*), who fly to Craig ($85 each way), where you can pick up a rental car without the $50 delivery fee.

Once out of town you can camp on any Forest Service land: the map in the *Explore Prince of Wales Island* brochure shows where private land is located, and also pinpoints several popular "dispersed" camping sites.

Almost everywhere you go on Prince of Wales Island there is someone keen to rent you a boat or take you fishing. What you don't see are the exclusive **fly-in lodges** dotted around the coast, some in abandoned canneries and most charging four figure sums for the privilege of spending two or three days there: if this is what you want, the visitor center in Craig can point you in the right direction.

Hydaburg and Klawock

From the dock at Hollis it is smooth asphalt all the way to Klawock and Craig. After twelve miles, Hydaburg Road runs twenty miles south past the trailhead for One Duck Trail (Mile 2), the Cable Creek Fish Pass (Mile 8), and the trailhead for Soda Lake Trail (Mile 12) to **HYDABURG**. This small waterside Haida town, established in 1911 when three local villages combined, is not known for its warm welcome to visitors, but you might call in to inspect the CCC **totem park** constructed in the late 1930s.

Sticking on the Hollis–Craig Highway, you soon reach the first-come, first-served *Harris River* **campground**, Mile 14.6 ($8 per vehicle), an attractive and organized site with toilets, pump water, and pleasant walks through the forest. At Mile 25.6 you can stop to see the workings of the community-run **Prince of Wales Hatchery** (daily 8am–5pm; donations appreciated), or continue a mile to **KLAWOCK**, which serves as the island's main intersection where Big Salt Lake Road heads north. The junction is marked by a modern mall with a post office, liquor store, supermarket, and a restaurant or two; the Native village of Klawock lies a couple of miles west. This was a very important place in the early years of American Alaska; one of the first canneries in Alaska was set up here in 1878, and two of Alaska's first three sawmills were constructed nearby. Now it is chiefly known for the collection of fifteen totem poles erected under the auspices of the CCC (see box, p.76) and displayed on a sloping hill beside a couple of roads; not the prettiest of spots but worth a look nonetheless.

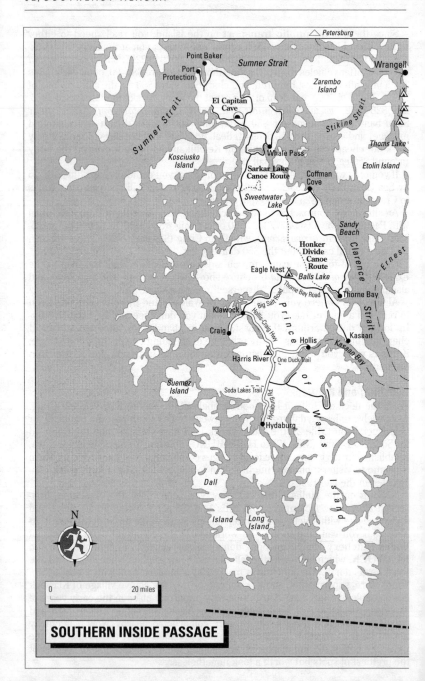

SOUTHERN INSIDE PASSAGE

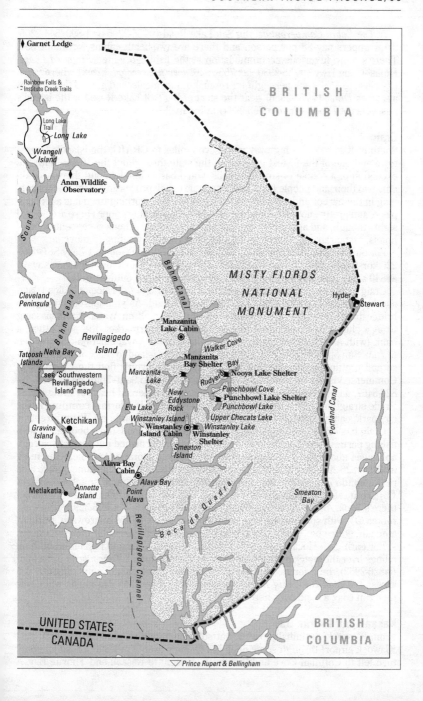

◆ **Garnet Ledge**

Rainbow Falls & Institute Creek Trails

BRITISH COLUMBIA

Long Lake Trail

Long Lake

Wrangell Island

▲ **Anan Wildlife Observatory**

Sound

Behm Canal

MISTY FIORDS NATIONAL MONUMENT

Hyder ● Stewart

Cleveland Peninsula

Revillagigedo Island

■ **Manzanita Lake Cabin** ◉

Walker Cove

Tatoosh Islands Naha Bay

see 'Southwestern Revillagigedo Island' map

Manzanita Bay Shelter ■ *Bay*

Manzanita Lake ◆ **Nooya Lake Shelter**

Rudyerd

New Eddystone Rock

Punchbowl Cove

■ **Punchbowl Lake Shelter**

Punchbowl Lake

Ella Lake

Upper Checats Lake

Winstanley Island

Winstanley Island Cabin ◉ *Winstanley Lake*

Winstanley Shelter ■

Smeaton Island

Ketchikan

Gravina Island

Portland Canal

■ **Alava Bay Cabin**

◉ *Alava Bay*

Point Alava

● **Metlakatla**

Annette Island

Smeaton Bay

Boca de Quadra

Revillagigedo Channel

UNITED STATES
CANADA

BRITISH COLUMBIA

▽ Prince Rupert & Bellingham

At *Log Cabin Campgrounds*, Big Salt Lake Road (☎755-2205 or 1-800/544-2205; ①), campers pay $8 per person and there are two-berth cabins for under $50. There's more luxurious accommodation at the fishing-oriented *Fireweed Lodge*, Hollis–Craig Hwy (☎755-2930, fax 755-2936, *www.fireweedlodge.com*) where you'll pay close to $150 each per night for room, hot tub, meals, and guided fishing. **Eat** at *Dave's Diner* (☎755-2986) near the start of Big Salt Lake Road, or the island's best pizza at *Papa's Pizza* (☎755-2244) in the mall.

Craig

South of Klawock, the highway runs seven miles to **CRAIG**, the island's largest town and one of the fastest growing in the state throughout the 1990s. With the exception of a couple of smallish malls, you'd barely know it, and there are still only two thousand people here. With a couple of fish processing plants, boats bobbing in the harbor and the hard-bitten tenor of a real working town it is a likeable place, and pretty enough to wander round on a sunny afternoon. There are no real sights though, and apart from making use of the island's densest concentration of hotels, restaurants, and bars, you'll soon find yourself wanting to move on.

For outdoor activities, get along to Log Cabin Sporting Goods, 1 Easy St (☎826-2205 or 1-888/265-0375, fax 826-2210), who rent out canoes for $20 a day, kayaks at $40 a day (doubles $50), and stock lots of fishing and outdoor gear.

Craig occupies Craig Island, linked by a short bridge to Prince of Wales Island and by a causeway to the smaller Graveyard Island. As you approach over the bridge from Prince of Wales Island you find yourself on Water Street passing Craig's cluster of minimalls where you'll find a supermarket, the post office, a bank (with ATM), *Papas Pizza*, *Burger King*, and the Voyageur Bookstore (open to 7pm, Sun 5pm; ☎826-2333), the best place on the island to relax over an espresso and muffin, or surf the Net. This is also where you'll find the Chamber of Commerce **visitor center** (Tues–Thurs 9am–4pm, Fri 9am–3pm; ☎826-3870, fax 826-5467, *www.princeofwalescoc.org*). The older commercial heart of Craig is half a mile straight on, and Graveyard Island, where there is informal **camping** in the city park, can be reached by following Hamilton Drive south, off Water Street.

Craig has easily the largest range of **hotels** on the island, most booked up with fishing parties. The cheapest rooms are the simply furnished but perfectly acceptable ones above the *TLC Laundry & Rooms*, Cold Storage Road near the minimalls (☎826-2966, fax 826-2932, *www.alaskarentals.com*; ②. The same people also rent a condo in Klawock sleeping five (⑤) and a cedar home suitable for eight (⑧), **rent skiffs** ($125–250 a day) and run the laundromat. More upmarket there's *Ruth Anne's Hotel* on Water Street (☎826-3878, fax 826-3293; suites ⑥, rooms ④), with spacious new rooms (⑤) equipped with TV, microwave, refrigerator, and coffee pot, plus older and smaller rooms that have a bit more character.

For **eating**, the locals favorite is *Ruth Anne's* with a bar and restaurant built on pilings over the water by the dock. Nearby there's *Jerzee's Take-n-bake* pizza joint (☎826-2952), best for takeout pizza (from $10), taco salads, and calzone; and across the road the *Craig Inn* is always animated and has live music whenever they can coax a band over here.

Kasaan and Thorne Bay

From Klawock, an initially paved, but subsequently dirt, road heads north past Klawock airport through some open hill country twenty miles to a road junction: turn left to Coffman Cove and the caves, or right to Kasaan and Thorne Bay. A couple of miles along the Klawock–Thorne Bay road you reach the lovely first-come, first-served *Eagle Nest* **campground** ($8 per vehicle), with well-spaced sites, some of which are walk-in platforms with lake views. Even if you're not staying, take a few minutes to stroll along the half-mile boardwalk around **Balls Lake**.

Beyond the campground a tortuous and boneshaking seventeen-mile road cuts southeast off the Klawock–Thorne Bay road to the tiny waterside village of **KASAAN**, one of Southeast's best (if least convenient) places to see totem poles. Though now mostly populated by whites, it was originally founded a century back when the lure of mining and fishing jobs attracted Haida here from the now-abandoned village of Old Kasaan. The only reason to come here is to visit the abandoned **totem park**, a mile west of the village. Park by the Community Hall, walk back towards the beach, and take the last track on the right. Follow this for twenty minutes or so through beachside woods to the next bay, perhaps the finest setting of any Alaskan totem park. The poles and clan house are the work of the CCC in the late 1930s, but its neglected state, the authentic feeling of its location, and the lack of any commercial trappings make it a wonderful spot. If you're here by yourselves, especially in the early morning or at dusk, it is particularly touching.

The beach is backed by the clan house with its platforms around the sunken fire pit, and powerfully carved roof supports only partly achieving their intended purpose as the forest gradually reclaims its own. In front, a superb pole faces out to sea, four feet thick at its base and over fifty feet tall, with bulbous eyes set in four-foot-high faces. Nearby, several other poles lurk in the woods, four of them in a ring almost swallowed by the undergrowth.

You have to return the way you came to get to **THORNE BAY**, until recently the site of the Ketchikan Pulp Company mill, set up here in 1962 when it moved from Hollis. Once described as the world's largest logging camp it is now mostly of interest to anglers, though you can stay in shared-bath rooms at *Welcome Inn B&B* (☎828-3950 or 1-888/828-3940; ④), and **campers** should stock up at the *Thorne Bay Market* before making for the bays to the north.

Coffman Cove and El Capitan Cave

North of Thorne Bay, the road deteriorates to a single lane and hugs the coast for ten miles passing some beautiful little bays. You can camp pretty much anywhere you like along here and probably the only people you'll see are those in the occasional RV parked in some pullout. **Sandy Beach**, six miles out, is the most popular spot with picnic table, toilets, and fire rings.

A former site of a Tlingit village and 1950s logging camp is now the village of **COFFMAN COVE**, which occupies an idyllic bay around thirty miles north of Thorne Bay. Again there's little to do but beachcomb and fish, perhaps best done while **staying** at *Oceanview RV Park and Campground* (☎ & fax 329-2015, *www.coffmancove.org/rvpark.html*), which has camping for $12, full hookup for $22, and basic trailers sleeping four for $35. It is nicely set by the sea, but is simple, and you might prefer *Rain Country B&B*, just as you enter on the road from the south (☎329-2274, fax 329-2254, *www.coffmancove.org/rcbandb.html*; ④), where plain rooms share a wonderful deck with great views across to Etolin Island and an outdoor barbecue to grill your catch. Skiff rentals are available at $75 a day. Since there are no restaurants for miles you'll want to avail yourselves of lunch and dinner for $15 a day extra.

Much of the north of the island is **karst landscape**, underlain by limestone riddled with dozens of caves, most of them barely explored (scientifically that is), if at all. The prize exhibit here is the **El Capitan Cave**, used by Native peoples as

---

HYDER

Not so long ago it was relatively cheap, though time consuming, to ride the AMHS ferry from Ketchikan to **HYDER** (pop. 70), a tiny outpost of Alaska at the head of the Portland Canal. Now the ferry service has stopped and Hyder seems entirely isolated from Alaska, far more closely linked with its British Columbian neighbor Stewart – just two miles away by road – with which it shares a Canadian phone code (☎250), Canadian currency and Canadian national holidays. Even the police are of the Mountie variety.

This southernmost and easternmost of Alaskan towns is a ramshackle place that only really attracts people visiting Stewart to say they've been to Alaska and to drink in one or both of its two bars. At the *Glacier Inn* the tradition is to pin a dollar to the wall in case you return broke and need a drink, and then toss back a shot of hard liquor in one and receive an "I've Been Hyderized" card. The result is many thousands of tacked dollars and the "world's most expensive wallpaper." It sounds a bit of a tourist carry-on, but if you arrive out of season there's a genuine warmth about the place that warrants its claims to be the "The Friendliest Ghost Town in Alaska." The bars are often open 23 hours a day and a couple of motels are on hand for you to take a break in: the *Sealaska Inn*, Premier Avenue (☎250/636-9003; ②), and the preferable *Grand View Inn* (☎250/636-9174; ③); both cheaper than their Stewart equivalents. If you want something to soak up the alcohol, make for the *Sealaska Inn Restaurant* (☎250/636-2486) for no-nonsense food.

From Ketchikan, you can fly here with Taquan Air (☎225-8800 & 1-800/770-8800).

---

long as 3400 years ago judging by charcoal left from torches. More recently, speleologists have discovered the El Cap Pit, which is the deepest known natural pit in the US with an initial drop of almost six hundred feet. The Forest Service run **guided tours** (late May to early Sept Thurs–Sun; free; ☎828-3304) several times throughout the day, but they're becoming popular and groups are limited to six, so you should book a couple of days in advance. To cope with muddy conditions and lack of formed trails you'll need sturdy footwear and warm clothing, and also have to make your own way to the site, which is towards the north of the island (see map, p.92), almost a hundred miles (3–4hr drive) from the ferry dock at Hollis. Freelance exploration is prevented by a locked gate fifty yards in, but you are welcome to explore the entrance area after negotiating the fifteen-minute access trail and its 370 steps.

Wrangell and around

The small fishing town of **WRANGELL** is the next ferry stop after Ketchikan and has an altogether quieter and more old-fashioned feel, with just a few relatively minor sights all easily accessible on foot. Right in the busy harbor and accessible by a short boardwalk is **Chief Shakes Island**, which holds an excellent collection of totem poles and a replica tribal house filled with Tlingit blankets. About a mile to the north, the ancient rock carvings at **Petroglyph Beach** defy explanation and have proven difficult to date, but are fascinating to seek, something possible any time except high tide.

Though Wrangell is by no means an unfriendly place, you sometimes feel there is a grudging acceptance of your presence in what is a fiercely independent town

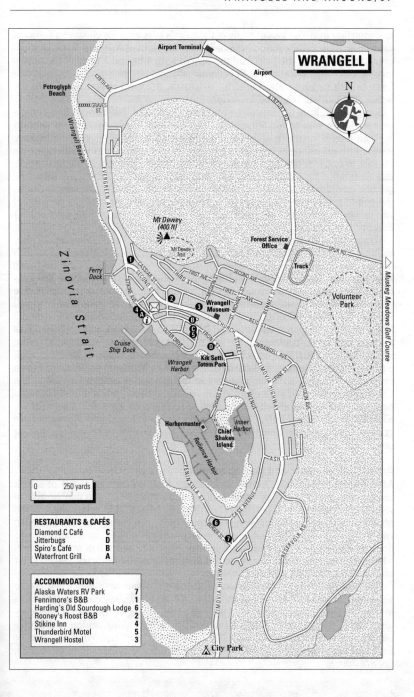

WRANGELL

N

Airport Terminal

Airport

Petroglyph Beach

FIFTH AVE.

GRAVES ST.

Wrangell Beach

Zinovia Strait

Mt Dewey (400 ft)

Mt Dewey Trail

EVERGREEN AVE.

Forest Service Office

SPUR RD

Track

Muskeg Meadows Golf Course

Ferry Dock

CASSIAR ST.

SECOND ST.

STIKINE AVE.

THIRD ST.

FIRST AVE.

SECOND AVE.

MCKINNON ST.

FIRST ST.

BENNETT ST.

Volunteer Park

①

②

③ Wrangell Museum

④ Ⓐ ⓘ

Ⓑ

Ⓒ ⑤

Ⓓ

OUTER DRIVE

FRONT ST.

CHURCH ST.

REID ST.

WRANGELL AVE.

ZIMOVIA HIGHWAY

PINE ST.

LENOIR AVE.

Cruise Ship Dock

Wrangell Harbor

Kik Setti Totem Park

CASE AVENUE

Harbormaster

SHAKES ST.

Chief Shakes Island

Inner Harbor

Reliance Harbor

PENINSULA ST.

CASE AVENUE

ASH ST.

RESERVOIR RD

ZIMOVIA HIGHWAY

⑥ BURGER ST.

⑦

0   250 yards

RESTAURANTS & CAFÉS

Diamond C Café	**C**
Jitterbugs	**D**
Spiro's Café	**B**
Waterfront Grill	**A**

ACCOMMODATION

Alaska Waters RV Park	**7**
Fennimore's B&B	**1**
Harding's Old Sourdough Lodge	**6**
Rooney's Roost B&B	**2**
Stikine Inn	**4**
Thunderbird Motel	**5**
Wrangell Hostel	**3**

△ City Park

still smarting from the loss of many of the town's jobs with the closure of the local sawmill in 1994. People round here believe in the right of Alaskans to make whatever use they can of the land, and the loss of both jobs and a third of the town's income has come as a shock both economically and psychologically. Always comfortable with its blue-collar workaday existence, the town now wrestles with the notion that tourism might be its savior.

Some people have no difficulty with the concept, and half a dozen tour companies are happy to take you out, either south to watch **bears gorging on salmon** at Anan Creek, or north and inland along the churning waters of the **Stikine River**, perhaps calling at the **Garnet Ledge**, where local children gather garnets for sale to tourists, or **Chief Shakes Hot Springs**, a perennially popular weekend destination for locals. Visitor numbers are still low here though – they only get one medium-sized cruise ship every week or two – and it can sometimes be difficult to gather enough people for a trip since they are arranged by demand. If you can get a group of four or six together you'll find your options (and prices) improve dramatically.

Wrangell claims to have been ruled by four nations; Tlingit, Russian, British, and the US. In the early nineteenth century, the Tlingit people were trading with the Russian-American company which feared the expansionism of the Hudson's Bay Company. To protect their rights to the sea otters hereabouts, the Russians established Redoubt St Dionysius in 1834, a small fort that soon drew local Native villagers to settle in and around Chief Shakes Island in the middle of Wrangell Harbor. To settle some trading dispute in 1840, the fort was leased to the Hudson's Bay Company, who renamed it Fort Stikine and helped established it as a supply post for fur traders and the first batch of gold seekers who headed up the Stikine River in 1861. When the United States purchased Alaska in 1867 they took control of the settlement and changed its name to Wrangell in honor of Baron Ferdinand Wrangel, a former manager of the Russian-American Company. The Canadian Cassiar gold rush came in the 1870s and thousands of miners brought heady days to this rural outpost, a situation repeated on a smaller scale with the Klondike gold rush of 1897. Canneries and logging followed and proved to have greater staying power, though Wrangell has long ceased to be a major fishing port, and now the mill has gone.

Arrival, information, and getting around

AMHS ferries (☎874-3711) don't usually stay long enough for much of a look around, though by grabbing a **taxi** (call Star Cab ☎874-3622) you may be able to see the petroglyphs, and perhaps Chief Shakes Island. The ferries dock at the northern edge of downtown Wrangell, from where you can easily walk into town and to most of the accommodation. The **airport** (☎874-3308), with daily connections to Ketchikan, Petersburg, and Juneau, is a mile and a half north of town, where you can **rent a car** from Practical Rent-A-Car (☎874-3975, fax 874-3911) for around $50 a day with unlimited mileage.

The **visitor center**, 107 Stikine Ave (Mon–Fri 10am–4pm and when cruise ships are in; ☎874-3901 or 1-800/367-9745, fax 874-3905, *www.wrangell.com*), is inside the *Stikine Inn*; if it's closed pick up a free *Wrangell Guide* from the ferry terminal or the museum. For information on hikes, cabins, and anything else out in the surrounding Tongass National Forest visit the Wrangell Ranger District **Forest Service office**, 525 Bennett St (Mon–Fri 8am–5pm; ☎874-2323, fax 874-7595).

Though it is easy enough to wander around the main sights in Wrangell, you might want to rent transport from Solo Cat Sports, 441 Church St (☎874-2920, fax 874-2923, *www.thetongass.com/solocat.htm*), who rent bicycles ($21–69 a day depending on sophistication), canoes ($42–50 a day), kayaks ($40–45 a day), and rafts ($90–150 a day), and organize a number of guided trips, pretty much to order. Breakaway Adventures (see "Listings", p.102) also rent single kayaks and canoes, for $40 a day; and Alaska Vistas rent single and double kayaks for $45 and $55 a day respectively.

There is something to be said for adding a little interpretation on a **local tour**, best done with Rain Walker Expeditions (☎874-2549, *www.rainwalkerexpeditions.com*), who run naturalist-guided walking and van tours. These start with a visit to the Petroglyph Beach (1.5hr; $15), which includes a rubbing kit for use on the replica glyphs, and a historic downtown tour (1.5hr; $12) including Chief Shakes Island, and range up to a half-day island exploration ($89).

Accommodation

For such a tiny place, Wrangell is fairly well supplied with accommodation, including a simple hostel, a couple of motels and several B&Bs. Camping is good too, with half a dozen designated places to camp along the road system; as well as the **campgrounds** and RV parks listed below there are several more free sites further along Zimovia Hwy at Mile 11, Mile 14, Mile 17, Mile 23, and Mile 28.

Alaska Waters RV Park, 241 Berger St (☎874-2378). Small and not especially attractive lot with just six power and water hookup sites for $15. Showers are $3 extra, and the city dump station is at the corner of Front Stand Case Ave.

City Park, 1.5 miles south on Zimovia Hwy. The nearest campground to town, well sited in woods beside the channel, with first-come, first-served sites available for a one-night maximum stay. There are shelters to cook under and marginal toilets but no showers. Free.

Fennimore's B&B, 312 Evergreen Ave (☎874-3012, fax 874-3697, *wrgbbb@seapac.net*). Comfy and friendly B&B conveniently sited by the ferry dock with two upstairs rooms with shared bath, and three downstairs rooms with private entrances and their own bathrooms. All are pleasantly furnished, have cable TV, and include a continental breakfast supplied in your room. ④.

Harding's Old Sourdough Lodge, 1104 Peninsula St (☎874-3613 or 1-800/874-3613, fax 874-3455, *www.akgetaway.com*). Large cedar log building at the southern edge of town with high-standard rooms in various sizes to suit individuals and small groups, and home-style meals for guests only (breakfast and lunch $10, dinner $20). The best deals are the wilderness and adventure packages such as two nights with one day spent either on the Stikine River, viewing bald eagles, whale-watching, or visiting the Anan Bear Observatory ($363 per person); two nights with car rental and green fees for Wrangell's nine-hole golf course ($298); and six nights, with five days spent kayaking the Stikine and flightseeing the LeConte glacier ($1350). Six-person suite ⑧, sauna room sleeping three ⑥, rooms ④.

Rooney's Roost B&B, 206 McKinnon St (☎874-2026, *rroost@seapac.net*). Attractive B&B, close to town with recently renovated rooms, phones, TV, antique furniture, clawfoot baths in the rooms with bathrooms, a large lounge and a full sit-down breakfast. Private bath ④, shared bath ③.

Shoemaker Bay Recreation Site, 4.5 miles south on Zimovia Hwy. Another free site with eight RV spaces, toilets, picnic tables, shelters, beach fishing, and a five-night maximum. Handy for the Rainbow Falls Trail.

Stikine Inn, Evergreen Ave (☎874-3388 or 1-888/874-3388, fax 874-3923, *www.stikine.com*). Wrangell's largest hotel, a little dated but right on the waterfront with spacious rooms all with cable TV. The waterside rooms are worth the extra $10. Suites ⑤, rooms ④.

Thunderbird Motel, 223 Front St (☎874-3322). Budget motel with fairly spacious phone- and shower-equipped rooms (ask for one with an external window) each with cable TV and some with refrigerator. ③.

Wrangell Hostel, 220 Church St (☎874-3534). Fifteen dollars seems like a lot for a foam mattress – and a thin one at that – on the floor of a room in the First Presbyterian Church, but if you want a cheap roof over your head here it is, and it is clean and central, with a good kitchen. There's usually a daytime lockout (though enforcement varies) and you're expected back by 11pm. Closed early Sept to mid-June. ①.

The town

It won't take long to notice the young garnet sellers clustered on the ferry docks with their red jewels from the Garnet Ledge (see p.103), but if buying garnets is of no interest, you've got forty minutes or so while the ferry is in port to grab a taxi (or walk very quickly) and make for **Petroglyph Beach**, just over half a mile north of the Ferry Dock along Evergreen Avenue to Graves Street. Of course, it is better to stay overnight and give yourself more time to explore the extensive new boardwalk which guides you down to the beach, where Southeast's most concentrated array of **ancient petroglyphs** are etched onto the rocks. Little is known about the purpose of these forty-odd shapes – spirals, birds, orca, faces, and masks – and even the age is uncertain. Numbers between a thousand and ten thousand years are bandied about; the range of designs from simple human forms to more detailed images resembling modern Tlingit iconography, indicate that they were produced in several eras, many predating the relatively modern Tlingit culture. Since they are located on an active beach, stratification studies to determine age are impossible.

It sometimes takes a few minutes to spy your first, but then you seem to see them everywhere. The most concentrated batch are around the high-tide line thirty to fifty yards to the right (north) of the boardwalk steps; don't miss the orca and owl forms close to the grass. The best time is usually as the high tide is receding and the glyphs are shiny and more visible (and photogenic). The low light of morning and evening is also helpful. Taking rubbings from the originals is strongly discouraged, and some replicas have been installed on the boardwalk for this purpose.

Some of the more portable glyphs have been removed for safekeeping to the **Wrangell Museum**, 122 2nd St (May–Sept Mon–Fri 10am–5pm, Sat and Sun whenever cruise ships are in port; $3), an eclectic community museum that's surprisingly extensive for such a diminutive town. The prize exhibit is the set of four very fine house posts, thought to be the oldest Tlingit house posts in existence and probably carved between 1775 and 1790 (but maybe as early as 1740). They're less stylized and more naturalistic in execution than many of the later models seen all over Southeast, and heavily weathered from the years they spent outdoors before being incorporated into the Chief Shakes Tribal House (see opposite) and subsequently moved here. Elsewhere, parts of totems are just piled in a corner as if waiting for their turn on display, there's a slab of rock from the Garnet Ledge with the garnets firmly embedded, and extensive coverage of the 1899 Harriman Expedition, in which railroad magnate Edward H Harriman rented a steamer and led a two-month-long combined family vacation and scientific expedition along the Alaskan coast with John Muir in tow.

Right downtown, at the corner of Front and Episcopal streets, you'll pass the **Kik.setti Totem Park**, a tiny grassed area created in 1987 on the original site of a long-lost pole known as Kik.setti. Noted carvers Steve Brown and Wayne Price used only traditional hand tools to re-create the Kik.setti totem – depicting the symbols of the Kik.setti people who settled Wrangell Island – which now stands in pride of place, backed by three others replicas of highly regarded poles. Among them is the **Raven totem**, with the raven creator at the top, just above what is known as the chief's box, which is said to have spiritual powers. Below that a young raven clasps a man between its wings signifying how Raven could change into a man at will. The lowest figure is Ha-ya-shon-a-gu, described as the "Native American Atlas" holding up the Earth.

Front Street continues south as Shakes Street to **Chief Shakes Island**, a small grass plot and the heart of the inner harbor, linked to the docks by a short boardwalk. Dominated by the Chief Shakes **Tribal House** ($2 when cruise ships are in port, and by appointment on ☎874-3747 when it is $10 each), and ringed by a forest of **totem poles**, it makes a wonderfully peaceful place to while away an hour or two. The replica high-caste clan house was rebuilt as part of the CCC project (see box, p.76) on the site of an ancient house, and dedicated in 1940 at one of the largest gatherings of Native people seen for many years. With the decline in traditional Tlingit ways in the early part of the twentieth century, there hadn't been a Chief Shakes (overall chief hereabouts) since 1916, and the potlatch – attended by the territorial governor – was seen as an opportunity to inaugurate the nephew of the last chief as Chief Shakes VII. Some 1500 people and several war canoes arrived from all over Southeast for what is generally regarded as the last great potlatch of the Tlingit people. Ancient house posts were incorporated into the building and only removed to the Wrangell Museum in 1982 when replicas were carved to replace them. If the house is open, nose around the adze-beamed

---

HIKES FROM WRANGELL

Though a couple of easy walks are close at hand, you'll need transport to get to the more challenging hikes out along the road system. The *Wrangell Guide* lists the more popular trails and the Forest Service are helpful with suggestions, and we've just given you a taster below. Topographic maps are available from the Forest Service for $4; if they're closed try Alaska Vistas on Front Street.

Mount Dewey Trail (1 mile round-trip; 30–40min; 300ft ascent). Pleasant and sometimes steep hike up through woods to the top of the hill that rises behind downtown Wrangell. There's a good observation point overlooking the town, undoubtedly also used by John Muir when he made the ascent in 1879. The trail starts on Third Street.

Rainbow Falls Trail (2 miles round-trip; 1hr; 300ft ascent). Moderate and sometimes boggy trail through the rainforest to the top of a waterfall. From here, keen and fit hikers can continue up what's known as **Institute Creek Trail** (4.5 miles round-trip; 2–4hr; 1200ft ascent) to the three-sided Shoemaker Bay Overlook Shelter atop a high ridge with long views. The trailhead is almost five miles south along Zimovia Hwy opposite the Shoemaker Bay Recreation Site.

Long Lake Trail (1.2 miles round-trip; 30–40min; negligible ascent). Easy boardwalk to a lake where there's a shelter, and a skiff with oars that's perfect for a little trout fishing. The trailhead is 27 miles southeast of Wrangell in the center of the island on Forest Road 6270.

Volunteer Park Trail (800-yard loop; 20min; flat). Easy nature walk along the edge of spruce forest with interpretive panels along the way. Starts near the ball park opposite the Forest Service office.

interior as the guide explains traditional life inside a clan house. Otherwise you'll have to make do with the intricately carved exterior and half a dozen poles, including the **Three Frogs totem**, a shame totem erected to mock the Frog clan who married slaves decades ago. Considered controversial, the Frog clan were distinctly put out by its raising in 2000.

Eating and drinking

There's nothing special about **eating** in Wrangell, but you won't go hungry and there's enough variety for the night or two you'll be here. Benjamin's Groceries on Outer Drive is reasonably well stocked and has an in-store bakery.

Diamond C Café, 223 Front St (☎874-3677). Standard diner that's always popular with locals for their good quality food at fair prices.

Jitterbugs, 309 Front St. Espresso to go.

Spiro's Café, 316 Front St (☎874-4422). The fairly antiseptic interior seems about right for a place that tries to specialize in Mexican, Indian, pasta, and American meals, but only achieves tolerable quality. It is fairly cheap though with entrees $7–13.

Waterfront Grill, inside the *Stikine Inn* (☎874-3388). About the best restaurant in town with good sea views, serving the usual menu of burgers, sandwiches, and Caesar salads while dinner ($14–21) ranges from pasta with mushrooms in a garlic and white-wine sauce to New York pepper steak.

Listings

Banks The National Bank of Alaska, 115 Front St, has an ATM.

Festivals The Garnet festival, 3rd week in April, celebrates the coming of spring and the gathering of bald eagles on the Stikine River with special boat trips and various events that have nothing to do with garnets; there's a king salmon derby from mid-May to mid-June; and a 4th of July celebration with the usual fireworks and parade, and a log-rolling competition in the harbor.

Internet access Free at the library.

Laundry and showers The Thunderbird Laundromat is at 225 Front St. The Community Center, next to the High School on 2nd St (☎874-2444; closed Sun) has a pool, weight room, and showers and costs $2 to get in.

Library Irene Ingle Public Library on 2nd St (Mon & Fri 10am–noon & 1–5pm, Tues–Thurs 1–5pm & 7–9pm, Sat 9am–5pm).

Medical assistance Wrangell General Hospital on Airport Rd (☎874-3356).

Post Office On Federal St. The **General Delivery** ZIP Code is 99929.

Taxes There's a seven percent city sales tax plus a $4 bed tax, all included within our price codes.

Tour operators Alaska Vistas (☎ & fax 874-3006, *www.alaskavistas.com*); Alaska Waters (☎874-2378 or 1-800/347-4462, *www.alaskawaters.com*); Breakaway Adventures (☎ & fax 874-2488 or ☎1-888/385-2488, *www.breakawayadventures.com*); Stikine Wilderness Adventures (☎874-2085 or 1-800/874-2085, *www.wrangell.com/business/harding.htm*); and Sunrise Aviation (☎874-2319 or 1-800/874-2311, *www.pnw.com/sunrise*).

Around Wrangell

Wrangell is well positioned to make the best of the local scenery and wildlife. Bear viewing is usually near the top of most people's list, and there are few places in Alaska you can get so close so cheaply as the **Anan Wildlife Observatory**, little more than a hide and viewing platform but a wonderful spot to commune with these awesome beasts.

BARNES & NOBLE BOOKSELLER
6050 EL CERRITO PLAZA
EL CERRITO, CA 94530
510 524-0087
04-22-03 S02113 R003

READERS' ADVANTAGE

Alaska   17.05
1858286883
DISCOUNT   18.95 - 1.90
Vancouver and Victoria f   14.39
0764553836
DISCOUNT   15.99 - 1.60

SUB TOTAL   31.44
SALES TAX   2.59
TOTAL   34.03
AMOUNT TENDERED
CASH   40.03

READERS' ADVANTAGE SAVINGS   - 3.50

TOTAL PAYMENT   40.03
CHANGE   6.00
        Thank You for shopping at
        Barnes & Noble Booksellers
#43482 04-22-03 02:29P Willie

The historic importance of Wrangell is its siting near the mouth of the **Stikine River**, the only passable break in the Coastal Range between Prince Rupert and Skagway. It became a major conduit for prospectors bound for the early gold rushes; first during the stampede to central BC as early as 1861, but significantly during the Yukon rush in 1897, when the Stikine became the so-called "back door" route to the Klondike. Riverboats that started during the gold rushes continued to run regularly on the river until 1969, a tradition now continued by jet boats that whisk tourists as far upstream as Telegraph Creek in British Columbia. Several companies in Wrangell (see "Tour operators", opposite) run trips on the Stikine and to Anan, and there are competitive packages offered by *Harding's Old Sourdough Lodge* (see "Accommodation," p.99).

Jet boats also run from Wrangell to the **LeConte Glacier** (covered under the Petersburg account, p.112) typically taking five to eight hours and costing $150.

Anan Wildlife Observatory

Potentially one of the most rewarding outings from Wrangell is to see the **bears feeding** at the **Anan Wildlife Observatory**, some thirty miles south of town and only accessible by boat or plane. Here, a waterfall a few hundred yards inland from Anan Lagoon slows the progress of one of the state's largest runs of "humpies" or pink salmon, and black bears (and a few browns) come to dine on the floundering fish. Come in July or August (particularly late July and early Aug when fish activity is highest) and you might see up to a couple of dozen bears, though patience is needed.

To provide more comfortable viewing conditions and limit the risk of bear–human contact the Forest Service have constructed an open-sided observation platform reached by a half-mile-long trail from the beach. Head half a mile in the other direction and the Forest Service's Anan Bay **cabin** ($35; book months in advance on ☎1-877/444-6777) is perfect if you want to stay a few days, perhaps watching bald eagles, or harbor seals out in the lagoon.

Access is by fifteen-minute flight, one-hour boat journey or a day or two in your own kayak. The cheapest way to get there is with Alaska Waters (see Wrangell "Listings"), who give you around four hours at Anan for $145; Alaska Vistas charge $165 for a full-day trip with six hours at the observatory; and Breakaway Adventures, who do a full-day trip by boat spending three to six hours at Anan for $170. Good-value flights can be had on Sunrise Aviation; $400 round-trip for up to four people, with as much time as you want at Anan.

Garnet Ledge

Wrangell's dockside garnet-selling industry is one of Southeast's more curious tales. Back in the 1860s garnets were found on the mainland, seven miles northeast of Wrangell, alongside a creek in an area that has become known as the **Garnet Ledge**. From 1907 to 1923, the Alaska Garnet Mining and Manufacturing Company – said to be the world's first corporation entirely run by women – was commercially mining the gems from the soft mica schist and making hat pins, watch fobs and the like.

By the 1930s, deft political maneuvering had left ownership in the hands of Wrangell mayor Fred Hanford, who subsequently (in 1962) deeded the Garnet Ledge to the local Boy Scouts with local children having the right to take garnets "in reasonable quantities." They decreed that children under sixteen had the sole right to gather and sell the sub-jewelry-quality garnets. When "mining" they must be accompanied by an adult, and enthusiastic parents often take their kids over to the Ledge in their skiff and let them fossick around, mining by hand. After all, a good session of selling to cruise ship and ferry passengers can easily net $200.

By paying $10 at the Wrangell Museum and committing ten percent of your find to the Museum (with proceeds to the Scouts) you can go fossicking yourself (though you are not allowed to sell your finds). Most of the boat operators running trips up the Stikine River (which pass by the Garnet Ledge) will have permits they can sell you. An hour will be enough for most people, but you can stay at the Forest Service **cabin** ($25; ☎1-877/444-6777).

Along the Stikine River

Wrangell sits seven miles south of the mouth of the **Stikine River** ("The Great River"), which is said to be the fastest navigable river in North America with peak flows around six miles per hour. From the mountains of British Columbia, it threads its way almost four hundred miles to the sea, with only the last thirty miles running through the Stikine–LeConte Wilderness in Alaska. It is a spectacular journey the whole way with dramatic mountains, canyons, glaciers, forests, and matchless wildlife, all observed from jet-boat trips or fly-in rafting expeditions. Despite the current, you can **kayak** up as far as the Canadian border by utilizing eddies and the slack-water sloughs marked on the Forest Service's excellent *Stikine River Canoe/Kayak Route Map* ($4), which also marks tent sites, cabins, and log jams.

The river reaches tidewater at the **Stikine Flats**, a broad and shallow delta full of small islands sprouting willows and cottonwoods. The surrounding mud flats are covered in spring and fall with **birds** – ducks, geese, sandhill cranes – resting along their migration route (known as the Pacific Flyway). The area around Mallard Slough, and the Mallard Slough cabin ($35) is particularly good in late May and early April for spotting shore birds, including huge flocks of **western sandpipers**. From late March to early May small oily fish called eulachon (usually bowdlerized to "hooligan") flood up the river, chased by the state's second largest concentration of **bald eagles**, often numbering well over a thousand.

The delta is a popular destination in summer when it can seem as though half of Wrangell is out here fishing, sightseeing, visiting the Garnet Ledge (see overleaf) or making for **Chief Shakes Hot Springs**, 28 miles by boat from Wrangell, for a soak in one of the redwood tubs (one enclosed).

The river is navigable for 160 miles upstream from the hot springs, to a small British Columbian town of Telegraph Creek, cutting through some wonderful scenery which John Muir favorably compared to his beloved Yosemite. Jet boat trips either stick to the delta and lower river, or head right up to Telegraph Creek. Most operators are prepared to take you and your kayaks, canoes, or rafts up there and leave you to float back down to Wrangell. Breakaway Adventures run a slew of trips including a trip around the delta visiting the Garnet Ledge, hot springs, and glaciers (5–7hr; $145), and multi-day trips upstream charged at $600 a day for a six-person boat. Alaska Waters take two days for their trip up to Telegraph Creek and back ($575), and most of the other operators have comparable trips.

If you are planning to enter Canada you'll need to call **Canadian customs** (☎250/627-3003 in Prince Rupert) to give them the details of your party, and will need to contact US customs (☎874-3415) as soon as possible after your re-entry into Alaska.

Petersburg and around

One of the highlights of riding the Inside Passage ferries is sitting up front to watch the boat negotiate the 46 slalom course turns of the 22-mile-long **Wrangell Narrows** between Mitkof and Kupreanof islands. It's a beautiful run by day when it feels like you can reach out and touch the steep-walled shore and crumbling wooden piers, and doubly so at night when it is baffling how the captain can pilot a course through the maze of lights from the marker buoys.

As the passage broadens, the starboard shore sprouts a straggle of jetties and wharves that run for a mile along the waterfront of **PETERSBURG**, with its canneries perched above the water on forests of poles. No prizes for guessing that Petersburg is primarily a fishing port, and the citizens are more interested in salmon, halibut, black cod, shrimp, crab, and herring than they are in tourists, which is a good part of the appeal. The larger cruise ships can't negotiate the Narrows, thus saving Petersburg from their hit-and-run attentions; no one is out to sell you anything, and it is refreshing to just saunter around the docks and gaze across Frederick Sound at the summit of **Devil's Thumb** on the US–Canada border.

Petersburg gets its name from Peter Buschmann, the Norwegian fisherman who, in 1897, decided that the abundant fish, free ice from the LeConte Glacier and relative proximity to markets made this a good place to found a fishing port. He proved to be very right, and many of his countryfolk followed his lead, giving some credence to Petersburg's claim to be "Alaska's Little Norway." Unless you are here on the third full weekend in May (nearest Norwegian Independence Day

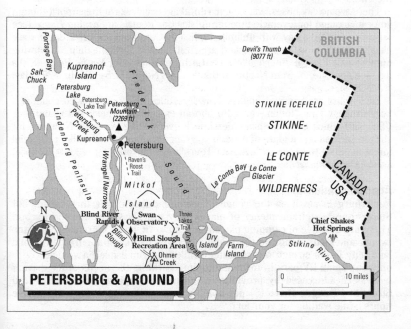

on May 17) for the **Little Norway Festival** when a model Viking longboat is trundled down the street, evidence is fairly scant, though several buildings have Norwegian-style scrolled detailing around windows known as **rosmaling**. Otherwise it is just a busy Alaskan fishing port where the streets are often filled with the thousand or so temporary cannery workers who significantly swell the ranks of this small town.

Sights are fairly thin on the ground, though anyone with a taste for the work of ancient civilizations shouldn't miss the easily accessible **fish traps** and **petroglyphs** at Sandy Beach. Further exploration requires transport, either along the road system to some gentle hikes, across Wrangell Narrows to the small settlement of Kupreanof from where more serious hikes begin, or by boat across the whale-rich waters of Frederick Sound to the **LeConte Glacier**.

Arrival, information, and getting around

Roughly daily AMHS ferries (☎772-3855) from Sitka and Wrangell arrive a mile west of downtown Petersburg on S Nordic Drive, an easy walk from town, though you could catch one of the waiting **taxis**, or call Maine Cabs on ☎772-6969. One southbound and one northbound Alaska Airlines **flight** per day lands at Petersburg airport (☎772-4255), a mile east of town on Haugen Drive. Again you can walk or catch a cab. LAB (☎772-430) do short-haul flights from Kake and Juneau.

The **visitor center**, 17 Fram St at 1st Street (mid-May to mid-Sept Mon–Sat 9am–5pm, Sun noon–4pm; mid-Sept to mid-May Mon–Fri 10am–2pm; ☎772-4636, fax 772-3646, *www.petersburg.org*), which also acts as the public face of the **forest service** (*www.fs.fed.us/r10/tongass*), has all the info you need and free copies of the *Viking Visitor Guide*.

There are no city buses, and no **car rental** agency desks at the airport, though you can arrange for a vehicle through Allstar Car Rentals at *Scandia House* (see opposite) for $50 a day with unlimited mileage. Cars from Avis at *Tides Inn* are usually a little more expensive and are best booked through their nationwide number (see Basics). Alternatively, **rent a bike** either from *Nordic House* ($10 a day, see opposite) or from Northern Bikes, 110 S Nordic Drive ($4/hr, $20 a day; ☎772-3978).

Local tours are run by Tongass Traveler Tours (☎772-4837), who conduct a brief cannery tour (45min–1hr; $10) and an extended cannery and island tour (3hr; $30) which ends on the owners' deck overlooking Wrangell Narrows, for shrimp cocktail and a glass of wine. If you fancy an educational walk in the rainforest south of town, go with Alaska Tours and Charters (3hr; $25; ☎772-4656, *hendyhut@alaska.net*).

Accommodation

Petersburg is small so the range of accommodation isn't that broad, but there's one hostel and plenty of places very prettily set beside the harbor. There are a couple of camping places close to town, and a more attractive one twenty miles out along the road, and while you can camp for free on public land, city limits stretch out seventeen miles, so you'll need a vehicle. With only one small RV park in town and limited parking, the needs of RV drivers have been addressed by providing a downtown **staging area**, corner 2nd Street and Haugen Drive ($1 per hour) where you can park for up to twelve hours while waiting for your ferry.

Bear Necessities Guesthouse, 18 Sing Lee Alley (☎772-2279, *www.alsaska.net/~bearbnb*). A single, self-contained, one-bedroom apartment with two double beds, cable TV, phone, and a kitchen filled with breakfast supplies. Although it is downtown on poles over the water, there's no view, and they prefer a two-night minimum. ④.

Broom Hus, Nordic Drive (☎772-3459, *www.alaska.net/~broomhus*). Well-equipped apartment (sleeping up to six) in the half-basement of an original 1920s house but with a separate entrance. Continental breakfast is provided and there's a lovely flower-filled deck out back for those occasional sunny afternoons. ④.

LeConte RV Park, cnr Haugen Drive and 4th St (☎772-4680). A cramped gravel lot large enough for half a dozen RVs and with a tiny semi-grassy patch for tents. Some traffic noise, and showers are $1.25 extra, but facilities are clean and it is central. Full hookup $25, water and electricity $15, tents $7.

Nordic House B&B, 806 S Nordic Drive (☎772-3620, fax 772-3673, *www.nordichouse.net*). Appealing B&B superbly sited close to the ferry dock with six comfortable rooms with shared bath. There is free use of the kitchen and large lounge which hangs right over the water. There's buffet breakfast, free local calls and Internet access for guests, and if you catch any fish they'll handle it for you, or you can just grill it on the sunny deck. Courtesy van from the airport or ferry and bikes rented at $10 a day. ④.

Ohmer Creek campground, Mile 22 Mitkof Hwy. Picturesque and very appealing Forest Service site on the southern shores of Mitkof Island with fire rings, a canopy of trees, stream water, and space for RVs and tents. May–Sept $6, Oct–April free.

Petersburg Bunk and Breakfast (☎772-3632, fax 772-2790, *www.bunkandbreakfast.com*). Welcoming hostel handily sited between downtown and the airport, with a couple of four-bunk rooms where bunk and continental breakfast costs $25. There are plenty of games and books to entertain you on wet evenings, but there's a lockout from 9am to 5pm and a 10.30pm curfew, though late ferry arrivals are catered for. The management requests you phone ahead for reservations and address. Closed mid-Sept to mid-May except by appointment. ①.

Scandia House, 110 N Nordic Drive (☎772-4281 or 1-800/722-5006, fax 772-4301, *scandia @alaska.net*). The best hotel in town with clean, modern rooms, all with cable TV, phone, coffee maker and a light continental breakfast. Some come with water views, others have kitchenettes (⑤), or are suites with jacuzzis (⑦) and there's a courtesy van. ④.

Tent City Campground, Haugen Drive (☎772-4224). Spacious site often used by prospective cannery workers, with tents pitched on wooden platforms, a covered communal area, and showers paid by the quarter. Closed Oct–April. $5.

Tides Inn, cnr Dolphin and 1st sts (☎772-4288 or 1-800/665-8433, fax 772-4286, *tidesinn@alaska.net*). Ordinary motel made more appealing if you can get a room with a view. All in any case come with bathtubs, cable TV, fax, and Internet access for guests. ④.

Twin Creek RV Park, Mile 7.5 Mitkof Hwy (☎772-3282). RV park with tent sites ($12), partial and full hookups ($15–19).

The town and Sandy Beach

If the weather behaves, there's nothing better to do in Petersburg than just wander the waterfront boardwalks as the fishing boats come and go and the ferry glides silently through the Wrangell Narrows. From the aptly named **Eagle's Roost Park**, north of downtown, it is all canneries and wharves through the center of town down to the single most striking section, **Sing Lee Alley**, a boardwalk built entirely over the water and named for a Chinese merchant who had his premises here in the early days. It is lined by shops and a couple of cafés on one side, and on the other by the town's only real bookshop, and the large white clapboard **Sons of Norway Hall**, built in 1912 as a meeting place for this fraternal organization. With its double-pitched roof design and subtle use of rosmaling around the windows it is easily the most distinctly Norwegian building in town. As though to further underline the connection, the adjacent parking lot is home

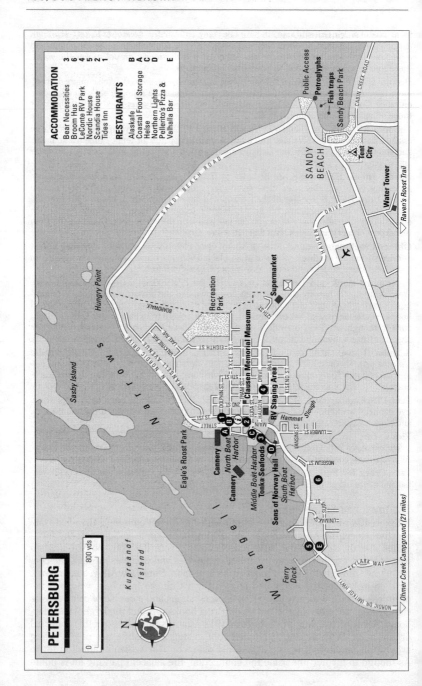

PETERSBURG

N

Kupreanof Island

Wrangell Narrows

Sasby Island

Hungry Point

Eagle's Roost Park

Recreation Park

BOARDWALK

Clausen Memorial Museum

Cannery
North Boat Harbor
Cannery
Middle Boat Harbor
Tonka Seafoods
Sons of Norway Hall
South Boat Harbor

Ferry Dock

RV Staging Area
Hammer Slough
Supermarket

SANDY BEACH

Tent City
Water Tower

Public Access
Petroglyphs
Fish traps
Sandy Beach Park

CABIN CREEK ROAD

⊳ Raven's Roost Trail

⊲ Nordic Dr (Mitkof Hwy)
⊲ Ohmer Creek Campground (21 miles)
⊳ SKYLARK WAY

ACCOMMODATION

Bear Necessities	3
Broom Hus	6
LeConte RV Park	4
Nordic House	5
Scandia House	2
Tides Inn	1

RESTAURANTS

Alaskafe	B
Coastal Food Storage	A
Helse	C
Northern Lights	D
Pellerito's Pizza &	
Valhalla Bar	E

800 yds

0

to a model Viking **longboat** used in the annual **Little Norway Festival** every third full weekend in May. Nearby, the ten-foot-tall bronze **Boyer Wikan Fisherman's Memorial** is the centerpiece of a small boardwalk "park" and was commissioned according to the will of one Bojer Wikan, a local fisherman deeply involved with the Sons of Norway. Both Hall and "park" stand on poles above **Hammer Slough**, a narrow estuary lined by brightly painted houses that seem to glow in the evening light.

Despite having two major canneries on and over the waterfront, it isn't easy to see what goes on inside. There is some compensation in being able to take an hour-long tour around the specialist **Tonka Seafoods** on Sing Lee Alley (Mon–Sat 1.30pm; $5; and by appointment on ☎772-3662 with a minimum $30 fee). Not exclusively a cannery, they also smoke and dry fish in what is really just two small rooms. The equipment isn't especially interesting to look at, but the tours are personal enough that you can direct the discussion to whatever interests you most, be it the life cycle of the fish, means of catching, fishery management, boat type, or processing. Of course there are free samples of the product and the opportunity to buy what you like.

HIKES IN AND AROUND PETERSBURG

Though there are a dozen or more good **hikes** around Petersburg, few are especially convenient unless you've got transport. Drivers and cyclists can get the best from several short trails out along Mitkof Hwy (see p.111), but serious hikers should think about two excellent trails a few hundred yards across Wrangell Narrows on Kupreanof Island. People have traditionally tried to hitch a ride, but local hospitality has been strained over the years, and it is advisable to arrange transport back to Petersburg before you head out – or risk being stranded over there. Rent a skiff from *Scandia Hotel* or contact the visitor center which will help you call around likely boat-charter companies. Expect to pay $25 to get over and back, and remember that there is no camping on the immediate Kupreanof side of the narrows as it is private property.

Forest Service cabins can be booked on ☎1-877/444-6777.

Petersburg Lake Trail (10.5 miles one-way; 4hr; 200ft ascent). Moderately difficult trail on Kupreanof Island leading left (west), over a low saddle then gradually ascending to Petersburg Lake and the *Petersburg Lake* cabin ($35), which is a good base for salmon and trout fishing, and bear viewing in fall. If you use a trailhead which is only accessible at high tide you can shorten the hike by four miles. Keen adventurers can continue beyond Portage Lake to a couple more cabins, though it is tough going and you'll need the latest information from the visitor center.

Petersburg Mountain Trail (5 miles round-trip; 4–6hr; 2750ft ascent). Challenging trail on Kupreanof Island leading right (east) from the dock opposite Petersburg to the summit of Petersburg Mountain from where there are long, long views down the Wrangell Narrows and across Frederick Sound to the coastal mountains and glaciers. The final section is a bit of a scramble.

Raven's Roost Trail (8 miles round-trip; 5–6hr; 2000ft ascent). An initial boardwalk leads to a sometime steep trail climbing up to alpine country and eventually the four-berth *Raven's Roost* Forest Service **cabin** ($35). Best done from mid-July to September when the likelihood of snow cover is least, though lack of water at the cabin means it is good to have some snow around. The trailhead is by the orange-and-white water towers just south of the airport.

Moving away from the waterfront, call in at the **Clausen Memorial Museum**, 203 Fram St at 2nd St (May to mid-Sept Mon–Sat 10am–4.30pm; $2), marked by the distinctive steel sculpture of salmon, halibut, and herring entitled *Fisk* – Norwegian for fish. There's not a great deal inside, but the staff are usually eager to help you interpret the small collection of Tlingit artifacts (particularly a large bentwood storage box), some great old photos of early Petersburg life, and what is reputed to be the largest salmon ever caught, though no one thought to weigh it before it was gutted; estimates put it at 126 pounds.

If you don't fancy tackling one of the more robust walks (see box, opposite), consider strolling north along the roads past Hungry Point to **Sandy Beach**, a pleasant little park-backed cove that's best visited at low tide when it is possible to see ancient Tlingit **fish traps** on the mud of the bay. They're not especially obvious to the untrained eye, but with some imagination you can pick out low ridges of rock formed into the shape of thirty-foot-diameter hearts. The pointy ends face the sea, and it is though that as the tide rapidly receded, fish swimming close to the beach would be guided into the traps and find themselves caught at the sharp end as the water level dropped. The rock formations are probably about two thousand years old, and unique to the immediate area around Petersburg. Later models used hemlock stakes, some of which are occasionally dislodged by the tide, and researchers claim that they are so well preserved by the mud that they still smell of fresh wood.

At the northern end of Sandy Beach, a large rock close to the high-tide line bears the marks of some poorly understood, but certainly old, **petroglyphs**. If you've already seen the petroglyphs at Wrangell you might be a little underwhelmed by what's on show here, but there are five faces etched onto the rock, one partly removed by recent vandalism. The petroglyphs can be seen at all water levels except high tide.

Eating and drinking

Despite Petersburg's efforts to promote its Norwegian heritage, the only herrings you'll see are those sold as bait, and there's nowhere to buy Norwegian bread. In fact the only bakery is in the Hammer & Wikan supermarket, on the edge of town, your best bet for groceries and deli items. Beyond that, there's a tolerable range of cafés, restaurants, and bars, but nothing special.

Alaskafe, cnr Nordic and Excel sts (☎772-5282). Relaxed café with sofas and Internet access at good rates. There's an impressive range of espresso coffees and teas plus soups, salads, panini, and pasta dishes. Live music jams and poetry readings on Saturday night. Closed Sun.

Coastal Food Storage, 306 N Nordic Drive (☎772-4177). An unusual establishment combining live-shellfish sales with takeout burgers and espresso. Tanks of live oysters, clams, and Dungeness crabs surround a couple of cramped tables where you can tuck into breaded oysters and fries ($8), a crab melt ($6) or a Greek style shrimp salad ($5).

Harbor Bar, 310 N Nordic Drive. A foot-to-the-floor drinkers bar always full of salmon canners and salmon fishers.

Helse Café, 17 Sing Lee Alley (☎772-3444). Vaguely health-oriented daytime and breakfast café with an imaginative range of salads, sandwiches, and burgers from around $6 plus daily specials and espresso. The bowl of soup and slice of homemade bread ($5) is a particularly good deal. Closed Sun.

Northern Lights, 28 Sing Lee Alley (☎772-3424). Reliable licensed restaurant perched out on stilts over the water with great views of the fishing boats and dazzling evening sun through the big windows if you're lucky. Burgers and sandwiches start at $7 and there are pasta dishes ($12 and up), fish and chips ($12), and prime rib ($14). They've got a couple of microbrews on tap and several bottled beers. Closed Tues.

Pellerito's Pizza, opposite the ferry terminal on S Nordic Drive (☎772-3727). A takeout pizza joint with a few tables for the under 21s who can't get into *Valhalla* upstairs where many patrons repair for a beer with their calzone. Good ice-cream cones too.

Valhalla Bar, opposite the ferry terminal on S Nordic Drive (no phone). Lively bar above *Pellerito's Pizza* with large windows overlooking the ferry dock and Wrangell Narrows. Order downstairs, and eat up here.

Listings

Banks There are a couple of banks downtown including First Bank, 103 Nordic Drive, which has an ATM.

Bookshop Sing Lee Alley Books, 11 Sing Lee Alley (Mon–Sat 10am–5pm, Sun noon–4pm; ☎772-4440)

Festivals The Little Norway Festival on the third full weekend in May is the town's celebration of its heritage. It is followed by a Salmon Derby on Memorial Day weekend.

Internet access Free access at the library is in heavy demand, and you may prefer the convenience of machines inside *Alaskafe* (see opposite) or the Macs at CHIPS, Sing Lee Alley (Mon–Sat 9am–10pm, Sun noon–10pm).

Laundry and showers You can also take a swim and shower ($3) at the Melvin Roundtree Pool (☎772-3304); Laundry is best done at Glacier Laundry, 313 Nordic Drive (daily 6am–10pm; ☎772-4144) where they also have showers ($2).

Library Petersburg Public Library, 12 S Nordic Drive (Mon–Thurs noon–9pm, Fri & Sat 1–5pm; ☎772-3349).

Medical assistance Petersburg Medical Center, 2nd & Fram sts (Mon–Fri 9am–5pm and 24hr ER; ☎772-4291).

Post Office 1400 Haugen Drive. The **General Delivery** ZIP Code is 99833.

Taxes Petersburg imposes a six percent sales tax plus a four percent bed tax, all included in our accommodation price codes.

Travel agency Viking Travel, 101 N Nordic Drive (☎772-3818).

Around Petersburg

The simplest way to get out of town is to rent a car and drive out along **Mitkof Hwy**, sixteen miles of paved two-lane road from which several roads fan out across the island. Fishing streams, easy boardwalk trails, picnic sites, a hatchery, and a seasonal swan viewing area are the main draws here.

Getting off the island involves getting on some kind of tour, either **kayaking**, **whale watching**, visiting the **LeConte Glacier** or fishing. Since tourists are few it can be difficult getting the numbers to make trips viable: befriending like-minded travelers on your way here and fronting up as a ready-to-go group of four or six can be a big advantage. Conversely, when the occasional cruise ship is in town you may find it hard to get a place on trips pre-booked by the ship. Many tours can be booked though Viking Travel (see above), and a quick visit here can save you a lot of phoning around. They're particularly helpful for hooking you up with one of the many fishing charters run from town.

Along the road system

Petersburg has a reasonably extensive road system, and if you rent a car there's a fair bit to keep you entertained, though nothing that's essential viewing. Renting a bike makes it all the more interesting, opening up miles of abandoned, dirt logging roads. Almost everything is along, or just off the paved Mitkof Hwy, which follows Wrangell Narrows for around fourteen miles then cuts inland to finish on the southern shores of Mitkof Island.

There are no specific sights until you reach **Blind River Rapids**, Mile 14, where there's a quarter-mile-long boardwalk along a stream where salmon come in to spawn and jump the rapids. Beyond here, the highway cuts inland along Blind Slough to the **Swan Observatory**, Mile 16, where a kind of primitive hide aids viewing trumpeter swans which call here on their way south from mid-October to December, a few dozen overwintering until around April. Salmon can also be seen in the stream. The asphalt ends, but the road continues a couple of miles to **Crystal Lake Hatchery**, Mile 18, where you can wander around and, between 8am and 4pm, ask the staff to explain what's going on. The adjacent **Blind Slough Recreation Area** is good for picnics and swimming (for the brave). There's no camping here, but you can pitch a tent four miles on at **Ohmer Creek campground** (see p.107), which acts as the trailhead for a mile-long path along a good trout and salmon fishing stream with some interpretive panels. Though the road continues an uneventful eleven miles along the island's south coast, you're better off driving to Mile 21 and heading northeast on Three Lakes Loop Road (Road 6235) which, after 21 miles, rejoins Mitkof Hwy at Mile 11. Roughly midway around the loop, you come to a series of three trailheads all interlinked as the **Three Lakes Loop Trail** (30min–3hr), where any number of boardwalk variations allow you to visit one or more of Crane, Hill, and Sand lakes, and access the sea along Ideal Cove Trail. A mile or so north of here the road passes the **LeConte Overlook**, the only place on the island where you can get a direct view across Frederick Sound to the face of the LeConte Glacier.

Kayaking, whale watching, and LeConte Glacier

At some point during their stay, most people want to get out on the water, and there are several companies happy to oblige. One prime destination is the **LeConte Glacier**, which peals off the Stikine Icefield, fifteen miles east across Frederick Sound. It is the southernmost tidewater glacier in the northern hemisphere, and Frederick Sound is usually dotted with small icebergs that get bigger the closer you are to the glacier, some with seals idling their day away. Often LeConte Bay is so packed with ice that you can't even penetrate far enough to see the face of the glacier, so you probably won't be able to see calving. Extended trips also continue a few miles south and visit the **delta of the Stikine River** (see "Wrangell," p.98), and wherever you go there is a chance of seeing **whales**, particularly the humpback whales that usually pass through from late June to early September.

About the most peaceful way to get on the water is by **kayak** with Tongass Kayak Adventures (☎772-4600, fax 772-4646, *www.tongasskayak.com*), who run four-hour trips ($55) around the Petersburg waterfront and across the Narrows to Petersburg Creek. Though very enjoyable, they are really a taster for their multiday whale watching and trips; relatively gentle affairs involving three to five hours paddling a day that need to be booked well in advance. Their Base Camp trips (3 nights for $700, 8 nights for $1800) fly you in to base camps beside Frederick Sound and near the LeConte Glacier from where you explore by day; the week-long Explorer Tours ($1400–1800) tend to move on to a new camp each day.

If you'd rather someone else did the work, join Hook & Eye Charters (☎772-3400, *www.alaska.net/~hookeye*), who run entertaining half-day **trips to LeConte Glacier** in a twenty-foot aluminum boat ($95) and also have whale watching and sport-fishing trips.

The visitor center has information about several other operators who do similar trips, usually for a little more money, with a full day of whale watching likely to cost $170; or you can go your own way with a skiff and forty-horse motor from *Scandia Hotel* (guests $125 a day, nonguest $150 a day).

Sitka and around

Perched on the seaward edge of the Inside Passage, **SITKA** ranks as one of Alaska's prettiest and most historic towns, with a bay chock full of tiny islands plumed with hemlock and spruce, and the looming presence of the Fuji-like **Mount Edgecumbe** volcano rising menacingly across Sitka Sound.

The appeal of the outdoors – hiking and kayaking in particular – is hard to pass up, but Sitka revels in its sixty-year reign as the political and cultural hub of Russian America. This is where Imperial Russian colonists established their capital, **Novaya Archangelsk** (New Archangel) in 1808, and their legacy is a major draw. When the United States bought Alaska, New Archangel became Sitka (a contraction of the Tlingit Shee Atika), and development since then has been relatively benign with the skyline still dominated by the cathedral as it was when Seward came here to formally receive the territory on Castle Hill on October 18, 1867.

Despite being the third largest town in Southeast, Sitka is still small enough to retain a compact and walkable core, and a relaxed and friendly ambience. Better still, it isn't as crowded as you'd expect, being off the main Inside Passage cruise ship lanes and lacking a dock deep enough for the big ships: passengers have to come ashore in lifeboats. Large ships still visit most days in summer though, ensuring steady interest in the tacky "Russiocana" – you'll find more nesting dolls here than the rest of the US put together.

Some history

Sitka's Kiksadi Tlingit clan have probably lived for 9000 years at their settlement Shee Atika, meaning village on the outside of Shee – their name for Baranof Island. In 1799, the Russian-American Company came to pursue fur trading and established the first European settlement in Southeast Alaska, seven miles north of Sitka in the grounds of what is now the *Starrigavan* campground. They continued to trade in sea otter pelts until the Kiksadi, living on the site of modern Sitka, got tired of their presence and stormed their fort killing nearly all the Russians. Alexander Baranov, the Chief Manager of the Russian–American Company in Kodiak got wind of this and, in 1804, returned with four ships and several baidarkas. The Kiksadi, under their leader Katlian, had established a fort at what is now the Totem Park, and the Russians sent a landing party of 150 to conduct the Siege of Shiskeenue. Tsarist ships pounded the stockade for six days. On the sixth night the Russians heard strange chanting and, next day, discovered ravens hovering over the fort. Though there were ample provisions, suggesting that there could have been a battle, the fort was empty except for the bodies of dead children – allegedly murdered so the Tlingit could retreat in complete silence. They burnt the fort, looted and burned the Tlingit community of Shee Atika and on the ashes

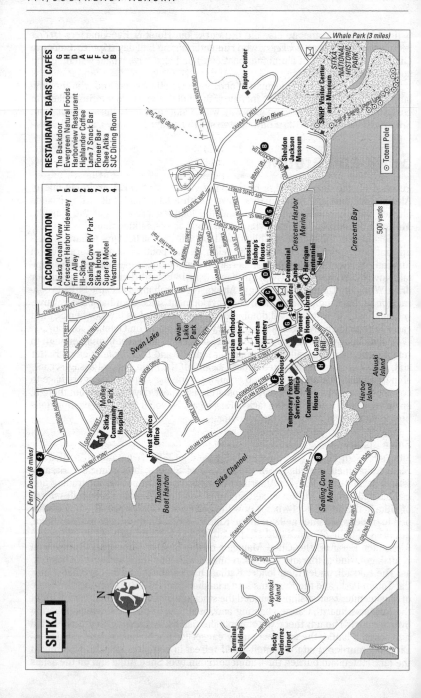

SITKA

△ Whale Park (3 miles)

RESTAURANTS, BARS & CAFÉS	
The Backdoor	G
Evergreen Natural Foods	H
Harborview Restaurant	D
Highlander Coffee	A
Lane 7 Snack Bar	E
Pioneer Bar	F
Shee Atika	C
SJC Dining Room	B

ACCOMMODATION	
Alaska Ocean View	1
Crescent Harbor Hideaway	5
Finn Alley	6
Hi-Sitka	2
Sealing Cove RV Park	8
Sitka Hotel	7
Super 8 Motel	3
Westmark	4

Raptor Center

SITKA NATIONAL HISTORIC PARK

SNHP Visitor Center and Museum

Indian River

Sawmill Creek

Sheldon Jackson Museum

Crescent Harbor Marina

Harrigan Centennial Hall

Centennial Canoe

Ceremonial

Russian Bishop's House

Cathedral

Pioneer Home

Library

Castle Hill

Russian Orthodox Cemetery

Lutheran Cemetery

Swan Lake

Swan Lake Park

Moller Park

Sitka Community Hospital

Forest Service Office

Blockhouse

Temporary Forest Service Office

Community House

Crescent Bay

Harbor Island

Aleutski Island

Thomsen Boat Harbor

Sitka Channel

Sealing Cove Marina

Japonski Island

Terminal Building

Rocky Gutierrez Airport

The Causeway

⊙ Totem Pole

△ Ferry Dock (6 miles)

N

0   500 yards

of the village built the stockaded settlement of New Archangel. The Tlingit didn't return for twenty years but eventually settled outside the palisades in an uneasy but workable relationship with the Russians.

In 1808, Novaya Archangelsk became the colonial capital with food imported from Fort Ross in California, and a social scene of dress balls and grand receptions. Still, those who described it as the "Paris of the Pacific" had obviously never been to Paris.

Its status survived the transfer of ownership to the United States, and Sitka continued as the capital of the territory of Alaska. As soon as America got hold of Alaska, adventurers flocked north, but gold drew people elsewhere. Capital status passed to Juneau in 1906, and Sitka was left to grow steadily on its fishing, and later logging. As fishing receipts ebb and flow, and logging returns are greatly diminished since the closure of the pulp mill here in 1993, tourism is increasingly filling the gaps.

Arrival, information, and getting around

To reach Sitka, AMHS **ferries** must pass through Segius Narrows and Peril Strait, narrow twisting watercourses which need to be negotiated at slack tide. Ferries often have to wait for three or more hours at the dock, seven miles north of town, for the tide to turn: call the Sitka terminal (☎747-8737) for details of particular sailings. Ferries are met by **shuttle buses** run by Sitka Tours (☎747-8443) who run downtown and to your accommodation ($5 one-way, $7 round-trip), and also conduct short **tours** (2.5hr; $12) for those who just want the flavor of the place before continuing on the ferry. If current plans come to fruition, there will be new fast ferries doing a daily run from Juneau by the summer of 2003.

The **airport** is on Japonski Island a mile or so from downtown, and sees Alaska Airlines (☎966-2266) jets direct from Juneau, Ketchikan, and Seattle. Again Sitka Tours meets planes and runs into town ($3 one-way, $5 round-trip); a ferry–downtown–airport sequence or vice versa is $7.

The **visitor center**, Harbor Drive (daily 8am–5pm; ☎747-3220, fax 747-8495, *www.sitka.org*) is inside the Harrigan Centennial Hall. For information on the surrounding Tongass National Forest, contact the **Sitka Ranger District Office**, 204 Siganaka Way (Mon–Fri 8am–5pm; ☎747-6671, fax 747-4253. *www.fs.fed.us/r10/tongass*), or their more convenient but supposedly temporary office at 201 Katlian St (Mon–Fri 8am–5pm; ☎747-4220).

Sitka has no permanent public transport system, though when large cruise ships are in port (4–5 days a week in summer) there's a Transit Bus ($5 all-day pass) making a half-hourly circuit from downtown to the Sheldon Jackson Museum, the Raptor Center, and back. In practice, you can walk to just about anywhere you are likely to want to go, **rent a bike** from Yellow Jersey Cycle Shop, 805 Halibut Point Rd (☎747-6317), or call a **taxi** such as Sitka Taxi (☎747-5001), who charge around $15 to the ferry terminal, $7 to the airport. **Rental cars** are available from AllStar Rent-A-Car at the airport (☎966-2552 or 1-800/722-6927) with your mileage only limited by the extent of the road system.

Apart from the **tours** run by Sitka Tours (see above), are those hosted by the Sitka Conservation Society (☎747-7509). Their gentle, guided forest walks emphasize understanding the history and ecology of the area and include the Indian River Guided Walk (mid-May to Aug Mon, Tues, Wed & Thurs 9–11am; $5), and the Family Fun Hike (mid-May to Aug Sun; free).

Accommodation

Sitka has a good range of **accommodation**, with a fine hotel, two dorm-style lodgings and several B&Bs. If you're looking for something a bit different, there are rental apartments on islands in Sitka Sound which make a great hideaway for a few days: get there either by water taxi or rent a kayak for a few days and explore.

There are no walk-in Forest Service **cabins** in the district, but almost two dozen beside salt water which can again be accessed by kayak or water taxi; we've listed some of the most convenient.

Hotels, motels, and B&Bs

Alaska Ocean View B&B, 1101 Edgecumbe Drive (☎747-8310, fax 747-3440, *www .sitka-alaska-lodging.com*). Very high standard B&B with all rooms featuring cable TV and VCR, CD stereo, data port, bath robes, and slippers. Guests also have the use of a patio spa pool and espresso machine, and there are facilities for business travelers. Beds are large and comfortable, the breakfasts generous, and the atmosphere's cheerful. ⑤.

Crescent Harbor Hideaway, 709 Lincoln St (☎ & fax 747-4900, *www.ptialaska.net/~bareis /b&b.htm*). Handily sited B&B with good water views from the common room, and very comfortable cable TV-equipped rooms and apartment. ⑤.

Finn Alley Inn B&B, 711 Lincoln St (☎747-3655, fax 747-5007, *www.ptialaska.net /~seakdist/finn.htm*). Well-located and large half-basement apartment with private entrance, full kitchen, and a continental breakfast delivered to the room. ④.

Sitka Hotel, 118 Lincoln St (☎747-3288, fax 747-8499, *www.sitkahotel.com*). Renovated historic town-center hotel offering good-value rooms with and without bathrooms and a touch of old-fashioned class. Very few rooms have views and fewer still have tubs. Suites ⑤, rooms with private bathroom ④, shared bath ③.

Super 8 Motel, 404 Sawmill Creek Rd (☎747-8804, 747-6101, *www.super8.com*). Spacious rooms, large TVs, free local calls, toast, donuts and coffee for breakfast, and the use of a big jacuzzi make this motel good value. ⑤.

Westmark Shee Atika, 330 Seward St (☎747-6241 or 1-800/544-0970, fax 747-5486, *www .westmarkhotels.com*). Sitka's best hotel with international-standard rooms made a little more interesting with Native paintings and trimmings. Harborview rooms are only slightly more expensive. ⑥.

Hostel and campgrounds

HI-Sitka, 303 Kimsham St (☎747-8661). An unusual hostel with camp beds in the basement of a Methodist church, but it actually works quite well, with good cooking facilities and spacious common area. Phone reservations are accepted and you probably won't be turned away even if they are full. They impose an 11pm curfew and there's a daytime lockout from 9.30am to 6pm, though this is flexible if there are ferry arrivals. Members $10, nonmembers $13. Closed Sept–May.

Sawmill Creek Campground, Blue Lake Rd (☎747-4216). Wooded Forest Service site seven miles east of Sitka and at the start of the Beaver Lake Trail. There's only creek water (treat it), pit toilets, and fire rings, and there are no sea views, but the price is right. Free.

Sealing Cove RV Parking, Airport Rd (☎747-3439). Asphalt parking lot ten-minutes' walk from downtown with water and electrical hookups for $21.

Sitka RV Park, Halibut Point Rd (☎747-6033). Parking lot next to the ferry dock with electrical and water hookups for $18.

Starrigavan Campground, Halibut Point Rd (☎747-4216). Rustic Forest Service campground 0.7 miles north of the ferry dock with secluded sites, shore fishing, easy hiking trails, water, and pit toilets. Tents (with 3 walk-in sites) and dry RV camping $8. Closed early Sept to late May.

Boat-access accommodation

Allan Point Cabin (☎1-877/444-6777). Large two-story Forest Service cabin sleeping up to fifteen and located on the sheltered Nakwasina Passage, 14 miles north of Sitka. Plenty of deer and brown bears in the area. $45.

Camp Coogan Bay Hideaway (☎747-6375). A secluded and private 72-foot float house sleeping up to ten ($155 for two; $180 for six or more) and located six miles paddle from Sitka. There's a kitchen with propane stove, living room with wood stove, bunks, futons and cots, an outhouse, sauna, double kayak for guests use and others available for rent. ⑥.

Fred's Creek Cabin (☎1-877/444-6777). Small A-frame Forest Service cabin ten miles west of Sitka on the southeast shore of Kruzof Island at the base of Mount Edgecumbe, and a good base for the summit hike. $35.

Kanga Bay Cabin (☎1-877/444-6777). Twelve miles south of Sitka, this chalet-style Forest Service cabinrests beside a beautiful cove and makes a good stopping point on the way to Goddard Hot Springs. $35.

Middle Island Recreation Cabin (☎747-5169, *www.norcov.com/~jgarey*). Cabin sleeping six on a small island five miles from Sitka. Everything is provided except food and sleeping bags, and you will need to arrange a water taxi or rent kayaks (though the owner will drop off and pick up for $75 total). ②.

Samsing Cove Cabin (☎1-877/444-6777). A rustic two-story Forest Service cabin six miles south of Sitka that's one of the most easily accessible around and is by a sandy gravel beach. $45.

Shelikof Cabin (☎1-877/444-6777). A-frame Forest Service cabin on Kruzof Island at the particularly gorgeous Shelikof Bay, an outside beach most easily accessed by a six-mile hike across the island from the sheltered Mud Bay. $35.

The town and around

Nowhere in Southeast Alaska has as many diverting cultural and historic sights as Sitka, all easily accessible on foot, and ranged conveniently along the waterfront. At its western end, the **downtown** area is overlooked by the rebuilt onion-domed **St Michael's Cathedral**, which, along with the immaculately restored **Russian Bishop's House** nearby, captures something of the spirit of Russian Alaska. Further east the **Sheldon Jackson Museum**, brings together a wonderful collection of Native crafts from around the state, and leads directly to the **Totem Park**, which forms the major component of the Sitka National Historic Park. Save time too for the **Raptor Center**, one of your few chances to get close and personal with a bald eagle, and the road system which provides access to the best local hikes.

Downtown

Getting to grips with Sitka's Russian past doesn't take much time. The best place to start is from the vantage point of **Castle Hill**, a rocky knob that was the original site of Tlingit Shee Atika. It subsequently became the site of Baranov's Castle, not a castle at all but a large wooden residence that was the nerve center of the Russian town, and was where William Seward came for the formal transfer of ownership of Alaska from Russia to the US on October 18, 1867. Baranov's Castle burnt down in 1894, but a plaque marks the spot, and the US, Alaskan, and Russian-American Company flags flutter above.

Vying with Castle Hill for dominance on the city skyline is **St Michael's Cathedral**, Lincoln Street (May–Sept 9am–4pm, when ships are in port and by appointment on ☎747-3560; $2), with its teardrop spire bearing a gold triple-bar

RUSSIAN ALASKA AND THE US PURCHASE

With a post-Cold War mindset it is easy to forget that Alaska – firmly part of the US in the American psyche – was once part of the Czarist Russian Empire. For well over a hundred years, from 1741 to 1867, Russia was the dominant power in the North Pacific, as it oversaw the near extinction of sea otters for their valuable pelts. The colonizing drive was never territorial expansionism, but a desire to top up the ever-draining coffers of the Imperial court. Though the Russian government enlisted Danish captain Vitus Bering to explore whatever was east of the Kamchatka Peninsula, they didn't subsequently run the show, leaving it up to *promyshleniki* – private fur traders – to reap huge profits under license. The Russian-American Company had already secured control of the entire coast from the Aleutians to Southcentral Alaska when, in 1799, Czar Paul granted them exclusive rights to Alaska and effectively granted them permission to subjugate the Aleut people.

About the only limitation put on the Russian-American Company was that they assist the Russian Orthodox Church in its proselytizing. And so began a symbiotic relationship with the Company providing logistical support and housing for the Church, while the priests educated and converted the Natives, thereby keeping them subservient and providing an underclass of semi-skilled workers. From 1790 to 1818, all this was overseen by Chief Manager **Alexander Baranov** (1747–1819), a failed Siberian fur businessman who arrived in Pavlovsk (Kodiak) ready to put his aggressive political skills to work. Supply routes were extremely long, and there was no military backing from St Petersburg, so Baranov was forced to cultivate cordial relations with British and American captains trading hereabouts. Nonetheless, in short order he expanded the company's domain right along the coast, and when the profitability of the fur trade declined around Kodiak in the early nineteenth century he decamped to fresh killing fields around Novaya Archangelsk, now Sitka. With untold riches at his behest he turned Sitka into the envy of the North Pacific. In his early seventies he retired, but never made it back to Russia, dying of fever on the ship home in 1819.

Under the second Chief Manager, **Ferdinand Wrangel**, and others, the sea otter and seal populations continued to decline. Meanwhile the Russian government was distracted by the Crimean War, and Russia began to look less favorably on its North American possessions. With the British-owned Hudson's Bay Company encroaching on their territory from the east, and American traders sailing out of the new settlements on the West Coast it became increasingly obvious that Russia wouldn't be able to hold on much longer. They found a willing buyer in the United States, still a relatively minor country politically. Many thought that the $7.2 million they paid was too much for this unexplored wasteland and dubbed it **"Seward's Folly,"** after the Secretary of State, William Seward.

The sale of land didn't cover private dwellings, warehouses, businesses, and the property of the Orthodox church – including the cathedral and Bishop's House – which kept its clergy in Alaska and continued to fund them from Russia until the Marxist Revolution in 1917. Russian residents were offered US citizenship, but most left taking their chattels with them and only leaving behind the racially-mixed children with their Native mothers.

Orthodoxy has turned out to be the most durable legacy of the Russian past, and apart from a couple of museums – in Sitka and Kodiak – the only significant reminders of their century-long presence in these waters are the onion-domed churches, filled with exquisite icons and topped with their triple-bar gold crosses.

cross. This fine piece of Russian architecture was built for Bishop Innocent, whose watchmaking skills were put to good use in the design of the church clock. It is in fact a faithful replica of the 1848 original which burned down on New Year's Day 1966 when a fire spread from a neighboring building to the cathedral tower. In the spirit of cooperation, the townspeople rallied to form a rescue line along which almost all the church's icons and religious treasures were passed in twenty minutes, though the irreplaceable library of books in Russian, Tlingit, and Aleut was lost. However they did save the chandelier, and eventually even the melted heap of bronze from the church bells was gathered up and recast as new bells. Inside is a priceless collection of icons, thought to be the best in the US, and all explained on the short tour. You are welcome to attend services (Sat 6.30pm and Sun 10am) which are held in English, Tlingit, and Old Slavonic.

Continue your explorations of the old Russian town by calling at the replica **blockhouse** (not open to the public), a two-story octagonal fort of thick logs on the site of one of the three that guarded the palisades which kept the Russians safe. They feared the Shee Atika Tlingits, whose land they'd stolen but who lived in an uneasy peace in the *ranche*, an area outside the stockade from where they would trade furs and food and accepted the benefits of education and religion. On the hill behind, the **Russian Cemetery** reveals a few triple-bar crosses and makes a pleasant place for a stroll.

Easily the most significant non-Russian building in town, and the one that gives Sitka the architectural solidity that is lacking from so many Alaskan towns, is the 1934 **Pioneers Home**. It is really just an old-folks home, and you'll see sourdoughs of both sexes sunning themselves on the porch. Outside a bronze statue of *The Prospector* stands resolute with staff, gun, pick, shovel, and the obligatory passage of Robert Service poetry (see box, p.177).

Walk back past the cathedral to get to the Harrigan Centennial Hall, which contains the visitor center and the **Isabel Miller Museum**, 300 Harbor Drive (May–Sept daily 8am–5pm; Oct–April Tues–Sun 10am–noon & 1.15–4pm; donations welcome), full of a little bit of everything, but nothing truly diverting, except perhaps the model of Sitka as it was at the time of the transfer. The fifty-foot-long Tlingit **ceremonial canoe** outside the museum was carved in 1967 as part of the centennial of the transfer, with an eagle at one prow and a raven on the other.

The Russian Bishop's House and the Sheldon Jackson Museum

With the loss of Sitka's original cathedral there are now just four buildings left in America from the Russian past: a private residence in Sitka, the museum in Kodiak, one building at Fort Ross in California, and the large mustard-colored **Russian Bishop's House** on Lincoln Street (May–Sept daily 9am–1pm & 2–5pm; rest of year by appointment on ☎747-6281; $3). It was completed in 1842 from Sitka spruce logs by Finnish shipwrights (who were then subjects of the Russian Czar), in style and color scheme aimed to create a little piece of St Petersburg in the North Pacific. After nearly collapsing from the rot induced by ninety inches of rain a year, the Russian Orthodox church (which maintained a bishop here until 1969) sold the house to the National Park Service in 1972. They then began a sixteen-year restoration, to re-create how the incumbent bishop maintained a lifestyle in keeping with a Russian nobleman. Reproduction wallpaper, sleigh beds, and even the original table, chairs, and sofa (which could be dismantled to travel flat) give a sense of the comforts of home.

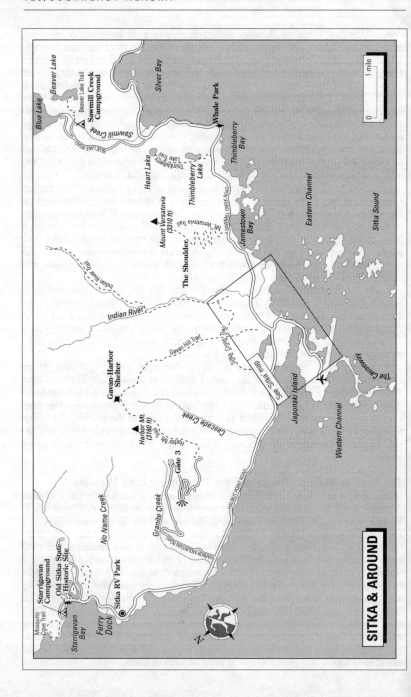

SITKA & AROUND

Such luxuries were rarely experienced by the house's first occupant, Ivan Veniaminov, who became **Bishop Innocent** of the Kamchatka Peninsula and the Russian-American Company's holdings on the Pacific Coast. He would often travel for months on end, spreading the word and learning Aleut and Tlingit. Back home he wrote a Russian–Aleut dictionary, recorded weather patterns, and became a skilled mason, blacksmith, and carpenter.

You can wander freely around the lower level of the house, which was used at various times as a grade school, seminary, orphanage, newspaper office, apartment, and tea house, and now contains a model of New Archangel as it was in 1845, the cutaway floor and wall revealing the ingenious insulation (sawdust in the walls and draft preventive joints), and several cases of artifacts and icons. Free guided tours (usually every 10–15min) lead you upstairs to the bishop's private apartments, a small library of original books, and the ornate one-room **chapel** that is still consecrated and used regularly.

The Russian Bishop's House is actually part of the Sitka National Historic Park, which continues half a mile east along Lincoln Street, just past the octagonal **Sheldon Jackson Museum**, 104 College Drive (mid-May to mid-Sept daily 9am–5pm; mid-Sept to mid-May Tues–Sat 10am–4pm; $4; ☎747-8981, *www.museums.state.ak.us/sjhome.html*), a compact but fascinating collection of Native artifacts. It was put together by the **Reverend Dr Sheldon Jackson**, a Presbyterian missionary who was Alaska's first General Agent for Education, though he turned out to be much more. Orthodoxy had never gained any widespread acceptance under the Russians, so on his wide-ranging travels throughout Alaska Jackson took it upon himself to divide the state up into a dozen broadly equivalent sections and encourage any religion he could interest to accept a kind of ecclesiastical monopoly within that region. The Presbyterians took the Arctic north and much of Southeast, Philadelphia Quakers got Kotzebue and a patch near Juneau, Methodists took the Aleutian Islands and so on, and for a long time these divisions remained.

Jackson also noted the change in Eskimo lifestyle as European presence altered hunting patterns and, ever eager to preserve Native culture, he pushed for the introduction of reindeer on the Seward Peninsula near Nome. The government initially wasn't interested, but he went ahead anyway and shipped 171 reindeer from Siberia in 1892. It was only ten years later when the government saw the benefits that they joined in and brought over another 1280 beasts. While all this was going on, he and his friends collected more than five thousand examples of Native work (useful, ceremonial, and decorative), always meticulously recording where and how the pieces were acquired. The first shack he built to house them soon filled up and in 1897 he built the current museum building, the first concrete structure in Alaska. Though small and a little old fashioned with its ranks of glass cases, it is packed to the rafters with exemplary works from throughout the state. Totems form the centerpiece, but all around are Tlingit items such as feast bowls made from alder, maple, and birch in bird and bear designs with decorative pieces picked out in bone. The wood-and-fur **Raven battle helmet** worn by the Kisadi leader, Katlian, in the 1804 conflict with the Russians vies for pride of place with armor made from leather and wooden slats, an Athapascan birch bark canoe, an Eskimo reindeer sled, and drawers full of smaller and more delicate items that could keep you occupied for hours.

The Totem Park and the Raptor Center

At the end of Lincoln Street, in a verdant copse between ocean and creek, you'll find the main section of the **Sitka National Historic Park** (known locally as just "Totem Park"). This wooded park bordered by totem poles occupies a small peninsula where the Shee Atika Tlingits established a fort in preparation for the return of the Russians after they'd been driven out the first time in 1802 (see "Some history" on p.113). The fort was subsequently destroyed by the Russians and all that's left is a grassy patch around a particularly striking totem pole. Somehow it seems a little out of character with the rest of the park, all brooding spruce and hemlocks swathed in almost incessant mist, out of which loom the poles gazing balefully out to sea. As elsewhere in Southeast, they're not originals, but replicas of nineteenth-century totems.

The park was first set aside in 1890 by President Benjamin Harrison, who recognized the cultural significance of such a battleground, and developed by Alaska governor John Brady, who chose this as the resting place for poles rounded up from all over Southeast for the Louisiana Purchase Exposition of 1904. None had actually come from here (most were from Haida villages on Prince of Wales Island) but with land already set aside, this seemed the most sensible place for them. As they continued to rot, the CCC (see p.76) began a program to replicate most of the thirteen poles now present. A couple are more recent creations, notably the Indian River Tlingit History Pole, by the visitor center, which was ceremoniously raised in 1996 after considerable debate within the Tlingit community about the Raven and Eagle appearing on the same pole.

In addition to inspecting the poles along the foreshore, check in at the **visitor center**, at the end of Lincoln Street (May–Sept daily 8am–5pm; rest of year by appointment on ☎747-6281; free), which has a small museum with well-chosen displays, good interpretive displays on what is commonly called the "Battle of Sitka," a ten-minute video on the last Native resistance to the coming of the white man, and workshops where you can chat to the Native craftspeople as they work.

Before returning to town consider a visit to the wooded, streamside confines of the nonprofit **Alaska Raptor Center**, 1101 Sawmill Creek Rd (daily: April–Sept 8am–4pm; Oct–March 8am–5pm; summer $10, winter free; *www.ptialaska.net /~arrc*). Here, wounded raptors – owls, hawks, peregrine falcons, and especially bald eagles – are cared for and released back into the wild, save those that are unable to fly or hunt, and are kept as "raptors in residence." The birds stay in large and thoughtfully constructed compounds and are introduced by the enthusiastic and well-informed staff who guide you around. When groups turn up (it pays to come on a day when there's a cruise ship in town) they'll even bring one of the bald eagles out; perhaps your only chance to come face to beak with one of these regal birds.

Along the road system

Unless you are camping or needing to reach distant trailheads there is little point in renting a car in Sitka: there are only about seven or eight miles of road in each direction from town, and not a great deal along them. Heading east along Sawmill Creek Road, you pass the trailhead for **Mount Versatovia Trail** at Jamestown Bay about three miles out; a mile further is **Whale Park**, three covered observation platforms linked by boardwalks. Another mile or so further west, the site of the pulp mill, which closed in 1993, marks Blue Lake Road, which leads to *Sawmill Creek Campground* and **Beaver Lake Trail**.

HIKES AROUND SITKA

Sitka is unusually well served with good hikes, from shoreside strolls to harder climbs up Gavan Hill and steep Mount Verstovia. Some of them are directly accessible from town, while others require transport to the trailhead; the Mount Edgecumbe Trail needs access by boat.

Beaver Lake Trail (1.5 miles-round trip; 1hr; 400ft ascent). Popular trail climbing steadily from *Sawmill Creek* campground through temperate forest then on a boardwalk across muskeg, dropping gently to the scenic Beaver Lake. Good mountain views if the clouds lift.

Gavan Hill Trail (6 miles round-trip; 4–7hr; 2400ft ascent). Beginning in town off Baranof Street (see map, p.114), this moderate trail leads to subalpine tops where you can hook up with the Harbor Mountain Trail, or continue into the Three Sister Mountains and some good high-country camping areas. The Gavan Hill and Harbor Mountain trails meet at the free-use **Gavan–Harbor Shelter**, which has no stove and is best treated as an emergency shelter: bring a tent if you want to stay up here.

Harbor Mountain Trail (8 miles round-trip; 4–6hr; 1500ft ascent). The narrow gravel Harbor Mountain Road twists five miles off Halibut Point Road to subalpine country at around 2000 feet. Unfortunately subsidence means that you can currently only drive the first three miles to Gate 3. To continue, follow the road on foot past an excellent overlook and a couple of picnic areas to the trailhead proper, were it is two miles up to the Gavan–Harbor Shelter (see above).

Indian River Trail (11 miles round-trip; 6–8hr; 500ft ascent). Long but fairly gentle and relaxing trail following the Indian River valley to the eighty-foot Indian River Falls below the Three Sisters Mountains. Lovely rainforest, and there's salmon in the river from midsummer. It starts right in town off Indian River Road (see map, p.114).

Mosquito Cove Trail (1.2 mile loop; 1 hr; 100ft ascent). New and easy trail partly following the coast then looping back through forest. Just one of several short trails which start from the Starrigavan Recreation Area, 8 miles west of Sitka.

Mount Edgecumbe Trail (13.5 miles round-trip; 7–10hr; 2600ft ascent). Climbs the prominent volcano on Sitka's horizon, requiring you to organize transport to the trailhead by the Forest Service's *Fred's Creek Cabin* ($35) on Kruzof Island. Water taxis will charge around $120 to drop off and pick up for up to six people. From *Fred's Creek Cabin* the trail crosses muskeg rising gently for the first four miles to where there's a three-sided emergency shelter. From there the path steepens to the tree line at 2000 feet then disappears. If there is low cloud, be absolutely certain you can retrace your steps across the unmarked upper slopes.

Mount Versatovia Trail (5 miles round-trip; 4–5hr; 2500ft). Arduous hike that is rewarding on a clear day. Beginning a couple of miles east of town off Sawmill Creek Road, it starts gently through an area logged by the Russians in the 1860; there's still some evidence of the charcoal pits they built. The trail soon climbs with ever-longer views to "the shoulder," which is as far as most people go. Enthusiasts can continue along the ridge to the northeast to the true 3310ft summit, roughly another hour on.

Thimbleberry–Heart Lakes Trail (0.5–2 miles round-trip; 30min–2hr; 50ft ascent). Short and relatively easy (though sometimes boggy) trail to a couple of good fishing lakes. The trailhead is at Mile 4 of Sawmill Creek Road.

Four miles west along Halibut Point Road you hit Halibut Point State Recreation Site, where there are some picnic tables and some short trails. More robust hikes can be found at the top of Harbor Mountain Road, which heads inland almost opposite. From here, Halibut Point Road continues to the AMHS **ferry dock** and, a mile beyond, the **Starrigavan Recreation Area**, which contains a campground and the **Old Sitka State Historic Site**, where barely discernable remains mark the original site of the Russian presence in 1799.

Cruises and kayaking

Sitka's setting, open to the ocean and yet hemmed in by myriad islands, is such that almost all your time on land is spent wishing you were on the water. That's easily rectified with Sitka Wildlife Quest (late May to early Sept; ☎747-8100 or 1-888/747-8101, *www.allenmarinetours.com*), who run educational and entertaining two-hour wildlife tours (Wed 6pm & Sat 9am; $49) out on Sitka Sound with every chance of seeing humpback whales (especially in the fall), sea otters, seals, and bears and deer along the banks of numerous islands. Their Sunday trip (9am; $49) goes instead to the sheer volcanic **St Lazaria Island**, a federal wildlife refuge at the mouth of Sitka Sound with cliffs that, during the summer months, are black with sea birds, notably comical puffins, murres, and petrels. The cliffs plunge so steeply into the sea that you can get within a few feet of the creatures. Trips leave from Crescent Harbor Marina.

Sitka has some of the best **sea kayaking** in Southeast, with mile upon mile of sheltered waterways, narrow channels, gorgeous coves, and tide pools. Paddle beyond the swanky homes that dot the islands near Sitka, and you can camp anywhere, or stay in one of the couple of dozen saltwater-accessible cabins (see "Boat-access accommodation," p.117). Even in a few hours you can explore **The Causeway**, a series of small islands south of the airport which were linked up during World War II to provide access to gun emplacements. Remnants are still visible, though hard to find, and it pays to ask whoever is renting you a kayak before you set out.

One popular destination is **Goddard Hot Springs**, seventeen miles to the south, where two covered hot tubs face out to sea. Don't expect to have the place to yourselves as it is a popular rest spot for commercial fishermen, but it makes an excellent destination for a kayak expedition (four days round-trip from Sitka). There is no cabin, though you can camp if you don't mind the mosquitoes; at their midsummer peak it is better to find spots on offshore islands.

Probably the best of the kayak businesses is Baidarka Boats, 201 Lincoln St (☎747-8996, fax 747-4801, *www.kayaksite.com*), who rent top-quality kayaks from $35 a day (doubles $50), a price which drops to $25/35 for five- to nine-day rentals. They also have folding kayaks ($60 1 day; $45 a day for over 5) which are ideal if you want to do a one-way paddle and fly back. Costs for guided trips depend on numbers, but four people in two double kayaks is going to cost $65 per person for a full day out with lunch.

Competitive rates are offered by Sitka Sound Ocean Adventures (☎747-6375, *www.ptialaska.net/~delongb*), who also rent kayaks and conduct guided kayak tours from as little as two hours ($50) around the Totem Park shoreline and out to the closer islands, and going up to full-day trips $100 and multiday affairs costing a little over $100 a day.

Eating, drinking, and entertainment

Sitka's **restaurants** aren't exactly going to set gourmet tongues wagging, though there are several reasonable places to dine out. For evening drinks, join the crowds in the *Westmark Shee Atika's* bar, or head along to the more colorful bars on Katlian Street.

Daytime entertainment is more varied with a couple of local dance troupes vying for your attention. The choice venue would have to be the Community House, 200 Katlian St, where the **Sheet'ka Kwaan Naa Kahidi Dancers** (May–Sept; $6; ☎747-7290 or 1-888/270-8687, *www.sitkatribal.com*), perform for half an hour in traditional costume, complete with a narration of local legends. Performance times (which are dependent on cruise ship sailings) are posted outside the 1997 replica clan house, beside the stridently painted Eagle and Raven design screen. The alternative is the **New Archangel Dancers**, Harrigan Centennial Hall ($6; ☎747-5516), who also do a half-hour show scheduled around the cruise ships, but concentrate on authentic Russian folk dances performed by local women.

Fans of chamber music will want to time their visit to coincide with the **Summer Music Festival** (*www.sitkamusicfestival.org*), which takes place throughout most of June and includes around eight evening concerts, mostly in Harrigan Centennial Hall, and featuring up to twenty artists of international renown. Tickets are available by calling ☎747-6774, or from Old Harbor Books, though you'll need to book in advance, or be content with sitting in on rehearsals, which are free.

The Backdoor, 104 Barracks St (☎747-8856). Daytime café with great coffee, plus tasty sandwiches, pastries, and light lunches. Access through Old Harbor Books.

Bayview Restaurant, upstairs at 407 Lincoln St (☎747-5440). Good restaurant with great sea views and well prepared standard Alaskan fare with additional Russian treats such as borscht.

Channel Club, 2906 Halibut Point Rd, 4 miles west of town (☎747-9916). If you've an appetite for steak, this is the only place to consider, and an enduring favorite with Sitka residents. Full service bar and a free shuttle from downtown.

Evergreen Natural Foods, 2a Lincoln St (☎747-6944). Organic produce store, and small café (only open weekdays until around 3pm) selling 95 percent organic juices, smoothies, and soups served with fresh-baked bread at low prices.

Highliner Coffee, Seward Square Mall, Seward St (☎747-4924). Daytime coffee shop with relaxing sofas, espresso coffee, good cakes, bagels, and Internet access.

Lane 7 Snack Bar, 331 Lincoln St (☎747-6310). Sitka's cheapest burger joint, with formica tables and the noise of bowling from next door.

Pioneer Bar, 212 Katlian St (☎747-3456). Down-to-earth bar with Alaskan maritime theme.

Raven Dining Room and Kadataan Lounge, 330 Seward St (☎747-6465). Smart restaurant and bar inside the *Westmark Shee Atika* hotel with good views of the water. The latter serves the usual range of burgers, sandwiches, and salads at slightly inflated prices, while the dining room dishes up the likes of seafood fettuccini ($16) and barbecue baby back ribs ($18).

Sheldon Jackson College Dining Room, David Sweetland Hall. The best bargain in town for diners on a budget. A simple cafeteria-style place with all-you-can-eat breakfast (6.30–8am; $5), lunch (11.30am–1pm; $5), and dinner (4.45–6pm; $10). They even have salmon for dinner. Follow the road opposite the entrance to the Sheldon Jackson Museum.

Listings

Banks The First National Bank of Anchorage at 318 Lincoln St has an ATM.

Bicycle rental and repair Southeast Diving & Sport Shop, 203 Lincoln St (☎747-8279); Yellow Jersey Cycle Shop, 805 Halibut Point Rd (☎747-6317, *yellowj@ptialaska.net*) rent bikes at $25 for 24hr.

Bookshop Old Harbor Books, 201 Lincoln St (☎747-8808, *oldharbr@ptialaska.net*).

Car rental Allstar Rent-a-Car, at the airport (☎966-2552 or 1-800/722-6927).

Festivals Apart from the Summer Music Festival (see overleaf) there's a salmon derby on the last weekend of May and first weekend in June; a lively Fourth of July parade and fireworks; a period costume ball, parade, and dinners to celebrate the lead-up to Alaska Day and the anniversary of the transfer on Oct 18; and a celebration of all things cetacean in the Whale Festival in the first week of Nov. It is also worth noting that the Russian Orthodox Church follows the Julian (rather than the standard Gregorian calendar) so religious festivals – Christmas and Easter in particular – are celebrated twice here, roughly twelve days apart.

Internet access The library has in-demand free access (reserve in advance), and for more immediate needs try Jeff Parker's Computer Center, 205 Harbor Drive (Mon–Sat 10am–5pm; ☎747-0600).

Laundry and showers The Hames PE Center at Sheldon Jackson College (early May to early Sept Mon–Fri 6am–8pm, Sat noon–6pm; ☎747-5231) has a pool, racquetball courts, and showers for $3. Duds N Suds, 906 Halibut Point Rd is the handiest for laundry.

Library Kettleson Memorial Library, Harbor Drive (Mon–Thurs 10am–9pm, Fri 10am–6pm, Sat & Sun 1–5pm).

Medical assistance Sitka Community Hospital, 209 Moeller Drive (☎747-3241) has emergency medical services and outpatient clinics.

Pharmacy White's Pharmacy, 705 Halibut Point Rd (☎747-5755).

Post Office there's a sub-post office downtown at 338 Lincoln St (Mon–Sat 8.30am–5.30pm) and the main on Sawmill Creek Rd out by the Raptor Center. The **General Delivery** ZIP code is 99835.

Taxes There's a 5 percent sales tax and an additional 6 percent bed tax, all included within our price codes.

Travel agency Totem Travel, 903 Halibut Point Rd (☎747-7474 or 1-800/478-3252, fax 747-7494).

Water taxi Sitka Sound Water Taxi (☎747-5970).

Minor Ports

All over Southeast Alaska there are small settlements of a few hundred people, sometimes Native villages that have survived intact, sometimes former logging camps or canneries that have developed enough momentum to exist beyond the death of the industry that spawned them. Many are off the main sea lanes plied by the AMHS ferries, while others get regular (though not especially frequent) visits; it is those we have covered here. None really warrants a special visit, and in most cases the hour you'll spend at the ferry dock is ample. Kayakers, however may want to paddle to one of these ports then catch the ferry back to their starting point: Petersburg to Kake and Sitka to Tenakee Springs are trips to consider.

Wherever you plan to stop, be sure to study the ferry schedule carefully to ensure you don't end up spending five nights in a place you only intended spending two.

Kake

Between Petersburg and Sitka, roughly two southbound and two northbound AMHS ferries a week call in at **KAKE**, an eight-hundred-strong Tlingit village on the west coast of Kupreanof Island. Fishing and subsistence hunting keep the town afloat, with the occasional visitor using the town as a springboard for kayak trips to Kuiu Island, or as a destination for a paddling expedition from Petersburg. Ferries dock a mile and a half from town, so you probably won't have long enough to closely inspect the town's 132-foot **totem pole**, carved for the 1970 World's Fair in Japan and said to be the tallest in the world. You can **stay** at the *Waterfront Lodge* (☎785-3472; ④), **eat** at the *Nugget Inn* (☎785-6469), and buy groceries from several stores.

Angoon

The Tlingit village of **ANGOON**, sixty miles southeast of Juneau, is the only significant settlement on Admiralty Island, and occupies one of the warmest and driest locations in Southeast on its western coast facing Chatham Strait. Its seven hundred residents survive on fishing and subsistence hunting and do nothing to encourage tourism, which only touches their lives when the AMHS ferries arrive every few days; and since the ferry dock is three miles from town the impact is very slight. About the only reason to stop is to do a little kayaking using *Favorite Bay Inn* (☎788-3123 or 1-800/423-3123, fax 788-3104, *favoritebayinn@juno.com*; ⑥) as your base.

Tenakee Springs

The ferry schedule occasionally allows visitors enough time to wallow in the soothing no-clothes **hot pool** (men 2–6pm & 10pm–9am, women at all other times) at **TENAKEE SPRINGS**, sixty miles southeast of Juneau. The stark concrete room containing the pool is at the base of the ferry dock just fifty yards from the boat, but the pressure of the soon departing boat makes it less than relaxing and you may not find yourself warmly welcomed by the locals. They're far from hostile; it's just that most of the hundred residents came here for a quiet life and can be easily overwhelmed by the masses. A case in point was the 1997 visit of a cruise ship, the *World Discoverer*, that disgorged a hundred-plus passengers onto the single car-free dirt path that serves as the town's main street. The people shut up shop and effectively hid until the ship went away promising never to return.

Individuals will feel much more welcome, yet, there's not a great deal to do except fall into the pattern of daily baths, perhaps do a little fishing, or hike eight miles east along the single road to the site of the old cannery, whose workers initially popularized the springs in the late nineteenth century.

If you want to **stay** you can **camp** for nothing at the undeveloped site a mile east of the ferry dock at the mouth of the Indian River. There are a few cheap cabins available through the *Snyder Mercantile* (☎736-2205; ①), at the foot of the dock opposite the hot pool, and there are meals to be had at the *Blue Moon Café*, behind the bathhouse. Hours can be erratic so it pays to bring some food and be prepared to self-cater.

Hoonah

Several ferries a week on the Sitka–Juneau run make the slight detour to **HOONAH**, a beachside Huna Tlingit fishing village on the north side of Chichagof Island, forty miles west of Juneau. Despite being the largest Native village in Southeast (with around 900 residents) there's little to see, though with a central ferry dock, it is easy to wander into town for a quick look around. All around the hillsides have been logged by a couple of Native corporations, but Port Frederick, as the bay is known, still has its most distinguished feature, the remains of the Hoonah Packing Company **cannery** around a mile north of town. If you have time, visit the Hoonah Indian Association **Cultural Center and Museum** (Mon–Fri 8am–4.30pm; free), on the hill behind the town, which has displays of local history and Native culture, including some interesting totem poles.

Pelican

The cheapest way to visit **PELICAN**, seventy miles west of Juneau, is to come from Juneau on the AMHS ferry that makes its run about every two weeks in summer, always on a Sunday ($64 round-trip). The two hours you get in Pelican is enough to get a flavor of the place as you stroll along the boardwalks, but the real appeal of the trip is the five-hour-each-way ferry journey which passes close to Glacier Bay, through Icy Strait, and around **Point Adolphus**, which is regarded as one of the world's best places for **watching humpback whales**: this can be the cheapest whale watching trip you are likely to get.

This tiny fishing village on the shores of Lisianski Inlet takes its name from the boat belonging to Finnish immigrant fisherman Charlie Raatikianen, who, with a few mates, established the town in 1938 to more conveniently process his catch. The setting proved favorable and the settlement added a post office in 1939, a cannery by 1943, and subsequently a school, a small sawmill, and a hotel. Most of the buildings stand on piles over the water, linked by boardwalks with only a couple of miles of roads.

If the ferry schedule doesn't suit, you can fly here daily from Juneau with Loken Air (☎789-3331 or 1-800/478-3360) for around $100. There are a few places to **eat and drink**, but most visitors seem to gravitate towards *Rosie's Bar and Grill*, on the boardwalk (☎735-2265; ③), which has rooms and a bar that's usually full of commercial fishermen.

Juneau

The sophisticated and vibrant city of **JUNEAU** (JUNE-oh) is unlike any other state capital in the nation. Accessible only by sea or air, it is exceptionally picturesque, hard against the **Gastineau Channel**, with steep, narrow roads clawing up into the rainforested hills behind. With no flat land to speak of, and a giant icefield blocking off any chance of land access to the interior, it would be hard to think of a less practical site for a state capital, but the vagaries of history and man's lust for gold swung the balance.

Waste rock from the town's gold mines was dumped into Gastineau Channel to create the flat downtown area where a ragged gold rush town sprung up with the usual complement of bars, churches, and brothels. Juneau had the good fortune to avoid a major fire – with towns built entirely of wood and many months of the year spent with stoves raging, fires were inevitable and few downtown areas avoided them entirely – and most of the older buildings remain leaving a viable sense of history and creating a harmonious focus for what has to be one of the most physically beguiling town centers in Alaska.

The trouble is, much of the beauty is often obscured by the weather. It is not so much the annual ninety-plus inches of rain, but the consistency with which it comes – on average two out of every three days. Even when it is not raining, it is often cloudy. That hasn't stopped Juneau from becoming one of the busiest cruise-ship ports in Alaska, creating a frenetic atmosphere with these huge floating hotels looming over the narrow central streets where diamond and emerald jewelry, handmade Swiss watches, and immaculately cut fur coats vie for shelf space with tasteless trinkets and mini totem poles. Still, it keeps the place lively, and makes a dramatic contrast with the languid evenings when the ships glide away, the streets empty out, and the buildings take on a glossy sheen as the low sun casts its last rays under the blanket of cloud.

Some history

Juneau was founded on gold. No one took much notice of the Auk Tlingit fishing village on Gastineau Channel until 1880 when George Pilz, a mining engineer from Sitka, dispatched Joe Juneau and Dick Harris there with Auk chief Kowee. Kowee had responded to Pilz's offer of a reward for divulging the whereabouts of gold, but these hapless drunken prospectors were unable to find much. Kowee insisted there was ore to be found and at the second attempt they unearthed "little lumps as large as peas and beans" at the head of Gold Creek. In no time, Alaska had its first gold rush and Harrisberg became the first American-established town in its new territory. Miners became disenchanted with Harris' dubious claim-staking practices and briefly switched the name to Rockwell before settling on Juneau in 1881.

Gold in the streams quickly ran out, but reef gold – locked in the hard rock below ground – was abundant. Early efforts at extraction from the Perseverance Mine (1885–1921) soon exhausted the best grade ore, and throughout most of Juneau's sixty-year gold mining era, its massive mines and crushing mills had to content themselves with low grade ore and could only turn a profit by mining on a massive huge scale; sometimes 28 tons of rock had to be crushed to yield a single ounce of gold. There were three main mines. The first and most enduring was the Alaska Juneau Mine (1887–1944), which hollowed out a hundred miles of tunnels in the hillside just south of downtown Juneau. You can still clearly see the scars left by its mill house where 12,000 tons of ore could be crushed in a single day by a thousand employees. Next was the Treadwell Gold Mining Company (1899–1922), in Douglas, which was briefly the most profitable of them all; and then there was the short-lived Alaska Gastineau Mining Company (1915–21), four miles south of Juneau.

Unlike the gold rushes elsewhere in Alaska, the feverish activity around Juneau was long-lived, and by 1906 the territorial capital had moved here from Sitka. As the gold became less profitable, the city shifted its focus to its legislative and administrative role, which it has hung onto despite periodic attempts to move it elsewhere (see p.181).

Arrival, getting around, and information

Though cruise ships dock conveniently downtown, most Juneau arrivals are inconvenient. The AMHS **ferry terminal**, Glacier Hwy (open for ferry arrivals; ☎789-7453), is fourteen miles northwest of downtown at Auke Bay, and since ferries often arrive at unearthly hours, getting into town can be a problem. Apart from taxis (see "Listings," p.145), which cost around $30 into town, the only transport is with the MGT shuttle (☎789-5460 between 6pm and 8pm only; *www.mightygreattrips.com*), which meets all ferries and charges $5 to downtown. The nearest local Capital Transit **bus routes** (#3 and #4; Mon–Sat 7.20am–10.50pm, Sun

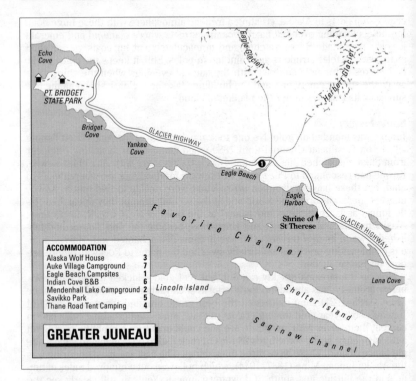

ACCOMMODATION

Alaska Wolf House	3
Auke Village Campground	7
Eagle Beach Campsites	1
Indian Cove B&B	6
Mendenhall Lake Campground	2
Savikko Park	5
Thane Road Tent Camping	4

GREATER JUNEAU

9.20am–5.20pm) are a mile and a half away at the junction with Mendenhall Loop Road.

Juneau **airport**, nine miles north of downtown (☎789-7821), is the main hub for flights around Southeast, with numerous Alaska Airlines arrivals and several from smaller local carriers. On arrival you'll find taxis outside ($20 downtown), and a small **visitor kiosk** that is open for all arrivals and is the place to go for directions to the bus stop. You'll need to walk about a quarter of a mile to the stop on Mallard Street, just behind the Nugget Mall.

Getting around

All the main points of interest (with the exception of the ferry terminal) can be reached using city **buses**, run by Capital Transit (☎789-6901), who operate four services, all costing $1.25, exact fare. The main routes (#3 and #4; hourly 7am–11pm) both run from downtown along the waterfront past Lemon Creek to the airport and then loop through the Mendenhall Valley. In addition, they operate a service (Mon–Sat 7am–10.30pm) from downtown over the bridge to Douglas: there are free bus transfers at the Federal Building stop. There's also an hourly **express service** (Mon–Fri 7.30am–6pm) between downtown and the university, about two miles short of the Auke Bay ferry terminal. The timetable is reasonably clear, and the *Understanding the Public Bus System* leaflet, available free from the visitor center, has detailed descriptions of how to get to various sights. Bikes travel free on the buses.

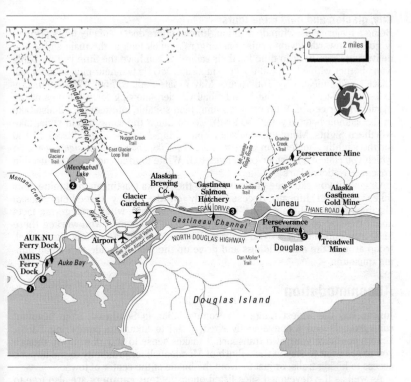

The bus system is infrequent enough, and the road system extensive enough that it makes sense to **rent a car** (see "Listings", p.144) for at least part of your stay. **Cycling** can also work well with a number of dedicated **bike routes** that hit all the main destinations. Pick up the free *Juneau Bike Routes* leaflet from the visitor center, and rent bikes for around $25 a day from Mountain Gears, 210 N Franklin St (☎586-4327), or Adventure Sports, Nugget Mall, Mendenhall (☎789-5696).

Information

The best source of information is the cramped Davis Log Cabin **visitor center**, 134 3rd St (May–Sept Mon–Fri 8.30am–5pm, Sat & Sun 9am–5pm; Oct–April Mon–Fri 9am–5pm; ☎586-2201 or 1-88/581-2201, fax 586-6304, *www.traveljuneau .com*), though during the day in summer there are handy **information booths** at Marine Park on the waterfront, and by the cruise-ship dock. There are also entertainment listings in the *Juneau Empire* newspaper, which has general city information on its useful Web site at *www.juneaualaska.com*.

For information specific to Glacier Bay, Tracy Arm Fjord, and the trails and cabins in Juneau's wooded surroundings, visit the joint National Park Service and **Tongass National Forest visitor center**, Centennial Hall, 101 Egan Drive (Mon–Fri 8am–5pm daily; ☎586-8751, fax 586-7928, *www.fs.fed.us/r10/tongass*), which has diverting displays and a wealth of videos on the region's ecology, geology, and ethnography.

City, glacier, and gold mine tours

Being a major cruise ship destination, Juneau offers dozens of city tours primarily geared towards giving cruise passengers a quick look at the main sights and delivering them back in time for their sailing. If you have the time you probably won't bother with a tour, but if you're in a rush MGT's two-hour-plus Mendenhall Glacier and Juneau City Tour (early May to late Sept; $17.50; ☎789-5460), provides low-cost access to the Mendenhall Glacier, allowing forty minutes at the glacier visitor center. With prior warning (and suitable interest) they'll also take in the salmon hatchery ($21.50 total). To do much the same trip in style, take Northern Sights' Mendenhall Glacier Tour (May–Aug 3–4 daily; $29.50, $19.50 for the slightly shorter 7pm tour; ☎1-877/479-8708, *www.northernsights.com*), on which you ride in a fourteen-passenger 1937 White touring car, originally used in Yosemite National Park.

One sight you can't see on your own is the Alaska Gastineau gold mine, four miles south of Juneau. Access is only on the pricey three-hour Alaska Gastineau Mill and Gold Mine Tour ($70; ☎789-9797), where staggering facts about the size of the mine and anecdotes about the people who worked there keep you entertained as you walk underground along a 360-foot flat tunnel, troop around the old buildings and drive up the mountainside to a small mining museum.

Accommodation

Juneau has the widest range of accommodation in Southeast, from beautiful campgrounds and a conveniently sited hostel to luxurious pampering B&Bs. Unless you have your own transport, it makes sense to stay downtown, though you might want to stay in the suburb of Mendenhall for proximity to the airport, access to hiking trails, or just to avoid the bustle of the center of town.

As well as the developed sites listed opposite, **tent campers** are also free to use undeveloped areas such as Echo Cove, forty miles north of downtown at the end of Glacier Hwy, and Eagle Beach, about thirty miles out in the same direction. **RV drivers** who just need a place to park up overnight can stay near the airport in the parking lots around Carr's at 3033 Vintage Blvd, K-Mart at 6525 Glacier Hwy, and Nugget Mall at 8745 Glacier Hwy, provided you park well away from the buildings.

Hotels and motels

Alaskan Hotel and Bar, 167 S Franklin St, downtown (☎586-1000 or 1-800/327-9374, *www .ptialaska.net/~akhotel*). Juneau's oldest hotel dates back to 1913 and truthfully claims to have "Styles & Rates of a bygone era," in fact, the cheapest rooms in town. They all have antique furniture of some sort, and around half of them have private bathrooms (④). TVs and kitchenettes are more randomly scattered, and some rooms are pretty small. Avoid the second floor rooms above the bar if you fancy an early night. ③.

Baranof Hotel, 127 N Franklin St, downtown (☎586-2660 or 1-800/544-0970, *www .westmarkhotels.com*). Now over sixty years old, this is Juneau's grandest hotel, though the rooms have become somewhat sanitized now that it is part of the statewide Westmark chain. All rooms are slightly different so ask to look at a few. Suites ⑧, rooms ⑦.

Driftwood Lodge, 435 Willoughby Ave, downtown (☎586-2280 or 1-800/544-2239, fax 586-1034, *www.driftwoodalaska.com*). Three-story motel one block from the waterfront, with large rooms including kitchenettes and some one-bedroom and two-bedroom apartments (both ⑤). Courtesy bus to airport and ferry, and bikes available for rent at $15 a half-day, $25 a day. ④.

Guesthouse Inn & Suites, 1800 Shell Simmons Drive, Mendenhall (☎790-8800 or 1-888/559-9876, fax 274-2152, *www.guesthousealaska.com*). New hotel opposite the airport made up entirely of two-room suites with all the expected in-room facilities, plus pool, spa, exercise room, and downtown shuttle. ⑥.

Prospector Hotel, 375 Whittier St, downtown (☎586-3737 or 1-800/478-5866 in Alaska, fax 586-1204, *www.prospectorhotel.com*). Pretty standard mid-range hotel (cable with HBO, phones, coffee and pastries for breakfast, etc), but with reasonable prices for its central location with water views from many rooms and suites (⑥). There are no nonsmoking rooms in the cheapest price bracket. ⑤.

Silverbow Guest Inn, 120 2nd St, downtown (☎586-4146 or 1-800/586-4146, fax 586-4242, *www.silverbowinn.com*). Attractive, small hotel linked to the restaurant and bakery of the same name, with smallish but nicely furnished and tastefully decorated rooms, each with TV and phone, and with a good continental breakfast included. Reasonable off-season rates, though in July and the first half of August there's a $10 supplement if you only stay one night. ⑥.

Super 8 Motel, 225 Trout St, Mendenhall (☎789-4858, fax 789-5819, *www.super8.com*). The cheapest accommodation near the airport – they run a complimentary shuttle, though it is only about five hundred yards away. Rooms are unexciting, but well equipped and were upgraded fairly recently. ⑤.

B&Bs

Alaska Wolf House, 1900 Wickersham St, downtown (☎586-2422, fax 586-9053, *www.alaskawolfhouse.com*). Spacious and very comfortable B&B in a large cedar-log house with views of Gastineau Channel where the emphasis is not so much on providing accommodation (though they do that admirably), but in helping their guests interpret the Juneau area. To this end the owners invite guests onto their 32-foot wooden boat for a day-long cruise ($150) viewing glaciers, shipwreck sites, and wildlife. Back at the B&B there is a range of individually styled suites (⑥) and tastefully decorated rooms (⑤), two with shared bath (④), and all with plenty of good books. Breakfasts are delicious.

Alaska's Capital Inn, 113 W 5th, downtown (☎586-6507 or 1-888/588-6507, fax 586-6508, *www.alaskacapitalinn.com*). One of the more luxurious of Juneau's B&Bs, in an elegantly restored 1906 mansion that holds a range of mostly large and varied rooms all with original features and beautiful fittings, and some with great views. The attic Governor's suite is superb. A five-course sit-down breakfast is served. Governor's suite ⑨, rooms ⑥.

Cashen Quarters, 315 Gold St, downtown (☎586-9863 or 1-888/543-5701, fax 586-9861, *www.cashenquarters.com*). Quiet but very central B&B with five comfortable rooms (two of them suites; ⑦) in a two-story house. The owners live next door and deliver to your room abundant ingredients for a self-made continental breakfast. Open all year with (②) winter rates. ⑤.

Indian Cove, Glacier Hwy, a mile north of Auke Bay (☎789-2726, *signell@email.msn.com*). Pleasant B&B where the main attraction is being (just) within walking distance of the ferry dock (particularly for late arrivals). It is right beside the water so there are good views and a continental breakfast is served. ③.

Pearson's Pond Luxury, 4541 Sawa Circle, Mendenhall (☎789-3772 or 1-888/658-6328, *www.pearsonspond.com*). Three very comfortable rooms in a spacious modern house a mile from Mendenhall Glacier, with CD and VCR, personal gyms, laptop, Internet access, kitchenettes with self-serve breakfasts, hot tubs, boating, bikes, in fact just about every amenity you can think of. Each room has a water or garden view and leads out to two communal hot tubs. ⑧.

Hostels and camping

Auke Village Campground, Mile 15 Glacier Hwy. First-come, first-served Forest Service campground 1.5 miles north of the Auke Bay ferry terminal and close to a scenic beach. RVs and tent sites have pit toilets and water and cost $8. Closed late Sept to April.

Eagle Beach Camp Sites, Glacier Hwy, Mile 28 Glacier Hwy, 15 miles north of the Auke Bay ferry terminal. A first-come, first-served state park campground that is picturesque even if it is only a gravel lot. Bring water. $3.

HI-Juneau, 614 Harris St, AK 99801 (☎586-9559, *juneauhostel@gci.net*). Costing just $7 for a bunk ($10 for nonmembers) this is an Alaskan bargain, but in return you have to put up with a daytime lockout (9am–5pm), an evening curfew (midnight), and limited office hours (7–9am & 5–10pm). Still, it is a comfortable, relaxed, and central place in an old Juneau home with separate floors for men and women, a spacious kitchen and lounge and laundry facilities. Reservations (necessary at least June–Aug) can only be made by mail and should include the first night's fee for each person. They'll reply by SAE or email. ①.

Mendenhall Lake Campground, Montana Creek Rd, off Mendenhall Loop Rd, 13 miles from downtown. A Particularly gorgeous first-come, first-served Forest Service campground within sight of the Mendenhall Glacier and with space for RVs (full hookup $20, water and electricity $18, dry $10), and some lovely lakeside tent sites ($10). Closed early Sept to mid-May.

Savikko Park, Savikko Rd, Douglas. Free space for four RVs to park with water and toilets nearby, located in Douglas, two miles south of the Douglas Bridge. Call at the Harbormaster's office on the water side of Egan Expressway in town. Maximum three-day stay.

Thane Road Tent Camping, Mile 1 Thane Rd. Small and primitive site with chemical toilets and stream water located just fifteen-minutes' walk south of downtown. First-come, first-served sites are only $5 but you'll have to put up with the all-night clatter from the docks nearby. Closed Oct–April.

The City and activities

Downtown Juneau is a faintly disturbing place, torn between the demands of herd tourism and the more prosaic needs of longstanding residents. Elderly cruise ship passengers are emptied into the tiny downtown core to window shop and poke around, but it is where you're likely to spend most of your time, especially on wet days when a couple of excellent museums, the State Capitol, and the Russian Orthodox Church provide suitably protected distraction. On better days the Mount Roberts Tram gives instant access to the high country above town, and it is easy to while away an afternoon wandering the precipitous streets and perhaps strolling out to the Last Chance Mining Museum.

Much of Juneau's real commercial life has moved nine miles north to **Mendenhall**, the largest piece of flat land around, left behind by the shrinking Mendenhall Glacier; you may well arrive here, and will likely return to visit the glacier and go hiking. Glacier Hwy and the roughly parallel Egan Drive freeway link downtown Juneau with Mendenhall, passing the fascinating, salmon hatchery, and Alaska's largest and most exalted brewery.

You'll have to cross Gastineau Channel by the Juneau–Douglas Bridge to reach the ruins of the Treadwell Mine, the most accessible of all Juneau's **gold mining remains**, one of which can only be visited on a city tour.

Downtown

By avoiding fires which plagued neighboring communities, Juneau has retained much of its original architecture, particularly in the **South Franklin Street Historic District** where the ageing upper frontages are in marked contrast to the glitz below. First stop here should be the excellent **Alaska State Museum**, 395 Whittier St (mid-May to mid-Sept Mon–Fri 9am–6pm, Sat & Sun 10am–6pm; mid-Sept to mid-May Tues–Sat 10am–4pm; summer $5, winter $4; *www.eed.state.ak.us/lam/museum*), which rivals the main museums in Anchorage and Fairbanks for its broad coverage of Alaska's culture and history. Much of the

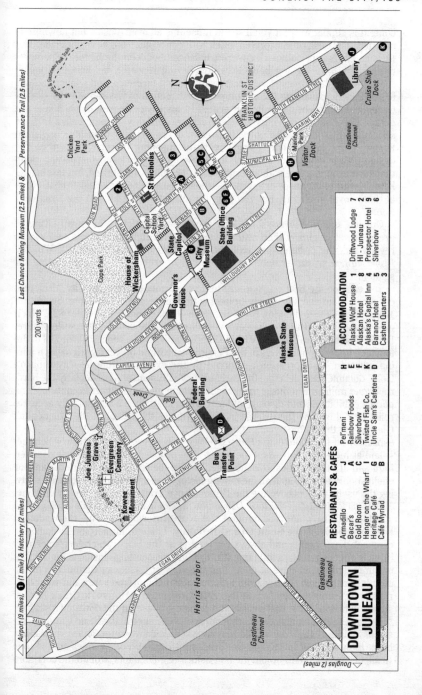

DOWNTOWN JUNEAU

0   200 yards

Airport (9 miles), ● (1 mile) & Hatchery (2 miles)

Evergreen Avenue

Last Chance Mining Museum (2.5 miles) & △ Perseverance Trail (2.5 miles)

N

FRANKLIN ST HISTORIC DISTRICT

Chicken Yard Park

Cope Park

House of Wickersham

Governor's House

State Capitol

City Museum

St Nicholas

Capital School Yard

State Office Building

Federal Building

Bus Transfer Point

Kowee Monument

Joe Juneau Grave

Evergreen Cemetery

Gold Creek

Alaska State Museum

Harris Harbor

Gastineau Channel

Douglas (2 miles)

Gastineau Channel

Cruise Ship Dock

Library

Visitor Park

Gastineau Channel

Marine Park

RESTAURANTS & CAFÉS

Armadillo   J
Bacar's   A
Gold Room   C
Hanger on the Wharf   G
Heritage Café   I
Café Myriad   B
Pel'meni   J
Rainbow Foods   E
Silverbow   F
Twisted Fish Co.   K
Uncle Sam's Cafeteria   D
  H

ACCOMMODATION

Alaska Wolf House   1
Alaskan Hotel   8
Alaska's Capital Inn   4
Baranof Hotel   5
Cashen Quarters   3
Driftwood Lodge   7
HI - Juneau   2
Prospector Hotel   9
Silverbow   6

content is similar to what you'll see in museums all over Alaska, but nowhere is it better displayed, or interpreted, often with conceptualizing text alongside. The Russian era is especially well covered, balanced between the historical perspective – they have the log book in which Bering reported his first sighting of Alaska – and the domestic, with samovars, period furniture, and some luminous icons. Panels explaining the circumpolar distribution of Eskimos (as far east as Greenland) stand beside a hunter seated in his kayak decked out in a seal gut parka. The Eskimo carvings are especially beautiful; very expressive in their simplicity. Elsewhere, the powerfully carved Frog House replicates one from Klukwan, the last Chilkat Village, with the meaning of each element in the design clearly explained. To reach the museum's upper level you follow a ramp that curls around a tree with an eagles nest. The birds are stuffed, but this is likely to be your best chance to appreciate the immense size of an eagle's nest. None of this is overwhelming, but you might want to take the kids to the Discovery Room.

Outside stands *Nimbus*, a modern sheet metal sculpture in an off shade of green. It was originally sited near the corner of 4th and Main streets, and was so reviled that the citizens eventually had it removed and replaced with *Windfall Fisherman*, a bronze sculpture of that Alaskan archetype, the bear fishing for salmon.

You can see the bear on your way up to the **Juneau–Douglas City Museum**, corner of Main and 4th streets (mid-May to Sept Mon–Fri 9am–5pm, Sat & Sun 10am–5pm; Oct to mid-May Fri & Sat noon–4pm; summer $3, winter $2), which gives a vivid picture of how Juneau's past fitted into the broader statewide picture. Drills, crucibles, ore samples, carbide lamps, assay scales, and a scale model of the fourteen underground levels of the Perseverance Mine reflect its origins as a mining museum, an impression reinforced by the excellent "Juneau: City Built on Gold" documentary detailing the early history of Juneau and particularly the hard-rock gold mining. But this is more than a mining museum. Apart from major temporary exhibitions and displays of local artworks, there's a wonderfully accurate relief model of how Juneau was in 1967 (witness the extent of the Mendenhall Glacier just thirty-some years ago), and plenty on the city's maritime past. Look especially for the photo of the *Princess May* which was wrecked on nearby Sentinel Island at high tide, and when the water level dropped the hull was left stranded high and dry thirty feet above the water. Notice the retouching where the anchor chain should have been. If all the mining history has ignited a spark, consider buying the useful leaflets covering the Perseverance Trail and to the Treadwell Mine.

Also pick up the free *Historic Downtown Juneau* leaflet, which has a self-guided walking tour to guide you around the rest of downtown. The slit-windowed bunker opposite is the **State Office Building**, home to numerous Alaskan government departments and always referred to as the SOB (which locals seem to think is amusing, if not a little risqué). The only reason to go inside is for the free organ recitals on Fridays at noon, and the view of Gastineau Channel from the eighth floor. Follow Glacier Avenue for a couple of hundred yards and you could ring Tony Knowles' doorbell at the 1912 **Governor's House**, a Greek Revival style antebellum affair that's easily the grandest house on the downtown skyline.

By the City Museum is the marble porticoed entrance of the **State Capitol**, corner of Main and 4th streets (mid-May to mid-Sept daily 9am–4.30pm), a six-story brick monster built in 1931 as the Territorial Capitol. Follow a self-guided tour (leaflet from reception) or join the half-hour free guided tour around the corridors of power. You'd have to have a deep interest in Alaskan politics to appreciate seeing the Finance Committee Room where they passed legislation establishing the Permanent Fund Dividend, or the chamber where, in 1945, Natives were given the right to sit in restaurants with whites, but it is made all the more interesting by a superb collection of Alaskan photos lining the walls. Outside there's a replica Liberty Bell which, at statehood, was struck seven times by seven people to denote the creation of the 49th state.

A couple of blocks east on 5th Street, the octagonal, onion-domed **St Nicholas Russian Orthodox Church**, 326 5th St at Gold Street (mid-May to Sept Mon–Sat 9am–6pm; $1 donation), is perhaps the most striking building in the city. Originally built in 1894, it was mainly used by Slavic immigrants and by Tlingits who, when virtually forced to accept Christianity, chose the only one with services in Tlingit. It was restored in the 1970s and continues in use today with Divine Liturgy sung in English, Tlingit, and Slavonic (Sat 6pm & Sun 10am). At other times, guides will explain the significance of the assorted icons and religious treasures.

Up the hill, the **House of Wickersham State Historical Site**, 213 7th St (May–Sept daily except Wed 8.30–10am & 1–5pm; $2 suggested donation; ☎586-9001, *www.dnr.state.ak.us*), is the historic home of Alaska's pioneering judge, statehood advocate, and general polymath. The enthusiastic and well-informed guide leads you around the house (kept much as it was when Wickersham purchased it in 1928), giving a flavor of the man and the times in which he lived. While you're up this way, skirt around past Cope Park and down to **Evergreen Cemetery**, which contains a monument to Chief Kowee and the **grave of Joe Juneau**. Following Glacier Hwy back to town you pass the **Federal Building**, 709 W 9th St, which contains the main post office, the bargain *Uncle Sam's Cafeteria*, a tiny and uninteresting museum, and a small room set aside as a time capsule. You can peer inside, but since it was only encapsulated in 1994 there's little surprising.

You'll have to go a couple of miles inland to see the **Last Chance Mining Museum** (mid-May to late Sept daily 9.30am–12.30pm & 3.30–6.30pm; $3), around forty-minutes' walk from downtown at the end of Basin Road. It is a hands-on museum featuring tools, machines, and infrastructure for what was the world's largest and most advanced hardrock gold mine. Buildings that once held the assay office, blacksmith shops, and locomotive repair shops now contain displays, antiques, minerals, and the 3-D glass map of the mine tunnels and massive "glory holes" inside the mountain.

For a bird's-eye view of downtown, and much more, take the **Mount Roberts Tramway**, 490 S Franklin St (mid-May to mid-Sept daily 9am–9pm; $20; ☎463-3412, *www.goldbelt.com*), which deposits you on a relatively level area 1700 feet up Mount Roberts. Here, several gentle and moderate walks fan out from a restaurant and nature center where an 18min video focuses on Tlingit culture – after all, the tramway is run by Goldbelt, the local Native Corporation. Your ticket is valid for as many rides as you want all day, but $20 will still seem like a lot and you might prefer to hike up (see box, p.140) then pay just $5 to ride down.

Towards Mendenhall, the Mendenhall Glacier, and points north

Three miles north of downtown, Egan Drive charges past the **Gastineau Salmon Hatchery**, 2697 Channel Drive (May–Sept Mon–Fri 10am–6pm, Sat & Sun 10am–5pm; $3; ☎1-877/463-2486, *www.alaska.net/~dipac*), one of the best places

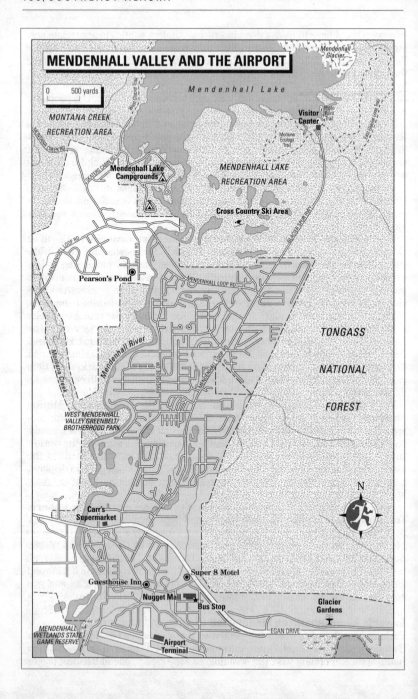

MENDENHALL VALLEY AND THE AIRPORT

0   500 yards

Mendenhall Glacier

Mendenhall Lake

MONTANA CREEK
RECREATION AREA

Visitor
Center

Mendenhall Lake
Campgrounds

MENDENHALL LAKE
RECREATION AREA

Cross Country Ski Area

Pearson's Pond

MENDENHALL LOOP RD

Mendenhall River

TONGASS

NATIONAL

FOREST

WEST MENDENHALL
VALLEY GREENBELT/
BROTHERHOOD PARK

Carr's
Supermarket

Super 8 Motel

Guesthouse Inn

Nugget Mall

Bus Stop

Glacier
Gardens

MENDENHALL
WETLANDS STATE
GAME RESERVE

EGAN DRIVE

Airport
Terminal

N

in the state to learn the intricacies of artificially rearing salmon. It is very much a working hatchery, responsible for stocking streams throughout the region, but was partly designed with visitors in mind. Inside, large saltwater aquariums are filled with local sea creatures in something akin to their natural environment, while outside you can follow walkways overlooking the entire hatchery process from pink and chum salmon struggling up the 450-foot-long fish ladder (the longest in the state), through various stages of development ready for release. The fish only run from late June to October, so in the early part of the season you are shown the incubation room instead. Anglers with the appropriate state license ($10 for one day, $15 for three) can dip a line in the water (rentals $5 an hour, $25 a day) with a fair chance of bagging their limit in double quick time. Ask the bus driver the best spot to get off and reboard.

City buses also pass through the suburb of Lemon Creek, five miles north of downtown, where you'll find the **Alaskan Brewing Co**, 5429 Shaune Drive (May–Sept Mon–Sat 11am–5pm; Oct–April Thurs–Sat 11am–5pm; free; ☎780-5866, *www.alaskanbeer.com*), which was one of the first microbreweries in the United States (in 1986) and is now Alaska's largest brewer. The twenty-minute tour mostly involves looking at half a dozen stainless steel tanks while they explain the process, but it does entitle you to a free tasting of their award winning brews.

A couple of miles further out, adversity has been channeled to good effect at **Glacier Gardens**, 7600 Glacier Way (May–Sept daily 9am–6pm; $15; ☎790-3377, *www.ptialaska.net/~ggardens*), the site of a devastating mudslide in 1984 and now a landscaped woodland garden. Most of the garden ranges up through the hillside spruce and hemlocks but you barely need to leave the parking lot to see the signature display of upturned tree trunks (salvaged from the mudslide) festooned with brightly colored bedding plants and hanging baskets. It is a curiously arresting sight, but the entry price seems high to see the rest of the garden, mostly visited on a golf-cart tour through the woods up to a good viewpoint high above Gastineau Channel.

There are certainly bigger and more spectacular glaciers in Alaska, but the twelve-mile-long, one-and-a-half-mile-wide **Mendenhall Glacier**, thirteen miles north of downtown, is one of the most accessible. You can drive to within a mile of the face and gaze across Mendenhall Lake at the huge sheet of white creeping down from the immense Juneau Icefield. When John Muir saw the glacier in 1879, it ended halfway down the valley where the suburb of Mendenhall now lies, but like most glaciers in Alaska, it has been retreating rapidly leaving all sorts of geological evidence of its passage. Should your knowledge of cirques and striations be a little rusty, there's detailed explanation, along with a wonderful relief map of the Juneau Icefield and an entertaining ten-minute video inside the Forest Service **visitor center** (early May to late Sept daily 8am–6pm; late Sept to early May generally weekends 10am–4pm; $3; ☎789-6640), located on a point occupied by the glacier as recently as 1940. If this inspires, consider joining one of the Forest Service's hour-plus nature hikes (late May to early Sept daily 10am & 2pm; free). The morning one being the better of the two follows the educational **Moraine Ecology Trail** (1.5-mile loop; 40min–1hr; negligible ascent) which, along with the handicap accessible **Photo Point Trail** (0.6 miles round-trip; 20min; negligible ascent) are the shortest of the local walks and therefore the most popular. Three longer trails are listed in the box overleaf.

Getting to the glacier without your own transport isn't too difficult: Capital Transit buses leave hourly from downtown and pass Glacier Spur Road, where you need to get off and walk the final mile or so. A visit to Mendenhall Glacier is

HIKES AROUND JUNEAU

Juneau is unmatched in Southeast for the number of top-quality trails accessible from the road system, many of them easily approached either from downtown or from the city bus out to the Mendenhall valley. Glaciers, forests, alpine high country, the remains of gold mines, and abundant wildlife make for a varied selection of trails, some easy and some fairly demanding.

If you are planning to spend a few days hiking in the area, it is definitely worth purchasing the new inch-to-a-mile *Juneau Area Trails Guide* ($4, plasticized version $10); otherwise make do with the free leaflets from the Forest Service visitor center.

Only one of the hikes listed below passes a Forest Service cabin, but there are loads of them in the area. The more accessible ones – whether on foot, on skis, by float plane, or boat – are all well used by Juneau residents, but getting one at short notice should be possible during the week; weekends are more difficult. The Forest Service visitor center (see "Information," p.131) has good information about the location of cabins and likely availability, but booking must be made through ReserveUSA (☎1-877/444-6777).

FROM DOWNTOWN JUNEAU

Perseverance Trail, Granite Creek Trail, and **Mount Juneau Trail** (1–10hr). The most popular and easily accessed system of trails in Juneau, suitable for a couple of hours of easy valley strolling, or an overnight hike along a rugged alpine ridge with stupendous views. The Perseverance Mine (3 miles round-trip; 2–4hr; 700ft ascent; $1 historic trail guide from the City Museum) follows Perseverance Creek to Silverbow Basin where the Perseverance Mine operated intermittently from 1885 to 1921. Be very careful when exploring the old mine workings. The Granite Creek Trail and Mount Juneau Trail both spur off the Perseverance Trail and can be linked up using the Mount Juneau Ridge Route creating a ten-hour expedition. There are no cabins along the way, but Granite Creek has a couple of lovely places to camp. The trailhead is 2.5 miles from downtown at the end of Basin Road. There's no public transport but you could grab a taxi or just walk from town.

Mount Roberts Trail (9 miles round-trip; 5–6hr; 3800ft ascent). A moderately difficult trail to the summit of Mount Roberts, switchbacking and climbing all the way but with increasingly good views and plenty of wildlife. You don't have to do

pretty much de rigueur on any of the Juneau city tours (see p.130): about the cheapest is with MGT (☎789-5460), who do a two-hour city tour for $17.50 and also provide a $5 each way shuttle service from downtown.

Beyond the suburb of Mendenhall and the airport, Glacier Hwy continues past Auke Lake and the University of Alaska Juneau campus, then passes the AMHS ferry dock at Auke Bay, eventually ending forty miles north of Juneau. It is only worth exploring if you've got your own transport, in which case you could call in at the **Shrine of St Terese**, Mile 23 (generally open daily 9am–5pm; donations appreciated), an attractive little church on a promontory accessed by a five-minute walk along a narrow spit. Built from beach stones in the 1930s and surrounded by the stations of the cross, it is now very popular for weddings and the spit is a favored spot for anglers keen to bag kings, silvers, and pinks from the shore.

The highway ends at **Point Bridget State Park**, Mile 40, a forested area overlooking Lynn Canal, with three short trails and a couple of rental cabins ($35; ☎465-4563).

the whole thing, since the trail passes the upper station for the Mount Roberts Tram (2 miles one-way; 1hr–1hr 30min; 1700ft ascent) where there's a nature center and a possible ride down in the tram for $5 (or $5 worth of purchases at the tram-top restaurant). Continue a little further on and you come to a wooden cross, a replica of one erected up here in 1908 by a local Jesuit priest, Father Brown. The trail starts downtown from the top of 6th Street.

FROM MENDENHALL

East Glacier Loop Trail (3.5-mile loop; 2–3hr; 400ft ascent). Moderate trail from the Mendenhall visitor center around the east of Mendenhall Lake with good views of the glacier, though more distant than from the West Glacier Trail. There's special interest in the remains of a old wooden flume and rail tram along the upper portion of the trail left over from a Nugget Creek hydro power project designed to provide power to the Treadwell Mill in 1911. The project was later taken over by the Alaska-Juneau Mine and the 600-foot tunnel drilled for the same project now spews the water that creates the A-J waterfall, viewed along the trail. Midway round the **Nugget Creek Trail** (add 5 miles round-trip; 3hr; 300ft ascent) spurs up Nugget Creek to the free-use Vista Creek Shelter.

    West Glacier Trail (7 miles round-trip; 4–6hr; 1300ft ascent). Excellent and fairly tough hike that skirts the northwestern side of Mendenhall Lake then climbs through alder and willow giving great views of icefalls, and even provides access to ice caves on the glacier for those who know what they're doing and have proper equipment. The trail is generally good but deteriorates until you are following rock cairns and ends at a scenic overlook. You can continue for another couple of miles to the summit of Mount McGinnis making it a full day outing. The trailhead is on Skaters Cabin Road, about a mile from the Capital Transit bus stop at the junction of Montana Creek Road and Mendenhall Loop Road.

ON DOUGLAS ISLAND

Dan Moller Trail (6.5 miles round-trip; 3–5hr; 1800ft ascent). A relatively easy trail ending high in an alpine cirque where there is a Forest Service cabin ($35; ☎1-877/444-6777). The trail starts close to the junction of Cordova and Foster streets (bus stop): follow Pioneer Street and the trailhead is by the fifth house.

Douglas and the Treadwell Mine

Downtown Juneau is connected by a road bridge to **Douglas Island**, a mountainous, forest-clad place that partly acts as a dormitory suburb for Juneau. There was a brief time around 1910 when the city of **DOUGLAS** was the largest in Southeast Alaska based on the employment opportunities at the Treadwell Mine. Like all of Juneau's mines, the Treadwell relied on economies of scale to turn a profit, processing huge quantities of low-grade ore to extract the valuable metal – $67 million worth between 1882 and 1922. At one stage it was the most extensive gold mining operation in the world, supporting a town of 15,000 people and burrowing 2800 feet down below Gastineau Channel. In 1917, a serious cave-in and the subsequent flooding closed all but one shaft, and work ceased by 1922, just four years before the whole place burned to the ground. Today most of the mine buildings have been enveloped by the regenerating alder and spruce forest with saplings sprouting from the moldering concrete shells of buildings, hulks of old machinery rusting quietly, and several rows of pilings from long-gone wharves running out into Gastineau Channel. The remains are threaded by the **Treadwell Mine Historic Trail**, a network of paths and numbered markers which are meaningless without the *Treadwell Mine Historic Trail* explanatory booklet ($2) available from the City Museum.

Capital Transit's Douglas **bus** runs every half-hour to downtown Douglas, from where you can wander past the Douglas boat harbor to **Sandy Beach Park**, a small strand created from the tailings from the mine. The Treadwell Mine Historic Trail starts at the southern end of the park. There are a couple of cafés in Douglas if you can't wait until you get back to town, but the only real reason to stick around is to attend a performance at the Perseverance Theatre (see "Entertainment," p.144).

Flightseeing, rafting, and kayaking

A visit to the Mendenhall Glacier only gives you a tiny sense of what lies behind the immense 1500-square-mile Juneau Icefield, which feeds close to forty glaciers, some creaking down the hills behind Juneau, others flowing the other way into Canada. The easiest and cheapest way to see all this is on a scenic plane flight with Wings of Alaska (☎789-0790, *www.wingsofalaska.com*), who charge $125 for a 45-minute flight. **Helicopter flights** are increasingly popular; Temsco (☎789-9501) offer a 55-minute Mendenhall Glacier Tour ($160) including a 25-minute glacier landing, and a ninety-minute variation ($230) with two glacier landings. Coastal Helicopters (☎789-5600, *www.coastalhelicopters.com*) and Era Helicopters (☎586-2030 or 1-800/843-1947) both do hour-long trips with glacier landing ($65 and $179 respectively), and North Star Trekking (☎790-4530) offer a helicopter flight with two hours spent hiking on the glacier for $289.

Further afield, there's tremendous **flightseeing over Glacier Bay National Park** (see p.148): Skagway Air Service (☎789-2006, fax 789-2054, *www.skagwayair.com*) run Glacier Bay overflights from Juneau ($160) and will include a diversion over Glacier Bay on their scheduled flight between Juneau and Skagway, also for $160.

Staying closer to Juneau, the Mendenhall River offers the only **rafting** in these parts, with a little low-grade white water and a good deal of even gentler stuff with guides explaining the local natural history. Auk Ta Shaa ($89; ☎586-8687 or 1-800/820-2628), and Alaska Travel Adventures ($97; ☎789-0052 or 1-800/478-0052) both run trips spending a couple of hours on the water.

Out on the Inside Passage, there are several opportunities for **kayaking**, either on guided tours, or just paddling around the islands in Auke Bay with kayaks rented locally (see p.145). Alaska Travel Adventures (see above) run gentle three-and-a-half-hour kayaking trips around Auke Bay (May–Sept; $72), mainly geared to cruise ship passengers; and Auk Ta Shaa (see above) organize six-hour trips ranging slightly further for $95. For more dedicated kayaking, go with Alaska Discovery (☎780-6226 or 1-800/586-1911), who have a good selection of multiday trips to Tracy Arm and Pack Creek, which we've covered in those sections.

Eating, drinking, and entertainment

As the largest town in Southeast Alaska, not to mention the state capital, you'd expect a decent range of restaurants and bars, but this is still only a town of 30,000 and your choices are fairly limited. Most of the worthwhile places are downtown, and there's little reason to go elsewhere, except perhaps to Douglas for the

Perseverance Theatre. However, there are enough **restaurants** to keep you well fed for a few days, and it is worth considering indulging in the salmon bake at the Gold Nugget Revue (see overleaf).

S Franklin and Front streets have so far resisted the downtown gentrification, and retain a number of dark **bars** where back-slapping camaraderie prevails. Of these, you may find the places we've listed more convivial than most.

For **entertainment listings**, the best source is the "Preview" section of Thursday afternoon's *Juneau Empire*.

Cafés and restaurants

Armadillo, 431 S Franklin St (☎586-1880). Justly popular Tex-Mex café and microbrewery where everything is freshly cooked from the *huevos rancheros* ($8) to the taco Laredo ($6) and chicken fajitas grande ($14). They also have their own microbrews, and sell bottles of the Alaskan Brewing Company's highly awarded (and hard to find) Smoked Porter.

Bacar's, cnr 4th and Franklin sts (☎463-5091). Quirky little restaurant that's not much to look at and hard to spot from the road, but worth seeking out for last-all-day breakfasts ($5–9), clam chowder and burger lunches ($8–10), and dinner that extends from a wonderful chicken fried steak ($19) to liver, bacon, and onions ($15). Closed Mon & Tues. No credit cards.

Gold Room, 127 N Franklin St (☎586-2660). One of Juneau's finest restaurants in a subdued sky-lit room in the heart of the *Baranof Hotel*, all white linen tablecloths and refined atmosphere. Start with New Zealand green-lipped mussels ($9) and follow with crab cakes ($21) or caribou medallions sautéed in port and peppercorns ($24).

Hanger on the Wharf, Merchants Wharf (☎586-5018). Mostly a place to drink (see overleaf), but also serving wraps and burgers at lunch, with the likes of jambalaya and halibut tacos ($8–11) at dinner.

Heritage Café, Emporium Mall, 174 S Franklin St (☎586-1087). About the best café in Juneau, with good espresso, lunch specials, soups, and sandwiches.

Café Myriad, 230 Seward St (☎586-3433). Imaginative fusion restaurant, bar, and Internet café (see "Listings", p.145) where dishes from around the world are prepared as a vegetarian (and usually organic) base, to which you can add tofu, barbecued pork, chicken breast, salmon, halibut, or whatever. Sounds odd but it works well with dishes as varied as Pad Thai, fettuccini alfredo, Tandoori chicken salad, and burgers, mostly $10–18.

Pel'Meni, 2 Marine Way (☎463-2630). Dave keeps threatening to expand his repertoire, but he currently serves just one item, a $5 helping of the Russian dish that gives this restaurant its name. These mini-dumplings are made from spicy ground sirloin wrapped in fresh pasta dough, then boiled and topped with hot sauce, curry powder, and cilantro; good anytime but especially popular after a drinking session at one of the Front St bars. The varied clientele also hangs out sipping espresso and selecting something from the eclectic collection of vinyl.

Rainbow Foods, cnr 2nd and Seward sts (☎586-6476). Wholefood and organic grocery also doing sandwich lunches and with an extensive noticeboard full of holistic classes and massage.

Silverbow Bakery and Restaurant, 120 2nd St (☎586-4146). Out front there's a wonderfully relaxed eat-in bakery and coffee bar with big windows that catch the morning sun (if you're lucky enough to see any). Traditionally boiled and baked bagels and superb pastries, bolster a menu of homemade breads used in hot and cold deli sandwiches ($5–11). The *Back Room* restaurant (closed Mon) has one of the most varied and imaginative menus in town from salads and soups ($6–9) to kielbasa and pierogies ($11), Indonesian peanut pasta with either tofu or chicken ($12), and pesto and red pepper burgers ($9); and some evenings you can even stick around for the movie (see overleaf).

Twisted Fish Company, 550 S Franklin St (☎463-5033). Bustling waterfront restaurant with a cosmopolitan feel and an extensive menu centered on fish and gourmet pizzas. Naturally salmon and halibut get a high billing whether eating inside or out at the salmon bake on the dockside. Personal pizzas and appetizers around $10, main courses $18–25.

Uncle Sam's Cafeteria, 2nd Floor, 709 W 9th St (☎586-3430). Low-cost dining with a view, inside the Federal Building. Open for breakfast ($4) from 7am, then lunches including daily specials ($6) such as taco salad or chicken fried steak. Closes 4pm.

Drinking

Alaskan Hotel & Bar, 167 S Franklin St. Ancient bar dating back to 1913 and still exuding a raucous atmosphere with live music on Friday and Saturday nights (anything from funk to bluegrass), open mic night on Thursday and plenty of bar propping anytime. During the day cruise ship crews often have impromptu jam sessions.

Hanger on the Wharf (see overleaf). Renovated, historic floatplane hanger right on the wharf with one wall made entirely of glass giving a tremendous view of the waterfront. There are over twenty beers on tap, pool tables on the mezzanine, and there's always a lively atmosphere, especially at weekends when there is live rock or jazz.

Red Dog Saloon, 278 S Franklin St (☎463-3777). Straightforward sawdust-on-the-floor tourist trap and merchandising empire masquerading as a raucous, historic bar. Musicians get the cruise ship crowd going from around 2pm. Pretty quiet once the boats leave.

Entertainment

Back Room Cinema, 120 2nd St (☎586-4146 or 1-800/586-4146). Part of the *Silverbow* hotel and bakery complex, this restaurant and movie theater in one shows cult, classic, and recent independent releases on Tuesday, Thursday, and Saturday nights. Best of all it's only $3, plus a minimum $5 food or drink order.

Gold Nugget Revue, Thane Ore House, Mile 4 Thane Rd (☎586-1462, *www.ptialaska.net /~holst*). A hokey but fun family show with cancan dancers and a stack of old-time merriment. It is $10 just for the show, $27 to add in the all-you-can-eat salmon, halibut, and ribs dinner, and there's free transport from town.

Perseverance Theatre, 914 3rd St, Douglas (☎364-2421). Alaska's largest professional theater and one of the nation's foremost regional houses, presenting revisions of classic texts, cutting edge works, and developing new plays by Alaskan playwrights. Paula Vogel's Pulitzer Prize winning *The Mineola Twins* premiered here in 1996.

20th Century Twin Theater, 222 Front St (☎586-4055). Shows first-run movies nightly.

Listings

Alaska Marine Highway System main ticket office, 1591 Glacier Ave (Mon–Fri 8am–5pm; reservations ☎465-3941, schedule info ☎465-3940).

Banks Several with 24hr ATMs in the downtown area, such as First National Bank of Anchorage, 228 Front St. There is currently nowhere to change foreign currency.

Bookshops The most extensive selection is at Hearthside Books, either downtown at 250 Front St or in the Nugget Mall close to the airport, good for whiling away an hour between flights. Also try Rainy Day Books, 113 Seward St (☎463-2665), which is good for new and used books.

Car rental Almost all the rental agencies are located at the airport but most will drop-off in downtown Juneau. Check the *Yellow Pages* under "Auto Rental" or call All-Star Practical (☎790-2414); Avis (☎789-9450); Evergreen Ford (☎789-9386); Payless (☎780-6004); or Rent-A-Wreck (☎789-4111). Rates are around $50 a day, though Rent-A-Wreck and All-Star sometimes have compacts for as little as $40 a day; book in advance.

Festivals The Alaska Folk Festival (☎364-2658) in mid-April involves a week of performances workshops, jams, and dances, mostly in Centennial Hall; the Juneau Jazz and Classics festival (☎463-3378) takes place during the third week in May and follows a similar program; and on July 3 Juneau sets off its fireworks to celebrate the arrival of July 4 and the ensuing parade and carnival.

Internet access The library (see below) has free use though you often need to reserve a day in advance. For more immediate needs try Surf Alaska, Emporium Mall, 174 S Franklin St (Mon–Sat 8am–10pm, Sun noon–8pm; ☎586-6559; *www.surfalaska.com*), which has modern PCs with fast connections; or *Café Myriad*, 230 Seward St (☎586-3433), where there are fast machines, and small discounts if you also eat a meal.

Kayak rentals Douglas-based Juneau Outdoor Center (☎586-8220, *alaska.kayak@gci.net*) rent out top-quality kayaks and skiffs and deliver anywhere in Juneau: rates are $35 for a single, $50 a double, and $150 a day for a skiff with a 40-horse outboard. Adventure Sports, near the airport at 8758 Glacier Hwy (☎789-5696) has comparable deals.

Laundry and showers Harbor Washboard, 1114 Glacier Ave, downtown (Mon–Fri 7.30am–9pm, Sat 9am–9pm, Sun 8am–6pm; ☎586-1133) has both laundry and showers ($2); The Dungeon, 4th and Franklin St (daily 8am–8pm; ☎586-2805). You can also shower at the *Alaskan Hotel* for $3.

Left luggage The HI hostel will store bags ($1 each) for nonguests, as will the *Alaskan Hotel* ($1.25). The Auke Bay AMHS terminal does not have useful lockers.

Library The Juneau Public Library, 292 Marine Way (Mon–Thurs 11am–9pm, Fri–Sun noon–5pm; ☎586-5249) has an extensive range of books and newspapers, Internet access and a great view of Gastineau Channel.

Medical assistance Bartlett Regional Hospital, 3260 Hospital Drive, 3 miles north of downtown (☎586-2611).

Outdoor equipment Foggy Mountain Sports, 134 N Franklin St (☎586-6760) stock top brand gear, and loads of it at slightly inflated prices.

Pharmacy Juneau Drug Co, cnr Front and Seward sts (Mon–Fri 9am–9pm, Sat & Sun 9am–6pm).

Post Office Inside the Federal Building, 709 W 9th St (Mon–Fri 9am–5pm). The **General Delivery** ZIP Code is 99801.

Taxes Juneau has a six percent sales tax; the bed tax is twelve percent and has been included in our price codes.

Taxi Capital Cab ☎586-2772.

Around Juneau

Though two or three days might suffice for seeing Juneau, you could easily use it as a base from which to make frequent forays into its hinterland by boat and plane. Day cruises head south to the hairline fjord of **Tracy Arm**, a vast granite and ice wonderland that also lends itself to extended exploration by kayak. When the salmon are running, **brown bears** find themselves sharing **Pack Creek** with humans eager to watch them gnawing on fish and fattening up for winter. Either drop in for a few hours during the day, or visit by kayak and spend a couple of days in the area camping nearby.

For extended trips away from Juneau, the prime destination is **Glacier Bay National Park**, often the destination around which people build their entire Alaskan vacation. The high-class B&Bs and lodges of bucolic **Gustavus** make a great base for wider exploration to the vast calving glaciers of Glacier Bay and the prime humpback whale watching territory of **Point Adolphus**.

Tracy Arm Fjord

If you are thinking of visiting Glacier Bay but don't really have the time or money, consider the cost-effective eight-hour trip to **Tracy Arm Fjord**, which cuts deeply

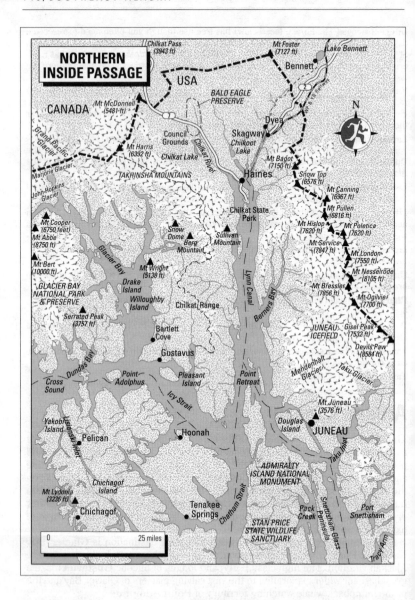

NORTHERN INSIDE PASSAGE

Chilkat Pass (3943 ft)
Mt Foster (7127 ft)
Lake Bennett
Bennett
USA
CANADA
BALD EAGLE PRESERVE
Mt McDonnell (5481 ft)
Grand Pacific Glacier
Council Grounds
Dyea
Skagway
Chilkoot Lake
N
Mt Harris (6392 ft)
Chilkat Lake
Chilkat River
Mt Bagot (7150 ft)
Marjorie Glacier
TAKHINSHA MOUNTAINS
Haines
Snow Top (6576 ft)
John Hopkins Glacier
Mt Canning (6967 ft)
Mt Cooper (6750 feet)
Mt Abbe (8750 ft)
Snow Dome
Berg Mountain
Chilkat State Park
Sullivan Mountain
Mt Pullen (6816 ft)
Mt Hislop (7620 ft)
Mt Poletica (7620 ft)
Mt Service (7847 ft)
Mt Bert (10000 ft)
Glacier Bay
Mt Wright (5138 ft)
Mt London (7550 ft)
Mt Nesselrode (8105 ft)
GLACIER BAY NATIONAL PARK & PRESERVE
Drake Island
Willoughby Island
Lynn Canal
Berners Bay
Mt Bressler (7856 ft)
Mt Ogilvie (7700 ft)
Serrated Peak (3757 ft)
Chilkat Range
JUNEAU ICEFIELD
Gisel Peak (7532 ft)
Bartlett Cove
Gustavus
Mendenhall Glacier
Taku Glacier
Devils Paw (8584 ft)
Cross Sound
Dundas Bay
Point Adolphus
Pleasant Island
Point Retreat
Yakobi Island
Lisianski Inlet
Icy Strait
Mt Juneau (3576 ft)
Pelican
Hoonah
Douglas Island
JUNEAU
Taku Inlet
Chichagof Island
ADMIRALTY ISLAND NATIONAL MONUMENT
Mt Lydonia (3236 ft)
Chichagof
Chatham Strait
Pack Creek
Snettisham Glass Peninsula
Port Snettisham
Tenakee Springs
STAN PRICE STATE WILDLIFE SANCTUARY
Tracy Arm
0   25 miles

into the Coast Mountains 45 miles south of Juneau. The glaciers may not be quite as spectacular, but the scenery is definitely on par with its more exalted neighbor. There's never more than a mile between the sheer waterfall-fringed cliffs that frame your approach to the head of the thirty-mile long fjord and the North Sawyer and South Sawyer glaciers. At any time these may be calving, but even if they're not there are always seals basking on the ice floes, mountain goats high up on the almost barren hills, and possibly dolphins and whales frolicking in the channels. John Muir was impressed when he visited in 1879; he said it reminded him of his beloved Yosemite, but then much of Southeast had the same effect on him.

The most popular way to go is with Auk Nu Tours (mid-May to early Sept daily at 9am; $109; ☎586-8687 or 1-800/820-2628, *www.goldbelttours.com*), whose 78-foot fast catamaran, *Keet*, departs from beside the cruise ship dock downtown, returning eight hours later. For a slightly more personal touch, go with Adventure Bound Alaska (☎463-2509 or 1-800/228-3875; $99) who run a smaller and single hulled boat from the north end of Marine Park. Being smaller, they can get in a little closer through the densely packed icebergs, but the single hull allows it to roll more and they go slower, extending the day from 8.15am–6pm.

The fjord is also a popular destination for kayakers; Alaska Discovery (see Basics, p.11) run a fairly adventurous seven-day paddling and camping trip here for $1900, including a charter-boat dropoff and pickup. You can also go it alone using rental kayaks (see "Listings", p.145) and getting dropped off in Tracy Arm on the Auk Nu Tours trip ($109 for drop off and pick up).

Pack Creek bear viewing

Douglas Island separates Juneau from the northern tip of Admiralty Island, a hundred-mile-long landmass of rugged 4000ft-high mountains cloaked in temperate forests known to the Tlingit as Kootznoowoo or "fortress of the bears." There is said to be a greater concentration of brown bears here than anywhere else in the world, and despite the town of Angoon sharing the island, the bears outnumber people. That's not to say you fall over them wherever you go – there is still only one per square mile – so in an effort to guarantee a sighting, most people head straight to the **Stan Price State Wildlife Sanctuary** at **Pack Creek**, on the east side of the island. From June to mid-September the pink and chum salmon are running and bears flock to the tidal flats around the Seymore Canal and to Pack Creek itself. Hunting was banned here back in the 1930s and brown bears have become used to having people watching them fish in what is considered a textbook case of low-stress habituation. The number of float planes landing each day does drive away some of the bears, but you can still expect to see three or four on an average day.

To help preserve this benign situation, the area has been designated for day use only, so most people visit from Juneau on a day-trip. You'll need a **permit** (just for viewing) from the Forest Service in Juneau (see p.131) which costs $50 per day (maximum 3 days) in peak season (July 5–Aug 25), $20 in shoulder season (June 1–July 5 & Aug 26–Sept 10). Outside these dates no permit is needed, but then there are no fish and no bears. Permits are offered from March 1 and you'll need to get in early to get specific dates, though four permits each day only become available three days before the date of your visit. It is often more effective to reserve early with one of the float-plane operators who drop off then pick up later in the day charging around $150 round-trip: try Wings of Alaska (☎789-0790, *www.wingsofalaska.com*).

One of the best approaches is on one of the kayaking trips run by Alaska Discovery (see Basics, p.11). On their one-day trip ($475) you fly in by float plane then kayak to Pack Creek for bear viewing and maybe hiking a mile and a half inland to the bear-viewing tower on Upper Pack Creek. The two-and-a-half-day trip ($895) follows the same pattern but includes two nights camped out near Pack Creek. Trips only run on certain dates and fill fast.

If you have your own boat or want to rent a kayak and paddle to Pack Creek, you'll need one of the permits described overleaf. Kayakers need to be moderately experienced particularly for the potentially rough crossing of Stephens Passage to Admiralty Island. Before setting off, ask for details of the tramway which aids your portage at Oliver Inlet and saves you having to paddle right around the Glass Peninsula. Once here, you can hang around for a few days by camping half a mile away, on the east side of Windfall Island, or staying at the Seymore Canal Cabin ($35; ☎465-4563) at the south end of the portage.

Pack Creek falls within the Kootnoowoo Wilderness, a section of the **Admiralty Island National Monument**, which covers most of the island. Even if you miss out on a Pack Creek permit, there are several other areas where bears congregate, and the adventure of going somewhere less populated can make your visit that much more appealing. The Forest Service in Juneau can provide details of likely destinations.

Glacier Bay National Park

When Captain George Vancouver sailed through Icy Strait in 1794, he didn't name **Glacier Bay**, largely because it didn't exist. Two hundred years ago, this 65-mile-long branched fjord was entirely taken up by the Grand Pacific Glacier, which was calving prodigious quantities of icebergs from its twenty-mile-wide four-thousand-foot-high face, almost choking Icy Strait. Today, the seaward end of Glacier Bay seldom sees bergs since the Grand Pacific has reeled back 65 miles, its retreat creating Glacier Bay in the process. Nowhere in the world have glaciers retreated so fast, a phenomenon noted by John Muir when he came up by canoe in 1879, finding it an "icy wilderness unspeakably pure and sublime." In the 85 years between Vancouver's and Muir's visits, the Grand Pacific had already receded 48 miles. As early as 1925, Calvin Coolidge designated it a National Monument; congress upgraded its status to **GLACIER BAY NATIONAL PARK** in 1980; and twelve years later the United Nations declared it a World Heritage Site.

All this receding ice has left behind a tranquil land of deep fjords lined by rock walls and encircled by towering mountains, in particular the 15,000-foot **Fairweather Range**, the tallest coastal mountains in the world. The various arms of Glacier Bay are fed by sixteen tidewater glaciers, a dozen of them calving on a regular basis. Huge sections of these intimidating walls of ice periodically come crashing down, captured by hundreds of video cameras onboard the cruise ships that make regular visits. In fact, if you've ever seen an image of a cruise ship dwarfed by the pure white face of a huge glacier, chances are that it will have been taken here in front of the **Marjorie Glacier**, which flows down the slopes of Mount Fairweather. It travels so swiftly it has little time to pick up the surface rubble typical of Alaskan glaciers making this the most pristine. It shares the barren West Arm of Glacier Bay with two other glaciers: the **Johns Hopkins Glacier**, which calves so much ice that boats can seldom approach within two miles of its ice cliffs; and the still-majestic remains of the **Grand Pacific Glacier**, which in the 1980s receded to the point where boats viewing the face from close quarters were technically in Canada. It has since advanced back into the US.

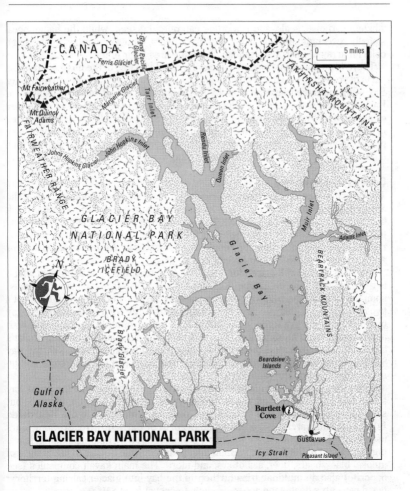

GLACIER BAY NATIONAL PARK

The glaciers' recession hasn't just left a strikingly beautiful landscape, it has created a living classroom for the mechanics of **plant succession** and **glacial rebound**. As the earth sheds the immense weight of the glaciers, the earth breathes a sigh of relief, and measurements reveal that the land is rising at a rate of an inch and a half per year. At the same time the newly uncovered land acts as a blank canvas for the progressive colonization by plant species. Near Bartlett Cove the earth was uncovered two centuries back and has a full cover of near-mature spruce forest, though the hemlocks seen elsewhere in Southeast are yet to establish themselves in any numbers.

You can see the succession process in reverse as you cruise up the bay, the spruce initially giving way to alder and cottonwoods, then stunted willows and finally the mosses and lichens that are the first to begin the colonization process. Animals have also been quick to populate the new habitat. In the water humpback whales, porpoise, seals, and sea otters can often be seen, while the banks occasionally reveal glimpses of brown and black bears, moose, mountain goats, and a colorful array of birds have quickly made the area their home.

There is no doubt that visiting Glacier Bay could be one of the most memorable parts of your time in Alaska, but it is going to cost you. Even a brief trip to Glacier Bay – spending perhaps one night in the settlements of either Gustavus or Bartlett Cove, and one day exploring the bay either on the *Spirit of Adventure* cruise boat or by kayak – will be a minimum of $250, more likely $400. If money is tight, you might get a better return for your dollar visiting Tracy Arm (see p.145), spending time around Prince William Sound, or viewing the glaciers on a flightseeing trip from Juneau, Haines, or Skagway.

Cruises and kayaking

The principal way of experiencing Glacier Bay's wonders is the day-cruise on the *Spirit of Adventure* ($157), a 250-seat launch with an on-board NPS ranger, a snack bar, and lunch provided. It leaves Bartlett Cove at 7.30am and makes its way through miles of bergs to the faces of the Marjorie and Grand Pacific glaciers, returning at 4.30pm in time for people to catch the *Auk Nu* ferry (see p.152) or Alaska Airlines plane back to Juneau that night.

Gustavus is also well-placed for cruises in Icy Strait, the most popular of which is the *Auk Nu*'s Wildlife Cruise ($139 from Juneau, $78 from Gustavus, reduced shoulder season pricing), which takes place in the afternoon between the boat's two daily visits to Gustavus. If you're coming on the *Auk Nu* from Juneau, just stay on board and you get three hours out in Icy Strait, around Point Adolphus, with almost guaranteed humpback whale watching and a fair chance of seeing Stellar's sea lions, sea otters, and orcas. Wolf Track Expeditions (half-day $90, full day $165; ☎ & fax 697-2326, *www.wolftrackexpeditions.com*) run more personal and in-depth trips in much the same area.

Everyone else goes **kayaking** which, if you're up for it, has to be the finest way to see Glacier Bay. **Guided day-trips** don't get anywhere near the glaciers, but stick close to Bartlett Cove or Gustavus, perhaps venturing into the **Beardslee Islands**, a small archipelago immediately north of Bartlett Cove. Six-hour tours usually involve instruction for the small group followed by gentle paddling, learning something of the flora, fauna, and tidal patterns while hoping to catch sight of moose, black bears, deer, sea otters, and more. The main kayak companies (see opposite) also do multiday trips further up the bay into glacier-calving territory: five days with a float-plane access is likely to cost at least $1600.

If you are confident about camping for several days in potentially inclement weather, you may want to go it alone with **rental kayaks**. No prior kayaking experience is needed, but you will need to attend one of the park rangers' two-hour orientation programs covering all aspects of kayaking in Glacier Bay, held at Bartlett Cove at 9am, and at 5pm for early departures the following morning. You'll also want to bring all your food supplies from Juneau.

Again, the Beardslee Islands make a good and easily accessible destination with excellent beach camping, plenty of wildlife for the patient, and gentle sheltered paddling with only the tidal currents (which need constant attention) to contend with. More ambitious paddlers will prefer to be dropped off close to more distant sections of Glacier Bay where motorized traffic is banned. To avoid potentially hazardous open-water crossings, organize transport with the *Crystal Fjord*, which departs from Bartlett Cove daily at 7.30am, setting kayakers down at five designated locations in **West Arm** between 10am and 2pm. The charge for kayaker (or camper) drop-off and pick-up is $84 each way, and there is a two-week "Bay Pass" ($188), which allows a sequence of up to five dropoff locations provided you don't double back. You can also do a one-way dropoff and then paddle back to Bartlett Cove over a week or so.

Alaska Discovery (☎1-800/586-1911, *www.akdiscovery.com*) have permits to go into Glacier Bay and run a two-hour evening paddle ($49), a six-hour day paddle ($125), a two-night trip ($750) specifically aimed at humpback whale-watching around Point Adolphus, and various longer trips. Spirit Walker (☎697-2266 or 1-800/529-2537, fax 697-2701, *www.he.net/~kayak*) conduct very worthwhile trips elsewhere in the region, mostly to Pleasant Island from the Gustavus Dock: half a day costs $70, it is $120 for a full day, $386 overnight, and $643 for two nights.

To go at your own pace, **rent kayaks** from Glacier Bay Sea Kayaks (☎697-2257, June–Sept fax 697-3002, Oct–May fax 697-2414, *www.he.net/~kayakak*), at Bartlett Cove; fiberglass kayaks cost $50 a day for a double and $35 a day for a single, reducing to $40/$25 for three- to nine-day rentals.

Bartlett Cove and Gustavus

The main access into Glacier Bay is from **BARTLETT COVE**, which consists of *Glacier Bay Lodge*, a campground, a Park Service visitor center and a dock for small cruise boats. It is a beautiful spot, best seen along some relatively easy trails: the mile-long **Forest Loop Trail** around the campground through hemlock and past small ponds; the **Bartlett River Trail** (two miles each way) along the intertidal lagoon where you might see shorebirds, waterfowl, and even bears; and the less popular and slightly more challenging **Bartlett Lake Trail** (four miles each way) through temperate rainforest to Bartlett Lake.

Most people stay ten miles away in **GUSTAVUS** (Gust-AY-vus), a thinly scattered former homesteading settlement that is now home to an airport, ferry dock, and a host of luxury inns. It can be a wonderfully peaceful spot with none of the frenetic activity engendered by cruise ship and major ferry arrivals, just a relaxed, almost genteel air. Unusually for Southeast Alaska it has a very spacious feel with plenty of flat ground on an alluvial fan, cut by a couple of meandering tidal rivers.

GUSTAVUS

0   250 yards

Bartlett Cove (6 miles)

TONG ROAD

MOUNTAIN VIEW

WILSON ROAD

Gustavus Airport

(3 miles)

Library

RESTAURANTS
Bear's Nest Café   B
Beartrack Inn   A

GOOD RIVER ROAD

GUSTAVUS ROAD

Gustavus Dray

STATE DOCK ROAD

ACCOMMODATION
Alaska Discovery Inn   2
Annie Mae Lodge   5
Bear's Nest B+B   3
Glacier Bay Country Inn 1
Good River B+B   4

Ferry Dock

Juneau (2 hr 15 min)

Icy Passage

There's very little to see in Gustavus, it is more a place to hang out at your lodge, perhaps borrowing one of their bikes or going for a stroll in the evening. You might wander down to the small boat harbor by the Salmon River, or past the **Gustavus Dray**, at the only crossroads in town. Even those who seldom play might fancy a round at Gustavus' nine-hole **Mount Fairweather Golf Course** on State Dock Road, where you just stick your $12 in the honesty box, plus another $3 if you need to borrow one of the bags of clubs leaning up against the shed. You can tee off with the setting sun glinting off the distant snow cap of Mount Fairweather, but remember that respecting the wildlife is one of the course rules, even if a moose blocks the fairway or a raven steals your ball.

Aside from the Glacier Bay cruises and kayaking, there are also a few Gustavus-based activities to tempt those with more time on their hands. Almost everyone you talk to seems to do fishing trips of some description; Wolf Track Expeditions (see p.150), run full-day mountain biking trips ($150) on old logging roads a short boat ride away, and they rent mountain bikes for $35 a day.

Arrival, getting around, and information

AMHS **ferries** don't go to Gustavus, so the cheapest way to get there is with Alaska Airlines who **fly** in once each afternoon in summer from Juneau (June to mid-Sept, currently arriving 4.45pm) for a bargain $32 each way. Smaller operators such as LAB (☎766-2222 or 1-800/426-0543) have more flights but charge around $60 to Juneau.

Perhaps the best solution is to fly one-way and travel in the other direction on the *Auk Nu*, (mid-May to early Sept daily; $45 one-way, $85 round-trip, bikes $10, kayaks $40, reduced shoulder season pricing; ☎586-8687 or 1-800/820-2628, *www.goldbelttours.com*), a fast passenger-only catamaran which makes the run out from Juneau in a little over two hours. They leave from their dock near the AMHS ferry dock in Auke Bay so you'll either have to find your own way out there or ride the Goldbelt Tours bus that picks up around downtown from 10am ($10) and the airport at 10.15am ($5) in time for the 11am boat departure. On its return, the *Auk Nu* departs Gustavus at 5.45pm and gets back to Auke Bay by 8pm where the Goldbelt bus runs people back to town for another $10.

Whether you **arrive** by boat or plane you'll be met by someone who will take you straight to your lodge or B&B. If you are heading direct to Bartlett Cove, catch the Glacier Bay Lodge bus ($10 each way), or hitch, which is usually possible. Alternatively, call the TLC Taxi (☎697-2239), which is good value for three people.

You can rent a car for around $60 a day from BW Enterprises Rent-a-Car (☎697-2403, fax 697-2789), but most people don't bother, relying on their kayaking company to pick them up in Gustavus. Many lodges have bicycles for getting around in the evening.

Gustavus has no visitor center though it is worth checking out the community Web site: *www.gustavus.com*. At Bartlett Cove there's a **park service visitor center**, upstairs in the *Glacier Bay Lodge*, and an information station down by the dock (mid-May to mid-Sept daily 7am–9pm; ☎697-2627, *www.nps.gov/glba*), where anyone going kayaking by themselves, or staying at the campground will be put through a short orientation program. Note that the park has **no entrance fee**, and although there is a post office in Gustavus, there are **no banks** or ATMs anywhere around here.

Accommodation, eating, and drinking

Many people arrive in Glacier Bay on all-inclusive packages run by the major lodges (particularly *Glacier Bay Lodge*) and kayaking operators that can offer small savings, particularly at either end of the season (mid-May to mid-June and the first ten days of Sept). All also accept independent visitors.

Accommodation at Bartlett Cove is limited to the *Glacier Bay Lodge* (closed Oct–April; rooms ⑦, dorm bunks ②), which is run by the park concessionaire, Glacier Bay Tours (☎586-8687 or 1-800/451-5952), who also handle bookings on the *Spirit of Adventure* and offer a bewildering array of package deals. Easily the largest of the lodges hereabouts, the *Glacier Bay Lodge* is the hotel of choice for most visitors, centered on a big cozy lounge (with large stone fireplace), a suitably stately restaurant, an excellent Park Service-run museum, and a great deck overlooking the cove. The rooms are comfortable if a little drab, though considerably better than the poky dorms which have no bedding, no cooking facilities, and still cost $28 per person. Public **showers** cost $1, and they'll do **bag storage** for $3 a day. The alternative is the free waterside first-come, first-served **campground**, with a warming hut, firewood, and bear-resistant food caches.

Many more people **stay** at one of two dozen or more lodges and B&Bs in **Gustavus**, most of which cost at least $80 a night for two and range up to swanky places charging $600 per person for a two-night all inclusive package. One of the best deals is *Bear's Nest B&B* (☎679-2440, *riddlephilip@hotmail.com*; ④), a completely self-contained and fully furnished circular cabin with a double bed upstairs and a single futon down. Breakfast ingredients are provided though you'll have to bring everything else from Juneau, or wander next door to the *Bear's Nest Café*. If you are kayaking with Alaska Discovery you'll probably be staying nearby at the *Alaska Discovery Inn* (☎697-2411; shared bath ④, private bath ⑤), a cozy lodge with comfortable rooms, a hearty breakfast, free use of bikes, and transport to the ferry and Bartlett Cove.

Good River B&B (☎ & fax 697-2241, *www.goodriver.com*; ④) is also at the cheaper end of the range with four rooms in the lodge, a rustic cabin nearby, a wholesome continental breakfast and free use of bikes. Another good bet is *Annie Mae Lodge* (☎697-2346 or 1-800/478-2346, fax 697-2211, *www.anniemae.com*; ⑧), a large house close to the Good River with attractive wood-paneled rooms, superb meals, free use of bikes, free local transportation for $215–245 a night for two ($130 single). At the upper end, the pick is *Glacier Bay Country Inn* (☎697-2288 or 1-800/628-0912, fax 697-2289, *www.glacierbayalaska.com*; ⑨), which has its own airstrip and concentrates on saltwater and fly fishing, but also has wonderful meals. Accommodation is either in very comfortable guestrooms in the main lodge ($165 per person including all meals) or in one of the luxury cabins nearby ($176 per person).

Eating in Gustavus mainly revolves around the lodge restaurants (usually open to nonguests if booked in advance), which vie to outdo each other and offer some of the best eating in Southeast. *Annie Mae Lodge* does superb three-course home-style dinners for $25, meals at *Glacier Bay Country Inn* are possibly even more outstanding for $30. The only stand-alone **café** worth its salt is the *Bear's Nest Café* (call to make sure they are open ☎679-2440), good for coffee, cakes, and home-baked bread. They also prepare a limited range of delicious meals from chicken burgers ($8) to Dungeness crab ($22) using organic ingredients and vegetables from the garden. Several of the larger lodges are licensed, but smaller places aren't, and there are no stores to buy **alcohol** in Gustavus, so if you fancy a glass of wine with your meal, bring some with you from Juneau. There are very limited **groceries** at the Bear Track Mercantile on State Dock Road.

Haines and around

The small service town of **HAINES**, 75 miles north of Juneau, occupies a narrow isthmus close to the head of the **Lynn Canal**, the longest and deepest in the US. It tends to be overshadowed by its brasher and more immediately arresting neighbor, Skagway, and certainly sees far fewer cruise ships, but in its own quiet way is an equally appealing place to spend a few days. Transport between the two towns is so frequent that some even base themselves here and visit Skagway on day-trips.

Populated by an interesting mix of rugged individualists and urban escapees from the Lower 48, Haines never seems quite sure whether it wants to be a real tourist destination or not. Its history is less dramatic than that of other Southeast communities, and its only major attraction, the mind-boggling congregation of up to four thousand bald eagles in the **Chilkat Bald Eagle Preserve** each November, happens well outside of the tourist season, making this feel very much like a genuine Alaskan town.

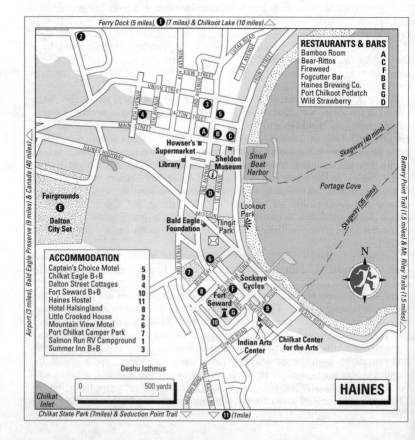

Ferry Dock (5 miles), ❶ (7 miles) & Chilkoot Lake (10 miles) △

RESTAURANTS & BARS

Bamboo Room	A
Bear-Rittos	C
Fireweed	F
Fogcutter Bar	B
Haines Brewing Co.	E
Port Chilkoot Potlatch	G
Wild Strawberry	D

Skagway (40 mins)

Battery Point Trail (1.5 miles) & Mt. Riley Trails (1.5 miles) ▷

Skagway (35 mins)

Airport (3 miles), Bald Eagle Preserve (9 miles) & Canada (40 miles) ◁

Howser's Supermarket

Library

Sheldon Museum

Small Boat Harbor

Portage Cove

Fairgrounds

Dalton City Set

Bald Eagle Foundation

Tlingit Park

Lookout Park

N

ACCOMMODATION

Captain's Choice Motel	5
Chilkat Eagle B+B	9
Dalton Street Cottages	4
Fort Seward B+B	10
Haines Hostel	11
Hotel Halsingland	8
Little Crooked House	2
Mountain View Motel	6
Port Chilkat Camper Park	7
Salmon Run RV Campground	1
Summer Inn B+B	3

Sockeye Cycles

Fort Seward

Indian Arts Center

Chilkat Center for the Arts

Deshu Isthmus

0   500 yards

Chilkat Inlet

Chilkat State Park (7miles) & Seduction Point Trail ▽   ▽ ❶ (1mile)

HAINES

With the waters of Lynn Canal lapping its shores, and glaciers spilling out of the **Chilkoot and Chilkat mountains** on both sides, its location is nothing short of spectacular, particularly on a clear day when some of the town's **hiking trails** reveal wonderfully long views.

History hasn't completely passed Haines by, its days as a military fort protecting the US border from marauding Canadians left the legacy of **Fort William H Seward**. Its dominant row of green-trimmed white mansions lend a certain weight and solidity to what would otherwise be a typically ragged Alaskan townscape.

Some history

Before the arrival of Europeans, this site at the mouth of the Chilkat River protected access to the Chilkat Valley, one of the very few glacier-free corridors to the Interior. Chilkat Tlingit fiercely guarded their trading rights along the route setting themselves up as middlemen between the Russian, American, and British traders along the coast and the Athapascans of the Interior. This continued after the arrival of the first traders and missionaries in the early 1880s, but as the Klondike gold rush got into full swing, one Jack Dalton decided to ignore traditional trading rights along the route and took it on himself to charge prospectors a toll to use the Chilkat Pass.

It was this lawlessness, and border disputes with the Canadians, that encouraged the US military to choose Haines for their new fort in 1903, though things rapidly calmed down and the fort never saw any military action. Troops soon got bored and Haines became one of the least sought-after postings, though things improved during World War II when the fort took an important role in the construction of the Haines Hwy over the Chilkat Pass to the newly built Alaska Hwy. Connection to the North American highway system didn't radically affect the town's fortunes, and Haines continued to bumble along surviving off fishing and, more recently, tourism.

Arrival and information

In summer the AMHS **ferry** *Malaspina* makes a daily run from Juneau to Haines, continues on to Skagway, an hour up the Lynn Canal, then returns to Juneau via Haines in the evening. These, and a couple of other AMHS services, dock at the terminal almost five miles north of downtown Haines. Shuttle services (roughly $5) run into town and various tour companies offer short tours while the ferry is in port (see overleaf); if you've booked accommodation you may be met by hotel courtesy transport; check ahead.

To get between Skagway and Haines you'll find it quicker and more flexible to travel with Chilkat Cruises & Tours (☎766-2100 or 1-888/766-2103, *www .chilkatcruises.com*) who run a passengers-only **fast ferry** (mid-May to mid-Sept 3 daily, 35min; $24 one-way, $36 round-trip), to the shuttle dock, near Fort Seward. For much the same price, the Haines–Skagway Water Taxi (mid-May to mid-Sept 3 daily; ☎766-3395 or 1-888/766-3395, *www.lynncanal.com*) will make the run from Skagway to the small-boat harbor often taking in a bit of sightseeing along the way and making stops if any wildlife should show itself.

Drivers can reach Haines along the 151-mile Haines Hwy which runs south from Haines Junction, Yukon, on the Alaska Hwy, and crosses from Canada into the US (for immigration details see "Crossing the border" box, overleaf). The

CROSSING THE BORDER

Those traveling on into Canada, or continuing to northern Alaska through the Yukon need to be aware that Canadian border controls are no less strict just because you are in transit. Everyone should carry a passport, though North Americans can get by with their birth certificate; a driver's license won't do. You are also supposed to carry sufficient funds to cover your expenses while in Canada and while $150 a day is recommended, they'll let you in with a lot less than this, and a credit card will often do the trick. As long as you look reasonably tidy you may not even be asked.

The Klondike Hwy border between Skagway and Fraser, BC, is open 24hr in summer (mid-May to Sept) and 8am to midnight: if in doubt call US Customs (☎983-2325) or Canadian Customs in Fraser (☎867/821-4111).

The Haines Hwy crossing is open 7am–11pm all year.

same route is followed by an RC Shuttles **minivan** (☎907/479-0079 or 1-877/479-0079, *rcshuttles@aol.com*), which does a once-weekly run from Fairbanks to Haines, stopping outside the *Mountain View Motel* (see "Accommodation", p.158). Currently there is only one service a week in each direction (from Fairbanks on Mon, from Haines on Tues), though if there are two or more people they'll do an extra run; call ahead. One-way fares from Haines are $30 to Haines Junction, $80 to Tok, and $130 to Fairbanks.

Alaska Airlines doesn't fly to Haines' tiny **airport** (☎766-3609), three miles north on Haines Hwy, though regional carriers fly from Skagway, Juneau, and Gustavus. Skagway Air Service (☎766-3233, fax 766-3237, *www.skagwayair.com*) fly from Skagway ($40 one-way, $70 round-trip), Juneau ($75/130), and Gustavus ($80/150); LAB Flying Service (☎766-2222 or 1-800/427-5966, *www.haines.ak.us /lab*) charge almost identical prices for the same routes.

The **visitor center**, 122 2nd St (June to mid-Sept Mon–Fri 8am–8pm, Sat 10am–4pm, Sun 1–5pm; mid-Sept to May Mon–Fri 8am–5pm; ☎766-2234, fax 766-3155, *www.haines.ak.us*) has material on everything you need to know about the district, including campgrounds and Forest Service cabins and trails. They also stock the free *Haines Visitor's Guide* newspaper and the *History and Walking Tour* leaflet for Fort Seward.

Getting around and tours

If you are staying close to town you can walk to most of the places you're likely to be interested in, though having your own transport opens up the fabulous road-accessible wilderness that's close at hand, and provides access to the Bald Eagle Preserve. **Bikes** can be rented from Sockeye Cycle Co, 24 Portage St (☎766-2869, *www.cyclealaska.com*), who charge $6 an hour, $20 a half-day, and $30 an eight-hour day, with discounts offered for two- and three-day rentals. Orca Gifts (☎766-2741), on Beach Road opposite the cruise-ship dock, have a limited range of slightly cheaper bikes. **Car rental** is cheapest from Eagle's Nest Rental Car (☎766-2891 or 1-800/354-6009, fax 766-2848, *fiddle@wytbear .com*) who charge $45 a day plus 35¢ a mile after the first hundred. The *Captain's Choice* motel (see opposite) and Avis at the *Hälsingland Hotel* (☎766-2733 or 1-800/478-2847) both have unlimited mileage vehicles for around $70 a day. Note that Canadian citizens are not allowed to drive vehicles rented outside

Canada into Canada; all others should have no trouble driving rental vehicles through the Yukon.

Haines now has a couple of dozen companies keen to take you on **tours** of some description, most of which are entertaining and educational enough, but over-priced and a bit staged, so it is best to stick to trips with a specific purpose. Two good options are the Alaska Nature Safari (several daily; $50) run by Alaska Nature Tours (☎766-2876, fax 766-2844, *kcd.com/aknature*), which goes either to Chilkoot Lake or the Bald Eagle Preserve; and the three-hour Chilkat Rainforest Nature Hike ($60), which takes you to the Battery Point trailhead for an educational hike with naturalists.

Sockeye Cycle Co (see opposite) allow you to **explore by bicycle** on a number of easy to moderate guided rides: the Chilkoot Lake Bicycle Adventure (3hr; $120) dawdles for eight miles around some flat dirt roads that are good for wildlife viewing; Chilkat Bicycle Adventure (1.5hr; $42) is a little more strenuous with the emphasis on local history; Glory Hole Bicycle Adventure (3.5hr; $90) is tougher again and visits the Chilkat Bald Eagle Preserve; and there's the Chilkat Pass Bicycle Adventure (8hr; $120) heading up into the Yukon's Tatshenshini/Alsek Provincial Park with an overnight camping option ($320).

Accommodation

Though Haines has no real luxury hotels, there is a reasonable selection of mid-range **places to stay**, and a decent hostel. For some reason, many of the hotels and B&Bs have an overly casual feel, but the hosts manage to carry the day either by going out of their way to help, or just by being entertaining characters. As an incentive to visit, during the bald eagle-watching season (mid-Oct to Jan) prices drop by a third, and the *Captain's Choice* motel does a room and rental car deal. There are also over a dozen campgrounds, the best of which we've listed below.

Hotels, motels, and B&Bs

Captain's Choice Motel, 108 2nd Ave (☎766-3111 or 1-800/478-2345, fax 766-3332, *www .capchoice.com*). Not the cheapest, but the nicest and most modern of Haines' motels with comfortable cable-equipped rooms, and some suites, one of them jacuzzi-equipped (⑦). There's a great view across the fjord from the sun deck and they do courtesy ferry pick-ups. Suites ⑥, rooms ⑤.

Chilkat Eagle B&B, Fort Seward (☎766-2763, fax 766-3677, *kcd.com/eaglebb*). Central B&B in an old Fort Seward building with comfortable rooms, and an entertaining and enthusiastic host who'll tell you all you ever wanted to know about Haines and more.

Dalton Street Cottages, 116 6th St at Dalton St (☎766-3123). Separate cottages sleeping up to four, centrally situated but on a quiet street and each with kitchenette, phone, and access to a hot tub. ④.

Fort Seward B&B, 1 Officer's Row (☎766-2856 or 1-800/615-6676, *www.haines.ak.us/norm*). Engaging B&B in what used to be the Chief Surgeon's house in Fort Seward, a three-story clapboard affair with a great veranda out front. There's courtesy ferry transfers, free use of basic bikes, a hearty breakfast, and a range of rooms. Rooms ⑤, shared-bath ④.

Hotel Hälsingland, 13 Fort Seward Drive (☎766-2000 or 1-800/542-6363 in US, 1-800/478-2525 in Yukon and BC, fax 766-2445, *www.haines.ak.us/halsingland*). The town's grandest hotel, though well past its prime with a rambling slightly run-down feel. Original features remain in some rooms, so ask for one with a clawfoot bath, or an original fireplace, or just a good view (though none have all three). They also run the *Officer's Inn* B&B next door which is more of the same but includes a breakfast voucher for the *Commander's Room* restaurant in the *Hälsingland*. B&B ⑤, rooms ④, shared bath ③.

Little Crooked House, 61 Helms Loop (☎766-3933, *button@wytbear.com*). Small low-key homestay with three shared-bath rooms, free ferry pickups, and a bargain price just creeping into this price code. The owners also run assorted town tours and rafting trips. ③.

Mountain View Motel, 57 Mud Bay Rd (☎766-2900 or 1-800/478-2902, *budget@mtnviewmotel .com*). Nine comfortable rooms with cable TV, free coffee, and most with functional kitchenettes. ④.

The Summer Inn B&B, 117 2nd Ave (☎766-2970, *www.summerinn.wytbear.com*). Immaculately kept and nicely decorated downtown B&B with shared-bath rooms, some with sea views and all including a good cooked breakfast. It has a very homey feel with clawfoot baths, quilts, and fresh flowers. ④.

Camping and a hostel

Chilkat State Park, 7 miles south of Haines on Mud Bay Rd. Beautifully set site near the south end of the Haines Peninsula looking west towards the Takhinsha and the Davidson and Rainbow glaciers. Thirty spaces for tents and RVs including three beachside tent sites, pump water, toilets, and a summertime campground host. $6.

Chilkoot Lake State Park, off Lutak Rd, 10 miles north of downtown. Fairly large site for RVs and tents, located beside the Dolly Varden-rich Chilkoot Lake and with pump water, toilets, and a boat ramp. $10.

Haines Hostel and **Bear Creek Cabins**, just over a mile south of Fort Seward on Small Tract Rd (☎ & fax 766-2259, *www.kcd.com/hostel*). Good hostel, that's a little inconveniently sited, but makes up for it with a coin-op laundry, bike rentals for $8 a day, no lockout or curfew, and $3 rides from the ferry terminal. Rates in the two dorms are $14, cabins cost $38 for two, and there's camping ($8 for one, $12 for two) which includes use of the hostel facilities. ①.

Port Chilkoot Camper Park, Mud Bay Rd beside Fort Seward (☎766-2000 or 1-800/542-6363, *www.haines.ak.us/halsingland*). Peaceful site among spruce trees despite being right in the heart of things. It is the best of the full-hookup sites ($20) but is also suitable for dry RV camping ($14) and tents ($8.50), and has pay-showers and a laundromat on site.

Portage Cove State Recreation Site, Beach Rd, half a mile southeast of Fort Seward. A small first-come, first-served tent-only site designed for backpackers and cyclists only, and with no overnight parking. It is right by the beach and has potable water. $6.

Salmon Run RV Campground, Lutak Rd, 7 miles north of downtown (☎723-4229, *salmonrunadventures.com*). Wooded RV park two miles north of the AMHS ferry dock, with dry camping ($12.50), camping cabins ($45), and showers, but no hookups.

The town and around

Much of the early prosperity of Haines was founded on the half-dozen canneries that sprouted along the coast nearby. One cannery in Letnikov Cove, a few miles south of town, still operates but it is off-limits to visitors and the only way you can get a sense of what goes on there is to visit the **Tsirku Canning Company**, 422 Main St at 5th Avenue (times vary according to cruise ship schedule; $13.50; ☎766-3474), an authentic canning line briefly operated to illustrate the process. It was recently rescued from an abandoned cannery in Kodiak, and after a ten-minute video they fire it up producing empty cans.

Just down the street is Haines' one essential indoor sight, the **Sheldon Museum & Cultural Center**, 11 Main St (mid-May to mid-Sept daily 1–5pm, extended when cruise ships are in port; mid-Sept to mid-May Mon, Wed & Sun 1–4pm, Tues, Thurs & Fri 3–5pm; ☎766-2366, *www.sheldonmuseum.org*; $3), which does a great job of showing how Haines fits into its Chilkat environment, and the wider Tlingit world. In few other places (if any) can you see such fine examples of the distinctive yellow-and-black Chilkat blanket in wolf, raven, and killer whale designs, as well as an intriguing example trimmed with pearl buttons and small "coppers." There are also superbly-carved bentwood boxes made from a single cedar plank made pliable by steaming with seaweed and hot rocks. Look too for the Tlingit armor, comprising a moosehide shirt with wooden slatted breastplate plus a thick wooden collar and wooden hat, the two combining to leave just a narrow slit. When threatened by some projectile the natural reaction is for the warrior to duck his head down between his shoulders, thereby closing the gap. Look too for the small Tsimshian box made from porcupine quills, and don't miss the hundreds of smaller works hidden away in the glass-topped drawers. Downstairs, there is less diverting coverage of Fort Seward and town life.

A stroll along the typically bustling Beach Road and up through Tlingit Park brings you to the home of the **American Bald Eagle Foundation**, corner of 2nd Avenue and Haines Hwy (May–Sept Mon–Thurs 9am–10pm, Fri 9am–5pm, Sat 10am–4pm, Sun 1–4pm; Oct–April Mon, Wed & Fri 1–4pm; $2.50; ☎766-3094, fax 766-3095, *www.baldeagles.org*), a nonprofit organization dedicated to maintaining the sanctity of the Bald Eagle Preserve. Their public face is this wildlife museum, essentially just one large room with specimens of over 180 species, all found in the immediate vicinity – bears, moose, seals, sea lions, mountain goats, even lynx. It's not particularly exciting but some enjoy seeing such creatures up close and danger free. They also promote the five-day **Bald Eagle Festival** (☎766-2202, *www.baldeaglefest.org*), a series of photographic workshops, naturalist guided excursions, and the like that takes place during the greatest gathering of eagles, and finishing on the second weekend in November.

A couple of hundred yards south is **Fort William H Seward**, less a fort than a large sloping grassy rectangle commonly known as the **Parade Ground**, surrounded by a dozen grand houses. It was established in 1903 in response to the general lawlessness of the gold-rush era, and territorial disputes with Canada. With the limited resources at their disposal, the army fashioned a formal military outpost that seems more California than Alaska – rows of huge white clapboard houses with shingle roofs and broad verandas. The Canadian threat receded, and by the end of World War II it had outlived its usefulness. Fortunately five war veterans and their families bought all 85 surplus buildings and proceeded to renovate them. Most are now put to good use as B&Bs, hotels, and condominiums, but you can wander round outside equipped with the free *History and Walking Tour* leaflet from the visitor center.

At the far southeast corner of the Parade Ground, a former cannery and warehouse now operates as the **Alaskan Indian Arts Center** (daily 9am–5pm and for cruise ships; free; ☎766-2160), with a gallery for locally produced sculpture, photos, and carving, and a back room where you can watch and chat to carvers as they work on huge totem poles. The center of the Parade Ground is dominated by the replica **Chilkat Tribal House**, scene of the salmon bake that takes place most nights in summer.

Back in 1989 Haines was chosen as the location for the filming of Jack London's *White Fang*. A set of **Dalton City** – really just one short section of street – was built on the fairgrounds and that's where it remains, partly put to use with a couple of shops, a microbrewery, and a restaurant.

Chilkat Bald Eagle Preserve

Local promotional material touts the annual congregation of bald eagles at the so-called Council Grounds in the **Chilkat Bald Eagle Preserve** around twenty miles

HIKES AROUND HAINES

Haines is blessed with several good trails right on its doorstep. The following hikes are all discussed more fully in the free *Haines is for Hikers* leaflet available from the visitor center.

Battery Point Trail (4 miles round-trip; 2hr; negligible ascent). Shoreline walk from the end of Beach Road, just south of Fort Seward, to Kelgaya Point. It initially parallels the beach through spruce then traverses meadows to headland where you are free to camp for up to two weeks.

Mount Ripinski Trails (8 miles round-trip; 4–5hr; 1760ft ascent). A forest and muskeg walk to the summit of Mount Ripinski, starting about two-thirds of the way along the Battery Point Trail. By using one of several different routes down you can turn it into a long and varied day out, walking all the way from town.

Mount Ripinski Trail (10 miles round-trip; 5–7hr; 3650ft ascent). An exhausting but very worthwhile all-day undertaking, following the distinctive skyline ridge to the north of town. Pick a clear day to get the best of the views, and if you want to avoid hiking through patches of snow, don't even consider it until late July. Experienced hikers can avoid having to retrace their steps by continuing beyond the North Peak of Mount Ripinski, and following the exposed ridgetop Skyline Trail to Peak 3920 from where you can descend to 7 Mile Saddle and the Haines Hwy. It will take ten hours for this extended hike and you'll finish about ten miles from Haines. Either arrange for a lift, or get down early enough to hitch back to town.

Seduction Point Trail (13.6 miles round-trip; 8–10hr; negligible ascent). Long but relatively easy beach and forest walk from Chilkat State Park (see "Camping", p.158) to Seduction Point, occasionally walking below the high-tide line (consult tide tables before starting). Camping is permitted along the route so you can make it an overnighter, and the mountain and forest scenery is gorgeous.

north along the Haines Hwy. Visit between late October and January (and especially Nov) and you'll see the world's largest gathering of bald eagles, perhaps three or four thousand, and up to two dozen in a single cottonwood tree, all here to feed on the extremely late run of chum salmon. By this time of year, most salmon rivers in Alaska are frozen and the fish long gone, but here water collects in alluvial gravels forming an underwater reservoir during the summer and, over time, percolates back into the river to keep it from freezing. The fish come to breed, the eagles come to eat them, and the people come armed with cameras and binoculars. The only problem is that, if you come at any other time of year there really isn't a great deal to see. You might spot a few resident eagles, but you can see a handful of bald eagles any day of the week in coastal Alaska, so there is little point in making a special journey.

The Preserve starts nine miles north of Haines and runs for thirty miles along the highway, but the main interpretive exhibits and the best viewing are around twenty-one miles north of Haines. During the summer, several of the city tours visit the Bald Eagle Preserve, but many people prefer to see the area from the water on a **raft**. There's no white water, so these are very much float trips specializing in a pleasant morning or afternoon looking for a few bald eagles and other wildlife along the shore. The main operator is the very professional Chilkat Guides (☎766-2491, fax 766-2409, *www.raftalaska.com*), who run half-day trips for $80, and you can also go with the recently established Eco Orca Tours (☎766-3933, *button@wytbear.com*) for $50.

Chilkat Guides also run major multiday expeditions on the Alsek and Tatshen-shini Rivers to the north (see Basics, p.57).

Eating, drinking, and entertainment

Considering its diminutive size, Haines has a decent offering of restaurants and cafés with a number of good places both downtown and around Fort Seward. Groceries are best sought at Howser's Supermarket at 211 Main St.

Bars tend to be straightforward drinking joints with little sophistication, though for something cultural you could attend the **Chilkat Center for the Arts**, in Fort Seward's recreational center (mid-May to mid-Sept Mon–Thurs at 7.30pm; $10; ☎766-2160), where the Chilkat Dancers do a forty-minute performance in tradi-tional costumes. It is an odd affair, promoted by a nonprofit corporation "dedicat-ed to the revival and perpetuation of the art and culture of the Northwest Coast Indian tribes," though most of the performers are white teenagers. At times it can feel like you're watching a school play.

While here you should try to sample some **birch syrup**, a poor relation to its maple-sourced cousin that's tapped from local trees and is available in many town gift shops.

Bamboo Room, 11 2nd St near Main (☎766-2800). Standard diner that is always popular for its well-prepared meals (especially the locally caught halibut and chip dinner) and fresh-baked pies.

Bear-Rittos, 14 Main St (☎766-2117). Chimichangas, burritos, and enchiladas with a choice of vege, chicken, beef, salmon, and halibut for $5–8 to eat-in at booths, or to take out.

Fireweed Bakery and Café, Building 37, Blacksmith Rd (☎766-3838). Convivial wood-floored place that's great for a coffee and one of their fresh pastries on the sunny deck, but equally good for more substantial dishes, often using organic ingredients. Eggs Benedict comes in half a dozen variations ($11–13), there's great pizza ($10 for a personal one), sand-wiches, gyros, falafel, daily soups, and things like roasted vegetable polenta and gnocchi al pesto ($15–17). Closed Sun.

Fogcutter Bar, 122 Main St. Favorite late-night drinking hole for locals and visitors with pool tables and sports on TV.

Haines Brewing Company, Southeast Alaska Fairgrounds (☎766-3823). Local microbrew-ery producing four mostly English-style ales for sale through the *Fogcutter Bar* as draft, and here in bottles for $7 a half gallon.

Mountain Market, 312 3rd Ave at Haines Hwy (☎766-3340). Combined natural food grocery and espresso bar that's one of the best places in town for a $6.50 bagel breakfast, similarly priced tortilla wraps (the falafel is especially good), or just a muffin with your mocha.

Port Chilkoot Potlatch, Parade Grounds, Fort Seward (☎766-2000). All-you-can-eat salmon bake on summer evenings (Mon–Thurs & Sat 5–9pm; $22).

Wild Strawberry, 138 2nd St (☎766-3608). Café, seafood restaurant, and deli with good espresso, fine chocolates, and good ice cream. The licensed restaurant serves salmon chow-der ($7), blackened halibut tacos ($15), and Cajun king salmon ($19).

Listings

Banks First National Bank, cnr 1st Ave and Main St, has an ATM.

Bookshop The Babbling Book, 225 Main St, is the best in town.

Festivals The community theater festival known as Actfest (☎766-2708) happens in late April in odd numbered years; cyclists racing in the 160-mile Kluane to Chilkat International Bicycle

Relay descend on Haines on the Sat nearest the summer solstice in late June; there are the usual parades and fireworks for the Fourth of July; and the cookouts, crafts, and log-rolling of the Southeast State Fair take place in the second week in Aug along with the Bald Eagle Music Festival which draws blues and bluegrass players from all over the state.

Internet access Free at the library (see below), and roughly $8 an hour at *Wild Strawberry* and *Mountain Market* (for both see overleaf). If you need to use your own disk, head to Northern Lights Internet Lounge, 715 Main St (Mon–Sat 9am–8pm, Sun 1–5pm).

Laundry and showers The Fort Chilkoot Camper Park has public showers by the quarter and a laundromat (7am–9pm).

Library The Haines Public Library, 103 3rd Ave (Mon & Wed 10am–9pm, Tues & Thurs 10am–4.30pm & 7–9pm, Fri 10am–4.30pm, Sat & Sun 1–4pm), has free Internet access.

Medical assistance Haines Medical Center, 131 1st Ave (Mon, Tues, Thurs & Fri 8.30am–5pm, Wed 9.30am–5pm; ☎766-3121).

Post Office cnr Haines Hwy opposite Tlingit Park. The **General Delivery** ZIP code is 99827.

Taxes Haines imposes a 5.5 percent sales tax and an additional 4 percent bed tax. Both have been included in our accommodation prices.

Travel agency The Travel Connection, 2nd Ave near Main St (☎766-2681 or 1-800/572-8006, fax 766-2585, *www.alaska4you.com*).

Skagway and around

SKAGWAY, the northernmost stop on the AMHS ferries, ranks as one of the best preserved gold rush towns in the US, a tiny kernel of century-old buildings that has a history to match. Throw in the superb **White Pass & Yukon Route** mountain train trip, a relatively dry climate, and the opportunity to emulate the Klondike gold prospectors hiking the challenging **Chilkoot Trail** (see box, p.174) and you've the makings of an enormously popular tourist destination.

But even when suitably forewarned, most people arrive unprepared for a place where, on a normal summer day, four or five huge boats will be moored at the foot of Broadway disgorging up to seven thousand passengers into a town with a year-round population of only eight hundred. In fact there are now ten times more people visiting Skagway each year than there were coming through during the Klondike gold rush, and it is not unusual to have five choppers and assorted fixed-wing planes in the air shattering the peace. It can seem as though everything that happens is conditioned by the presence of the cruise ships. Even the stores seem quite out of keeping with the pioneer tenor of the place; all high-class furs and glitzy diamond jewelry sold by slick men in suits and cuff links. Still, for most, the pleasures far outweigh the downsides.

This narrow, steep-sided valley at the mouth of the Skagway River was known to the Chilkoot Tlingit as Skagua, meaning "a windy place," though that didn't stop the town springing up overnight to satisfy the needs of stampeders bound for the Klondike. Having grown from one cabin to a town of twenty thousand in three months, Skagway, rife with disease and desperado violence, won the reputation of "hell on earth." It boasted over seventy bars and hundreds of prostitutes, and was controlled by organized criminals, including the notorious **Jefferson "Soapy" Smith**, renowned for cheating hapless prospectors out of their gold (see box p.165). Territorial governor John Brady complained to Washington that "gamblers, thugs and lewd women" were taking control of Skagway and the nearby town of Dyea. In response, the government sent the 14th Infantry to maintain

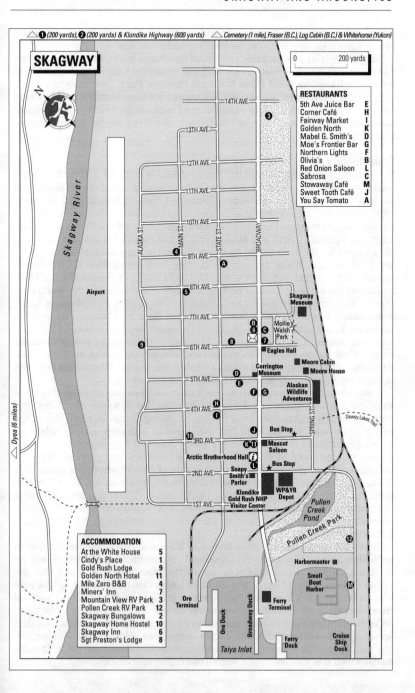

SKAGWAY

0   200 yards

RESTAURANTS

5th Ave Juice Bar	E
Corner Café	H
Fairway Market	I
Golden North	K
Mabel G. Smith's	D
Moe's Frontier Bar	G
Northern Lights	F
Olivia's	B
Red Onion Saloon	L
Sabrosa	C
Stowaway Café	M
Sweet Tooth Café	J
You Say Tomato	A

14TH AVE

13TH AVE

12TH AVE

11TH AVE

10TH AVE

9TH AVE

8TH AVE

7TH AVE

6TH AVE

5TH AVE

4TH AVE

3RD AVE

2ND AVE

1ST AVE

Skagway River

Airport

△ Dyea (6 miles)

ALASKA ST
MAIN ST
STATE ST
BROADWAY
SPRING ST

Skagway Museum

Mollie Walsh Park

Eagles Hall

Moore Cabin
Moore House

Corrington Museum

Alaskan Wildlife Adventures

Dewey Lakes Trail

Bus Stop

Mascot Saloon

Arctic Brotherhood Hall

Bus Stop

Soapy Smith's Parlor

WP&YR Depot

Klondike Gold Rush NHP Visitor Center

Pullen Creek Pond

Pullen Creek Park

Harbormaster

Small Boat Harbor

Ore Terminal

Ferry Terminal

Ore Dock
Broadway Dock

Ferry Dock

Cruise Ship Dock

Taiya Inlet

ACCOMMODATION

At the White House	5
Cindy's Place	1
Gold Rush Lodge	9
Golden North Hotel	11
Mile Zero B&B	4
Miners' Inn	7
Mountain View RV Park	3
Pollen Creek RV Park	12
Skagway Bungalows	2
Skagway Home Hostel	10
Skagway Inn	6
Sgt Preston's Lodge	8

order. Things gradually settled down and Skagway became the first incorporated city in Alaska on June 28, 1900, beating Juneau by one day.

Skagway retains a remarkable number of structures from its heyday in the late 1890s, encompassed in downtown's Skagway Historical District, and most being part of the **Klondike Gold Rush National Historic Park**. Over the years, buildings have been restored, wood-plank sidewalks have been installed and frontages have been gussied up to try to maintain (and increasingly reinvent) the original appearance of the town. None of this, though, detracts from the general harmonious impression.

Some history

No single image better conjures the human drama of the 1898 gold rush than the lines of prospectors struggling over the Chilkoot Trail desperate to get to the gold fields of the Klondike. Gold was first discovered there in August 1896, but word didn't reach the outside world until eleven months later when the steamship *Excelsior* pulled into San Francisco laden with gold. The gold rush was on. Within days every passage north was booked and Seattle rapidly became the main supply entrepot for the routes used by ninety percent of Yukon-bound gold seekers, the Chilkoot and White passes. Prospectors took steamships up the Inside Passage to the Lynn Canal from where they had a choice of disembarking at Dyea and taking the Chilkoot Trail, or landing at Skagway and following the White Pass Route. Once through the coastal mountains, the two routes met at **Bennett Lake**, from where it was 550 miles down the Yukon River to Dawson City and the Klondike. In the winter of 1897–98, thirty thousand hopefuls reached the frozen waters of Bennett Lake and the town of Bennett grew up as the gold seekers set about felling the trees for miles around and whipsawing planks for their boats. Break-up came on May 29 and within a week seven thousand boats had departed Bennett for Dawson City leaving the place almost deserted.

It was a tough journey, and seems even more so when you consider that there were few maps, nowhere to get supplies en route, harsh winter conditions, and people generally had no idea what they were getting themselves into. About the only reliable news was the word that the Canadian Mounties – who established ad hoc border posts in the absence of a widely accepted frontier – were enforcing a rule which required all stampeders entering Canada to carry a year's supplies, roughly a "**ton of goods**." Introduced because of chronic shortages in the gold fields, the ruling probably saved many lives in the long run, but laid enormous hardship on the backs of the stampeders. Altogether 22,000 prospectors made it over the Chilkoot Pass, many carrying their ton of supplies on their backs, sometimes making as many as fifty journeys through temperatures of –60°F and eighty feet of snow fall.

Before the rush, Skagway (then known as Mooresville) was just one hut owned by William Moore, who helped the Canadian Government pioneer a new route from the coast, through the mountains to the interior from Skagway up and over the **White Pass** to Bennett Lake. It was ten miles longer than the Chilkoot, but the pass was six hundred feet lower and had a gentler gradient, so it became the route of choice for prospectors wealthy enough to buy horses. Overuse, along with the sharp rocks, boulder fields and muskeg made it very heavy going and over three thousand horses died on what soon became known as the "Dead Horse Trail." Neither trail was the slightest bit appealing, and as one experienced stampeder put it "It didn't matter which one you took, you'd wished you'd taken the other."

THE REIGN OF SOAPY SMITH

Jefferson Randolph "Soapy" Smith and his gang of conmen and cutthroats had a short but lucrative career preying on gullible stampeders until Soapy got his comeuppance nine months after his arrival in Skagway. Soapy came by his name after a con trick he'd pulled years before in Colorado where he sold $5 bars of soap, some containing large denomination bills. From the skeptical crowd, Soapy's accomplices emerged to buy the first few bars which, miraculously, contained a $20 or even $50 bill. The ensuing buying frenzy revealed that few of the remaining bars contained even a $1 bill.

In Skagway, Soapy established a saloon from which he ran his empire of up to a hundred henchmen posing as newspaper reporters, priests or savvy sourdoughs to ensnare greenhorns arriving at the docks. Victims would soon be swindled at one of Soapy's businesses: crooked gambling halls, bogus freight companies that simply commandeered your consignment, an army enlistment tent where they'd steal your clothes and possessions while you visited the "doctor," and a telegraph office that had no telegraph link but which returned requests for money from loved ones back home. Soapy could, of course, arrange to have the money wired for you.

Soapy got his cronies to do the dirty work and established himself as a solid, philanthropic citizen, funding Skagway's first church and starting an adopt-a-dog program at a time when Skagway was full of discarded pull-nothing dogs. Many saw through the veneer, but he had the support of much of the business community and he even stood next to the Governor of Alaska during the 1898 Independence Day parade.

Things came to a head four days later when the vigilante "Committee of 101" gathered to discuss the situation at the Juneau Company wharf, led by one Frank Reid. Fearful of mob rule, Soapy went to address the meeting only to find himself in a gun battle with Reid. Soapy was shot in the heart and died immediately; Frank Reid died twelve agonizing days later from a gunshot wound to the groin. Both are buried in the Gold Rush Cemetery and, though Reid was no saint, it is obvious from the relative size of the monuments where the town's allegiances lay.

Everything changed with the July 1900 completion of the White Pass & Yukon Route railway which broadly followed the White Pass Trail. As one local newspaper noted "what was formerly an all-winter's job for the gold seeker can now be achieved in four hours, for less than one tenth the financial outlay." By now, the gold rush had subsided, but Skagway survived by maintaining the railway and supporting tourists who were coming to see this gold-rush town – the first tour boat arriving in 1900. Skagway got a new lease of life as a supply route for the construction of the Alaska Hwy during World War II, and continued as the main port for Yukon mineral-ore exports. Low returns for metals eventually closed the railway in 1982 but the rising influence of tourism saw it revived in 1986.

Arrival, information, and getting around

The daily AMHS **ferry** (☎983-2229 for recorded schedule, 983-2941 for the office) from Juneau and Haines arrives two hundred yards from the main thoroughfare, Broadway. This is marginally the cheapest way to get here from Haines, though a couple of local companies run more frequent (at least 3 daily) and very competitive trips, and do special deals on the WP&YR train: Haines-Skagway Water Taxi (☎766-3395 or 1-888/766-3395, *www.kcd.com/watertax*) take roughly an hour, charge $22 one-way ($35 round-trip) and show you different scenery in each direction with stops if wildlife is spotted; Native-owned Chilkat Cruises and Tours (☎766-2100, or 1-888/766-2103, *www.chilkatcruises.com*) are a bit quicker (40min between ports) and charge $24 one-way and $36 round-trip.

Bus routes to Skagway all come through Whitehorse in the Yukon: Alaska Overland (☎867/667-7896, *www.yukon.net/alaskaoverland*) is the cheapest ($30 one-way, $40 round-trip) running Monday to Saturday from Whitehorse in the morning to the corner of 2nd and Broadway, and returning that afternoon; *Alaska Direct* (☎1-800/780-6652) runs daily in summer from Whitehorse to Skagway and back ($35 one-way, $70 round-trip) and has connections three days a week from Tok ($40), Anchorage ($145), and Fairbanks ($120); Alaskon Express (☎983-2241 or 1-800/478-6388) offers a similar service ($45 each way from Whitehorse) arriving at the *Westmark Inn* on 3rd Avenue.

Though the WP&YR (see p.170) is primarily a tourist **train** service, it can be combined with Alaskon Express so that you travel from Whitehorse by bus to Log Cabin, BC, from where you ride the train into Skagway at a cost of $95.

It may also be worth considering **flying** to Skagway, especially if you want to visit Glacier Bay. You can fly (or catch the ferry) from Juneau to Gustavus, then avoid returning to Juneau by flying on to Haines or Skagway with a Glacier Bay overflight included (see "Local tours, cycling and flightseeing," p.173).

The best source of general information is the **visitor center**, Broadway at 2nd (daily: May–Sept 8am–6pm; Oct–April 8am–5pm; ☎983-2854 or 1-888/762-1898, fax 983-3854, *infoskag@aptalaska.net, www.skagway.org*), though there is also the Klondike Gold Rush National Historic Park **visitor center**, Broadway at 2nd Avenue (see p.168), and the Trail Center (see box, p.175).

The downtown area is eminently manageable on foot, but the SMART **bus** (May–Sept; ☎983-2743) tours downtown ($1 per journey; correct change needed), and is useful for a run up to 23rd Street ($2), a ten-minute walk from the cemetery.

Accommodation

Growth in tourism has meant a rise in standards for Skagway's accommodation. Prices tend to be quite high, but they generally offer good value: it is pretty much essential to reserve in advance in July and August and advisable a month either side.

As well as the **campgrounds** listed opposite, you can camp on the trails out of town, though if you are still within city limits (such as at Lower Dewey Lake) you are required to alert the Skagway police (☎983-2232) of your presence. There are also two Forest Service **cabins** on the trails hereabouts (see box, p.171).

Hotels, motels B&Bs, and cabins

At the White House, Main St at 8th (☎983-9000, fax 983-9010, *www.skagway.com /whitehouse*). High standard B&B in one of Skagway's original homes, restored from its fire-damaged state and now with fully modernized rooms, some particularly spacious (⑥). All have phone, cable TV, ceiling fans, and super-comfy beds. A full buffet breakfast is served and there's always tea, coffee, and home-baked cookies on hand. ⑤.

Cindy's Place, Mile 0.2 Dyea Rd, two miles from downtown Skagway (☎983-2674 or 1-800/831-8095, *www.alaska.net/~croland*). A beautiful spot in the woods with three cabins, one budget and two more luxurious log-built examples with private bathrooms (one with a wood-burning stove), phone, and cooking equipment. The budget Arctic Poppy cabin is small but good value with indoor toilet, sink, microwave, fridge, kettle, and toaster, but no shower. It sleeps two ($53), but is perfect for one ($38) and you can save $5 per person by using your own bedding and towels. All guests have free use of the hot tub and mountain bikes. Thoughtful little touches like fresh baking in the afternoon, a dozen varieties of tea and coffee in the cabins, and homemade jams and jellies for breakfast make this place special. Slight reductions for stays of two nights or more. Deluxe ⑤, budget ①/②.

Gold Rush Lodge, 6th Ave at Alaska St (☎983-2831, fax 983-2742, *www.alaskaone.com/goldrush*). Immaculately kept and tastefully decorated motel, the smallness of the rooms compensated by appointments which extend to cable TV with VCR, phone, fridge, microwave, and coffee pot. Courtesy transfers available. ④.

Golden North Hotel, Broadway at 3rd (☎983-2294 or 1-888/222-1898, fax 983-2755, *www.goldennorthhotel.com*). Alaska's oldest and Skagway's most famous hotel, recently restored with considerable aplomb; all antique furniture, somber tones, and floral Victorian wallpaper, but never oppressive. It is a place to splurge a little on one of their spacious deluxe rooms (⑥), some with wicker chairs in sunny alcoves, but the standard rooms (⑤), all with clawfoot baths, are good too, and there's nothing wrong with the shared-bath rooms (④). Everyone has access to a gracious lounge. ④–⑥.

Mile Zero B&B, Main St and 9th (☎983-3045, fax 983-3046, *www.mile-zero.com*). Modern, purpose-built B&B with large rooms each with a private entrance and a continental buffet breakfast in the communal lounge area, which is where you'll find the TV. ⑤.

Miner's Inn, Broadway at 6th (☎983-3303 or 1-800/764-7670, fax 983-3304, *mitchels@aptalaska.net*). Seven of the cheapest rooms in town. They're simple with sloping floors, but are pleasant and share the use of three bathrooms. There's even a tiny TV lounge where morning coffee and muffins are served, and they'll pickup from the ferry, though they're so central it is hardly necessary. Closed Oct–April. ③.

Sgt Preston's Lodge, 6th Ave at State St (☎983-2521, fax 983-3500, *sgt-prestons@usa.net*). Decent downtown motel with Standard, and much nicer Deluxe, rooms (at opposite ends of the price code) all with cable TV and pickups by courtesy van. ④.

Skagway Bungalows, Mile 0.2 Dyea Rd (☎983-2986, fax 983-3986). A couple of large cabins in the woods next to *Cindy's Place* (see above), each with king bed, futon couch, an inside bathroom, big deck out front, and croissants and fruit delivered for a make-your-own breakfast. ⑤.

Skagway Inn, Broadway at 7th (☎983-2289 or 1-888/752-4929, fax 983-2713, *www.skagwayinn.com*). Turn-of-the-century former bordello now operating as a boutique B&B hotel with comfortable shared-bath rooms decorated with old furniture and each bearing the name of an erstwhile occupant. Rooms vary considerably so ask to see a few, or simply go for one of the larger rooms (also ⑤), particularly the spacious, streetfront "Alice." Fresh-baked breakfasts (included) are served in the restaurant downstairs. ⑤.

Hostel and campgrounds

Mountain View RV Park, Broadway at 12th (☎983-3333 or 1-888/778-7700, fax 983-2444, *www.alaskarv.com*). Large RV dominated site with all the expected facilities, full RV hookup ($21) and dry RV sites ($15.50). The few wooded tent sites ($12.50) are in high demand.

NPS Dyea Campground, at Dyea, nine miles northeast of Skagway. Simple and attractive first-served, first-served Park Service campground (not recommended for RVs) beside the Taiya River with fire rings, picnic tables, pit toilets, and water which should be treated. Free.

Pullen Creek RV Park, Congress Way (☎ & fax 983-2768 or 1-800/936-3731). RV and tent park right by the harbor and with some trees. Showers are $1 extra. Closed Oct to mid-April. Tent $12, tent and car or dry RV $16, full hookup $22.

Skagway Home Hostel, 3rd Ave at Main St (☎983-2131). Meals are shared at this traditionally run hostel in a century-old building with an honesty box for your contribution for breakfast ($3) or a (typically) vegetarian dinner ($5). If you are cooking there are ample supplies, and often fresh bread and fruit for a small contribution. Bunks in fairly spacious single-sex dorms are $15 per night, and there's one private room for $40: sheets are extra, or bring your sleeping bag. No daytime lockout, but office hours are 5.30–10.30pm and there is an 11pm curfew. The biggest inconvenience is that they don't confirm reservations by phone so you'll need to send payment (particularly in July and Aug, and essential in winter) to Box 231, Skagway, AK 99840. ①.

The town and around

Almost everything in **downtown Skagway** happens on, or just off, Broadway, a half-mile-long strip lined with hotels, restaurants, a few bars, old buildings restored as museums, and a lot of swanky shops. It is a strange blend that can be unsettling at first though you can come to terms with it all using the free and widely available *Skagway Walking Tour* leaflet. This is where you'll spend your time between forays on the WP&YR railway, out to the **Gold Rush Cemetery** (walkable, though plenty of tours go there), and further afield to the scant remains of Dyea, the starting point for the multiday Chilkoot Trail hiking path.

Downtown Skagway

Most people arrive by boat and find themselves at the foot of Broadway, an area typically dominated by passengers disgorging from the White Pass & Yukon Route railroad. A small park by the tracks contains an old snow-blowing locomotive once used on the line, and a statue of a Tlingit guide and prospector built to commemorate the town's Centennial in 1998.

Many of Skagway's important historic buildings come under the auspices of the **Klondike Gold Rush National Historic Park**, including the **visitor center**, Broadway at 2nd Ave (May & Sept daily 8am–6pm, June–Aug 8am–8pm; ☎983-2921, *www.nps.gov/klgo*), in what was the original WP&YR depot. There are plenty of information panels, and park rangers ready to answer any questions, but it is best to time your visit to coincide with the excellent thirty-minute *Days of Adventure, Dreams of Gold* video (on the hour, most hours; free) telling the tale of the gold rush prospectors' struggles over the passes to the Klondike. The center also runs ranger talks (10am & 3pm; free) and walking tours of the downtown historic district (9am, 10am, 11am, 2pm & 3pm; free). In a separate room there are great photos of those heady days a century back along with a sample "ton of goods", a lot more than you'd fancy hauling over the Chilkoot Trail.

Opposite the visitor center, a small building contains the **Chilkoot Trail Center** (see box, p.175), the first stop for all Chilkoot Trail aspirants, but otherwise of little interest. Around the corner stands **Soapy Smith's Parlor**, from where he ran his short-lived empire. The building is an 1890s original, though it was moved to this site in 1964 and is not currently open to the public. Across 2nd Avenue, the **Red Onion Saloon** is another transported building, though it is very much open for business (see p.177). Liquor was only one of the commodities formerly sold here, and you can now join the fifteen- to thirty-minute **Brothel Tour** (May–Sept daily roughly hourly 11am–4pm; $5), a tongue-in-cheek but historically accurate walk through what is left of the upstairs rooms (one of them restored) guided by "girls," suitably dressed in push-up bodices and feather boas, who stay in character throughout and come with a stack of entertaining tales. If this inspires you, consider the two-hour **Haunted Red Light** walking tour ($26, including a glass of bubbly), also done in costume with more entertaining

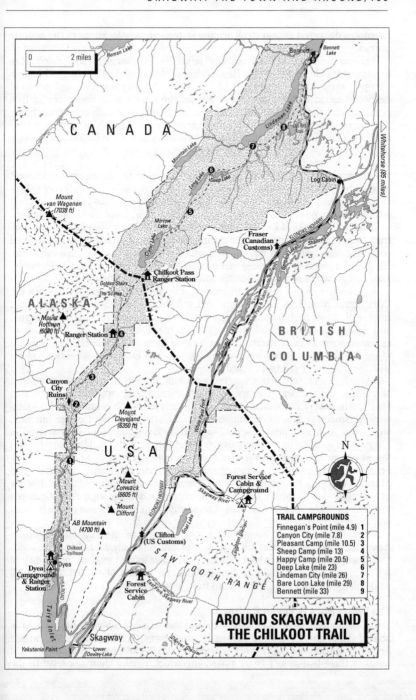

0   2 miles

Homan Lake

Bennett

Bennett
Lake

9

CANADA

Mountain Lake

8

Cut-off
Trail

Lindeman Lake

7

Mount
van Wagenen
(7038 ft)

Long Lake

6

Deep Lake

Log Cabin

KLONDIKE HIGHWAY

5

Morrow
Lake

Fraser
(Canadian
Customs)

Shallow Lake

Crater Lake

Chilkoot Pass
Ranger Station

Bernard Lake

Golden Stairs

The Scales

White Pass & Yukon Route Railroad

ALASKA

Mount
Hoffman
(6080 ft)

Ranger Station 4

Skagway TRAIL

BRITISH

3

COLUMBIA

Canyon
City
Ruins 2

Mount
Cleveland
(6350 ft)

Walsh Park Fork

USA

1

Mount
Cormack
(6605 ft)

Forest Service
Cabin &
Campground

N

Mount
Clifford

Skagway River

AB Mountain
(4700 ft)

KLONDIKE HIGHWAY

Goat Lake

Chilkoot
Trailhead

Clifton
(US Customs)

Dyea

SAW TOOTH RANGE

Dyea
Campground
& Ranger
Station

Forest Service
Cabin

East Fork Skagway River

Taiya Inlet

Skagway

Lower
Dewey Lake

Yakutania Point

W White Pass

▷ Whitehorse (85 miles)

TRAIL CAMPGROUNDS

Finnegan's Point (mile 4.9)   1
Canyon City (mile 7.8)   2
Pleasant Camp (mile 10.5)   3
Sheep Camp (mile 13)   4
Happy Camp (mile 20.5)   5
Deep Lake (mile 23)   6
Lindeman City (mile 26)   7
Bare Loon Lake (mile 29)   8
Bennett (mile 33)   9

AROUND SKAGWAY AND
THE CHILKOOT TRAIL

anecdotes delivered as you stroll around sixteen ghostly locations in the historic district.

Pressing on along Broadway you pass the eye-catching and much photographed facade of the **Arctic Brotherhood Hall**, built in 1899 by gold miners who paid their dues in nuggets, and decorated with over ten thousand pieces of driftwood nailed to the front. It now houses the town's main visitor center (see p.166). Across the road is the **Mascot Saloon** (May & Sept daily 8am–6pm; June–Aug 8am–8pm; free), which had its heyday as a bar and gambling den from 1897 to 1916, finally closing with prohibition. It's been renovated to its 1910 state, complete with a tableau of a bar scene, the marvelous mirror-backed bar patronized by several mannequins.

A couple of blocks up Broadway, turn right into 5th to the birthplace of Skagway, marked by Moore Cabin and **Moore House**, 5th Avenue at Spring Street (May–Sept daily 10am–noon & 1–5pm; $2). It was here that sixty-five-year-old founding settler, Captain William Moore, set up his cabin in 1887, prophesying an imminent gold rush, though he'd have to wait ten years to see it. Despite tales to the contrary, Moore made a small fortune during the gold rush, running the sawmill and collecting dues from what was the best wharf in Skagway. The original cabin (not open) and a much larger house that started out as a simple cabin in 1899, but by 1904 had grown to accommodate his whole family, still stands.

Back on Broadway, it is worth popping into the craft store that harbors the **Corrington Museum**, Broadway at 5th (mid-May to mid-Sept daily 9am–7pm; free), with its six-foot mammoth tusk, fossilized mastodon tooth, and spruceroot and baleen basketware, all thoroughly upstaged by the huge collection of engraved walrus tusks. There are over forty of them along with the tools custom made for carving scenes from Eskimo legends and European adventures along with the obligatory cribbage boards.

Seventh Street spans the spectrum of cultural life in gold-rush Skagway. Northwest of Broadway you are in what became the town's Red Light District after brothels were consolidated here in the early twentieth century; to the southwest of Broadway lies the granite-built mock-Gothic McCabe College building, which was built as a private school in 1899, before public schooling arrived in Skagway. After roles as a courthouse, jail, and City Hall, the building now houses the **Skagway Museum and Archive** (May–Sept daily 9am–5pm; $2; ☎983-2420, *info@skagwaymuseum.org*), recently refurbished, and containing the Trail of 98 Museum covering the stampede years. There's excellent material on the history of Skagway, the Klondike, the WP&YR railroad and fascinating collections put together by early Skagway families. Ethnography on all of Alaska gets a look in, and the collection of Native basketware is one of the finest in the state.

If the historical stuff seems a bit dry, venture to the **Alaskan Wildlife Adventure**, Spring Street at 4th (mid-May to mid-Sept daily 9am–6pm; $19; ☎983-6360), where guided tours lead you along boardwalks and explain the history of Alaska through a mountain of memorabilia and dozens of stuffed animals, all while hokey country music blares out from loudspeakers.

The White Pass & Yukon Railroad

Undoubtedly the most stately way to see the dazzling scenery hereabouts is aboard the **White Pass and Yukon Route** railway (WP&YR: early May to late Sept; 3–7 departures daily; ☎983-2217 or 1-800/343-7373, *www.whitepassrailroad .com*), a three-foot-wide narrow-gauge line which climbs from sea level to the

HIKES AROUND SKAGWAY

To enjoy the good **hiking** available around Skagway, firstly equip yourself with the useful *Skagway Trail Map*, available free from the visitor center, with detailed descriptions of a dozen walks in the area, the best of which are described below. These can all be tackled in a day, though you could make use of the two Forest Service cabins in the area: since there is no Forest Service office in Skagway you'll need to book through their reservation service (☎1-877/444-6777, *www .reserveUSA.com*). Camping along the local trails is also possible, though you need to be fully self-sufficient and must register at the local police station (☎983-2232).

AB Mountain (9.5 miles round-trip from downtown; 6–8hr; 4700ft ascent). Strenuous hike up the southwest ridge of the prominent mountain immediately north of town which provides panoramic views from the alpine meadows near the summit. The trailhead on Dyea Road is most easily reached by the Yakutania Point Trail (see below). Some claim the name comes from the Arctic Brotherhood, while others contend it is for the letters A and B which were once picked out in the melting snow: you can see them on old photos such as one in the *Mascot Saloon* on Broadway. Recent tree growth means you'll need a lot of imagination to see them these days, your best chance being in May and early June.

Denver Glacier (7 miles round-trip; 4–6hr; 1200ft ascent). Moderate hike in the shadow of the magnificent Sawtooth Range to the scrubby terminal moraine of the Denver Glacier. The trailhead is six miles north of downtown Skagway and is accessed by the WP&YR railroad, which runs a summer hiker flag-stop service (mid-May to mid-Sept; $26 round-trip) departing from Skagway daily at 8am and 12.40pm, with Skagway-bound services passing the trailhead at 11.40am and 4pm. By the trailhead there is an old railway caboose which operates as a Forest Service cabin ($35).

Dewey Lakes Trails (1–8 miles round-trip; 40min–6hr; 500–3600ft ascent). A varied system of trails straggling up the hills to the south of town to pretty, subalpine lakes and tumbling waterfalls, starting near the end of 3rd Avenue. A steep ten-minute walk gets you to a great viewpoint over town, though it is worth continuing to Lower Dewey Lake (0.7 miles). If you're fairly fit, press on to the muskeg meadows around Upper Dewey Lake (3 miles), where there's a primitive free-use cabin, or even on to Devil's Punchbowl (4.2 miles) where there's a small alpine lake.

Laughton Glacier (3 miles round-trip; 1hr–1hr 30min; 200ft ascent). Easy stroll following the Skagway River ending in a wonderful "rocky amphitheater" surrounded by hanging glaciers. It is a short walk, but consider staying overnight, either camping or in the Forest Service cabin ($35) about half a mile from the trailhead and a mile from the glacier. The trailhead is fourteen miles north of Skagway and is accessed by the WP&YR railroad, which runs a summer hiker flag-stop service ($52 round-trip) departing from Skagway daily at 8am and 12.40pm, with Skagway-bound services passing the trailhead at 11am and 3.30pm.

Yakutania Point (30–40min round-trip; 1.5 miles; negligible ascent). Gentle stroll to the pleasant picnic area at Yakutania Point or on a few minutes further to another at Smuggler's Cove. Start by following the path and footbridge at the western end of 1st Avenue.

2865-foot White Pass in just twenty miles making it one of the world's steepest train routes. Along the way it follows the tumbling Skagway River, trundling over precarious bridges, hugging precipitous cliffs and tunneling through the granite of the Sawtooth Range. It is a stunning journey with waterfalls, ice-packed gorges, a thousand-foot wooden trestle bridge, all seen from rolling stock in matching 1890s style; some very recent, some older than the railway itself, having been imported from elsewhere.

As with almost everything else around here, its construction was driven by gold. The relatively easy gradient of the White Pass made it amenable to the construction of a train line, and as thousands slogged their way to the goldfield over the Chilkoot and White passes, private interests were at work on Alaska's first railroad. In the two months from May 1898 four miles of track were laid. Things slowed considerably as workers had to be slung from ropes on the steep terrain to place blasting charges and enormous bridges had to be built. Nonetheless, the entire 110 miles to Whitehorse was completed in an astonishing 26 months. Altogether 35,000 workers were employed building the railroad, but never more than 2000 at once, ample evidence of just how transient the population was at this time. It had cost its backers $10 million, but despite being completed after the great Yukon stampede was over, it soon recouped the capital as prospectors abandoned both the Chilkoot and White Pass trails in favor of the railroad.

As the flood of gold-seekers abated the WP&YR settled into a more staid existence shipping metal ores from mines around Whitehorse to the sea at Skagway, and acting as a supply route during the wartime construction of the Alaska Hwy. Services were suspended in 1982, only to be revived six years later with a view to tapping the cruise-ship market. Initially there were limited services to the pass, but since 1988 services have expanded with daily trains running as far as Bennett Lake, forty miles from Skagway. For the summer of 2001, WP&YR are planning to reopen the line a further 28 miles along the shores of Bennett Lake to Carcross, probably running a train from Carcross to Bennett on Friday, Saturday, and Sunday from June to August, though details are sketchy.

Unfortunately, this unmissable trip doesn't come cheap, and with heavy bookings from the cruise ships you seldom have the luxury to wait for a fine day then travel on the spur of the moment. The most popular run – and the one which most cruise passengers are funneled onto – is the three-hour White Pass Summit Excursion (early May to late Sept 2–3 daily; $78 round-trip), which runs from the **station** at the junction of Broadway and 1st Avenue, twenty miles up to the Canadian border at the top of White Pass and back: sit on the left going up. As with most service, the train is hauled by a **steam engine** for the first couple of miles then by diesel after that. There's also the eight-hour Bennett Lake Adventure (June–Aug 4 weekly; $128), which continues beyond White Pass to Bennett Lake, British Columbia (the end of the Chilkoot Trail hiking route), where stampeders built boats before launching them five hundred miles down the Yukon to Dawson City. You get a couple of hours by the lake at Bennett to eat your box lunch (included) and be shown around the evidence of those frenetic two years. The Saturday service to Bennett Lake ($156) is hauled by an ancient steam engine. In addition there is the Skagway–Whitehorse Train+Bus service (mid-May to mid-Sept daily; $95 one-way to Whitehorse) on which you ride the train as far as Fraser (the Canadian border) then transfer to a bus for the run past Carcross to Whitehorse. This service doubles as access for hikers wanting to get into Denver and Laughton glaciers (see box, p.171).

Gold Rush Cemetery and Dyea

No exploration of Skagway's gold-rush heritage would be complete without a visit to the **Gold Rush Cemetery**, the final resting place of many of the stampeders. Among them are Skagway's most famous outlaw, Soapy Smith, and his nemesis, Frank Reid, who according to his gravestone "gave his life for the honor of Skagway." Local prostitute Ella Wilson is also interred here, with the cheeky epitaph "she gave her honor for the life of Skagway." It fits nicely in a cemetery full of gentle conceits: most of the signs marking graves are modern additions put here when the cemetery was revamped for the benefit of tourists. It is a pleasant enough place to idle away half an hour; while there, be sure to take the short stroll to the 300ft-high **Reid Falls** which cascade down the hills behind the graveyard.

Those prospectors who weren't in Skagway trying to cheat death on the White Pass route to the Klondike were chancing their luck at the start of the Chilkoot Trail (see box, overleaf), nine miles away at the mouth of the Taiya River in **DYEA** (Dy-EE). At the height of the rush this was a bustling town where gold seekers stopped off just long enough to prepare for the three-month journey ahead, ferrying goods over the Chilkoot Pass. For a short time the typical gold-rush inducements of Dyea prevailed over Skagway's, and it ranked as the largest town in Alaska, but it went into rapid decline after the opening of the WP&YR railway. Most of the buildings were torn down, but a few foundations remain along with rotting stumps from the two-mile-long wharf, and the **slide cemetery**, mass burial place for the victims of a Chilkoot Trail avalanche that took sixty-odd lives at The Scales in April 1898. There's little else to show for the place, but it is a lovely spot to wander around, admiring the wildflowers and spotting birds, guided by interpretive panels and paths constructed by the Park Service. They even operate a primitive campground here (see p.167).

Local tours, cycling, and flightseeing

It is easy enough to stroll around the downtown area, and even hike out to the Gold Rush Cemetery but for more extensive exploration you might want to join one of the **local tours**. About the cheapest is with Klondike Tours ($30; ☎983-2075 or 1-888/983-2075) taking up to three hours to make the run around the local sights (including the cemetery) and out past the Canadian border to the top of White Pass. Most of the rest cater largely to the cruise ship set including Frontier Excursions, Broadway at 7th Avenue (☎983-2512, fax 983-3512, *www.ptialaska.net /~frontier*), who do a White Pass Summit and City Tour (2.5hr; $31) which also visits the cemetery, a Dyea Nature Tour (2.5hr; $31), and a drive into the Yukon as far as Carcross (6hr; $73).

Sockeye Cycle Co (see "Bicycle rental", p.178) offer a couple of local guided **cycling tours**, neither requiring much effort on your part: the Klondike Bicycle Tour (2hr; $69) involves a narrated van ride up to the 3300-foot Klondike Pass then a moderately graded descent back to Skagway with negligible pedaling; the Dyea Bicycle Adventure (2.5hr; $69) also starts with a van ride, this time to the start of the Chilkoot Trail followed by ninety minutes gentle riding on the dirt roads around Dyea.

Flightseeing trips from Skagway are understandably popular; the glacial scenery immediately around town is certainly impressive, and you're only a few minutes' flight from Glacier Bay and all the majestic wonder that that entails. Some of the most popular local trips are with Temsco Helicopters (☎983-2900, *www.temscoair.com*), who do a flightseeing circuit with twenty-five minutes

HIKING THE CHILKOOT TRAIL

Alaska's most famous and popular trail, the 33-mile **Chilkoot Trail**, is a three-or-four day journey through a giant wilderness museum, tracing the footsteps of Klondike-bound prospectors from the coast at **Dyea** through temperate rainforest, alpine tundra and the bare rocks of the Chilkoot Pass, to **Bennett Lake** in British Columbia. The entire route is littered with haunting reminders of the past: ancient boilers that once drove aerial tramways, twisted metal fittings, collapsed huts, glass bottles, old boots, wooden tramway pylons, and even a stash of canvas and wood boats that were never used. Leave everything as you found it and try not to step on fragile relics.

The trail has an iconic status in the north and is consequently used by over three thousand hikers a year, many of whom would never consider any other multiday hike. Keen hikers shouldn't find it too challenging, though the less fit find it tough going, especially the much-hyped 45-degree scramble from "The Scales" to the top of the pass – 2500 feet of ascent in one seven-mile day – which some people struggle to finish in twelve or fourteen hours. All this is made considerably more intimidating if the weather turns inclement, as it can do in any month of the year.

You need to be entirely self-sufficient, and must camp in one of the nine approved **campgrounds**, each equipped with demarcated sites (sometimes on wooden platforms), pit toilets, and a central eating area overlooked by twenty-foot poles for hanging food out of bears' reach. With the exception of the one long day mentioned above, most campgrounds are spaced less than four hours apart, so you can take the whole trail at a leisurely pace.

THE ROUTE

Most people hike from Dyea to Bennett, which keeps the strong prevailing winds at your back, and makes for an easier scramble up the slippery rocks to the pass. From the trailhead you hike through temperate rainforest following the Taiya River past campgrounds at Finnegan's Point (Mile 4.9), Canyon City (Mile 7.8), and Pleasant Camp (Mile 10.5) before reaching **Sheep Camp** (Mile 13), the last before the big day over the pass. Get an early start from Dyea and it is easy enough to hike to Sheep Camp in one day: late risers should aim to cover the distance in two days. Leaving Sheep Camp at 4am or 5am ensures you get over the pass and past an avalanche danger zone early in the day when it is safest. You initially climb through forest and tundra to the former tent city of "The Scales," where prospectors marshaled their gear before the arduous ascent of "Golden Stairs," a five-hundred-foot, hands-and-feet clamber over rocks to the top. At the pass there's an occasionally-manned **Canadian border post** and a warming hut where you can brew up and gather your strength for the long hike down to **Happy Camp** (Mile 20.5). In June you'll have to cross extensive snowfields, but the stunning alpine scenery easily compensates. If you've got the strength you might want to continue on to the campground at Deep Lake (Mile 23), beautifully set beside some rapids, or even on to the lakeside campground at Lindeman City (Mile 26), where some prospectors built their boats. An early start from here takes you along a ridge parallel to Lindeman Lake and gets you to Bennett (Mile 33) in time for the train back to Skagway, though it is worth spending an extra day here exploring what is left of Bennett, basically a wooden church and a lot of junk the prospectors left behind.

From Bennett it is a seven-mile hike along the tracks to the highway at Log Cabin, but you can take a **cut-off trail** by Bare Loon Lake, midway between Lindeman City and Bennett, which saves about four miles but means you never see Bennett.

RESERVATIONS AND PERMITS

The trail is open all year, though most visit during the **hiking season** (late May to early Sept) when rangers patrol the trail, warming huts are open and poles mark the route; though you can still expect to encounter snow up until the first or second week of July. An advance **information pack** (Can$5, refunded with a subsequent reservation) can be ordered by calling the **reservation system** (☎867/667-3910 or 1-800/661-0486 between 8.30am and 4pm Pacific Standard Time, which is one hour ahead of Alaska time), or write to Chilkoot Trail National Historic Site, 205–300 Main St, Whitehorse, Yukon, Y1A 2B5. Throughout the hiking season Parks Canada limits the number of hikers crossing the Chilkoot Pass into Canada to 50 per day, of which 42 places can be booked in advance (Can$11; money order or credit card) by calling the reservation system (see above). The remaining 8 places are offered on a first-come, first-served basis after 1pm on the day before you plan to start the trail from the Skagway **Trail Center**, Broadway at 1st Avenue (late May to early Sept daily 8am–4.15pm). The busy season is July and the first two weeks of August: outside this time you probably don't need to make a reservation.

All hikers need to go to the Trail Center to buy a **permit** ($40), sign a register (for customs purposes) and consult the weather forecast. You'll need to carry **identification**, which means a birth certificate for North Americans (a driver's license is not acceptable) and a passport for everyone else. You may be required to deal with Canadian Customs at the Chilkoot Pass ranger station but more likely you'll do it after your hike at the Alaska–Canada border post at Fraser or in Whitehorse.

If you have made an advance reservation, you'll already have the Canadian Parks Service's *Chilkoot Trail* **map** (otherwise $2 from the Trail Center), which is about the best available.

TRANSPORT AND SUPPLIES

To get to the start of the trail, nine miles northwest of Skagway at Dyea, you could arrange a lift or walk, though it isn't a very pleasant hike, and hitching isn't usually very successful. Otherwise you'll have to engage the services of one of the **shuttle buses** ($10): Dyea Dave (☎983-2731) goes on demand, Frontier Excursions (☎983-2512) have dropoffs at 8am, 9am, noon, and 2pm.

The trail finishes at Bennett where you can get boats from Tutshi Charters (☎867/821-4905) to take you across Bennett Lake to Carcross (Can$65) to meet the Whitehorse-bound Alaskon Express bus. Alternatively you can walk the eight miles to the highway at Log Cabin (there's a shortcut off the trail which avoids Bennett) and meet up with one of the shuttle buses ($25 for a combined dropoff and pickup); or **return to Skagway** on the WP&YR railroad. Riding the rails is the perfect complement to the hike, giving a sense of how important the train was to the prospectors. In June, July, and August there is the Chilkoot Trail Hikers Service (departs 1pm Alaska time; $25 one-way to Fraser, $65 to Skagway) which is either a railcar, or one carriage of the Bennett Lake Excursion that's specially designated for smelly hikers. Remember to buy your **tickets** at the WP&YR office in Skagway before you set off on the trail otherwise you'll have a $15 fee added to the ticket price for the convenience of buying your ticket on the train; and note that for customs reasons the train doesn't stop at Log Cabin.

When setting out from Skagway be sure to take wet-weather gear, matches, some method of water treatment, sunscreen, sunglasses, a flashlight, and **thirty feet of rope** so that you can sling your food, toothpaste, and any scented items over the bear poles at each campground. Rope is available from Skagway Hardware Co, Broadway and 4th Avenue. Early in the season when there's plenty of snow about, consider **gaiters**, which can be rented from The Mountain Shop in Skagway (see "Outdoor gear," p.178).

Almost all accommodations in Skagway offer free **gear storage** for their guests while they hike the trail.

stopped on a flat section at the foot of one of the local glaciers (55min; $160), and will whisk you up onto the Denver Glacier (1.5hr; $300) where they've installed several dog teams that will take you on a brief sled ride.

Planes lack the agility of choppers, but are cheaper to run and have a longer range, so you tend to get a longer trip for your money and flights over Glacier Bay are possible. Three companies operate tours including Skagway Air Service, 420 Broadway (☎983-2218, fax 983-3318, *www.skagwayair.com*), who start off with their Gold Rush Tour (45min; $65) around the White and Chilkoot passes, Bennett Lake, and the Juneau Ice Field, and do an excellent Glacier Bay Tour (1.5hr; $125) with views down to the main glaciers and sometimes straying as far as the Fairweather Range. They also fly to Skagway from Juneau (direct, 45min; $80; with a Glacier Bay overflight, 1.5hr; $160), and from Gustavus ($90).

Eating, drinking, and entertainment

Most of Skagway's **bars** and **restaurants** lie in the touristy part of Broadway where a five-minute stroll will reveal almost everything the town has to offer. As befits such a touristy town, the range is pretty decent, and Skagway even has a *Starbucks*, though the fast food franchises haven't moved in yet. For **groceries** and trail supplies head to the Fairway Market, State Street at 4th Avenue, or for more exotic (and healthy) goods, visit You Say Tomato, State Street at 9th Avenue (☎983-2784).

Evening entertainment mainly revolves around the bars (all on Broadway), though you shouldn't pass up the opportunity to see Buckwheat Donahue's highly entertaining **Robert Service Poetry** performance (June–Aug Mon & Tues 7pm; free) held in the Historic Park Service Auditorium, Broadway and 2nd Avenue. More Service can be heard in the Eagle Hall at the *Days of '98 Show*, Broadway at 6th Avenue (May–Sept daily at 10.30am, 2.30pm & 8pm; $12, evening show $14), where the story of Soapy and Frank (see box, p.165) is acted out in a gold-rush saloon atmosphere (only without the drinking). Evening show is preceded by an hour of fake gambling.

Corner Café, State St at 4th Ave (☎983-2155). Often smoky daytime diner that's much favored by Skagway's outdoor set and a good break from the press of people on Broadway just a couple of blocks away. Stuffed croissants with salad or soup for $7, or halibut burger for $8.

5th Avenue Juice Bar, 5th Ave and Broadway (no phone). Hectic spot to pop in for a juice combo ($5), fruit smoothie ($6), or fruit salad plate ($6) while you surf the Net.

Golden North Restaurant, Broadway at 3rd Ave (☎983-2294). Popular restaurant chiefly notable for sidewalk seating that catches the afternoon sun, and a good range of micro-brewed beer made on the premises. Be warned that a service charge of fifteen percent is automatically added to the check.

Mabel G Smith's, 342 5th Ave at Broadway (☎983-2609). Low-key espresso bar with the best coffee in town, glazed pumpkin cookies with a reputation throughout the north, and a relaxed vibe.

Moe's Frontier Bar, Broadway at 4th Ave (☎983-2238). The place for straightforward drinking.

Northern Lights, Broadway, between 4th and 5th (☎983-2225). Family restaurant that's always popular for its range of pizza (12" from $13), pasta dishes such as shrimp parmigiana ($17), Mexican favorites like a chile relleno dinner ($18), and even souvlaki ($17).

Olivia's, Broadway at 7th Ave, inside the *Skagway Inn* (☎983-3287). Probably the finest dining in Skagway, all linen tablecloths and napkins, polished wine glasses, and deferential waiters…and the food's very good too. The menu is imaginative starting with, perhaps, Asian spring rolls or a curried carrot soup and continuing with Sitka rockfish fillet, but hoping you've left room for the signature white chocolate bread pudding. For three courses, expect to pay $40 plus wine.

Red Onion Saloon, Broadway at 2nd Ave (☎983-2222). An 1898 wood-floored bar and former bordello (see p.168) where the bar staff don period dress and engage in role play that would be horribly cheesy if it wasn't done with such enthusiasm. It is an approach much loved by cruise ship passengers who flock in during the day, often with the ships' band in tow, ready to strike up a few jazz tunes. The girls who once plied their trade upstairs have

ROBERT SERVICE

With the possible exception of Jack London, no literary figure is more closely associated with the sub-Arctic North than English-born poet **Robert Service** (1874–1958), whose lilting, well-crafted rhymes captured the essence of the Klondike gold rushes. This "Bard of the Yukon" had only tenuous contact with Alaska – he traveled through Skagway and on the WP&YR railway to Whitehorse – but the material he dealt with, and the spirit with which he imbued his poetry, rings just as true in Alaska as it does in the Yukon. It certainly has no trouble crossing over in the public perception, and Service has been wholly adopted by the Alaskan tourist machine. All over the state you'll find crowds of visitors flocking to hear performers reciting Service's more crowd-pleasing Klondike works: "The Shooting of Dan McGrew," "The Cremation of Sam McGee," and "The Spell of the Yukon."

Service's work is often derided by the literary establishment, who barely consider him a "real" poet let alone a "great" one, but, despite the unfamiliarity of his subject matter, he spoke to the average reader in language understood by all, his vibrant imagery delivered with a dramatic, almost metronomic intensity. Undoubtedly a people's poet, he once claimed "The only society I like, is that which is rough and tough – and the tougher the better. That's where you get down to bedrock and meet human people." His sympathies certainly rested with the common people, but he was never the archetypal starving poet, and after the publication of his Yukon poems he quickly became very wealthy, some claiming that "The Shooting of Dan McGrew" alone brought in half a million dollars.

His three most famous poems were written in Whitehorse during a prolific few months at the end of 1906, eight years after the Klondike rush, a phenomenon that Service had missed entirely as he drifted around the southwestern US and Mexico. By 1904 he had returned to his original profession as a bank clerk and been transferred to Whitehorse, a town in decline as prospectors had moved on to richer Alaskan strikes leaving the old claims to be worked over by mechanical dredges. Still, there were enough sourdoughs left to tell the tale, and when the local paper, who knew of his poetic leanings, asked for "something about our own bit of earth," he quickly tapped into a rich vein. Overheard yarns, shaggy-dog stories, and snippets gleaned from every source were woven together and soon became his first and most celebrated book, *Songs of a Sourdough*.

Numerous other books followed, some even being turned into films, but none of his later work captured the zeitgeist to the same degree, nor have any had the same enduring popularity. Service spent the rest of his long life pursuing all manner of interests, and doing pretty much as he pleased, freed by the nest egg he had created in those few months in Whitehorse. He traveled the world, worked as a war correspondent, settled in Paris with a French woman, flirted with Marxism, narrowly escaped the German Army after mocking Hitler in a poem he wrote for a newspaper, and died of a heart attack at his retreat in Lancieux, France, at the age of 84.

unwittingly given their names to the excellent pizza, a theme followed with the named sandwiches washed down with the town's best selection of draft beers. Evenings can be a good deal quieter, though the Thursday night blues band is usually a winner.

Sabrosa, Broadway at 6th Ave (☎983-2469). Daytime café and bakery tucked in behind the gift shops that's great for breakfast (from $4) and lunches of burritos ($7), vegetarian chili (cup $3, bowl $6) and tarragon, pecan, and chicken salad ($8).

Stowaway Café, 205 Congress Way (☎982-3463). Stop by during the day for top-quality takeaway meals such as hot soup (from $3), French bread sandwiches, wraps or a blackened-chicken Caesar ($5.50) from a window known as the *Go-Away Café* (11am–4pm). In the evening head inside for seafood file gumbo ($17), prawns gorgonzola ($23), sweet and sour vegetables ($15), and pecan pie ($6) all served in a congenial atmosphere with views of the small boat harbor.

Sweet Tooth Café, Broadway at 3rd Ave (☎983-2405). Popular traditional American-style café, serving breakfast along with lunches of Reuben sandwich ($6.50), halibut burgers ($6–8) and ice cream.

Listings

Banks The National Bank of Alaska, Broadway at 6th (Mon–Fri 9.30am–5pm) has 24hr ATMs and there's another ATM inside the WP&YR depot.

Bicycle rental Sockeye Cycle Co, 5th Ave 7 Broadway St (☎983-2851, *www.cyclealaska.com*) charge $6 an hour, $20 a half-day, and $30 an eight-hour day, with discounts offered for two- and three-day rentals; Sourdough Car Rentals (see below) rent basic runabouts for $10 a day.

Bookshop Skaguay News Depot, Broadway at 3rd Ave (☎983-3354, *www.skagwaybooks.com*) has lots of Alaskana, a small selection of other books and magazines, and out-of-state newspapers.

Car rental The cheapest cars are offered by Sourdough Car Rentals, 6th Ave at Broadway (☎983-2523 or 1-800/478-2529, fax 983-2553, *www.ptialaska.net/~renta*) who have compacts for $59 (plus 30¢ a mile after first 100) and a four-hour unlimited mileage special for around $40. They also do one-way rentals as far as Whitehorse at $69 a day (plus 22¢ a mile after first 100, plus $50 dropoff fee). Avis, inside the *Westmark Hotel* at 3rd Ave and Spring St (☎983-2247, fax 983-2753) charge around $65 a day in high summer with unlimited mileage.

Internet access Currently three places have Internet access, all fairly expensive and with a half-hour minimum. The cheapest is at the *5th Avenue Juice Bar*, 5th Ave at Broadway (roughly daily 7am–7pm), though *Skagway E-mail Café*, Broadway at 3rd (daily 9am–7pm) has faster machines and a less frenetic atmosphere.

Laundry and showers Pay-by-the-quarter showers next to the Harbormaster's office on Congress Way. Laundry at Services Unlimited, cnr State and 2nd (daily 8am–8pm), and at *Garden City RV Park*, State St at 16th St.

Left luggage Nothing formal, so when hiking the Chilkoot you'll have to rely on your hotel or hostel: most are amenable but it pays to ask.

Library Skagway Public Library, State St at 8th Ave (Mon–Fri 1–9pm, Sat 1–5pm).

Medical assistance Dahl Memorial Health Center, 11th Ave at Broadway (Mon–Fri 9am–5pm; ☎983-2255). After hours call ☎983-2418.

Outdoor gear The Mountain Shop, 355 4th Ave (☎983-2544) sells major brands and rents tents (first night $18, subsequent nights $9), sleeping bags ($18/9), cooking stoves ($6/3), packs ($12/6), foam pads ($4/2), snowshoes ($5), sea kayaks ($40 a day), and more.

Post Office Broadway at 6th Ave (Mon–Fri 8.30am–5pm). The **General Delivery** ZIP code is 99840.

Taxes There's a four percent sales tax in Skagway; the tax on hotels amounts to eight percent, which we've already included within our price codes.

travel details

With the exception of the 372-mile loop between near neighbors Haines and Skagway, none of the towns in Southeast are connected by road, so ferries (for more details see Basics, p.33) and planes take the load. The following ferry frequencies only apply from May to September, though there are limited services throughout the winter.

Alaska Airlines link most of the main Southeast towns using Juneau as the main hub but running several daily frequent-stop "milk runs" such as: Juneau–Petersburg–Wrangell–Ketchikan–Seattle; Anchorage–Cordova–Yakutat–Juneau–Seattle; and Anchorage–Juneau–Sitka–Ketchikan–Seattle.

BUSES

Haines to: Fairbanks (1 weekly; 13hr); Haines Junction (1 weekly; 3hr); Tok (1 weekly; 9hr).

Skagway to: Anchorage (3 weekly; overnight with a stop at Beaver Creek, Yukon; Beaver Creek, Yukon (3 weekly; 12hr); Haines Junction (3 weekly; 6–7hr); Tok (3 weekly; overnight with a stop at Beaver Creek, Yukon; Whitehorse (1–2 daily; 3hr).

FERRIES

Angoon to: Kake (1–2 weekly; 4hr); Sitka (3–5 weekly; 4hr); Tenakee Springs (2–3 weekly; 2hr 30min);

Bellingham, WA to: Ketchikan (weekly; 37hr).

Haines to: Juneau (1–2 daily; 4hr 30min); Skagway (1–2 daily; 1hr).

Hollis to: Ketchikan (8 weekly; 2hr 45min).

Hoonah to: Juneau (3–4 weekly; 3hr 15min); Tenakee Springs (2–3 weekly; 3hr 15min).

Juneau to: Angoon (2–3 weekly; 10hr 30min); Bellingham, WA (weekly; 72hr); Haines (1–2 daily; 4hr 30min); Hoonah (2–4 weekly; 3hr 15min); Kake (1–2 weekly; 13hr 30min); Ketchikan (roughly daily; 21hr); Pelican (every 2 weeks; 4hr 30min); Petersburg (roughly daily; 8–18hr); Prince Rupert, BC (almost daily; 53hr); Seward (one a month; 50hr); Sitka (3–5 weekly; 9hr); Skagway (1–2 daily; 5hr 30min); Tenakee Springs (1–3 weekly; 7hr 30min); Valdez (one a month; 36hr); Wrangell (5–7 weekly; 12hr).

Kake to: Angoon (1–2 weekly; 4hr); Sitka (1–2 weekly; 8hr).

Ketchikan to: Bellingham, WA (weekly; 37hr); Hollis (8 weekly; 2hr 45min); Metlakatla (6 weekly; 1hr 15min); Petersburg (roughly daily; 10hr); Prince Rupert, BC (6–7 weekly; 6hr); Wrangell (5–7 weekly; 6hr).

Metlakatla to: Ketchikan (6 weekly; 1hr 15min).

Pelican to: Juneau (every 2 weeks; 4hr 30min).

Petersburg to: Juneau (roughly daily; 8–18hr); Kake (3–5 weekly; 4hr); Sitka (3–5 weekly; 10hr); Wrangell (4–6 weekly; 3hr).

Prince Rupert, BC to: Ketchikan (6–7 weekly; 6hr).

Sitka to: Angoon (3–5 weekly; 4hr); Juneau (3–5 weekly; 9hr); Petersburg (3–5 weekly; 11hr); Tenakee Springs (2–3 weekly; 9hr).

Skagway to: Haines (1–2 daily; 1hr); Juneau (1–2 daily; 5hr 30min).

Tenakee Springs to: Angoon (2–3 weekly; 2hr 30min); Hoonah (2–3 weekly; 3hr 15min).

Wrangell to: Ketchikan (5–7 weekly; 6hr); Petersburg (4–6 weekly; 3hr).

FLIGHTS

Glacier Bay/Gustavus to: Juneau (1 daily; 25min).

Juneau to: Anchorage (5 daily; 1hr 40min–3hr 15min); Cordova (1 daily; 2hr); Fairbanks (2 daily; 2hr 25min); Glacier Bay (1 daily; 25min); Ketchikan (2–3 daily; 1–2hr); Petersburg (1 daily; 40min); Seattle (10–12 daily; 2hr 30min–4hr 40min); Sitka (3 daily; 40min); Wrangell (1 daily; 1hr 30min); Yakutat (1 daily; 40min).

Ketchikan to: Anchorage (1–2 daily; 4–5hr); Craig (3 daily; 45min); Juneau (2–3 daily; 1–2hr); Metlakatla (15 daily; 10min); Petersburg (1 daily; 1hr 20min); Seattle (5 daily; 1hr 40min); Sitka (1 daily; 40min); Wrangell (1 daily; 30min).

Petersburg to: Anchorage (1 daily; 3hr); Juneau (1 daily; 40min); Ketchikan (1 daily; 1hr 20min); Seattle (1 daily; 3hr 50min); Wrangell (1 daily; 20min).

Seattle to: Juneau (10–12 daily; 2hr 30min–4hr 40min); Ketchikan (5 daily; 1hr 40min); Petersburg (1daily; 3hr 50min); Petersburg (1 daily; 3hr 50min); Sitka (4 daily; 2–3hr); Wrangell (1 daily; 2hr 50min); Yakutat (1 daily; 3hr 40min).

Sitka to: Anchorage (1 daily; 2hr 50min); Juneau (3 daily; 40min); Ketchikan (1 daily; 40min); Seattle (4 daily; 2–3hr).

Wrangell to: Anchorage (1 daily; 3hr 40min); Juneau (1 daily; 1hr 30min); Ketchikan (1 daily; 30min); Petersburg (1 daily; 20min); Seattle (1 daily; 2hr 50min).

Yakutat to: Anchorage (1 daily; 2hr); Cordova (1 daily; 45min); Juneau (1 daily; 40min); Seattle (1 daily; 3hr 40min).

CHAPTER TWO

ANCHORAGE

A quarter of a million strong, **ANCHORAGE** is Alaska's only true city, home to some forty percent of Alaskans and four times the size of Fairbanks, its nearest challenger. It is the state capital in all but name: branches of state government have even relocated here from Juneau. The influence Anchorage has in the state can easily be attributed to oil, Alaska's lifeblood, which is neither tapped, shipped, nor pumped anywhere near the city, but oil companies have established offices here, and oil-generated wealth has a tangible presence in the city. However, this is only part of the reason why the city fosters resentment; Anchorage is actually almost reviled by just about everyone who doesn't live in the big city. It is cited as the very antithesis of all things archetypally Alaskan, with gleaming cars, designer labels, and gourmet goodies present here in a way you

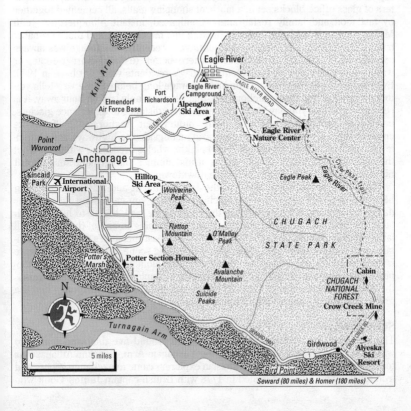

Seward (80 miles) & Homer (180 miles) ▽

ACCOMMODATION PRICE CODES

All accommodation prices in this book have been coded using the symbols below. Note that prices are for the least expensive double rooms in each establishment. For a full explanation see p.44 in Basics.

① up to $50	④ $80–100	⑦ $160–200
② $50–65	⑤ $100–130	⑧ $200–250
③ $65–80	⑥ $130–160	⑨ $250 and over

won't find anywhere else in the state. Nonetheless, every so often there is a move to relocate the political capital away from Juneau to somewhere more central and accessible: Anchorage is the obvious choice, but for fear of concentrating even more power, the rest of the state will never let that happen.

Flying into the **Anchorage Bowl** – the common term for the city and its immediate surroundings – you're instantly struck by the majesty of the setting, seated at the foot of the snow-capped Chugach Mountains on the edge of a great wilderness and girt by the shimmering water of Cook Inlet. Trouble is, the civic planners seem to have turned their backs on the location and managed to produce a replica of just about any American city west of the Great Plains: a couple of clusters of glass office blocks set in a fabric of shopping malls, all cemented together by fast food and family restaurants. "Condensed, instant Albuquerque" John McPhee called it in his 1977 classic *Coming into the Country*, and that's probably truer today than it was then. Indeed, until very recently, Anchorage was always considered a stepping stone to somewhere better (usually more remote, or warmer), and some seventy percent of today's residents were not here in 1980. Even today, it's likely you won't be in Anchorage long before some wag tells you that the great thing about Anchorage is that Alaska is only half an hour away. It is certainly true that you have to travel only a short distance to experience glaciers, precipitous mountains, and wild bush country, but Anchorage itself has its charms. What other city has moose grazing alongside the highways and chomping through suburban flower gardens; belukha whales breaching within yards of the coastal bike trail; or twenty hours of midsummer sunlight and magnificent hiking trails just a couple of miles from downtown?

Thanks to the warming effect of the Japan Current and the rain-shadowing beneficence of the Kenai and Chugach Mountains, you can spend the summer days in shorts and a T-shirt cycling the coastal bike trail, hiking to hilltops with fabulous views of the Alaska Range, or even swimming in one of the city's small lakes. There are more urban attractions too, not least the state's most cosmopolitan, and tolerably affordable, **dining and drinking** scene. As well, coffee culture is as strong here as in any West Coast city. That alone is enough to justify stopping for a couple of nights, but there are also a couple of excellent **museums** – the Anchorage Museum of Art and History and the Heritage Museum – and the ground-breaking Alaska Native Heritage Center.

Some history

The banks of Cook Inlet were first discovered around five thousand years ago when proto-Eskimos occupied sites along Turnagain Arm. Dena'ina Athapascans took their place by the time early Russian explorers came to exchange copper and iron for fish and furs, and traded in 1778 with British captain **James Cook** who was in search of the Northwest Passage. Later, the ever humble Cook named the whole inlet after himself, then dubbed one branch **Turnagain Arm** as he about-faced and tacked off to search further west.

By Cook's time, the **Russians** were well established in Alaska, and their influence twenty miles north of Anchorage in the Russian Orthodox church at Eklutna was the largest settlement in the region. It wasn't until 1912 that Congress sensed the need for greater access to the strategic coal fields and sanctioned the construction of a railway linking the port of Seward and the navigable rivers of the Interior. Construction was centered on the ice-free shores of Cook Inlet, a flat and barren spot that soon sprouted the fledgling tent city of **Anchorage**. Within weeks Anchorage was home to two thousand construction hopefuls. Five months later it was gone, the surrounding land was auctioned off in gridded lots leaving the creekside mud flats for the rail yards and docks. Some 650 lots were sold with the stipulation that any lots used for gambling, prostitution, or liquor production would be forfeited. The US post office used a literal description of the site and called the place **Anchorage**, a name which the residents failed to dislodge despite holding a referendum and picking Alaska City as the name for their new home. Since then Anchorage has been characterized by rapid but sporadic growth. By the beginning of the 1940s the city still had only 3500 residents but was soon to see the effect of a developing infrastructure, and a spinoff from the influx of New Deal settlers in the Mat-Su Valley. With the arrival of the military during World War II, Anchorage was firmly established as Alaska's dominant city, and statewide events – such as the construction of the Alaska Hwy – only served to reinforce its

MONEY FOR NOTHING – THE PERMANENT FUND DIVIDEND

Alaskans pay no income tax, and on top of that they reap the benefits of the **Permanent Fund Dividend**, paid out in the first week in October each year to every man, woman, and child who has spent ten months of the previous calendar year in Alaska. In recent years it has consistently topped $1500 (in 2000 it was $1963), so for a family of five it might form a quarter of their annual income, and provide an opportunity to stash some away for the kids' education, or just get frivolous. By mid-September, Alaskan companies start tapping into the mini-boom luring customers with attractive offers: airlines offer multiflight trips in return for the dividend check, and with winter approaching snow machine dealers do a roaring trade in their latest models. For people eking out a hand-to-mouth existence in the woods from hunting, trapping, and a little gold panning, the PFD is even more important. For them it is the only time in the year they have enough cash to stock up on spare parts, fishing lures, ammunition, fuel, and basic groceries.

Alaska took a smart approach to its oil revenues by instituting a state constitutional amendment in 1976 to set aside a quarter of all oil royalties as a kind of nest egg to be used as oil revenues declined. Very quickly the account reached embarrassing proportions and in 1982 the state made its first payment to residents in which ten percent of the interest gained (averaged over the last five years) was distributed among those who qualified. The payment has become such a staple of the Alaskan year that it would be political suicide to drop or substantially cut it – a strange situation in a state where anything that has the faintest whiff of socialism is widely reviled and ridiculed.

With the bull markets of recent years the Permanent Fund is now valued at over $28 billion a sum which, bizarrely, generates more revenue from interest than the state receives from its oil revenue.

high ranking position. The population jumped to 47,000 by the completion of the road link to Seward in the early 1950s – just in time for the discovery of oil on the Kenai Peninsula. This, statehood in 1959, and the establishment of Anchorage's international airport – which, being equidistant from New York and Tokyo, soon became a kind of sub-polar crossroads for long-distance flights – set an optimistic tone for the new decade. Confidence was soon rocked by the 1964 **Good Friday Earthquake** (see box, p.195), which destroyed an entire suburb, wrecked the city, and imprinted itself on the memories of a generation.

During the 1950s, a small oil drilling operation had been established on the Kenai Peninsula, so when enormous quantities of black gold were discovered at Prudhoe Bay in Alaska's arctic north, it made sense for oil companies to consolidate their operations In Anchorage. Fairbanks was the base for the construction of the Trans Alaska Pipeline (see box, p.454) but Anchorage continued to benefit from the new pool of skilled workers both fueling the demand and providing the wherewithal for continued development. When oil revenues started pouring in so fast they couldn't be spent, the benefits were divided proportional to the population, so it was Anchorage that got a slew of new and grandiose buildings downtown – library, sports arena, civic center, and more. But much of the money was diverted into the Permanent Fund (see box, overleaf) which helped ease the hardships brought on by low oil prices in the late 1980s. Today, Anchorage continues to grow, gradually shaking off its boom-and-bust persona and gaining a level of maturity as it copes with the economic difficulties thrown up by the decline in oil revenues.

Arrival, information, and city transport

As Alaska's major gateway city, Anchorage is the destination point for a sizeable portion of the state's international arrivals. If you're not driving the Alaska Hwy or cruising up through the Inside Passage you'll almost certainly arrive here. You're most likely to arrive **by air** from Seattle or Vancouver: get a right-side window seat for views of the inside passage, fjords, and glaciers prior to the magnificent descent into Anchorage airport – recently retitled the Ted Stevens International Airport, after Alaska's senior senator. Direct flights from outside North America (and all Delta flights) arrive at the North (international) Terminal, which only has a small visitor desk (daily 9am–3pm); to get to the main terminal board the airport shuttle which runs every 10 to 15 minutes.

Most visitors arrive at the main South (domestic) Terminal which, along with the usual restaurants and shops, has a **visitor information** desk (daily 9am–4pm) in the baggage claim area, ATMs (but no foreign exchange facilities), courtesy phones to some hotels, and luggage storage (see "Listings," p.214).

The airport is only five miles southwest of central Anchorage, so **getting downtown** is quick and fairly painless: taxis cost about $15 and are lined up outside the terminal. During the summer, bus #6 serves both airport terminals hourly (early May to early Sept daily 10am–6pm; $1); during spring, winter, and fall, the nearest city bus is #7, which picks up at the junction of International Airport Road and Spenard Road (over a mile away) hourly (6am–9pm; less frequently on weekends).

On the whole your best bet is with the **Borealis Airporter Shuttle** (☎1-888/436-3600 or 276-3600, *www.borealisshuttle.com*), which runs door-to-door and charges around $8 to the downtown area for the first person and $2 for every extra person to the same destination: there's a courtesy phone in the baggage claim area.

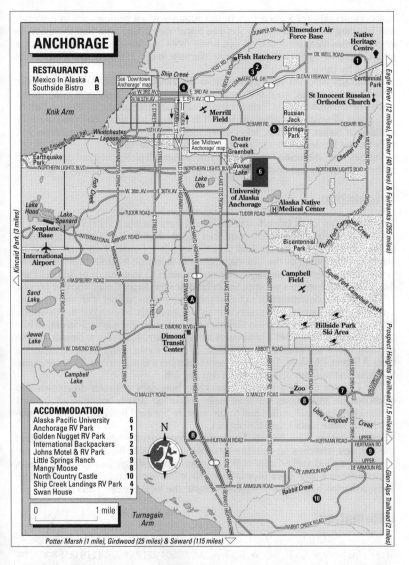

ANCHORAGE

RESTAURANTS
Mexico In Alaska	A
Southside Bistro	B

ACCOMMODATION
Alaska Pacific University	6
Anchorage RV Park	1
Golden Nugget RV Park	5
International Backpackers	2
Johns Motel & RV Park	3
Little Springs Ranch	9
Mangy Moose	8
North Country Castle	10
Ship Creek Landings RV Park	4
Swan House	7

0   1 mile

Potter Marsh (1 mile), Girdwood (25 miles) & Seward (115 miles)

For your first night's accommodation (or last night before departure), it is also worth considering staying at one of the places closest to the airport (see "Midtown and the airport" accommodation, p.191), which offer a courtesy airport pickup and dropoff. Drivers picking up **rental cars** will find desks for the major car rental agencies in the South Terminal (see p.213) while the smaller companies will actually meet you at the airport if you have a confirmed reservation – always a good idea in the summer when vehicles are in demand, and booking ahead will usually get you lower rates. Also note that these smaller companies frequently offer much lower rates in return for slightly older cars and off-airport agencies can charge slightly lower rates by avoiding a tax imposed by the airport authorities.

Anchorage owes its very existence to the construction of the rail line from Seward to Fairbanks, so it is no surprise that the **train station** is bang in the center of downtown on 1st Street, a fairly easy walk from all the downtown hotels: taxis meet all trains. Services are limited to a couple of trains a day (and are fully detailed in Basics p.36); the ticket office (daily 5.30am–5pm) fields inquiries and sells tickets for departures to Seward, Denali, and Fairbanks.

Various **long-distance buses** serve Anchorage, all picking up and dropping off at the main hotels and hostels (for more details see "Buses" in p.213).

Orientation

The city sits on Cook Inlet, 150 miles inland from the open waters of the Gulf of Alaska on a nub of land which splits two thirty-odd-mile-long fingers: Knik Arm to the north and Turnagain Arm to the south. It is bounded on three sides by water and the fourth by the Chugach Mountains, whose foothills provide the elevation for the city's more sought-after real estate. The vast woods of Kincaid Park drape over Anchorage's western tip; behind lies the airport, then the city proper.

The gridplan **downtown** area lies at the city's northern limit with avenues running east–west increasing numerically as you go south. Streets run north–south, those west of A Street progress alphabetically (though there is no J Street), while those east of A Street get alphabetical names – Barrow, Cordova, Denali, and so on. Addresses are numbered according to their eastern and western direction from A Street (think of A Street as zero); numbers along streets increase going south so that number 320 is between 3rd and 4th.

The Chester Creek greenbelt marks the boundary between downtown and **midtown**, an amorphous smear of malls and broad streets bounded on the east by the city's two universities and to the west by Spenard Road as well as the suburb of the same name), and the airport.

Beyond Tudor Road, **South Anchorage** comprises the whole southern half of the city, and stretches up onto the wealthier suburb of **Hillside**.

To gain a good appreciation of the city and surroundings, join up to five others on the full-day **Killer Tour** (April–Sept; $80; ☎258-7999), a minivan trip guided by Tony, a marine biologist who's passion about the local ecology runs deep.

Information

Anywhere accessible from Anchorage on a day-trip is considered within the scope of the **Anchorage CVB**, 524 W 4th Ave, AK 99501-2212 (☎276-4118 or 1-800/478-1255, fax 278-5559, *info@anchorage.net*, *www.anchorage.net*), who are happy to provide information in advance (but no drop-ins). Once in the city try the log-cabin **visitor center** corner of W 4th Avenue and F Street (daily: April, May & Sept 8am–6pm; June–Aug 7.30am–7pm, Oct–March 9am–4pm; ☎274-3531), a model for visitor centers throughout Alaska with a sod roof sprouting Jacob's ladder and wild onions in springtime. Here you can pick up the free, listings-packed *Anchorage Visitors Guide* and stacks of other visitor publications. Immediately behind the log cabin you can find a broader selection of leaflets, plus free direct-dial phones to a range of places to stay and tour companies.

Across the road you'll find the consolidated **Public Lands Information Center**, 605 W 4th Ave at F Street (June–Aug daily 9am–7pm; Sept to May Mon–Fri 10am–5.30pm; ☎271-2737, fax 271-2744, *www.nps.gov/aplic*), which manages recreational and conservation land throughout the state. As well as supplying you with brochures and maps they can provide cabin, camping, boating, fishing, hunting, and hiking information for central Alaska. There's also an Alaska Marine Highway information desk, and copies of *Ridgelines*, a handy newspaper (50¢) with details on hikes, camping, and day-use activities in the Chugach State Park which surrounds Anchorage.

For more on Anchorage's daily and weekly newspapers, as well as bookshops, map outlets, and the Internet, see "Listings," p.213.

City transport

Anchorage is a city designed around the car, but you can see the major sights, eat in good restaurants, and get back to your accommodation using no more than your own feet and the city bus system. Try to do anything in a hurry though and you're out of luck; possibly the best argument for **renting a car** in Alaska. Once equipped with a vehicle, getting used to Anchorage's traffic is rarely a problem. **Parking** is easy; every mall has a huge parking lot, and even downtown you'll find low-cost parking meters just a couple of blocks from where you need to be.

Buses

For such a spread out and thinly populated city the "People Mover" (*www.people-mover.org*) **bus system** does a remarkably good job of covering a lot of ground, though the limited hours of operation can be frustrating (Mon–Fri 6am – 10pm, Sat 8am–8pm, Sun 9.30am–6.30pm). However, some of the less popular routes shut down as early as 7pm, so be sure to find out what time the last bus is really going to come by. You can purchase your ticket from the driver (correct change only, bills accepted): $1 per ride, 10¢ for a transfer, or $2.50 for an all-day pass which can be purchased at the Transit Center (see below) and most Tesoro 2 Go stores, but not from the driver. All buses are equipped with **racks for bikes**.

Most routes start at the **Transit Center**, 6th Avenue and G Street (the 24-hr Rideline ☎343-6543 has operator assistance available Mon–Fri 8am–5pm), where you can obtain *The Ride Guide* ($1) detailing timetables for all routes, and the *Bus Map* route guide (50¢). South Anchorage is further served by the **Dimond Transit Center**, behind the Dimond Center Mall, five miles south of downtown.

The downtown "DASH" will scoot you around Anchorage's **free-travel zone** along 3rd and 9th avenues between Ingra and L streets (Mon–Fri 9am–3pm & 6–8pm), but it's of limited use since waiting for a bus often takes longer than walking.

You might also find some use for the **4th Avenue Trolley Tours**, 630 W 4th Ave (mid-May to mid-Sept 7–8 daily; ☎257-5609), highly orchestrated bus tours that provide useful transport to places ill served by the city buses. All tours start at $10, but go up to $15 if you wish to get on and off throughout the day; the best deal is the $20 three-day pass valid on all routes. From outside the 4th Avenue Theatre, the West Trolley Tour loops southwest to Kincaid Park, the Aviation Museum, Point Woronzof, Earthquake Park, and Westchester Lagoon. The South Trolley tour is most useful for the zoo and the Glen Alps Trailhead (see box, p.201), and you are only likely to need the East Trolley Tour to get out to the Alaska Native Heritage Center.

Cycling

Although **bike paths** in Anchorage are wonderful, they're seldom the shortest route between two points, and a bike as your only transport option is not a great idea. Anchorage's main roads are four-lane drag strips hogged by drivers whose lack of bike-awareness threatens cyclists very existence: **wear a helmet**. Fortunately, green "Bike Route" signs herd riders onto the sidewalk; not exactly a bike path but the total absence of pedestrians makes it safer than the road.

Cycling in Anchorage is best following one of the **bike trails** – smooth, paved affairs also open to walkers, rollerbladers, and roller skiers. Foremost among them is the **Tony Knowles Coastal Trail** (see p.198) running from downtown to Kincaid Park (12 miles). At Westchester Lagoon, just south of downtown, the Tony Knowles Trail joins the **Chester Creek Trail**, a streamside meander through midtown verdure towards the university campuses. Keen mountain bikers should make for the undulating terrain, beaver pools, and mud of **Far North Bicentennial Park**, or the steep trails of the Chugach State Park just beyond.

There are several **bike rental** places around town, most offering fairly high-quality machines for $20–25 a day including, helmet, lock, and a map of good routes. About the most convenient outlet if you are downtown is Downtown Bicycle Rental, 333 W 4th Ave (mid-May to mid-Sept daily 9am–7pm, sporadically in winter; ☎279-5293), which rents bikes on a first-come, first-served basis and requires a major credit card: rates are $15 for 3hr and $29 for 24hr; tandems go for $43 a day. In addition, there are retail and repair shops, and several other reputable bike rental agencies in midtown; see "Listings," p.213.

Accommodation

Anchorage must have more **places to stay** than the rest of the state put together, but since most visitors to the state spend at least a couple of nights here places fill up fast. From the beginning of June until the end of August it is critical to have something booked weeks ahead. May can be busy too; by mid-September things quiet down considerably.

Campers and RV drivers will find sites scattered all around the city, but everyone else ends up either **downtown**, in **Spenard** close to the airport, or on **the Hillside**, Anchorage's swanky suburb and home to some of the best B&Bs.

Prices strictly follow demand. In summer, hotels can pretty much charge what they like, and they do. Even quite modest motels go for over $100 a night, while the big hotels let their most basic room for upwards of $250, the same price you'd pay for the presidential suite in winter. B&Bs vary their prices less, but they play to the same rules: expect thirty to forty percent reductions on summer rates once winter rolls around. Visitors in early May, late September, and October can expect shoulder season prices somewhere between these extremes. Hostels and campgrounds tend to hold their prices year round making them less competitive in the off season, especially if you are traveling in a small group: in winter four people can stay at the *Sheraton* for little more than a dorm bed each at a hostel.

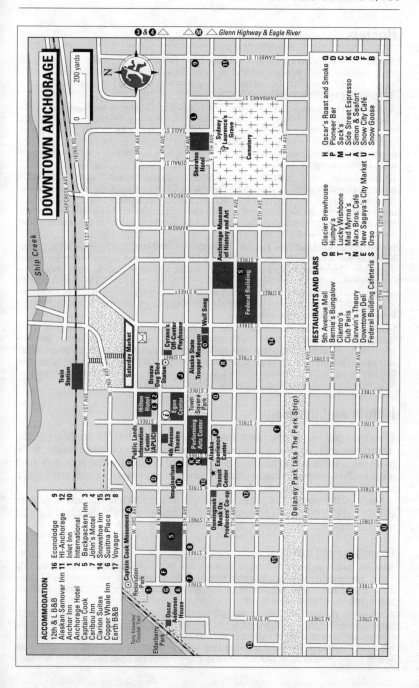

DOWNTOWN ANCHORAGE

3 & 4 △   △ Ⓜ △ Glenn Highway & Eagle River

N

0   200 yards

Ship Creek

Train Station

Saturday Market

Bronze Dog Sled Statue

Cyrano's Off-Center Playhouse

Anchorage Museum of History and Art

Wolf Song

Alaska State Trooper Museum

Federal Building

Sheraton Hotel

Sydney Laurence's Grave

Cemetery

Hilton Hotel

Egan Center

Town Square Park

Public Lands Information Center (APLIC)

4th Avenue Theatre

Performing Arts Center

Alaska Experience Center

Imaginarium

Transit Center

Oomingmak Musk Ox Producers' Co-op

Delaney Park (aka The Park Strip)

Captain Cook Monument

Resolution Park

Oscar Anderson House

Elderberry Park

Tony Knowles Coastal Trail

ACCOMMODATION

12th & L B&B	16
Alaskan Samovar Inn	11
Anchor Inn	1
Anchorage Hotel	2
Captain Cook	7
Caribou Inn	4
Clarion Suites	14
Copper Whale Inn	6
Earth B&B	13
Econolodge	9
HI-Anchorage	12
Inlet Inn	10
International	3
Backpackers Inn	5
John's Motel	15
Snowshoe Inn	5
Susitna Place	6
Voyager	8

RESTAURANTS AND BARS

5th Avenue Mall	O	Oscar's Roast and Smoke	Q
Bernie's Bungalow	R	Pioneer Bar	D
Cilantro's	T	Sack's	C
Club Paris	J	Side Street Espresso	K
Darwin's Theory	N	Simon & Seafort	G
Downtown Deli	E	New Sagaya's City Market	F
Federal Building Cafeteria	S	Snow City Café	I
Glacier Brewhouse	O	Snow Goose	B
Humpy's	R		
Lucky Wishbone	M		
Mad Myrna's	L		
Marx Bros. Café	A		
New Sagaya's City Market			
Orso			

Hostels

Alaska Pacific University, 4101 University Drive (☎564-8238 no sooner than mid-April). From mid-May to July twin-bedded student rooms are available at $38 per person. It's not in a very convenient location and you have to bring your own sleeping bag or sheets, but in the tight summer season it may be your best option. ①.

Anchorage Guesthouse, 2001 Hillcrest Drive (☎ & fax 274-0408; *www.akhouse.com*,). This upscale backpacker-style hostel, just over a mile from downtown, is handy for midtown and the Coastal Trail (bikes available for $10 a half-day). Other perks include sheets, towels, breakfast, use of kitchen, free gear storage, free local calls, and Internet access. They offer dorms with bunks and single beds ($24) as well as private rooms with double or king-sized beds. Dorms ①, rooms ②.

HI-Anchorage, 700 H St (☎276-3635, fax 276-7772, *www.alaska.net~hianch*). A functional hostel in a great location – a block from the Transit Center – though the afternoon lockout (from noon to 5pm), and 1am curfew are less than appealing. Kitchen, laundry, luggage storage ($1 a day per bag), and shuttle services (dropoff and pickup) are available. There's a four-night maximum stay in summer. Dorm beds $16 for members, $19 for nonmembers, private rooms ① – reserve well in advance.

International Backpackers Inn, 3601 Peterkin Ave (☎274-3870). The *Inn* is actually a collection of five suburban homes operated as a backpacker hostel a couple of miles east of downtown. There's no lockout or curfew, rooms are shared with up to three people, and there's access to the kitchen, laundry, and TV-equipped common area. The neighborhood's not great, but it's not dangerous either; take the #45 bus (every 30min, hourly at weekends) to Bragaw & Peterkin, and walk west three blocks. Camping on the grounds costs $10; dorms beds are $15 (max three per room). ①.

Spenard Hostel International, 2845 W 42nd Pl (☎248-5036, fax 248-5063, *www.alaskalife.net/spnrdhstl/hostel*). Friendly hostel about 1.5 miles from the airport and four from downtown with bikes for rent ($5 a day). Most dorms are separate sex, there are no private rooms, and you'll be expected to do a small chore, but at $15 a bed it's great value. Also features a garden with barbecue, spacious communal areas, low-cost baggage storage, Internet access, and no lockout. Accessible by bus #6 or taxi ($7). ①.

Hotels and motels

There are two major concentrations of hotels and motels. In the heart of the **downtown** area business hotels predominate, some all-out five-star affairs, some more modest but still attractive. A few blocks to the east, as the high rises melt away to the low-rent and semi-industrial areas around Merrill Field, you'll find a concentration of cheaper motels, the best of which we've listed below.

Many of the rest of the places – a couple of large hotels and lots of smaller motels – are in the **Spenard** neighborhood, close to much of the city's nightlife and the airport; all places offer airport pickups.

Downtown and north

Alaskan Samovar Inn, 720 Gambell St at 6th Ave (☎277-1511 or 1-800/478-1511, fax 272-5192). A reasonably priced motel within an easy walk of downtown, with large rooms, cable TV, and spa baths. Better still, they've got suites with a jacuzzi in the room, a bottle of champagne, and breakfast supplied. ④–⑦.

Anchorage Hotel, 330 E St at 4th Ave (☎272-4553 or 1-800/544-0988, fax 277-4483, *anchoragehotel@alaska.net*). This small hotel (once frequented by painter Sydney Laurence) has been around since the birth of Anchorage and acts as a counterpoint to the over-the-top business hotels surrounding it. The decor is understated and the overall feel is personal and relaxed but with all the business facilities, plus free newspaper, and continental breakfast. Suites ⑧, rooms ⑦.

Captain Cook, 4th Ave at K St (☎276-6000 or 1-800/843-1950, fax 343-2298, *www.captaincook* *.com*). Formal and somber in tone, it is the oil-man's hotel of choice with every luxury imaginable – five restaurants with well-stocked bars, fabulous views (one at $1500 a night), health club with pool, and all the trimmings. Suites $30–50 above normal room rates of $260. ⑨.

Caribou Inn, 501 L St at 5th Ave (☎272-0444, fax 274-4828, *caribou@alaska.net*). It is well worth stepping up from the cheaper hotels to these ageing but comfortable rooms (some with private bath ⑤), which come with complimentary airport and train station shuttle, HBO, and a free breakfast. ④/⑤.

Inlet Inn, 539 H St at 6th Ave (☎277-5541, fax 277-3108, *inletinn@alaska.com*). Undoubtedly the cheapest hotel rooms downtown, and the complimentary airport and train station shuttle, cable TV, and free local calls make it a real bargain, though it can be noisy. The public areas and some of the decor leave a fair bit to be desired, but all rooms have private bath. ③.

Snowshoe Inn, 826 K St (☎258-7669, fax 258-7463, *showshoeinnak@aol.com*). Immaculately maintained and reasonably priced, nonsmoking hotel where all sixteen rooms – ask for one with an outside window as some look into a courtyard – come with cable TV and VCR, microwave, and a continental breakfast. Despite the odd piece of antique-styled furniture it still has a slightly sterile feel. Suites ⑥, rooms ⑤.

Voyager, 501 K St at 5th Ave (☎277-9501 or 1-800/247-9070, fax 274-0333, *www.voyagerhotel* *.com*). The best of the mid- to upper-range hotels featuring spacious rooms (with kitchenette) and all the amenities of the stuffy business hotels without the stuffiness. Entirely nonsmoking. Reserve well in advance in summer. ⑦.

Midtown and the airport

Arctic Inn Motel, 842 W International Airport Rd (☎561-1328, fax 562-8701). Good-value motel that's close to the airport (about $7 in a taxi) and local restaurants but a little noisy at the front. Rooms are somewhat drab but spacious and clean and come with HBO, a microwave, and fridge. ④.

Puffin Inn, 4400 Spenard Rd at Turnagain Blvd (☎243-4044 or 1-800/478-3346, fax 248-6853, *www.puffininn.net*). The most appealing of the mid-priced motels close to the airport. Well maintained with simple but attractive decor, free local calls, cable TV, complimentary newspaper, coffee and muffins, and free airport transfers. ⑤.

Qupqugiac Inn, 640 W 36th Ave at Arctic Blvd (☎562-5681, *www.qupq.com*). Excellent inn that falls somewhere between a hostel and a hotel, with simply furnished but attractively decorated and well-priced private double and twin rooms. All share baths and rooms at the front can be noisy, but each has cable TV, and the rate includes a bagel-and-latte breakfast in the *Q Café* downstairs (see p.207). ②.

Spenard Motel, 3960 Spenard Rd (☎243-6917, fax 248-4614, *spenardjohn@gci.net*). Clean and comfortable motel convenient for the airport with a courtesy phone in baggage claim and free pickup anytime. All rooms have private bath, cable TV, and free local calls, and some come with spa baths. ④.

B&Bs

Anchorage's B&B market is booming with new places opening all the time to cater to the massive summer influx. They range from modest houses to palaces where the attention to details borders on fanatical. The two main concentrations of B&Bs are **downtown**, within easy walking distance of just about everywhere (including the bus station for ventures further afield), and in **the Hillside** area, over five miles southeast of the center on the flanks of the Chugach Mountains and close to the hiking trailheads. You really need a car to stay out here, but if you have one and don't mind the slight inconvenience of having to drive everywhere, this is the place to be – scenic and quiet. It is worth bearing in mind that B&Bs aren't allowed roadside signs and city ordinances limit the size of signs that are permitted, so you may need to look hard to find your bed for the night. Also, there is an increasing tendency to charge a premium (around $20) for one-night stays: ask when you book.

Downtown and north

Anchor Inn, 326 L St (☎277-2624, fax 279-2063, *anchorin@alaska.net*). Small B&B with tree-obscured views of Cook Inlet and comfortable rooms each with a large bed, sofa, cable TV, and most with a kitchenette. There's an enticing deck out front and Internet access is available. ⑤.

Copper Whale Inn, 440 L St (☎258-7999, fax 258-6213, *www.copperwhale.com*). Large and welcoming B&B ideally situated in the center of downtown. Rooms are comfortably furnished and have fitted blackout shades – a boon on the long summer evenings – but (intentionally) come without phones or TVs. An extensive buffet-style breakfast is served in the lounge which overlooks Cook Inlet. Private bath ⑦, shared bath ⑤.

Earth B&B, 1001 W 12th Ave (☎279-9907, fax 279-9862, *www.alaskaone.com/earthbb*). Enthusiastically and liberally run this is home away from home for Denali-bound climbers during the season and a broad cross-section the rest of the year. It's basic but very accommodating with a garage for drying and sorting gear, bikes to use, a barbecue out back and flexible deals for groups. Continental breakfast included and owner Margriet runs her own tour business (see "Basics," p.10). Bus #3, #36 or #60 from downtown. Private bathroom ⑤, shared bathroom ④.

Susitna Place, 727 N St (☎274-3344, fax 272-4141, *www.alaska.net/~suplace*). Central lodge with a comfortable communal area overlooking Cook Inlet and Mount Susitna. Rooms range from smallish shared-bath affairs (just ④), to larger rooms with private baths, some with sun deck and water views, to the huge, and always popular, Susitna Suite with magnificent views, whirlpool tub and a private deck with views of Denali. Suite ⑦, sea view ⑤, rooms ④.

12th and L, 1134 L St (☎276-1225, fax 276-1224, *www.anchorage-lodging.com*). Quite simply, this is a lovely, well-maintained B&B just a few blocks walk from downtown. Cable-equipped rooms are tastefully furnished, there's a self-serve continental breakfast, and liberal daytime use of the kitchen is available. Plus, guests get half-price bikes from Downtown Bicycle Rental. Bus #3, #36 or #60 from downtown. Large suite ⑥, rooms ⑤.

The Hillside and around

Little Springs Ranch, 8324 E 130th St (☎345-9499, fax 345-3331, *www.alakan.com /littlesprings*). Spacious and welcoming home right on the edge of the Hillside almost in the Chugach Mountains and with long views over Cook Inlet. Rooms are fairly plain but come with private bath, robes, and cable TV – plus there's an outdoor hot tub, though if you go for the suite (⑦) you get a jacuzzi tub in the room. ⑥.

Mangy Moose, 5560 E 112th St (☎346-8052, fax 346-8053, *www.bedandbreakfastnetwork .com/mangymoose*). Neither the prominent moose's head in the lounge nor the rest of the house is the slightest bit mangy; in fact, this is one of the nicest B&Bs around. Attractive wood-paneled rooms either share bathrooms or have private facilities and everyone meets in the communal lounge with TV, VCR, and a self-serve kitchenette. Good breakfasts too. ⑤.

North Country Castle, 14600 Joanne Court (☎ & fax 345-7296, *www.customcpu.com /commercial/nccbnb*). Excellent value if a little distant from the sights, this is a modern, informal home (as little like a castle as you could imagine) tucked in among the white spruce at the southern limit of Anchorage. The smaller rooms share a bathroom and views of Flattop Mountain; the suite (⑥) sports a wonderful view over Turnagain Arm from its private deck and has its own fireplace. ⑤.

Camping and RV parks

Tent campers are not well catered for in Anchorage: the nearest place that is at all pleasant to pitch a tent is *Centennial Camper Park*, five miles (a half-hour bus ride) east of downtown. With your own vehicle you might find it more pleasant commuting into the city from *Eagle River Campground* (opposite) or at the wooded sites 27 miles south at Bird Creek. **RV drivers** are better served with several full service (and pricey) places close to town.

Anchorage RV Park, 7300 N Muldoon Rd (☎338-7275 or 1-800/400-7275, fax 337-9007, *www.anchrvpark.com*). Very large, well-organized, and well-appointed RV park with wooded landscaping and pull-through sites with cable TV. No tents. $29.

Eagle River Campground, Glenn Hwy, Eagle River. A first-come, first-served Alaska State Parks campground twelve miles north of Anchorage with fire pits, water, and outhouses, and fishing, white-water rafting, and short hiking trails right on the doorstep. $15. Take the Hiland Rd exit off the expressway.

John's Motel & RV Park, 3543 Mountain View Drive (☎277-4332 or 1-800/478-4332, fax 272-0739, *www.johnsmotel.com*). Mostly a gravel lot next to a busy road, but good value with a laundromat and free showers. Full hookup $22.

Ship Creek Landings RV Park, 150 N Ingra (☎227-0877 or 1-888/778-7700, fax 425/882-2479, *www.alaskarv.com*,). Very central RV and campground that's close to the train tracks and yet still quite secluded. Tent sites on specially constructed sand pads ($11), RV sites from dry ($13) to full hookup pull-through ($27).

The City

In their eagerness to hightail into the "real" Alaska, visitors tend to overlook Anchorage as a destination. There is, however, plenty to see in town, and it's worth spending some time here experiencing your only taste of big-city Alaska. The best introduction is simply to wander around downtown, in the northwest corner of Anchorage, getting a flavor for a city grown too fast; a blend of old and new, urban blight and rural parks that can still have something of a shanty town feel to it. As you walk around, you can't miss how the boom and bust nature of Anchorage's development has evidenced itself, even if the glitzy high-rise **Phillips 66 Oil Building** – which critics half-jokingly refer to as the State Capitol – still looks out of place next to prefabricated clapboard houses and abandoned lots. The benefit of oil revenue is evident in the Performing Arts Center, and the museum, both seen by walking around the downtown area and taking in other key sights: the salmon waters of **Ship Creek** where the original tent city sprung up, the **cemetery** full of the headstones of prominent sourdoughs, and the **Anchorage Museum of Art and History**.

The central business district is contained to the south, below the **Park Strip** (aka Delaney Park), a former air strip and golf course as well as the site of the 50-ton statehood bonfire in 1959. Today, it mainly supports summer evening softball and soccer games. Further south you're into the malls of **midtown**. You'll most likely find yourself here during the day buying books, renting outdoor equipment, eating, and visiting the **Heritage Museum**, then again at night for the bars of the Spenard district.

Immediately north of downtown, the city butts up against Elmendorf Air Force Base and Fort Richardson Military Reservation. There is no room for downtown to grow while the military retain their presence – and there is little reason to suggest they won't. The Glenn Hwy skirts the southern flanks of the bases on its way north to the celebrated **Alaska Native Heritage Center**.

Of course, you probably won't spend long on the highways and sidewalks of Anchorage, one of the best things about the city is the opportunity to be **outdoors** – away from cityscapes and pavement. On a fine day it's hard to beat a late afternoon stroll (or cycle) along the waterside **Tony Knowles Coastal Trail** or, more adventurously, the encircling Chugach Mountains and the stiff hikes up Flattop and Wolverine Peak. The wilder country beyond hides the city's hiking gem, the two-day **Crow Pass Trail** which terminates by the delightful Eagle River Nature Center. There's plenty more to do in and around the city with such things as **rock climbing** and **swimming** covered fully in "Listings," p.213.

The big city peters out beyond the limits of the Anchorage Bowl, but there are a few places you might consider as **day-trips from Anchorage**: to the south, Girdwood (p.220) and Portage Glacier (p.223) lie within an hour's drive along Turnagain Arm; and to the north Eklutna (p.326), Palmer (p.330), and the Independence Mine at Hatcher Pass (p.338) are all easily accessible by car.

Downtown Anchorage

A good place to begin exploring downtown is from the front door of Anchorage's major Art Deco building, the classic pastel-toned **4th Avenue Theatre**, 630 W 4th Ave. Already architecturally dated when it was built in the early 1940s, it remains a fine example of the style, all mahogany and Italian marble, ziggurats and chevron friezes, and a proscenium flanked by floor-to-ceiling relief panels depicting Old and New Alaska scenes – uplifting and positive in true Deco fashion. It spent much of its life as Anchorage's premier cinema and, though now little used, is often open during the day so you can wander in and take a peek.

On the corner of 4th Avenue and D Street is the striking **Wendler Building**, Anchorage's only corner turret structure, which overlooks a bronze sculpture of a sled dog – the ceremonial starting point of the Iditarod (see box, p.336) and the real start for numerous races. Taking F Street north, you'll notice that the road slopes down a dozen feet – a consequence of subsidence in the 1964 quake – to 3rd where a parking lot between here and C Street transforms itself into the **Saturday market** (mid-May to mid-Sept 10am–6pm), selling everything from oversized Mat-Su vegetables to arts and crafts, some of it really good, some just cheap souvenirs. A block north lies the **Statehood Monument**, a bronze statue depicting Eisenhower's head being attacked by a bald eagle – or so it seems from some angles. Below, the hillside drops away to the site of the original tent city, now occupied by rail yards and the restrained Art Deco form of the **train station**. Beyond it flows **Ship Creek**, often flanked by folk fishing for king salmon just yards away from the city offices – some workers even cast away their lunch hour down here.

Second Avenue runs west from the Statehood Monument past a handful of Anchorage's original homes – nos. 542, 605, 610, and 618 (none open to the public) – to the start of the Tony Knowles Coastal Trail (see p.198). There's more to be seen at the corner of 3rd Avenue and L Street where a nest of steps and viewing platforms known as **Resolution Park** is surmounted by the **Captain Cook Monument**, a regal statue of the great navigator. The waters which once bore his ship, the *Resolution*, now bear his name and stretch away to Mount Susitna and the Alaska Range. On a clear day the dominant peaks of Mount Foraker and Denali can be seen presiding over the city in the distance.

Those who expect verdure in their parks should weave south to Elderberry Park, a grassy quadrant cut off from the water by the rail line and the Coastal Trail. Alongside is the 1915 **Oscar Anderson House Museum**, 420 M St (June to mid-Sept Tues–Sat 11am–4pm; $3), a lovely two-story, which was once the

GOOD FRIDAY EARTHQUAKE

The confidence and hope for the future nurtured by statehood in 1959 took a devastating blow at 5.36pm on March 27th, 1964, when Southcentral Alaska was rocked by the **Good Friday Earthquake**, the most powerful earthquake ever recorded in North America. It was centered below Miners Lake on the northern edge of Prince William Sound, some forty miles west of Valdez, and about eighty miles east of Anchorage, rating an astonishing 8.6 on the Richter Scale (compared to 8.3 for the 1906 San Francisco quake). Even more fearsome, it lasted close to five minutes and was followed by numerous devastating aftershocks.

All over Southcentral, whole blocks of buildings were flattened, railroad lines were kinked, roads were uplifted at 45 degrees, and cars were pitched into shop windows with their tail fins pointing skyward. In Anchorage, there is a twelve-foot drop between 3rd and 2nd avenues, and **Earthquake Park** now stands on land which liquefied – virtually swallowing the suburb of Turnagain Heights. All the houses have been cleared away but explanatory panels and a rucked-up landscape tell the tale. An underwater landslide in Prince William Sound produced huge waves, which swept over Cordova, Valdez, Whittier, Seward, and Kodiak Island, accounting for 119 of the 131 deaths that were attributed to the earthquake. **Valdez** was devastated to the point that the site was abandoned and the town had to be completely rebuilt four miles away on more stable ground. Further along the coast, **Kodiak** lost its boat harbor and a fishing boat was pitched over waterfront buildings to be left high and dry two streets back.

home of Oscar Anderson, a Swedish butcher who was the eighteenth resident of early Anchorage. Guides lead you through period-furnished rooms of what was the city's first privately built wood-frame residence, completed soon after the town's lots were auctioned off.

Back in the center of town, the **Alaska Experience Center**, 705 W 6th Ave at G Street (daily: mid-May to mid-Sept 9am–9pm; mid-Sept to mid-May noon–6pm), projects an eminently missable movie on the state and its wonders onto a 180-degree wraparound screen ($7). There's also a considerably more diverting earthquake exhibit ($5, joint entry $10) with displays on the 1964 quake (see box, above), and a 15-minute film (and jolting quake simulation) featuring a wonderfully Germanic-sounding professor expounding the geophysics of it all and linking poignant tales from Anchorage residents. Kids will be better off at the nearby **Imaginarium Science Discovery Center**, 737 W 5th Ave at G Street (Mon–Sat 10am–6pm, Sun noon–5pm; $5), packed with hands-on experiments using prisms, pendulums, gears, and a contraption which makes giant soap bubbles around you, along with a tide pool full of local marine life and instructional material on earthquakes and the northern lights.

Big shows and the few top-flight bands that make it to Alaska all play the acoustically impressive **Alaska Center for the Performing Arts**, 6th Avenue between F and G streets (aka PAC; tickets ☎1-800/478-7328 or 263-ARTS, *www.carrstix.com*). You might consider popping in to see either **Sky Song** (late May to mid-Sept daily 9am–9pm; $7), a forty-minute northern lights and wildlife slide show put to classical music, or more temptingly, one of two IMAX films (mid-May to late Sept daily 2–9pm; one film $10, both $14). The staple IMAX is *Alaska Spirit of the Wild*, shown every second hour with some impressive footage of breaching whales, bears catching salmon, polar bears reclining in the snow, and glaciers calving at something close to actual size. On alternate hours they show *Bears* (the title gives the subject away) shot mostly in Alaska and Churchill, Canada.

Out front is the **Town Square Park**, a riot of blooms in summer overlooked by a whales-in-the-arctic mural by renowned environmental community artist WyLand.

You'll need to have fairly special interests to be attracted by the **Alaska State Trooper Museum**, 320 W 6th Ave at D Street (Mon–Fri 10am–5pm, Sat noon–4pm; free), which celebrates law enforcement in the state. The star exhibit, a 1952 Hudson Hornet in State Trooper livery, is visible through the window as you pass en route to **Wolf Song of Alaska**, 6th Avenue at C Street (June–Aug Mon–Fri 10am–7pm, Sat 10am–6pm, Sun noon–5pm; rest of year Mon–Fri 11am–6pm, Sat 11am–5pm, Sun noon–5pm; $3; *www.wolfsongalaska.org*), the public face of a non-profit organization aiming to educate the masses on Alaska's most intriguing and misunderstood mammal – the wolf. They're committed to building a 500-acre wolf study and observation facility in Anchorage in the near future, but in the meantime you'll have to make do with this homage: wildlife dioramas, radio collars, and some wonderful photos and prints.

Continuing east past the back of the Anchorage Museum of History & Art (see below) you come to the **Anchorage Memorial Park Cemetery** (open daily), where Alaskans of note wish to be buried. Highly respected pioneers ended up in plots along the north perimeter along with artist Sydney Laurence, who is marked with a palette-shaped headstone. Elsewhere the upright whalebone ribs marking Inupiat graves mix with propeller blades of pioneer aviators and three-bar Russian Orthodox crosses. It would be a peaceful place to idle away half an hour if not for the constant drone of small planes from nearby **Merrill Field**, one of the nation's busiest airfields – only a mile from downtown – with more than 230,000 takeoffs and landings annually.

Anchorage Museum of History & Art

Even if you're only spending a night or two in Anchorage, be certain to visit the **Anchorage Museum of History & Art**, 121 W 7th Ave at A Street (June to mid-Sept Sun–Fri 9am–9pm, Sat 9am–6pm; mid-Sept to May Tues–Sat 10am–6pm, Sun 1–5pm; $6.50; *www.ci.anchorage.ak.us*), an enjoyable museum easily covered in a couple of hours. Time your visit to take in one of the free **museum tours** (10am, 11am, 1pm & 2pm), and one of the **films** in the auditorium, both included with your entry ticket and usually well worth a few minutes of your time.

The legacy of the 1970s oil windfall is immediately apparent in the museum's opulent central atrium with its expensive fine-grained wood, preserved totem pole, and arresting sculptures mainly by Native Alaskan artists. Museum displays occupy the upper floor moving chronologically through the state's history, beginning with exquisite dioramas of village life. These lead on to full-size re-creations of Native houses along with an 1830 Russian blockhouse relocated from where it once defended St Michael near the Yukon delta, and mock-ups of a goldminer's hut, a 1920s Anchorage home, and a wartime Quonset hut. All this is given some context in well laid-out cases which, though light on artifacts, illustrate the changes that Alaska has undergone during the last two centuries. Here too are gorgeous examples of carved walrus ivory: cribbage boards, candle holders, even an engraved map of the Yukon. Alongside there's a small but instructive collection of Native **basketware**: exemplary pieces illustrate the open-weave Yup'ik coiled-grass style, Tlingit spruceroot weaves, and Kobuk River woven birch-bark designs, plus super-fine Aleut baskets with up to 1000 stitches per square inch, and Iñupiat vessels constructed from whale baleen, a material that is traditionally worked only by men. Note the presence of Russian, and later American, influence as European patterns get worked into the designs.

The upper floor catches up to the present with discussions on the role of telecommunications in modern Alaska, the pivotal part played by air travel, logging displays with a rather camp looking timber worker, and, inevitably, paeans to the oil industry with scale models of petrochemical installations and a slice of the pipeline.

The **lower floor** is given over to **Alaskan art**, mostly works by **Alaskan** (or adoptive Alaskan) artists but also paintings of an Aleut man and woman from the late eighteenth century done by John Webber, ship's artist on James Cook's third voyage. Art-loving Alaskans all but genuflect at mention of **Sydney Laurence**, widely regarded as the most accomplished historical painter of the Alaskan landscape. He remains largely unknown outside the Pacific Northwest, but his masterwork, *Mount McKinley*, is given pride of place, the ice-white peak of Denali shining back at you through the alpenglow. Born in Brooklyn in 1865, he spent time developing his style in Europe – there's a selection of his works in an adjoining room along with a portable painting kit – but initially came to Alaska in 1904 to prospect for gold. Limited success gradually forced him into photography, his Anchorage studio supporting frequent painting forays into the wilds. By the mid-1920s his reputation, built on a lifelong passion for painting Mount McKinley, effectively gave him a monopoly on its depiction in oil. He died in 1940 and is buried in the Anchorage Cemetery (see opposite).

Despite having over two dozen Laurence works on display, the museum has nothing on display by his Detroit-born near contemporary, **Eustace Ziegler** (or "Zieg" as he was usually known). His landscapes are less the subject than the frame in which to set his subjects – trappers, fishermen, Native Alaskans – often shown outside the stereotypical roles common in Alaskan art of the time.

In more recent times, Laurence and Ziegler have been joined by **Fred Machetanz**, probably the most popular artist in Alaska today. His ascendancy is partly on the back of purchases by large corporations who find his anodyne canvases – with recurrent motifs of polar bears, blue water and sky, and alpenglow – perfect for large public spaces and company boardrooms. *Serenity, Where Men and Dogs Seem Small* and others can seem little more than adult painting-by-numbers, but it is helpful when viewing them in the gallery to look at some of his earlier works to see how his painting developd from early oils of sourdoughs and native life.

Modern painters to look out for in the gallery include **Spence Guerin**, represented by his luminous cloudscape *Moon over Matanuska*, and **Rosemary Redmond** whose abstract landscape *Somewhere East of the Sun and West of the Moon* stands in stark contrast to Sydney Laurence's *Mount McKinley* just along the wall. Look too for paintings and sculpture by Native Alaskans, particularly Lawrence Beck's humorous *Punk Walrus Spirit* and Lawrence Ullaq Ahvaliana's more sensitive *Waiting for the Wolf Dance*. There's so much to take in here it's easy to spend several hours and you might want to take a break in the excellent atrium restaurant, and offshoot of downtown's *Marx Bros Café* (see p.206).

Midtown and the coastal trail

Provided you're not in a tearing hurry to get someplace in midtown (and especially if you are cycling), the best approach is along the **Tony Knowles Coastal Trail**, which runs twelve paved miles along Knik Arm from the western end of 2nd Avenue downtown to Kincaid Park (see "South Anchorage" below). On any fine day you'll be among power walkers, cyclists, rollerbladers – and, in winter, skiers and ski-jorers – all making the best of the long views over tidal flats to **Mount Susitna**, locally known as The Sleeping Lady: it takes some imagination, but apparently she has her arms crossed over her chest. A mile south of downtown you weave around **Westchester Lagoon**, a waterfowl sanctuary usually alive with ducks and geese. Here, the **Chester Creek Trail** cuts inland through the Chester Creek Greenbelt effectively separating downtown from **midtown**. Staying on the Coastal Trail you pass **Bootleggers' Cove**, where stills supplied Anchorage's speakeasies from the city's founding until the end of prohibition in 1933. This whole coastline was affected by the 1964 Good Friday earthquake (see box, p.195), but nowhere more so than **Earthquake Park**, three miles from downtown, the site of Anchorage's most extensive and destructive landslide. Ninety seconds into the quake the clays underlying the Turnagain Heights suburb effectively liquefied, destroying 75 homes and killing four people. There is a blockish sculpture, fenceposts, and concrete barriers, all designed in jagged forms, alluding to the effects of the quake. Nearby, explanatory panels fill in the details, but to actually see the results you'll need to ferret among the birch trees where the ground appears as scrunched paper on a grand scale. The Coastal Trail continues past the teenage hangout of **Point Woronzof** and on to Kincaid Park, but if you are midtown-bound you'll need to cut inland from Earthquake Park following Northern Lights Boulevard (the fairly frequent #36 bus comes within half a mile of Earthquake Park, except Sun).

If you are driving head south from the city to Aircraft Drive and the western end of **Lake Hood**, believably claimed as the largest floatplane harbor in the world with up to eight hundred takeoffs and landings on a peak summer day, and a record 1200 on one day in 1984. Any time the water isn't frozen there is a constant drone of taxiing Cessnas, and on a sunny day it can be surprisingly pleasant to hang out here and dream of the planes' exotic destinations: remote lakes and tiny Native villages probably well outside your budget.

The *Fancy Moose* bar in the *Regal Alaskan* hotel at the eastern end of Lake Spenard makes for more comfortable plane-watching, but aviation fanatics won't want to pass up the **Alaska Aviation Heritage Museum**, 4721 Airport Drive (daily: mid-May to mid-Sept 9am–6pm; limited winter hours call ahead; $8; ☎248-5325), perched on the shores of Lake Hood right by the airport. Grabbing visitors' attention a couple of hangars devoted to the lives and machines of the pilots who played such a pivotal role in making Alaska what it is today, stuffed with hagiographic displays on these heroes and heroines. There are intricate scale models of just about every plane in the state, and extensive coverage of Alaska's role in World War II provide the framework for the crown jewels of Alaskan aviation, a couple of dozen pre-1950 planes mostly restored on site. Their pride and joy is the 1928 Stearman C2B that did the run to Nome during the diphtheria epidemic (see p.468), made the first landing and rescue on Mount McKinley in 1932, and was flown by a roll call of Alaska's aviation pioneers – Noel Wien, Carl Ben Eielson, Harold Gillam, and Joe Crosson, to name just a few.

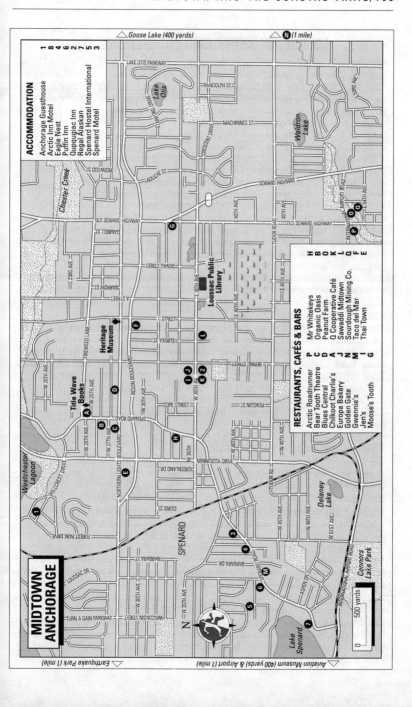

△ Goose Lake (400 yards)   △ Ⓝ (1 mile)

MIDTOWN ANCHORAGE

△ Earthquake Park (1 mile)

△ Aviation Museum (400 yards) & Airport (1 mile)

ACCOMMODATION

1 Anchorage Guesthouse
8 Arctic Inn Motel
4 Eagle Nest
6 Puffin Inn
2 Oupuguiac Inn
7 Regal Alaskan
5 Spenard Hostel International
3 Spenard Motel

RESTAURANTS, CAFÉS & BARS

Arctic Roadrunner P
Bear Tooth Theatre C
Blues Central D
Chilkoot Charlie's A
Europa Bakery J
Golden Gate N
Gwennie's M
Jen's I
Moose's Tooth G

Mr Whitekeys H
Organic Oasis B
Peanut Farm O
Q Cooperative Café K
Sawaddi Midtown L
Sourdough Mining Co. Q
Taco del Mar F
Thai Town E

HIKING IN THE CHUGACH MOUNTAINS

Contrary to expectations, Alaska is not overly endowed with good, maintained hiking trails. Much of the state is either too remote, too steep, or too boggy. One major exception, the **Chugach Mountains**, rises immediately behind Anchorage, the western end forming part of the Chugach State Park which, at half a million acres, is the third largest state park in the country. The **major hikes** – all with fabulous views over the city, Cook Inlet, and north to the Alaska Range – start from trailheads within half an hour's drive of Anchorage. Most can be tackled in a day and some can be combined into multiday affairs. The best source of information is the *Ridgelines* newspaper (50¢ from the Public Lands Information Office), which contains the latest trail information: for more details consult *55 Ways to the Wilderness of Southcentral Alaska* (The Mountaineers), which covers all walks in the Chugach State Park, including some south of Anchorage along Turnagain Arm.

You can hike from the beginning of May, but most trails aren't free of **snow** until the beginning of June and stay clear until around the end of September. **Bikes** are not generally allowed along these trails with the exception of the run from the Glen Alps parking lot to the Powerline Trail, and the 13 miles along the Powerline Trail from Prospect Heights to Indian; hikers always have right of way. Without a car or bicycle, your access to the hills is limited to the 4th Avenue Trolley to the Glen Alps Trailhead (see "Buses," p.187), and taxis. The listed distances and times are for the round-trip, unless stated otherwise.

FROM THE EAGLE RIVER NATURE CENTER

The Nature Center is the base for a couple of gentle nature trails (see p.205), and the finishing point for the Crow Pass Trail (see opposite). Sections of the Crow Pass Trail can be walked from this end, for example the relatively easy **Heritage Falls Trail** (9 miles round-trip; 4–5hrs; 100ft ascent) and the stiffer **Twin Falls Trail** (18 miles round-trip; 8–10hrs; 300ft ascent), which involves some stream crossings but rewards with beaver ponds and the Twin Falls themselves. To reach the Center follow the Glenn Hwy twelve miles north of Anchorage, then follow Eagle River Road ten miles east. There is a parking fee of $5 for every twelve hours.

FROM PROSPECT HEIGHTS TRAILHEAD

The Prospect Heights Trailhead (1050ft) is a 25-minute drive south of downtown Anchorage, reached by following O'Malley Road east until it becomes Upper O'Malley Road then turning left into Prospect Drive and following it 1.3 miles to the parking lot, which has a $5 per day parking fee. No useful bus access.

Middle Fork Trail (13 miles; 8–10hr; 1600ft ascent). Easy to moderate trail which again starts on the Near Point Trail then cuts right after 1.3 miles. It can get muddy underfoot as you gently climb through mountain hemlock and spruce towards beautiful alpine lakes set amid the open tundra under the precipitous face of Mount Williwaw. Anyone not needing to return to their own vehicle can vary the return journey by descending down a different path to the Glen Alps trailhead. Gets the early sun but is in shadow later in the day.

Wolverine Peak Trail (10.5 miles; 8–10hr; 3400ft ascent). Moderately strenuous trail which initially follows the Near Point Trail for two miles then spurs up towards the bush line. The way up to the triangular, 4450ft summit of Wolverine Peak is clear enough but you need to be sure where the path re-enters the bush on the way down. Besides the fabulous views and possible animal sightings –

moose, sheep, and arctic ground squirrel – you can spot parts of a wrecked plane near the summit.

FROM THE GLEN ALPS TRAILHEAD
The Glen Alps Trailhead (2250ft) is located at close to the tree line above Anchorage's swanky Hillside suburb, twenty-minutes' drive south of downtown Anchorage: turn off Hillside Drive and follow Upper Huffman Road for 2.6 miles to the parking lot. There is a $5 per day parking fee. The 4th Avenue Trolley's "South Trolley Tour" runs here in summer (8 daily; all-day pass $15).

Flattop Mountain (3.5 miles; 2–3hrs; 1300ft ascent). Good views over Anchorage and to the Alaska Range from the most climbed peak in Alaska, a fairly steep hike through mountain hemlocks out onto the tundra that requires some attention: hikers higher up can dislodge rocks.

Powerline Trail to Indian (11 miles one-way; 5–6hr; 1300ft ascent). Easy to moderate walking gradually gaining open tundra that's good for berry picking in fall. Start early in the day as it goes into shadow in the afternoon.

Williwaw Lakes (12 miles; 6–8hr; 740ft ascent). Easy to moderate walk that's best started early in the day to catch the sun. It climbs through spruce woods and mountain hemlock joining the Middle Fork Trail (see opposite) for the climb above the tree line to Williwaw Lakes.

FROM THE CROW PASS TRAIL
The trail starts at the end of Crow Creek Road some 37 miles southeast of Anchorage along the Seward Hwy then winds 8 miles inland, and finishes at Eagle River Nature Center. Take one of the Kenai-bound buses to Girdwood then either walk or hitch the five miles to the trailhead. At the other end, hitch from the Nature Center to Eagle River and pick up bus #74, #76, or #102 back to Anchorage.

The single best hike in the Anchorage area is the **Crow Pass Trail** (26 miles one-way; 2–3 days; 2500ft ascent, 3500ft descent), a dramatic grind up a steep pass overhung by glaciers then down a narrow wildlife-rich wooded valley strung with waterfalls and passing the gorgeous Raven Gorge where the fledgling Raven Creek plunges into a chasm sculpted into channels, chutes, and cauldrons. It also goes by the name of the "Historic Iditarod Trail" in recognition of its service as the winter track used, until the completion of the railway in 1918, by miners to get from the north side of Turnagain Arm to Knik. Nowadays it is best done in summer and fall when avalanche danger is negligible.

Despite its length it isn't an especially arduous hike, though bad weather can turn it into a nightmare for the ill-prepared. The one objective difficulty is crossing the glacial Eagle River, a simple but cold calf-deep wade at times, but a wide and impassable waist-high torrent especially after a series of warm days when glacial run-off is greatest: call the Nature Center for the latest information. Memorize the route before you leave and you're unlikely to get lost, but if you've any doubts at all, obtain the inch-to-a-mile Anchorage A6 and A7 quad maps.

For maximum flexibility (and the pick of the campsites) carry a stove, but there are numerous primitive **campsites** where campfires are allowed and a 12-berth **cabin** atop Crow Pass at Mile 3 ($35 plus an $8 reservation fee per night for the whole place; book up to 6 months in advance through the Forest Service ☎1-800/280-2267).

The contiguous lakes Hood and Spenard form the western limit of the **Spenard** district, a region once synonymous with sleaze and still the raunchiest part of town. The only sight in the traditional sense is the **NBA Heritage Library & Museum**, 1st floor National Bank of Alaska building, corner of C Street and Northern Lights Boulevard (Mon–Fri noon–5pm; free), just one compact room which perfectly complements the contextual slant of downtown's History & Art museum. The emphasis here is on the pieces themselves, almost without exception beautiful works and many of Native origin. Don't miss the bird parka made from the skins of over fifty murres, or the fragile-looking kayak and bleached seal-gut parka trimmed with auklet feathers and beaks. Though brittle when dry, seal gut becomes soggy and clingy in the sea yet remains breathable – Eskimo Gore-tex, and only three ounces are needed. Blankets sold to Tlingit people by the Hudson's Bay Company were also turned into clothing, here fashioned into a ceremonial coat used for potlatches with the owner's crest picked out in buttons. Basketware too is well represented along with matchless ivory carving – from simple stylized seals to whole whaling scenes enacted along the length of a walrus tusk or of a seascape made on a whale vertebra. Look too for the ivory scale model of the *Bear*, a locally famous revenue cutter (effectively the Alaskan coast guard in the late nineteenth century) which, patrolled Alaskan waters for forty years and, among other deeds, first brought reindeer to Alaska in 1885. Elsewhere there's a small collection of Russian icons, and the walls are hung with oils by leading Alaskan artists such as Laurence, Ziegler, and Machetanz.

Northern Lights Boulevard continues east until it meets the Chester Creek Greenbelt near **Goose Lake** (see "Swimming" p.214) on the northern flank of Anchorage's two universities – the University of Alaska Anchorage and Alaska Pacific University – neither of special interest to visitors. North of the universities lie the urban hiking and biking trails of **Russian Jack Springs Park**, which also contains the municipal greenhouse known as the **Mann Leiser Memorial Gardens**, 5200 DeBarr Rd (Mon–Fri 8am–3pm, Sat & Sun 9am–3pm; free; ☎343-4717). Keen horticulturists, however, are better off south of the universities at the **Alaska Botanical Garden**, Campbell Airstrip Road (June–Aug daily 9am–9pm; free), boasting pleasant paths around perennial gardens, wildflower trails, herb gardens, and trails into the nearby woods.

The Botanical Gardens lie within the **Far North Bicentennial Park**, a vast forested area butting up against the Chugach State Park, and an ideal spot for mountain bikers.

South Anchorage

It's not that hard to see Alaskan animals in the wild, but if you're not feeling too adventurous you can always check out the **Alaska Zoo**, 4731 O'Malley Rd (May–Sept daily 10am–6pm; Oct–April daily except Tues 10am–5pm; $7), which specializes in Alaskan fauna along with a few camels and llamas. Beyond the zoo, O'Malley Road continues to climb through the plush houses of the Hillside to the open flanks of the Chugach Mountains. The **Prospect Heights and Glen Alps trailheads** (see box, p.200) give access to the widest range of hikes, and the latter offers expansive city and sea views from a viewing platform.

Twelve miles south of downtown the New Seward Hwy (Mile 115) arcs away from the Chugach foothills, effectively creating a sea wall between Turnagain Arm and the 564 acres of **Potter Marsh** (unrestricted entry). Since 1971 it has been part of the **Anchorage Coastal Wildlife Refuge**, which (particularly late May to early June and late Aug to early Sept) acts as a stopover for more than two hundred species of migratory birds: Canada geese, mallards, pintails, green winged teal, widgeons, canvasbacks, shovelers, and scaup are common, definitely more so than the trumpeter swans, bald eagles, northern harrier, snow geese, and short-eared owls also occasionally present. A boardwalk with interpretive displays provides a vantage point for viewing king salmon running below, but is too close to the highway to be really relaxing.

Just as you leave the wetlands behind, an ancient snow-clearing locomotive marks the Potter Section House Historic Site where the 1929 section house, once a maintenance depot for a stretch of the railway, now serves as the **Chugach State Park Headquarters** (Mon–Fri 8am–noon & 1–4.30pm; ☎345-5014, fax 345-6982, *chugstpk@alaska.net*). A couple of wagons attached to the engine contain the **Kenai Peninsula visitor center** (June–Aug daily 8am–5pm; ☎336-3300, *www.kpvc.org*), which stocks leaflets on the whole peninsula and gives access to the interior of the snow plow.

From here the Seward Hwy continues to Girdwood, Portage Glacier, and the Kenai Peninsula; our account continues on p.219.

North Anchorage: the Alaska Native Heritage Center and Eagle River

The city's northern boundary is marked by the original townsite on Ship Creek which, during the salmon runs, is lined with anglers eager to land the fish returning to the **Elmendorf State Fish Hatchery**, Post Road at Reeve Boulevard (unrestricted access). Every year almost two million king and silver salmon are raised here for sport fishing around the state and while there's not a lot to see, the creek is usually full of spawning salmon.

Since downtown is perched on the extreme northern edge of Anchorage, leaving town along the Glenn Hwy gives the odd sensation of being out in the countryside just a few blocks from the central business district. Just before you leave the city completely, there's one essential (though expensive) sight, the **Alaska Native Heritage Center**, 8800 Heritage Center Drive (mid-May to late Sept daily 9am–6pm; closed winter; $20; infoline ☎330-8095, *www.alaskanative.net*). For years, there was a glaring absence of any pan-Alaska recognition of its tribal heritage, but this finally changed in 1999 with the opening of the Center, a celebration of the traditions of Alaska's five main Native groups. Unfortunately, the whole place takes a fairly broad, almost simplistic, approach, and important issues in modern tribal life are barely addressed at all. However, as an introduction to the people and their lives it is hard to beat; not least because it is staffed almost entirely by Native Alaskans. Kick off with the excellent twenty-minute film, *Stories Given, Stories Shared*, which really gives a sense of a people whose culture is finally starting to be accorded the respect it deserves. This leads on to a small museum, sparsely displayed with some lovely artifacts – ivory work, spirit masks, beadwork – and interpreted by a series of case studies and images that give a real sense of what it is like to be a Native Alaskan in modern Alaska. All this is reinforced by the main body of the center, five outdoor compounds arranged around a small lake, each representing a major tribal group – Athapascan, Yup'ik, Iñupiaq, Aleut, and Tlingit/Haida/Tsimshian. Each compound focuses on a house, built in the appropriate style from traditional materials, and surrounded by plantings typical of that region. Inside, guides interpret the lifestyles of their people, and it is all too apparent that much of this knowledge has been specially learned, rather than passed down as it once was, bringing a certain artificial tone to the information. Look out too for the Native crafts being pursued each summer (traditional clothing in 2001, medicine and healing in 2002), and try to break your wanderings at some point to catch one of the cultural performances – Native dance, storytelling, music – taking place in the main auditorium.

The Center is seven miles northwest of the city: from downtown, head north along the Glenn Hwy and take the Muldoon exit; or ride the 4th Avenue Trolley which departs from outside the 4th Avenue Theatre (8 daily; $26 round-trip including Center entry).

Eagle River

The Glenn Hwy expressway, twelve miles north of Anchorage, hurtles straight through the strip-mall suburb of **EAGLE RIVER**, which you might skip through too save for the **Eagle River Nature Center** (May–Oct Tues–Sun 10am–5pm; Nov–April Fri, Sat & Sun 10am–5pm; parking $5 for each 12hr period; ☎ 694-2108, fax 694-2119, *www.ernc.org*), at the edge of Eagle River Road. It is in a gorgeous setting, nestled below 7000-foot peaks and surrounded by forest. Extensive outdoor decking and a cozy telescope-equipped lounge to let you view Dall sheep,

---

WINTER IN ANCHORAGE

Once high season ends and the days start getting shorter, everyone starts (at least mentally) preparing for winter. The bike trails are all of a sudden thick with enthusiasts on roller skis hoping to get into shape before the snow falls sometime in late October. There are two **downhill skiing** venues in town – Hilltop, in south Anchorage, and Alpenglow, just north of downtown – but neither is particularly challenging and most head to Alyeska Resort (see p.220) 35 miles south. In Anchorage, when people talk skiing they mean cross country.

Cross-country skiers are spoilt for choice with backcountry skiing trails all around. The twelve-mile-long **Tony Knowles Coastal Trail** is flat and groomed with excellent views of Cook Inlet and the city all the way to **Kincaid Park**, where over thirty miles of well-maintained trails await. In less busy areas – East Anchorage's Bicentennial Park, for example – you'll find people **ski-joring**, a variation on cross-country skiing in which a dog, harnessed to your chest, takes the strain. Lakes freeze to produce eight outdoor **iceskating** rinks and occasionally paths are cleared across the ice of Westchester Lagoon. **Snow machine** riders head for five areas of the Chugach State Park set aside for their noisy activities; more retiring types huddle over holes in local lakes **ice fishing**.

Spectator-oriented events focus on the citywide Anchorage Fur Rendezvous (aka **Fur Rondy**), which runs for ten days between the second and third weekends in February and stems from the city's early days when trappers made one of their rare appearances out of the bush to sell their furs (See "Festivals" in Basics). But the highlight of the winter calendar is the ceremonial start of the 1100-mile **Iditarod** (see box, p.336) at 10am on the first Saturday in March.

eagles, coyote, and occasionally bears – moose come so close there's no need for magnification. The nature center sells coffee and a very limited supply of snacks, and offers bountiful information on surrounding **walks**. Easiest of these is the gentle **Rodak Nature Trail** (half-mile loop; 15–30min; 50ft ascent), which slopes down to an attractive salmon-viewing deck on stilts over a small lake. For something a little more strenuous, try the **Albert Loop Trail** (3-mile loop; 1–2hr; 100ft ascent) through the forest and across gravel bars of the glacial Eagle River, or the **Crow Pass Trail** (see box, p.201).

If you want to spend a night or two out here you've got a few possibilities. There is plenty of **free camping** at very basic sites (really just wide patches in the trail) along the Crow Pass Trail, and the nature center manages a modern eight-berth **cabin** and two **yurts** (one four-berth, one six), deep in the woods just over a mile from the center with sleeping platforms, wood stoves, firewood, and a lake for water. They each cost $55 a night and are often booked well in advance, especially at weekends and school vacations; check availability through the Web site.

Eating

Nowhere in Alaska will you find a more diverse range of places to eat – restaurants, cafés, bars, and brewpubs – than Anchorage. That's not to say you'd make a special journey for its culinary wonders, but you'd have to have fairly specific tastes to find the city wanting; indeed, after a few weeks in the Interior it can seem like heaven. As the state's population (and sophistication) has increased, so has the enthusiasm of food importers, to the point where the stock in exotic supermarket-cum-delis such as New Sagaya's City Market ranks with the best in the Northwest. Add to that the bounty of Alaska's seas and rivers and you've got the basis for some pretty wonderful eating. What's more, competition means that **prices** here are some of the lowest in the state, though newcomers to Alaska will still get a shock.

There are superb places to eat all over the city but the **downtown** area still has the largest concentration; in fact it has seen a burst of activity in recent years with new places popping up every few months. **Midtown** has a good stock too, and there are a few worth seeking out in the south of the city.

Buying **groceries** is easy enough with your own wheels, but without a car you're a bit stuck. There is nowhere to buy ordinary groceries downtown, only the New Sagaya's City Market. For lower prices you'll have to get yourselves to Carr's at the junction of Northern Lights Boulevard and Minnesota Drive (bus #3, #4, or #36).

Downtown

Cilantro's, 611 W 9th Ave (☎279-8226). Budget, authentic Mexican with a wide range of traditional favorites, and great seviche.

Club Paris, 417 W 5th Ave between D and E sts (☎277-6332). Well-established restaurant that survived the 1964 earthquake and flourished during the oil-boom years, specializing in what are undoubtedly Alaska's finest steaks ($15 "mini" sirloin to the $33 four-inch-thick filet mignon), served in the dim recesses of leather booths. Alaskan seafood is top-notch too, lunches (Mon–Sat only) come in at modest prices and you can follow with key lime pie or creme caramel.

Downtown Deli, 525 W 4th Ave (☎276-7116). The city's premier diner, owned by Governor Tony Knowles (seldom seen serving these days), and a longstanding Anchorage favorite for bagels, sandwiches, and the full range of breakfasts. A bit pricey but in summer there are seats outside.

The Federal Building Cafeteria, 222 W 7th at C St (☎277-6736). Breakfast and lunch cafeteria that's about the best budget eating downtown, and certainly a cut above the fast-food joints around. A large bowl of clam chowder or one of their entrees from a daily changing menu will only set you back $5.

Glacier Brewhouse, 737 W 5th Ave (☎274-2739; *www.glacierbrewhouse.com*). Typically rowdy, hectic, and hugely popular restaurant, bar, and microbrewery that nonetheless serves wonderful food and drink. There is always at least half a dozen toothsome house-brewed beers on tap (a shot-glass sampler of five of them costs $4.50), and the brewing grains go on to *Europa Bakery* (see opposite), returning as scrumptious bread served with an olive oil dip. It is tempting to fill up on that treat, leaving no room for the alder-wood baked gourmet pizza ($10), the spit-grilled three-peppercorn prime rib ($21), or the steamed Alaskan king crab legs ($30). Finish off with outstanding bread pudding: there is usually a supply of sticky wines which will stand up to it.

Humpy's, 610 W 6th Ave (☎276-2337). Though it functions primarily as a bar (see p.209) *Humpy's* also produces some of the best-value meals in town: the likes of char-broiled salmon, burgers, soups, and salads, all much better than you'd expect in a bar. The halibut burger with a small Caesar salad is about $10.

L'Aroma at New Sagaya's City Market, 900 W 13th Ave at I St. This is *the* place to get your groceries and deli takeouts, and prices match its trendiness, but the selection is great – varied organic selection, unusual vegetables, great cheeses, on-site bakery – and it is about the only place to buy such things anywhere near downtown. It is also good for eat-in meals (around $8) in the café with Thai dishes, sushi and sashimi, pizza, wraps, sandwiches, and good coffee. Mon–Fri 6am–9pm, Sat 7am–9pm, Sun 8am–7pm.

Lucky Wishbone, 1033 E 5th Ave (☎272 3454). Anchorageites have been coming to "The Bone" since 1955 for its classic diner decor and a menu chiefly noted for its lightly battered pan-fried chicken (dishes mostly around $7). For the real enthusiast, they often have gizzards, livers, and giblets.

The Marx Bros Café, 627 W 3rd Ave (☎278-2133). The best all-round fine dining downtown; gourmet cuisine served up in a historic house with views of the water. Start on the sautéed alligator with crawfish tails ($9) or Neapolitan seafood mousse ($12), and follow it up with yellow-fin tuna in a black-bean ginger *beurre blanc* with stir-fried baby *bok choy* ($25), or their signature dish, baked halibut rolled in a macadamia-nut crust and curry sauce and chutney ($25).

Orso, 737 W 5th Ave (☎222-3232). Fine dining in a grand baronial setting where smartly dressed staff serve tempting Northern Italian dishes. *Crostini di funghi* is done quite well, as is the salmon and mushroom ravioli, and their chocolate torte with sambuca syrup. Expect to pay $40–50 plus wine, which starts around $20 a bottle.

Oscar's Roast 'n Smoke, 508 6th Ave. This Internet café is the most relaxing place in town to sip a latte while surfing, provided you don't mind smoke drifting through from the cigar room.

Sack's, 328 G St (☎274-4022, *www.sackscafe.com*). An appealing and modestly priced favorite. Everything is made with care from the Thai chicken marinated in a spicy peanut sauce ($7 and $9) to the Caesar salad ($6). Entrées might include a lamb red curry or seared sea scallops ($20), and they do Sunday brunches (11am–3pm) with a south-of-the-border variation on eggs Benedict.

Side Street Espresso, 412 G St. Coffee is pretty much all they do, and they attract a loyal following for doing it right. Have your caffeine and browse the magazines. Mon–Fri 7am–7pm, Sat 7am–5pm, Sun 8am–5pm.

Simon and Seafort's, 420 L St (☎274-3502). Consistently one of Anchorage's better restaurants serving meals such as beer-battered fish and chips ($10) in the bar (see p.209) and beautifully prepared American favorites – steaks, ribs, salmon, etc – in a *c*.1900 saloon with wonderful views of Cook Inlet. Expect about $40–50 for three courses.

Snow City Café, 1034 W 4th Ave (☎272-6338). Foremost among the city establishments that successfully manage to draw the coffee set, lunching office workers, and pre-theater diners. Relax over a pot of Earl Grey, get breakfast all day – eggs florentine for $8, French toast for $6, or granola for $3.50 – or have a full-blown meal: grilled mahi, seafood primavera, or vegetarian lasagna. There's usually some form of live music on Friday night. Closes 4pm on Mon & Tues.

Snow Goose Restaurant and Brewery, 717 W 3rd Ave (☎277-7727). Bustling brewpub and restaurant that's great for supping one of their half-dozen excellent ales on the deck overlooking Cook Inlet, or tucking into dishes of, say, steamed clams ($10) followed by wild-mushroom pizza ($10). On Friday and Saturday nights they run a great oyster bar.

Midtown

Arctic Roadrunner, 5300 Old Seward Hwy at International Airport Rd (☎561-1245). An eat-in and takeout Anchorage staple since 1964 that is regularly voted as serving the best burgers in town. Few fancy trimmings here, just good no-nonsense food, and a floor-to-ceiling photo gallery of (almost) famous past customers. Closed Sun.

Bear Tooth Theatre Pub, 1230 W 27th Ave (☎276-4200, *www.beartooththeatre.net*). Top-notch combination restaurant, bar, and cinema where, for $2 on top of your meal price, you can dine while watching a movie (see "Listings," p.213). Menu has a wide range – Caesar salads ($4), burritos and tacos ($5–8), and gourmet pizzas ($15 for a 16-inch) and the microbrews made on the premises are excellent.

Europa Bakery, 601 W 36th Ave (☎563-5704). Superb bakery where the utmost care is taken in producing all manner of loaves including a spent-grain variety using the leftovers from the *Glacier Brewhouse*'s beer brewing. The breads are then used in excellent sandwiches ($7) either to take out or eat in. It is also a popular place for omelette breakfast on weekends, and produces fine pastries and cakes.

Golden Gate, 3471 E Tudor Rd (☎561-4274). Basic Chinese joint that's inconveniently sited away from where you're likely to be, but worth a drive for heaving plates at bargain prices; the Mongolian beef ($5.50) is excellent, and they do combination dinners for one from $9.50.

Gwennie's Old Alaska Restaurant, 4333 Spenard Rd at Forest Rd (☎243-2090). Something of an Anchorage institution; two busy floors decorated with Alaskan memorabilia and old photos providing a family setting for all-day breakfasts – the sourdough pancakes are outstanding – as well as the usual range of burgers and sandwiches.

Jen's Restaurant, 701 W 36th Ave at Arctic Blvd (☎561-5367). Combined fine-dining restaurant and wine bar that's highly fashionable with a well-heeled crowd. The menu, which reflects the chef's Danish heritage, varies daily but you might expect to start with king salmon and king-crab paté ($12) followed by pan-fried medallions of marlin on mango, jalapeño and citrus *beurre blanc* ($20). The wine list is equally impressive and there's always a convivial atmosphere. Closed Sat lunch, Mon evening and all day Sun.

Moose's Tooth, 3300 Old Seward Hwy at 33rd Ave (☎258-2537, *www.moosestooth.net*). A perennial favorite, always alive with diners tucking into some of the town's best gourmet pizza (in 42 variations) or imbibing one of a dozen or so house-brewed beers at the bar. On the first Thursday of the month they celebrate First Tap Thursday (9pm–1am), offering a band, a party, and an opportunity to meet the brewer over a glass of that month's new creation.

Organic Oasis, 2610 Spenard Rd (☎277-7882). Earthy and reasonably priced lunch spot that's great for soups and organic dishes that are mostly vegetarian or vegan (though not exclusively). Daily full meal specials for $15. Closed Sun.

Q Cooperative Café, 640 W 36th Ave at Arctic Blvd (☎563-5634). Locally known simply as the *Q Café*, the curvaceous interior is the best spot in midtown to relax over a coffee (organic available) or something more substantial from their meat-free menu. Open until around 9pm daily. Closed Sun in winter.

Sawaddi Midtown, 300 W 36th Ave (☎563-8335). A basic Thai restaurant with little in the way of atmosphere, but good for the daily buffet (11am–2.30pm; $8), which includes an all-you-can-eat salad bar.

Taco del Mar, 343 W Benson Blvd (☎563-9097). Northern outpost of this small Seattle-based chain serving enormous burritos, stupendous Baja fish tacos, and other Mexican staples at low prices. Plenty of vegetarian and vegan choices.

Thai Town, 1780 W Northern Lights Blvd at Minnesota (☎272-8696). Uninspiring decor and low prices give little indication of the top quality and authenticity of the dishes served: all the typical Thai favorites including an excellent Tom Yum Kai soup (hot and sour with lemon grass and mushrooms; $6), and plenty of vegetarian dishes.

South Anchorage

Mexico in Alaska, 7305 Old Seward Hwy at 73rd (☎349-1528). Anchorage's most authentic Mexican restaurant though still slightly sanitized for northern tastes. Nonetheless, you won't find better dishes than the *camarones Veracruzana* ($20) or the *chaquiles* done in a savory chocolate (mole) sauce for $11. For the budget conscious, the $9 weekday lunch buffet is worth considering, and there are always bottles of the excellent Bohemia beer.

Southside Bistro, 1320 Huffman Park Drive (☎348-0088). Some of the finest dining in the south of the city, particularly noted for its seafood, fresh pasta, and hardwood-baked flat-bread pizza. Main courses in the $20–25 range. Closed Sun & Mon.

Drinking and entertainment

Good bars abound in downtown Anchorage, and the atmosphere varies as much as the clientele. You don't need to dig far to find dark, block-built hideaway lounges left over from the oil-boom Seventies when they were meeting places for shady deals; and late at night, the main drag of **4th Avenue** can seem like a sur-real slalom course as you swerve to avoid the terminally drunk. But, in recent years, the downtown area has rebounded and now harbors half a dozen or more genuinely appealing places to drink, and even a little **live music**, most reliably at *Humpy's*.

The other lively area is **Spenard** – along Spenard Road between Northern Lights Boulevard and International Airport Road – which has long since shaken its reputation for sleazy excess, earned during the freewheeling oil days of the late 1970s, but still retains an edge. It can be a lot of fun as long as you are sensi-ble though, women travelers may not find the wilder side of macho Anchorage quite as endearing as many locals seem to think it is, evident in some innocent-looking bars turning out to be strip joints. Here, too, you'll find live music, either at *Blues Central* and *Chilkoot Charlie's*, or after the main show at *Mr Whitekeys*.

Beer drinkers should be very happy in Anchorage, which currently has more top-quality microbreweries than any city of comparable size in the US. Breweries worth trying are the *Moose's Tooth*, *Bear Tooth*, *Glacier Brewhouse*, *Snow Goose*, and even *Humpy's*, which doesn't brew its own, but has a vast range on tap.

There isn't a great deal of live **theater** in Anchorage, particularly during the summer when it takes something really special to lure Alaskans indoors. For the rest of the year, the Alaska Center for the Performing Arts (aka PAC; ☎263-2900) puts its exemplary acoustics to the test with a variety of shows, plays, and concerts, and hosts both the Anchorage Opera (☎279-2557) and the Anchorage Symphony Orchestra (☎274-8668).

It's a major step down in formality, though not ambition or invention, to the quirky Cyrano's Off-Center Playhouse, 413 D St at 4th Avenue (☎274-2499, *www.cyranos.org*), which fashions itself a "cultural mini-mall" with a bookstore filled with artbooks (see overleaf), an offbeat 44-seat cinema (see "Listings," p.213), and a theater which puts on a lively range of material from locally-penned plays to the more edgy classics and frequently stages works performed by their resident troupe, the Eccentric Theater Company. They also have a 3D gold-rush movie ($7) shown daily every hour (10am–9pm in summer), plus there are frequent runs of classic films and mini festivals.

To find out what's on at any of the places listed below, consult the *Anchorage Daily News* – particularly Friday's comprehensive "8" entertainment supplement – or Thursday's free weekly *Press*, a kind of cafés and bars newsletter found all over town. Both also give a rundown of the first-run movies and occasional art-house flicks at the profusion of multiscreen **cinemas** in suburban malls (see "Listings," p.213).

Tickets for almost any major show can be bought from the CarrsTix office in the foyer of the Performing Arts Center (Mon–Sat noon–4pm) or by calling ☎263-2787 or 1-800/478-7328.

Downtown

Bernie's Bungalow, 626 D St at 7th Ave. Very un-Alaskan; a chic cocktail bar fashioned from an old wooden house that shimmies to cool Latin and jazz grooves. They have an ever-expanding deck for the long summer evenings, but indoor seating is in short supply so come early and dress sharp.

Darwin's Theory, 426 G St at 4th. Straightforward bar for moderately priced boozing and beery encounters with colorful local characters.

Humpy's Great Alaskan Alehouse, 610 W 6th at F St (☎276-2337; see p.206). An ever-popular watering hole with a strong college bar feel and what must be Alaska's widest selection of Pacific Northwest microbrews (over 30) as well as some expensive English and Belgian bottled beers. Whiskey drinkers are also well catered for with more than thirty single malts, and there is live music nightly, often acoustic or Irish.

Mad Myrna's, 530 E 5th Ave (☎276-9762). Anchorage's main gay dance club usually open Wed–Sun from 9pm, with regular drag acts and karaoke. Small cover charge at weekends.

Pioneer Bar, 739 W 4th Ave (☎276-7996). Traditional dark, downtown bar that has traded in its seedy reputation in favor of boisterous youthful drinking.

Simon and Seafort's, 420 L St (☎274-3502). Mainly an upmarket restaurant (see p.206), but the saloon bar is a great spot for cocktails or scotches and bourbons (over 100 varieties), especially if you can steal a seat close to the picture windows with unsurpassed views of Cook Inlet and Mount Susitna.

Midtown

Blues Central, 825 W Northern Lights Blvd at Arctic Ave (☎272-1341). A restaurant mainly notable as Anchorage's premier blues venue, operating every night until 2am, with a very popular jam session on Sunday night. Cover charge Tues–Thurs $2, Fri–Sat $3, Sun free.

Chilkoot Charlie's, 2435 Spenard Rd (☎272-1010). OK, so it's not everyone's idea of a good night out, and can be a cattle market, but "Koots" is Alaskan through and through. Every night this sawdust-strewn barn of a place packs them in for a wide range of pricey drinks, pool, foosball, two floors of DJ-led dance and a band from 9.30pm. "We screw the other guy and pass the savings on to you!" they claim, but still have a cover charge ($2–5) on weekends.

Mr Whitekey's Fly By Night Club, 3300 Spenard Rd, at 33rd St (☎279-7726). Zany cabaret and live music venue which, throughout summer, hosts *The Whale Fat Follies* (June to mid-Sept Tues–Sat 8pm; $12–18; 16 and over only), a satirical and occasionally bawdy slant on Alaska and its people which you'll understand and appreciate all the more at the end of your time in the state. There's usually live music after the show on weekends (around 10.30pm; free) and there's food, too, featuring SPAM in ways you never thought possible.

Peanut Farm, 5227 Old Seward Hwy at International Airport Rd (☎563-3283). Straightforward sports bar, always lively and open very late.

Shopping

For Alaskans, Anchorage offers the best shopping this side of Seattle, and is often the only place you can get your hands on the goods. As a visitor, shopping is likely to be fairly low on your list of priorities, though with no state sales tax to pay, it can be a good place to buy **books** and **outdoor equipment** if you plan on being in the wild. As well you should consider putting some cash aside for **Native craftwork**, some of it is tasteless souvenir junk, but much of it is beautiful and superbly made. Of course there are prices to match, but some judicious shopping around can turn up affordable pieces.

Books

Wherever you are in Alaska you'll have no problem finding books about the state or by Alaskan authors, but if you've got specific needs (and we've made plenty of recommendations in the "Books" section of Contexts, p.504), Anchorage is by far your best bet.

Borders, 1100 E Dimond at Old Seward Hwy (books ☎344-4099, music ☎344-4453). Giant chain bookstore with a solid selection of new books and newspapers from all over the world and around Alaska. Daily 10am–midnight.

C & M Used Books, 215 E 4th Ave (☎278-9394). Downtown secondhand bookstore where, amid the apparent chaos, they've got some good books available at half the cover price (quarter price with a similarly priced trade). Mon–Sat 9am–5pm, closed Sun.

Cook Inlet Book Co, 415 W 5th Ave at D St (☎258-4544, *info@cookinlet.com*). Anchorage's handiest source for new books, strong on Alaskan titles and stocks a wide selection of *Rough Guides* for your onward travels. Daily 8.30am–10pm.

Cyrano's, 413 D St (☎274-2599). Specialist bookstore with a good line in the arts, literary fiction, and the classics. The owner is particularly well versed in their stock of Alaskan titles. Mon–Sat 9am–5.30pm.

Title Wave, 1068 W Fireweed Lane (☎278-9283 or 1-800/598-9283, *www.wavebooks.com*). Wondrous midtown emporium with the widest selection of used books in the city and a modest selection of remaindered new titles. Mon–Sat 10.30am–6.30pm, Sun noon–5pm.

Camping and outdoor equipment

If you are planning to spend a fair bit of time exposed to Alaskan outdoor conditions, you'll need the right gear. Your best bet is to head to Anchorage's outdoor supply ghetto – at the junction of Spenard Road and Northern Lights Boulevard, in midtown – where you'll find pretty much everything you need; canoes, tents, climbing tackle, fishing gear, and bicycles, some of it also available for renting (see "Listings," p.213).

Alaska Kayak, 6921 Brayton Drive, South Anchorage (☎522-7710). Anchorage's specialist canoe and kayak store which rents canoes and whitewater kayaks from $50 for 2 days.

Alaska Mountaineering & Hiking, 2633 Spenard Rd (☎272-1811, fax 274-6362, *www .alaskan.com/amh*). Rock climbers and mountaineers are best served here at AMH, which also covers hiking needs, rents mountaineering and ski equipment at competitive rates, and has a used-equipment board. Mon–Fri 9am–7pm, Sat 9am–6pm, Sun noon–5pm.

Barney's Sport Chalet, 906 W Northern Lights Blvd (☎561-5242). A little more personal than REI, strong on top-quality tents, backpacking equipment and, in winter, cross-country ski equipment. Mon–Fri 10am–7pm, Sat 10am–5pm.

Great Outdoor Clothing Co, 1200 W Northern Lights Blvd (☎277-6664). The best spot for low-cost fleeces, hats, and thermal underwear. Daily 10am–6pm.

REI, 1200 W Northern Lights Blvd (☎272-4565, fax 274-5102, *www.rei.com*). This one-stop specialist store stocks Alaska's widest selection of camping, hiking, canoeing, climbing, and skiing gear plus clothing, footwear, and freeze-dried foods. They also do an extensive range of rentals. A single lifetime family payment of $15 gives you membership in the co-op and substantial discounts on retail and rental gear. Daily 10am–9pm.

The Windy Corner, 434 K St (☎278-3100). This North Face specialist is a small shop stocking camping essentials, the only downtown outfitter not geared towards hunting and fishing.

Crafts

Most of the tourist-oriented shops in Anchorage stock the usual array of garish T-shirts and overpriced rubbish, not much of it kitsch enough to even be enticing. Amongst the dross you will find some excellent **Native crafts**, and Anchorage has the best selection in the state since craftspeople visiting the big city from outlying villages tend to bring in their work for sale. When buying here you lose some of the satisfaction of dealing directly with the artisan and will probably pay more than you would at source. Before buying anything containing parts of endangered animals, read the box on taking your purchases outside the US (see overleaf).

Most likely you'll notice how Alaska hasn't quite shaken its Russian influence and there are several shops downtown stocking **Russian-made goods**, particularly fine-porcelain tea sets from Lomonosov in Saint Petersburg, and nested Matreshka dolls (the wooden ones that fit into each other) in traditional designs and modern variations: American football teams, *South Park* characters, and political genealogies from Lenin to Putin.

Alaska Native Medical Center, 4315 Diplomacy Drive, off Tudor Rd (☎729-1122). Serious buyers should definitely make for the craft shop on the ground floor of this hospital. Items are brought in by folk from Native villages when they come to visit recuperating friends and relatives. Good range and modest prices. Open Mon–Fri 10am–2pm.

Alaskan Ivory Exchange, 700 W 4th Ave (☎272-3662). A small shop chock-full of carved walrus ivory and fossilized whalebone products; some simple and fairly cheap, others more intricate and pricey.

Anchorage Museum of History & Art, 121 W 7th Ave at A St (☎343-4326). The museum shop in the foyer (no entrance fee) stocks a wide selection of quality Native crafts along with Russian lacquerwork and Alaska books.

Antique Gallery, 1001 W 4th Ave, Suite B (☎276-8986, fax 278-6260, *www.theantiquegallery .com*). A real treasure trove, packed to the rafters with pre-twentieth-century artifacts you'd normally only see in museums; and everything's for sale. Avoid sticking your foot through the thousand-dollar canvases that line the aisles, and browse through $1500 baskets woven

---

TAKING NATIVE CRAFTS BACK HOME

In an attempt to preserve traditional lifestyles, particularly in remote villages, Native Alaskans are allowed to trade in raw materials otherwise proscribed by the Convention on International Trade in Endangered Species (CITES). While it is perfectly legal to buy Native artifacts such as walrus-tusk cribbage boards, spirit masks, whalebone sculpture, etched pieces of baleen, and the pelts of wolves, otters, walruses, seals, and bears, the customs people back home may not look too kindly on you importing such items.

Strictly speaking, it is illegal to export from the US products containing parts of bears (black and brown), cormorants, eagles, loons, puffins, ravens, sea lions, snowy owls, waterfowl, and whales of any kind. In practice, you are unlikely to be stopped leaving the country, but may be questioned when entering another – even in transit to the Lower 48 through Canada. Many people manage to carry stuff through customs without any problem, but it is worth being aware that your souvenirs may be confiscated.

In addition to the animal products listed above, most Western countries also ban the import of lynx, otter, walrus, wolf, and wolverine, though it is often possible to import these with the appropriate paperwork. Any reputable shop will provide a US Department of the Interior CITES Personal Property Exemption form and preferably documentation of who made the item and where.

If you think you are likely to buy Native crafts, the best bet is to check import restriction before you leave home. One publication worth checking out is *A Customs Guide to Traditional Alaska Native Handicrafts*, which includes a country by country list of which species are legal, permissible with paperwork, or illegal.

---

from whale baleen, Tiffany lamps, suits of armor, Ormolu clocks, stacks of shotguns and pistols, Russian icons, and even the occasional $40,000 oil by Laurence, Ziegler, or Machetanz.

Aurora, 713 W 5th Ave (☎274-0234). Colorful store with a wide range of Native arts and crafts, much of it quite expensive but top quality.

Kobuk Coffee Company, 504 W 5th Ave (☎272-3626, *www.kobukcoffee.com*). Mainly a coffee and tea emporium – free samovar tea to sample – but also selling beautiful Russian tea services.

Oomingmak Musk Ox Producers Cooperative, 604 H St (☎272-9225, *www.qiviut.com*). Small shop selling garments knitted from qiviut, the under-fur of the musk ox, by natives of western Alaska, where each village has a distinctive design. Most products are fawn; a scarf going for $200–300, a hat for $100–150. For more on this organization and these ancient beasts see Palmer, p.332.

Listings

Airlines Alaska (☎266-7200 or 1-800/426-0333); American (☎1-800/433-7300); Delta, in *Hotel Captain Cook* and 3830 W International Airport Rd (☎1-800/221-1212); ERA Aviation, 6160 Carl Brady Drive (☎1-800/866-8394); Korean Air, 4600 Postmark Drive (☎243-3329); Northwest, 319 F St (☎1-800/225-2525); Peninsula Airways, 6100 Boeing Ave (☎1-800/448-4226); Reeve Aleutian, 4700 W International Airport Rd (☎243-4700 or 1-800/544-2248); TWA, (☎1-800/275-4892); United (☎1-800/241-6522).

American Express American Express Travel Service, Suite 104, 5011 Jewel Lake Rd, near the airport (Mon–Fri 9am–6pm; ☎266-6600, fax 266-6689) operates as a travel agency, exchanges foreign currency, and handles client mail.

Banks and currency exchange Banks are located all over town, many of them drive-thru. ATMs are even more abundant, some even located in bars. Downtown there's a First National Bank of Anchorage branch at 646 W 4th Ave between F and G sts. The best bet for exchanging foreign bills and travelers' checks is Thomas Cook, 311 F St between 3rd and 4th aves (Mon–Fri 9am–6pm, Sat & Sun noon–4pm; ☎278-2822 or 1-800/287-7362, fax 278-0687).

Bicycle repair, retail, and rental The best of the bike retail and repair shops are in mid-town among the camping and outdoor shops near the junction of Spenard Rd and Northern Lights Blvd (see "Shopping," p.211): Paramount Cycles, 1231 W Northern Lights Blvd (☎277-2453) probably has the most comprehensive retail section and does repairs on most machines; The Bicycle Shop, along the street at #1035 (☎272-5219) does much the same and also offers bargain bike rental with mid-range mountain bikes for $20 for the first 24 hours then $15 a day thereafter.

Buses (long distance) All the following services operate from mid-May to mid-Sept, though it pays to book ahead at the end of the season when services may not run if there are too few customers. Alaska Backpacker Shuttle (☎1-800/266-8625) picks up at the *Anchorage-HI* hostel and runs daily to Seward and Fairbanks; Alaska Direct Bus Line (☎1-800/770-6652; in Anchorage ☎227-6652) depart from *Days Inn*, 321 5th Ave, and the *Anchorage-HI* hostel for Whitehorse, Yukon (Wed, Fri, and Sun only) via Palmer, Glenallen, and Tok; Alaskon Express (☎1-800/478-6388 or 277-5581), picks up at the *Hilton*, *Westmark*, and *Sheraton* hotels for runs to Denali, Valdez, Seward, Whittier, Skagway, and Whitehorse; Parks Highway Express (☎1-888/600-6001) picks up at the *Anchorage-HI* hostel and goes to Fairbanks.

Camping and outdoor equipment rental REI (see p.211) rents tents from $18 for the first day, $7 thereafter; sleeping bags $15/$6; cooking stoves $6/$4; canoes $28/$18 and more. In summer a lot of this stuff is reserved in advance, so phone or fax early.

Car rental Affordable New Car Rentals, 4707 Spenard Rd at Breezewood (☎243-3370 or 1-800/248-3765, fax 243-3543, *www.ancr.com*), have first-come, first-served subcompacts ($39 a day), and reservable compacts starting at $50, all good for gravel roads; Airport Car Rental, 502 W Northern Lights Blvd (☎562-0897, fax 561-1437, *www.alaskan.com/airportcarrental*), rents compacts from around $50, are good for drivers under 25, and sometimes allow one-way rentals between Anchorage and Fairbanks; Rent-a-Wreck, 5610 Old Seward Hwy (☎563-2558 or 1-800/965-6547, fax 562-7885), also allow their cars on gravel roads and charge low rates. Other low-cost agencies worth trying are: Ace Rent-a-Car, 512 W International Airport Rd (☎562-8078 or 1-888/685-1155, *kiskaak@alaska.net*); Denali Car Rental, 1209 Gambell St (☎276-1230 or 1-800/757-1230, fax 272-3731, *lptheprez@akcache.com*); and Levi Car Rental, 1135 E Dowling Rd (☎563-2279, fax 5652-4918, *www.levicarrental.com*). All major agencies are listed in Basics, p.41.

Cinemas Cyrano's Off-Center Playhouse, 413 D St at 4th Ave (☎274-2499, *www.cyranos.org*; $5) usually has something unusual or art-house on. Or try the *Bear Tooth Theatre Pub* (see p.207), which plays movies a couple of months old and often has film festivals and classic-movie nights, all for a couple of bucks. The remaining movie theaters are mainstream multi-screen ventures in the suburbs: closest to downtown is the Fireweed Cinemas, 661 E Fireweed at Gambell (☎566-3328), otherwise try Century 16, 301 E 36th Ave (☎929-FILM; $8, early shows $5); the nine-screen Dimond Center, Dimond Center Mall, cnr Old Seward Hwy and Dimond Blvd (☎566-3327); University Six, 3901 Old Seward Hwy (☎566-3338); or the ten-screen Totem Cinemas, 3131 Muldoon Rd (☎566-3329).

Consulates Canada (☎333-1400); UK, 3211 Providence Drive (☎786-4848).

Gay and lesbian helpline ☎258-4777; daily 6–11pm.

Internet access For free email visit the Loussac Library (see overleaf) where you can get an hour (reserve in person) at no charge, but you can't use floppies to down- or upload information. Downtown try Custom CPU, 245 W 5th Ave (☎277-6969; Mon–Sat 9.30am–6pm), or *Oscar's Roast 'n Smoke*, 508 6th Ave (daily noon–9pm; ☎274-1344).

Laundry K-Speed Wash, 600 E 6th Ave (open Mon–Sat 7am–10pm; ☎279-0731).

Left luggage There is luggage storage (daily 5am–2am) at the airport's main domestic (South) terminal. For up to 24 hours storage they charge $5 for a suitcase or backpack and $12 for a set of antlers.

Library ZJ Loussac Library, 3600 Denali St at 36th St (Mon–Thurs 10am–8pm, Fri & Sat 10am–6pm, Sun 1–5pm; closed Sun in summer), has a huge selection of books with plenty on Alaska, Internet access (see overleaf) and an on-site café. Buses #2 and #60 are most convenient from downtown.

Maps The Maps Place, 601 W 36th Ave (☎562-7277, fax 562-7334) stocks a wide selection of topo and other maps. Topographical and geotechnical maps are also available from USGS Earth Science Information Center, 4230 University Drive, in Grace Hall at Alaska Pacific University (☎786-7011, fax 786-7050) but are probably more detailed than you need.

Medical assistance Alaska Health Care Clinic, 3600 Minnesota Drive at 36th Ave (Mon–Fri 8am–7pm, Sat 10am–4pm; ☎279-3500); Anchorage Medical & Surgical Clinic, 718 K St (Mon–Fri 8am–5.30pm; ☎272-2571); Alaska Regional Hospital, 2801 DeBarr Rd (☎276-1131).

Newspapers The morning paper is the *Anchorage Daily News*, which provides Alaska's most comprehensive coverage of local and world events. It prints daily movie listings and on Friday publishes the more comprehensive "8" entertainment supplement. Better still, for listings and offbeat entertaining coverage, pick up a free copy of Thursday's weekly *Press* (*www.anchoragepress.com*) at bookshops and cafés all over town; something of a clubs and cafés newsletter, but a refreshing alternative with some excellent cartoons and a lively spin on what's going on, and a weekly global round-up of bizzaro stories in News of the Weird.

Pharmacy There's a 24-hour pharmacy in Carr's, cnr Minnesota Drive and Northern Lights Blvd (☎297-0560); Fred Meyer's, 1000 E Northern Lights Blvd (☎264-9633) has a pharmacy open daily 8am–11pm.

Photographic supplies Stewart's Photo Shop, 531 W 4th Ave between E and F sts (Mon–Sat 8.30am–6pm; ☎272-8581), caters to pretty much all film and camera needs.

Post Office The most central post office (Mon–Fri 10am–5.30pm) is located downstairs in the mall on W 4th Ave between C and D sts and is the best place to use as **General Delivery** (ZIP 99510).

Road conditions A 24-hour prerecorded message on Alaskan road conditions can be found at ☎273-6037.

Rock climbing The nearest rock climbing to the city is the quarried embankment alongside the Seward Hwy and train line between fifteen and thirty miles south of the city. It is close enough for locals to pop out after work: if you want to join them just drive along and look for likely spots or purchase the local guidebook *The Scar* (see "Books," p.504). Indoors, there's the Alaska Rock Gym, 4840 Fairbanks St (daily noon–10pm; ☎56-CRANK) which charges $12 a visit.

RV rental See our general comments about RV rentals in Basics (p.41).

Swimming Cook Inlet isn't suitable for swimming but a couple of lakes are: Spenard Beach Park, at the eastern end of Lake Spenard (bus #7 or #36) has a roped-off area patrolled by lifeguards and a beach with picnic tables and volleyball; Goose Lake, off Northern Lights Blvd, just east of Lake Otis Parkway has similar facilities (buses #3 or #4). To swim indoors, the best pool is on the UAA campus ($5; ☎786-1231).

Taxes There is no sales tax in Anchorage, but the city does impose an eight percent bed tax which is already included in our accommodation prices.

Taxi Alaska Cab ☎563-5353; Checker Cab ☎276-1234; The Taxicab Co ☎278-8000. Expect $5 for a journey downtown, $8 between downtown and midtown and $12–15 from downtown to the airport.

Travel agency New World Travel, 1200 W Northern Lights Blvd (☎276-7071).

travel details

Anchorage is the heart of Alaska's land and air transport networks and you'll almost certainly find yourself passing through even if you're not interested in the city. All the following journey frequencies apply to the summer season and are greatly reduced in winter.

Trains make one round-trip a day each to Seward and Whittier, and there's one service a day in each direction between Anchorage, Talkeetna, Denali and Fairbanks. **Bus routes** are more extensive, with individual lines fanning out to Seward, Homer, Valdez, and Tok, and several companies running from Anchorage to Denali, some continuing to Fairbanks. Most **planes** run along simple there-and-back flight schedules, though the strung-out nature of Southeast Alaska, and the importance of Seattle makes long multistop runs more suitable. Major towns – especially Juneau, Ketchikan, and Seattle – have direct nonstop services while smaller places are reached on multistop routes such as: Anchorage–Juneau–Sitka–Ketchikan–Seattle; Anchorage–Cordova–Yakuta–Juneau–Seattle; and Anchorage–Juneau–Petersburg–Wrangell–Ketchikan–Seattle.

TRAINS

Anchorage to: Denali Park (daily; 7hr 30min); Fairbanks (daily; 12hr); Seward (daily; 4–5hr); Talkeetna (daily; 3hr 10min); Wasilla (daily; 1hr 30min); Whittier (daily; 2hr 30min–3hr).

BUSES

Anchorage to: Beaver Creek, Yukon (3 weekly; 11hr); Denali/Glitter Gulch (4 daily; 5–6hr); Fairbanks (1 daily; 9–10hr); Girdwood (2 daily; 1hr 15min); Glenallen (1–2 daily; 4–5hr); Homer (3–6 weekly; 5hr); Nenana (2 daily; 7hr); Ninilchik (3–6 weekly; 4hr); Palmer (2 daily; 1hr); Seward (2 daily; 3–4hr); Skagway (3 weekly; overnight with a stop at Beaver Creek, Yukon); Soldotna (3–6 weekly; 3hr 30min); Talkeetna (2–3 daily; 3hr); Talkeetna Junction (2 daily; 3hr); Tok (6 weekly; 8–9hr); Valdez (daily; 10hr); Wasilla (2 daily; 1hr 15min); Whitehorse (3 weekly; 16hr).

FLIGHTS

Anchorage to: Barrow (2–3 daily; 3hr); Cordova (2–3 daily; 50min); Dillingham (4–5 daily; 1hr 10min); Dutch Harbor (3 daily; 2hr–2hr 50min); Fairbanks (10–12 daily; 1hr); Homer (6 daily; 40min); Juneau (5 daily; 1hr 40min–3hr 15min); Kenai (14–18 daily; 25min); Ketchikan (1–2 daily; 4–5hr); King Salmon (5–8 daily; 1hr–1hr 20min); Kodiak (6–8 daily; 50min–1hr 10min); Kotzebue (2–3 daily; 1hr 30min); Nome (2–3 daily; 1hr 30min–3hr); Petersburg (1 daily; 3hr); Prudhoe Bay/Deadhorse (1 daily; 1hr 40min); Seattle, WA (20–25 daily; 3hr 20min); Sitka (1 daily; 2hr 50min); Valdez (2–3 daily; 40min); Whitehorse, Yukon (1 daily; 3hr); Wrangell (1 daily; 3hr 40min); Yakutat (1 daily; 2hr).

CHAPTER THREE

SOUTHCENTRAL ALASKA

SOUTHCENTRAL ALASKA drapes around the Gulf of Alaska from Cordova in the east to Homer in the west, a two-hundred-mile arc packed with a little of almost everything Alaska has to offer: tidewater glaciers, whale watching, outstanding halibut and salmon fishing, entertaining small towns, accessible hiking, and much more. It is a region that lacks any truly unifying characteristic, except perhaps for its proximity to Anchorage. This has helped make it one of the most densely populated rural areas of the state, as well as one of the best connected, with a train line, a relatively dense network of roads, and good ferry services. These factors combine to make this one of the most popular parts of Alaska and the region that people choose in order to see as many sights as possible in a short amount of time. The pressure on accommodation can be a problem in summer, but having a lot of people around can be a benefit as the increased demand for all kinds of trips – flightseeing cruises, kayaking, etc – means you'll find more companies running a wider range of trips to more unusual destinations.

The region divides neatly into three sections. Leaving Anchorage, road and rail follow **Turnagain Arm**, a broad finger off Cook Inlet that provided access for late nineteenth-century prospectors. The only town that has seen much activity in recent times is **Girdwood**, an easygoing place that is home to Alaska's premier downhill **ski resort** and the best preserved of the old gold mines. From here you've a choice: continue around the head of Turnagain Arm to the Kenai Peninsula; or turn onto Portage Road past **Portage Glacier** to the unusual former military port of **Whittier**. Ferries and cruises then become the main transport around **Prince William Sound**, the sheltered, ninety-mile-wide body of water brought to world attention by the *Exxon Valdez* oil spill. You would never know now, as this is once again one of the most fruitful areas for **whale watching** and seems alive with sea otters, seals, and seabirds. Prince William Sound's

---

ACCOMMODATION PRICE CODES

All **accommodation prices** in this book have been coded using the symbols below. Note that prices are for the least expensive double rooms in each establishment. For a full explanation see p.44 in Basics.

① up to $50	④ $80–100	⑦ $160–200
② $50–65	⑤ $100–130	⑧ $200–250
③ $65–80	⑥ $130–160	⑨ $250 and over

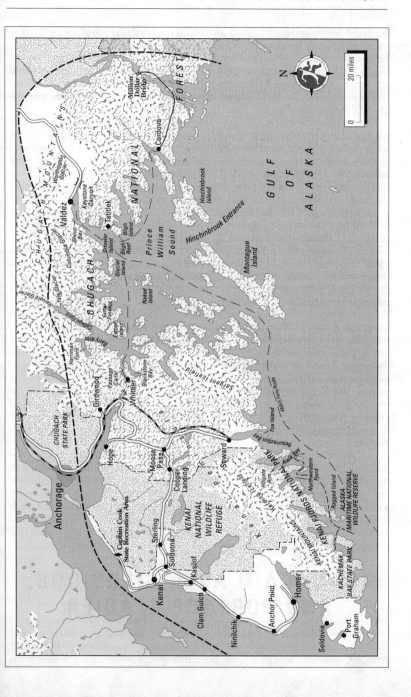

fjords cut deeply into the Chugach Mountains to reveal massive **glaciers**, parts of which periodically break off and choke the waterways. Cruises link Whittier with **Valdez**, where oil that has flowed eight hundred miles through the trans-Alaska pipeline is finally transferred to tankers. It is not as industrial as it might sound and makes a great base for kayaking trips and cruises. Further east, **Cordova** stands as a gateway to the **Copper River Delta** with its vast wetlands, and the glaciers feeding icebergs into the Copper River.

Prince William Sound is also linked by ferry to the **Kenai Peninsula**, though most people explore by car, stopping first at **Seward**, another port with first class whale watching and glacier viewing trips. Much of the center of the peninsula devotes its summers to salmon fishing, specifically the record-breaking **king salmon** that fight their way up the Kenai River – the most famous salmon river in Alaska – trying to avoid the hundreds of lures that are cast their way. The end of the road is **Homer**, always popular for its easy pace, magical scenery, and access to some of Alaska's best **halibut fishing**. Boats then run across Kachemak Bay to **Halibut Cove** with its galleries and popular restaurant, and to **Seldovia**, one of the most alluring places around for spending a couple of relaxing days.

In pre-European times, Southcentral was occupied by four great Native cultures. In the east, the Eyak people lived around the Copper River Delta and traded inland with the Ahtna, and along the coast with the Chugach who settled around the shores of Prince William Sound. Most of the Kenai Peninsula was Dena'ina country, populated by the Kenaitze subtribe. Whatever balance they had achieved between themselves was turned upside down by the arrival of Russians who first set foot in Alaska in 1741 on Kayak Island, fifty miles southeast of Cordova. The Russians eventually established a small town on the Kenai Peninsula, but once under US control the area was virtually ignored until gold was found along Turnagain Arm in 1897. Attention soon shifted to the copper deposits inland from Cordova, and switched again when Alaska's first oil was drilled in 1957 on the west of the Kenai Peninsula. That small find was soon overshadowed by far greater finds elsewhere, but Kenai retains its gas production platforms and oil refinery. A very different instinct was at work in 1907 when President Theodore Roosevelt established one of the country's first national forests, the **Chugach National Forest**, which cloaks much of Southcentral, specifically the whole of Prince William Sound, the eastern third of the Kenai Peninsula and much of the land up towards Anchorage. After Southeast's Tongass National Forest it is America's largest and, like the Tongass, the issue of logging is highly controversial. The difference here is that large sections of forest, particularly in the southwestern corner of the Kenai Peninsula, have been attacked by the **spruce bark beetle**, which kills trees in their thousands. These then become a fire hazard and have to be felled, providing plenty of work for Kenai's forestry companies and clogging up the docks at Homer with logs.

TURNAGAIN ARM, GIRDWOOD, AND PORTAGE GLACIER

Drive twelve miles south of downtown Anchorage and you are already a world away from the city, hemmed in between the Chugach Mountains and **Turnagain Arm**, a 45-mile-long tendril of Cook Inlet, that separates the Chugach Mountains from the Kenai Peninsula. Its glistening, opaque waters have the second greatest tidal range in North America, something which helps create a **tidal bore** (see box, p.220) that sweeps up the Arm on extremely low tides. The bore is best seen from roadside pull-outs also used as vantage points for spotting the white **belukha whales** that can occasionally be seen chasing salmon. At low tide the broad expanse might look enticing, but the **mudflats are dangerous** and you should steer well clear of them. The glacial silt here is so fine that once you break the surface crust your leg sinks in and is almost impossible to remove; then the tide comes in, quickly.

Turnagain Arm first saw white men in the 1890s when a small gold rush erupted, with bursts of activity at Independence Mine, Sunrise City, Resurrection Creek, and Hope City. By the summer of 1901 the strike in Nome had lured miners elsewhere, but a couple of small mines remain as testaments to the dreams of prospectors in an unmapped and untamed land. The best of these is just outside **Girdwood**, a growing dormitory community for Anchorage with its own downhill ski resort – Alyeska – and enough rat-race refugees to give it a bohemian tenor.

Turnagain Arm finally narrows to a point at the old town of Portage, now abandoned after the land around here dropped by six to eleven feet as a result of the 1964 earthquake. From here a road runs inland to the relatively unspectacular but always popular **Portage Glacier**, and continues through a combined road and rail tunnel to Whittier (see p.225).

The Seward Hwy

From Potter Marsh wildlife refuge, twelve miles south of Anchorage, the **Seward Hwy** runs for nearly forty miles along the shore of Turnagain Arm to Portage and the junction for Portage Glacier and Whittier. All along the highway there are great views across the water to the snow-capped Kenai Mountains, but none better than from **McHugh Creek Wayside**, Mile 112 some four miles south of Potter Marsh (daily 9am–9pm), where a refreshing waterfall cascades past the start of several hiking trails (see box, p.221) and some barbecue areas.

In recent years, the numbers of belukha whales in Cook Inlet has rapidly decreased, perhaps as part of a natural cycle, though some blame overzealous Native hunting. The frequency of sightings has dropped accordingly, but your best chance of spotting them as they chase salmon up the inlet from May to August is at the **Beluga Point Interpretive Site**, Mile 110. This is also a prime location for viewing Turnagain Arm's **tidal bore** (see box, overleaf).

Anchorage rock climbers hone their skills on the roadside cliffs on the way to the tiny settlement of **Indian**, Mile 104, the turnoff for the Indian Valley Trail (see box, p.221), and the site of the **Indian Valley Mine** (mid-May to mid-Sept daily 10am–7pm; $1), which captures the area's mining history from 1920 to 1939 though a small collection of artifacts found at the site and displayed (along with a gift shop) in the original assay office. You can pan for gold ($3) and see the old underground mine entrances, but little else.

A mile further south, the trailhead for the Bird Ridge Trail heralds **Bird Creek**, scene of frenetic summer "combat fishing" where anglers are shoulder to shoulder along the riverbank casting for silver and pink salmon. The *Bird Creek* campground,

Headlights are required at all times along the Seward Highway.

TURNAGAIN'S TIDAL BORE

When low tides are extremely low, it is possible to see Turnagain Arm's **tidal bore**, a broken wave of foaming whitewater up to six feet high that sweeps up the Arm towards Portage once every tide. It is a rare phenomenon that only occurs in perhaps sixty places around the world, two of them in Alaska, this large one on Turnagain Arm, and a smaller one on Knik Arm, just to the north of Anchorage. Bores are caused by a combination of extreme tidal variation (almost 39 feet in Turnagain Arm) and the local marine geography, here accentuated by the funneling effect of Turnagain Arm. It is at its most impressive a day or so either side of full moon, when the tidal variation is at its greatest: under less auspicious conditions the bore is barely noticeable. The best time for viewing – and possibly seeing keen board-riders surf the bore – is an hour and a quarter after low tide in Anchorage at Beluga Point: check tide times in the *Anchorage Daily News* and look for a low tide of minus 4.5 feet or lower.

Mile 101, just east of the Bird Creek bridge ($10; pump water), has tent sites away from the RV parking, but you'll need to arrive early to get a site away from the highway. The excellent *Bird Creek Café and Bakery*, Mile 101, renowned for its burgers, espresso, and fruit pies, is handily less than a mile further on. From here, the highway continues to hug the coast for the next eleven miles to Girdwood.

Girdwood and Alyeska Resort

Almost forty miles southeast of Anchorage, Turnagain Arm and the Chugach Mountains briefly release their grip on the Seward Highway, which now runs across broad wetlands. This was the original site of Girdwood which was abandoned after it sank six to eight feet during the 1964 earthquake. In the process the roots of hundreds of black spruce were immersed in the brackish waters of Turnagain Arm. They soon died, but remain standing in a semi-petrified state and are now afforded some degree of legal protection.

GIRDWOOD (*www.girdwoodalaska.com*) relocated a couple of miles inland and has developed into a modest woodland community popular with neo-hippies, outdoor enthusiasts, and escapees from Anchorage. It sits among the spruce below the 3939-foot summit of Mount Alyeska, the low-rise sprawl given some focus by the presence of the **Alyeska Resort** (snow hotline ☎754-7669, ski school ☎754-2280, *www.alyeskaresort.com*), Alaska's premier downhill ski complex. This is the lowest-elevation ski resort in the world, with tows that start just 250 feet above sea level, and yet it manages a six-month season (Nov to mid-April, and sometimes to the end of May) courtesy of an average annual snowfall of nearly fifty feet. Factor in a healthy range of runs (including three perilously steep double black diamond descents), stupendous views, relatively mild temperatures (usually in the twenties) plus the chance to see the aurora borealis, and an Alaskan skiing holiday here takes on considerable appeal. Until 1993 Alyeska resembled one of the small municipal resorts in the Rockies, but a huge influx of cash has given it many new downhill runs, a first-class hotel, and an extensive night-skiing operation (Christmas–New Year and weekends Jan–March, until 9.30pm). Lift **tickets** cost $44 a day ($17 at night) and you can rent basic downhill equipment for $20 a day; quality ski gear or snowboard and boots cost $27.

From around mid-June to September the relatively snow-free slopes make decent hiking country, notably along the ridge-crest Alyeska Glacier View Trail, which can be followed as far as your fitness allows. It is accessed from the *Alyeska Prince* by the **Alyeska Tramway** gondola (late May to mid-Sept daily 10.30am–9.30pm; $16) which swoops you up to *Seven Glaciers* and *Glacier Express* restaurants perched high on the mountain. If you are also planning to dine up here, expensive menus can be offset to some degree by buying a Tram & Lunch Combo ($19) which includes a bite to eat in the *Glacier Express* restaurant. The top of the tramway also serves as a launch pad for rides with Chugach Tandem **Paragliding** ($150; ☎754-2108). Low-level hiking is best done along the **Winner Creek Trail** (3 hours round-trip; 7 miles; 100ft ascent), which heads east from the base of the tramway and weaves through moss-carpeted hemlock and spruce to a plunging gorge. Resident outdoor enthusiasts base Class V Whitewater (☎783-2004, *www.alaskanrafting.com*) here, running a range of **rafting** trips through the summer months from gentle scenic float trips on the Portage River (3hr; $50) to serious whitewater on the Six-Mile Creek (see p.249).

HIKES FROM TURNAGAIN ARM

With the Kenai Peninsula drawing you on it is tempting to skip the hikes beside the Seward Hwy, but the sparking views from sea level, and steep slopes rising straight from the road offer hikes for all abilities. Hikes are listed in order of distance from Anchorage.

Turnagain Arm Trail (9.4 miles one-way; 5–6hr; negligible ascent). Easy coastal trail following a path forged by Dena'ina Natives and consolidated by gold miners. The views of Turnagain Arm are tremendous and you might see spring wildflowers or Dall sheep among the crags. It runs from the Potter Section House to Windy Corner passing numerous access points making it easy to do in shorter stretches. Since this trail runs along the highway, you can easily make this a one-way hike, arranging someone to pick you up or hitch a ride back to the trailhead.

McHugh Lake Trail (14 miles round-trip; 6–8hr; 2750ft ascent). Moderately stiff hike which leads from the McHugh Creek Wayside up McHugh Creek to the tundra-girt McHugh Lake and the larger Rabbit Lake below the rugged form of Suicide Mountain.

McHugh Scenic Overlook (2 miles round-trip; 1hr; negligible ascent). Wheelchair-accessible paved path with handrails and seating offering views of Turnagain Arm and wind-sculpted trees.

Indian Valley Trail (12 miles round-trip; 5–7hr; 2100ft ascent). An easy to moderate trail on a well-graded path climbing out of the tall coastal woods to a pass among alpine tundra and back. Hardy hikers can continue beyond the pass and link up with the Ship Creek Trail behind Anchorage (in winter this becomes a cross-country ski trail). The trailhead is just over a mile off the Seward Hwy (Mile 103.1) at the end of a gravel road.

Bird Ridge Trail (8 miles round-trip; 4–6hr; 2500ft ascent). A steep trail following Bird Ridge from a trailhead parking lot (Mile 102.1) up onto the alpine tundra. Once again, the views are wonderful, the chances of spotting Dall sheep are high, and wildflowers carpet the ground in early spring, replaced by berries in the fall. Note that it is exposed above the tree line and can be windy.

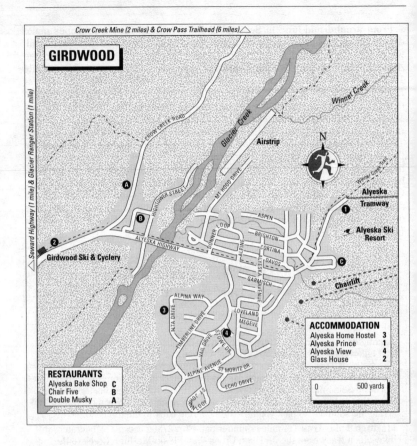

GIRDWOOD

Crow Creek Mine (2 miles) & Crow Pass Trailhead (6 miles)

Seward Highway (1 mile) & Glacier Ranger Station (1 mile)

Winner Creek

Crow Creek Road

Glacier Creek

Airstrip

N

Winner Creek Trail

Alyeska Tramway

Hightower Street

MT HOOD DRIVE

Alyeska Ski Resort

Alyeska Highway

Girdwood Ski & Cyclery

DONNER LOOP

ASPEN

BRIGHTON

CORTINA

ALYESKA AVENUE

DAVOS

GARMISCH

Chairlift

ALPINA WAY

ALTA DRIVE

TIMBERLINE DRIVE

VAIL DRIVE

STOWE DR.

LOVELAND

MEGEVE

ST MORITZ DR.

Alpine Avenue

ECHO DRIVE

HOFFER ST. LOOP

ACCOMMODATION

Alyeska Home Hostel	3
Alyeska Prince	1
Alyeska View	4
Glass House	2

0   500 yards

RESTAURANTS

Alyeska Bake Shop	C
Chair Five	B
Double Musky	A

A mile back towards the Seward Hwy from Alyeska, the unimproved Crow Creek Road penetrates five miles further into the heart of the Chugach Mountains. After three hundred yards you pass the *Double Musky Inn* (see p.223) and press on three miles to **Crow Creek Gold Mine** (mid-May to mid-Sept daily 9am–6pm; $3, $5 with gold panning; ☎278-8060). The mine was established here in 1898 and soon became the most productive of the Turnagain Arm gold strikes. The so-called Crow Creek Boys instituted hydraulic mining operations to scour away the gold-bearing gravels and left in their wake all manner of detritus which today litters the valley. It is still worked on a small scale but is mostly set up for tourists with eight of the mine buildings still on their original foundations and prettied up with planters, moose racks, and aging artifacts.

The trailhead for the **Crow Pass Trail** lies four miles beyond the mine up Crow Creek Road.

Practicalities

The closest thing to a visitor center in these parts is the Forest Service's **Glacier Ranger Station** (Mon–Fri 8am–5pm; ☎783-3242), at the start of Alyeska Hwy, which concentrates on hiking and outdoor activities in the region. Since there is no public transportation, anyone without a car should visit Girdwood Ski and Cyclery, Mile 1.5 (☎783-2453; closed Mon & Tues), who rent mountain **bikes** ($25 a day), and cruisers ($15) which are adequate for the immediate surroundings. In winter and spring they rent telemark and backcountry equipment for $25 a day.

Rack rates at the eight-story *Alyeska Prince* (☎754-2111 or 1-800/880-3880, fax 754-2200, *www.alyeskaresort.com*; ⑦) are outside most budgets, but throughout the summer there are deals offering two nights plus a tramway ride for $250 per person. Even if you can't afford a room, you may want to treat yourself to a meal in one of the restaurants or check out the health spa ($10) complete with pool, hot tub, and views up to Mount Alyeska.

More affordable **accommodation** starts with $10 bunks at the tiny *Alyeska Home Hostel*, Alta Drive (☎783-2099; ①), open year-round and has mountain views, cooking facilities, and a sauna to make up for the lack of a shower. Several **B&Bs** fall under the umbrella of the Girdwood B&B Network (☎222-4858): the Austrian-run *Alyeska View B&B*, Vail Drive, off Timberline Drive (☎ & fax 783-2747, *alyeska-view-bb@gci.net*; ④), is both good and cheap; while *The Glass House*, Mile 1.2 Alyeska Hwy (☎754-1470, fax 754-1100; ⑤), has tastefully decorated rooms illuminated by some of the finest modern stained glass in Alaska, all made by your host. There is also basic **camping** up by the Crow Creek Mine ($5).

Skiers, mountain bikers, in fact just about anyone with a hunger for tasty low-cost **food** should make for the *Alyeska Bake Shop* (☎783-2831) on Olympic Circle at the base of the ski tows. The soup and sourdough bread are legendary and they serve great breakfasts until 1pm. *Chair Five*, Lindblad Ave (☎783-2500, *www.chairfive.com*), is good for gourmet pizza, fresh seafood, and microbrews and is moderately priced, but the restaurant that really draws the Anchorage foodies is the *Double Musky Inn*, Crow Creek Rd (closed Mon, no reservations). It has been an institution since 1962, and its dark bar and airy conservatory are always bustling with diners eager to get their lips around the Louisiana Cajun cuisine and tender steaks. Expect halibut seviche, scallop-stuffed mushroom Rockefeller, rack of lamb, and salmon in green peppercorns and brandy and set aside $40 apiece.

Portage Glacier

The five-mile-long, mile-wide **Portage Glacier** is the single most visited sight in the state. The impressive calving which earned its reputation is a thing of the past, but proximity to Anchorage – just fifty miles away – and assiduous promotion by Gray Line Tours ensures that it remains *the* destination for day-trips from the city. Not so many years ago visitors could see the glacier from the access road, but its retreat has been so profound that it can now only be seen by taking an hour-long **cruise** across the lake its retreat has created. Throughout the summer, tour buses decant their passengers onto the *Ptarmigan* (mid-May to mid-Sept 10.30am–4.30pm every 90min; $35; day-trip from Anchorage with Gray Line $62; ☎1-800/544-2206), which shoulders its way through small icebergs and spends half an hour patrolling the face of the glacier as everyone hopes for a display of calving. A measure of how much it has retreated can be gauged by the location of the **Begich, Boggs Visitor Center**, Mile 5.5 (June–Sept daily 9am–6pm; Oct–May Sat & Sun 10am–4pm; ☎783-2326), built on the moraine which marks the furthest extent of glacial advance a century ago, now two and a half miles from the face. Even when the visitor center was built in the mid-1980s you could spot the glacier from the huge picture windows, something no longer true. Still, the center is a sheltered spot from which to admire the surrounding glaciers, mostly bearing the names of British poets – Burns, Shakespeare, and Byron. For closer inspection, strike out along the trail to the base of **Byron Glacier** (0.7 miles one-way) where you can sometimes see slender, black **iceworms** living on the surface of the glacier. To learn more about this intriguing wee beastie – which many believe only exists in a poem by Robert Service – you can join the free, two-hour **Iceworm Safari** (usually on Sat and one weekday; call in advance) from the visitor center.

Practicalities and the road to Whittier

Portage Glacier lies six miles off the Seward Hwy (Mile 80) and is reached from a junction marked by a copse of salt-damaged trees which make an especially picturesque backdrop for a couple of dilapidated buildings slowly sinking into the mire, both victims of the 1964 earthquake. From here, Portage Road runs up the Portage Valley passing two **campgrounds** – *Blackbear*, Mile 3.7 ($10; pump water) and the very pleasant *Williwaw*, Mile 4.2 ($12; pump water). Beside the latter, reds and chums come up to spawn from mid- to late summer below a platform at the **Williwaw Salmon Viewing Area** (Mile 4.3).

Beside Portage Lake there's the visitor center and boat dock (roughly a mile apart) and the *Portage Glacier Lodge* (mid-May to mid-Sept daily 9am–7pm), a gift shop and decent **café** with hearty soup, sandwich, pie, and drink lunch specials for $8. Just behind, the 400-yard **Moraine Nature Trail** is an easy way to get away from the tour-bus crowds and has a viewpoint fine for a picnic. In spring and fall it might also be a good place for **bird-watching**, since the forested and steeply-sided valley is used as a flyway for birds spending the summer in western Alaska.

Until June 2000, this was the end of the road, but a single-lane road (toll $15) now continues through a combined road and rail tunnel to Whittier: delays mean that you will have to park in the staging areas close to the visitor center.

PRINCE WILLIAM SOUND

If you've come to Alaska hoping to see huge chunks of ice crashing into deep fjords where harbor seals loll on icebergs and mountain goats dot the hillsides then **PRINCE WILLIAM SOUND** is the place for you. Of course, it is also the perfect place to kayak to small islands and scan the horizon for breaching whales. Either way it is hard to surpass these sheltered waters with their three thousand miles of convoluted coastline and myriad uninhabited islands. Many compare the Sound favorably with Southeast's Glacier Bay, citing a larger number of glaciers and ease of access, though that same accessibility robs Prince William Sound of some of the isolated qualities of Glacier Bay.

Prince William Sound is also where the *Exxon Valdez* went aground on Bligh Reef in 1989, spilling millions of gallons of oil and killing numerous birds and sea mammals. Many species have yet to fully recover, but there are no longer any visual reminders of those shameful days, just sparkling blue water, abundant birdlife, and orcas cruising the waterways.

You'll likely approach the Sound from one of the three towns on its shores: **Whittier**, a strange former military port that has been recently connected by road to Anchorage; the port of **Valdez** with its oil-terminal tour and extreme skiing, and isolated **Cordova**, which gives wonderful access to the birdlife of the Copper River Delta and the famed Million Dollar Bridge. All are interesting in their own right, but most serve as bases for getting out on the water.

Money, time. and your taste for adventure will determine how you explore Prince William Sound, an experience which could be as little as a ferry trip between Whittier and Valdez (see box, p.228), which gives a good sense of the region's beauty, affords distant views of glaciers, and may offer a few sightings of seals and perhaps whales. If you have the time, go **kayaking**, an activity that can be as easy-going as you wish and gives a much more realistic sense of the scale of everything than you get from on a big cruise boat.

Birds and sea mammals seem so abundant that it hardly matters where you go, but cruises and kayak trips tend to focus on particular areas. Around Whittier the prize destinations are **College Fjord**, with its collegiate tidewater glaciers, Harvard and Yale, and the nearby **Harriman Fjord**, almost entirely encircled by icy, glacier-feeding mountains. King of all the Prince William Sound glaciers is the **Columbia Glacier**, the largest tidewater glacier in Southcentral Alaska. It is an astonishing sight, protruding forty miles from the peaks of the snowbound Chugach Mountains out into Prince William Sound where its three-mile-wide face is forever calving off huge bergs. Actually, icy chunks are falling off faster than they are being replaced, and the glacier's terminus has retreated almost ten miles over the last twenty years leaving behind a huge bay choked solid with bobbing hunks of ice. Usually it is impossible to get close enough to see any impressive calving, but it is a brilliant place to spend time listening to the popping of melting ice. Understandably it has become the focus of numerous cruise and kayaking itineraries.

One of the first Europeans to gain a sense of what lay behind the sheltering belt of islands here was **James Cook**, who sailed through in 1778 naming it Sandwich Sound, in honor of his patron the Earl of Sandwich. On Cook's return to England the Earl was out of favor and the House of Lords changed the name to recognize the king's son. Spanish explorer, **Don Salvador Fidalgo** arrived in 1790, also looking for the Northwest Passage. He took longer to decide he hadn't found it, and in the process named Cordova, Galena Bay, and Puerto Valdes, renamed Valdez during the Spanish-American War at the end of the nineteenth century. He approached Colombia Glacier but turned away as he thought the load roar and spray of calving icebergs was the action of a live volcano.

Whittier

The tiny port of **WHITTIER**, sixty miles southeast of Anchorage, is a bizarre place, effectively a sprawling rail depot hemmed in by heavily glaciated mountains. Almost all of the town's three hundred residents live either in the single tower block, or the scruffy low-rise Whittier Manor. Until recently it had only been reachable by sea or by train, an isolating state of affairs shattered by the recently constructed rail and road tunnel (at 2.5 miles the longest highway tunnel in the US). It remains unknown just how the townsfolk (many of whom opposed road access) are going to cope with the new parking lots, plans to double the size of the small boat harbor, and the new businesses itching to spring up. However, for the time being, the expected influx of visitors has failed to materialize.

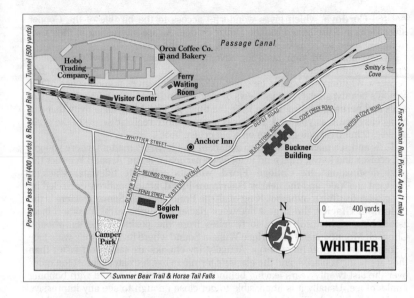

Whittier was founded as an alternative ice-free port during World War II when the profusion of boats waiting to unload cargo onto the Alaska Railroad at Seward was seen as an easy target for Japanese bombers pressing eastward from the Aleutians. Its location at the head of Passage Canal Fjord, and the almost permanent cloud cover made it a prime candidate, so a sequence of two tunnels was bored through the surrounding mountains, and by 1943 a rail link was established to Portage and Anchorage. Soon after the end of the war, the army began consolidating their position by building the six-level **Buckner Building**, now a hollow shell but once known as the "city under one roof" with living quarters, shops, rifle range, hospital, cinema, bowling alley, and swimming pool. The all-in-one design dramatically reduced snow removal problems in an area notorious for heavy dumps, and the same principle was applied when they built the fourteen-story, flesh-toned **Begich Tower**, which is now home to over half the town's residents. The army pulled out in 1960 and the town ticked over serving the railroad, the AMHS ferries to Valdez and Cordova, and a few tourists looking to take glacier cruises. The new road could well signal Whittier's renaissance, though as one tourist recently put it "I went through the longest tunnel in North America and all I got was Whittier."

Cruises

The mountains, glaciers, and occasionally glistening fjord make a dramatic first impression, but there is really nothing to do in Whittier. This isn't a problem for most visitors who either hop on the AMHS ferry for Valdez or Cordova, or are bundled straight onto a glacier cruise (for discussion of ferry routes and cruises across Prince William Sound, see box on p.228).

Biggest and slickest of the local cruises (which are all timed to coincide with train arrivals) is the 26 Glacier Cruise (5hr; $119; ☎276-8023 or 1-800/544-0529,

Cruise ship and glacier

Orca breaching

Bald eagle

Interior of an ice cave, Mendenhall Glacier, Juneau

Deep Lake, Chilkoot Trail, Skagway

Sawyer Glacier, Tracy Arm Fjord

St Michaels Russian Orthodox Church, Sitka

Fishing boat, Ninilchik

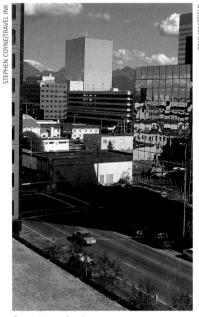

Downtown Anchorage

Totem pole, Anchorage

Portage Glacier

Caribou migration across Kobuk River

College Fjord, Prince William Sound

www.26glaciers.com) on a speedy catamaran, briefly viewing all 26 of the glaciers in Harriman and College fjords (see p.225). Slightly less pressured big-boat cruises include the Wilderness Explorer (6hr; $109; ☎1-800/992-1297, *www .princewilliamsound.com*), which calls at the world's second largest salmon hatchery, winds through the hairline Esther Passage, and spends time around the tidewater glaciers in Barry Arm; and the excellent-value and more leisurely Glacier Lovers Cruise (5.5hr; $99; ☎274-7300 or 1-800/764-7300, *www.majormarine.com*), which travels slower and can include an all-you-can-eat buffet ($10 extra) as you visit Blackstone and Beloit glaciers. These all tend to be fairly crowded and cursory, and you'll get much more intimate contact with the aquatic environment (and more time on the water) with marine wildlife biologist, Gerry Sanger of Sound Eco Adventures (☎ & fax 472-2312, ☎1-888/471-2312, *www.alaskan.com/ecotours*). He covers the main calving-glacier territory on trips into College Fjord (8hr; $155), Barry Arm (5–6hr; $134), and Blackstone Bay (over 3hr; $69); but also ranges into more peaceful waters either whale watching (10hr; $170), viewing sea birds on remote islands (8hr; $155), or catching fjord wildlife at its most active in the early morning (over 4hr; $89). It is best to book in advance, and is essential if you fancy a four-day marine wildlife trip ($2100 for two; $2400 for three; $2700 for four). In most cases there are discounts for groups of five or six.

Kayaking

In the calm waters of Prince William Sound you really need no prior experience to go on guided **sea-kayaking** trips such as those run by Alaska Sea Kayakers (☎472-2534 or 1-877/472-2534, *www.honeycharters.com*): the Kittiwake trip (at noon daily; 3hr; $60) is essentially an extended introduction to the sport; the Shotgun Cove trip (5hr; $115) involves an outbound charter and a paddle back along the fjord shore; and the Blackstone Bay trip (full day; $250) gives you the opportunity to paddle around calving tidewater glaciers.

Some proof of experience is necessary when renting kayaks (double $60 a day; single $40; every fifth day is free) to spend a few days exploring the area around Blackstone Bay, or heading north into Harriman Fjord and College Fjord. To save a bit of slog getting there, it may be worth sticking your boat on a water taxi. Sound Eco Adventures (see above) will oblige: they often try to match parties up to reduce costs and will recommend someone else if they're not available.

Hiking around Whittier

If you've got a couple of hours between ferry and train, you might as well hike out and see a little of the surrounding scenery. The easiest **short walk** is to **Smitty's Cove** (half a mile round-trip) at the eastern end of town where you can gaze across at the kittiwake rookery and get tolerable views of Billings Glacier. You'll get a better angle on the glacier and tremendous fjord views along the walk to **First Salmon Run** picnic area (2 miles round-trip; 1hr) reached along the gravel Shotgun Cove Road heading east. In June and late August the river is alive with king and silver salmon (respectively), as is Second Salmon Run a further three miles east along the fjord.

If you can organize your schedule accordingly it is worth setting aside some time to hike the **Portage Pass Trail** (8 miles round-trip; 4hr; 700ft ascent), maybe **camping** beside Divide Lake near the top of the pass, which presents great views back down the fjord, only superseded by those down to the Portage Glacier. This is the route taken by many gold prospectors, who would climb to the pass and descend across Portage Glacier, a route no longer feasible as the glacier has receded to form Portage Lake. The trail begins at the western end of town near the tunnel entrance.

CRUISES AND FERRIES ACROSS PRINCE WILLIAM SOUND

Whittier and Valdez both have excellent cruises, but some of the grandeur of plunging fjords and calving glaciers can also be seen on a ferry or cruise that crosses Prince William Sound and has the additional benefit of providing transport between the two towns.

The cheapest passage between the two towns, and the only option if you're driving, is one of the AMHS **ferries** which visit the Prince William Sound ports during the summer months. Much the most frequent being the *Bartlett*, which plies a seemingly random pattern between Whittier, Valdez, and Cordova that ensures a ferry at least every couple of days to each destination. Valdez also gets visits from the *Tustumena*, with almost-weekly connections out of Prince William Sound to Seward, Kodiak, and Homer. Finally, the *Kennicott* runs once a month between Juneau and Valdez – the so-called "Inter-tie" trip. If you are not planning to take one of the dedicated glacier cruises, at least do the ferry run between Whittier and Valdez, which passes within sight of the Columbia Glacier. It is a popular run and while foot passengers seldom have trouble getting a space, drivers should **reserve in advance**. Ferry fares are roughly half the cruise fares and are listed in Basics (see p.34).

The biggest day-cruise operator in the region is Prince William Sound Cruises & Tours (☎1-800/992-1297, *www.princewilliamsound.com*) who run several Whittier- and Valdez-based trips (see town accounts), and link the two with their Prince William Sound Crossing (between Valdez and Whittier; mid-May to mid-Sept daily; $119), which visits the Columbia Glacier, and calls for lunch at their camp at Growler Island. Six-hour crossings depart Valdez at 7.15am and Whittier at 2.15pm.

GROWLER ISLAND

Named for the car-sized icebergs that wash up on the beach from the Columbia Glacier thirteen miles away, **Growler Island** lies beside a narrow channel and lagoon populated by seals and bald eagles, and wonderfully sheltered for kayaking and canoeing. There's just a handful of buildings linked by boardwalk to a central dining area, and it is almost always peaceful, often with great views across the sound. The company's cruises call in during the day either for an eat-your-fill salmon and halibut bake or to dropoff guests who **stay** either in A-frame alpine-style cabins or in platform tents equipped with functional beds ($125 per person including all meals).

Between cruise visits you've got the place to yourself with free use of canoes and pedalboats to paddle around the lagoon; for something more organized join Alaskan Wilderness Sailing and Kayaking (☎835-5175, fax 835-3765, *www.alaskan-wilderness.com*) for very professional sailing and guided kayaking ($65 a half-day; full day $94) past melting icebergs, out around some wooded coves and visiting a sea lion haulout on Glacier Island. The kayaks and one-person trimarans are both easy to handle and can be combined with overnight camping around Prince William Sound on multiday paddling and sailing trips ($175 a day). Experienced paddlers can also **rent kayaks** (single $45, double $65, 20 percent reduction after first day) at Growler Island saving you having to paddle or transport a rented kayak out here from Valdez or Whittier.

Practicalities

Despite the conversion of the rail tunnel to joint road use, the easiest way to reach Whittier is still by rail. Passenger **trains** run once daily direct from Anchorage ($45 one-way; $52 round-trip) and drop you right in the heart of Whittier two and a half hours later. By taking a glacier cruise and returning on a later train it is possible to treat Whittier as a day-trip destination from Anchorage. Train schedules take precedence over **road traffic** through the tunnel, which must stop to let the train through, then wait half an hour for fumes to clear before being allowed to proceed. The tunnel (6am–11pm; $15 toll on Whittier-bound cars and motorbikes, RVs $40; *www.dot.state.ak.us/whittiertunnel*) is only wide enough for traffic in one direction which further increases delays to the point where the twelve-mile drive from Portage to Whittier can take up to two hours if you time it badly. To get here from Girdwood, hop aboard the Whittier **shuttle bus** ($17 one-way; $30 round-trip; 3 daily; ☎224-7239). Cars, buses, and trains all emerge from the tunnel right by the Whittier **visitor center** (June–Aug daily 10am–5pm; ☎472-2379), which occupies a disused rail car close to the station, a mere ten-minutes' walk from anywhere in town.

With well-integrated boat and train timetables it is unlikely you'll have to spend more than a couple of hours (and possibly just a few minutes) in Whittier. If you find you need **to stay**, the best bets are the **campground** (early June to Sept; $5 per site; showers at the Harbor office for $3) tucked in behind the Begich Tower, and *June's Whittier B&B* (☎472-2396 or 1-888/472-2396, fax 472-2503, *www.alaska .net/~junebbak*; ④) spread over several condos inside the Begich Tower. *June's* has an office on the waterfront. The scruffy *Anchor Inn* (☎472-2354 or 1-877/870-8787, fax 472-2394, *anchjoe@aol.com*; ④) is the only other place in town with rooms.

It is more likely you'll need something **to eat**, and several places close to the dock fit the bill. Best known is the *Hobo Trading Company*, (mid-May to mid-Sept daily except Tues 11am–7pm; ☎472-2374), run by Babs, a "local renegade" deeply embroiled in area politics. Burgers, sandwiches, pies, and ice cream (among other things) are served in a glassed-in cabin overlooking the small boat harbor. Other good bets are *Frankie's Deli* (☎472-2477), with an extensive menu and imported beers, and *Orca Coffee Co and Bakery*, a cozy spot with a good view up the fjord.

Should you need them there is a **post office** (variable hours but often Mon, Wed & Fri 11.30am–5.30pm) on the first floor of the Begich Tower, a **medical clinic** (Thurs–Mon 10am–6pm) in apartment 301, and a grocery store and hair salon, but **no bank** or ATM.

Valdez and around

VALDEZ (pronounced Val-DEEZ) owns one of the most remarkably picturesque settings in Alaska, nestled under some of the world's tallest coastal mountains on the shores of Valdez Arm, a curving tentacle threading twelve miles north off Prince William Sound. It is a small town without a great deal to actually see, though it easily makes up for this by its proximity to some wonderful cruising and sea-kayaking waters, and the stupendous **Columbia Glacier**.

There are fewer than five thousand residents in Valdez, but its status as North America's northernmost ice-free port has brought it considerable prosperity, largely as the **southern terminus for the trans-Alaska oil pipeline**. Tankers seem almost perpetually moored across the water at the Alyeska Marine Terminal, a constant reminder that the **Exxon Valdez disaster** (see box, p.234) happened just a few miles away. But this was only the latest chapter in a catalog of grim events to have befallen Valdez over the years.

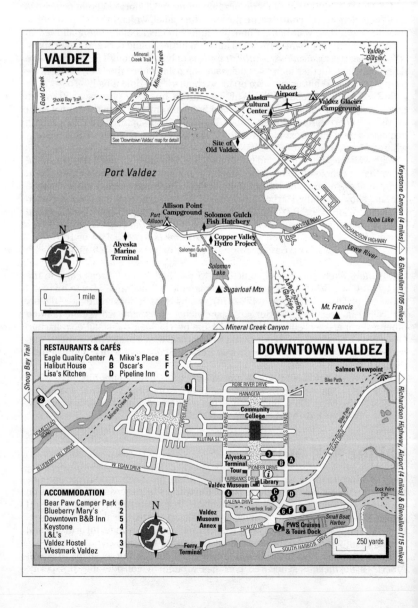

The first was in 1897, soon after gold was discovered on the Klondike. Gold seekers were already wary of Canadian regulations and taxes on the White Pass and Chilkoot trails from Skagway to the Yukon, so there was a ready audience when the *Seattle Post-Intelligencer* reported that the **All-American Route** from Valdez Arm to the Interior was not only two hundred miles shorter than other routes but "altogether in American territory…and said to be not difficult." No one mentioned the complete lack of facilities in Valdez, nor the need to cross the Valdez and Klutina glaciers, a twenty-mile route riddled with killer crevasses. Altogether around 3500 set off from the mud flats and tents that constituted Valdez. As one prospector put it, "It was a wonderful sight to stand on the summit of that glacier 5000 feet above the sea and look back eighteen miles to the coast and see the black serpent of humanity winding its way over the snow and ice like a huge snake." Gold fever outweighed prudence and most set off entirely unprepared, hundreds dying of starvation and scurvy. Those who tried to hike during the day struggled desperately through the soft snow or succumbed to snow blindness, and groped unseeing into gaping crevasses. Most were forced to travel at night with minimal protection from the terrible cold, and few reached the Klondike in time to stake a paying claim.

A boost came in 1900 with the discovery of huge deposits of copper at Kennicott (see p.383), a hundred miles to the northeast. When a railroad was proposed to transport the copper to a port, Cordova and Valdez battled over the privilege, a gunfight even taking place in Keystone Canyon between rival rail companies. Valdez eventually lost the battle and life ticked by quietly until 1964 when it was struck by the **Good Friday earthquake**, the most powerful in North American recorded history (see box, p.195). The ensuing tsunami took 33 lives, washed away the waterfront and destroyed the town, which was subsequently rebuilt on more stable ground four miles to the west.

A few old buildings were relocated to the new town, but the overall effect is modern and faceless. The layout comes with dead-end streets, a devilish design for snow plows struggling to cope with some of the **highest snowfalls in the state**: the 7000-foot barrier of the Chugach Mountains causes an average of 27 feet (and a record 46 feet) of snow to fall on the town each winter.

Valdez boomed again in the mid-1970s during construction of the huge oil terminal where North Slope crude could be loaded from the trans-Alaska pipeline into waiting tankers. One fully laden tanker, the *Exxon Valdez*, catapulted Valdez into world headlines on Good Friday 1989, when it struck Bligh Reef at the entrance to Valdez Arm exactly 25 years after the 1964 earthquake. Since then, Valdez has settled back into a fairly sleepy existence.

Arrival and information

AMHS **ferries** (for discussion of routes see box, p.35) dock at the **ferry terminal** (☎835-4436), a quarter of a mile west of downtown Valdez, while the cross-sound cruise pulls in at the small boat harbor, right in the center.

Arriving **by road** you'll be negotiating the towering Chugach Mountains on the most dramatic section of the Richardson Hwy: our account starts in Glenallen (p.375) and continues north on p.387. It is a gorgeous run served by Alaskon Express **buses** (☎835-4391) from Anchorage, and the Parks Highway Express (☎1-888/600-6001) from Fairbanks: both terminate downtown at the *Westmark Hotel*, 100 Fidalgo Drive. If you're leaving Valdez by bus there are early departures with connections at Glenallen for Tok (with Alaskon), but you arrive in Glenallen too late in the day to get the Kennicott Shuttle into the Wrangell-St Elias National Park.

The only scheduled **flights** into Valdez are with ERA Aviation (☎1-800/866-8394) who fly three times daily direct from Anchorage ($100 one-way, $160 seven-day APEX round-trip) to **Valdez airport**, four miles east of town along Airport Road. A **taxi** into town with Valdez Yellow Cab (☎835-2500) will cost $10. For more flexibility visit the airport **rental-car** office of Valdez-U-Drive (☎835-4402 or 1-800/478-4402 in Alaska, *valudrive@alaska.net*) who charge as little as $44 a day, or Hertz (☎835-44378, fax 835-2761) who charge a little more for larger cars and allow one-way rentals.

Once in town, everywhere is accessible on foot from the central **visitor center**, 200 Fairbanks St (late May to early Sept daily 8am–8pm; ☎1-800/770-5954 or 835-4636, fax 835-4845, *www.valdezalaska.org*), which has a free map of town. Outside there is a freecall phone linked to some of the town's B&Bs, and in winter information is available from the **CVB** (Mon–Fri 8am–5pm) in the same building.

Accommodation

Traditional **accommodation** is fairly expensive in Valdez though you'll find more satisfying and cheaper rooms at the assortment of downtown and neighborhood **B&Bs**, the descendants of the city's first crop which sprung up during the clean-up of the *Exxon Valdez* when there weren't enough beds to go round. In high summer, downtown is swamped with RVs occupying soulless but well-placed gravel lots. The nearest leafy **campground** is five miles away, and signs downtown discourage free camping, but for one-night stays creative campers should find a quiet spot a mile or so west along Mineral Creek.

Hotels and B&Bs

Blueberry Mary's, 810 Salmonberry Way (☎835-5015, *www.alaska.net/~bmary*). Secluded B&B a mile from town with stupendous views of Valdez Arm, comfortable rooms, a sauna, and a breakfast of pancakes with blueberries from the local hillside. ④.

Downtown B&B Inn, 113 Galena Drive (☎835-2791 or 1-800/478-2791, fax 835-5406, *www.alaskaone.com/downinn*). Slightly shabby hotel but with some newer rooms with private bath (⑤). Handy downtown location with good rates which include a substantial continental breakfast. ④.

Keystone, 144 Egan Drive (☎835-3851 or 1-888/835-0665, fax 835-5322, *www.alaskan.com/keystonehotel*). Recently renovated hotel with industrial-looking steel-clad exterior, and well-appointed rooms that are comfortable, though some are small. All come with private bathrooms and a complimentary continental breakfast. ④.

L&L's, 533 W Hanagita St (☎835-4447, fax 835-4797, *www.alaskan.com/lnlbnb*). Comfortable five-room B&B with shared bathrooms in a modern home ten-minutes' walk from the center but with a couple of free bikes to get around. Good self-serve breakfast. ③.

Westmark Valdez, 100 Fidalgo Drive (☎835-4391, fax 835-2308, *www.westmarkhotels.com*). Valdez' top hotel with all the expected facilities and a great waterside location, though the best views are reserved for the restaurant/bar. ⑤.

Hostels and campgrounds

Allison Point Ocean Front Campground, Mile 5 Dayville Rd (mid-May to mid-Sept; ☎835-2282). Gravel RV sites with water and outhouses, most sites wedged between Dayville Rd and the waters of the bay. Oil terminal traffic makes it less than peaceful, but the view is great. $10.

Bear Paw Camper Park, 101 N Harbor Drive (☎835-2530, fax 835-5266, *www.alaska.net /~bpawcamp*). Not the cheapest of the downtown RV parks ($17 dry, $22 full hookup) but it is in a great location, has a heated sitting area with modem jacks and there is an adult-only camping area ($18) in the alders away from the RVs.

Valdez Glacier Campground, Mile 2.3 Airport Rd (mid-May to mid-Sept; ☎835-2282). Valdez's only rural campground; large, spacious, leafy and located five miles east of town by the airport. Sites are well spaced with picnic tables and fire rings. $10 per site.

Valdez Hostel, 139 Altina St (☎835-2155, *www.alaska.net/~nckcs*). The only hostel in town, and handily sited close to everything. A little cramped but there's only three bunks to a room ($22 per person), free tea and coffee and excellent cooking facilities. Some bedding available for rent but it's best to bring your own. ①.

The town and around

With its mountain-girt setting perched beside a deep fjord, Valdez can be a great place just to walk around, perhaps walking along the Overlook Trail or the Dock Point Trail (see box, p.236) to gain a better vantage or heading for the small boat harbor later in the day when huge halibut are landed and strung up.

About the only distraction in town is the **Valdez Museum**, 217 Egan Drive (late May to mid-Sept Mon–Sat 9am–6pm, Sun 8am–5pm; mid-Sept to late May Mon–Fri 10am–5pm, Sat noon–4pm; $3; *www.alaska.net/~vldzmuse*), an eclectic regional collection with the old fresnel lens from the Hinchinbrook Lighthouse in Prince William Sound, a field gun from Fort Liscum, which closed in 1922 and is now the oil terminal, and the superb mirror-backed Pinzon Bar from pre-quake Valdez. Notice the copper panels covering the holes in the bar that were cut for soda siphons during prohibition. Photos of yesteryear show the effect of the earthquake, while others from the big-snow year of 1989–90 illustrate just how much of a problem snow clearance can be. There's even a three-quarters-of-an-inch-thick piece of the hull from the *Exxon Valdez*, which sounds rugged enough, until you consider that it was the only thing between 53 million gallons of crude and a pristine marine environment.

The associated **Valdez Museum Annex**, 436 S Hazelet St (June–Aug daily 9am–4pm; $1.50), is more focused than the Valdez Museum, with much of the floor space taken up by a huge and historically accurate model of Valdez as it was in 1963, before the earthquake. Impressive as it is, the earthquake displays demand more of your time, particularly if you have patience to watch the whole of the 45-minute *Though the Earth Moved* video. It is worth it, if only to see the 8mm footage shot from aboard the *Chena*, which was moored at Valdez dock. Despite being buffeted by huge waves then having the sea sucked out from under them, two crew members kept filming throughout. Elsewhere there are interactive displays, and a working seismograph with its sensor in College Fjord, epicenter of the 1964 quake.

On a warm afternoon it is a pleasant wander half a mile out along East Egan Drive to the **Crooked Creek Salmon Viewing Platform** (unrestricted access), on the site of a former hatchery and still a good place to spot pink and chum salmon, especially from mid-July to early September. There's an underwater camera, so you can watch the spawning inside the adjacent **Crooked Creek information Site** (June–Aug daily 9am–6pm), which, outside the spawning season, shows a video of last year's performance.

Around Valdez Arm

Almost everything else is out of town and you really need your own vehicle, though you can get a fair idea of the local layout by joining the two-hour **Alyeska**

THE EXXON VALDEZ AND ITS LEGACY

In the American public consciousness the name Valdez isn't so much associated with the town as with the 987-foot tanker *Exxon Valdez*, which struck Bligh Reef, 25 miles to the southwest, and spilled eleven million gallons of North Slope crude all over Prince William Sound in 1989 – the biggest and most catastrophic oil spill in US history. Images of oil-smothered birds and slick black beaches flashed around the globe, and the State of Alaska looked on as if paralyzed. Twelve years later, Prince William Sound looks as unspoiled as ever, but scratch below the surface (at least on the beaches) and evidence of the ongoing effects is easy to find, a realization revived every time a new round of legal wrangling over settlement is wrapped up.

On the evening of March 23, 1989, the *Exxon Valdez* left port with a full load and within a couple of hours had to take evasive action to avoid an iceberg that had calved off the Columbia Glacier. After issuing instructions, hot-shot tanker captain, Joseph Hazelwood had gone below – a common enough practice with all the paperwork to complete – leaving an inexperienced third mate in charge. At 12.04am Hazelwood reported "We've fetched up hard aground north of Goose Island off Bligh Reef, and evidently leaking some oil." As soon as the disaster happened, Exxon hired a PR company who locked onto Hazelwood as a convenient scapegoat, especially when it was reported that he had been drinking at the *Pipeline Inn* immediately before taking command. Remedial action would have been more useful, but the sole response barge was under fourteen feet of snow so the response team was laid up for three days while the barge was dug out. A tenth anniversary report on the incident stated that "11 million gallons of oil spread slowly over open water during three days of flat calm seas. Despite the opportunity to skim the oil before it hit the shorelines, almost none was scooped up...Even if [the response barge] had responded, there were not enough skimmers and boom available to do an effective job. Dispersants were applied, but were determined to be ineffective because of prevailing conditions. Even if dispersants had been effective, however, there was not enough dispersant on hand to make a dent in the spreading oil slick." The State of Alaska's 1993 report described it as "a botched response."

Altogether 1500 miles of coastline were befouled (200 miles badly) and some slicks found their way to shore almost 500 miles from Bligh Reef. Animal population studies estimate that as a direct result of the spill almost 3000 sea otters perished along with 300 harbor seals, up to 22 orcas and a quarter of a million seabirds, including 250 bald eagles. Salmon streams as far away as Kenai and

Marine Terminal tour, 212 Tatitlek St (May to mid-Sept 2–4 tours daily; $16; ☎835-2686, fax 835-8986), which is the only way you'll get to see anything of the terminal. In the wake of the *Exxon Valdez* oil spill, and ongoing criticism of safety standards, Alyeska are keen to put on a promotional face, but this is kept tolerably in check. After browsing around the assorted promotional displays and the model of a pump station, you are put through security procedures (and are asked to leave any cameras behind), and then board a bus to the site. The huge tanks and gleaming pipes are vaguely impressive, but once inside the site you are only allowed out of the bus briefly at a high viewpoint with a great perspective over the terminal towards Valdez.

Drivers can take East Egan Drive four miles to Mile Zero of the Richardson Hwy, where Alaska Avenue runs four hundred yards down to the **Old Townsite**, little more than a couple of building foundations and a memorial

Kodiak were even affected. Of the 28 species affected by the oil spill, only two are considered to have fully recovered; bald eagles and river otters. The rest are all affected in some way, one study showing that hydrocarbons present in crude oil at concentrations as low as one part per billion can harm herring and salmon eggs.

To clean the mess up, ten thousand people were involved at a cost to Exxon of around $2 billion. Only eleven percent of the oil was recovered and the futility of the clean-up was highlighted by Alutiiq village chief, Walter Meganack, who described spending "all day cleaning one huge rock, and the tide comes in and covers it with oil again. Spend a week wiping and spraying the surface, but pick up a rock and there's four inches of oil underneath."

Commercial fishermen were badly hit. The 1989 fishing season never opened and fish stocks were negatively affected for years. Some say stocks are still suffering, though with the passage of time, widespread overfishing and a number of other factors, it is becoming increasingly difficult to apportion blame. Subsistence hunting for seals and the harvest of herring eggs on kelp in Native villages were ruined for years, and many residents fled to Valdez, some getting jobs as oil-spill response crews.

Change has been forced by new federal and state laws, and the creation of monitoring organizations such as the Prince William Sound Regional Citizens' Advisory Council (*www.pwsrcac.org*), a permanent industry-funded citizens' council which struggles to maintain its independence from industry lobbyists. Prince William Sound now has more weather buoys than any similar body of water in the world, the Coast Guard monitors a much wider area, an innovative iceberg detection system is being tested, boats must now be tethered to a powerful and highly maneuverable escort tug as far as the entrance to Prince William Sound, tanker captains are drug and alcohol tested before sailing, oil skimming and storage capability is much improved, and regular response drills are conducted.

Meanwhile, Exxon have wrestled in the courts over restitution. In 1991, Exxon, the Federal Government, and the State of Alaska reached an out-of-court settlement requiring Exxon to pay the other two parties $100 million in criminal restitution for fish, wildlife, and lands; and $900 million as a civil settlement with payments spread over ten years. Forty thousand commercial fishers and other parties who suffered as a result of the spill then joined forces in a class-action suit against Exxon, and in 1994 a jury awarded them $5.2 billion. Exxon immediately appealed and, though this money has been put in escrow and is gaining interest, the fishers have seen none of it, and probably won't for many years to come.

plaque. On the other side of the Richardson Hwy, Airport Road runs a mile to the airport, where you'll find the **Alaska Cultural Center** (June–Aug daily 11am–7pm; Sept–May Mon–Sat 9am–6pm, $4, call for winter opening hours on ☎834-8931), which contains one of the finest collections of sculpted ivory and Eskimo artifacts in the state. The enormous stuffed bull moose, caribou, bison, and polar bear loom over beautifully made mukluks, a parka made from ground squirrel pelts, another made from murre skins, and a large umiak which uses whale baleen for its ribs. Two moose hides with mountain scenes are hung next to each other to illustrate the changing Alaskan landscape; the images are thought to be of the same place, the first (undated) with a cabin in the newly tamed wilderness, the second a few years later (1913) with the cabin in disrepair and moose reclaiming the territory. The ivory room is crammed with pieces veering well away from the typical walrus-tusk cribbage boards, ranging from grotesque figures traditionally used to ward off evil spirits, to a model of a Pan-Am 747 carved in the 1970s.

Some seven miles out of town along the Richardson Hwy (Mile 2.9), Dayville Road cuts around the head of the bay to the Alyeska Marine Terminal. The buildings along the waters' edge four miles along Dayville Road are the **Solomon Gulch Hatchery** (unrestricted entry) where you can pick up a leaflet and follow a free self-guided tour along waterside boardwalks passing tanks of salmon in various states of growth. It is hoped that the salmon will be here in large enough numbers to support the commercial fishery once the oil stops flowing. A similar forward-looking policy helped the creation of the diminutive **Copper Valley Hydro Project**, which channels water from high-country lakes through turbines providing power to Valdez and Glenallen. The penstocks above the power station can be seen on the **Solomon Gulch Trail** (see box, below) which starts a mile further on by the Allison Point RV park. The road finishes at the Alyeska Marine Terminal, built on the site of the former Fort Liscum, the terminus of the WAMCATS telegraph wire to Eagle (see box, p.408) from 1900 to 1923. There is no access to the terminal from here, just a few information boards about the operations, and a monument to the workers who built the pipeline, inscribed with "We didn't know it couldn't de done."

HIKES AROUND VALDEZ

Much of the best hiking around Valdez requires a vehicle for access, but there are a couple of good hikes which start right in town. These should be largely snow free from early June to late September.

Dock Point Trail (1 mile loop; 30min; 100ft ascent). A peaceful nature walk on gravel trails and boardwalks with interpretive signs. It leads from the east end of the small boat harbor to a knoll and a couple of viewpoints looking across the bay.

Mineral Creek Canyon (2 miles round-trip; 1hr; 100ft ascent). A good one for mountain bikers mostly because it starts at the end of a rough six-mile road that is all but impassable for low-slung vehicles and is boring to walk. From the trailhead it continues a mile to the abandoned gold stamp mill of Hercules Mine near the base of the Johnson Glacier.

Overlook Trail (100 yards; 5min; mostly steps). A flight of steps up to a good shelter with great views over town and Valdez Arm.

Shoup Bay Trail (24 miles round-trip; 1–2 days; mostly flat). Beautiful, easy (but long) hike along the shores of Port Valdez to Shoup Bay where there are three beautifully-sited six-bunk State Park cabins looking at the face of Shoup Glacier ($50; book through APLIC in Anchorage ☎269-8400, check availability on *nutmeg.state.ak.us/ixpress/dnr/parks/index.dml*). The hike is particularly good for keen birders though direct access to the shores of the fjord is limited.

Solomon Gulch Trail (3.8 miles round-trip; 1.5–2.5hr; 620ft ascent). Starting thirteen miles from Valdez on the road to the Pipeline terminal, the trail initially follows the gravel road laid atop the penultimate mile of the oil pipeline as far as Solomon Gulch. Here, surplus tubing from the pipeline was used as penstocks for the Solomon Gulch hydro station. These are then followed to the glacial waters behind the Solomon Gulch Dam overlooked by Sugarloaf Mountain (3484ft) and a distant glacier at the end of the lake.

Cruising and paddling

Valdez is superbly placed for cruises and kayak trips out into Prince William Sound, and to the equally popular kayaking destination of **Shoup Glacier**, which drains out into Valdez Arm eight miles west of Valdez. Like most Alaskan glaciers, this is currently retreating, but over the centuries has made two significant advance and retreat cycles, leaving two terminal moraines which have created **Shoup Bay**. At high tide you can paddle up from Shoup Bay to the lake immediately below the glacier and paddle close (but not too close) to the face of the glacier. As you bob around on the opaque gray-green water thick with brash ice, it feels like you're paddling in a giant frozen margarita. Through most of the summer, one prominent rock is completely covered by some seventeen thousand black-legged **kittiwakes** who nest here. It is even possible to stay in one of the three Alaska State Parks cabins nearby (see box, opposite).

The most popular **cruises** are those with Prince William Sound Cruises & Tours (☎835-4731 or 1-800/992-1297, *www.princewilliamsound.com*), who run a daily trip across the sound to Whittier via Columbia Glacier and Growler Island (see box, p.228), and a couple of circular Valdez-based cruises. The Columbia Glacier Cruise (May–Sept; 6hr; $69) mainly visits the glacier but there's usually plenty of time for watching whales or whatever else makes an appearance; the Columbia and Meares Glacier Excursion (9hr; $119) also takes in the advancing Meares Glacier and stops for a buffet lunch at Growler Island; and if you're prepared for a 7am start you can cruise out to the Columbia Glacier and Growler Island, spend half a day kayaking or yachting and return to Valdez ($165). For a smaller boat, a more personal approach and plenty of whale watching try a five-hour cruise aboard the *Lu-Lu Belle* (☎1-800/411-0090; $75) which also visits the Columbia.

Two companies (with offices along North Harbor Drive) handle most of the **kayaking** trips along Valdez Arm and out to Prince William Sound, both with short day-trips and longer kayak camping or boat-supported expeditions. Anadyr Adventures (☎835-2814 or 1-800/865-2925, *www.alaska.net/~anadyr*), offer four- and six-hour paddles exploring the local flora and fauna ($49/$79) and several trips to more distant locales with initial access by water taxi: Shoup Glacier (8hr; $139); Galena Bay (10hr; $169); and Columbia Glacier (10hr; $169). Extended, guided camping trips range from two days around Shoup Glacier ($239, with meals $299) to a twelve-day exploration of Prince William Sound's highlights ($1469/$2289), and there are "mothership" tours either using a sailboat (3 days for $889, 5 days $1499) or motor yacht (2 days $769, 6 days $2500). **Kayak rentals** (single $40, double $60) reduce by $5 a day after the second day. Pangaea (☎835-8442 or 1-800/660-9637, *www.pangaeaadventures.com*) run a similarly wide-ranging set of trips for almost identical prices, though their rentals are marginally more expensive.

Fishing, rafting, and helicopter flightseeing

During summer Valdez holds three **fishing derbies**; for halibut (mid-May to early Sept), pink salmon (late June–July), and silver salmon (Aug to early Sept). The big winnings are for the largest silver salmon ($10,000 plus smaller daily prizes), but unlike most of the halibut derbies held in coastal towns around the state, the idea here isn't to land the biggest halibut but to land one within that week's specified weight range which puts you in line for the end of season draw (also $10,000). You have to enter to win, and that will set you back $6 for one day, $15 for three. The small boat harbor is full of boats ready to take you out to catch

WINTER IN VALDEZ

Valdez likes to promote itself as "**Snow Capital of Alaska**" and it has every right to. After all, each winter it does get more snow than any other seaside town in the world. A few miles inland in the Chugach Mountains, the average almost triples, and the dense, wet nature of coastal snow makes this perfect territory for extreme skiing in ludicrously steep chutes, and some wonderful heli-skiing on more forgiving slopes. No one has built any permanent downhill skiing facilities, but there is plenty of scope for snow machining and dog mushing around Valdez, or ice climbing on the waterfalls of Keystone Canyon. For a full list of operators, obtain the **free annual Valdez Winter Guide** from the Valdez visitor center (or visit *www.valdezalaska.org/events .html*).

If you want to provide a focus for your activities, try to organize your visit to coincide with one of the winter festivals, which start on Presidents weekend in mid-February with the **Alaskan Local Snowboarding Champs** (*www.alaskagold.com/aklocalsnow*), followed in early March by the **Valdez Ice Climbing Festival** (*www.alaskagold.com/ice*), and a couple of weeks later by the **World Extreme Skiing Championships** (*www.wesc.com*), held on the near-vertical powder-filled chutes at Thompson Pass. Around the same time there's the **Mountain Man Snowmachine Hill Climb**, immediately followed by the **King & Queen of the Hill Snowboard Tournament** which lasts until mid-April. Actually seeing any of the extreme skiing and snowboarding up close is nearly impossible, but just being in town for the associated activities and partying is excuse enough.

that winner; try Aurora Charters (☎835-2140, *www.alaska.net/~redbird*), who charge a competitive $80 for half a day salmon fishing, and $165 for the full day necessary to get out to good halibut waters.

The Interior rivers also present opportunities, notably with Keystone Raft & Kayak Adventures (☎835-2606 or 1-800/328-8460, *www.alaskawhitewater.com*), who run whitewater **rafting** trips on the Lowe River through Keystone Canyon (June–Aug; $35) with an hour on the water tackling predominantly Class III water and floating under dramatic waterfalls, and longer trips in Class IV rivers including the Tsaina (3hr; $70), the Tonsina (all day; $85), and the Tana, in the Wrangell Mountains (4 days; $925).

For **flightseeing**, go with ERA Helicopters (☎835-2595 or 1-800/843-1947, *www .era.aviation.com/helicoptertours*), who run the Glacier Exploration Tour (1hr; $179) with a **glacier landing** high above Valdez, and their Prince William Sound Safari (1hr; $199), which heads out over the Columbia Glacier and lands briefly beside Shoup Bay.

Eating and drinking

There's little special about dining in Valdez, but there are several perfectly adequate places (some with harbor views) and a couple of dark bars to keep you entertained in the evening. **Groceries**, along with deli selections, baked goods, and espressos are available from the two supermarkets, the best being the Eagle

Quality Center, corner of Pioneer Drive and Meals Avenue. For wholefoods, visit
A Rogue's Garden Natural Foodstore, 354 Fairbanks Drive.

Halibut House, cnr Fairbanks St and Meals Ave (☎835-2788). Budget halibut sandwiches,
salmon wedges, chicken nuggets, and assorted fried goodies, mostly for under $5 and served
in spartan surroundings.

Lisa's Kitchen, cnr Egan Drive and Fidalgo Drive (☎835-5633). Fast food from a roadside
cart selling soft tacos for under $4, chimichangas for $6, a taco salad for $7.50 (all available
in vegetarian formats), plus burgers and fries. Closed Sun.

Mike's Palace, 201 N Harbor Drive (☎835-2365). Good Italian-oriented restaurant on the
waterfront, though in true Alaskan fashion they also do burgers and Mexican dishes. Their
lasagna ($12) is super tasty, the pizzas (from $10 for a 12") are reliable and a couple of enchiladas can be had for $9.

Oscar's on the Waterfront, 143 N Harbor Drive (☎835-4891). Probably the best all-round
restaurant with a varied menu and harbor views. Their breakfast of eggs, reindeer sausage, and
Klondike potatoes (home fries grilled with onions, and blanketed with cheddar) is particularly
good, and there are sandwiches, burgers, steak, and seafood entrees plus a wide range of
desserts with your espresso. Through summer there's a nightly all-you-can-eat $15 barbecue.

The Pipeline Inn & Club, 112 Egan Drive (☎835-4332). Dim booths in a room off the main
bar lend a suitable ambience for this survivor of the oil boom times. It is still a favorite of the
tanker crews who come for the menu composed entirely of top-quality steak and seafood
such as the 12oz filet mignon dinner ($27), the salmon, shrimp, halibut, and scallop combo
($22), or the Pipeline Pu Pu house special of sliced steak sautéed with onion, bell pepper,
tomatoes, and soy sauce on a bed of rice (a bargain at $15). Burgers and sandwiches are also
sold at the bar, which is the most likely place to find live music and dancing.

Listings

Banks and exchange Valdez only has two banks: the National Bank of Alaska, 337 Egan
Drive (☎835-4745), and First National Bank, 101 Egan Drive (☎834-4800). Both have 24hr
ATMs.

Camping equipment Beaver Sports, 316 Galena (☎835-4727) sell high-quality hiking, camping and general outdoors gear. The Prospector, along the street at #117 (☎835-3858) is aimed
more at the hunting and fishing set but stocks good standard gear that can work out to be a
bargain.

Festivals Most of the major annual events happen in winter (see box, opposite), but during
the second week in June the town's Convention Center plays host to the **Edward Albee
Theatre Conference** (☎835-2421, fax 835-2694) which is getting a reputation beyond the
state border: Albee himself usually attends. New plays by Alaskan writers are read and performed along with an Albee piece or two.

Internet access See Library (below), and Macs and PCs at Mac Copies, 354 Fairbanks
Drive (Mon–Fri 8am–6pm, Sat 11am–5pm).

Laundry and showers Like Home Laundromat, Valdez Mall, 121 Egan Drive (daily 8am–
9pm; ☎835-2913) has washers and dryers; the Habormaster's office on North Harbor Drive
offers ten-minute showers for $4.

Library Valdez Library, 200 Fairbanks Drive (Mon & Fri 10am–6pm, Tues–Thurs 10am–
8pm, Sat noon–5pm, Sun 1–5pm) has a good selection of books and free Internet access
bookable by the hour.

Medical assistance Valdez Medical Clinic, 100 Meals Ave (☎835-4811) for walk-in care; and
Valdez Regional Health Authority, 911 Meals Ave (☎835-2249), for more serious attention.

Pharmacy Village Pharmacy, cnr Pioneer Drive and Meals Ave (Mon–Thurs 9am–6pm, Fri
9am–7pm, Sat 11am–2pm).

Post Office cnr Galena St and Tatitlek St (Mon–Fri 9am–5pm, Sat 10am–noon; ☎835-4449).
The General Delivery ZIP code is 99686.

Taxes There is no sales tax in Valdez, a hotel tax of six percent has been included in our prices.

Travel agency US Travel, inside *Guesthouse Inn*, 100 Meals Ave (☎835-8373 or 1-877/835-8374, fax 835-3735, *www.ustravelak.com*).

North of Valdez: along the Richardson Hwy

The old Valdez townsite marks the beginning of the **Richardson Highway** (for more on the origins of this important artery see box, p.376), sections of which constitute some of the finest road in the state, particularly the southern eighty miles or so where it winds from Valdez through the steep rock walls of Keystone Canyon and up over the seemingly impenetrable rock-and-ice barrier presented by Thompson Pass. Much of the rest crosses drier, open country studded with permafrost-stunted spruce, often with stupendous views east to the snow-shrouded Wrangell Mountains. It is a good year-round paved road, occasionally dotted with roadhouses, some with cabins, plus primitive RV and camp sites, food, and usually fuel. That said, it is best to fill up in Valdez and stock up with food if you're planning to make use of some lovely **campgrounds** along the way.

The Richardson Hwy initially traces the right bank of the Lowe River, heavily braided at first then, thirteen miles outside Valdez, constrained by **Keystone Canyon**, a narrow four-mile-long defile cutting through angled bedrock. This proved one of the most difficult obstacles on the route into the Interior and during 1898 many preferred the hazardous route over the Valdez Glacier. All this changed in 1899 when the army cut the Goat Trail high on the cliffs 200–300 feet above the north bank, and just wide enough for two horses to pass. Most drive straight through pausing only long enough to photograph **Horsetail Falls** (Mile 13.5) and the five-leap 400-foot **Bridal Veil Falls** (Mile 13.8). If you feel like stretching your legs, you can follow part of the **Goat Trail** from a turn-out opposite Bridal Veil Falls. The best section is the short climb up to the **Bridal Veil Falls overlook** (400 yards each way), but the trail then contours along for a couple of miles high above the canyon floor. Though pleasant enough, it is less exciting than it might be with restricted views, no relics of the gold days, and no way to turn it into a loop. Following the success of the Goat Trail, several companies tried to push a train line along the bottom of the canyon. None were ever completed, but the remains of a hand-cut tunnel can still be seen at Mile 15.

As you emerge from Keystone Canyon, the country opens out again, this time into broad river flats hemmed in by mountains spilling glaciers down their flanks towards the road. The Richardson then begins its steep climb towards **Thompson Pass**, a 2771-foot alpine saddle between six-thousand-foot craggy peaks. Midway up, a mile-long access road leads to *Blueberry Lake State Recreation Site*, Mile 24 ($12; pump water), one of the finest campgrounds in the state, with ten popular sites high on a ridge with 360-degree views of sawtooth mountains and creaking crystalline glaciers – though many sites remain snow covered well into June. From here it is only a couple of miles to the crest of the pass where grayling and rainbow trout fill a number of small lakes. The low tundra around the lakes is spotted with stunted willow and makes inviting territory for a half-hour **hike**, which should see you up at the snow line even in late summer. The majestic grandeur of the area is only spoilt by maintenance sheds for the pipeline which crosses the mountains here, and road-clearing equipment needed to keep the Richardson open in winter when it sees some of the heaviest snowfall

Our account of the **Richardson Hwy** continues with Glenallen (p.375). **Wrangell-St. Elias National Park** coverage starts on p.376.

in the state (a record 81 feet in the winter of 1952–53), though the road is largely safe from avalanches. For southbound travelers the pass will give you your first glimpse of the mountains to the south, but little indication that Valdez and the sea are only twenty miles away.

The descent through the northern foothills of the Chugach Mountains is more gradual, initially passing the three-pronged **Worthington Glacier**, Mile 28.6, which threatens to envelop the highway. You can drive to within two hundred yards of the glacier, and follow a short trail along the lateral moraine almost to its face. *Tsaina Lodge*, Mile 34.7 (☎835-3500, fax 835-5661; ②), set amid majestic sawtooth ridges, is the first roadhouse on the Richardson offering a restaurant, bar, cabins, and a bunkhouse. The first (or last) **gas** is at *Tiekel River Lodge*, Mile 56 (☎822-3259, fax 822-5669; cabins ①, with private bath ④; closed Jan & Feb) which has dry RV and tent camping ($10) and cabins. Campers may well want to push on beyond the pipeline's **Pump Station 12**, Mile 64.7, to the diminutive *Little Tonsina State Recreation Site*, ($10; pump water) where you can fish for Dolly Varden using small hooks and salmon eggs; or the forest-girt *Squirrel Creek State Recreation Site*, Mile 80.3 ($10; pump water) with some nice water-side sites.

Cordova and around

CORDOVA can feel like a town displaced: it is on the eastern shores of Prince William Sound and yet seems a world apart from the day-cruise bustle of Whittier and Valdez; it is tentatively linked to the Interior by an old railroad up the Copper River valley, and yet you can only get here by boat or plane; and with its water-front canneries and large fishing fleet it has a lot in common with Southeast Alaska over four hundred miles away.

The residents (2500 in winter, twice that in summer) go quietly about their business, balancing the day-to-day needs of a small town with the demands of a busy port and the fledgling tourist industry. With less than one cruise-ship visit a week in summer, and a ferry schedule that is infrequent enough to discourage many visitors, Cordova has remained off the main tourist circuit, and there is a definite charm to wandering the streets (some still with wooden boardwalks) which straggle up the hillside, or strolling past the waterside canneries perched on rows of forty-foot stilts, their sides all rusted corrugated iron spot-painted in half-hearted patch jobs. Much of the time all this is blanketed in low cloud and damp mist, giving a suitably ethereal atmosphere to the surrounding spruce-specked islands.

Much of downtown dates back to 1909 when Irish railroad engineer, Michael J Heney, selected this cannery site as the place to export copper from the mines at Kennicott, and began forging a railroad between the two. He named the place after his favorite Spanish city. Cordova boomed and continued to prosper with its docks, railroad, and canneries until 1939 when the mines and railroad closed for good. In recent years, the biggest threat to the town's livelihood came when a big slick from the *Exxon Valdez* destroyed most of the fishery.

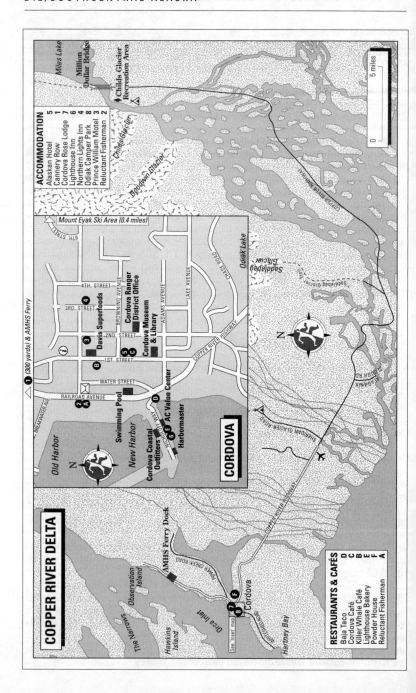

COPPER RIVER DELTA

CORDOVA

ACCOMMODATION

Alaskan Hotel	5
Cannery Row	1
Cordova Rose Lodge	7
Lighthouse Inn	6
Northern Lights Inn	4
Odiak Camper Park	8
Prince William Motel	3
Reluctant Fisherman	2

RESTAURANTS & CAFÉS

Baja Taco	D
Cordova Café	C
Killer Whale Café	B
Lighthouse Bakery	E
Powder House	F
Reluctant Fisherman	A

Mount Eyak Ski Area (0.4 miles)

Childs Glacier Recreation Area

Million Dollar Bridge

Miles Lake

Goodwin Glacier

Childs Glacier

Saddlebag Glacier

Odiak Lake

COPPER RIVER HIGHWAY

SHERIDAN GLACIER ROAD

FAIRBANKS

SLOUGH RD

COPPER RIVER HIGHWAY

WHITSHED ROAD

POWER CREEK ROAD

Hartney Bay

Cordova

AMHS Ferry Dock

Observation Island

The Narrows

Hawkins Island

Orca Inlet

Hartney Bay

See Inset map

5 miles

4TH. STREET
3RD. STREET
2ND. STREET
1ST. STREET
WATER STREET
RAILROAD AVENUE
BROWNING AVENUE
ADAMS AVENUE
LAKE AVENUE
CHASE ROAD
6TH STREET
BREAKWATER AVE.

Cordova Ranger District Office
Davis Superfoods
Cordova Museum & Library
AC Value Center
Harbormaster
Cordova Coastal Outfitters
Swimming Pool
New Harbor
Old Harbor

(300 yards) & AMHS Ferry

Long after the railroad closed down, the route was turned into the Copper River Hwy, which provides access to the immense birding wetlands of the **Copper River Delta**, the partly destroyed **Million Dollar Bridge** over the Copper River, and the **Childs Glacier** right by it.

Arrival and information

Arriving by **ferry** (☎424-7333 in Cordova) from Valdez or Whittier you'll be dropped an easy half-mile walk north of the town center. If you can't be bothered call Wild Hare **taxi** service (☎424-3939), or leap straight on the Copper River and Northwest Tours bus which sets off on a six-hour tour of the Copper River Delta (see p.246). Usually, the *Bartlett* is only here for an hour or so on Monday and Wednesday, but on Friday stays in port for nearly six hours before returning to Valdez making it possible to visit on a long day-trip from Valdez.

Alaska Airlines (☎1-800/225-2752), Jim Air (☎243-5161), and ERA Aviation (☎1-800/426-0333) all run daily scheduled **flights** to Anchorage, with Alaska Airlines also flying south to Cordova, Yakutat, Juneau, and Seattle. They land at the Merle K "Mudhole" Smith International Airport (☎424-7151), named after an early bush pilot, located thirteen miles east of town along the Copper Delta Hwy. The Airport Shuttle (☎424-3272; $10 each way) meets each plane and runs into town.

You might also want to **rent a car** either from JB Transportation at the *Reluctant Fisherman Hotel* (☎424-3272 or 1-800/770-3272; $75 a day unlimited mileage) or from Cordova Car Rental (☎424-5982, fax 424-5961, *www.ptialaska .net/~cars*; $65 a day unlimited mileage) who have slightly older cars and are based at the airport but will drop off in town or at the ferry. **Bikes** are also a viable option, even for exploring the Copper River Hwy: rent from Cordova Coastal Outfitters (see, p.245; $15 a day).

The main **visitor center** is the Chamber of Commerce, 404 1st Ave (variable hours, roughly Mon–Fri 11am–6pm; ☎424-7260, fax 424-7259, *www.polarnet.com /~cchamber*): if they're not open, check out the booth at the museum. Information on hikes, cabins, and wildlife is best sought at the Forest Service's **Cordova Ranger District office**, 610 2nd Ave (Mon–Fri 8am–5pm; ☎424-7661, fax 424-7214), which has a few mildly interesting displays on the local natural history.

Accommodation

Cordova's accommodation is fairly varied, and most people should find somewhere that suits, although there is **no hostel**, and limited **camping** close to town. There are, however, plenty of good places along the Copper River Hwy for those with transport.

Alaskan Hotel, 600 1st St (☎424-3299, *hotleak@ptialaska.net*). Old and fairly low-standard hotel, though the price is right, with shared-bath rooms at around $40 and ones with private bath for a little more (②). ①.

Cannery Row, 1 Cannery Row (☎424-5920, fax 424-5923, *canrow@ptialaska*). Former cannery manager's home right on the old dock, with wood floors and a 1920s feel. It has been converted to a gorgeous self-catering apartment which sleeps up to six but is still good value for two. ⑤.

Cordova Rose Lodge, 1315 Whitshed Rd (☎424-7673, *www.alaskan.com/cordovarose*; ③). Excellent B&B a mile south of downtown, that's been imaginatively converted from a barge landlocked by the shores of Odiak Slough. They've kept the nautical theme throughout, the rooms feeling somewhat like cabins each with its own character, and all sharing a communal lounge with library, TV/VCR and a great view. There's also a separate three-room self-contained annex with a fishing theme. ④.

Northern Lights Inn, 500 3rd Ave (☎424-5356, fax 424-3291, *orca.cordovanet.com /~alaskan*). Spacious and attractively decorated rooms in one of Cordova's original 1910 homes, all with private bathroom, cable TV, and phone, and most with kitchenettes and harbor views. The owners don't provide breakfast, though you can prepare your own. Great value. ③.

Odiak Camper Park, Whitshed Rd (☎424-6200). Just a gravel lot next to the town dump with token-operated showers and a view of town, that is fine for RVs ($12) but not especially pleasant for campers ($3).

Prince William Motel, 501 3rd St (☎424-3201 or 1-888/796-6835, fax 424-2260, *orca.cordova .com/~pwmotel*). Modern, spacious, block-built motel, some rooms having kitchenettes (⑤) and all coming with cable TV and phones with free local calls. ④.

Reluctant Fisherman Inn, 407 Railroad Ave (☎424-3272 or 1-800/770-3272, *www.cordovaak .com*). Cordova's best hotel with comfortable (if ageing) rooms, many with views over the small-boat harbor, a restaurant and bar plus business facilities, their own travel agency, airport shuttle service, and car-rental agency. Sea- and mountainview rooms ⑤, others ④.

The town and around

The self-guided **Cordova Historic Walking Tour** (free leaflet from the visitor center) is a pleasant way to spend an hour, getting a sense of how rapidly the town developed as the railhead for the Copper River and Northwestern Railway. The town center still has plenty of original buildings from 1908 that give Cordova a fairly harmonious townscape. When the clouds open, make for the **Cordova Historical Museum**, 620 1st St (June to early Sept Mon–Sat 10am–6pm, Sun 2–4pm; early Sept to May Tues–Fri 1–5pm, Sat 2–4pm; $1 donation appreciated), and spend half an hour watching the ageing but still relevant thirty-minute video on the region's history (ask if it isn't already playing). You then have the context for a few minutes poking around the eclectic collection spanning Aleut and Tlingit artifacts, the local fishing industry, photos of the annual iceworm festival, and minor paintings by Eustace Ziegler and Sydney Lawrence (see p.197) who both lived here during the early years of the twentieth century. Note especially the display on the railroad, with a couple of lovely aquatints – a coastal section of track, and the mill at Kennicott – track-laying equipment, and jewelry cut from high-grade copper ore.

That's about it for genuine sights, though if you fancy seeing the inside of a working cannery you can ask at the visitor center and see if anyone is currently running tours. Equally, you can get a sense of what fishing means to Cordova by strolling around the not-so-small **small boat harbor**, very much the heart and soul of the town and always abuzz with commercial seiners and gill-netters going about their business, and charter boats heading out with their complement of tourists.

Cordova even has a downhill ski slope at the **Mount Eyak Ski Area**, complete with an antique chair lift built in 1936, and moved here in 1974 from Sun Valley, Idaho. It works in a chunking and grinding, slow but magisterial way and is operated by the local ski club who require at least six people to fire it up (common enough in midsummer), and charge $87 for the ride to the top. From the top of the chair there are wonderful views right across the Copper River Delta around to Orca Bay and Prince William Sound.

Anyone who is interested in wading birds and has a vehicle should definitely drive the seven miles out along Whitshed Road to the **Hartney Bay Shorebird Viewing Area**, especially from late April to mid-May and again from September through October, when numbers are at their greatest.

Cruising, kayaking, and rafting

One essential stop for any active visitor to Cordova is Cordova Coastal Outfitters, Nicholoff Way (☎424-7424 or 1-800/357-5145, *www.cdvcoastal.com*), who rent bikes, canoes, and kayaks, provide trailhead transport, and run tours. Their Wildlife and Natural History **cruise** (2hr; $50) heads out into Orca Inlet with local history filling in between sightings of sea otters, seals, seabirds, and occasionally Sitka black-tailed deer, Stellar sea lions, and maybe orca. Keen birders will be better served by the Copper River Delta "On the Mud" tour (4hr; $55), which partly floats down Eyak River and spends time sitting by the mud flats within sight of the mountain ranges hoping to spot perhaps twenty or thirty species – sandpipers, dunlins, jaegers, harriers, and many more. They also do **guided kayak tours** on Orca Inlet (half-day $65; full day $95) paddling among sea otters, harbor porpoises, and maybe sea lions. If you'd rather go your own way, they **rent sea kayaks** (single $35 a day; double $50), canoes ($30), 30HP outboard-equipped skiffs ($85, $60 for second and subsequent days), and fishing and camping gear.

An excellent way to see something of the Copper River Delta and get in a little **rafting** is to join one of the trips run by Alaska River Rafters (☎424-7238 or 1-800/776-1864, *www.alaskarafters.com*). Perhaps the best is the full-day Million Dollar Run (early June to late Aug; $250) involving a flight to a sand bar in the Copper River followed by a fifteen-mile float down a Class II–III section of the Copper River and through the icebergs in Miles Lake to the Million Dollar Bridge, then a drive back to town. They need six people to run a trip so it may help to coax others into joining. The same company also does half-day rafting ($65) and kayaking ($75) trips immediately below Sheridan Glacier, the rafting including some Class II–III water; and multiday trips on the Copper River (3 days for $875, 5 days for $1475, and 10 days all the way from McCarthy for $2495).

A superb way to see the local marine environment and combine it with transport from Whittier is to join Sound Eco Adventures (☎ & fax 472-2312, ☎1-888/471-2312, *www.alaskan.com/ecotours*) who run four-day Spring Birding and Wildlife trips ($2100 each for two people, $2400 for three, and $2700 for four) to coincide with the Copper River Delta Shorebird Festival on the first weekend in May. There's one from Whittier to Cordova just before, and one back just after, and there is plenty of time for exploring off the beaten track with your marine ecologist skipper.

Eating and drinking

If you are cooking your own meals or surviving on snacks, make use of the large AC Value Center **supermarket** on Nicholoff Way, which has the best selection including a good deli counter and bakery, and is open to 9pm or later nightly; Davis Superfoods at 512 1st Ave is more convenient but stocks less. For more substantial **meals** there's a reasonable selection of places in town, the *Powder House* a couple of miles "out the road," but nothing beyond that.

Baja Taco, Nicholoff Way (☎424-5599). Alfresco dining on quality Mexican staples selected from the menu pinned to a surfboard and served out of an old red school bus. A fajita plate goes for $7, a tamale for $3, and there's good low-cost espresso too. Open daily, and open late on weekends.

Cordova Café, 604 1st St inside *Cordova Hotel* (☎424-5543). Windowless greasy spoon that looks closed most of the time but is usually full of fishers tucking into $4 stacks of sourdough pancakes and diner favorites.

Killer Whale Café, 507 1st St (☎424-7733). Tables and benches on a couple of mezzanines inside Orca Books where you will find three-egg omelette breakfasts ($7.50), sandwiches on a choice of French stick, wholewheat or croissant ($8), imaginative salads ($8), and good coffee. A favorite with Cordova's slackers. Open to 4pm, closed Sun.

Powder House, Mile 2 Copper River Hwy (☎424-3529). Restaurant and bar built in a former gunpowder storage shed from CR&NW railroad days, now with a deck overlooking Eyak Lake. Come for the local blues and country bands in the evening or stop in for a meal on the way back from the Million Dollar Bridge.

Reluctant Fisherman, Railroad Ave (☎424-3272). The town's most formal restaurant, though still fairly casual and with great views over Orca Bay and the boat harbor. Check out the beaten-copper ceiling in the bar while ordering dishes such as Copper River king salmon fillet ($22), Alaskan halibut or Alaskan scallops served with vegetables, rice, and soup or salad ($22), grilled halibut sandwich ($8), or just a hearty bowl of salmon chili for $5.

Listings

Banks The National Bank of Alaska, 510 1st St (☎424-3258) has an ATM, as does the AC Value Center supermarket.

Bookshop Orca Books and Sound, 507 1st St (☎424-5305).

Festivals The Cordova Ice Worm Festival takes place in mid-Feb with a traditional annual march of the ice worm (a 100ft-long costume with dozens of feet sticking out) down the main street; in the first weekend of May the Copper River Delta Shorebird Festival attracts birders from all over.

Internet access See Library.

Laundry Whirlwind Laundromat, cnr Railroad and Adams avs (daily 8am–8pm; ☎424-5110)

Library Cordova Public Library, 620 1st St (Tues–Sat 1–8pm; ☎424-6667) has a free book-swap and free Internet access.

Medical assistance Cordova Community Medical Center, Chase Rd (☎424-8000).

Post Office Railroad Ave and Council Ave (Mon–Fri 10am–5.30pm, Sat 10am–1pm). The **General Delivery** ZIP code is 99574.

Showers Harbormaster Office ($3 for 10min, token available, Mon–Fri 8am–5pm); the Bob Korn Memorial Pool on Railroad Ave costs $5 a session for swimming and use of the facilities.

Taxes A six percent sales tax is also added to hotel rates, and has been included within our price codes.

Travel agency Cordova Travel Service, 407 Railroad Ave (☎424-7102 or 1-800/267-3682, fax 424-7101, *cdvtravel@ptialaska.net*) located inside the *Reluctant Fisherman Inn*.

The Copper River Delta and the Million Dollar Bridge

You should really spend at least one of your days in Cordova driving the fifty-mile-long **Copper River Hwy**, and if you are equipped for camping then two or three days would be better: pick up the Chugach National Forest's free *Copper River Delta* leaflet from the visitor center. There's plenty to explore, not least the

Copper River Delta, the largest intact wetland on the Pacific coast, stretching for sixty miles east of Cordova. It is a wonderfully rich area of marshes, ponds, and sloughs fed by the outwash from half a dozen glaciers, myriad channels of the mighty Copper River, and more than 160 inches of rainfall. Almost every stream offers opportunities for patient **fishers** with Dolly Varden and cutthroat trout biting throughout the summer (cutthroat from mid-June only), and more seasonal runs of red (late May to mid-July), and silver salmon (Aug to mid-Sept). **Birdwatchers** are even more richly rewarded, especially in spring (late April to late May) for the massive migration of around twenty million waterfowl and shorebirds, including almost the entire world population of western sandpipers.

The highway is laid on the old bed of the **Copper River and Northwestern Railway** (see box, p.380), which linked the ice-free port of Cordova with the copper mines at Kennicott by way of the Copper River valley. When the copper mines closed in 1938 the railway was pulled up, and Cordova boosters have since promoted the idea of using the trackbed to connect their town with the outside world. Congress appropriated funds to lay a road on the old trackbed in 1954, but since its partial destruction in 1964, the Million Dollar Bridge has been an eternal thorn in their side.

For maximum freedom you really need a car, though it is also rewarding (if often wet) to explore by bike, which can be rented in Cordova (see p.243). Allow at least a day in each direction to the end of the Copper River Hwy, or arrange to get dropped off there (around $25 per person; min 3), and ride back. The next best way to get a quick look at the region is to join Copper River and Northwest Tours (late-May to early-Sept four times weekly; $45; ☎424-5366) who turn the Copper River Hwy into a five-hour sightseeing and wildlife spotting outing complete with a box lunch at road's end.

Along the Copper River Highway

The Copper River Highway leaves Cordova past the *Powder House* restaurant, then bursts out of the mountains which hem in the town. From here on there are broad views on all sides as you drive across outwash fans from the Scott, Sheridan, and Sherman glaciers, all visible off to the left. With streams and ponds all about, you seldom seem to be on firm ground for long, except around Cordova's airport (Mile 12). Here the asphalt gives out, though it remains a good, fast road all the way. A couple of miles on, Sheridan Glacier Road runs four miles inland to the trailhead for the often wet **Sheridan Mountain Trail** (3hr round-trip; 6 miles; 600ft ascent), which climbs gradually up through the forest to open country for tremendous views of Sheridan and Sherman glaciers. At the trailhead there's an attractive little streamside **campground** (officially one-night stays only; free) with fire rings, picnic tables, and stream water.

Back on the Copper River Hwy you soon come to Alaganik Slough Road (Mile 16.8), a three-mile access road to a picnic area and a three-hundred-yard long **wetland boardwalk**, which leads to a raised platform that's perfect for viewing waterfowl. Between Mile 21 and Mile 25 you are again on firm ground, and a couple of side roads provide access to several easy hiking trails, then the highway begins eleven miles of island hopping to get across the multiple broad, gray channels of the Copper River. The final few miles (sometimes not clear of snow until early June) end at a point unnervingly close to two glaciers – the Miles and the Childs – both feeding icebergs into the Copper River. This is where railroad maestro, Michael Heney, chose to build his huge, four-span, steel and concrete

Million Dollar Bridge, one of the biggest engineering headaches during the construction of the CR&NW Railway between 1908 and 1910. Heney was undaunted, boasting "give me enough dynamite and snoose and I'll build a road to hell." He did manage to build a railroad to Kennicott, though only just, and died of exhaustion just months before its completion. As his workers battled temperatures of minus 60°F, winds reaching 95mph, and 34 feet of snow a year, the Childs Glacier unexpectedly began advancing at around 35 feet per day and threatening to destroy the bridge. By feverish hacking away at the ice and a fortuitous halt in the glacier's advance, the bridge was saved, only to succumb to the big earthquake in 1964. The northernmost span was dislodged so that the trackbed now drags in the river, though a ramp has been rigged up so that pedestrians, bikes and even high-clearance vehicles can cross the downed span and explore the two miles of unmaintained road on the other side.

The highway ends at the south side of the bridge at the **Childs Glacier Recreation Area**, only separated from the three-mile-long face of the Childs Glacier by the quarter-mile-wide river. Enormous snowfalls in the Chugach Mountains feed the twelve-mile-long glacier which bulldozes its way east, only kept in check by the undercutting currents of the Copper River. Stay alert as you wait for ice to calve into the river as large chunks periodically break off creating powerful ten-, twenty-, or even forty-foot-high waves which have been known to wash small icebergs into the day-use area and salmon into the trees. People have been injured, so you might feel safer on the viewing platform on high ground away from the river's edge. Wherever you stand, this is about as close as you are going to get to a large calving glacier and it is a magnificent and underrated sight. Nearby, in a more protected spot, there's a good **campground** (late May or early June to Sept; $10; water and outhouses).

THE KENAI PENINSULA

The **KENAI PENINSULA** (KEEN-eye) is sometimes lauded as Alaska in a nutshell, and it is certainly true that a lot of what is great in Alaska can be found here shoehorned into what, by Alaskan standards, is a tiny area. Certainly you miss out on the extreme conditions of the Interior, the towering mountains of the Alaska Range, the full span of the state's cultural mix, and a lot more besides, but if you can only spend time on one part of Alaska then this is probably your best bet.

Only two hours out of Anchorage **Seward** is a place where you can stand next to a glacier or cruise about looking for whales as icebergs calve into the fjord nearby. The aquatic world will even come to you at the classy SeaLife Center. Stay in the mountains and there are hundreds of miles of first-class **hiking trails** just waiting for you to strap on your boots, and peaceful campgrounds where you can while away a warm afternoon. Follow the Sterling Hwy south and you enter serious **salmon fishing** territory where some of the world's largest and most combative salmon are caught, particularly around the towns of **Soldotna** and **Kenai**. The whole peninsula is alive with moose, bears, mountain goats, and other large game, but few places in greater concentrations than the **Kenai National Wildlife Refuge**, good canoeing and hunting territory. Further south, the **razor clamming** beaches of Clam Gulch and Ninilchik are only marginal distractions from the main goal, easy-paced **Homer**, with its bohemian air and exemplary halibut fishing trips. It sits beside Kachemak Bay, a beautiful mountain-backed sound where water taxis and short cruises provide access to great hiking and the gorgeous village of **Seldovia**.

All of this is within five-hours' drive of the big city, and therein lies a problem. With so much to do and such ease of access, everyone gets the same idea and you can sit on the highway for two hours behind a line of RVs only to end up at a packed campground. As ever, it only takes a little imagination to beat the crowds, but forewarned is forearmed.

Northeastern Kenai Peninsula

The northeastern third of the Kenai Peninsula is mostly mountainous country, the Chugach and Kenai mountains meeting around the head of Turnagain Arm. Numerous peaks top four thousand feet and a few soar up over five thousand creating a near impenetrable barrier to the lusher flatlands to the south. Only the Seward Hwy finds a passage by climbing Turnagain Pass and continuing to Seward, while the Sterling Hwy peels off east through the Central Kenai to Homer. In summer, the high country beside the highway is used by **hikers** and **bikers** here to tackle some of the excellent trails, and nearby Six-Mile Creek gets crowded with **rafters**, risking some superb whitewater.

The only real destination is **Hope**, a former gold town on the shores of Turnagain Arm that's great for just kicking back for a couple of days, perhaps doing a little **gold panning** in Resurrection Creek.

Turnagain Pass and rafting Six-Mile Creek

At the head of Turnagain Arm, Portage Road turns off for Portage Glacier and Whittier, but the Seward Hwy hugs the water for a few more miles before turning inland for the steady five-mile climb up to the 1000-foot **Turnagain Pass**. The altitude and shadowing effect of the surrounding four thousand-foot peaks means that spring comes late up here. At weekends, you'll see people from Anchorage cross-country skiing well into June. It is a broad and fast road right through here with nothing in the way of services, so it is tempting to hurry on straight to Hope, Seward (about 60 miles away), or Homer (around 170 miles). Still, the scenery is striking with highwayside alpine meadows threaded by glacial streams, so you might want to stop a night or two in one of the campgrounds and consider tackling some of the long hikes (see box, p.264).

Leaving Turnagain Pass at Mile 68, milepost numbers continue to decrease towards Seward passing a couple of first-come, first-served Forest Service campgrounds in the next five miles – *Bertha Creek*, Mile 65 ($10), and *Granite Creek*, Mile 63 ($10) – both handy for one-day forays up part of the **Johnson Pass Trail**, which leaves the highway between the two.

At Mile 57, the highway sweeps high across **Six-Mile Creek**, immediately before the junction for Hope Hwy, which runs sixteen miles to the small town of Hope (see overleaf), passing the negligible remains of the gold rush town of Sunrise at Mile 8. More importantly, it runs alongside the wild **rafting** waters of Six-Mile Creek. Just off the Seward Hwy, a mile along the road to Hope, rafters amass for the wildest stretch of commercially rafted water in Alaska that doesn't require expedition logistics. The three rafted canyons – all beautiful with crisp, clear, and very cold water – increase in difficulty so you can just do the first Class

III canyon, or stay onboard for the Class V section, though they requires you to have had some previous experience and be over sixteen for the toughest section. Class V Whitewater (☎783-2004, *www.alaskanrafting.com*) have 9am and 3pm starts either meeting at the river or with pickups in Girdwood: first canyon (Class III; 1.5hr on the water; $65), first two canyons (Class IV; 2.5hr; $90), and all three (Class V; 3.5hr; $130). The other main operator is Nova (☎1-800/746-5753, *www.novaalaska.com*) who run the top two canyons (9am; $75) or all three (noon; $135). The main season is mid-June to August.

Hope

At the end of a sixteen-mile asphalt spur off the Seward Hwy, the small former gold-rush town of **HOPE** sits quietly beside the south shore of Turnagain Arm. It is mostly populated by loners and rat-race refugees but is close enough to Anchorage to draw in hikers, fishers after salmon (particularly pinks from mid-July to mid-August), and even gold seekers. In the last five years of the nineteenth century the whole of this area was alive with gold prospectors; the town survived well after the gold did, leaving a dusty collection of picturesque weather-worn log buildings. To get a sense of what it was like at its peak, visit the small **Hope and Sunrise Historical Mining Museum**, in the old town (late May to early Sept Fri–Mon noon–4pm; free), full of old-time photos and gold-mining paraphernalia. There's still **gold** in the creeks too, and if you've got a pan, you're free to make use of the Forest Service's claim close to the start of the Resurrection Pass Trail (see box, p.264).

Hikers who aren't up for something as taxing as the Resurrection Pass Trail (see "Northern Kenai Trails" box, p.264) should drive to the *Porcupine* campground (see below), at the end of the Hope Hwy, which marks the beginning of the gentle and heavily-used **Gull Rock Trail** (10 miles round-trip; 5–6hr; 620ft ascent). It follows an old wagon road along Turnagain Arm through spruce, birch, and aspen woods, and past an old sawmill to a viewpoint atop Gull Rock, and can be tackled any time from May to October, though late summer is good for low-bush cranberry picking.

Practicalities

At the first major junction as you drive in along the Hope Hwy, a left turn leads five miles up Resurrection Road to the start of the Resurrection Trail. Straight on at the junction, the new *Discovery Café* marks the start of the old town, reached down the road on the right. This eventually rejoins the Hope Hwy for the final mile to the road end *Porcupine* campground.

The best all-round place to **stay and eat** is the *Seaview Café*, Main Street in the old town (closed Oct–April; ☎782-3300, fax 782-3344, *www.home.gci.net/~hopeak*; ①), in a cluster of 1896 buildings, nicely sited close to Turnagain Arm. There are rustic cabins without running water but sleeping up to four ($40), a rather exposed place to camp ($19 for full RV hookup, $14 for power and $5 for tents), a great restaurant noted for its baked goods, especially the apple pie, and a bar that stays open to midnight. They even have a sunny deck outside. **Campers** have other options: just over a mile beyond Hope the *Porcupine* campground ($10; pump water), has neatly tended sites among the woods with fire rings, picnic tables, and even some Turnagain Arm views, but it is often full; budget tenters who don't mind being over four miles up Resurrection Road can camp beside the river for nothing near the start of the Resurrection Pass Trail, and pan for gold while you're there.

There's also a very comfortable fully equipped cabin sleeping five at *Hope Gold Rush B&B* (☎248-463, *fayrene@alaska.net*; ④), where a hearty breakfast is included; and new streamside cabins with access to a hot tub at *Discovery Cabins* (☎782-3725, fax 782-3725, *cabins@advenalaska.com*; ④).

Apart from the *Seaview*, eating is best at the *Bear Creek Lodge*, Mile 15.7 Hope Hwy (☎782-3141).

The Seward Highway: south from Turnagain Pass

South of Hope, the Seward Hwy continues past the first-come, first-served *Tenderfoot Creek* campground, Mile 46 ($10), which has creekside sites and pump water, then reaches **Tern Lake**, Mile 37, where the Sterling Hwy turns right and runs 143 miles through the central Kenai Peninsula to Homer. The Seward Hwy stays straight on past the *Tern Lake* campground, Mile 37 ($10), close to the lake and with a salmon-viewing platform.

Around Mile 29, the scattered community of **MOOSE PASS** comprises little more than a few cabins in the woods and a post office, all beautifully set beside Upper Trail Lake. A few of the cabins operate as B&Bs, and there's even a grocery, a couple of places to eat, a lodge, and an RV park, but outside the summer solstice when the town holds the Moose Pass Summer Festival, with cook-outs, craft stalls, and all sorts of kids' games, there's not much real action.

Along the last half-hour drive into Seward there are a few more fine campgrounds, and the trailheads for a couple of hikes listed in the box on p.264.

Seward and the Kenai Fjords National Park

There's a beguiling charm to **SEWARD** (pronounced SOO-erd), nestled between the shores of Resurrection Bay and the icy wastes of the Kenai Fjords National Park, 127 miles south of Anchorage. It is a small town, with a good deal less bustle than Homer and yet a perfect balance of distractions. It is also a strategic spot as the southern terminus of the Alaska Railroad and a major port (at least by Alaska's modest standards) with cruise ships coming and going on a fairly regular basis, though never adversely affecting the slow pace of life.

With a couple of minor exceptions, it is Seward's proximity to the **KENAI FJORDS NATIONAL PARK** which makes it so appealing. Only created in 1978, it remains a little known park almost entirely covered in ice, much of its western portion composed of the **Harding Icefield**, a vast icy tableland thought to be up to four thousand feet thick in places and spreading over almost 300 square miles. The ice at the edges spills over the mountains as steep glaciers – 38 of them in all – which forge down U-shaped valleys. **Exit Glacier** comes so close to Seward that they've built a road to its terminus. Spectacular though it is, few can resist joining one of the **cruises** that visit some of the eight tidewater glaciers that regularly calve icebergs into the fjords along the park's southeast flank. Cruising the waterways and fjords only nibbles at the fecund edges of the park and to really get a sense of its barren, icy immensity you need to fly over it (see "Flightseeing", p.261), or hike up beside Exit Glacier for a glimpse of this sheet of white

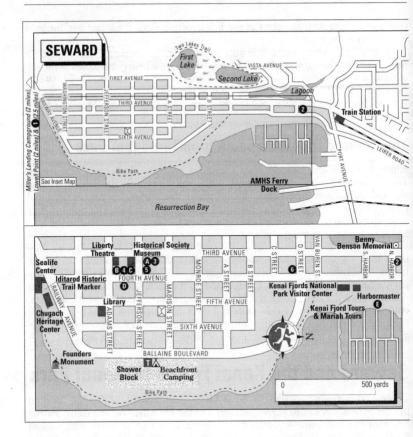

punctuated by bare pyramidal mountains known as nunataks, or "lonely peaks" in Eskimo.

The park's marine environment however is readily on view in Seward in the form of the **SeaLife Center**. This sits close to the spot where, in 1903, **John Ballaine** established his railroad to serve a new port on the shores of Resurrection Bay. Ballaine called the place Seward, in honor of the man who was responsible for the US purchase of Alaska from Russia, and although there were already two towns called Seward in Alaska, Ballaine's petitioning prevailed and this became the true Seward. Around the same time Seward was the gold-shipping port at the end of the Iditarod trail, huge quantities arriving by sled from Nome and the Interior. The railroad went through several incarnations before being incorporated into the construction of the Alaska Railroad, in 1915, after which it continued to prosper as a railhead and port for both goods and commercial fishing. Everything looked set to change when the 1964 earthquake caused whole chunks of the waterfront to slide into the bay and set the town ablaze, but everything was rebuilt and Seward continues, building on its fishing and tourism industries.

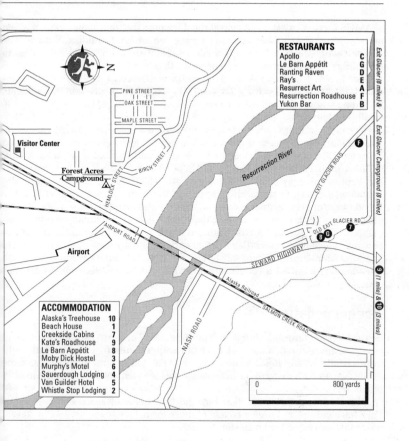

Arrival, local transport, and information

Seward is remarkably well connected, with ferries, buses, trains, a good highway, and even a network of long-distance hiking trails ending not far from town. The four-hour **train** journey from Anchorage (mid-May to early Sept daily; $86 round-trip, $50 one-way; ☎1-800/544-0552) reaches Seward's desolate platform, a couple of hundred yards north of the small boat harbor, at 11am; the daily departure time is 6pm. It is considerably cheaper and quicker to travel by **bus** and two companies run daily from Anchorage in summer: Seward Bus Line (in Seward ☎224-3608, in Anchorage ☎563-0800), and the slightly more expensive Park Connection (☎245-0200 or 1-800/208-0200, *www.alaska-tour.com*), which continues its run through Anchorage to Denali. Homer Stage Line (☎224-3608) runs from the Seward Bus Line depot to Homer at least three times a week (currently Mon, Wed & Fri; $40 one-way), and Kachemak Bay Transit (☎235-3795 or 1-877/235-9101, *info@jbrtransport.com*) call in daily on their run between Homer and Anchorage stopping at various points in town around noon in both directions.

AMHS **ferries** (☎224-5485) stop at the dock near the train station twice a week; once westbound to Valdez, and once on the return run to Kodiak. With all that choice **flying** seems a luxury; FS Air (☎224-5920 or 1-800/478-9595) flies to Anchorage from the airport a mile or so north of town.

Once in Seward, **getting around** the central sights is easy on foot, but you might want to make use of **Seward's Trolley** (May–Sept daily 10am–7pm every 30min; $1.50 one-way, $3 all day), which makes a loop from the SeaLife Center past the small boat harbor, the ferry dock, and the visitor center (see below). For further explorations (to Exit Glacier for example) **rent a bike** from Seward Bike Shop (☎224-2448), which has cruisers for $12 a half-day and full-suspension mountain bikes for $32 a day, and is located in the corral of railcars close to the train station.

The **visitor center** (mid-May to mid-Sept Mon–Sat 8am–6pm, Sun 9am–4pm; mid-Sept to mid-May Mon–Fri 8am–5pm; ☎224-8051, fax 224-5353, *www.seward .net/chamber*) on the approach to town at Mile 2 on the Seward Hwy, holds a broad range of general information, and there's also an **information booth** in an old railcar at 401 3rd Ave (June–Aug daily 9am–5pm). For outdoor-oriented information visit the **Kenai Fjords National Park visitor center**, 1212 4th Ave in Seward's small-boat harbor (late May to early Sept daily 8am–7pm; early Sept to late May Mon–Fri 8am–5pm; ☎224-3175, fax 224-2144, *www.nps.gov/kefj*), which provides maps, shows a couple of worthwhile videos and slide shows and has details on regional hikes.

Accommodation

Seward has **accommodation** to suit most people. There are two **hostels** (one in town, one more rural), a wide selection of **campgrounds** (one conveniently right in the center beside Resurrection Bay), motels, and several good B&Bs, some downtown, though many of the best places are inconveniently sited for those without a car.

A bit further out, Resurrection Bay and the shores of Kenai Fjords National Park have **cabins** and even a couple of more formal lodges accessible by kayak, water taxi, or cruise (see p.260 for details).

Hotels, motels, and B&Bs

Alaska's Treehouse, Forest Rd (☎224-3867, fax 224-3978, *www.seward.net/treehouse*). Very attractive and welcoming B&B in a large timber house seven miles out along the Seward Hwy (turn into Timber Lane Drive then Forest Rd). There's one room with a private (but separate) bathroom, and a suite which sleeps up to five; and everyone gets a full sourdough pancake breakfast and access to a hot tub out on the deck among the spruce trees. ④.

The Beach House, Lowell Point, 2.5 miles south of Seward (☎224-7000). Just one self-catering apartment with space for up to seven though compact enough to be comfortable for two. Good bay views, peaceful location, and good walking to Caines Head nearby. ⑤.

Creekside Cabins, Old Exit Glacier Rd, 3.5 miles from town (☎ & fax 224-3834, *creekside @seward.net*). Four attractively set log cabins in the woods, each with heating, refrigerator, coffee maker (coffee and juice provided), and outdoor fire pit, and access to a streamside sauna. There are also a couple of walk-in campsites for $15. ②–④.

Le Barn Appétit, Old Exit Glacier Rd, 3.5 miles from town (☎224-8706, fax 224-8461, *lebarn @arctic.net*). More of an experience than just a place to stay and somewhere that won't be to everyone's taste. You'll spend time with Janet Van Driessche and her very outgoing husband Yvon and a constant stream of foster children who help run the on-site restaurant (where you'll eat breakfast; see p.261) tend the gardens, hang out on the big sunny deck, or in the activity room with musical instruments. Varied accommodation is either in a room (②/③), three-room apartment (⑧), or a separate tree house (⑤) that's perfect for two adults and two kids. ②–⑧.

Murphy's Motel, 911 4th Ave (☎224-8090, fax 224-5650, *www.murphysmotel.com*). Well-kept motel close to the small boat harbor with great bay and mountain views from many rooms especially those in the new block (⑥). Older rooms are also good with microwave, fridge, and cable TV. ⑤.

Sauerdough Lodging, 225 4th Ave (☎224-8946 or 1-877/224-8946, *www.sauerdoughlodging .com*). The pick of the downtown B&Bs with imaginatively decorated rooms (all different and highly individual) in a historic former trading post built in 1908. The smaller rooms share a bathroom, but there are also suites with clawfoot baths, twelve-foot ceilings, and even an especially large suite sleeping up to seven (⑧). A sumptuous continental breakfast is served downstairs or, in the suites, delivered on an antique tray. Suites ⑥, rooms ④.

Van Guilder Hotel, 308 Adams St (☎224-3079 or 1-800/204-6835, *www.landsendvanguilder .com*). Original 1916 hotel right in the heart of town that's been fully restored and now has modern rooms, cable TV, and dataports. Avoid the cheapest rooms in favor of those with a full bath and a view. Suites ⑦, rooms ⑤.

Whistle Stop Lodging, 411 Port Ave (☎224-5050, *sandefursandy@netscape.net*). Just two rooms unusually sited in a reconstructed World War II railcar close to the small boat harbor and with great views of the fjord. Rooms aren't luxurious but are comfortable and come with private bath, A kitchenette costs $20 extra. ⑤.

Hostels and campgrounds

Beachfront campground, Ballaine Blvd (☎224-4055, fax 224-4088, *campsprd@seward .net*) Excellent central campground that's so close to the shores of Resurrection Bay you can almost fish from inside your tent. There are separate designated tent sites ($6) away from the RVs (dry $10, power and water $15), and coin-operated showers ($2) but open fires and alcohol are banned. Closed Oct to mid-April.

Exit Glacier campground, at Exit Glacier, 13 miles northwest of Seward. First-come, first-served walk-in tent sites with outhouse, pump water, fire rings, and bear-resistant food storage. Free.

Forest Acres campground, Hemlock Ave, a mile north of the small boat harbor. Pleasant wooded site with some grass but no views. Reasonably convenient if Beachfront is full. Tents $6, dry RV sites $10.

Kate's Roadhouse, Mile 5.5 Seward Hwy (☎224-5888, *katesroadhouse@hotmail.com*). Comfortable and welcoming hostel with a five-bed hostel room (no bunks; $17) and a private double (②) in the house, plus three lovely cabins out back ($29 for one person, otherwise ③) each with its own little outdoor seating area. Bedding and a buffet breakfast is included and everyone has access to the kitchen with use of garden herbs, free bikes, a barbecue area with free charcoal and freezer space for your catch. It is inconveniently sited if you don't have a car, but they run a free shuttle service into town. Internet access, no credit cards. ①–③.

Miller's Landing campground, Lowell Point, 2 miles south of Seward (☎224-5739, *www .seward-alaska.com/millers*). One of the best organized campgrounds around with RV spots ($25) beside the beach and tent camping ($20) in the woods, plus cozy cabins (from $40), fishing charters, and kayak rental. Closed Oct–March.

Moby Dick Hostel, 432 3rd Ave (☎224-7072, *www.mobydickhostel.com*). Slightly cramped downtown hostel handily sited on the trolley route with bunks ($16.50), limited kitchen facilities, and small private rooms (②; some with kitchenettes, ③). Closed Nov–March. ①–③.

The town and around

The center of town is small and short on sights except for the superb **SeaLife Center**; from there it's a stroll down to the **small boat harbor**, site of most of the offices for companies running cruises and kayaking trips out onto Resurrection Bay and beyond into the **whale watching** and glacier-fed waters of the **Kenai Fjords National Park**. At some point everyone finds their way to **Exit Glacier**, one of the few glaciers in Alaska that you can walk right up to. Fewer people make it out to the World War II gun emplacements at Caines Head State Recreation Area, partly because of the long walk and need to monitor the tide times.

Downtown

Before taking a cruise to the Kenai Fjords National Park, consider spending a couple of hours on Seward's waterfront at the **Alaska SeaLife Center**, 301 Railway Ave (early May to Sept daily 8am–8pm; mid-Sept to April daily 10am–5pm; adults $12.50, $10 children; *www.alaskasealife.org*), a unique attempt to integrate research, rehabilitation, and public education under one roof. It owes its genesis to the *Exxon Valdez* oil spill (see box, p.234), which both highlighted the need for a coldwater marine research facility in the western hemisphere and provided the bulk of the funds. When marine mammals and seabird populations were severely harmed by the spill, the lack of baseline information hampered attempts to measure just how severely. Altogether some $37 million was diverted from the various civil and criminal settlements against Exxon and funneled into this nonprofit facility.

The SeaLife Center was opened in 1998 and has since firmly established itself on the tourist circuit, not as some bells-and-whistles marine circus, or even an aquarium in the traditional sense, but as a genuine educational and research facility. It can sometimes feel too earnest, but generally balances its priorities well. Certainly there are nicely displayed tanks of fish, but all the marine specimens are native to this part of Alaska and displayed in context, usually to illustrate some facet of the local marine environment. The impact of the oil spill is covered, along with the conflict between commercial fishing and the well-being of marine mammals, and the need for habitat protection in old-growth forests to protect the purity of salmon spawning streams. As you stroll around you are confronted with windows overlooking wet labs and outdoor compounds where you might see sea lions recovering from illness or measurements being taken from coho salmon which swim up a fish ladder from Resurrection Bay. The main concession to entertainment is a series of tanks with underwater viewing windows; one containing Stellar sea lions, another harbor seals, and a third with captive-bred pigeon guillemots, tufted puffins, and common murres. There are no shows as such, but aquarium habits die hard, and everyone flocks to the appropriate tank or window when feeding is announced. If closer views of a working research facility seem enticing, call several days ahead to get on the daily **Behind the Scenes Tour** ($4).

Follow 3rd Avenue a couple of blocks north to the Resurrection Bay Historical Society **museum**, 336 3rd Ave (mid-May to mid-Sept daily 9am–5pm; $2), which is full of moderately interesting displays on Seward's early days, including its role as a Russian shipyard at the turn of the eighteenth century, treatment of its rail heyday, and coverage of the devastating effects of the 1964 earthquake. More detail can be gleaned a few blocks away at the library, 238 5th Ave, where **slides** of the 1964 earthquake are shown (Mon–Sat 2pm; $3). Returning to the waterfront, at the foot of 4th Avenue there's a small marker indicating the **start of the Iditarod Trail**, a route now mostly associated with the Anchorage to Nome sled dog race, though at the beginning of the twentieth century it was the overland trail to the gold fields of the Interior. Nearby, the original 1917 train station has been restored and put to use as the **Chugach Heritage Center**, 501 Railway Ave (May–Sept daily except Tues 10am–6pm; ☎224-5065), an outlet for local artists and craftspeople with a small theater that occasionally sees live performances. From here, follow the bike path along the shore, past a concrete **obelisk** to Seward's founders, and taking in the Bay views all the way to the **small boat harbor**, often a more lively place than downtown. Though there are no sights as such, you'll find a few places to eat, and it can be a pleasant place to spend an afternoon planning the rest of your stay and watching the day's catch come in. Nearby at the corner of 3rd Avenue and N Harbor Street, the **Benny Benson Memorial** remembers the orphaned Aleut thirteen-year-old who designed the state flag in 1927 when he was studying here. From 142 competition submissions, a panel immediately selected his simple design of a deep-blue background adorned with golden stars – the Pole Star and the seven stars of the Big Dipper, its Latin name (*Ursa major*: the great bear), a further allusion to iconic Alaska.

Exit Glacier

One of the most popular activities in Seward is to drive thirteen miles to **Exit Glacier** (never closed; $5 per car, $2 per hiker or biker, both valid 7 days), a four-mile-long tongue of ice poking out from the Harding Icefield, that is one of the few glaciers in the state you can approach by car. During early explorations of the Harding Icefield in the 1960s the glacier was found to be equally convenient as an "exit" route from the icy wastes above.

To get there, follow the Seward Hwy four miles north then turn onto the partly gravel Exit Glacier Road (snow-free mid-May to mid-Oct) beside the Resurrection River. Along the approach, date markers beside the road indicate the location of the glacier's terminus as it has retreated at an average of fifty feet a year: the 1790 marker is two miles from the current face of the glacier. Though the ice moves forward at roughly two feet per day, it melts back slightly more, leaving a broad outwash plain of gravel in its wake.

The road ends at the *Exit Glacier* campground (see p.255) and a ranger station, from where an easy half-mile trail leads to the glacier. Compared to the calving glaciers out in the fjords it is not especially impressive, but there are wildlife viewing opportunities – moose, bears, and mountain goats especially – and a couple of other short loop trails giving a more elevated view into deep-blue crevasses. Rangers lead free nature walks (late May to early Sept daily at 11am, 1pm, 3pm & 5pm) around the base of the glacier, and occasionally (usually July & Aug Sat 9am, but call ☎224-3175 to check) guide all-day treks up the Harding Icefield Trail (see box, overleaf).

Those without a car may want to cycle, or come with Glacier Quest Eco-Tours (☎224-5770 or 1-877/444-5770, *www.alaskaecotours.net*) who run an Exit Glacier shuttle (4 daily in summer; $20 includes entry fee) with pickups all over Seward and a schedule which allows you to spend up to eight hours at the glacier.

Lowell Point and Caines Head State Recreation Area

South of downtown, Lowell Point Road runs a couple of miles south along the fjord to **Lowell Point**, a small scattered community with the *Miller's Landing* campground (see p.255), some B&Bs (we've listed one on p.254), and a couple of kayak-rental places (see p.260). Close to the end of the road a 4.5-mile tide-dependent hiking trail follows old army roads to **Caines Head State Recreation**

MOUNT MARATHON AND OTHER HIKES AROUND SEWARD

The event of the year in Seward is the Fourth of July race up **Mount Marathon**, the big chunk of rock that looms over 3022 feet above Seward. The race is a big deal with up to eight hundred competitors from all over the state and beyond training specifically for the steep, taxing, and frequently dusty conditions, the winner often featuring on the front page of the *Anchorage Daily News* the next day.

The event allegedly started with a barroom wager in 1909, when a couple of sourdoughs speculated as to whether it was possible to climb the mountain and return in under an hour. They just failed, but the event soon became an annual fixture with times rapidly dropping to under 53 minutes by 1928, and 43 minutes 23 seconds in 1981 when eight-time winner Bill Spencer set the current record. The women's record holder is Nancy Pease who took 50 minutes 30 seconds in 1990.

The race route starts and finishes on Lowell Canyon Road, just west of 1st Avenue, and follows the steep ridge, returning down an obvious line of loose rock and scree. A gentler and more scenic **route up Mount Marathon** (3.5 miles round-trip; 3–4hr; 3000ft ascent) starts by a gate at the western end of Monroe Stand and follows a jeep track up to the town's former reservoir, then skirts north around the flank of the mountain to Scheffler Creek waterfall, where you gain a skyline ridge to "Race Point," where competitors turn back. You'll probably want to follow their example, but it is possible to hike higher to the true 4603ft summit of Mount Marathon.

OTHER HIKES

There are a few interesting trails in Seward's immediate vicinity, ranging from the short and gentle Two Lakes Trail right in town to the stiff Harding Icefield Trail. As well as those listed below, there is a coastal trail from Lowell Point to Caines Head (see opposite) and a stack more a few miles back up the Seward Hwy around Moose Pass and Cooper Landing (see box, p.264).

Harding Icefield Trail (5–7hr; 7 miles; 3000ft ascent). A taxing but superbly gratifying hike up a steep and occasionally slippery trail on the north side of Exit Glacier, providing wonderful views of the glacier itself and, once you get high enough, of the Harding Icefield ice. It is usually free of snow from late June to mid-October, and starts near the base of Exit Glacier at the beginning of the Lower Loop Trail. Take water and be prepared for all kinds of weather.

Lost Lake Trail (3hr one-way; 7 miles; 1800ft ascent). Moderately difficult and very scenic trail starting in Lost Lake subdivision at Mile 5.3 of the Seward Hwy and winding through spruce forest. Four miles along there is a 1.5-mile side path to Clemens Memorial Cabin ($35), though day-hikers should continue up above the tree line at Mile 5 to Lost Lake. From here you can either return the way you came, or follow the **Primrose Trail** (3–4hr one-way; 8 miles; 1500ft descent) north, mostly following an old mining road to *Primrose* campground, beside Kenai Lake, rejoining the Seward Hwy at Mile 17. This makes a good loop but leaves you twelve miles along the Seward Hwy from where you started; hitch back or plan your hike to coincide with the bus schedule.

Two Lakes Trail (1 mile loop; 20–30min; 100ft ascent). Easy and enjoyable downtown trail encircling two small lakes and passing a salmon spawning creek. Starts at the back of a parking lot near the junction of 2nd Avenue and B Street.

Area, a site occupied by **Fort McGilvray** during World War II. On a strategic headland 650 feet above the tide with mountains and alpine meadows all about, the fort still has the remains of gun emplacements and ammunition magazines used to defend the southern terminus of the Alaska Railroad. Many people arrive by boat (water taxi or kayak), but if you **hike** (2–3hr one-way; 4.5 miles; 700ft ascent), you'll need to take into account the tide, which must be at its lowest ebb on the middle section of the hike: set off (and head back) two hours before low tide. Unless low tides fall in the early morning and late evening you'll have to stay overnight, either at one of several free campsites, or at either of the two **cabins** ($50 each; book through the Natural Resources Public Information Center in Anchorage on ☎269-8400), Derby Cove or Callisto Canyon, both at the northern end of the recreation area around four miles from the trailhead.

Resurrection Bay and Kenai Fjords cruises

A visit to Seward wouldn't be complete without time spent on the water. The shorter and generally cheaper **cruises** travel around **Resurrection Bay**, where you might expect to see harbor seals, Dall's and harbor porpoises, sea otters, mountain goats on the hillsides, and large numbers of birds – bald eagles, puffins, black-legged kittiwakes, murres, and more. It is definitely worth the extra expense and time to go beyond the limit of the bay into the **Kenai Fjords National Park**, where, in larger open bodies of water, there's a better chance of seeing humpback and gray whales, orcas, and maybe the huge fin whales. The longer trips to Northwestern Fjord also visit the **Chiswell Islands Wildlife Refuge**, at the mouth of Aialik Bay, a major summer nesting site for fifty thousand birds from eighteen species such as tufted and horned puffins, storm petrels, common murres, and auklets. This is also the only Stellar sea lion pupping area in Alaska that you can legally approach and observe. This is particularly special since, for reasons as yet undetermined, numbers of Stellar sea lions have dropped rapidly in recent years and they are now protected under the Endangered Species Act. In the fjords themselves boats visit **tidewater glaciers** which may put on a display sending towers of ice crashing into the water.

The biggest and most popular of the cruise companies is Kenai Fjords Tours (☎1-800/478 8068, *www.kenaifjords.com*), who offer a huge array of trips, some calling at their simple wilderness lodge on **Fox Island** (June to early Sept), fourteen miles south of Seward in Resurrection Bay. There's no road access and there's only electricity when they fire up the generator, but they manage to provide salmon buffet meals for the cruises that call in, provide accommodation, and have kayaks stationed there for cruise/kayak combos. If you want to stroll the pebble beaches you can combine a cruise with one or more nights in rustic but comfortable cabins with proper beds, wood stove, and solar-powered lighting. A two-day combination Kenai Fjords cruise and a night on Fox Island and all meals goes for $319 ($160 each extra night), and you can kayak while there ($70 for three hours, $89 for four hours).

Kenai Fjords Tours' cheapest cruise (3hr; $54) covers Resurrection Bay and comes in variations that stop for lunch or dinner on Fox Island (4–5hr; $59–74). Trips out into the Kenai Fjords National Park include a six-hour trip into Holgate Arm ($109), and the mighty nine-hour Northwestern Fjord Cruise ($139). These all run from late May to early September with a couple of them extending a week or two at either end of the season. Early season visitors can enjoy the Gray Whale Watch Cruise (late March to early May; 5hr; $69), which hopes to catch some of the twenty thousand California gray whales as they pass on their spring migration to the arctic.

Under the guise of Mariah Tours (☎224-8623 or 1-800/270-1238, *www.kenaifjords .com*) the same company also runs **small boat cruises** trading some boat stability and speed for more personal attention and slightly lower cost. Their main trip is to Northwestern Fjord (10hr; $115).

The main opposition is Major Marine Tours (☎224-8030 or 1-800/764-7300, *www.majormarine.com*), who visit Holgate Glacier, not quite as far nor as spectacular as Northwestern Fjord, but cheaper (8hr; $89), though you should definitely consider spending the extra $10 for a buffet salmon and chicken lunch.

Kayaking and boat-accessible cabins

Resurrection Bay and the Kenai Fjords National Park both make wonderful **seakayaking** territory and there is a wide range of tours offered by Sunny Cove Sea Kayaking Co (☎224-8810 or 1-800/770-9119, *www.sunnycove.com*), who are based at Lowell Point, two miles south of Seward. Direct from their base they run guided paddles on Resurrection Bay ($59 for 3hr, $99 for 7hr) including a three-hour evening paddle at 7pm. They also team up with Kenai Fjord Tours to offer a cruise, a meal at Fox Island, and two to four hours of kayaking ($140–160). To paddle among icebergs you'll need the cruise-and-paddle trip to Aialik Bay (10hr; $259), or join one of their many overnight trips: paddling to Caines Head and spending the night there ($280); two nights in Aialik Bay ($750); or four nights in Northwestern Fjord ($1300).

Kayak & Custom Adventures, at the *Miller's Landing* campground at Lowell Point (☎224-3960 or 1-800/288-3134, *kayak@arctic.net*) also run guided trips around Resurrection Bay (7hr; $99) and offer a **beginners instruction course** including overnight camping (2 days; $195) for folks who want to go it alone. Those suitably experienced can **rent kayaks** from them (single $30 first day, $15 thereafter; double $55/$45) and explore at will. Relatively close destinations include two **cabins** in Caines Head State Recreation Area (see overleaf), and *Kayakers Cove* (☎224-8662, *kayakerscove@hotmail.com*; ①/②), a lodge (bunks $20) with kitchen surrounded by cabins ($60 for up to three) on the mainland close to Fox Island: bring your own food and sleeping bag. You can also get here by water taxi from Seward ($45 per person round-trip), and rent kayaks by the day (single $20, double $30) while you're there.

Further afield there's great paddling around the fjord-indented coast of Kenai Fjords National Park, particularly around Aialik Bay. The more remote Northwestern Fjord is less visited, though possibly less varied unless you are skilled enough to venture out around the more exposed mouth of Harris Bay. The best approach is to get a charter boat to deliver you and your kayak: typical fares are: $250 per person round-trip for Aialik Bay; more like $350 for Harris Bay or Northwestern Fjord. You can then spend several days either hopping from one campsite to another or basing yourself at one of several water-accessible **cabins** ($35). The Kenai Fjords visitor center handle bookings and have a stack of good advice to help your trip planning.

Eating, drinking, and entertainment

The presence of a significant number of tourists raises Seward's culinary scene a little above the Alaskan small-town norm with several worthwhile **restaurants** spanning the spectrum. Most are downtown, though there are a few around the small-boat harbor and a couple of distant places worth seeking out. The majority of the restaurants listed below are licensed, but a handful of good **bars** also exist around the waterfront end of 4th Avenue. Entertainment is limited to second-run **movies**, nightly at the Liberty Theatre at 304 Adams St, though most people are content to eat then spend the long evenings wandering along the waterfront or paying a late visit to Exit Glacier.

For **groceries**, the best selection and prices are at the Eagle Quality Center at Mile 2 on the Seward Hwy, close to the visitor center, though Bob's Market at 207 4th Ave is more convenient.

Apollo, 229 4th Ave (☎224-3092). Reliable cover-all-the-bases Alaskan-style dining where you can get a wide range of Italian and Greek specialties ($12–15) along with sandwiches and burgers ($7–10), seafood dishes ($18), steaks ($21), and great pizza (from $12) surrounded by images of Greek gods.

Le Barn Appétit, Old Exit Glacier Rd (☎224-8706). Some of the most lovingly prepared food in Seward is served here in warm and lively family surroundings. Usually healthy, often vegetarian, and always imaginative; breakfast might consist of three-egg omelettes, Belgian waffles, or French toast washed down with good espresso. Home-baked eight-grain breads are used for sandwiches, served with hearty soups, and in the evening there are full meals (from meatloaf to salmon) served with rice pilaf or sautéed red potatoes. Moderate prices.

Ranting Raven, 238 4th Ave (☎224-2228). Gift shop with attached bakery and café serving tasty and good-value quiches, pastries, croissants, bagels, and espresso in a sunny wooden-floored room.

Ray's Waterfront, 1316 4th Ave (☎224-5606, *www.alaskaone.com/waterfront*). Fine dining by the small-boat harbor in a building distinctively topped by a fake lighthouse. Take in the great mountain views as you tuck into the likes of roasted elephant garlic ($9), crab cakes ($11), and pan-seared Thai scallops ($21), all beautifully cooked using herbs grown in the small greenhouse alongside. Closed Nov–March.

Resurrect Art Coffee House, 320 3rd Ave (☎224-7161). Seward's best café, in a former church with seating on the main floor surrounded by quality local arts and crafts, and up in the choir where there are books and board games. Good coffee, cakes, and light meals at agreeable prices, and many evenings there is acoustic music, book readings, or whatever. Open daily to 10pm.

Resurrection Roadhouse, Mile 0.7 Exit Glacier Rd (☎224-7116). Cavernous log-built restaurant and bar offering day-long casual dining on Denver omelette ($8), Pork mole wrap ($8), shrimp Veracruz ($20), and a selection of burgers and pizzas.

Yukon Bar, 201 4th Ave at Washington (☎224-3063). Lively bar with a good range of beers and frequent rowdy music particularly towards the weekend.

Listings

Banks There are several around town with 24hr ATMs including First National Bank, 303 4th Ave.

Car rental Hertz, 604 Port Ave (☎224-4378); U-Save, 13881 Bruno Rd (☎224-7271).

Flightseeing Scenic Mountain Air (☎288-3646, *www.scenicmountainair.com*) run flightseeing trips from Seward airport: over the town and to Exit Glacier (15min; $29); out over Kenai Fjords and the Harding Icefield (30min; $69); an extended version over the same area (1hr; $129); and more.

Internet access The free thirty-minute sessions at the library are in high demand so you might find it easier to visit Grant Electronics, 222 4th Ave (Tues–Sat 10am–6pm; ☎224-7015), where rates are reasonable.

Laundry Seward Laundry and Dry Cleaning, 804 4th Ave (Mon–Sat 8am–8pm; ☎224-5727) has coin-op and service laundry.

Library Seward Community Library, 238 5th Ave (Mon–Sat noon–8pm; ☎224-3646) has free Internet access.

Medical assistance Providence Seward Medical Center, 417 1st Ave at Jefferson St (☎224-5205).

Pharmacy Seward Drug Co, 220 4th Ave (☎224-8989).

Post Office 507 Madison St at 6th. The **General Delivery** ZIP code is 99664.

Showers The Harbormasters office by the small boat harbor has coin-op showers for $2, and Seward Laundry (see overleaf) has showers with towel and soap for $4.

Taxes The two percent city tax is charged in all purchases; the nine percent hotel tax has been included in our price codes.

Travel agency World Express Travel, 300 4th Ave (☎224-5554, fax 224-5403).

Water taxi Miller's Landing at Lowell Point (☎224-5739, fax 224-5975, *milland@ptialaska.net*).

Western Kenai Peninsula

Nowhere in Alaska can there be a more dramatic change of scenery than the transition from the tight-bound, almost claustrophobic, mountains of the northwest to the flatlands of the **western Kenai Peninsula** just twenty-odd miles to the south. Almost the entire western half of the peninsula is low and swampy country studded with shallow lakes ringed by spruce trees. In fact this is one of the largest areas of flat, useable land in Alaska; only the Mat-Su valley and the region around Fairbanks have comparable acreages. This has its benefits with numerous interconnected lakes and level portages forming superb canoe routes, but has also left the region open to unfettered development. Much of the area around the towns of Kenai and Soldotna was developed with no thought of town planning. The coast north of Kenai is also one of Alaska's most industrialized on account of the oil and natural gas sucked out of the ground underneath Cook Inlet.

Depressing though that may sound, it mars only a small area, and the vast majority of the region is wonderfully pristine, much of it falling under the control of the **Kenai National Wildlife Refuge**. A tranche running through the center of the peninsula from the far northern tip to Kachemak Bay was originally set aside by Franklin Roosevelt in 1941 as a moose-hunting preserve, and then expanded into the Kenai National Wildlife Refuge in 1980. Very little has highway access, making its trails and lakes some of the least visited in the region, though it does get busy in the campgrounds along the Skilak Lake Loop Road (see below). Much the best source of detailed information is the park visitor center in Soldotna (see p.266).

In summer **Soldotna** is overrun by Alaskans and outsiders seeking some of the world's best **king salmon fishing**. Nearby **Kenai** is popular for its fish, but has some history too, best seen in its beautiful **Russian Orthodox church**. Get anywhere near the coast on a fine day and it is hard to be unimpressed by the sight of the two conical volcanoes – Redoubt and Iliamna – across the water, though the best views are south of Soldotna where the highway runs close to the clifftops past the state's finest **razor clam** beaches.

Cooper Landing and around

Tern Lake Junction marks the point where the Sterling Hwy splits off from the Seward Hwy, the mileposts confusingly starting at Mile 37, reflecting the distance

KENAI

0 500 yds

8TH AVE.
4TH AVE.
3RD AVE.
2ND AVE.
1ST AVE.
BIRCH DRIVE
DRIVE
SPRUCE
CORAL ST.
COHE AVE.
FLOAT PLANE ROAD
MAIN STREET
BARNACLE WAY
WILLOW STREET
TRADING BAY RD.
CANDID
1ST
BLUFF ST.
BROAD ST.
LAKE ST.
C.ST. S.W.

Library

Russian
Orthodox
Church
Fort
Kenay
Chapel
COOK AVE.
Beluga Whale Lookout

A **2** **B**
3
1
i

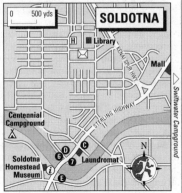

SOLDOTNA

0 500 yds

H Library

KENAI SPUR HWY.
Mall

Centennial
Campground

STERLING HIGHWAY

Swiftwater Campground

Soldotna
Homestead
Museum
i
Laundromat

D **C**
6
7
E

▽ *Kenai NWR Visitor Center (1 mile)*

Discovery
CAPTAIN COOK STATE RECREATION AREA
Bishop Creek

Cook Inlet

EAST
FORELAND
LIGHTHOUSE
RESERVE

NORTH KENAI ROAD

KENAI NATIONAL
WILDLIFE REFUGE

see
Kenai
inset

KENAI SPUR ROAD

see
Soldotna
inset

Cook
Inlet

KALIFONSKY BEACH ROAD

STERLING HWY

4
5

KENAI NATIONAL
WILDLIFE REFUGE

Kasilof
River
SRS

Tustumena
Lake

Tustumena
Lake

CLAM
GULCH
STATE
RECREATION
AREA

0   2 miles

**WESTERN KENAI
PENINSULA**

ACCOMMODATION

Aksala	4
Alaska's Log Cabin	5
Beluga Lookout RV Park	2
Goodnight Inn Lodge	7
Harborside Cottages	3
Kenai Merit Inn	1
Kenai River Lodge	6

RESTAURANTS

Acapulco	D
Old Town Village Restaurant	B
Sal's Klondike Diner	C
Tides Inn	E
Veronica's	A

NORTHERN KENAI TRAILS

The mountains of the northern Kenai Peninsula are laced with the most extensive network of multiday hiking trails in Alaska, over two hundred miles in total. With little difficulty and minimal money it is quite possible for experienced hikers to spend a week or ten days piecing together a circular loop, or hiking across the peninsula from Hope, on the shores of Turnagain Arm, to Seward on Resurrection Bay. While all are long, none are especially arduous or involve long steep climbs, though there is some logistic difficulty in that none of the trails finish close to where they start. The whole region falls within the bounds of the Chugach National Forest, which manages fifteen first-come, first-served forest campgrounds in the region, along with seventeen public-use cabins ($35–45; reserve on 1-877/444-6777, *www.reserveusa.com*), the more popular being available for three-day stays, while you can stay in others for a week.

It is worth remembering that the Kenai mountains typically receive a lot of snow, so don't expect the upland sections of any of these trails to be snow-free until early June, or later. The first significant snowfall of the winter usually arrives late in September.

Johnson Pass Trail (2–3 days one-way; 23 miles; 1000ft ascent). Particularly beautiful trail with a predominance of treeless subalpine country with wondrous long views. From the north trailhead at Mile 64 on the Seward Hwy (close to the *Granite Creek* campground) it climbs steeply through hemlock, willow, and alder then, as the trail levels out, there's more wildflowers and shrubs and great camping spots. At the highest point of the trail around Johnson Pass the terrain is open enough for you to explore away from the trail pretty much as you please. The trail finishes just west of Moose Pass at Mile 32.5 on the Seward Hwy.

Resurrection Pass Trail (3–5 days one-way; 39 miles; 2200ft ascent). Superb and justly popular trail following the long valley of Resurrection Creek up to Resurrection Pass then down to the Sterling Hwy near Cooper Landing. It was the

from Seward in the days before these roads were connected to Anchorage. With the exception of a couple of campgrounds, there is very little in the way of facilities along the Sterling Hwy until **COOPER LANDING**, another one of those strung-out Alaskan highway towns where you're never quite sure if you've arrived or not, until you've passed through. It was named for Joseph Cooper who sought gold here in 1884 and set up a trading post, though the place never really got off the ground until salmon-**fishing** enthusiasts began to congregate here for the red-salmon run on the Russian River (mid-June to late Aug), and various runs on the Kenai River. Hikers might prefer to explore the first few miles of some of the region's trails (see box, above), or try some fairly gentle **rafting** on the Kenai River with great opportunities for spotting eagles and moose. Alaska Rivers Co, Mile 50 (☎595-1226), run raft-fishing trips on the Kenai River (half-day $85, full day $135); and pure rafting trips; either two hours (Class II; $42), or the seven-hour run through a canyon and across Skilak Lake (Class III; $85). They'll also run $35 guided hikes along the Russian Lakes Trail (see box, above) and rent rustic but comfortable cabins (④), one by the river. There's nothing shoddy about Alaska Rivers' trips, but there's an altogether slicker, more professional approach to those run by Alaska Wildland Adventures, Mile 50 (☎595-1279 or 1-800/478-4100, fax 595-1428, *www.alaskarivertrips.com*). Most of their business is all-inclusive packages, such as four nights in their comfortable lodge and three days

scene of frenetic activity in 1888 when this was the site of a brief but intense gold rush, during which the prospectors forged the trail now used by hikers. It is mostly fairly easy going with a gradual grade, and is well maintained, though it can be boggy with June snowmelt. Apart from the superb mountain scenery – about a third of the distance is above the tree line – there's abundant wildlife and good fishing in three lakes towards the southern end of the trail; take a rod and a license. You can camp in the many designated camping spots (usually just off the trail), though there are also eight cabins, evenly distributed along the route.

Without an amenable driver, you'll have to hitch from the Seward Hwy fourteen miles into Hope then hitch (or more likely, walk) the four miles up Resurrection Road to the trailhead. The southern trailhead is at Mile 52 on the Sterling Hwy near Cooper Landing from where you can pick up passing buses to your next destination, hitch back to Hope if your car is there, or continue hiking along the Russian Lakes Trail.

Mountain bikers can also tackle the Resurrection Pass Trail in around ten to twelve hours making it possible to do it in a day, leaving your gear with someone who can meet you at the other end. Bikes, panniers, and camping gear can be rented from Girdwood Ski & Cyclery in Girdwood (see p.222).

Russian Lakes Trail (2–4 days one-way; 21 miles; 1100ft ascent). A less arduous alternative to the Resurrection Pass Trail, again fairly gently graded and well maintained most of it through spruce forests well below the timber line. It may not be as dramatic as some of the other hikes, but it's good for spotting moose, bears, Dall sheep, and even wolves. Fishing again is rewarding especially for rainbow trout in upper and Lower Russian lakes. Without transport, access is a problem as the best starting point is twelve miles off the Sterling Hwy (Mile 48) at Cooper Lake, where there's the *Cooper Lake* campground (and $5 trailhead parking). The trail finishes at Mile 52 of the Sterling Hwy close to Cooper Landing.

salmon and trout fishing ($1350), though they also do rafting (2hr float, $45; 7hr canyon, $110), and day-fishing trips on the upper Kenai (9hr; $195).

Fishing trips are also available from *Gwin's Lodge*, Mile 52 (☎595-1266, www.ool.com/gwins), a classic roadhouse that has been serving diner meals for almost fifty years, around the clock during the red-salmon run. Their driftboat fishing trips are either half-day ($95–125) or full day ($145–185) and they also do fly-in trout fishing at remote streams from as little as $110.

Gwin's has **accommodation** in the form of basic fisherman's cabins ($35), and more salubrious affairs with plumbing and proper beds (⑤), as well as RV hookups ($20). Campers are also well served with campgrounds beside red-salmon spawning grounds: *Cooper Creek*, Mile 50.7 (tents $10, RVs $15), and the larger and enormously popular *Russian River*, Mile 52.6 ($13, RVs $20).

On from Cooper Landing you enter the **Kenai National Wildlife Refuge** and pass the campground at *Kenai-Russian River Recreation Area*, Mile 55 ($6), typically full of RVs and anglers, who use a small passenger **ferry** ($5 round-trip) to get to favored spots on the far bank. A couple of miles on, the trailhead for the **Fuller Lakes Trail**, Mile 57 (5–6hr round-trip; 8 miles; 1700ft ascent) heralds the **Kenai National Wildlife Refuge visitor station** (mid-May to mid-Sept daily 10am–7pm), where you can pick up information on the nineteen-mile gravel **Skilak Lake Loop Road**. This temporarily diverts off the Sterling Hwy (rejoining it at Mile 75) and runs close to Skilak Lake and a handful of **camp-grounds**, three of them free, the others $5–10.

From Mile 80 of the Sterling Hwy, **Sterling** sprawls on either side of the road for eight miles, with no center of focus, and is best left behind.

Soldotna

There is hardly anywhere in Alaska that fishing isn't a big deal, but nowhere is it quite so all-consuming as **SOLDOTNA**, 47 miles west of Cooper Landing. The town sits on the banks of the Kenai River which, in summer, is the single busiest salmon river in Alaska, and for good reason, as it regularly produces some of the **largest king salmon ever caught**. The current record, caught in 1985, is a 97-pound monster now mounted and on display in the visitor center, and fish over 80 pounds are not uncommon. In fact, the Kenai River is so renowned for its king salmon that the statewide minimum weight of 50 pounds is here raised to 75 pounds.

Fishing aside, Soldotna is a dull place characterized by strip-mall sprawl of supermarkets and fast-food restaurants, having grown up since being home-steaded by returning World War II soldiers in the late 1940s. Veterans were given first preference, and flocked here despite the lack of roads and the need to either fly in or make the difficult hike from the coast at Kenai.

It is this homesteading connection that provides Soldotna's only tangible sight, the **Soldotna Homestead Museum** (mid-May to mid-Sept Tues–Sat 10am–4pm, Sun noon–4pm; donations appreciated), around the corner from the visitor center, a classic example of showcasing Alaskan "history," which mostly happened less than half a century back. It occupies six original log cabins that have been moved to the site, their interiors arranged to illustrate homesteading life with everything from beds and stoves to oil lamps and preserving jars. One cabin was the former schoolhouse, built by the teacher and pupils' parents.

Though the Kenai National Wildlife Refuge is scattered over the peninsula's western lowlands, Soldotna is home to the main **KNWR visitor center** (June to early Sept Mon–Fri 8am–5pm, Sat & Sun 9am–6pm; early Sept to May Mon–Fri 8.30am–4.30pm, Sat & Sun 10am–5pm; ☎262-7021), a mile off the Seward Hwy at Mile 58, near the Soldotna visitor center. Pop in for the extensive displays about the region, wildlife videos in the theater, and the opportunity to stroll along a couple of easy **woodland trails**.

Salmon fishing, however, is king here, and not all the wilderness experience you might expect: with kings, reds silvers, pinks (in significant numbers only in even-numbered years), rainbow trout, and Dolly Varden all spawning in the river it is busy throughout most of the summer, but the main peak is from mid-May to early July when the first run of kings come in. A combination of the deep and wide Kenai River, and the sheer size of the fish means that they keep to the middle, so successful anglers fish from boats, and the river can be thick with people zipping back and forth with their outboard skiffs. On average, it takes 31 hours of fishing to get a king, though odds can be improved threefold with a guide. Not only do they know the best spots and techniques, they're also up with the byzantine regulations (which differ from the rules on other rivers). For a recorded fishing report (and the latest regs) call ☎262-6737.

The visitor center can put you in touch with fishing guides and boat-rental places, but if this all sounds too complicated and expensive you could always just wet a line from the boardwalk just in front of the visitor center, or fish the Kasilof

River, fifteen miles south, where the fish are a little smaller but can be caught from the bank.

Practicalities

Kachemak Bay Transit (☎235-3795 or 1-877/235-9101) and Homer Stage Lines (☎262-4584 in Soldotna) pass through Soldotna and will dropoff at the **visitor center**, 47900 Sterling Hwy (May–Sept daily 9am–7pm; Oct–April Mon–Fri 9am–5pm, Sat noon–5pm; ☎262-1337, fax 262-3566, *www.soldotnachamber.com*), beside the Kenai River at Mile 69, which has all you need to know about fishing in the area and holds brochures for dozens of B&Bs scattered around. For **accommodation**, try *Kenai River Lodge*, 393 Riverside Drive (☎262-4292, fax 262-7332, *www.alaskais.com/kenailodge*; ⑤), directly across the river from the visitor center, which has deluxe motel rooms all with river views, and fishing from the hotel grounds. The *Goodnight Inn Lodge*, 44715 Sterling Hwy (☎262-4584 or 1-800/478-4584 in Alaska; ④) across the highway is less salubrious but cheaper. There is no budget accommodation, but **campers** can stay close to the river at the wooded *Centennial Park Campground* (☎262-5299; $10), which is large but still manages to fill up early in the day from around mid-May to mid-July, or the similarly busy *Swiftwater Park Campground* on E Redoubt Avenue ($10).

There's a good selection of **places to eat** in Soldotna with everything visible along the highway. The major fast-food chains are represented, but everyone seems to end up visiting *Sal's Klondike Diner*, 44619 Sterling Hwy (☎262-9065), which serves home-style dishes like biscuits, gravy, and two-egg breakfast ($4) or a veggie skillet ($7) followed by one of their ridiculously large and sticky cinnamon rolls ($3.50). On a sunny day try the riverside deck of the *Tides Inn*, 44789 Seward Hwy (☎262-1906), where you can get a burger and brew for as little as $7, or the *Acapulco Restaurant*, 44758 Sterling Hwy (no phone), which does reasonably priced Mexican, and pizza.

There are **banks** along the highway, as well as the Alpine Laundromat, 44669 Sterling Hwy (daily 8am–10pm), which has showers, and a **library** at 235 Binkley Street with free **email**.

Kenai and around

On initial acquaintance, **KENAI**, eleven miles north of Soldotna, is little better than its southern sibling, suffering from the same unplanned development – in fact both have spread so far they almost join. That said, it can be a pretty place, especially on clear days when there are wonderful views of Iliamna and Redoubt volcanoes across Cook Inlet. There is also a tangible sense of history, though perhaps less than you would expect in what is the second oldest permanent European settlement in the state.

The Russians arrived in 1791 looking to obtain sea-otter pelts, and built Redoubt Nikolaevsk (Fort St Nicholas) to protect their interests. Despite a battle over fur trading with the local Dena'ina Athapascans in which a hundred people were killed, the Russians stuck around, building a productive brickworks in 1841 and a school in 1864, just three years before they sold Alaska to the United States.

Apart from a few homesteaders and fishermen, no one took much notice of the place until 1957 when oil was discovered along the Swanson River. Subsequently natural gas was found under Cook Inlet and there are now over a dozen production platforms sending oil and gas to the refinery north of town.

Stop first at the **Kenai Visitors and Cultural Center**, corner of Kenai Spur Hwy and Main Street (June–Aug Mon–Fri 9am–8pm, Sat & Sun 11am–7pm; Sept–May Mon–Fri 9am–5pm, Sat 10am–4pm; ☎283-1991, fax 283-2230, *www.visitkenai.com*), where the cultural center ($3), usually has some top-quality exhibition to bolster an already fascinating section on local history with good examples of baleen and ivory baskets, and an Athapascan necklace fashioned from shells and Russian trade beads. You can also pick up the free *Old Kenai Town Walking Tour* leaflet then walk a quarter of a mile to the **historic part of town** on a bluff overlooking Cook Inlet and the mouth of the Kenai River. This is the remains of the Russian settlement built around the striking **Holy Assumption of the Virgin Mary Orthodox Church**, Mission Street (June–Aug Mon–Sat 11am–5pm; $1 donation appreciated; ☎283-4122 at other times), with its three, blue onion domes representing the father, son, and holy spirit. The interior is beautiful and dominated by a huge chandelier that came from Irkutsk in 1875, and an ancient Bible brought here by Father Nicolai (see below). The walls all around are covered in icons and religious images, some dating back two hundred years: look particularly for the image of Alexandr Nefsky (on the doorway to the left of the altar), the man who was instrumental in bringing the Russian Orthodox Church to Alaska.

Nearby is the bare-wood **Chapel of Saint Nicholas**, built in 1906 over the grave of Father Nicolai, much loved locally for his dedication in administering the smallpox vaccine while Natives in other communities were dying by the hundreds. It is said that he presided over such a wide area that it would take a year to complete his "circuit" of baptisms.

Across the road from the church is the site of the US army barracks of **Fort Kenay**, Mission Avenue, though the buildings (closed to the public) are reconstructions built in 1967 for the Alaska Centennial. Continuing southeast along Mission Avenue you come to the **Beluga Whale Lookout**, corner of Mission Avenue and Main Street, a clifftop viewing platform that provide the chance – increasingly rare these days – to spot white belukha whales chasing salmon.

Practicalities

You really need your own transport to get the best out of Kenai, though Homer Stage Lines **buses** (☎235-7847 in Homer, ☎224-3608 in Seward) stop in Kenai once in each direction on their run between Seward and Homer. With Homer (or Seward, or even Anchorage) beckoning, there is really not much reason to **stay** in Kenai; RV drivers at the end of a long day might want to hookup at *Beluga Lookout RV Park*, 929 Mission Ave (☎283-5999; $16) right by the church. Almost equally handy are the *Kenai Merit Inn*, 260 S Willow St (☎283-6131 or 1-800/227-6131; ④), which has comfortable rooms, complimentary breakfast and a restaurant; and *Harborside Cottages*, 813 Riverview Drive (☎283-6162 or 1-888/283-6161, *cottages@ptialaska.net*; ④), where you stay in individual cottages with great views of the Kenai River mouth. A couple of B&Bs about three miles away are also worth trying: *Aksala*, Karluk St (☎283-9233, fax 283-1646, *www.alaskaone.com/aksala*; ④) which has waterside cabins among the trees; and *Alaska's Log Cabin Inn*, Mile 5.5 Kalifonsky Beach Rd (☎283-3653, fax 283-3653, *www.ptialaska.net/~tedtitus*; ④) with very comfortable upstairs rooms, less salubrious rooms in a half-basement, and some cabins outside. **Campers** are better served at the Captain Cook State Recreation Area (see opposite).

For something to **eat**, *Veronica's Coffee House*, 604 Peterson St (☎283-2725), is well placed opposite the church and has outdoor seating as well as places inside where you can read magazines over a good coffee, or tuck into soups, sandwiches, and quiches. On weekend evenings there is sometimes live acoustic music. Nearby, the *Old Town Village Restaurant*, 1000 Mission St (☎283-4515), has a standard Alaskan menu of burgers, pasta dishes, and halibut and chips, plus an all-you-can-eat Sunday brunch for $10.

For other practical needs there are **banks** across the road from the visitor center, and the Kenai Public Library, 163 Main Street Loop (Mon–Thurs 10am–8pm, Fri & Sat 10am–5pm, Sun noon–5pm; ☎283-4378), offers **Internet** access.

Captain Cook State Recreation Area

North of Kenai the suburban sprawl bleeds easily into **Nikiski**, which in turn fades out as the highway briefly brushes the coast. Take a quick look at the volcanoes across Cook Inlet before your view is blocked by the oil refinery, and the fertilizer plant, which uses natural gas from the rigs dotted out to sea. The road then weaves inland through trees until, 25 miles north of Kenai, it hits the **Captain Cook State Recreation Area**, a peaceful area with road access to lake swimming, camping, and some wonderful canoeing. Though approached from here, the multiday Swanson River and Swan Lake canoe routes fall within the Kenai National Wildlife Refuge: for details call at their visitor center in Soldotna (see p.266).

You first come across the small *Bishop Creek* campground ($10), which has walk-in tent sites, paths down to the beach, and potable water, and is an easy walk from the **swimming** beach on **Story Lake**. Three miles on, the larger *Discovery* campground ($10) has the best Cook Inlet views and spacious drive-in campsites in the trees. Limited supplies are available at the *Bishop Creek Bar* and liquor store, a couple of miles back down the highway, but it is best to stock up with supplies in Soldotna or Kenai.

South of Soldotna

The Sterling Hwy makes its final 84-mile run to Homer mostly following the western coast of the Kenai Peninsula along the shores of Cook Inlet, a wonderful drive on a clear day when the snow-capped volcanic peaks of Iliamna and Redoubt dominate the views across Cook Inlet. There are a handful of small settlements along the way – the most interesting being **Ninilchik** with its Russian Orthodox church – but the coast is really known for its **clamming beaches**. At almost any low tide you'll see dozens of people up to their knees in mud digging out **razor clams**, sharp-edged bivalves that burrow a foot or two under the sand and make especially good eating if you can catch them. They're typically around three to four inches long (though sometimes up to seven) so although the daily limit is sixty, you only need a dozen or so each for a good meal, either lightly pan-fried or in clam chowder. The best source of information about the rules and necessary skills for clamming is the free *Kenai Peninsula Razor Clams* leaflet available widely, but specifically from the Soldotna office of Fish and Game at 34828 Kalifonsky Beach Rd. Essentially you need to equip yourself with a state sport-fishing license, knee-high rubber boots, rubber gloves, a narrow-bladed shovel, and a bucket, all available to buy or rent locally. Wait for a low tide (the lower the better), look for a dimple in the sand and quickly dig just on the seaward side of it to avoid breaking its fragile shell. After two or three shovels, dig around with your hand and grab the clam before it scuttles away. Dump them in salt water and they'll naturally clear themselves of sand, saving you a lot of trouble. For more information on clamming visit *www.dnr.state.ak.us/parks/units/clamglch.htm*.

Kasilof and Clam Gulch

The Seward Hwy and Kalifonsky Beach Road converge at **KASILOF**, fourteen miles south of Soldotna, a small fishing community mainly of interest for its collection of simple **campgrounds**, beside lakes or fishing streams, the best being the small *Kasilof River State Recreation Site*, Mile 109 ($10) and the *Tustumena Lake Campground* ($10), located beside the Kasilof River, six miles inland along Tustumena Lake Road from Mile 110.

Ten minutes further south, **CLAM GULCH**, Mile 117, is really just a post office, and a few cabins beside the most northerly of the major clamming beaches. With its broad, gently shelving strand, Clam Gulch is widely regarded as one of the best hunting grounds, and has the double convenience of the *Clam Gulch State Recreation Area* (day-use $5, camping $10) right by the beach, and *Clam Shell Lodge* (☎262-4211 or 1-800/808-1699; ③), where they'll rent you a shovel for $5 and sell you tasty bowls of clam chowder.

Ninilchik

Down the coast another seventeen miles you reach **NINILCHIK**, a loosely defined community spread for a couple of miles along the highway and centered on the mouths of two rivers, the Ninilchik River to the north and the Deep Creek a mile to the south. Most visitors come for the exemplary **clamming**, but there is interest too in the picturesque **Russian Orthodox church** and cemetery superbly set atop the hill overlooking town. It was built in 1901, some eighty years after employees of the Russian-American Company first established a town here. Unlike many Russian communities, Ninilchik wasn't deserted when the Russians sold Alaska to the US, and the descendants still live hereabouts.

After admiring the exterior of the church, head down the highway to **Old Ninilchik Village**, a collection of cabins and engagingly dilapidated shacks bounded on three sides by a bend in the Ninilchik River where old fishing boats rest on the shore. Much of the village was lost when the ground sank three feet during the 1964 earthquake, but you can still visit the restored nineteenth-century cabin known as the **Village Cache**, a quality craft shop where you can pick up the free *Tour of Ninilchik Village* leaflet. Spend a few minutes here before walking round to the main beach where the best of the clamming happens.

South from Ninilchik the only significant settlement is the fishing town of **Anchor Point**; best to press on the remaining 23 miles to Homer.

PRACTICALITIES

When the weather is good, Ninilchik is certainly appealing enough to make you want to stay the night, and if you're here for the clamming it seems in the spirit of the enterprise to **camp** by the beach. This is easily done either on gravel sites at the exposed *Ninilchik Beach* campground ($5) or a mile south at the larger *Deep Creek State Recreation Site* ($10), which is heavily used by clammers (day-use $5). There are also more sheltered and secluded $10 sites inland close to the highway at *Deep Creek* and *Ninilchik River*, and also at the small *Ninilchik View* campground ($10), high up and with great volcano views from some sites.

Right on the beach, there are simple **rooms** at the *Beachcomber Motel* (☎567-3417; ③), and about three miles inland there's the *HI-Ninilchik* **hostel** (aka The Eagle Watch), Mile 3 Oilwell Rd (mid-May to mid-Sept; office 8–10am & 5–10am; ☎567-3905; members $10, nonmembers $13), sited on a high bluff above a meandering creek where moose often graze. It is a spotless and well-organized hostel in a family home with separate men's and women's dorms, and a communal kitchen, downstairs. Tea, coffee, and some kitchen necessities are supplied, they'll pick up from the highway ($1) with prior warning, and run clamming sessions ($5 if you stay at the hostel the night before) when the tides are low enough and four people can be rounded up.

There isn't much choice for **eating**, but about the best place is the *Boardwalk* (no phone), almost opposite the *Beachcomber Motel*, where you can sit inside or out admiring the view as you dine on build-your-own subs, burgers, halibut dishes and, of course, clam chowder, all at moderate prices. Most of Ninilchik's limited services are a mile south of here, including surprisingly excellent coffee at *Electric Beach Espresso & Tanning*, 15555 Sterling Hwy (☎567-3269), the **library** (☎567-3333) which stocks some local information, an **ATM** at the Ninilchik General Store and not a lot else.

Homer and around

HOMER, 44 miles south of Ninilchik, exerts a strong pull on Alaskans and visitors. Its combination of superb location, fairly mild climate, and proximity to **Kachemak Bay** have long drawn a mix of people, from 1960s dropouts to the so-called Old Believers who rejected reforms of the Russian Orthodox Church and came seeking religious freedom. Artists in particular have taken to its relative isolation and slow-paced charms, adding a creative element to the communities that seem at the same time more varied and more integrated than you find elsewhere in Alaska.

Arriving on a day of low cloud coverage, the town's beauty can seem over-hyped, but as you discover the range of diverting activities, the place grows on you and you can easily fall under its relaxed spell. The area across the bay, too, provides welcome retreat in places like **Seldovia** and **Halibut Cove**. You can also take a water taxi to some of the fine hiking on the south side of Kachemak Bay, and try to **catch a halibut** big enough to win the halibut derby.

The first whites to come to Kachemak Bay were Russians who arrived in search of sea otters. They found plenty and nearly wiped them out, but the otters have rebounded in such numbers that you'll likely see several on any bay cruise. No significant settlements were established until the end of the nineteenth century when an English company developed a mine to exploit coal seams on the north shore of the bay.

Homer was founded in 1898 at the tip of the Spit by **Homer Pennock**, something of a con man who had convinced a fifty-strong party of men to come here to look for gold. Little was discovered, but they stayed on and set up an isolated community based on herring fishing and coal. As the herring-salting industry took off in the early years of the twentieth century, communities sprang up around Kachemak Bay, notably Seldovia, which soon became the main town of the region. After 1951, when new gravel roads connected Homer to the rest of the state highway system, Homer began to take over that mantle, a position consolidated by the effects of the 1964 earthquake, which virtually destroyed Seldovia. The Homer Spit sank six feet, swamping a stand of spruce and the fields where cows once grazed, and making the end of the Spit an island at high tide. It has since taken considerable effort to restore and maintain road access along its length, something justified by the thriving commercial port and tourism based around the small-boat harbor.

Arrival, information, and getting around

You'll most likely arrive in Homer by car or on one of the **bus**es run by Homer Stage Lines and Kachemak Bay Transit, giving you a sweeping view of Kachemak Bay, the Spit, and Homer itself from high on a bluff just before you enter town. The highway continues almost five miles out to the end of the Spit, the western limit of the continuous US highway system. The terminal here (☎235-8449 or 1-800/382-9229, *www.akms.com*) is where the **AMHS ferry** *Tustumena* docks on its thrice-weekly run to Kodiak, and weekly service to Seward. Visitors in a hurry might want **to fly** from Anchorage to Homer's airport on Kachemak Bay Road with ERA Aviation (☎235-5205 or 1-800/866-8394) or Southcentral Air (☎283-3926 or 1-800/478-2550), which both charge around $100 one-way and around $150 for an advance-purchase round-trip.

Once here it is quite possible to walk around downtown and around the Spit, but to span the four miles between the two you'll need to ride the **Homer Trolley** (June–Aug daily 10am–6pm), though service is infrequent and it may be quicker to hitch. Better still, **rent a bike** from Homer Saw and Cycle, 1532 Ocean Drive, at the head of the Spit road (☎235-8406, *homersaw@xyz.net*), who charge $15 for half a day ($25 all day) for quality off-road machines, and also rent **rollerblades** ($7/hr). **Car rental** is available from Polar Car Rental, at the airport (☎235-5998), for $50 a day with a hundred miles free ($55 unlimited). Hertz, also at the airport (☎235-0734), are a little more expensive and do allow one-way dropoffs from Anchorage, though the cost is prohibitive.

Information

The town's **visitor center**, 135 Sterling Hwy (late May to early Sept Mon–Fri 9am–8pm, Sat & Sun 10am–6pm, early Sept to late May Mon–Fri 9am–5pm; ☎235-7740, fax 235-8766, *www.xyz.net/~homer*), is the place to pick up free advertising-laden magazines, consult with the knowledgeable staff, and to make reservations on their free phone service. Homer is also the headquarters for the **Alaska Maritime National Wildlife Refuge**, a vast tract of Alaska covering large sections of the Alaska Peninsula, the Aleutian Islands, and the Pribilof Islands, that was set up mainly to protect seabirds – all 40 million of them. Although none of the refuge is particularly close to Homer, the Alaska Maritime NWR visitor center, 451 Sterling Hwy (late May to early Sept daily 9am–6pm; ☎235-6961, fax 235-7469,

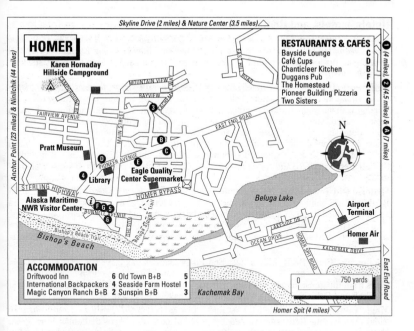

www.r7.fws.gov/nwr/akmnwr), is full of informative displays, interactive CDs of seabirds, and a video on the refuge. Throughout the summer they also run free hour-long **guided birding walks** (mid-May to mid-Sept Wed & Sun 1pm) and free tide-pooling beach walks along Bishop's Beach on days which have the lowest tides: dates are posted at the visitor center.

Accommodation

Accommodation in and around Homer is about as diverse as you'll find anywhere in Alaska, from **camping** on the beach to excellent **B&Bs** with spectacular views across to the Kenai Mountains, **waterside cabins** across in Kachemak Bay State Park, and even some **exclusive lodges** just half an hour away by water taxi. In any of the B&Bs and hotels, **reservations are essential** during July and worthwhile a month on either side.

For many, the quintessential place to stay in Homer is on the **Spit**, either in one of several RV parks that line the road, or in the tent sites with the so-called "Spit Rats," seasonal workers who live in makeshift tents all summer long. Sitting around a driftwood fire as the sun dips below the horizon around 10pm is one of the pleasures of time spent in Homer: getting nearly blown off the beach in heavy rain is not.

Apart from places in the camping section overleaf, tenters and **RV drivers** should check out the *Driftwood Inn*, and hostelers might also consider the *Sunspin Guesthouse*. It is also worth looking at the accommodation around Kachemak Bay (in our account starting on p.279), which may not be good for exploring Homer, but may form a large component of your time in the area.

Hotels, motels, and B&Bs

Chocolate Drop Inn, Mile 6 East End Rd (☎235-3668 or 1-800/530-6015, fax 235-3729, *www .chocolatedropinn.com*). Homer's finest inn, located on a hillside facing Kachemak Bay and with a spacious lounge, recreation room, sauna and hot tub, and gorgeous breakfasts. One room ⑤, mostly ⑥/⑦.

Driftwood Inn, 135 W Bunnell Ave (☎1-800/478-8019 or ☎ & fax 235-8019, *www .thedriftwoodinn.com*). Characterful older hotel with an extensive and varied range of rooms starting with fairly small and individually styled shared-bath rooms, and ranging up through their so-called "shipsquarters" rooms with built-in beds and a distinctly nautical feel, to spacious motel-style rooms. There's also an on-site RV park with full hook-up ($25) and plenty of space for cleaning fish then cooking them up on the sunny deck. The cheaper rooms have no TV but there is a communal TV lounge with video library. Breakfast is not included, though there is free tea and coffee and breakfast is available. Private bath ③–⑤, shared bath ②/③.

Historic Old Town B&B, 106 W Bunnell Ave (☎235-7558, *www.xyz.net/~oldtown*). Beautiful B&B in a 1936 building in the oldest part of Homer, with three rooms all with wooden floors and a restrained decor of antiques, quilted bed covers, and old-fashioned bathroom fittings. Two have tremendous seaviews (one with a private bathroom; ④), and all are reached by a seriously crooked staircase from beside the *Two Sisters* bakery, which is where breakfast is served. ③.

Kachemak Kiana B&B, Mile 5 East End Rd (☎235-8824, fax 235-8349, *www.alaskan.com /~ams/kiana*). Very hospitable B&B occupying the upper floor of a modern house with great views from the guest lounge and some rooms. There's also a great little cabin out the back, a hot tub under the stars, and a full continental breakfast is served. ④.

Magic Canyon Ranch, Mile 5.5 East End Rd (☎ & fax 235-6077, *www.magiccanyonranch .com*). Welcoming B&B surrounded by peaceful countryside (with llamas) and great Kachemak Bay views. Rooms are quite comfortable and tastefully decorated, all having en-suite or semi-private bathrooms. The best is the Glacier View Suite with its antique four-poster, clawfoot bath and a good view of Grewingk Glacier. Breakfasts to remember. ④.

Sunspin Guesthouse, 358 E Lee Drive (☎235-6677 or 1-800/391-6677, fax 235-1022, *www .sunspin.com*). Large B&B in a spacious hillside house offering a range of accommodations from a shared bunkroom ($28 per person) to shared-bath private rooms (③), and considerably more appealing rooms with private bath (④). There's a large deck with a barbecue for guest use, and rates include airport or ferry pickup and a large breakfast ($6 extra if you are in a bunkroom). ①–④.

Hostels and camping

Homer Spit Camping (☎235-1583). Several locations, mostly along the western shore of the Homer Spit with spots on the beach (mostly tents) and round the fishing hole (mostly RVs). Within a short walk of each site you'll find drinking water, toilets, and fish-cleaning tables, and there are dump stations nearby. Fees of $6 for tents and $10 for RVs are payable at the office by the fishing hole. Rules forbid late-night rowdiness (and generator use), and homemade tents are proscribed, though that doesn't seem to prevent "Spit Rats" there for the summer adding extensions of driftwood and blue plastic tarps.

International Backpackers Inn/Hostel, 304 W Pioneer Ave (☎235-1463). Convenient, centrally located hostel in a converted home where you sleep in made-up beds and bunks ($18), some in slightly cramped dorms, and relax in a big lounge with TV/VCR and a great view of the mountains. There's no curfew, lockout or chores and there are often provisions for couples and families.

Karen Hornaday Hillside Campground, Campground Rd (☎235-1583). Wooded sites (some with views) on the slopes above Homer and away from the bustle of the Spit. There's potable water, toilets, picnic tables, and fire rings on site but no hookups or showers. Tents $6, RVs $10.

Seaside Farm Hostel, Mile 5 East End Rd (☎235-7850). One of the best hostels in Alaska, set on a small farm that runs down to the shores of Kachemak Bay. Dorms (bunks $15) are in the main house which makes the best of Alaska's long summer days by having a large outdoor cooking and lounge area. There are cabins all around ($40), and a quarter of a mile away there's also the cozy almost-waterside Sea Shell Cabin (②) which sleeps two and has a small deck. There's even camping ($6), and organic milk for sale. Closed Oct to May. ①/②.

The Town

The only real sight as such in town is the **Pratt Museum of Homer**, 3779 Bartlett St (mid-May to mid-Sept daily 10am–6pm; mid-Sept to mid-May Tues–Sun noon–5pm; $6; *www.prattmuseum.org*), a highly informative and well presented trawl through local and natural history – mounted examples of sea mammals, tide pools, the handiwork of the Peninsula's Native peoples – with special attention to major issues of recent years. For example, one room is devoted to the *Exxon Valdez* oil spill, where you can hear the deadpan communication between Captain Hazelwood and the US Coast Guard immediately after the ship struck the Bligh Reef, and listen to the reaction of Native people to the mess. Elsewhere there's material on the **spruce bark beetle** which has ravaged the Kenai Peninsula's forests in recent years, and discussion of the economically devastating crash in king crab and shrimp stocks since the late 1980s. One of the best sections covers the Kachemak birdlife, particularly that of **Gull Island** (see p.281) which is now equipped with a remote-controlled camera giving unsurpassable close-ups of nesting glaucous winged gulls, murres, puffins, and cormorants. Buttons allow you to pan and zoom in on whichever birds attract your attention. It is cheap enough to go on a cruise and see Gull Island for yourself, but the bear-watching grounds of McNeil River Game Sanctuary (see box p.309) are a lot more expensive to visit. Fortunately, during the peak season of July and August there's a camera focused exclusively on **McNeil River bears** catching salmon. Outside, a **homesteaders cabin** hosts old-timers telling tales of bygone days, and the museum also runs ninety-minute afternoon **walking tours of the spit** (June–Sept Fri–Sun; $10) starting by the *Salty Dawg*: call for times.

Elsewhere, the work of Homer's strong community of **artists**, potters, sculptors, and craftspeople fill numerous **galleries**. Pick up the free *Downtown Homer Art Galleries* leaflet and choose from such longstanding favorites as the nonprofit Bunnell Street Gallery, 106 W Bunnell St (☎235-2662), which exhibits often-challenging work by a changing roster of cutting-edge artists, and Ptarmigan Arts, 471 E Pioneer Ave (☎235-5345), which takes a more commercial and craft-oriented approach, often with artists in residence.

With your own transport, it is also worth taking a drive five miles from downtown up East Hill Road to Skyline Drive, which runs along the top of a series of bluffs a thousand feet above town. The views across the glistening waters of the bay to the glaciers and mountains beyond can be tremendous, but even when clouds are low it is worth calling in at the **Carl E Wynn Nature Center**, E Skyline Drive (early June to early Sept daily 10am–6pm; $5; *www.akcoastalstudies.org*). Here, the Center for Alaskan Coastal Studies has gone to considerable lengths to interpret the local flora and fauna both through displays in their small visitor center and outside along gentle and well-formed trails, wildflower meadows, and spruce forests. To appreciate more of the mushrooms, lichens, and mosses, or learn to identify the animal tracks you come across, join one of the naturalist-led **tours** (10am, noon, 2pm & 4pm).

Homer Spit

Homer's defining feature is **the Spit**, a narrow bank of gravel that runs for over four miles out into Kachemak Bay almost cutting off the inner bay from Cook Inlet. For a place that is one of Alaska's most powerful tourist magnets, it is oddly ugly: the shimmer of the water is often outdone by the sheet-metal glare of hundreds of RVs, the snowy mountains have to compete with the rusting machinery of a working port, and large gravel areas are likely to be stacked high with logs, felled after falling victim to the spruce bark beetle.

Nonetheless, it has become activity central for Kachemak Bay: this is where you'll come to catch ferries to Seldovia or Halibut Cove, and to organize day-cruises, halibut-fishing trips, and kayak rentals (all covered in our Kachemak Bay account starting on p.279). Charter-company offices, fishing-tackle shops, espresso bars, restaurants, small fish-processing operations, and even an email shack are arranged in a series of short rows raised off the beach on pilings and linked by boardwalks. You can spend a good part of the day wandering around here, though there are no real sights. Perhaps the biggest lure is the **fishing hole** (open mid-May to mid-Sept), a small man-made harbor stocked with hatchery-raised salmon which return here to spawn and find nowhere to go. Visitors stand cheek-by-jowl hoping to land one of the late-run kings (late July to early Aug) which have been known to top sixty pounds, or smaller pinks and silvers.

Towards the end of the Spit stands the **Seafarer's Memorial**, a statue remembering Homer residents lost at sea, but there's considerably more interest nearby at the *Salty Dawg* saloon, comprising three relocated huts from the early days of Homer and topped by a wooden lighthouse tower. It is a spit-and-sawdust kind of place with the emphasis on drinking and telling tall tales, but is also firmly on the tourist tick list.

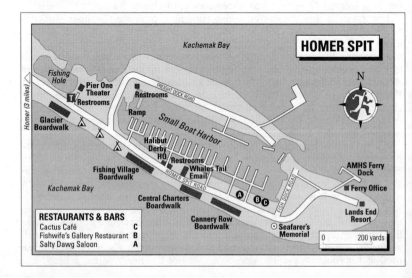

HOMER SPIT

Kachemak Bay

Fishing Hole

Homer (3 miles)

Pier One Theater
Restrooms
Restrooms
FREIGHT DOCK ROAD
Ramp
Glacier Boardwalk
Small Boat Harbor
Halibut Derby HQ
Restrooms
Fishing Village Boardwalk
Whales Tail
Email
HOMER SPIT ROAD
Kachemak Bay
Central Charters Boardwalk
Cannery Row Boardwalk
Seafarer's Memorial
FISH DOCK ROAD
AMHS Ferry Dock
Ferry Office
Lands End Resort

N

0   200 yards

RESTAURANTS & BARS
Cactus Café	C
Fishwife's Gallery Restaurant	B
Salty Dawg Saloon	A

HIKING AND BIKING AROUND HOMER

The most exalted hikes hereabouts are those in the Kachemak Bay State Park on the south side of Kachemak Bay, but if you just want a good walk and don't fancy paying $50 just to get to the trailhead, there are a couple of moderately interesting hikes right on the doorstep. Starting at the eastern end of Bunnell Avenue the **Beluga Slough Trail** (200 yards) runs along a boardwalk beside some wetlands, then continues with the **Bishop Beach Trail** (as long as you want to make it), which heads north along the beach and is best done at low tide when hiking is easier and tide pools more numerous. The beach is passable for around eleven miles, with good sea views all the way, a popular spot for sea otters to raft up offshore after three miles, and highway access at seven miles.

The visitor center has free leaflets detailing how to access the **Homestead Trail** (6.7 miles; 3hr one-way), a route mostly on car-free dirt roads that link Roger's Loop Road to Skyline Drive near the Bridge Creek Reservoir. You gain height quickly and get great views to the west and south, but it is a fairly long walk and you may have to do it twice unless you can talk someone into driving your car to the end trailhead.

A **bicycle** is an ideal way to get around Homer, and you can challenge those thigh muscles riding up to the bluff-crest Skyline Drive, which is relatively flat once you get up there. There is no biking in the Kachemak Bay State Park, but you can take your machine over to Seldovia or Jakolof Bay and ride the old road over to the Gulf Coast.

Eating, drinking, and entertainment

Homer has a better range of **restaurants** than most Alaskan small towns, some of them located out on the Spit where you can sit and watch the sun go down over a late dinner. If you catch a huge halibut you may just want to cook up your own feast with **groceries** bought from the Eagle Quality Center close to the beginning of the Sterling Hwy.

In the long summer evenings it is a pleasure just to stroll around and take it easy, though there are a few bars, none of them very fancy, if you're looking for nightlife. It is also worth considering a visit to the Pier One Theater (June–Aug Thurs–Sun; $9; ☎235-7333, *www.xyz.net/~lance*), a quality community theater that occasionally sees touring shows.

Downtown and around

Bayside Lounge, 453 Pioneer Ave (☎235-9921). Straightforward boozing bar with a pool table and good jukebox.

Chanticleer Kitchen, 432 E Pioneer Ave (☎235-3282). The best place downtown for good espresso (in real cups – no styrofoam), great cakes, smoothies, and a wide selection of tasty and lovingly prepared savories. Try their sautéed vegetable, egg, and home fries wrap for breakfast ($6), a fish taco ($6), or more substantial meals from Wednesday to Saturday when they serve dinner.

Café Cups, 162 W Pioneer Ave (☎235-8330). Justly popular licensed restaurant, unmissable with its two huge sculpted cups above the door, good for lunch or dinner inside or on the small deck. They do a good Reuben sandwich ($8), along with imaginative dishes such as vegetarian Yaki Soba with a sesame cilantro ginger dressing ($8), shrimp and scallop satay ($10), and braised lamb shanks ($15).

The Homestead, Mile 8.2 East Rd (☎235-8723). One of Homer's top restaurants, open nightly for dinner which might be crab-and-shrimp cakes ($13) followed by Mediterranean pasta ($20), half a pound of king crab ($23), sautéed scallops ($21), or something from the extensive specials board.

Pioneer Building Pizzeria, 265 E Pioneer Ave (☎235-3663). Drab family pizza restaurant mainly of interest for the $5 pizza-and-soda lunchtime specials and the $8.50 all-you-can-eat buffet (Mon–Sat evenings only).

Smith Family Restaurant, 412 E Pioneer Ave (☎235-8600). Reliable mainstream dining with filling bacon, eggs, and hash browns breakfast for $7, burger and sandwich lunches and, after 5pm, steak, halibut, and prawn dishes for $15–20.

Two Sisters Espresso/Bakery, 106 W Bunnell Ave (☎235-2280). Great little spot for that morning coffee either in the diminutive bakery or at tables out on the small deck. Good too for pizza, soups, and quiches at moderate prices.

Waterfront Bar, 120 W Bunnell Ave. Rowdy bar with live rock music most nights from Wednesday to Saturday.

The Spit

Cactus Café (☎235-0721). Great cheap eats where you place your order at a hole in the wall and retire to a kind of cabaña walled with plastic sheeting to await your halibut burrito ($6), ginger curry tofu wrap ($6), fruit smoothie ($3.50), or espresso. Dine in or take out. Closed Sun.

Fishwife's Galley, 4460 Homer Spit Rd (☎235-4951). Diminutive restaurant with multicolored tables outside by the small-boat harbor serving delicious dishes at modest prices. Try the excellent New York-style corned beef sandwich, or the halibut chowder served with their great homemade bread (the rye is especially tasty), but there's plenty more including pizzas and authentic tamales (Thurs to Sat only). Closed Wed.

Salty Dawg (no phone). No self-respecting drinker should pass up a few jars in the *Dawg* with its dark interior, life preserver vests pinned to the wall, and what is reliably claimed to be the only surveyors' benchmark located in a bar in the US.

Listings

Banks Branches of the National Bank of Alaska at 203 W Pioneer Ave, and 4014 Lake St; and First National Bank on the Homer Bypass at Heath St: all with 24hr ATMs.

Bear viewing Homer makes a convenient starting point for bear-viewing trips to Katmai National Park (see p.303), and at McNeil River State Game Sanctuary (see box p.309), both on the Alaska peninsula, less than an hour's float-plane flight away. From mid-May to Sept, there are bears to be found somewhere as they gorge themselves on salmon swimming up their spawning streams; the air-charter companies always know the best spots. Trips typically cost close to $500 per person for the flight there and back, and around six hours on the ground viewing: try Bald Mountain Air Service (☎235-7969), Emerald Air Service (☎235-6993), or Homer Air (☎235-8591).

Bookshop The Bookstore, Eagle Center Mall (Mon–Sat 10am–7pm, Sun noon–5pm).

Festivals The Kachemak Bay Shorebird Festival (☎235-7337), over the first weekend of May, coincides with the Wooden Boat Festival but they are really only worth the journey if you're a keen birder.

Horseback Riding Trails End, Mile 11.2 East End Rd (☎235-6393) have horseback rides at $20 an hour, $65 for four hours and $110 for a full day along the river flats and the shores of Kachemak Bay.

Internet access There's free email at the library, but only two machines, so it may be quicker to go to The Whales Tail, 4245 Homer Spit Rd #6 (daily 10am–8pm; ☎235-9791) on the spit.

Laundry Washboard Laundromat, 1204 Ocean Drive (☎235-8586) has laundry and showers.

Library The Homer Public Library, 141 W Pioneer Ave (Tues & Thurs 10am–8pm, Wed, Fri & Sat 10am–6pm; ☎ 235-3180, *www.xyz.net/~hpl/*).

Medical assistance South Peninsula Hospital, 4300 Bartlett St (☎235-8101).

Post Office on Sterling Hwy at Lake St. The **General Delivery** ZIP code is 99603.

Taxi Kache Cab ☎235-1950.

Around Homer

Even tourists on a busy schedule often spend a week **around Homer**, not so much for what the town offers, but for its access to wonderful country nearby. Most people's focus is **Kachemak Bay**, a forty-mile-long and eight-mile-wide tongue of water with a southern shore that has been carved by the glaciers that still peel off the Kenai Mountains behind.

Kachemak Bay is almost divided in two by the Homer Spit, its central position and deep harbor making it the nerve center for activities around the bay and a staging point for day-cruises, ferries, and water taxis. Boats crossing the bay almost always spend a few minutes bobbing around in the waters off **Gull Island**, a guano-encrusted rock three miles off the tip of the Spit that is typically alive with

---

HIKING IN KACHEMAK BAY STATE PARK

The south side of Kachemak Bay has some wonderful hiking along a forty-mile series of interlinked trails, none penetrating far into the interior of the Kenai Mountains, but most providing access to shoreline walks, fishing streams, small lakes, seasonal berry picking, and the Grewingk Glacier. Those listed here are just a taster of the sixteen trails currently included on the *Kachemak Bay State Park Hiking Trails* leaflet ($1), which also pinpoints a dozen simple, trail-accessible **campsites** (first-come, first-served; no permits required; free) and five **cabins** ($50; sleep 6–8), bookable through the Web site or the State Park office (☎235-7024, *www.dnr.state.ak.us/parks*). There are three cabins at the head of Halibut Cove Lagoon (Lagoon Overlook, Lagoon East, and Lagoon West), the China Poot Lake Cabin beside China Poot Lake and the Sea Star Cove cabin on the western shore of Tutka Bay.

Access is by water taxi (see p.282) and costs $45–60, depending on the distance between the Homer Spit and your destination.

Glacier Lake Trail (1hr–1hr 30min one-way; 2.2 miles; negligible ascent). A very easy trail with good Grewingk Glacier views that links the Glacier Spit and Saddle trailheads and has a number of potential (longer) variations. The Rusty's Lagoon **campsite** is close to the Glacier Spit trailhead.

Grewingk Glacier Trail (4–6hr round-trip; 13 miles; 500ft ascent). Easy and relatively flat trail with superb views of the glacier and surrounding area. Makes a good day-trip from Homer getting dropped at Glacier Spit with an evening pickup at the Saddle trailhead, though there are good campsites along the way.

Wosnesenski River Trail (8–10hr one-way; 11 miles; 300ft ascent). One of the longest hikes in the park and one of the most scenic, starting from the Haystack Trailhead in China Poot Bay and following a broad river valley through cottonwoods before climbing over a low ridge to a series of three lakes. It finishes at China Poot Lake, where there is a cabin and a choice of trails to reach Halibut Cove Lagoon.

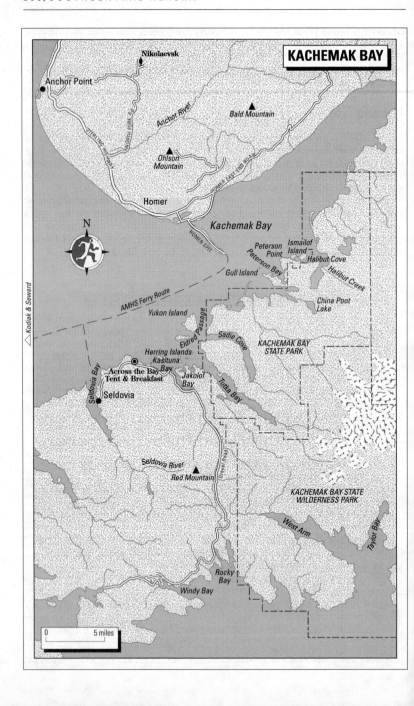

KACHEMAK BAY

Nikolaevsk

Anchor Point

Anchor River

STERLING HIGHWAY

NORTH FORK RD.

Bald Mountain

Ohlson Mountain

HOMER EAST END ROAD

Homer

N

Kachemak Bay

HOMER SPIT

Peterson Point

Peterson Bay

Ismailof Island

Halibut Cove

Halibut Creek

Gull Island

AMHS Ferry Route

Yukon Island

Eldred Passage

Sadie Cove

China Poot Lake

KACHEMAK BAY STATE PARK

Kodiak & Seward

Seldovia Bay

Herring Islands

Kasituna Bay

Across the Bay Tent & Breakfast

Jakolof Bay

Turka Bay

Windy Bay

Seldovia

Seldovia River

Red Mountain

KACHEMAK BAY STATE WILDERNESS PARK

West Arm

Taylor Bay

Rocky Bay

Windy Bay

0   5 miles

up to sixteen thousand squawking, screeching, seabirds: glaucous-winged gulls, black-legged kittiwakes, tufted puffins, pelagic, and red-faced cormorants, and perhaps common murres rafting up offshore ready to wing in and lay their eggs among the rocks. The boats get right up close to the steep cliffs, so you get a great view, aided by the binoculars many boats make available. The birds almost certainly appreciate the super-rich waters of the bay, something which is also dear to the hearts of anglers who have made Homer something of a **halibut-fishing** mecca.

The surrounding mountains give Kachemak Bay a relatively mild and dry climate with conditions further enhanced by the Homer Spit, which provides some protection from swells. Nonetheless, **kayakers** largely stick to the even more sheltered fjords of the **Kachemak Bay State Park**, which encompasses most of the southern shoreline and the hill-country inland. Easy multiday trips are possible making use of several free campsites along the shore and kayak-accessible cabins, which are also used by **hikers** (see box, p.279).

Just outside the State Park lie the two most popular and highly picturesque destinations around Homer: **Halibut Cove**, with its tiny boardwalk community, art galleries, and *The Saltry* restaurant; and the larger **Seldovia**, a peaceful former herring-canning town where there is not a great deal to do, and that's just perfect.

Cruises, kayaking, and water taxis

The Homer Spit is packed with companies keen to get you out on the water. We've covered halibut fishing (overleaf), and transport to Halibut Cove (p.283) and Seldovia (p.284) separately, but there are also several cruises, some operated by companies which double as water taxis, as well as a handful of companies running guided kayaking trips and renting kayaks. Most of the people offering trips operate through one of the small number of agencies along the boardwalks at the end of the Spit: the biggest is Central Charters, 4241 Homer Spit Rd (☎235-7847 or 1-800/478-7847, *www.ptialaska.net/~central*).

The most visited spot in the Kachemak Bay is **Gull Island**, which can be seen inexpensively on the Gull Island cruise (1hr 30min; $20) run by Rainbow Tours (☎235-7272, fax 235-7446, *www.rainbowtours.net*). To get an additional hour exploring Kachemak Bay, join the trip run by St Augustine's Charters (2.5hr; $37; ☎235-6126), or commit the whole day on the excellent-value Natural History Tour run by the nonprofit **Center for Alaskan Coastal Studies** (9hr; $63; ☎235-6667, reservations through Rainbow Tours ☎235-7272). The organization promotes appreciation and conservation of Kachemak Bay by broadening people's understanding of the marine and forest ecosystems with a visit to their field station in Peterson Bay. Here, you can explore the beaches and intertidal life, walk through the forest or learn something of the local flora, fauna, and first peoples.

There's greater intimacy with the surroundings when **kayaking**, best done with True North Kayak Adventures (☎235-0708, *www.jakolofferryservice.com /kayak.html*), who make a point of being ecologically sensitive. Their basic trip ($125) involves a water taxi ride to their base across the bay on Yukon Island, followed by around six hours paddling, including a break for a tasty lunch. For something more ambitious, go for the two-day Eldred Passage Overnight ($290) with extended paddling around Tutka Bay, Sadie Cove, and Eldred Passage (see p.283) and camping somewhere on a beach (save $40 if you have your own camping and cooking gear). Custom multiday wilderness expeditions cost around $325 for three days and $125 for each extra day. Experienced paddlers can **rent kayaks** (doubles $60 first day then $55, singles $35/$30); those less sure of their abilities can join a one-day trip and head off solo afterwards. Similarly priced kayaking trips can be booked through Central Charters and with Seaside Adventures Ecotours (☎235-6672), both of which use water taxis to get you across the exposed Kachemak Bay and into the sheltered waters of the far shore.

Visitors staying in one of the luxury lodges, planning to spend the night in a state park cabin, or just going hiking for the day on the other side of the bay, need to engage the services of a **water taxi**. Competition keeps the prices steady at around $45 per person round-trip to the closest bits of the Kachemak Bay State Park; more like $60 for the more distant corners. Again Central Reservations can be of help, though two of the most active and reliable operators are Mako's Water Taxi (☎235-9055, *mako@xyz.net*), who also runs a short $45 cruise to Gull Island and makes a point of causing minimal disturbance to the birds, and Jakolof Ferry Service (☎235-2376, *www.jakolofferryservice.com*), which runs a number of services along the bay.

Halibut fishing

Homer and its surrounding environs has become inextricably tied to its reputation for halibut. The very biggest ones aren't caught here, but a combination of good halibut waters close to town, and the lucrative summer-long halibut derby have created enough of a buzz that it seems every RV driver wants an ice chest full of the succulent white flesh. Wander along the Spit in the late afternoon and you'll see small groups of people lined up for photos behind the boat's catch of the day. Two-hundred-pound fish are relatively common, and three-hundred-pounders get landed each summer, but something in the twenty to forty pound range is more common. Even at this modest size it can be quite a strain reeling the thing in.

Every year there are sob stories about people who bagged a huge halibut that would have claimed a $30,000 jackpot prize in the annual **Halibut Derby** (May 1–Labor Day; *www.homerhalibutderby.com*), but had failed to buy a derby ticket. With prizes for landing various tagged fish, as well as monthly prizes, and an overall biggest-fish jackpot, you really should buy an $8 ticket from the Derby Headquarters (daily 5.30–8am & 3–7pm), a log cabin by Ramp 4 at the small-boat harbor on the Spit.

Trips are typically all-day affairs with boats powering about an hour out into the bay then bobbing around for about six hours as some try to land halibut while (on rougher days) others hang over the back inflicted with sea sickness. The going rate is $145–165 depending on the season (mid-June to mid-Aug being the most expensive) and you can add $25 if you also want to go after saltwater king salmon as they make their way towards the spawning streams. With all the charter companies located close to each other on the Spit it is worth spending a few minutes wandering around to get the best deals, asking about the size and speed of the boat, comfort, number of other customers, amount of fish cleaning and filleting they'll do, lunch and so on.

There is really no need to book anything in advance, but you could try Homer Ocean Charters (☎235-6212 or 1-800/426-6212, *www.homerocean.com*), or call Rainbow Tours (☎235-7272) who do a half-day trip for $85.

Halibut Cove

One of the most popular day-trips from Homer is to the small private community of **HALIBUT COVE**, a gorgeous enclave of boardwalks, art galleries, a restaurant, and some accommodation (but no roads), on Ismailof Island, eight miles east of the tip of the Homer Spit on the southern shore of Kachemak Bay. It was once the site of a herring industry which peaked in the 1920s when there were over a thousand people here working 36 salteries. It petered out to the point where there were just a few old bachelors left when, in the late 1940s, fisherman Clem Tillion and his artistic wife Diana were spellbound by the isolation and beauty and decided to stay. Their presence encouraged others to stay and revived the community, by the late 1970s other artists were arriving and today, with a hundred-strong residents, there continues to be an overall creative tenor to the place.

It is hard not to be enchanted as you stroll the boardwalks, follow the paths through Sitka spruce forests or just mooch around the three high-quality **art galleries**. Those who aren't buying tend to spend time at the only **restaurant**, *The Saltry* (late May to early Sept; reservations recommended ☎296-2223), where you can sit on the deck on pilings over the water and dine on seviche or sushi (both $10), a large bowl of fish chowder with freshly baked bread ($8), or Kachemak Bay clams steamed in garlic, white wine, and butter (market price), all washed down with wine or microbrews.

You can get there using the Jakolof Ferry Service (☎235-6384), which allows you to visit Halibut Cove from Seldovia ($45 round-trip) or one of the luxury lodges along the coast, but most people arrive direct from Homer on the *Danny J* (mid-May to mid-Sept; book through Central Charters ☎235-7847), a quaint old fishing boat which leaves from behind the *Salty Dawg Saloon* twice a day. One sailing leaves at noon (returns 5pm; $44 round-trip) and takes in Gull Island en route to Halibut Cove where you get two and a half hours to have lunch and wander the boardwalks. The second, more direct, sailing is at 5pm (returns 10pm; $22 and you must have a dinner reservation or a room booked, but the savings on the price of the boat journey just about pays for your dinner (typically $15–25). During the middle of summer, the press of visitors during the day can rob the place of some of its tranquility, something circumvented by **staying at Halibut Cove**. The cheapest option is the self-catering *Cove Country Cabins* (☎296-2257, *www.xyz.net/~ctjones*; ④) which have no running water or indoor plumbing, though the cabins are perfectly decent. If you've got the budget, go for the *Quiet Place Lodge* (☎296-2212, fax 296-2241, *www.quietplace.com*; ⑧) where you get a luxurious cabin, a sumptuous breakfast, and free use of their rowboats. They cook dinner four nights a week ($30) or they'll take you across to *The Saltry*.

Ismailof Island sits in a body of water somewhat confusingly also known as **Halibut Cove**. The head of the cove is Halibut Cove Lagoon, part of Kachemak Bay State Park and a popular spot for the hiking trails that surround it and the three State Park cabins at the head of the lagoon. Water taxis aren't allowed to run you to *The Saltry*, but they can bring you here (around $50 round-trip), dropping you at the trailhead close to the **Halibut Cove Lagoon Ranger Station**, which is staffed full time from mid-May to mid-September.

Sadie Cove, Tutka Bay, and Eldred Passage

Moving further southwest along the southern shores of Kachemak Bay, you pass **Peterson Bay** with its Center for Alaskan Coastal Studies field station, accessible on day-cruises (see p.281). The wide mouth of the bay opens onto Gull Island, visited on just about every local cruise, and provides access to **China Poot Bay**, a sheltered spot for paddling and the starting point of some good hiking trails (see box, p.279). To get around to **Sadie Cove** and **Tutka Bay**, you have to pass through **Eldred Passage**, a broad channel with the mainland on one side and

Cohen Island, **Yukon Island**, and **Hesketh Island** on the other. This is some of the most gorgeous paddling and cruising territory with plenty of wildlife (especially sea otters, seals, and sea lions), steep beaches for camping, and even some caves around the high-tide line on the north shore of Yukon Island.

Exploring the region doesn't necessarily mean camping out. The state park maintains a **cabin** ($50) on the western shore of Tutka Bay, there are more salubrious fully self-catering log cabins on Hesketh Island (☎235-9449; ⑤) with a sauna and bathhouse on the beach, and there are a couple of **luxury lodges** only accessible by sea or float plane. The slightly cheaper of the two is the elegant yet rustic *Sadie Cove Wilderness Lodge* (☎235-2350 or 1-888/283-7234, *www.sadiecove.com*; ⑨), where the nightly fee of $225 includes all meals, lodging in private cabins and use of fishing tackle and a kayak, but you'll have to pay for the water taxi to get here ($60 round-trip). You'll be up for the same access cost, and be required to stay a minimum of two nights at the *Tutka Bay Wilderness Lodge* (☎235-3905 or 1-800/606-3909, fax 235-3909, *www.tutkabaylodge.com*), which ranks as one of the finest wilderness lodges in Alaska, with comfortable cabins linked by a series of boardwalks in a beautiful setting. Plenty of beach walking, tide pooling, and fishing and sightseeing excursions also available.

Just around the point from Tutka Bay is **Jakolof Bay**, which is linked by the only road on the south side of Kachemak Bay to Seldovia.

Seldovia

SELDOVIA seems a world away from the bustle of Homer, just fifteen miles across Kachemak Bay. This maze of peninsulas, sloughs, lakes, and steeply raked beaches manages to balance seclusion and sophistication, with superb B&Bs and a couple of good places to eat ensuring that you're not deprived of civilization as you slow to the pace of the place. It is a tremendously picturesque spot, draped around its small-boat harbor with snow-clad mountains behind, a view of Redoubt and Iliamna volcanoes across the bay and a few remaining vestiges of the boardwalks that once made the place famous. In the quaintest section, brightly painted houses are artistically perched on pilings over the slough and when the weather plays ball there's nothing better to do than sit on the boardwalk trying to spot sea otters, or lean over the rails of the bridge encouraging a salmon to bite on your hook.

This is the oldest port on Kachemak Bay, and was named Zaliv Seldovoy, or Herring Bay by a Russian captain in 1852. Initially the trade was in sea-otter pelts, but the eponymous herrings soon had their day and several canneries sprang up during the 1920s when many Scandinavians came here, staying on to fish for salmon, halibut, and crab over the next forty years. Wooden boardwalks along the waterfront were built during this time to facilitate travel between the dozens of buildings built on pilings. With the closure of most of the canneries, Seldovia went into decline, something hastened by the 1964 earthquake, which dropped the land around here by four feet and caused the destruction of much of the town. A new town was created on landfill and only short sections of the boardwalk survived, but much of the character was retained.

GETTING THERE, ARRIVAL, AND INFORMATION
Almost everyone reaches Seldovia by boat or plane from Homer. The cheapest way is on the car-carrying AMHS **ferry** *Tustumena* ($18 each way; ☎234-7868 in

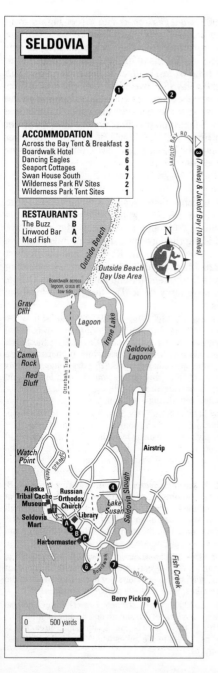

SELDOVIA

ACCOMMODATION

Across the Bay Tent & Breakfast	3
Boardwalk Hotel	5
Dancing Eagles	6
Seaport Cottages	4
Swan House South	7
Wilderness Park RV Sites	2
Wilderness Park Tent Sites	1

RESTAURANTS

The Buzz	**B**
Linwood Bar	**A**
Mad Fish	**C**

Seldovia), which makes the ninety-minute crossing twice a week. It usually returns to Homer straight away, though in summer the Tuesday run gives you around four hours in Seldovia. Once a month (usually second Tues of the month) it continues to Kodiak, staying in Seldovia for a couple of hours, which is long enough for a quick look round. You'll see a lot more of the surrounding country-side by taking one of the two cruise-boat ferries: Seldovia Tours (☎235-7847 or 1-800/478-7847; $45 round-trip, $25 one-way), and Rainbow Tours (☎235-7272, fax 235-7446; $45, $55 via Gull Island). Both leave Homer in the late morning and take a little over an hour to get there (around two hours if also visiting Gull Island), then spend a couple of hours there before setting off back around 3pm. Both allow you to split your journey and spend as many nights as you wish in Seldovia. Water taxis do not run from Homer to Seldovia, but several run to Jakolof Dock ($45 round-trip), twelve miles by road from Seldovia, which may be handy if you are planning to do some cycling over here. Try the Jakolof Ferry Service (☎235-2376) who do a scenic trip to Jakolof Dock and can connect with South Shore Tours to Seldovia (☎234-8000). Another option is to travel with Mako's Water Taxi (☎235-9055) to Jakolof, take a taxi to Seldovia, lunch there, then fly back to Homer, all for $75.

Locals who can't hitch a ride on a neighbor's fishing boat usually **fly** from Homer, a scenic twelve-minute flight best done with Homer Air (see p.278), who charge $30 one-way and $50 for the round-trip. Great Northern

Airlines (☎243-1968 or 1-800/243-1968, *www.gnair.com*) run direct flights from Anchorage for around $100 each way.

Nowhere in Seldovia is more than half a mile from the dock or airstrip, so **getting around** is easy on foot, but there are dozens of miles of gravel roads in the vicinity and you may want to **rent a bike** from *The Buzz Coffee House*, 231 Main St, who rent functional hybrids for $20 a day ($30 overnight).

There is currently no **visitor center**, but everything you need to know is on the widely available *Map of the City of Seldovia* leaflet, and you can check it out online at *www.xyz.net/~seldovia*. In town you'll find a **post office**, corner of Main Street and Seldovia St, a sporadically-open **library**, 260 Seldovia St, and free **Internet access** at SKIAP, 274 Main St (Mon–Fri 1–5pm; ☎234-7807), but **no bank or ATM**: most businesses accept credit cards.

ACCOMMODATION

Seldovia specializes in quality B&Bs, which sets the perfect tone for taking in the area at a leisurely pace. There's great **camping** too at the *Wilderness Park*, Mile 1.5 Jakolof Bay Rd, where RVs get sites ($8) among the trees. Tent campers are better off at tent sites ($5) scattered along the foreshore a quarter-mile from the RV sites. There is pump water and outhouses near the RV sites, and the nearest **showers** are at Harbor Laundry, 226 Main St (daily 11am–8pm; $4 including towel and soap). Before heading out to camp, register and pay at the City Office, 346 Dock Street (☎234-7643) by the state ferry dock. The five percent local tax has been included in our price codes.

Across the Bay Tent & Breakfast, Kasitsna Bay, Mile 8 Jakolof Bay Rd (May–Sept ☎235-3633, Oct–April ☎345-2571, *www.tentandbreakfastalaska.com*). A collection of canvas-walled platform tents (with fresh flowers, hot showers, and a wood-fired sauna) beside the beach eight miles east of Seldovia, that is a great place to hang out for a while, perhaps taking a guided sea-kayaking trip ($95), or doing a little bike riding (rentals $25 a day). *Across the Bay* will pick you up from either Seldovia or Jakolof Dock, and charge you $58 each for tent and breakfast, or $85 if you also want them to provide their excellent seafood-based meals. Everyone chips in with the evening entertainment. Bring a sleeping bag. ⑤.

Boardwalk Hotel, Main St (☎234-7816 or 1-800/238-7862, fax 234-7699, *www.alaskaone.com /boardwalkhotel*). Seldovia's main hotel has only fourteen rooms, many flaunting great harbor views (⑤, deluxe queen ⑥). There are savings to be made by taking either the One-Night Package (from $129), which includes a cruise over and a scenic flight back to Homer; or the Two-Night Kayak Special (from $236) adding a day of kayaking and an extra night at the hotel. ④–⑥.

Dancing Eagles (☎234-7627, fax 278-0289, *www.dancingeagles.com*). Superbly sited B&B, perched on rocks right above the water. The rooms (shared-bath) in the lodge are great value, but the real star is the fully self-contained "cabin" with fabulous views and enough room for six ($40 extra per person). There's free use of an outdoor hot tub and you get a breakfast basket to either take to your room or eat on the sunny (weather permitting) and secluded deck. Cabin ⑥, rooms ⑤.

Seaport Cottages 313 Shoreline Drive (☎234-7483, *www.xyz.net/~chap*). A little cluster of ageing but attractive and well-priced fully self-contained cottages that are perfect if you want to cut costs and prepare your own meals. There are no sea views but it is a short walk to the harbor and you can explore using the free bikes. Suite that sleeps five ⑤, cottages ③.

Swan House South (☎234-8888 or 1-800/921-1900, *www.alaska.net/~swan1*). Large and spacious B&B featuring a beautiful deck with great views of the slough and Mount Iliamna. The interior is light and airy, rooms come with all the comforts, and a substantial breakfast is served up on cue. Luxury is taken to the next level in the suites which also get a VCR and free use of mountain bikes. Suites ⑦, rooms ⑥.

THE TOWN

Seldovia is mostly a place suited for hanging out: maybe strolling around the harbor, stopping somewhere for coffee and browsing some of the better-than-average craft shops. Easily the most scenic section is along the **old boardwalks** at the southern end of Main Street, where you can walk the plank streets high above the water past wonderfully picturesque brightly painted houses perched on stilts over the slough. These are the scant remains of the extensive system of boardwalks that made Seldovia famous before they were destroyed by the 1964 earthquake.

Late July to mid-September is **berry-picking** time, and the best hunting ground for the abundant salmonberries and blueberries, but also cranberries, mossberries, and lowbush cranberries is along Rocky Road to the south of town (see map, p.285). Labor Day weekend marks the **Blueberry Festival** when everyone scours the hills and fills their baskets with rich fruit.

Saint Nicholas Russian Orthodox Church is Seldovia's only traditional sight, idyllically set on a knoll above the harbor. It was built in 1891, and restored in 1981 but is usually closed. If you want to go inside, try to rouse the priest who lives in the trailer next door. At the foot of the knoll there's the **Alaska Tribal Cache Museum**, Main Street (June–Aug Mon–Sat 10am–5pm, Sun noon–5pm; free), which contains a tiny assortment of ivory, a whalebone bowl, and a samovar, but most of all is a good spot to buy homemade berry jam.

If you're looking to do some light exercise follow Main Street and duck up Spring Street to the start of the **Otterbahn Trail** (1hr one-way; 1.5 miles; 100ft ascent), a track through the coastal forest and over lagoon boardwalks diligently carved out by local high school students. It reaches Kachemak Bay at a diminutive, steeply shelving beach then rounds a headland to **Outside Beach**, reached by crossing a tidal slough which may be impassable at high tide (or require some wading). Check the tide tables at the Harbormaster office or on a board by the trailhead. Outside Beach has a day-use area, and can also be easily reached by road (see map, p.285).

ACTIVITIES

If you sign up for a **kayaking** trip in Homer, the first thing they'll do is bring you across to Seldovia for the miles of protected bays, coves, and islands to explore, especially around Eldred Passage, Sadie Cove, and Tutka Bay. Guided kayaking trips here are run by Kayak'atak (☎234-7425, *www.alaska.net/~kayaks*), who work out of the Herring Bay Mercantile store on Main Street and run a local tour (5–6hr; $110; $90 each for groups of four or more), which includes a gourmet lunch. For their overnight trips ($180 each, discounts for three or more) you'll need your own sleeping bag and rain gear, and departures for both trips are designed with the ferry schedules in mind. More confident paddlers can rent kayaks at $50 for a single and $75 for a double ($35 and $55 respectively for second and subsequent days). To speed your passage to the best paddling waters it may pay to organize transport along the road to Jakolof Bay with South Shore Tours (☎234-8000).

With several miles of former logging roads, **mountain biking** may appeal, either with a bike rented here or one brought over from Homer. The road to Jakolof continues south to the Gulf of Alaska coast via **Red Mountain**, a huge lump of chromium ore that was once mined and now cloaked in stunted vegetation rather than the huge trees found elsewhere. It is about 35 miles to the end of the road and while it can be done in a long Alaskan day, an overnight trip is better. Before you go, ask about local conditions and obtain a permit ($1 a day; $10 per season) from the SNA office at 328 Main St (☎234-7625).

For a little **fishing**, consider a full-day halibut trip with Mad Viking Charters ($160; ☎234-7838), or just hang off the bridge over the slough where there is always something running after mid-May: consult the sport-fishing regulations posted at the head of the gangway to the boat harbor.

EATING AND DRINKING

Soon after stepping off the boat you'll spot the licensed *Mad Fish Restaurant* (☎234-7676), a great place to watch harbor life go by while savoring freshly made salmon cakes ($11), deep-fried oysters in pita bread ($9), or lightly sautéed vegetables on field greens and blueberry vinaigrette. For the best coffee in town, stroll across the road to *The Buzz*, 231 Main St (☎234-7479), which has a wonderful deck almost overhanging the harbor where you can tuck into homemade cakes and quiches. For **groceries**, head along Main Street to the *Seldovia Mart*, which has fairly limited supplies.

Long sunny evenings in Seldovia can be beautiful, but if it is raining, head for the *Linwood* **bar**, 257 Main St.

travel details

TRAINS

Seward to: Anchorage (daily; 4–5hr).

Whittier to: Anchorage (daily; 2hr 30min–3hr).

BUSES

Girdwood to: Anchorage (2 daily; 1hr 15min); Seward (2 daily; 2hr); Whittier (3 daily; 1hr–1hr 30min).

Homer to: Anchorage (3–6 weekly; 5hr); Seward (3 weekly; 4hr); Soldotna (6–9 weekly; 1hr 30min).

Seward to: Anchorage (2 daily; 3–4hr); Girdwood (2 daily; 2hr); Homer (3 weekly; 4hr).

Soldotna to: Anchorage (3–6 weekly; 3hr 30min); Homer (3–6 weekly; 1hr 30min).

Valdez to: Anchorage (daily; 10hr); Delta Junction (3 weekly; 5hr 30min); Fairbanks (3 weekly; 7–8hr); Glenallen (1–2 daily; 3hr 15min).

Whittier to: Girdwood (3 daily; 1hr–1hr 30min).

FERRIES

Cordova to: Valdez (3 weekly; 5hr 30min); Whittier (2 weekly; 7hr).

Homer to: Kodiak (2–3 weekly; 9hr 30min); Port Lions (weekly; 10hr); Seldovia (2 weekly; 1hr 30min).

Seldovia to: Homer (2 weekly; 1hr 30min).

Seward to: Juneau (one a month; 50hr); Kodiak (weekly; 13hr 15min); Valdez (weekly; 11hr).

Valdez to: Cordova (3 weekly; 5hr 30min); Juneau (one a month; 36hr); Seward (weekly; 11hr); Whittier (4 weekly; 6hr 45min).

Whittier to: Cordova (2 weekly; 7hr); Valdez (4 weekly; 6hr 45min).

FLIGHTS

Anchorage to: Cordova (2–3 daily; 40–50min); Seldovia (4 weekly; 1hr 15min); Valdez (2–3 daily; 40min).

Cordova to: Anchorage (2–3 daily; 40–50min); Juneau (1 daily; 2hr); Seattle (1 daily; 5hr); Valdez (2–3 weekly; 30min); Yakutat (1 daily; 45min).

Homer to: Anchorage (6 daily; 40min); Seldovia (several daily; 12min).

Kenai to: Anchorage (14–18 daily; 25min).

Seldovia to: Anchorage (4 weekly; 1hr 15min); Homer (several daily; 12min).

Valdez to: Anchorage (2–3 daily; 40min); Cordova (2–3 weekly; 30min).

CHAPTER FOUR

SOUTHWEST ALASKA

E ven by Alaska's standards, few places are as isolated as **Southwest**, a vast region that stretches 1600 miles from Anchorage, along the Alaska Peninsula and out to the tip of the Aleutian Chain. From its southern shore, the Alaska Peninsula rises steeply to its snowy backbone, the Aleutian Range, then drops away to the north towards the swampy lowlands of the Lake Clark and Katmai national parks. Further west the Peninsula tapers off until breaking up into the string of Aleutian Islands, each the top of a volcano rising from the sea bottom. Altogether less than 25,000 people call this home.

The weather bears much of the blame for its inhospitable reputation, as arctic winds whip up ferocious seas and warm currents from Japan generate dense fogs that can hang around for days. Yet those who can stick it out are often rewarded – fishermen working two short seasons in these rich waters can haul in over $100,000 a year – a temptation that's hard to resist.

With these quick returns, there's a healthy proportion of transient workers who fly into Kodiak or Dutch Harbor from the Lower 48, stay six weeks, then head somewhere warm until the next seasonal opening. Visitors come too, but in low numbers, which adds to the region's appeal. Because of the high cost of transportation it is only the dedicated and those with an adventurous spirit that bother to make the effort to experience Southwest Alaska. For those that do, there are substantial rewards, not least the striking topography of almost fifty **volcanoes**, many of them classic snow-capped cones: **Spurr**, on Anchorage's doorstep; **Redoubt** and **Iliamna** in the Lake Clark National Park; **Augustine**, an island at the mouth of Cook Inlet; **Novorupta** in Katmai National Park; **Shishaldin**, at the end of the Alaska Peninsula, which erupted as recently as 1999; **Makushin** on Unalaska Island; and many more.

At over 10,000 feet, Redoubt and Iliamna are two of the tallest, overlooking the **Lake Clark National Park** where exclusive fishing lodges allow keen anglers to hook salmon on their way upstream from Bristol Bay. The salmon-rich rivers are used by rafters and experienced canoeists who tackle one of the three designated "Wild and Scenic Rivers" within the park's bounds. People also come to fish for salmon in **Katmai National Park**, but here most folks prefer to see the fish eaten

---

ACCOMMODATION PRICE CODES

All **accommodation prices** in this book have been coded using the symbols below. Note that prices are for the least expensive double rooms in each establishment. For a full explanation see p.44 in Basics.

① up to $50	④ $80–100	⑦ $160–200
② $50–65	⑤ $100–130	⑧ $200–250
③ $65–80	⑥ $130–160	⑨ $250 and over

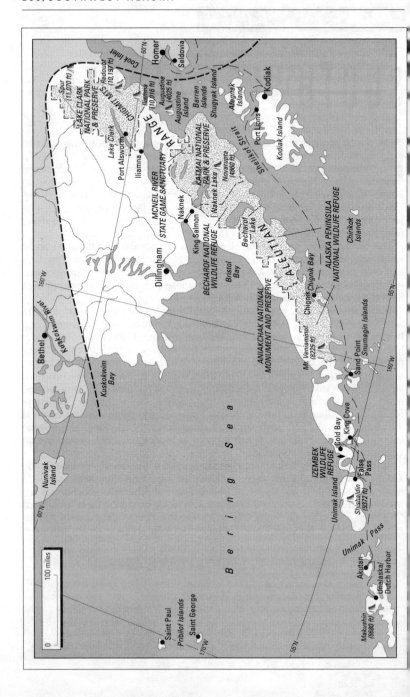

by hungry brown bears congregating around Brooks Falls. If you can score a position on the platform there's a chance of getting the ultimate in Alaskan wildlife photography: a snap of an open-jawed bear about to snag a leaping salmon.

Both parks can only be reached by expensive flights, however the rest of Southeast can be reached by ferry, with frequent services visiting **Kodiak Island** in particular, with its concentration of enormous Kodiak bears. This is where the Russians set up their first capital while enslaving the Native Aleut people to ensure a profitable supply of sea otter pelts. The ferry continues further to the southwest calling at tiny fishing ports en route to **Unalaska/Dutch Harbor**, near the start of the Aleutian Chain; California gray whales can sometimes be seen migrating here, heading north in April to the Bering Sea, and Mexico-bound in September. The rest of the long Aleutian Chain, strung out beyond Dutch Harbor, is barely inhabited, expensive to get to and usually well off the tourist itinerary, though specialist bird-watching trips occasionally venture out here.

To the north, the **Pribilof Islands** stand apart from the Aleutian Chain, their treeless tops covered with lush grass and wildflowers in spring. There's a windswept beauty to the place, but the few visitors who make it here come specifically to admire the sea cliffs, that are alive with thousands of nesting birds, and the rocks and beaches below, usually packed with basking seals.

Kodiak Island and the archipelago

On most days an ethereal mist wreaths the green hummocky hills of **KODIAK ISLAND**, a ragged, once-glaciated slice of the state adrift in the Gulf of Alaska. At a hundred miles long and sixty wide it ranks behind only Hawaii's Big Island as the largest in the US.

Most of the residents are tucked into the top-right corner, around the town of Kodiak, leaving the rest of the island to some three thousand of the biggest brown bears in the world. Weighing in at anywhere from 800 to 1500 pounds, they are so large they even get a separate name, **Kodiak bears**. Their size is a product of their rich diet; in fact, so abundant are the salmon here that bears often only bother with the fattiest, most nutritious parts (the skin and the roe) and discard the rest. With such a comfortable lifestyle, it is hardly surprising that the island supports as many bears as there are grizzlies in the whole of the Lower 48. Most of the bears are deep within the **Kodiak National Wildlife Refuge**, which encompasses the entire western two-thirds of Kodiak, all of neighboring Uganik Island, and parts of Afognak Island to the north. The refuge is also home to Sitka black-tailed deer, mountain goat, red fox, Roosevelt elk, and plenty of bald eagles, but not a single moose. Come during the salmon runs between mid-June and early September for the best chance of seeing bears, and set aside a good wad of cash for the flights required.

Human settlement began with the Alutiiq people who have occupied sites around here for upwards of seven thousand years, gradually developing a sophisticated culture based on fishing and hunting. That all changed in the middle of the eighteenth century when **Russian fur traders** arrived and, by forcefully separating families, kidnapping, and even burning villages, forced the Natives to hunt sea otters for sale rather than for their own needs. So profitable was the trade that by 1784 the enterprising Siberian merchant, **Gregorii Shelikov**, along with his wife and over a hundred Russian men, established Alaska's first white settlement at Three Saints Bay, halfway down the east coast of Kodiak Island. After a couple of years, word of his

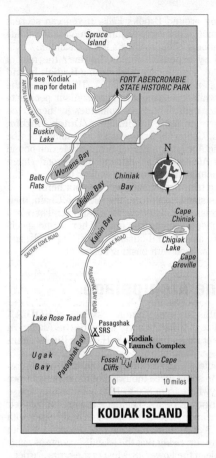

ruthless methods got out and he was recalled to Russia, only to be replaced in 1792 by **Alexandr Baranov**. After a tsunami nearly destroyed the Three Saints Bay settlement, Baranov set up Pavlovsk at St Paul Harbor, the current site of Kodiak, as the new Russian-American Company headquarters. Pavlovsk's golden period only lasted a decade, and as the region's sea otters were killed off the focus of Russian interest shifted towards Sitka where Baranov moved his capital of Russian Alaska in 1804. (For more on Alaska's Russian period see p.489.)

Today, Kodiak Island has some wonderful kayaking and good hiking, all within easy reach of the historic and attractively set town of Kodiak. Add in a busy fishing fleet, a few good festivals throughout the year, the possibility of surfing at road-accessible beaches, and you can easily fill a few enjoyable days, possibly supplemented by joining an archeological dig on **Afognak Island** to the north, and more remote kayaking around **Shugyak Island** still further north. Be warned though that the **weather** throughout the archipelago is cool and wet most of the summer with low clouds covering the island.

Kodiak

The town of **KODIAK** was transformed on March 27, 1964, when the huge earthquake that rocked Southcentral and parts of Southwest Alaska caused a thirty-foot tsunami to sweep over the town. The wave was so powerful that fishing boats were washed onto dry land, one fisherman reporting to a state trooper "It looks as though I'm behind the Kodiak schoolhouse, about six blocks from the waterfront"; a plaque on Lower Mill Bay Road still marks the spot. Much of the town was destroyed in the process, but land uplifted in the quake created a new flat surface that turned out to be perfect for the reconstruction of downtown, a largely modern place with a couple of Russian-era buildings contributing the only architectural interest.

As the big wave drew out it sucked the water from the channel between Kodiak and the offshore Near Island, but the fishing harbor survived and is as busy as ever, almost eight hundred boats calling Kodiak home. King crab used to be the big-money catch, but they have been mostly fished out, and today the boats go out for salmon, halibut, Dungeness and Tanner crab, and bottom fish such as gray cod, pollock, and sole. The day's catch is brought to channel-side canneries, such as the one built around the *Star of Kodiak*, a World War II ship, brought here after the 1964 tsunami as emergency accommodation and subsequently converted for fish processing.

After its days as the capital of Russian Alaska, Kodiak ticked by quietly until World War II whereupon the **navy** moved in, setting up a huge base south of town and constructing a decoy Kodiak topped with lights to draw enemy fire away from the blacked-out town. During World War II 25,000 people lived here, but the population has now dropped to around 10,000 with most living off fishing and fish processing. In the last twenty years, high wages have attracted immigrants from the Philippines, Laos, Vietnam, Mexico, Hawaii, Samoa, and elsewhere, and Kodiak has taken on a fairly cosmopolitan tenor.

Although quite easy to reach from Homer, Kodiak sees relatively few tourists, and it can be refreshing to wander the streets stopping into the excellent **Baranov and Alutiiq museums**, checking out Near Island's **Fisheries Research Institute**, and visiting the moody clifftop forest of **Fort Abercrombie State Historic Park**.

Getting there and arrival

You can reach Kodiak either by scheduled flight, ferry or on one of the short but convenient and good-value Anchorage-based **tours** run by Alaska Airlines Vacations (☎1-800/468-2248): the two-day "Emerald Isle Tour" (late May to early Sept; $410 double occupancy) or the three-day "Kodiak Island Tour" ($465), both with accommodation at the *Kodiak Inn*.

The *Tustumena* **ferry** from Homer ties up at the dock right in the heart of town beside the AMHS office (Mon–Fri 8am–5pm, Sat 8am–4pm; ☎486-3800). Normally there are three ferries a week: on Sunday and Monday the ferry is only in town for an hour or two before heading back to Homer, but on Wednesday you have the full day (from 9am to 4.30pm) to explore, making a round-trip from Homer a great short cruise, especially if you see whales and other marine mammals that frequently show themselves around the Barren Islands north of Kodiak. About every fourth Wednesday sailing continues west along the Alaska Peninsula to Unalaska/Dutch Harbor (see p.312), after first spending the day in Kodiak.

ERA Aviation (☎487-2663) and Alaska Airlines (☎266-7600) jointly dispatch eight **flights** a day from Anchorage to Kodiak airport: fares vary a fair bit but can often be as low as $250 round-trip with Alaska Airlines. Flight delays due to bad weather are not uncommon. The airport is five miles south of Kodiak town, and the local bus (see p.295) only runs downtown roughly every ninety minutes (not Sun), so you might prefer to catch one of the waiting taxis, or call A & B Taxi (☎486-4343), and pay around $6 into town.

Information and getting around

The main **visitor center**, 100 Marine Way (mid-June to mid-Sept Mon–Fri 8am–5pm, Sat & Sun dependent on ferries; mid-Sept to mid-June Mon–Fri 8am–noon & 1–5pm; ☎486-4782, fax 486-6545, *www.kodiak.org*) is downtown right by the ferry dock. For information on the **Kodiak National Wildlife Refuge** call at their **visitor center**, 1390 Buskin River Rd (April–Sept Mon–Fri 8am–4.30pm, Sat noon–4.30pm; in winter call ☎487-2600), close to the airport, four miles south of town. It is an essential stop before any trip into the refuge and worth a call anyway for the mounted animals and seventeen-minute video about the island and its wildlife.

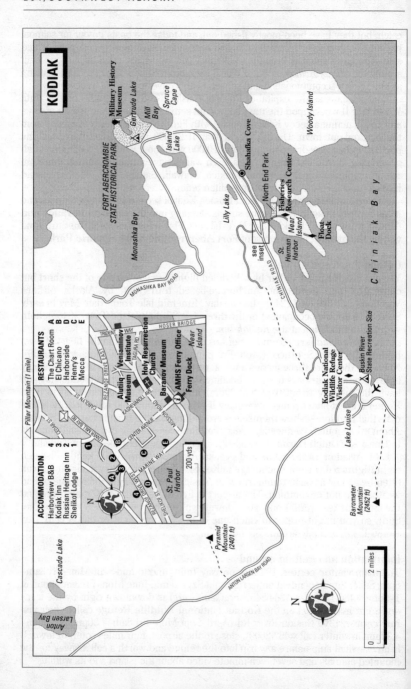

KODIAK

Military History Museum
Gertrude Lake
Mill Bay
Spruce Cape
Woody Island

FORT ABERCROMBIE STATE HISTORICAL PARK

Monashka Bay
Island Lake

Monashka Bay Road

Lilly Lake

Shahafka Cove
North End Park
Fisheries Research Center

see inset

St. Herman Harbor
Near Island
Float Dock

CHINIAK ROAD

C h i n i a k   B a y

Kodiak National Wildlife Refuge Visitor Center
Buskin River State Recreation Site

Lake Louise

Barometer Mountain (2452 ft)

Pyramid Mountain (2401 ft)

ANTON LARSEN BAY ROAD

Cascade Lake

Anton Larsen Bay

0   2 miles

N

Pillar Mountain (1 mile)

ACCOMMODATION
Harborview B&B   4
Kodiak Inn   3
Russian Heritage Inn   2
Sheilkof Lodge   1

RESTAURANTS
The Chart Room   A
El Chicano   B
Harborside   C
Henry's   D
Mecca   E

HOSER BRIDGE
TRIDENT WAY
TAGURA RD
REZANOF DRIVE EAST
CAROLYN ST
CEDAR ST
LOWER MILL BAY RD

Alutiiq Museum
Veniaminov Institute
Holy Resurrection Church
Baranov Museum
AMHS Ferry Office
Ferry Dock

Near Island

KASHEVAROF AVE
MISSION ROAD
CENTER AVENUE
MARINE WAY
SHELIKOF ST
REZANOF DRIVE WEST

St. Paul Harbor

N

0   200 yds

The downtown sights can all be seen on foot, without recourse to the KATS **bus** system ($2; ☎486-8308), which operates two routes: the In-Town route around the main shopping and residential areas, and an Express route covering the same ground more quickly and running out to the airport. Unfortunately this won't get you to any trailheads so you may want to **rent a car**. Rent-a-Heap, inside Kodiak Gifts in The Mall (☎487-4001, fax 487-2261, *carrent@ptialaska.net*), charge $30 a day plus 29¢ a mile for a subcompact, though $51 unlimited mileage cars from Budget, at the airport (☎487-2220), can work out cheaper. Alternatively, **rent a bicycle** from 58° North, 1231 Mill Bay Rd, a mile from town (☎486-6294, *thowland@ptialaska.net*), who charge $35 per day (full 24 hours) for their front-suspension mountain bikes which are ideal for the gravel surfaces anywhere outside downtown. If you don't want to rent a bike or car, but still want to see something of the island, consider joining Custom Tours of Kodiak (☎486-3920 evenings) for a **bus tour** of the town and surrounds (half-day $30; full day $80).

Accommodation

As in most of Alaska you'll need to book in advance to secure a room during the peak three months of summer. The two local **campgrounds** are usually less busy and, though distant from town, are accessible on the city bus. The finest is *Fort Abercrombie State Historical Park*, four miles north ($10; potable water), with campsites, fire rings, and picnic tables dotted among the Sitka spruce with World War II fort remnants all around. Four and a half miles southwest of town, and close to the airport, lies the *Buskin River State Recreation Site* ($10; potable water), adjacent to the Kodiak National Wildlife Refuge Visitor Center and its associated nature trail.

Kodiak has **no hostel**, and the eleven percent local tax hikes up the already high room rates. The cheapest **hotel** rooms are at *Shelikof Lodge*, 211 Thorsheim Ave (☎486-4141, fax 486-4116, *www.ptialaska.net/~kyle*; ③), and *Russian Heritage Inn*, 119 Yukon St (☎486-5657, fax 486-4634, *www.ak-biz.com/russianheritage*; ④), both offering adequate rooms with private bath. There's little to choose between them and they are next door to each other so it won't take you a moment to compare. The *Best Western Kodiak Inn*, 236 W Rezanof Drive (☎1-888/563-4254 or 486-5712, fax 486-3430, *www.ptialaska.net/~kodiakin*; ⑤), has the flashest rooms in town, with all the expected amenities.

In most cases, you're better off in a **B&B**. *Harborview*, 312 W Rezanof Drive (☎486-2464 or 1-888/283-2464 &, fax 486-3486; *www.ptialaska.net/~kodiakfk*; ④), is well located and offers home-cooked breakfast, cable TV, and one room (⑤) with a wonderful view of the harbor. Another good bet is *Shahafka Cove*, 1812 Mission Rd (☎486-2409, fax 486-2301, *www.ptialaska.net/~rwoitel*; ④), over a mile north of town but with a huge waterside deck, views over the channel, and a full breakfast.

Outside town there is a limited range of accommodation. **Campers** looking to explore the area should make for *Pasagshak State Recreation Site* (free), 45 miles south of town. Inside the Kodiak National Wildlife Refuge you can charter a float plane to take you into one of the seven **public-use cabins** ($35 in summer, $25 in winter), each of which comes with a kerosene heater, a pit toilet, and sleeping platforms for at least four people: you'll need to carry everything else including a cooking stove. In practice it can be hard to get a place as the cabins are made available by lottery several months in advance. If there are spaces after the lottery is drawn, the cabins are let on a first-come, first-served basis: for details contact the refuge visitor center.

There are also some forty **wilderness lodges** dotted around the archipelago, almost all in gorgeous remote locations with canoes and kayaks to get out and about. Many are pitched towards the rod and gun set, but will also cater to birders, wildlife photographers, and those who just want a few days complete relaxation. All require float plane access and most charge $200–400 per person a day: the Kodiak visitor center has a full list and you can check out many of their Web sites through the "Wilderness Lodges" section of *www.kodiak.org*.

The town

Opposite the visitor center stand Kodiak's two most architecturally harmonious buildings, both Russian in design and execution. Straight ahead is **Erskine House**, a white-weatherboard building with green trim, built as a fur warehouse and office for the Russian-American Company around 1808, making it not only the oldest building in Alaska but the oldest extant structure on the West Coast of North America. It houses the **Baranov Museum**, 101 Marine Way (June–Aug Mon–Fri 10am–4pm, Sat & Sun noon–4pm; Sept–May Mon–Wed & Fri 10am–4pm, Sat noon–3pm; $2), a small but intriguing collection of Native and Russian pieces from intricate woven grass baskets and a kopek note printed on seal skin to a three-place bidarka made from sea lion hides. One room is filled with high-quality furniture from the Russian era, illustrating just how much money was being made from the sea otter pelts. Elsewhere there's a corner devoted to local Aleut boy **Benny Benson**, who designed the Alaska state flag (see p.257).

Behind Erskine House is the **Holy Resurrection Russian Orthodox Church** (closed except for tours and services, Thurs 6.30pm and Sun 9am), another weatherboard structure, prim and white but for two flamboyant blue onion-dome cupolas. Sadly it is neither on its original site, nor is it authentic, the original having burnt down in 1943. To the right of the main entrance lie some of the original bells, cast here between 1794 and 1796, the first on the West Coast.

Across the street, the **Alutiiq Museum**, 215 Mission Rd (June–Aug Mon–Fri 9am–5pm, Sat 10am–5pm; Sept–May Tues–Fri 9am–5pm, Sat 10.30am–4.30pm; $2; *www.alutiiqmuseum.com*), plays a crucial role in preserving the history of Kodiak's native people by facilitating interaction between the local Native community, anthropologists, and archeologists. When the Russians arrived in Alaska they assumed the Alutiiq people were the same as the Aleuts they'd encountered further west, failing to recognize the cultural and linguistic associations that united them more closely with the Yupik further north. Some confusion is perhaps excusable since Kodiak has long been something of a cultural crossroads, and archeologists have unearthed sites dating back to 7500 years ago. Some of these sites have come under threat since the *Exxon Valdez* disaster; hose spraying during the beach cleanup washed away precious evidence, and newly uncovered sites were vandalized.

The upside of the oil spill is the Alutiiq Museum and the Dig Afognak (see p.301) project, both the result of a hefty settlement. There are only a few artifacts on display but all are beautiful including a six-inch-high fertility doll with distended belly that was found with human hair attached, dated to about five hundred years ago. The portrait masks are lovely, too, and less stylized than the Yup'ik spirit masks you may have seen elsewhere; and on a more mundane level you can see how sea-otter, land-otter, and spotted-seal pelts compare for softness.

Further north, the St Herman's Russian Orthodox Theological Seminary houses the **Veniaminov Institute and Museum**, 414 Mission Rd (daily 1–4.30pm; free), with displays of samovars, icons, and ancient Bibles left open to reveal the intricate work within.

Near Island and Fort Abercrombie State Park

A narrow channel separates Kodiak from Near Island, reached over the modern **Hoser Bridge** (aka "The Bridge to Nowhere"), named not for some local dignitary or dead general, but for the Kodiak fire department's Dalmatian who, shortly after the bridge's completion, took a suicide leap off the middle span.

Near Island is now home to Kodiak's second commercial fishing harbor, St Herman's, the float plane dock, and the **Kodiak Fisheries Research Center**, 301 Research Court (Mon–Fri 8am–5pm; free), easily reached from town in twenty minutes on foot. There isn't a lot to see, but the building is beautifully sited by the ocean and what's on display is well presented, particularly the cylindrical aquarium stocked with several species of crab, assorted starfish, colorful anemones, mussels, and more. Behind is the touch tank, a riot of purples, reds, blues, and oranges: dip your hand in to feel the silky-smooth sea cucumbers and inspect at close quarters the scarlet blood star. Notice too the panel showing where various species of salmon spend their lives before returning to Alaskan rivers to spawn.

By far the best short outing from town is to ride the city bus to Mill Bay and walk the last half-mile to **Fort Abercrombie State Historic Park**, four miles north of downtown. The prominent headland of Miller Point is now shrouded in towering, moss-covered Sitka spruce, but this was once an important defense position developed following the Japanese attack on Pearl Harbor in 1941. Stroll through the wooded parkland and you will come across moldering, but neatly labeled, World War II remains: ammunition magazines, searchlight bunkers, observation platforms, and the shattered mounts for a couple of eight-inch guns. It is a great place to idle away some time, with orchids and wildflowers blooming in spring, and an opportunity to view bald eagles, puffins, and humpback whales (mid-May to mid-Aug) migrating past at the **Miller Point headland**. Here you'll also find the largest of the ammunition bunkers, at the **Kodiak Military History Museum** (sporadically in summer and by appointment ☎486-4700), which concentrates mainly on World War II history. There's also a small visitor center (Mon–Fri 8am–4.30pm; ☎486-6339), and walking tracks which lead around **Lake Gurtrude**, good for tidepooling and even swimming for the very keen.

With wheels you might fancy driving up the anonymous gravel road to the top of **Pillar Mountain** (1270ft) immediately behind town. The wide selection of radar and communications towers on top aren't especially pretty, but turn your back on them and you can see down to the town and harbor and inland across the lumpy interior.

Kayaking and fishing

The Kodiak archipelago has some of the finest **sea kayaking** around. **Near Island** and its acolytes, just across the channel from the town, have all sorts of narrow straits and shallow coves where you can bob around looking down through crystal clear water at brilliantly-colored starfish and anemones. Contact Wavetamer Kayaking (☎ & fax 486-2604, *wavetamer@gci.net*), who run two-hour novice trips ($40) and four-hour guided outings ($85) for the more experienced, or Mythos Expeditions (☎486-5536, *www.ptialaska.net/~mythosdk/mythos*) who have rentals (doubles $55 a day, $50 for 4–7 days) and run a two-hour beginners trip ($50) and an extended four-hour trip ($100) either in the harbor or out where you might see whales.

There are so many people prepared to take you **fishing** it is hard to know where to start, but Kodiak Fish Konnection (late May to late Sept; ☎486-2464, *kodiakfk@ptialaska.net*), will take you out for a full day of salmon or halibut fishing for $175 including processing (gutting, filleting, freezing, and packing) what you catch. If they don't do the sort of thing you're after they'll put you in touch with someone who does.

Kodiak is also said to have some of the best roadside **salmon fishing** in the state: the Alaska Department of Fish and Game, 211 Mission Rd (☎486-1880, *www .state.ak.us/local/akpages/fish.game/adfghome.htm*), have a list of guides, know the regulations and can sell you a license.

Eating, drinking, and entertainment

The range of restaurants in Kodiak is adequate for a few days, and grocery prices from the Value Center downtown are only around ten percent higher than in Anchorage. About the only regular entertainment is the **Kodiak Alutiiq Dancers**, 713 E Rezanof Drive (June to early Sept daily 3.30pm; $15; ☎486-4449), an hour-long celebration of traditional dance that takes place in a *barabara*, the adopted Russian term for a partly subterranean sod-built house once typical in the Aleutians and on Kodiak.

The Chart Room, 236 W Rezanof Drive inside the *Best Western* (☎486-5712). Kodiak's most formal dining, with good harbor views as you enjoy $30 king-crab legs, or $17 halibut steaks. Don't miss the photos of the 1964 tsunami aftermath in the hallway.

El Chicano, 103 Center Ave (☎486-6116). The menu might not look too inspiring but the food is good, whether it's huevos rancheros, Mexican-style sandwiches, or plates of chorizo, eggs, rice, and beans for under $10.

Harborside Coffee and Goods, 216 Shelikov St (☎486-5862). Just the spot for hanging out over an espresso to watch the harbor activity out the window, or tucking into the town's best selection of soups and muffins.

Henry's Great Alaskan, 512 Marine Way (☎486-2522). A kind of sports bar and restaurant selling salads, sandwiches, burgers, and halibut and fries all around $8–10.

Mecca, 302 Marine Way. Typically lively bar often with live music and even the occasional touring band.

Listings

Air-charter companies Andrew Airways (☎487-2566, *andrewair@aol.com*); Highline Air (☎486-5155, *highline@ptialaska.net*); Kodiak Air Service (☎486-4446, *wehall@camai.com*); PenAir (☎487-4014, *info@penair.com*); Sea Hawk (☎486-8282 or 1-800/770-4295); Uyak Air Service (☎486-3407, *uyakair@ptialaska.net*).

Banks There are several around town including Key Bank, 422 E Marine Way, in The Mall. All banks and the supermarkets have ATMs.

Books Several places around town have free book swaps including the *Harborside Coffee and Goods* and the PenAir office at the airport.

Car rental The best deals are Rent-a-Heap, inside Kodiak Gifts in The Mall (☎487-4001, fax 487-2261, *carrent@ptialaska.net*), who charge $30 a day plus 29¢ a mile for a subcompact, and Budget, at the airport (☎487-2220), who rent unlimited mileage compacts for $51.

Festivals In late March there's the Pillar Mountain Golf Classic (☎486-6445), a one-hole par-70 course in which you have to hit 1400 feet up Pillar Mountain in the depths of winter snow, with ball-spotters allowed but no radio communication or dogs; Memorial Day weekend draws enthusiasts from Anchorage and elsewhere for the Kodiak Crab Festival (☎486-5557), with all manner of races, a blessing of the fishing fleet, crab eating, and music; mid-July's Bear Country Music Festival (☎486-6117) has over fifty bluegrass, folk, and country bands from around the state; and on Labor Day Weekend there's the Kodiak State Fair.

HIKING ON KODIAK

Hiking in Kodiak is limited to forest walks and a few trails up hills close to Kodiak town. Out in the **Kodiak National Wildlife Refuge** hiking trails are few, and you'll be pretty much making it up as you go along. If you fancy engaging the services of a guide, you'll find a list of operators at the refuge visitor center.

Remember that Kodiak weather is fickle even by Alaskan standards, so you'll need to be well prepared. If you need to rent gear (or extra gear), contact Kodiak Kamps (☎486-5333).

Barometer Mountain (5 miles round-trip; 3–4hr; 2500ft ascent). The most popular hike on the island climbs to the summit of this 2452-foot peak by the steep east ridge with views improving all the way up. The trail starts almost opposite the end of the airport runway a hundred yards south of a sharp bend in the road. After heading into the brush it switchbacks up to a fork where you branch right along a gravel road for 500 yards until the path up the ridge heads off on your left.

North End Park (half a mile; 20min; 100ft ascent). Easy shoreline trails starting beside the Hoser Bridge on Near Island, ideal for an evening stroll and for salmonberry picking in July and August.

Pillar Mountain (2.5 miles round-trip; 1–2hr; 800ft ascent). A moderate hike to the summit beginning at Pillar Mountain Road on the left just past the quarry a third of the way up the mountain. From the summit, a second trail leads three miles southwest towards the Tie substation, where a gravel road leads down to the highway a mile or so north of the airport.

Pyramid Mountain (4 miles round-trip; 3–4hr; 2200ft ascent). This hike starts at the ski area on Anton Larson Road, a couple of miles past the golf course. From the parking lot it climbs steeply through brush to a broad shoulder on alpine tundra. The views are great from here, but the more adventurous will want to press on to the top.

Internet access *Sweets N More* on W Rezanof Drive has commercial Internet access; the library (see below) has free research access but they discourage email.

Laundry Ernie's, 218 Shelikof St has laundry and shower facilities.

Library 319 W Rezanof Drive (Mon–Fri 10am–9pm, Sat 10am–5pm, Sun 1–5pm).

Medical assistance Kodiak Island Medical Center, 1915 E Rezanof Drive (☎486-3281).

Post office The main post office is at 419 Lower Mill Bay Rd (Mon–Fri 9am–5.30pm), but the Value Center has a handier branch inside (Mon–Sat 10am–6pm). The **General Delivery** ZIP code is 99615.

Taxes Kodiak has a six percent sales tax (primarily to pay for the Hoser Bridge) and an additional five percent bed tax.

Travel agency US Travel, 340 Mission Rd (☎486-3232, fax 486-4272).

Around the island and the archipelago

Outside the main town, things on Kodiak Island get pretty quiet. There are a few small communities dotted throughout the indented coastline, but most are only accessible by boat or float plane. Kodiak's **road system** barely tops a hundred miles (mostly gravel), and doesn't really contain any essential sights, but if you've come this far it is worth renting a car for a day and exploring, especially if you strike a clear, sunny day. To see more than just the roads you'll need to go **flightseeing**, and most flights set off with the express aim of seeing some of the island's huge **bears**, observed from riverbank platforms erected for the purpose.

Kodiak Island is the largest in an archipelago, significantly outranking Afognak Island immediately to the north. They're separated by Kupreanof Strait, on the shores of which lay the Native village of Afognak, until it was destroyed by the 1964 tsunami. The site is now the location of **Dig Afognak** where you can join in an archeological excavation for a week or more. There is gorgeous coastal scenery all around, but nowhere more so than that surrounding **Shugyak Island**, north of Afognak, a perfect destination for keen kayakers.

Along the road system

Heading south of town, **Anton Larsen Bay Road** branches to the right just before the airport and winds twelve miles over a low mountain pass to Anton Larsen Bay where there's a dock used by residents of **Port Lions**, a village just across the water.

At the airport junction, **Chiniak Road** runs south past the entrance to the former military base at Women's Bay, now the nation's largest **Coast Guard station** with over two thousand personnel patrolling the fishing grounds and providing search and rescue for the whole of Southwest Alaska. About ten miles south of town, you'll see the last of the Sitka spruce trees that blanket the eastern third of the archipelago, and break into more open country. The road passes Bell's Flat (once the island's dairy farm), and hugs the coast where there's occasional beach access, and bald eagles nesting in cottonwood trees, and continues to the Pasagshak Road junction. Chiniak Road continues, through a residential area where you'll find the *Road's End Restaurant* (☎486-2885), to the Chigiak airstrip, in service from World War II until 1967 and surrounded by abandoned bunkers and gun emplacements.

Pasagshak Road runs eight miles south of Chigiak Road to **Lake Rose Tead**, filled with red salmon in August and home to a variety of birds, especially swans, throughout the year. Nearby is the **Pasagshak State Recreation Area**, good for beach walking and camping (free). The road then continues six miles to the fossil-filled cliffs of Narrow Cape and the Kodiak Launch Complex, a private site for launching low-orbit polar satellites that saw it first launch in 1998.

Bear viewing and flightseeing

For many, the reason to come to Kodiak is to view some of the 3000 Kodiak bears as they fish the salmon streams. Highway sightings are rare, and city ordinances have recently put an end to the practice of bear viewing at the city dump, so you now need an expensive flight into the **Kodiak National Wildlife Refuge**. These typically cost around $400, and air-charter operators are so confident you'll spot a bear, they promise to take you up again if you don't. From June to August (and sometimes Sept and even Oct) they'll go out on four-hour runs spending a fair bit of time on the ground at several locations viewing at reasonably close quarters. Common destinations are **Frazer Lake**, where there is a fish ladder a mile down the Dog Salmon River, and **Karluk Lake**, both in the south of the island. There are half a dozen companies (see "Listings", p.298, for details) to choose from.

Any of the companies will also do flightseeing – possibly offering distant views of the bears – but the trip to go for is with PenAir, who fly a couple of rare 1940s Grumman Goose seaplanes on daily mail routes around the archipelago briefly landing at native villages, old canneries, and remote wilderness lodges. There are usually only a handful of passengers, so you've a fair chance of getting the co-pilot's seat. Some flights run all year but from mid-May to mid-September there's a Kodiak Island loop (daily; 2hr; $130) calling at Alitak, Moser Bay, and Olga Bay; an Afognak Island loop (twice weekly; 1hr 30min; $90) around Kitoi Bay, Port Williams, and Seal Bay; and another loop (twice weekly; 1hr 20min; $85) landing at Amook, West Point, and Zacher Bay.

Dig Afognak

Afognak Island, immediately north of Kodiak Island, offers the unique opportunity to be part of an archeological excavation with a professional team alongside Alutiiq people, visiting scholars, and guest speakers. **Dig Afognak** is the site of an Alutiiq village continually settled for 7000 years until abandoned after the 1964 tsunami, with old house structures, middens, even an overseer's building from the Russian era still visible. Here you can learn field techniques, cultural traditions, natural history, and have formal sessions with guest speakers. It is not cheap though: $1650 for seven days including transport from Kodiak to the field camp, accommodation in platform tents, and simple, hearty cooking. There is no whip cracking, but you are expected to put in at least four hours a day.

The season runs from late June to mid-August and only twelve people can be accommodated each week, so book at least a couple of months in advance through Afognak Adventures, Dig Afognak (☎486-6014 or 1-800/770-6014, fax 486-2514, *www.afognak.com/dig*).

Shugyak Island

Shugyak, the northernmost island in the archipelago, lies forty minutes by float plane northwest of Kodiak. Cloaked in virgin Sitka spruce, it is entrusted to the Shugyak Island State Park, which protects a deeply incised network of passages and islands encompassed by Big Bay, Western Inlet, Carry Inlet, and Shanigan Bay. This is ideal territory for **intermediate and experienced kayakers**; pick up the sea-kayaking leaflet detailing several loop paddles from one of the visitor centers on Kodiak. This region has four well-equipped shoreline **cabins** sleeping eight ($50 a night, contact Alaska State Parks ☎486-6339, check availability at *nutmeg.state.ak.us /ixpress/dnr/parks/Kodiak*), accessible by kayak, and some linked by short trails.

Access to Shugyak is usually by air charter, the smallest planes costing $200–250 for dropoff, the same for pickup. Kayaks are expensive to transport, so consider bringing a folding model, or better yet rent from Wavetamer in Kodiak (see "Kayaking and fishing," p.297) who usually have kayaks already stationed at the island and have a three-day minimum rental.

Lake Clark National Park

Considering **LAKE CLARK NATIONAL PARK** (*www.nops.gov/lacl*) is only a hundred miles west of Anchorage and has scenery to match any in the rest of Alaska, it is surprisingly little visited. With no dense congregations of bears or calving glaciers, it is left off many itineraries, and yet this is quintessential Alaskan parkland. Modest numbers of anglers come to remote lodges to fish for the abundant sockeye salmon in what is one of the most important spawning grounds for the Bristol Bay fishery, but apart from that, only a few hardy hikers and teams of rafters taking on the three federally-designated "Wild and Scenic" rivers seem to get up this way.

The park gets its name from the fifty-mile-long **Lake Clark** in its southwest, and features two conical snow-capped volcanoes – **Redoubt** (10,197ft) and **Iliamna** (10,016ft) – both visible from Anchorage and dominating the western horizon along the Kenai Peninsula's Cook Inlet coast. They form part of the Pacific Ring of Fire and are sporadically active, Redoubt as recently as 1990, when it spewed clouds of ash that briefly closed Anchorage airport. The volcanoes lie between Cook Inlet and the **Chigmit Mountains**, a jagged and glacially-sculpted geological jumble where the Alaska Range meets the Aleutian Range. Glaciers still peel off the slopes feeding rivers which either cut into the wild interior of the park, or tumble steeply through Sitka and white spruce to the coastal cliffs.

It is a spectacularly diverse park with a remarkable range of plant communities from coastal rainforest to boreal forest typical of Interior Alaska and alpine tundra. Fauna is equally varied, from the seabird rookeries on the Cook Inlet seacliffs to the moose, black and brown bears, Dall sheep, and caribou of the interior of the park.

Hiking and rafting

The only community inside the park is **PORT ALSWORTH**, on the southern shores of Lake Clark, which is where the park's one well-formed trail leads to the **Tanalian Falls** (2 miles one-way) and on to **Kontrashibuna Lake** (3 miles one-way). After that you're on your own. Keen hikers prepared to follow an unmarked route over rugged terrain can tackle the **Telaquana Trail** (50 miles one-way), which follows an old Dena'ina route later used by trappers and miners during the early 1900s. It runs north from Lake Clark through boreal forest and across alpine tundra, and requires fording glacial rivers that can at times be impassable.

Almost all the **rafting** in the park takes place on three rivers classed as "Wild and Scenic." It is an appropriate description since most of your trip will be spent watching the scenery with patches of Class III and IV whitewater in between. All rivers are raftable from June to September (with the highest water being in July and Aug), and all require float-plane access and egress. The *Lake Clark Inn* in Port Alsworth (see opposite) **rents rafts** for $50 a day.

The easiest is the **Mulchatna River** (Class II–III), usually run from Turquoise Lake (about thirty miles north of Lake Clark), from where it descends into a shallow and rocky bed through the Bonanza Hills for a couple of days, then eases to a gentle float down to its confluence with the Chilikadrotna River; perhaps five days in all. The **Chilikadrotna River** (Class III), is a slightly tougher four-to-five day proposition running sixty miles down from Twin Lakes on the western flanks of the Alaska Range. Windsong Wilderness Adventures, PO Box 513, Sterling, Alaska 996762 (☎260-5410, *www.alaska.net/~twinlake/adventure.html*) run guided trips here with flights from Kenai, a couple of nights at their lodge at Twin Lakes and four nights on the river for $2600.

The put-in for the **Tlikakila River** is Summit Lake, a good hiking area on the eastern edge of the park that is easily reached direct from Kenai or Anchorage. From there it is 51 miles down to Lake Clark through a densely forested valley with occasional sections of Class III and one section of potentially Class IV (depending on water levels), though this can be portaged.

The weather in the park is cool, rainy, and unpredictable, so come prepared for anything (including bugs); bugs tend to be less evident in August and September which are the best months for hiking, and for rafting too if there's enough water.

Practicalities

Before traveling to Lake Clark, get detailed information and advice from the park headquarters in Anchorage (4230 University Drive, Suite 311, Anchorage, AK 99508; ☎271-3751). In Port Alsworth, the park **field headquarters** (May–Oct daily 8am–5pm; ☎781-2218, fax 781-2119) has interesting natural history displays, puts on slide and video programs and conducts nature walks and hikes on request.

Almost everyone **flies** into the park, either direct to one of the expensive lodges, or by air taxi from either Port Alsworth or Iliamna, thirty miles to the southwest. Both of these small towns have frequent flights from Anchorage: Iliamna is served by ERA (☎1-800/866-8394) who fly daily for around $290 round-trip; Port Alsworth is reached by Lake Clark Air (☎1-800/662-7661) for $275 round-trip.

It is best to organize an air charter to your desired destination and not hang around either town, though both have **places to stay**. In Port Alsworth there's *Wilder House B&B* (☎781-2228; ④) and the *Lake Clark Inn* (☎781-2224, fax 781-2252, *www.lakeclark.com*; ⑥). In Iliamna, try the *Airport Hotel* (☎571-1276; ⑨) which includes full board for $160 a night.

Katmai National Park and McNeil River

Although there are several places in Alaska where bears congregate in large numbers, only **KATMAI NATIONAL PARK** (*www.nps.gov/katm*), some 250 miles southwest of Anchorage, combines the close bear viewing with wonderful scenery, relatively easy access, convenient accommodation, and a stock of other activities in case viewing bears begins to pale. None of this comes cheap, but it is hard to put a value on standing twenty yards from a large brown bear as it stands atop the five-foot Brooks Falls ready to chomp on any sockeye salmon that is foolish enough to leap within striking distance.

Throughout July, the Brooks River is so thick with sockeyes that up to forty bears might be scattered along its mile-and-a-half length. This is also the busiest time for visitors, coming to a head again in September when the bears gather at Brooks Falls to feast on dying fish. You won't see bears catching fish in mid-air at this time, but you will see enormous bears fattened up for winter, sometimes topping a thousand pounds.

For many years, Katmai was only known for the most violent volcanic eruption of the twentieth century, when **Novorupta** (Latin for "newly erupted") spewed out seven cubic miles of ash and pumice for three days beginning on June 6, 1912. The cloud of ash drifted as far as North Africa, and northern hemisphere temperatures dropped a couple of degrees effectively creating a year without a summer. People a hundred miles away in Kodiak were wading knee-deep through volcanic ash and couldn't see their outstretched hand for two days. Close to Novorupta, intensely hot ash settled to a depth of up to seven hundred feet blanketing the volcanic gases and vaporizing streams. As the steam and gases forced their way to the surface, they created an unearthly landscape described by National Geographic geologist Robert Griggs, in 1916, as looking like "all the steam engines in the world, assembled together, had popped their safety valves at once and were letting off surplus steam in concert." As the Novorupta fireworks emptied the underground magma chamber, the summit of nearby **Mount**

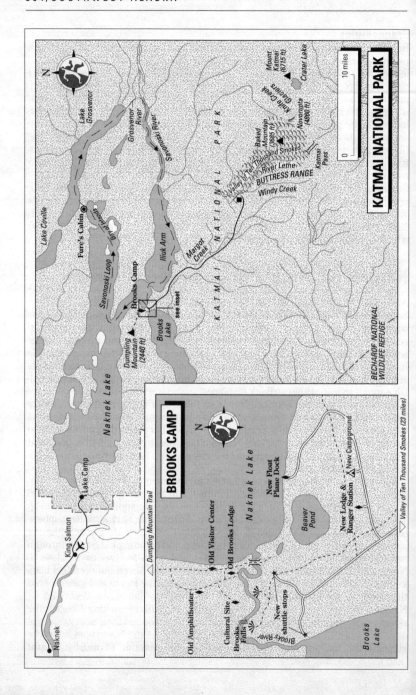

KATMAI NATIONAL PARK

BROOKS CAMP

Katmai collapsed to form an almost perfectly circular crater lake. Two years later the **Valley of 10,000 Smokes** became the centerpiece of the Katmai National Monument.

As the underground temperatures subsided and the gases escaped, the number of active vents diminished until none were left. The park languished until the 1940s when Ray Petersen set up five remote fishing camps in the park, the most popular being at **Brooks Camp**. Here the abundance of sockeye salmon was just as much of a lure for brown bears, which rapidly became the main attraction.

Now, Brooks Camp is the single most popular bear-viewing spot in Alaska, and one which warrants at least a few days of your time, whether camping and hiking in the Valley of 10,000 Smokes or spending more time kayaking the Savonoski Loop.

If seeing bears is your sole objective, you may want to enter the lottery for an opening at **McNeil River State Game Sanctuary** (see box, p.309) on the northeastern fringe of Katmai, where bears are equally concentrated, though without the press of visitors.

Practicalities

Almost everyone visiting Katmai National Park does so from Anchorage on an all-inclusive package (see below) or a connecting sequence of flights to Brooks Camp, thereby avoiding unnecessary time spent in the small town of King Salmon. With the appropriate reservations you'll be met at the King Salmon airport, driven a mile to the float docks on the Naknek River, and flown in to Brooks Camp.

Alaska Airlines jets and PenAir (☎243-2323 or 1-800/448-4226) twin-props **fly** from Anchorage to King Salmon, usually for around $400–450 round trip, though by booking well in advance it is possible to get fares as low as $260. From there you'll pay around $140 round-trip to fly to Brooks Camp by air taxi: try Katmai Air, run by Katmailand (see below). PenAir allow you to book right through to Brooks Camp from Anchorage for $500 (14-day advance fare) round-trip.

Alternatively you can get between King Salmon and Brooks Camp using a **bus/boat combination** (mid-June to mid-Sept; 1hr; $125 round-trip). A shuttle bus leaves the *Quinnat Landing Hotel* (see below) at 7am for Lake Camp where you pick up the *Katmai Lady II* to take you to Brooks Camp. You get around five hours in Brooks (though your return ticket is still valid if you want to return on a later date), and there's a boat/fly combo for $135.

The park concessionaire, Katmailand, 4125 Aircraft Drive, Anchorage 99502 (☎243-5448 in Anchorage, 246-3079 in King Salmon, or 1-800/544-0551, fax 243-0649, *www.katmailand.com*), operates *Brooks Lodge*, rentals and trips at Brooks Camp, and Katmai Air. They sell competitive inclusive packages with round-trip flights from Anchorage, accommodation at *Brooks Lodge*, and park fees, but not meals: one night ($652); two nights ($928); three nights ($1046); four-night early-season special (June 1–June 16; $1056); and others. If you don't mind staying in King Salmon at the *Quinnat Landing* and commuting into the park, consider Alaska Airlines Vacations (mid-June to mid-September; ☎1-800/468-2248) packages: a two-day affair ($670 double occupancy), and a more leisurely three-day trip ($785), both including bear viewing at Brooks Camp.

King Salmon and Naknek

The small bush community of **KING SALMON**, scattered between its airport and the broad tidal Naknek River 250 miles southwest of Anchorage, was once a

Cold War military base and is now the main service town for the region. There's no reason to be here except as a staging point for Katmai, or as access to some remote fishing. If you get stranded or have an hour to spare, call in at the King Salmon **visitor center**, right by the airport terminal (sporadic, but nominally Mon–Sat 9am–5pm; ☎246-4250), with interesting and informative displays, or wander a hundred yards along the street to the King Salmon Mall where, upstairs, you'll find the **NPS visitor center** (Mon–Fri 8am–4.30pm; ☎246-3305), which has specific information on Katmai and Lake Clark national parks. The Mall also has a **bank** (Mon–Thurs 10am–5pm, Fri 10am–6pm) with an ATM, and *Mel's Diner*, which serves lunch, good **espresso**, and has **Internet access**.

Accommodation in King Salmon is expensive, though if you have a sturdy, bug-proof tent you can easily find a quiet spot to **camp**. The cheapest rooms are at *Antlers Inn*, just behind the Mall (☎246-8525 or 1-888/735-8525, fax 246-6634, *antlers@bristolbay.com*; apartments ⑦, rooms ⑤), which has self-contained apartments, and smaller rooms that share bathrooms and a communal kitchen. They also have a camping area ($12 per person) with washing facilities and use of bug-free barbecue area. The only other possibilities are the *King Ko Inn* (☎246-3377, *www.kingko.com*; ⑧), which has fairly new and comfortable cabins, and the top-of-the-range *Quinnat Landing Hotel* (☎272-6300 in Anchorage or 1-800/770-3474, *www.quinnat.com*; ⑨), with international-quality hotel rooms.

King Salmon is pricey and **eating** options are limited to the two hotels, which serve similar menus with salads ($12), pasta dishes ($18), and steaks, salmon, and halibut ($20–30). There's a lively bar at the *King Ko*, though the view overlooking the Naknek River from the restaurant/bar at the *Quinnat* is better.

If you are self-catering and haven't brought everything you need from Anchorage (as you should), pick up **groceries** from the limited supply at the City Market supermarket/deli/liquor store beside the Mall.

Fourteen miles downstream, the Bristol Bay fishing village of **NAKNEK** is the scene of the world's largest sockeye run with some twenty million fish passing between mid-June and the end of July (peaking in the first two weeks of July). Around seventy percent of all the world's red salmon are caught in Bristol Bay and three-quarters of those are caught in and around Naknek. Once the fishing season opens in late June commercial fishing boats are gunwhale-to-gunwhale trying to be first to get their nets in the water, and both King Salmon and Naknek are alive with fishermen.

To get there, contact Redline Taxi (☎246-8294), who charge around $15 for the ride from King Salmon, **rent a truck** from the *Antler Inn* ($65 a day), or join Bristol Bay Tours (mid-June to mid-Sept; $40; ☎246-4218), a two-hour-plus minibus tour that picks up in King Salmon and visits Naknek, accompanied by loads of history and local anecdotes, and maybe a visit to a commercial cannery in action.

Brooks Camp and around

Bears are all over Katmai National Park, but your best chance of seeing them in any number is at **Brooks Camp** ($10 per day-user fee), 47 miles east of King Salmon. It is essentially just a lodge, campground, and ranger station on the north side of the Brooks River, and a couple of bear-viewing platforms – one by Brooks Falls on the south bank. An undesirable (and occasionally worrying) amount of bear–human interaction has prompted the Park Service to move all the visitor facilities to **Beaver Pond Terrace** south of the river (see map inset, p.304), supposedly by the summer of 2002. Currently everyone walks around Brooks Camp, but the authorities have decided to introduce buses to shuttle people between the new float dock, the new lodge, and Brooks Falls. With a maximum of fifteen-minutes' walk between points of interest this sounds like a backward step in such a pristine environment.

Your first day is likely to be spent hanging around **Brooks Falls** watching and photographing up to a dozen bears, though you'll have to be patient since only forty people are allowed on the main platform, and rangers have to limit the time people can stay there so that everyone gets a chance. Even on the platform there's considerable jockeying for position as video cameras are poked between ranks of professional photographers and their tripods.

Things tend to be quieter early and late in the day when day-trippers are absent, and the middle of the day can be spent tackling the **Dumpling Mountain Hike** (8 miles round-trip; 4–5hr; 2400ft ascent), which follows the only formed trail hereabouts and climbs to the mountain's summit passing an overlook about half way. The Park Service also run a daily guided hike (free) going part the way up.

Kayaking and **canoeing** are superb ways to see more of the area, either on the Savonoski Loop (see box, below) or shorter trips using boats rented (and booked in advance) from *Brooks Lodge*: double kayaks $7 an hour, $50 a day, $245 a week; canoes $6, $36, and $168 respectively. There's plenty of interest within a couple of hours' paddle, but if you are equipped for camping you could head twenty miles to the Bay of Islands (see box, below), one to two days paddle away, or ten miles to the islands around the mouth of Margot Creek, an area with a reputation for its bears. Either camp on the islands or turn it into one very long paddling day.

Fishing is also stupendous around here and many visitors are happy to spend their day doing guided trolling for lake trout, and arctic char ($135 a half day);

SAVONOSKI LOOP

Anyone with experience in backcountry camping and with moderate kayaking or canoeing skills shouldn't have too much trouble completing the **Savonoski Loop**, an 86-mile lake and river paddle which can be done in as little as three days by fit kayakers, though most people take seven to ten days. That said, it is a true wilderness experience and help may be days away, so you need to be able to handle braided rivers with sweepers, and whitewater up to Class II. There's also one strenuous portage, and high winds can whip up across the lakes so you need to be prepared to pitch camp and wait for bad weather to pass.

Almost everyone follows a clockwise course from Brooks Camp into the North Arm of Naknek Lake and the **Bay of Islands**, myriad small islands with great camping spots, separated by crystal-clear water with good pike and trout fishing. Accommodation is available at **Fure's Cabin** (reservations through NPS visitor center in King Salmon; free), which is located at the start of the mile-long portage to **Lake Grosvenor**. At the southern end of the lake you enter the Class I **Grosvenor River** which typically has excellent wildlife viewing. As you enter the Class I–II **Savonoski River** the wildlife is most likely to be bears, and you're advised to press through this section in one day to avoid camping among the bears. To complete the loop back to Brooks Camp you've then only got to cross **Iliuk Arm** which is exposed and best traversed along its south shore passing. Pick a campsite away from the mouth of Margot Creek, which has a reputation for bears.

taking a boat on Naknek Lake ($200 a day each); or employing a river guide for rainbow fishing ($50 an hour, $150 a day).

Activity at Brooks Camp revolves entirely around the presence of bears, so it is only open to the public from June 1 to September 18. On arrival, rangers will put you through a twenty-minute **orientation program**, partly to help you avoid having to deal with bears, and partly to instill some commonsense rules so that up to three hundred sightseers and photographers can go about their business in relative harmony.

The only **rooms** at Brooks Camp are those available on package deals (see p.305) at *Brooks Lodge*, which fills up almost a year in advance for the prime viewing month of July. Everyone else stays at the **campground** ($15 per person, includes the $10 daily park fee), which has fire rings and bear-resistant food caches, and also fills up early: book through Biospherics (☎301/722-1257 or 1-800/365-22667 6am–6pm, *reservations.nps.gov*).

If you are **cooking** your own meals you'll need to bring a camp stove and an empty fuel bottle: white gas (but not propane) is available in Brooks at the Katmai Trading Post, which also stocks a few snacks, film, and fishing gear, but little else. **Meals** are only available at *Brooks Lodge* where they lay on all-you-can-eat buffet affairs (breakfast $10; lunch $12; dinner $22) open to all.

The Valley of 10,000 Smokes

Having forked out the cash to get to Brooks Camp it seems penny-pinching not to also visit the **Valley of 10,000 Smokes**, a virtually plant-free expanse of red, yellow, and tan wasteland some three miles wide and twelve long, deeply incised by river-carved gorges a hundred feet deep. It is reached along a 23-mile dirt road by Katmailand's "Natural History Tour" (9am–4.30pm; $72 round-trip, $42 one-way for hikers), which uses a 4WD bus for the ninety-minute run to Three Forks Overlook, where there's a wonderful view over the desolate landscape and a shelter to protect you from the wind and the volcanic ash it carries. The onboard ranger then leads an instructive three-mile round-trip hike (700ft ascent) down the **Ukak Falls Trail** to the confluence of Knife, Lethe, and Windy creeks, and the spectacular falls themselves. The tour is often full throughout the summer, so it pays to sign up at *Brooks Lodge* when you arrive.

You can also see the Valley on an hour-long **flightseeing** trip from Brooks Camp (around $200), cycle the road on **mountain bikes** rented from *Brooks Lodge* for $35 a day, or even walk the road, although you must be at least five miles from *Brooks Lodge* before camping.

To really explore the area, spend a few days **hiking**, best done in late August and early September when the weather is relatively benign, most snow cover has melted, and bugs are at their least menacing. Most hikers spend their first day heading southeast through the Valley of 10,000 Smokes to reach some abandoned US Geological Survey **cabins** (free) on the flanks of Baked Mountain. There are nicer campsites further to the southeast but the cabins have the advantage of providing shelter from the wind, though there's no water source. By setting up a base camp you are then free to explore the half-mile-wide crater of **Novorupta**, **Mount Griggs** with its nested craters from successive eruptions, the 2600-foot **Katmai Pass**, which was used as a mail route during the Nome gold rush, and the turquoise, ice-encrusted crater lake of **Mount Katmai**. The latter requires crampons, ice axe, and glacier travel skills, and if you have these you may also want to play around on **Knife Creek Glaciers**, now stagnant and

---

MCNEIL RIVER STATE GAME SANCTUARY

If you want to see a lot of bears without the crowds, try to visit **McNeil River State Game Sanctuary**, 110 miles west of Homer. From early July to mid-August, brown bears come to feast on chum salmon struggling up **McNeil River Falls**, a mess of rocks and whitewater a mile inland from Cook Inlet. Here you might easily see twenty or thirty bears at one time, and perhaps a hundred over the course of a day. In June, slightly smaller numbers congregate for the sockeye run at **Mikfik Creek** a few miles away.

The trouble is, you are unlikely to experience this firsthand, since only ten people are allowed to come here on any one day (between June 7 and Aug 25), with places given only to winners of an annual lottery. What's more each place is valid for four days, so the turnover is low. If that is not deterrent enough, you have to pay $25 simply to enter the lottery (where your chances are around one in ten), then a further $350 ($150 for Alaska residents) for the permit if your name is drawn, plus around $350 round-trip for the flight from Homer. If you are staying overnight you'll have to be self-sufficient for camping at McNeil River, and should bring hip waders. There are also four standby places (again distributed by lottery: $25 for the application, $175 for the standby permit) so that there are people on hand if someone fails to show or doesn't take their full quota of four days. On a more hopeful note, Kachemak Air Service (☎235-8924), who fly to McNeil River from Homer, usually hear about any places that do come free: call them and you might be able to grab a spur-of-the-moment opportunity.

To enter the **lottery**, send an application before March 1 to ATTN: McNeil River, Alaska Department of Fish & Game, Division of Wildlife Conservation, 333 Raspberry Rd, Anchorage, Alaska 99518-1599 (☎267-2182). A full set of lottery rules and an application form can be found at *www.state.ak.us/adfg/wildlife/region2 /refuge2/mr-home.htm*.

---

slowly melting since the 1912 collapse of Mount Katmai robbed them of the ice fields which fed them.

With the rapid erosion in the area, conditions change rapidly and you'll need to get the latest information and route guides from the NPS visitor center in King Salmon where they'll issue free backcountry and fire permits, and sell you the Trails Illustrated *Katmai National Park and Preserve* topo map. They'll also tell you where you can get water and warn you about hazardous river crossings, since very deep narrow gorges can often fill up and appear to be shallow pools, the bottom invisible through the silty water. Ferocious ash-laden winds occur quite frequently so, along with a strong tent, you'll want protective goggles or wraparound sunglasses and perhaps a bandana to breathe through. Bear-resistant food canisters can be obtained free of charge from the NPS visitor centers in Brooks Camp and King Salmon.

The Alaska Peninsula and the Aleutian Islands

Beyond the vast national parks of Lake Clark and Katmai, and west of Kodiak, lies the **Alaska Peninsula**, a slender arm reaching out to Asia and separating the

Bering Sea from the north Pacific Ocean. It ends 800 miles southwest of Anchorage, but the mountainous spine effectively continues as the **Aleutian Islands** (pronounced *al-OO-shun*), an 1100-mile-long necklace of volcanic islands along the seam of the American and Pacific plates and stretching to within five hundred miles of Russia's Kamchatka Peninsula. The whole arc of the peninsula and islands is an isolated, windswept, and almost treeless place where fierce gales, earthquakes and vulcanism add a spectacular component to a region as often as not cloaked in silent mist.

Few people live out this way. The Native Aleut (*AL-ee-oot*) wrested a living from the sea around small villages throughout the region, then Russian fur traders began more substantial towns as bases for their operations. Ultimately it was the Japanese occupation of the two westernmost islands – Attu and Kiska – during World War II, and the subsequent military buildup that brought the first modern development to the region, something consolidated by the fishing industry. Now almost every community lives off the sea, either subsistence fishing and hunting in the remaining Native villages, or commercial fishing from **Dutch Harbor** – the US's most productive fishing port – or smaller ports along the peninsula.

There are only two realistic ways to visit this area. You can fly direct to Dutch Harbor, where you could easily spend a week, though two or three days is more likely, or take the **three-day ferry journey** to Unalaska/Dutch Harbor aboard the *Tustumena* from either Homer or Kodiak. It briefly calls at all the isolated fishing communities along the southern shore of the Alaska Peninsula giving a real sense of just how isolated these places are. Unless you've a highly developed sense of adventure, and a fat wallet, you probably won't see any of the Aleutians beyond Unalaska, though birding fanatics occasionally take specialist cruises out to the more distant islands to add Asiatic accidentals to their life list.

The Alaskan Peninsula ferry trip

Any trip to Alaska should have at least one real adventure, and the best value has to be riding the AMHS ferry *Tustumena* along the southern coast of the Alaska Peninsula to the beginning of the Aleutian Chain. Once a month from April to October the ferry leaves Homer for Kodiak, then continues west (typically leaving Kodiak on the second Wed) for the two-and-a-half-day trip to Unalaska/Dutch Harbor, arriving early Saturday morning. The town warrants more of your time than the five or six hours you'll get, but the only solution is to stay for a while and then fly back to Anchorage: it'll cost you more, but may be preferable to spending another three days on the boat getting back to Homer or Kodiak (especially if the weather forecast is foul).

Along the journey the ferry sails parallel to the treeless grassy lowlands of the Alaska Peninsula, which periodically rise up to lofty volcanoes, some of which let out small eruptions from time to time. Catch it all through a fine patch with calm seas and blue skies and it can be glorious, but the "Trusty Tusty," as it is often called, has to regularly weather rough waters, and can spend the whole journey easing its way through dense fog with the coastline barely discernible: bring a good book just in case. There's no guarantee of good weather but the June, July, and August sailings are probably the best bets, and also have an onboard naturalist helping interpret the vegetation, marine, and birdlife you might encounter along the way.

The *Tustumena* is no cruise ship, but a working ferry with a mission to call in at the half-dozen fishing ports along the way to drop off vehicles, people, and supplies. Much of the adventure is the sense of isolation you get sailing overnight to get to the next god-forsaken fishing community. All the villages have small airports, but the ferry remains the lifeline, and just chatting to those on board can be half the fun. The ferry seldom stops for long but the hour or two you spend in port is enough to make a brief inspection and be on your way.

The ferry passenger **fare** from Homer to Unalaska is currently $242 each way ($202 from Kodiak), with Alaska Airlines charging around $380 (14-day advance purchase) for the one-way fare back to Anchorage. If you live outside the US and buy your ticket in advance, you can take advantage of the "Best of the West Airpass" (see p.32) and fly back to Anchorage for $99.

The *Tustumena* is one of the smaller ferries in the AMHS fleet, but still big enough to have a car deck, restaurant with meals at fair prices, and cabins (Homer to Unalaska from $274). There is no solarium or reclining chairs, but you can save money on a cabin – if you don't mind the discomfort – by sleeping on the floor and taking full advantage of free showers and free hot water for tea, noodles, or whatever you bring with you.

Chignik and Sand Point

From Kodiak, the ferry heads northwest between Kodiak and Afognak islands, threading through Whale Pass to reach the **Shelikof Strait**, which separates Kodiak from the Alaskan Peninsula. From there it swings southwest, conveniently making the only open-water passage through the night. By morning you're hugging the coast, jagged white mountains stretching as far as you can see on the starboard side. Towards noon the ferry enters Chignik Bay surrounded on three sides by snow-capped mountains and approached past the soaring spires and plateau rock of Castle Cape. The hour-long stop in **CHIGNIK** (pop. under 200) is all you need to go ashore and briefly inspect the outside of the fish-processing plants and the few dozen houses strung along the shore.

It is another nine hours to **SAND POINT**, reached at about 10pm. It sits on Popof Island, where the Russians first established a community in the nineteenth century, and now has a permanent population of almost 1200, giving it the feel of a real town. There are even a couple of bars, and since you should have a couple of hours in port there is time enough to hike into town, look at the bald eagles that are almost always in the trees, and join the locals for a game of pool in the *Sand Point Tavern*.

King Cove and Cold Bay

An overnight passage brings you to **KING COVE**, yet another small community entirely dependent on fishing and fish processing. Use your two-hour layover to walk into town where (as in many remote communities) the school is by far the biggest and best-kept building. Nearby there is a Russian Orthodox Church, modern in execution but equipped with icons and exterior bells moved here in the 1980s from the now abandoned town of Belkofski, twelve miles to the southeast.

The shortest hop on the whole trip passes through a narrow channel surrounded by beautiful mountains and the conical form of Morzhovoi Volcano to **COLD BAY**, a tiny settlement with a level of importance that outweighs its hundred-strong population. In 1941, this became Fort Randall, a major base from which the war in the Aleutians was orchestrated. During the army's occupation as many as twenty thousand troops were stationed here in Quonset huts, some contributing to the construction of the third longest airport runway in the state. Cold Bay is now an air hub for the Aleutian and Pribilof islands, an alternative airport when Anchorage is socked-in, and even (it is said) a last ditch alternative landing zone for the space shuttle. This ability to handle big planes has brought controversy to the region: residents of King Cove have demanded the construction of a thirty-something-mile road to Cold Bay so that in poor weather, when their own small airport is closed, they can still fly out from the larger airport. Medical emergency is cited as the reason, though cynics suggest that easy access to good hunting is a stronger driving force. None of this would be contentious except that the proposed road would cross critical wetlands within the **Izembek National Wildlife Refuge**. Alternatives are being considered and it remains to be seen whether the road gets built.

The refuge attracts 142 species of birds, but was originally set aside for brant geese, the entire North American population of 100,000 feeding on the world's largest eelgrass beds during the spring and fall migrations. Catch one of the fall ferry sailings and you may also see some of the 70,000 Canada geese who migrate through here. Unless you are an enthusiastic birder, you'll probably only stop at Cold Bay for a few minutes, enough to hike the half-mile length of the jetty and back, should you wish.

False Pass and Akutan

Later that afternoon you'll hit tiny **FALSE PASS**, which marks the entrance to the 150-foot-wide channel between the end of the Alaska Peninsula and the easternmost of the Aleutian Islands, **Unimak**. For centuries Aleuts had used the channel to travel between the Bering Sea and the Gulf of Alaska, and the Russians followed suit, but large American ships found the strait too perilous and named it **False Pass** to encourage shipping to go around the western end of Unimak Island. The community that built up around the early twentieth-century cannery took on the name of the pass and now supports under a hundred people.

Outbound ferries chug through the night straight to Unalaska, but the eastbound service stops very briefly at **AKUTAN**, three hours after leaving Unalaska. Akutan hunkers below the 4275-foot Akutan Volcano which last erupted in 1978. It was established in 1878 as a fur-storage and trading port, though cod fishing soon took precedence. The residents here were evacuated to Ketchikan during World War II and few returned, but those that did have recently been nursing their dying language, which looks to be on the cusp of recovery. Hop off to see the historic **Alexandr Nevsky Chapel**, a Russian Orthodox structure built in 1918 to replace an 1878 original. The ferry only spends 45 minutes here then skips False Pass but calls at all the other ports on its way back to Kodiak.

Unalaska and Dutch Harbor

In a state full of remote spots, it is hard to outdo **UNALASKA/DUTCH HARBOR**, located on a foggy, windswept, and treeless Aleutian island rising out of the North Pacific, eight hundred miles southwest of Anchorage. The nearest town of any size is Kodiak, nearly six hundred miles away, and yet here you'll find the eleventh most populous locale in Alaska, as big as Homer and bigger than heavyweight names such as Seward, Cordova, and Skagway. The reason is simple: this has been the United States' most productive **fishing port** for most of the

---

UNALASKA OR DUTCH HARBOR?

No one much cares whether you call the contiguous settlement **Unalaska or Dutch Harbor**, and the terms are used pretty much interchangeably, except among local residents. For them, the settlement on the island of Amaknak is Dutch Harbor, now linked by "The Bridge to the Other Side" to Unalaska Island and the town of Unalaska. Residents on both sides of the bridge all live within the bounds of the "city" of Unalaska, which is where mail gets sent and even where the ferry schedule says it is taking you. However, while ferries officially arrive in Unalaska, the nearby airport is in Dutch Harbor, so you have the unlikely situation where planes land at Dutch Harbor and ferries go to Unalaska.

---

last decade, both in terms of weight and dollar value. The four-thousand-strong town almost doubles in size for the winter fishing and crabbing season when storm-tossed trawlers and six-hundred-foot-long factory ships periodically call in to offload their catch. From August to November, and again from January to March the season is open on some of the world's richest fishing grounds – salmon, crab, cod, pollock, yellowfin, mackerel – and the town is alive with Mexicans, Filipinos, Russians, Vietnamese, Americans up from the Lower 48, in fact just about anyone who's after a quick buck.

Short-stay profiteering and the eternally erratic nature of the fishing industry do little to foster a developed community and there's a certain frontier spirit to the place, but less than you might imagine. Taxes on fishing-boat catches have made Unalaska a wealthy town, so most of the roads are paved, health and public services are maintained to a high standard, and you can sleep in a top-class hotel. Even the fish-processing factories are conveniently tucked away from view (many in Captains Bay) and only the container port gives any kind of an industrial tenor to the place.

In summer, when most visitors arrive, the commercial fishery gives way to lively bouts of **sport fishing**, primarily for huge halibut. In the last few years the world mark has twice been broken around Dutch Harbor and the record now stands at a whopping barn-door-sized 459 pounds. There's plenty of hiking, mountain biking and kayaking to take advantage of, and wildlife fans will appreciate the whales passing by each spring and fall, the sea mammals which amass in huge numbers hereabouts, and the unusual seabirds that turn up. Birders come especially to see the **crested auklet** which is seldom found anywhere else.

There's interest too in the legacy of three nations – Aleut, Russian, and American – which have combined to leave a fascinating history, though not a great deal of tangible evidence. The Aleuts have been here for close on nine thousand years, but much of their culture was suppressed by the Russian fur traders. The US military helped complete the near-genocide during World War II (see box, p.316), and left behind hilltop bunkers and the shells of Quonset huts still visible in the hills. Fortunately, something of Aleut culture has been preserved in the **Museum of the Aleutians**, and local language and culture is again being taught at the local school.

History

Evidence from archeological digs around Unalaska indicates that the Unangan people (see box, p.316) have lived here for around nine thousand years, but

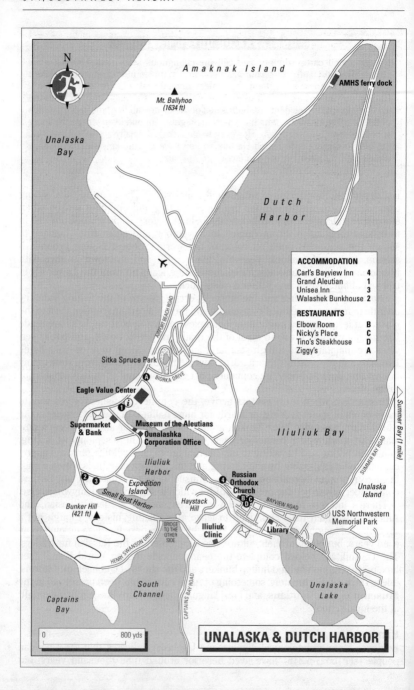

UNALASKA & DUTCH HARBOR

Amaknak Island

AMHS ferry dock

▲ *Mt. Ballyhoo (1634 ft)*

Unalaska Bay

Dutch Harbor

ACCOMMODATION

Carl's Bayview Inn	**4**
Grand Aleutian	**1**
Unisea Inn	**3**
Walashek Bunkhouse	**2**

RESTAURANTS

Elbow Room	**B**
Nicky's Place	**C**
Tino's Steakhouse	**D**
Ziggy's	**A**

△ *Summer Bay (1 mile)*

Sitka Spruce Park

BIORKA DRIVE

Eagle Value Center

Supermarket & Bank

Museum of the Aleutians

Ounalashka Corporation Office

Iliuliuk Bay

Iliuliuk Harbor

Expedition Island

Small Boat Harbor

AIRPORT BEACH ROAD

Bunker Hill (421 ft) ▲

Haystack Hill

Russian Orthodox Church

BAYVIEW ROAD

Unalaska Island

SUMMER BAY ROAD

USS Northwestern Memorial Park

BROADWAY

Library

Iliuliuk Clinic

BRIDGE TO THE OTHER SIDE

HENRY SWANSON DRIVE

CAPTAINS BAY ROAD

South Channel

Captains Bay

Unalaska Lake

N

0	800 yds

recorded history doesn't begin until Stephan Glotov led a crew of fur buyers here in August 1759. They stayed for three years and laid the groundwork for what became a key link in the chain of Russian settlements along the American coast as far down as northern California. Ultimately, their main legacy was the Russian Orthodox Church, which remains the most important religion among the Aleut.

Under US government, Dutch (as it is often known) became the base for seal harvesting in the Pribilof Islands and subsequently a coal-supply depot for Yukon-bound ships during the Klondike gold strike. As prospectors flocked to the beaches of Nome a few years later, Dutch was where boats amassed as they waited for the ice to break up in Norton Sound. Then when fuel oil replaced coal, the need for restocking the bunkers disappeared and the town declined until 1939 when the government started fortifying the area against possible attack. It came on June 3–4, 1942 when this became the only place in the US to be bombed during World War II, except for Pearl Harbor. Subsequently Dutch was the headquarters of the battle for the Aleutians: almost all the roads you now see were built then, and up to 40,000 troops were stationed here.

Military involvement aside, Unalaska/Dutch Harbor was still a small town until the 1970s when super-lucrative crab fishing, and the get-rich-quick attitude that it engendered, turned it into the most productive seafood port in the nation. As successive fisheries declined, different species were targeted and the boom and bust cycle has been repeated several times. A quota system has recently been introduced in the hopes of stabilizing the situation.

Arrival and tours

There's no better way to reach Dutch Harbor than on the AMHS **ferry** *Tustumena* (see p.310), which arrives around the middle of each month (April–Oct only) early Saturday morning. It stays in port a little over five hours, so if you are heading back on the boat the best bet is to join one of the town **tours**, which won't cost you a lot more than a taxi ride into town and back. The best deals are with the Native-run Aleut Tours (June–Aug Mon–Sat; $40; ☎ & fax 581-6061), which visit the main sections of town including the interior of the Holy Ascension Cathedral, and Extra Mile Tours (June–Aug daily; ☎ & fax 581-6171, *xmitours @arctic.net*), which skips the cathedral on the two-hour trip ($40) and heads out along some of the rougher roads into the surrounding countryside; there's also an extended four-hour trip for $75.

Alaska Airlines and PenAir (both ☎581-1383) jointly run daily **flights** direct from Anchorage with extortionate spur-of-the-moment prices, two-week advance purchases come down to $750 round-trip ($380 one-way) and occasional specials can be as low as $270 round-trip: shop around especially if your dates are flexible. Foreigners who book before leaving home can get excellent use out of the "Best of the West" Airpass (see p.32) flying for $99 each way.

Getting around and information

The twin towns are spread out, but fairly flat so it is quite possible to **get around** on foot, though if arriving with luggage you may want to engage the services of one of the many taxis which charge almost $20 to get into town from the ferry: try Blue Checker Taxi (☎581-2186). Rental cars are available from Northport Rental (☎581-3880) and Aleutian Truck Rental (☎581-1576, fax 581-2285), both at the airport, for $45–50 a day with unlimited mileage for a compact, and $70–85 for a pickup or Explorer. You can also **rent mountain bikes** from Aleutian

THE ALEUT: KAYAKS, SLAVERY, AND INTERNMENT

The US government has a far from exemplary record in dealing with its Native people, but one of the most shameful events took place during World War II in the conveniently out of sight Aleutian Islands. The **Unangan** people (or Aleuts as they've become known since Russian times) had lived for centuries in this barren treeless land, relying almost entirely on the sea, using their finely honed hunting skills, expertly crafted iqax (kayaks), and unmatched knowledge of the sea. In their semi-subterranean sod and driftwood huts they spent long winter nights around the seal-oil lamp creating some of the most finely woven baskets seen anywhere, stitching seal gut into wonderfully light and waterproof hunting jackets, and perfecting sophisticated knowledge of medicine, acupuncture, and even the art of mummification.

They lived in a tenuous balance with their natural surroundings until the arrival of the **Russians** in the 1750s seeking sea-otter pelts to sell on the Chinese market at exorbitant prices. The Russians virtually enslaved the Aleut, holding family members hostage in order to force the men to hunt. Within fifty years of Russian contact, disease, warfare, starvation, and enslavement had literally decimated the original population of about fifteen thousand, something only reversed with the increasing influence of the Russian Orthodox church.

After the US purchase in 1867 the Aleut were neglected by the territorial authorities, but regained some degree of self-determination by returning to their traditional lifestyles, occasionally supplementing their income by working for wages on fox farms. The US government only started to take interest when the US entered World War II and preparations were made to evacuate the Aleut from what was now considered a prime Japanese target. Evacuation didn't take place until after Dutch Harbor was bombed and the westernmost Aleutian Islands of Attu and Kiska were captured in June 1942. The offensive was only a failed diversion from the real battle at Midway, but the Japanese found that the Americans became so intent on regaining their territory that they dug in and were only ousted eleven months later in an intensely bloody, and largely pointless, battle.

Meanwhile, ostensibly for their own safety, Aleuts on Atka, Umnak, Sedanka, Unalaska, and Akutan islands, plus those on the Pribilof islands of St Paul and St George, were shipped to Southeast Alaska. They were housed in abominable conditions in old and dilapidated herring and salmon canneries which were not insulated for winter use. Only the goodwill of the local Tlingit provided them with the means to fish and the transport to attend church. The radical change in climate, unfamiliar surroundings, primitive housing and negligible medical care took its toll and in some places a quarter of evacuees died during the three-year internment. Still, that was only half the death rate of the people of Attu, who had been captured by the Japanese and spent the rest of the war on Hokkaido.

Some men were allowed to return in 1943 and were put to work harvesting fur seals, but most waited in the camps until 1945. On their return they discovered their homes looted and destroyed and whole villages burned. Many villages were never rebuilt, and some islands remained under military control, principally Adak, about halfway along the chain. This was still in operation until 1995 when it was finally handed over to the local Native corporation, a small but significant step in the restitution of Aleut culture.

Adventure Sports (see p.319), who have a booth on the wharf for ferry arrivals in the summer.

The **visitor center** (Mon–Fri 9am–5pm, and some Sats in summer; ☎581-2612, fax 581-2613, *www.arctic.net/~updhcvb*) is inside the *Grand Aleutian Hotel* about a mile from the airport. Many visitor facilities are congregated nearby including the two supermarkets, each with a bank and ATM, and the main **post office** (Mon–Fri 9am–5pm, Sat 1–5pm). There's another post office branch downtown, on Airport Beach Road, a few steps away from the **Iliuliuk Clinic**, 34 LaVelle Court (☎581-1202), a **laundromat** at 111 Blue Fox Alley, and the **library**, (Mon–Fri 9am–9pm, Sat & Sun 2–6pm), which has free **Internet access**.

Accommodation

High- and moderate-standard **accommodation** is available in Unalaska but nowhere comes cheap, and there are no campgrounds, though camping is possible in the hills all around (see p.319). There is no hostel as such, but fish-factory **bunkhouses** cater to the cheaper end of the market, none demanding the kind of communal sleeping arrangements the name might imply. Handiest and best value is the *Walashek Bunkhouse*, 103 Gilman St (☎581-4357, fax 581-6247; ②), which is often full with fishermen and construction crews, but has singles for $42 and offers fixed-menu breakfast ($5), lunch ($5), and dinner ($10) to its guests. You'll find it more convenient and much more comfortable at the modern and slightly chintzy *Carl's Bayview Inn*, 606 Bayview (☎581-1230 or 1-800/581-1230, fax 581-1880; ⑤), with some bayview rooms (⑦), and studio kitchenettes (⑥), all with cable TV and free airport transfer. In the same price range you'll find the decidedly faded *Unisea Inn* on Gilman Street (☎581-1325, fax 581-1633; ⑤); it's a step up to its younger sister the *Grand Aleutian*, 498 Salmon Way (☎581-3844 or 1-800/891-1194, fax 581-7150, *www.grandaleutian.com*; suites ⑧, rooms ⑥), an imposing three-story four-star hotel that's so out of keeping with the general tone of the area it is sometimes referred to as the "Grand Delusion."

The town

Easily the most imposing building in Unalaska is the **Russian Orthodox Cathedral of the Holy Ascension**, its green onion-dome tower endlessly reproduced on postcards and tourist brochures, usually with one of the town's abundant **bald eagles** regally perched on top of the triple-bar cross. It ranks as the oldest existing Russian Orthodox church in the state, built on the site of a church built in 1808, and a later model jointly built by Father Ivan Veniaminov and the local Aleut in 1826. The current structure was built in the mid-1890s and survived considerable neglect to rise gloriously restored in 1996. You can normally only go inside for services (Sat 6.30pm & Sun 10am) and on a town tour (see p.315), but you should make the effort to see one of the finest collections of **religious art** in Alaska. There are almost seven hundred icons and relics amassed over the years as the other half-dozen village churches on Unalaska Island closed when the villages were abandoned. Adjacent is the small **Bishop's House**, which was originally built in San Francisco in 1882 and subsequently reassembled here. It is currently being restored and is not open to the public.

The cathedral looms over Unalaska's sweeping arc of gravel beach, which is backed by the heart of downtown. Stroll to the far eastern end of the beach where there's a memorial to the **USS Northwestern**, a retired former freighter pressed into use during World War II as civilian accommodation but bombed by the Japanese. After burning for five days the boat was later scuttled, and its steel prow can still be seen rising above the waters at the head of Captains Bay. The propeller was recovered for the fiftieth anniversary and now forms the centerpiece of the memorial. Beyond here, Summer Bay Road leads three miles to Summer Bay where there's good beach walking, a small lake, and a hike across an isthmus to Agamgik Bay (see opposite).

West of downtown Unalaska, the "Bridge to the Other Side" crosses South Channel onto Amaknak Island, once five separate islands now joined by landfill. Immediately over the bridge, a dirt road runs left around the base of Quonset huts, then up to the summit of **Bunker Hill** (aka Hill 400; 421ft), the commanding site of a World War II gun emplacement. It only takes about fifteen minutes to hike up the road past the remains of Quonset huts (long semicircular sheet-metal huts used in military World War II installations), ammunition stores, and tunnel entrances to reach the summit with its concrete bunkers and circular turntable for directing the 155mm guns at anything approaching.

Back on the main Airport Beach Road, turn right onto Gilman Road to reach the recently opened **Museum of the Aleutians**, 314 Salmon Way (June to mid-Sept Mon–Sat 10am–5pm, Sun noon–5pm; $2; *www.aleutians.org*), built on the existing foundations of a World War II warehouse which provides the terrazzo flooring of the entrance area. Inside, temporary displays augment the permanent collection which aims to interpret the history and culture of Unalaska Island and the Aleutian region. There's coverage too of the Russian involvement in the area, the herring salteries which flourished in the 1920s, and World War II military buildup, represented here by the lower two-thirds of a Tlingit-style totem pole carved by bored servicemen stationed on Kiska. Artifacts include a four-thousand-year-old pumice mask unearthed from Margaret Bay, a seal-gut wallet handmade in the 1930s, and seal-bone harpoon points dating back 2000 years.

It is very much a working museum employing a team of archeologists who conduct research programs on a couple of sites, notably an important two-acre dig right outside the door and just behind the *Grand Aleutian Hotel*. More than 100,000 artifacts – harpoons, oil lamps, semi-subterranean houses – uncovered since 1996 show that several successive Unangan villages have occupied the site. Ongoing laboratory work can be seen through a window in the museum, and visitors may join in the dig through the **Margaret Bay Ecotourism Project** (mid-June to mid-Aug), which involves staying and eating at the *Grand Aleutian* for a reduced rate (around $260 a day each),working at the site or lab, and listening to evening lectures. There may also be opportunities to volunteer on a day by day basis for short-term visitors. For more details contact Rick Knecht, Museum of the Aleutians, PO Box 648, Unalaska, Alaska 99685 (☎581-5150, *knecht@arctic.net*).

Sitka Spruce Park, a short walk to the north, contains three trees which remain from the Sitka Spruce Plantation, laid out by Russian settlers around 1805. Nearby, and around the flanks of Mount Ballyhoo you'll see all manner of remnants of military activity during World War II, mostly abandoned but in some cases incorporated into modern functions: an old torpedo production facility is now a six-lane bowling alley.

Hiking, biking, and kayaking

With miles of treeless terrain right on the town's doorstep there is plenty of scope for hiking, either along the small number of accessible trails or heading off wherever you please. There's also an extensive network of old World War II roads that make wonderful mountain biking territory. Bring a sturdy tent and you increase the scope of your explorations immeasurably, but all the land hereabouts is private and you need to obtain **permits** from the Ounalashka Corporation, 400 Salmon Way, Margaret Bay Subdivision (Mon–Fri 9am–5pm; ☎581-1276).

Currently it costs $6 a day for hiking or mountain biking, and an additional $5 a day if you plan to camp.

Camping is possible close to town, though it is hard to find anywhere that is flat, dry, protected from the wind, and relatively inconspicuous on these bald hills. You also need to take account of the weather which can whip up seventy-mile-per-hour winds in no time: locals even suggest taking a packet of balloons so you can ensure the fly and inner stay separated.

June is a good month for **hiking**. You will still encounter snow on the tops, the 120 varieties of wildflower are magnificent, and the summer grass is not yet too tall. July and August are likely to have better weather (and juicy salmonberries and blueberries) though you still need to keep to the ridge if you want relatively dry feet, and should carry a compass since the fog comes in quick and thick. It is also worth noting that, despite an extensive clean-up in recent years, there is still a slim possibility you may come across **unexploded ordnance** left over from World War II; don't disturb any rusted-up bits of metal. After all these warnings it is comforting that there are no bears, and the bugs aren't too bad.

The easiest of the local hikes is up **Mount Ballyhoo** (4 miles round-trip; 3hr; 1600ft ascent), which rises behind the airport and offers views to Makushin Volcano and the rest of Unalaska Island. Much of the mountain falls within the **Aleutian WWII National Historic Area**, essentially a lot of detritus left over from World War II that is more fully explained in leaflets available locally. The hike can be extended by continuing north along the ridge to Ulakta Head. The **Agamgik Bay Trail** (8 miles round-trip; 3–5hr; 500ft ascent) is also worthwhile though it starts an inconvenient four miles from town at Summer Bay, reached along Summer Bay Road.

The twin towns have 38 miles of regular roads, but many more disused tracks from World War II, challenging terrain that is perfect for **mountain biking** using front-suspension machines rented from Aleutian Adventure Sports (☎581-4489 or 1-888/581-4489, fax 581-6458, *www.aleutianadventure.com*) for $25 a half-day, and $35 for the full day. The same company also rents kayaks (double $85 a day, single $65) and leads a wide range of excellent **guided kayak trips** from the Harbor and Captains Bay tours (3–4hr; $55 and $65 respectively) that are open to complete novices, to the more demanding paddle northwest to Wide Bay (10–12hr; $145) and four- to six-day extended trips ($550–1100). **Guided hiking and mountaineering trips** take place through the summer months including a visit to Akutan Volcano and nearby hot springs (four days; $1100), and one to the snow-capped 6680ft summit of Makushin Volcano on Unalaska Island.

Halibut fishing and birding

Keen birders and halibut fishers usually fly in on Anchorage-based packages, a couple of the best offered in conjunction with the *Grand Aleutian Hotel* (see p.317), which provides accommodation and meals. Their "Whiskered Auklet Tour" comes in three variations each with round-trip flights from Anchorage and day-charters out to see these rare birds, along with tufted and horned puffins, petrels, jaegers, and all sorts of marine mammals: two nights for $1268, three nights for $1698, and four nights for $2129.

Halibut Heaven (June–Aug) has two-night packages for $1268, and one-night increments up to seven nights for $3420 with charters each day. If you are here, and just fancy a day **halibut fishing**, expect to pay around $170 a day (minimum two people), and go with Shuregood Adventures (☎581-2378, *shuregood@ansi.net*), or F/V Lucille (☎ & fax 581-5949). Between June 1 and September 15 you can also enter the **halibut derby** and hope to land one of the weekly, monthly, or overall prizes, or perhaps break that 459-pound world record.

Eating, drinking, and entertainment

Unalaska is reputed to have a cost of living almost thirty percent higher than Anchorage, so you can expect **eating** to be pricey. The best way around this is to prepare your own food with groceries from the huge Eagle Value Center near the *Grand Aleutian*, which has good deli and bakery sections and sells espresso.

Nearby, *Ziggy's Restaurant*, corner of E Point Road and Airport Beach Road has a diverse menu from soups, salads, and burgers to seafood mains ($13–20), Mexican dishes ($12–15), and Polish specialties plus craft beers and wines by the glass. The *Grand Aleutian* has some of the finest food around, as expensive as expected, with a good-value Sunday brunch for $22.

In downtown Unalaska, *Nicky's Place* on Front Beach (Mon–Sat 10am–6pm, Sun 1–5pm; ☎581-1570) is good for espresso while browsing new and secondhand books and maps. *Tino's Steakhouse*, 11 N 2nd St (☎581-4288), does good steaks and much more, including fairly authentic Mexican dishes – chicken fajitas for $17, *camarones a la diabla* for $20, and a whopping *carne asada* burrito meal for $20 – as well as excellent breakfasts from waffles to omelettes and reindeer sausages and eggs.

There was a time when a survey declared that the *Elbow Room* (☎581-1271) was the second roughest **bar** in the US with tales of near-constant fights and people left bleeding out in the snow. It is considerably toned down now (at least in summer when most visitors arrive and the fishermen are away) and makes a good place for a lively evening, though there's often more action down the road in the large dark bar at *Carl's Bayside Inn*.

The Pribilof Islands

Nature enthusiasts might salivate over visiting the **PRIBILOF ISLANDS**, an archipelago of two inhabited volcanic crests – St Paul Island and St George Island – and assorted islets rising from the bed of the Bering Sea 900 miles west of Anchorage and 200 miles north of Dutch Harbor. It is a bleak place of treeless tundra-covered hills saddled with the wet and misty weather typical of the Aleutians, and an average summer temperature below fifty degrees. Unappealing as this may sound, the islands have two major drawcards: an incredibly rich gathering of honking seals and some of the most densely packed **seabird cliffs** found anywhere.

The islands were uninhabited when Russian Gerassim Pribylov discovered the fur-clad bounty he was looking for in 1786. It wasn't long before Aleutian Islands natives were virtually enslaved and shipped to the Pribilofs to harvest the seals, in time reducing seal numbers to the brink of extinction. Nonetheless, pickings were still healthy enough for the United States to look to the islands to recoup some of their costs after the 1867 purchase from Russia. The US continued the enslavement of the Aleuts manipulating virtually every aspect of their lives until World War II when the Pribilof Aleuts were evacuated to southeastern Alaska. Since their return to the islands, the Aleut have managed to gain some degree of self-governance.

By 1910, seal numbers were down to around 125,000 and stayed low until 1957 when the United States, Japan, Canada, and the Soviet Union created the North Pacific Fur Seal Commission to control indiscriminate killing. Seal harvesting finally stopped in 1986 and now every summer some 800,000 northern fur seals (three-quarters of the world population) vie for space at the breeding rookeries on the rocky beaches, accompanied by harbor seals, Stellar sea lions, walruses, and sea otters. Camouflaged viewing hides have been set up along the beaches, and if your attention should waver you can always wander along the hiking trails to other positions with a better angle on the nesting seabirds that cram onto every available ledge and squeeze into impossible crevices. The islands attract around two million birds from over two hundred species; mostly murres, puffins, fulmars, kittiwakes, cormorants, and auklets, but also small numbers of Asiatic vagrants which turn up mostly in May. Come a little later in the season and the endless summer days bring out blankets of wildflowers. Only the most curmudgeonly of city types could fail to be impressed by this spectacular convergence of birds, seals, and flowers, but the cost of getting and staying here puts many off.

Most visitors end up on **ST PAUL**, which at fourteen miles by eight is the larger of the two inhabited islands, supporting a population of eight hundred Aleuts, the world's largest such community. Their spiritual center is the **Sts Peter and Paul church** its plain exterior giving little hint of the rich Russian Orthodox interior, all icons and fuschia-colored carpet. Basic roads and hiking trails ring the island providing access to half a dozen bird cliffs and seal-viewing areas.

ST GEORGE only has a couple of hundred Aleut residents, its own impressive church, **St George the Martyr**, and a few seals; but excels when it comes to seabird cliffs, some of which rise a thousand feet from the crashing waves. It's small enough to hike around and find your favorite viewing spot.

Practicalities

The Pribilofs can be reached independently on scheduled flights from Anchorage with Reeve Aleutian (☎243-4700 or 1-800/544-2248) and PenAir (☎243-2323) but with fares close to $800 ($900 to St George) and the limited scope for independent travel, it usually works out better to join an organized tour. The most frequently run (and easiest to squeeze into a tight schedule) are those operated by Alaska Birding & Wildlife Tours, 1500 W 33rd Ave, Anchorage, AK 99503 (☎1-877/424-5637, fax 278-2316, *www.alaskabirding.com*) who from mid-May to late August run frequent trips including flights from Anchorage to St Paul, accommodation at the *King Eider*, and a naturalist guide: stay durations range from two nights ($1069) to seven nights ($1999) including everything except meals. The Pribilof weather frequently disrupts flight schedules for days at a time, so be sure to **allow some flexibility in your schedule**, and have some cash spare for those extra nights at the *King Eider*.

Once on the islands, choices are few and neither island allows camping. On St Paul Island the only **place to stay** is the plain but comfortable *King Eider Hotel* (☎546-2477; ④); meals are available from the cafeteria of the local fish-processing plant and will set you back around $40 a day. On **St George Island** you can sleep at the *St George Tanaq Hotel* (☎272-9886; ④), which has shared bathrooms and a kitchen where you can prepare food, best brought from Anchorage but available locally at a price. There are no restaurants on St George.

travel details

With the exception of a fourteen-mile road from King Salmon to Naknek, no Southwest towns are linked by road. Transport is predominantly by air, though the *Tustumena* sails to Kodiak from Homer three times a week and continues along the Alaska Peninsula to Unalaska/Dutch Harbor once a month in summer.

FERRIES

Chignik to: Kodiak (one a month; 18hr 30min); Sand Point (one a month; 9hr 15min).

Cold Bay to: False Pass (one a month; 4hr 15min); King Cove (one a month; 2hr).

Dutch Harbor to: Chignik (one a month; 37hr); Cold Bay (one a month; 17hr); False Pass (one a month; 13hr); King Cove (one a month; 19hr); Kodiak (one a month; 61hr); Sand Point (one a month; 27hr).

False Pass to: Cold Bay (one a month; 4hr 15min); Dutch Harbor (one a month; 13hr).

King Cove to: Cold Bay (one a month; 2hr); Sand Point (one a month; 6hr 30min).

Kodiak to: Chignik (one a month; 18hr 30min); Cold Bay (one a month; 42hr); Dutch Harbor (one a month; 61hr); Homer (2–3 weekly; 9hr 30min); False Pass (one a month; 48hr); King Cove (one a month; 39hr); Port Lions (weekly; 2hr 30min); Sand Point (one a month; 30hr); Seward (weekly; 13hr 15min).

Port Lions to: Homer (weekly; 10hr); Kodiak (weekly; 2hr 30min).

Sand Point to: Chignik (one a month; 9hr 15min); King Cove (one a month; 6hr 30min).

FLIGHTS

Anchorage to: King Salmon (5–8 daily; 1hr–1hr 20min); St George (1 weekly; 4hr 20min); St Paul (3 weekly; 3hr 30min).

Dillingham to: Anchorage (4–5 daily; 1hr 10min).

Dutch Harbor to: Anchorage (3 daily; 2hr–2hr 50min).

King Salmon to: Anchorage (5–8 daily; 1hr–1hr 20min); Brooks Camp (4–8 daily; 20min).

Kodiak to: Anchorage (6–8 daily; 50min–1hr 10min).

CHAPTER FIVE

THE INTERIOR

Interior Alaska is the Alaska of popular imagination – a land of wild and untamed beauty spreading out from the Canadian border to the deserted western reaches of Denali National Park. For the most part, it is a low plateau of permafrost swampland only feebly drained by small streams. Wherever you go, you'll feel the presence of the mountains, either as a barrier to where you're trying to get to or as an icy backdrop to broad river valleys. Four major ranges ruck up the landscape – the Chugach and Wrangell mountains across the south, the Talkeetnas north of them, and the Alaska Range arcing in a great crescent around the top, with Mount McKinley as its crown.

It is a region settled over the last century by **miners**, **hunters**, and **trappers**, and though towns have grown up to serve the scattered communities, the pioneer spirit shows itself in the modern-day sourdoughs who chose it as their home. Originally this was **Athapascan** country, populated by Native Americans who share their heritage with the Navajos and Apaches of the American Southwest. Their presence is still strong in the area, though they mainly keep to themselves in villages off the beaten track, and you're more likely to run into somewhat sanitized vignettes of their lifestyle presented for tourists all over the region.

People are hugely outnumbered by animals – moose, Dall sheep, grizzly bears, and herds of caribou sweep over seemingly endless swaths of taiga and tundra. Day-to-day weather can vary enormously with even more severe seasonal variations: in winter, temperatures can drop to -50°F for days at a time, while summer days reach a sweltering 90°F. However, the major problem during the warmer months is large quantities of huge **mosquitoes**; don't set off without insect repellent.

In the lowland **Mat-Su Valley**, there's considerable interest in the depression-era farming colony that kick-started Alaska's limited arable tradition, but it is the hills that draw you on, principally to **Hatcher Pass** and the magnificently sited ruin of **Independence Mine**. But this is small cheese compared to what's to come, the 20,000-foot **Mount McKinley** screaming up from the 2000-foot tundra is the greatest vertical rise of any mountain anywhere. It is known to many as **Denali**, probably a Dena'ina word for "the Great One," and to say that it dominates the Alaska Range is an understatement. There are few other ranges in the

---

ACCOMMODATION PRICE CODES

All **accommodation prices** in this book have been coded using the symbols below. Note that prices are for the least expensive double rooms in each establishment. For a full explanation see p.44 in Basics.

① up to $50	④ $80–100	⑦ $160–200
② $50–65	⑤ $100–130	⑧ $200–250
③ $65–80	⑥ $130–160	⑨ $250 and over

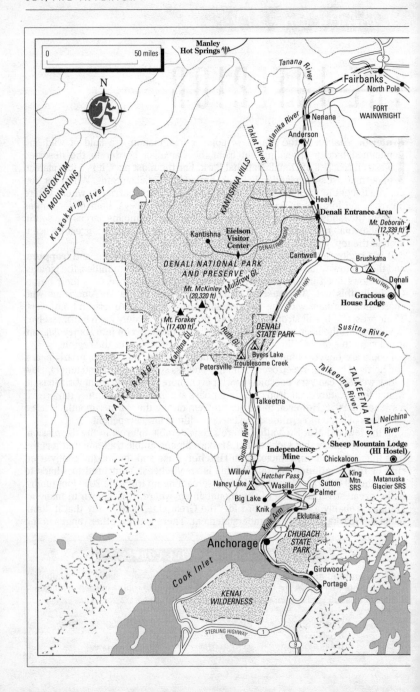

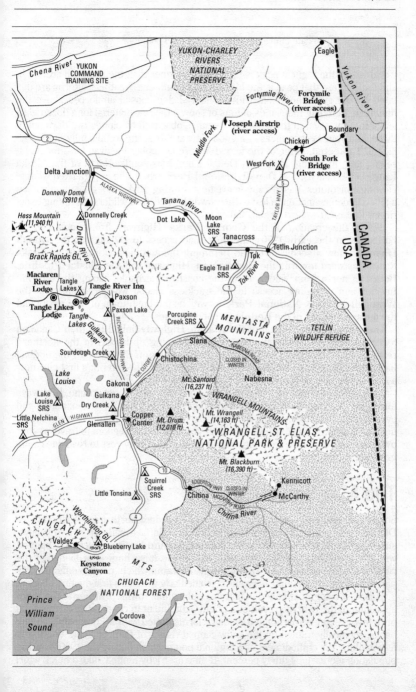

For up-to-date information on Interior road conditions call ☎456-7623.

world where the highest peak is fifty percent higher than the peaks all around it, and none where that peak is the highest on a continent. Weather patterns are dictated by the giant mountain, with moisture-laden coastal air forced above the mountain, dumping thousands of tons of snow – the raw material for a dozen glaciers – into the area. In the summer, Denali is obscured by clouds two days out of three, and your best chances of a good view are from the wonderfully quirky village of **Talkeetna**, home of the famed Moose Dropping Festival, base for flight-seeing and, in spring, alive with Denali summit aspirants. North of the Alaska Range is the heartland of **Denali National Park**, where the unparalleled wildlife viewing constitutes Alaska's single greatest drawing card – though you only need a pinch of determination to leave the crowds behind for a wilderness hiking experience that is little short of spiritual.

Before the creation of the **George Parks Highway** from Anchorage to Fairbanks in the early 1970s, the only road access to Denali was the **Denali Highway**, now a scenic dirt road hemming the southern skirts of the Alaska Range eastward towards the **Richardson Highway** and the **Alaska Pipeline**. Both run north from Valdez along the coast to Fairbanks slicing through the Interior and providing access to the trackless glacial wonderland that is the **Wrangell–St Elias National Park**, as well as the bush town of **McCarthy** and the decaying wreck of the **Kennicott** copper mines.

The wartime construction of the **Alaska Highway** linked the then Canadian territory with the Lower 48 road system, opening up access to the northern reaches of the Interior. The **Taylor Highway** spurs off this through the oddball hamlet of **Chicken** up to the Yukon River and **Eagle**, the Interior's first city, now a fascinating historical remnant.

Uniquely for Alaska, the Interior is a region that's easy to get around. Highways form the main lines of communication, so get hold of a **car** if you can: buses, and even a train line, do exist but services are skeletal and infrequent (see "Travel details," p.409). With your own transport you'll have the freedom to travel at your own pace and, if you are camping, will allow much better access to roadside campgrounds.

The Mat-Su Valley

Somewhat criminally overlooked by tourists speeding north from Anchorage to Denali, the glacially contorted **Mat-Su Valley** is in fact made up of two valleys, shaped by the erosive powers of the **Matanuska and Susitna rivers** and spotted with lakes, open plateaux, and towering mountains. It is a huge area divided by the rugged granite forms of the **Talkeetna Mountains** which, despite only just topping 7000 feet, are an impressive sight, particularly with fall's first dusting of snow.

This vast catchment contains just two substantial towns. **Palmer** is the more appealing of the two, the result of a grand experiment in cooperative farming. Its prim town center is surrounded by dairy farms dotted with Midwest-style colony barns, scenically framed by the snow-capped ridges of Pioneer Peak. **Wasilla** is less inviting, the embodiment of a regional boom which during the 1990s saw the population increase by thirty percent. If time is strictly limited, take a quick whirl through the Palmer back roads checking out the colony barns, then follow one of the loveliest alpine drives in the state to **Hatcher Pass** and the dramatic remains of the **Independence Mine**.

Mileposts for both the Glenn Hwy and the George Parks Hwy start in Anchorage. They go their separate ways 35 miles north of there at the "Y" junction; the Glenn going east through Palmer to Glenallen (our account begins on p.373), the George Parks running north through Wasilla to Fairbanks. Half a mile north on the Parks lies the **Matanuska-Susitna CVB**, Mile 35.5 Parks Hwy (mid-May to mid-Sept daily 8.30am–6.30pm; closed in winter; ☎746-5000, fax 746-2688, *www .alaskavisit.com*) the main visitor center for the region.

It is worth noting that you really need to be **independently mobile** to get the best from the region and, though there are **ATMs** further north, Wasilla's malls have the last banks before Fairbanks.

Eklutna

Heading north out of Anchorage, it would be easy to race past the hamlet of **EKLUTNA**, 25 miles to the north; but this would be a mistake. Eklutna was a Native settlement long before Anchorage was even thought of, the Russian influence which followed is apparent by the 1830 construction of the Saint Nicholas Russian Orthodox Church – a low-built, log-shaped structure with a shingle roof sporting three triple-barred crosses. It is the oldest extant building in the Anchorage area and houses rare icons brought from Russia before the 1867 sale to the United States. It forms the centerpiece of **Eklutna Historical Park** (mid-May to mid-Sept daily 8am–6pm, last tour 5.15pm; $6; ☎688-6026; *www.eklutna .com*), a fascinating blend of Russian and Athapascan culture, with a cemetery, densely packed with the state's finest collection of **spirit houses**. There are more than eighty of these mostly waist-high huts, their yellow, red, blue, green, or even candy-striped pitched-roofs topped with a crenellated crest in technicolor. In place of the familiar headstone, tradition requires that when an Orthodox Russian Athapascan dies a new blanket is placed over the grave and a three-bar Orthodox cross is planted at the foot. Forty days after burial, the deceased's family builds a "spirit house" over the grave using the family's traditional colors to denote who is interred. Other clues to look for are a small house within a larger one, thought to indicate joint burial of a mother and her child, and a house surrounded by a picket fence indicating that the dead person was neither Tanaina or Russian Orthodox.

The same exit from the Glenn Hwy accesses **Thunderbird Falls**, a pretty 200-foot, two-leap cataract (an icefall in winter) at the end of a mile-long trail through birch forest. Wilder scenery is on hand nearby at the end of the ten-mile, unpaved Eklutna Lake Road, which winds east into the heart of Chugach Mountains. It ends at **Eklutna Lake**, a bush-girt mountain reservoir which provides tap water to half of Anchorage. It is bordered by the sizeable *Eklutna Lake* campground ($10 includes parking fee; pump water; fire rings), a summer-only ranger station, and the Eklutna Lake Recreation Area (parking $5 a day), where you can **rent kayaks and bikes** (late May to early Sept Mon–Fri 11am–7pm, Sat & Sun 10am–8pm). Cyclists typically make for the gentle **Eklutna Lakeside Trail** (12.7 miles one-way; 300ft ascent), which follows an abandoned roadbed for seven miles to the head of the lake and is open to ATVs from Sunday to Wednesday. On Thursdays, Fridays, and Saturdays bikers and hikers have it to themselves. Walkers can continue beyond the end of the abandoned roadbed along Eklutna

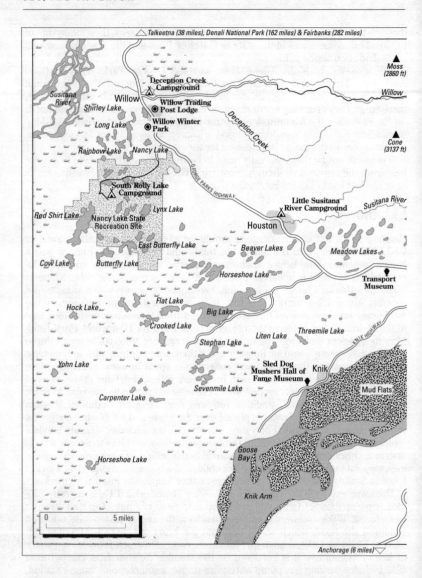

△ Talkeetna (38 miles), Denali National Park (162 miles) & Fairbanks (282 miles)

Glacier Trail, which turns rockier and tougher as you approach the snout of the Eklutna Glacier across glacial gravel bars which were under hundreds of feet of ice as little as fifty years ago. Here, the Mitre and Benign Peak rise over 6000 feet above you and views of steep canyon walls and waterfalls surround. The Lakeside Trail provides access to two further trails: five miles along Eklutna Lake you can strike off north up the arduous **Bold Ridge Trail** (7 miles round-trip; 4–6hr; 2500ft ascent), which climbs up to open tundra inviting further exploration for the

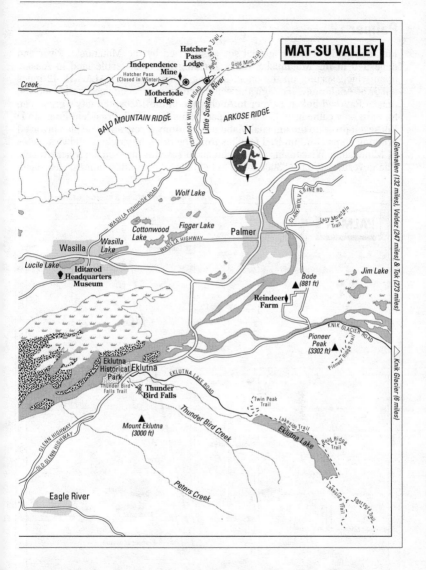

committed; and at the 10.5-mile mark the narrow **East Fork Trail** (13 miles round-trip; 6–8hr; 700ft ascent) spurs off along, unsurprisingly, the East Fork of the Eklutna River fording numerous streams.

The whole area is perhaps best explored by spending a night in one of the simple **backcountry camping** areas, each equipped with fire rings and nearby stream water. Two sites are located along the Glacier Trail and there's another at the southern end of Eklutna Lake.

Palmer

For thousands of years, glacial silt was carried by the Matanuska River and deposited in the Matanuska Valley, creating the most fertile land in Alaska, upon which sprung up the small farming community of **PALMER**, 42 miles north of Anchorage. Though the soil's fertility was recognized early, and the Alaska Railroad linked Palmer to Anchorage in the 1920s, the city's great leap forward only came in 1935 when, as part of his New Deal, President Franklin D Roosevelt drew up the unusual Matanuska **Colony Program**. The plan involved bringing some two hundred families from the drought-stricken Midwest states of Minnesota, Wisconsin, and Michigan to resettle here on forty-acre tracts. The government gave $3000 loans to help the settlers build homes, clear land,

PALMER

N

△ Musk Ox Farm (7 miles), Hatcher Pass (20 miles) & Glenallen (144 miles)

WEST ARCTIC AVENUE — EAST ARCTIC AVENUE

Pioneer Motel

■ Laundromat

W. BLUEBERRY AVE.

E. BLUEBERRY AVE

E. BLUEBERRY AVE

W. BIRCH AVENUE

E. BIRCH AVE

W. COTTONWOOD AVE.

E. COTTONWOOD AVENUE

W. CEDAR AVE

W. DOGWOOD AVENUE

E. DOGWOOD AVENUE

Vagabond Blues ■

W. DAHLIA AVENUE

E. DAHLIA AVENUE

Bank

W. EVERGREEN AVENUE

Library

Colony Memorial ●

Colony Inn & The Inn Cafe ●

E. ELMWOOD AVENUE

W. ELMWOOD AVENUE

ⓘ Visitor Center & Pioneer Museum

W. FIREWEED AVENUE

E. FIREWEED AVENUE

GLENN HIGHWAY

S. COBB STREET

BAILEY STREET

S. ALASKA STREET

S. BONANZA STREET

E. CEDAR AVENUE

S. VALLEY WAY

S. DENALI STREET

S. EKLUTNA STREET

S. DENALI ST.

S. LUCAS STREET

S. DIMOND STREET

COLONY WAY

PALMER-WASILLA ROAD

DARON DR.

Wasilla (12 miles) ◁

▷ Matanuska River Park (800 yds), A Lazy Acres (7 miles) & Reindeer Farm (7 miles)

0 — 400 yds

State Fairground ▽ (2 miles) & Anchorage (42 miles)   ▽ State Fairground (2 miles)

MAT-SU'S MEGA-VEGGIES AND THE ALASKA STATE FAIR

The happy convergence of twenty hours of summer sunlight and a deep, rock-less bed of glacial loess (a type of glacial soil) allows the Mat-Su Valley to produce **gargantuan vegetables**, notably freak cabbages weighing in at close to a hundred pounds, as well as six-pound onions, eight-pound carrots and once, a single pea pod weighing a quarter of a pound. Astoundingly, the record pumpkin for the area is almost 350 pounds.

Produce that is merely huge can be bought from pick-your-own farms all round the district – peaches, apples, and other fruit work out at bargain prices – but to see record-breakers you'll need to go to Palmer's **Alaska State Fair** (Mon–Fri noon–10pm, Sat & Sun 10am–10pm; $6 weekdays, $8 weekends; ☎1-800/850-3247, *www.alaskastatefair.org*), held at the State Fairground two miles south along the Glenn Hwy, on the ten days leading up to Labor Day. Though it is really just Palmer's annual fair, it fights off all contenders to the "state" title by being by far the biggest around, with just about every sector of the Alaskan economy and arts scene represented; in fact it is hard to find a band playing anywhere else in the state when the fair is on. Expect everything from staples like monster-truck displays, rodeo, and lumberjacking competitions to Native dance and blanket tossing, and oddball events like the Husband Holler, the potato-stacking contest and a competition in which the organizers grow a potato patch, then contestants dig as fast as they can striving to fill their two-gallon bucket first. Some kind of historical authenticity is lent by the homesteading events like wood splitting and water hauling, but highlight for the valley growers is the giant vegetable weigh-off.

and eat until their first crop came in. In return the government received $5 an acre for the land and ran a highly un-Alaskan cooperative system whereby the crops grown became the property of the group who shared the profits. Though glad to escape their dusty farms back home, many felt the disapproval of the original homesteaders who believed the newcomers were getting something for nothing.

The newcomers eschewed the log-cabin customs, and constructed frame houses and gambrel-roofed barns of their home states, each with jutting eaves supporting winch jibs. These **colony barns** and their associated grain silos are very much a feature of Palmer today, but improved transportation made goods shipped in from Seattle and elsewhere increasingly competitive and farms were steadily sold off and subdivided. Much of the best farm land in the state is now prime real estate and, though Alaskan supermarkets stock local dairy products, most of the ingredients now come from the Lower 48.

One crop you won't find on display, but which undoubtedly thrives due to the same beneficial agricultural conditions, is **Matanuska Thunderfuck**, revered throughout the land as some of the strongest marijuana anywhere.

The town and around

Palmer is an Alaskan rarity in that it has a real living center with a neatly maintained train station, visitor center and a grid of small streets with shops and a steady trickle of pedestrians. Almost everything worth seeing lies outside town, but you can pass a pleasant few minutes in the small, free pioneer **museum** downstairs in the visitor center (see overleaf), then follow a self-guided walking tour through the town. Outside the visitor center, there's a demonstration patch of oversized vegetable (see box overleaf), and across the road the **Colony Memorial**, a sculpture dedicated to the first 202 families.

The place that really draws visitors to these parts is the **Musk Ox Farm**, Glenn Hwy Mile 50, just east of town (May to late Sept daily 10am–6pm; tours every half-hour; $8; *www.muskoxfarm.org*), where you are guided past a few dozen of these ancient straggly beasts grazing on the lush pasture. They're often pretty inactive in the warmth of a Mat-Su summer day – early morning is best to see them move about – but they manage to look cute enough in a dopey sort of way. They aren't just here for tourists to pet though. In 1930, anthropologist John Teal envisaged helping the people of the Arctic to maintain some financial independence by setting up a cottage industry based on **quiviut**, the uniquely warm and soft under-wool shed each spring by musk oxen. These ancient animals were long since extinct in Alaska when Teal introduced 34 specimens from Greenland and set about breeding them and reintroducing them into the wild: 3000 of their descendants now roam the arctic tundra. Gathered quiviut is spun into fine yarn and sent, undyed, to scattered western Alaskan villages where knitted garments are produced using patterns individual to that village and based on motifs once common on clothing and baskets made there. Altogether about 3000 garments are made and sold through the shop here at the Musk Ox Farm and at Oomingmak Musk Ox Producers Cooperative in Anchorage (see "Shopping," p.210). They often sell out, but you might not find yourself too disappointed at missing out on that $300 fawny-brown shawl.

Domesticated wild animals are also on display some seven miles south of Palmer on one of the original Colony farms now operating as the **Reindeer Farm**, Bodenburg Butte Road, off the Old Glenn Hwy (May–Sept daily 10am–6pm; $5), where hand feeding and photo-taking is very much the order of the day. The journey out here is made considerably more worthwhile by the short hike up **Bodenburg Butte** (see box, opposite), which starts along Bodenburg Butte Road, almost opposite.

A further three miles south, the Old Glenn Hwy crosses the Knik River and the unpaved 11-mile Knik Glacier Road runs up beside the river past the **Pioneer Ridge** trailhead (see box, opposite) towards Knik Glacier, which can be visited on four-hour airboat tours run by Knik Glacier Adventures (☎746-5133; $65).

Practicalities

Alaskon Express (daily from Anchorage and Valdez; ☎1-800/478-6388) and Alaska Direct (Wed, Fri & Sun between Anchorage and Tok; ☎1-800/770-6652) **buses** will dropoff on request, but without your own transport there is little point stopping in Palmer. Both stop outside the **visitor center**, 723 S Valley Way at Fireweed Avenue (May to mid-Sept daily 8am–7pm; mid-Sept to April Mon–Fri 9am–5pm; ☎745-2880, fax 746-4164, *www.palmerchamber.org*), which is close to some good central **accommodation**. One option is the basic but clean and cable-equipped *Pioneer Motel*, 124 W Arctic Ave (☎745-3425, fax 746-0777; ③), and there's also the superior *Colony Inn*, 325 E Elmwood (☎ & fax 745-3330 or 1-800/478-7666; ④), a lovingly restored teachers' dormitory from the Colony days, with attractive rooms dressed in unfussy period decor. There are several good B&Bs hereabouts, not least the very friendly and welcoming *A Lazy Acres*, Helmaur Place (☎745-6340; ④), seven miles northeast of town up on Lazy Mountain; consider, too, staying at *Hatcher Pass Lodge*, up by the Independence Mine (see p.338). **Campers** should make for *Matanuska River Park*, 350 E Arctic Ave ($10) with wooded sites, showers for $2 and a day-use area all located half a mile east of town on the Old Glenn Hwy.

HIKES AROUND PALMER

The proximity to towns and farms makes Palmer an unusual hiking area in the Alaskan context, but the trails listed here (and those in Hatcher Pass, see box, p.339) easily justify an extra day or so in the area. The listed distances and times are for the round-trip.

Bodenburg Butte (2 miles; 1hr–1hr 30min; 800ft ascent). The shortest of the local hikes, and steep too, but with a lower vantage point giving great views of virgin forest and the surrounding mountains. The trailhead is right by the Reindeer Farm, (see opposite). Parking $3 per car.

Lazy Mountain Trail (5 miles; 3–5hr; 3600ft ascent). The best and most convenient hike near Palmer offers outstanding views of the valley and farmland. Parts can be pretty steep but it is worth it. The trail can be turned into a full day of hiking by combining it with other trails described in the free *Lazy Mountain & Morgan Horse Trails* leaflet available from the Palmer visitor center. To reach the trailhead take Arctic Avenue east across the Matanuska River, then a mile along Clark–Wolverine Road and right onto Huntley Road. The trailhead is at the end, a mile or so along.

Pioneer Ridge Trail (12 miles; 6–8hr; 5100ft ascent). A fairly tough day-long hike requiring reasonable fitness to slog up through steep underbrush, though it eases as it reaches alder thicket and becomes almost gentle on the subalpine tundra approaching the high point of 5300 feet on the ridge below Pioneer Peaks. Progress beyond here requires rock-climbing skills and tackle, but it is still a rewarding hike with long views to the north and west, and the chance to see Dall sheep, moose, and black bears. The trailhead is four miles along Knik Glacier Road.

There are several reasonable **places to eat** in the vicinity, but few really worth seeking out. The big surprise is *Vagabond Blues Café*, 642 S Alaska St (☎745-2233), a cool, bohemian kind of place with a huddle of old worktables (one dedicated to chess playing) for sipping good coffee or tucking into great salads and soups, many of them vegetarian. At weekends this is the place to come for live music, usually acoustic and sometimes with a small cover charge. *The Inn Café*, 325 E Elmwood Ave (☎746-6118), in the *Colony Inn* building, is more formal, even touching on prim, but they bake their own pies and pastries, and serve good-value lunch and dinner specials ($8 and $10 respectively); entrees such as New York steak or Cajun shrimp stir fry go for $17–22.

Downtown Palmer has a **bank** and ATM at 110 S Colony Way; a laundry at 127 S Alaska St; a **library** with free **Internet access** at 655 S Valley Way; a **post office** at the corner of S Cobb Street and W Cedar Avenue; and levies a three percent sales **tax** plus a five percent bed tax.

Wasilla, Knik, and around

At first glance **WASILLA** (pronounced Wa-SILL-a), forty miles north of Anchorage, embodies all that is wrong with the kind of urban sprawl so prevalent in America today: countless strip malls line almost eight miles of the Parks Hwy north of the "Y" junction, and the only indication it has any center at all is the presence of a train station. The blight though is only skin-deep, with some beautiful lakes just off the highway and a couple of good museums nearby. Provided you've got wheels it can make an agreeable place from which to explore the Mat-Su

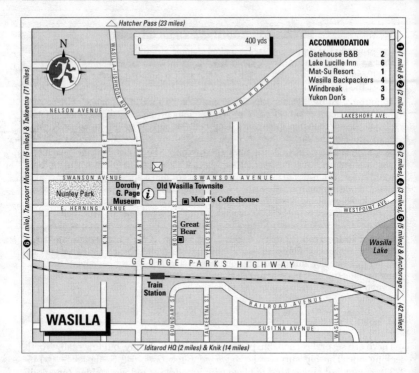

Valley: after all you are only ten miles west of Palmer and Hatcher Pass is close at hand.

Wasilla started out in the late nineteenth century as a way station and service center on the Carle Wagon Road between Knik – then a significant tidal port – and the mines at Hatcher Pass. With the advent of Anchorage and the construction of the railway, Knik's *raison d'être* disappeared and Wasilla became just a minor stop on the Anchorage to Fairbanks line. That all changed with the construction of the George Parks Hwy in the early 1970s, and the threat of the capital moving to Willow (see p.340). All of a sudden this moribund village became hot property and Wasilla began its rampant growth fueled by the overspill from Anchorage.

The blue-ribbon event on Wasilla's calendar is the **Iditarod Restart**, held the day after the first Saturday in March when dogs, sleds, and mushers all get bundled off the trucks that have brought them from the previous day's ceremonial run to Eagle River, and kick off the race proper (see p.336).

Museums

The **Dorothy G Page Museum**, 323 Main St (mid-May to mid-Sept Tues–Sat 10am–6pm; $3; ☎373-9071), does a good job of capturing and presenting historic Wasilla. The main body of the museum comprises an eclectic assortment of everything from a Native sealskin coat with patchwork trim to a translucent white raincoat made from walrus intestines, to simple dogsleds and material on Balto, the dog famed for his role in the epidemic-busting serum run (see p.468). In the basement there's all manner of gold paraphernalia including a mock hard-rock mine akin to those up at Hatcher Pass and an assay office where the quality of the gold was measured. The most diverting stuff is out the back in the **Old Wasilla Townsite**, a corral of half a dozen mostly log-built structures relocated here from around the region. Alongside Wasilla's first one-room schoolhouse and huge sauna and community bathhouse is the Capital Site Cabin prematurely built for Governor Jay Hammond at Willow when it was thought the state capital was going to move there.

Five miles north of town, the privately run **Museum of Alaska Transportation & Industry**, Mile 47 Parks Hwy (May–Sept daily 9am–6pm; Oct–April Tues–Sat 9am–5pm; $5; *www.alaska.net/~rmosrris/mati1.htm*), hoards just about everything imaginable to do with transport in the state: a Native umiak, homesteading sleds, the first motorized pump fire engine to work in Anchorage, the first hang glider to be launched off the summit of Denali, and a line of restored railroad carriages. It can all be a bit overwhelming, unless you can engage the deeply passionate and knowledgeable owner in some contextualizing conversation.

Back by the train station in Wasilla, Knik Road runs fourteen miles southwest to the tiny settlement of **KNIK** (ka-Nick), a former Russian mission site and one-time transport and supply hub for the gold towns of the Interior. Stop along the way at the **Iditarod Headquarters**, Mile 2.2 Knik Rd (mid-May to mid-Sept daily 8am–7pm; mid-Sept to mid-May Mon–Fri 8am–5pm; donation appreciated), the state's foremost shrine to the Iditarod Sled Dog Race (see box, overleaf). One wall is like a giant scrapbook of newspaper clippings reporting on the 1925 Serum Run and the early years of the Iditarod; there's also a sled with the traces that attach to the dog team and the large bag for carrying gear, myriad trophies – including the winner's trophy which is always kept here – and the 23-minute video *Beyond Courage*, which successfully captures the spirit of the race. Look too for the immortalized Togo, stuffed and displayed nearby, who led the final sprint across the ice into Nome during the Serum Run. Outside, beside a cabin decked-out like an Iditarod checkpoint, you can board a wheeled sled ($5) and get towed around a set course through the woods.

If the Iditarod Headquarters has whetted your appetite for more, continue twelve miles to Knik itself and the **Knik Museum and Musher's Hall of Fame** (June–Aug Wed–Sun noon–6pm; $2; to visit off-season call ☎376-2005), its lower floor packed with pioneer artifacts that seem little different from what your grandmother might have used, illustrating just how young Alaska is. The more diverting material is upstairs in the Iditarod Hall of Fame, a homage to the race which annually comes right past the door of the museum. Trophies, cups, and medals abound along with maps of the two main routes, some excellent photos of mushers in action, charcoal drawings of the winners up to 1984, and the winning sled from the first full-blown Iditarod in 1973, a lightweight sporty-looking affair.

Practicalities

If you are traveling by train or bus there is little point getting off: you'll find yourself stranded a fair distance from anywhere you want to be, though you could walk to the Dorothy Page Museum and visit the primitive **visitor center** inside (same hours). **Accommodation** is reasonably priced, and often nicely sited beside the lakes off the highway. There's the low-cost *Wasilla Backpackers Hostel*, 3950 Carefree Drive (☎357-3699, *www.wasillabackpackers.com*; closed Oct–April; beds $22, room ②), in a spacious home surrounded by birch trees about fifty yards off the Parks Hwy at Mile 39. It is clean, the atmosphere is relaxed, dorms have beds

THE IDITAROD

On the first Saturday in March, the world's press descends on downtown Anchorage for the start of the **Iditarod**, the highlight of Alaska's winter calendar and the world's longest dog-sled race, across the barren wastes of the Interior to Nome on the Bering Sea. Every year since its inception in 1973 mushers from all over the US – mostly Alaska but also many of the northern Lower 48, and from countries as far afield as Scotland, Spain, and Australia – have got behind their teams of up to sixteen dogs. The "official" length is 1049 miles – a round thousand plus a reminder that this is the 49th state – but it is actually considerably longer: the shorter northern route through Ruby, followed in even-numbered years is around 1150 miles, while the 1180-mile southern route traced in odd-numbered years passes through the gold-rush ghost town of Iditarod – a mispronunciation of "Hidedhod," Ingalik for "a distant place."

For mushers it is the culmination of weeks of logistical preparation on top of several years learning how to handle and care for their dogs. Breeding plays a major part; only the perfect team will do for negotiating this winter-only route over two mountain ranges, across muskeg, along 150 miles of the frozen Yukon River and across the iced-in Norton Sound. Temperatures well below freezing are often exacerbated by gale-force winds reducing the visibility on days already short of daylight, but competitors are rewarded by wonderful scenery and the overwhelming sense of accomplishment. Certainly the financial rewards are not the motivation for most, though the first prize is about $50,000 and a shiny new truck. Only a handful of mushers make a viable living from their kennels and winnings, and despite a purse distributed between the first twenty teams only a few might hope to recoup their costs for running the race. The cost of maintaining a support crew and supplying dog food along the route typically exceeds $15,000.

The Iditarod had its genesis around the beginning of the twentieth century when fledgling gold towns were linked by a winter mail and supply route – mail and food in, gold out – from the ice-free port of Seward, through the Interior mining camps to Nome. By the late 1960s, four decades of reliable air transport had done away with the need for regular dog-sled routes to remote communities, and the advent of affordable snow machines was threatening to hammer the final nail in the dog-sledding coffin. Then in 1967, historian **Dorothy Page** sought to enliven the Wasilla-Knik Centennial commemoration by running a dog-sled race: a 56-mile sprint was run for a purse of $25,000. She soon joined forces with local musher, **Joe Reddington Senior** – the "Father of the Iditarod" – and together they began promoting their idea of retracing the old mail route and capturing the spirit of the Serum Run (see box, p.468) when an influenza vaccine was whisked across the Interior to Nome by a relay of dog teams during an epidemic in 1925.

Finally in March 1973 the first full-blown Iditarod set off along more or less the modern route from Knik to Nome. Twenty-two mushers (around half the field)

rather than bunks, and you can rent bikes ($10 a half-day) and surf the Net. The lakeside *Mat-Su Resort*, 1850 Bogard Rd (☎376-3228, fax 376-7781, *www .alaskan.com/matsuresort*; ④), offers luxury rooms along with pedalboat and jet-ski rental. Further along the same road, about a mile and a half from the train station, nestles the equally appealing *Gatehouse B&B*, 2500 Bogard Rd (☎376-5960 or 1-888/866-9326, fax 376-6756, *www.gatehousealaska.com*; ④), where the best spot to rest your head is the lakefront cabin. Fairview Loop Road, which leaves the

astounded doubters by completing the course that year. Though they were most definitely races, in the early years they were also endurance events; just completing the course was regarded as an honorable achievement. Today, everything has become much more professional, the degree of organization (at least in the eyes of some critics) taking away from the true musher spirit and turning it into a carefully managed series of short sprints. The criticism is overly harsh, but some purists prefer the rigors of the Yukon Quest (see "Winter in Fairbanks" box, p.424), or other long races such as the Kuskokwim 300.

Since 1983 the race has started in Anchorage, something of a circus with truckloads of snow being dumped along 4th Avenue for the teams which set off at two-minute intervals. The absence of a suitable route north of Eagle River means that teams are then trucked 35 miles to Wasilla for the staggered start the following morning. The last checkpoint accessible on the road system is Knik, fourteen miles southwest of Wasilla, but there is more than just wilderness up ahead. The trail is broken by volunteers on snow machines, and check points are attended by volunteers supported up by a fleet of bush planes ferrying race organizers and veterinary staff. Far fewer women compete than men, but from 1985 to 1990 all but one race was won by a woman, four of them by Susan Butcher, a record only beaten by Rick Swenson, who has won five times, with victories in three separate decades.

Prizes aren't only awarded at the finish line. There's one for the first to Unalakleet, the first to the Yukon River gets a seven-course meal from the chef of a top Anchorage hotel, and there's another prize for the first to the halfway point, considered the halfway jinx – only three of its recipients subsequently went on to win at Nome. In recognition of one of the great mushers of the Serum Run, the Leonhard Seppala Humanitarian Award is presented to the musher who exhibits the most concern for his animals, according to the votes of fellow mushers. In fact **animal care** is a sensitive issue. For the vast majority of mushers, the dogs are their lives, but the occasional death has led to usually-unfounded accusations of mistreatment. Consequently regulations require mushers to always have a supply of booties for the dogs' feet and enforce compulsory layovers – two of eight hours and one of twenty-four – as well as insisting the sleds carry a heavy sleeping bag, an axe, snowshoes, a cooking stove, a pot, a veterinarian notebook and dog food at all times; the last remaining nod to self-sufficiency.

Over the years the Iditarod has developed it's own lore. As the mushers leave Anchorage the "Widow's Lamp" is lit in Nome and attached to the official finish line, the Burl Arch. To honor all who complete the course, it remains lit until the last musher – known as the "red lantern" – arrives, a link to the days when dog teams were the only means of transport and a guiding light was hung in the window of roadhouses.

The official Iditarod Web site, loaded with information on its history, the course, and past winners is at *www.iditarod.com*.

Parks Hwy further south at Mile 38, leads a mile and a half to *Yukon Don's* (☎1-800/478-7472 or ☎ & fax 376-7472, *www.yukondon.com*; ④), one of Alaska's best-known B&Bs set in a converted milk barn with a couple of lovely large suites (⑤), four themed shared-bath rooms (④; go for the Iditarod one), a cozy cabin, and a spacious lounge with panoramic views of the surrounding valleys and mountains. The cheapest hotel rooms are just south of town at the *Windbreak Hotel*, Mile 40.5 Parks Hwy (☎376-4484; ③), which has ten clean, simple rooms and a café renowned for sating serious appetites with low-cost specials. Elsewhere, **eating** is largely a matter of choosing your favorite franchise, though there are a few alternatives. For coffee, cakes, soups, sandwiches, and Internet access visit *Mead's Coffeehouse*, 405 E Herning St (☎357-5633), just behind the Dorothy Page Museum; try the *Great Bear*, 238 N Boundary (☎373-4782) just nearby, for burgers, salads, substantial entrees ($15–18) and tasty made-on-site microbrews; or drive out to *Lake Lucille Inn*, Mile 43.5 Parks Hwy (☎373-1776), a Best Western hotel with a lovely deck overlooking the water, for a relaxing meal; choices include beef teriyaki, stir-fried scallops, sandwiches, and burgers. For **entertainment**, try *Mead's*, which occasionally has live music.

Hatcher Pass and Independence Mine

Even if you don't plan to stop in the Mat-Su area, set aside half a day to drive the **Hatcher Pass** road, which twists and turns for fifty mostly unpaved miles through picturesque valleys, then high above the tree line among the shattered granite peaks of the Talkeetna Mountains, topping out in the high tundra of the 3886-foot pass.

The route was built as a wagon road to serve hard-rock gold mines now preserved in the **Independence Mine State Historic Park** (June to early Sept daily 11am–7pm; $5 per vehicle; ☎745-2827), a cluster of semi-dilapidated houses and mine workings spread 3500-feet up in a beautiful alpine bowl twenty miles north of Palmer. It is a spectacular place, the fragile timbers and winding gear cast long shadows in the late afternoon sun while the silver-and-red paintwork of the old bunkhouses stand in dramatic contrast to the blue of the sky and the snow-capped peaks. Prospectors in the Matanuska Valley first found rough flakes of gold in Willow Creek in 1897 and surmised its source lay high in the mountains. By 1906 the first shafts were being sunk and miners were ferreting along tunnels in search of gold-bearing quartz veins. Large scale investment soon put the grub-stake miner out of business, and before long the whole area was riddled with holes and humming with activity.

It all came to a halt in 1942 when the government decreed that gold mining was not essential to the war effort, and pretty much overnight the place was abandoned, leaving everything where it stood. Over the decades much was allowed to artfully rot away, but since the 1980s various bunkhouses and workshops have been restored. The former manager's house is now the **visitor center** and the place to head for some town history. Guided tours (daily: 1.30pm & 3.30pm, weekends additional tour at 4.30pm; $3) start here and give you a chance to explore inside some of the buildings otherwise out of bounds to those who just choose to wander around outside.

Palmer–Fishhook Road and Wasilla–Fishhook Road head north from their respective towns and join to become Fishhook–Willow Road at the Little Susitna River. For the next six miles it passes through some gorgeous country with the tumbling waters of the river framed by rocky spires poking up through aspen and cottonwood. The *Motherlode Lodge*, Mile 14 Palmer–Fishhook Rd (☎746-1464 or 1-877/745-6171, *www.motherlodelodge.com*; ④), offers a solid bed and continental breakfast, as well as fine dining at weekends, and marks the start of **Gold Mint Trail** (see box, opposite).

A mile before the mine lies *Hatcher Pass Lodge*, Mile 18 Fishhook–Willow Rd (☎745-5879, fax 745-1200, *www.hatcherpasslodge.com*; cabins ⑤, rooms ③), a

---

HIKES AROUND HATCHER PASS

Hatcher Pass, and the area around the Independence Mine in particular, invites freelance exploration: equip yourself with food, drink, sunscreen, and a camera and head for the hills. Dangerous old mine workings and loose rocks are hazards, but if you keep your eyes open and act sensibly you can have a fabulous afternoon up here. Lower down there are a couple more formal trails accessed from the Fishhook–Willow road. The listed distances and times are round-trip.

Gold Mint Trail (12 miles; 4–6hr). An easy and delightful trail which follows the right bank of the Little Susitna River through a gently sloping valley past the ruined remains of the Lonesome Mine and on to the river's source at Mint Glacier. The trailhead is opposite *Motherlode Lodge*.

Reed Lakes Trail (7 miles; 3–5hr). Another fairly easy hike starting along a broad track then climbing to the head of the valley and Reed Lakes. The trailhead is just over a mile up Archangel Road which leads up Archangel Valley half a mile uphill from *Motherlode Lodge*.

---

group of modern and spacious cabins with limited facilities (but with a separate sauna building) clustered around an A-frame restaurant (open all day, all year) fabulously sited on the rim of the valley looking down to Palmer far below. The rooms are very popular with folk up here for the **Nordic trail skiing** in winter, as is the restaurant, where the stupendous view easily justifies the slightly inflated price of coffee, gourmet pizza, soup, and assorted vegetarian dishes.

To continue over Hatcher Pass (typically open late June to mid-Sept but sometimes longer) **to Willow** take the road opposite *Hatcher Pass Lodge* which climbs steeply up to the pass and Summit Lake, a beautiful high-country tarn. From here the road descends, largely following the cascading Willow Creek through beautiful open mountain scenery, past the *Last Chance Coffee House & RV Park* then rejoining the tarmac for the last ten miles to the George Parks Hwy.

Along the George Parks Highway: Big Lake, Nancy Lake, and Willow

There's not a lot in between Wasilla and Fairbanks, some three hundred miles north, save the Alaska Range, Denali National Park, a lot of spruce forest and some beautiful lakes. The most popular of these is **BIG LAKE**, on a side road fifteen miles west of Wasilla (at Mile 52.3), a large sheet of water lined by log houses and vacation homes typically with a float plane or boat tethered alongside. It's big with weekenders from Anchorage but unless you've specifically come to motor about on the water (in which case you'll need your own gear) then there isn't a lot of reason to leave the highway: there are prettier and quieter lakes not far ahead.

Campers may want to rest up at the large, wooded, and peaceful *Little Susitna River* campground, Mile 57.3 Parks Hwy ($8; tap water), at the hamlet of **Houston**, or press on to **Nancy Lake State Recreation Area**, accessed by a good gravel road off the Parks Hwy at Mile 67.2. Rolling hillsides make up the landscape, with the low ridges and hummocks providing glimpses through the trees of an almost unfathomable network of small lakes and sloughs linked by small creeks. If you are equipped with camping gear and mosquito repellent this makes perfect canoeing country and is good too for a little fishing or easy hiking. The large and beautifully sited *South Rolly Lake* campground, six miles off the highway (well water; outhouse; fire rings), is the place to base yourselves either for the day (parking $5) or overnight ($10 camping fee includes day-parking). **Hikers** should find the nearby trailhead for **Red Shirt Lake Trail** (6 miles round-trip; 3–4hr), the pick of several well-signposted local trails, which sticks to higher ground and ends up at a primitive campsite by Red Shirt Lake. Here you can continue using **canoes** secured at the lakeside and rented from Tippecanoe ($18 for 8hr, $25 per 24hr day, $70 for up to 7 days; ☎ & fax 495-6688, *www.paddlealaska.com*), who have a hut by the *South Rolly Lake* campground, and an office at Mile 66.6 of the Parks Hwy. Canoeing on Red Shirt Lake opens up access to four highly popular, six-berth backcountry **cabins** ($35 a night; reserve through the Public Lands Information Center in Anchorage ☎269-8400), each with a wood stove but little else: bring everything but your tent.

There are enough waterways here to keep you entertained for a week or more, but most will be satisfied with the popular two-day loop of the **Lynx Lake Canoe Route** which pieces together fourteen lakes by means of short well-marked portages and starts at the Tanaina Lake Canoe Trailhead 4.6 miles off the Parks Hwy. Primitive campsites and backcountry cabins (including an especially beautiful one beside James Lake) dot the route, which can be extended almost infinitely.

Willow and north to Talkeetna Junction

Periodically, pretty much everyone except Juneau residents raise the issue of moving the state capital to somewhere more accessible. Every few years a referendum gets defeated, but in the mid 1970s – when the state was flushed by the promise of untold oil riches – this process went further than usual and **WILLOW**, at Mile 69 on the Parks Hwy, was selected as the preferred site for state headquarters. Its location between Anchorage and Fairbanks, and the proximity to the rail line and the newly completed highway swung the decision away from other contenders. However, opponents distorted the projected costs into the billions and the electorate soundly defeated the funding referendum in 1982. John McPhee's book *Coming into the Country* has extensive coverage of the issue.

Despite Willow's ambitions, you'll barely notice the town as you drive through and on a clear day you are much more likely to gaze out at Denali. Nonetheless, Willow refers to itself as "Alaska's State Capital – of recreation," a half-joking promotion of its boundless opportunities for fishing and winter activities. Though shared by several other towns, its claim to be "Alaska's dog mushing capital" is a justified one, with numerous successful kennels hereabouts including that of DeeDee Jonrowe, currently the state's top female musher.

Willow strings along the highway, where you'll find a grocery, an ATM, gas, and a post office – the very definition of small town. Being close to the western approach to Hatcher Pass you might want to spend the night here, and about the best **place to stay** is *Willow Winter Park*, Winter Park Road, at Mile 68.1 (☎495-7547, fax 495-7638, *winterpark@matnet.com*; ④), a pleasant B&B that has a beautiful deck (with hot tub) overlooking the calm Winter Park Lake. The last bit of Willow to remain by the tracks is the lakeside *Willow Trading Post Lodge*, Mile 69.5 Parks Hwy (☎495-6457 or 1-888/239-6679, *www.denalics.net/~keby*; rooms ④, cabins ①, RVs $15, tents $5), a traditional roadhouse with simple cabins, very spacious rooms, space for RVs and tents, sauna, laundry, and a bar. The restaurant sells reasonably priced and filling meals, though food gourmands are better served at the

Pioneer Lodge, Mile 71.4 Parks Hwy (☎495-6883, fax 495-6884; cabins ②, hookups $18, camping $12), an RV park, bar, and restaurant that produces surprisingly excellent food. Steaks, halibut, and salmon are still the staples but they're served with wild rice and fresh, al dente vegetables; the chicken masala is especially good and they have a selection of gourmet pizzas all for very reasonable prices.

North of Willow and the turnoff for Hatcher Pass (at Mile 71) it all gets pretty quiet for a while. You could stop at Lucky Husky Racing Kennel, Mile 80 (May–Sept daily 10am–6pm; ☎495-6470, fax 495-6471, *www.luckyhusky.com*), for a look around the kennels where all aspects of sled-dog rearing are covered ($6), or ride a wheeled sled around the kennel's three-quarter-mile course for $24. Alternatively, your kennel tour is included when staying at *Susitna Dog Tours B&B*, Mile 91.5 (☎495-6324, fax 495-6325, *susdog@matnet.com*, ④), a good spot for wintertime dog mushing (Dec to mid-March; $85). Otherwise, just continue on to Mile 98.7 where a side road leads you to one of Alaska's most inviting towns, Talkeetna.

Talkeetna

With dirt roads, log cabins, and an international flavor lent by the world's mountaineers congregating to take on Denali, **TALKEETNA** makes for an unusual and essential stop. The intimate downtown area, two blocks long and one wide, makes it the perfect place to kick back for a few days and stroll through the woods or along the sandy river banks.

Rumor has it that this eclectic hamlet was the model for Cicely in *Northern Exposure* and residents claim they can identify the source of every character – bar the retired astronaut. To its credit, Talkeetna doesn't use this as tour-bus bait, but that's not to say the tourists aren't coming. Several years as a hot destination on the travelers' grapevine have finally had an impact on the tourism mainstream spawning a head-in-a-moose photo opportunity and an abundance of tacky souvenir shops. Some years back, the big tour-company lobbyists got a new bus-accessible train station built on the edge of town, though a backlash has kept buses barred from the main street.

Apart from the charm of the town itself, the biggest attraction is **flightseeing around Mount McKinley**, though if you can time it right, drop by for the major summer celebration, the **Moose Dropping Festival** (☎733-2487), on the second weekend in July. The mention of the event caused one outraged citizen in Florida to reach for the phone and demand that the Chamber of Commerce tell him how far they actually drop the poor moose. However, the festival in fact focuses on the brown droppings that are revealed in their millions with the spring snow-melt and are sold throughout the town (complete with a heavy coat of varnish) for use as earrings, necklaces, and Talkeetna's iconic moose-dropping-on-a-stick "lollipoop." In addition to these lumps of Alaskana, the festival features dancing, drinking, and a moose-dropping throwing competition.

Talkeetna – rivers of plenty in Dena'ina – lies at the confluence of the Talkeetna, Chulitna, and Susitna rivers where the search for gold brought early prospectors in 1896. By 1910, Talkeetna had established itself as a riverboat station supplying miners and beaver trappers, and would have slipped into river-port obscurity were it not for its selection in 1915 as the local headquarters for the construction of the new Seward to Fairbanks railway. With the completion of the line, **President Warren Harding** visited Nenana to drive in the golden spike then

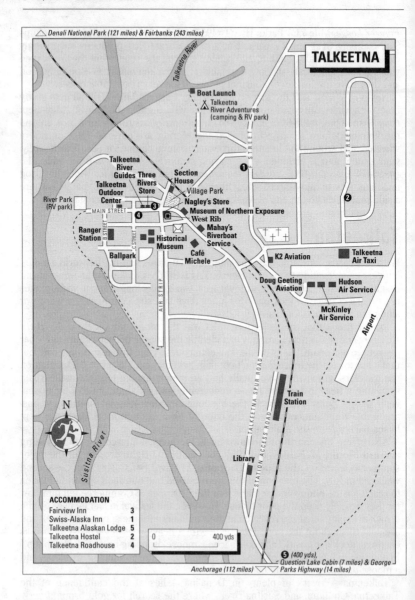

△ Denali National Park (121 miles) & Fairbanks (243 miles)

TALKEETNA

Boat Launch

△ Talkeetna River Adventures (camping & RV park)

Talkeetna River Guides

Three Rivers Store

Section House

Talkeetna Outdoor Center

Village Park

River Park (RV park)

Nagley's Store

MAIN STREET

Museum of Northern Exposure

West Rib

Ranger Station

Historical Museum

Mahay's Riverboat Service

Ballpark

Café Michele

K2 Aviation

Talkeetna Air Taxi

Doug Geeting Aviation

Hudson Air Service

McKinley Air Service

Airport

AIR STRIP

TALKEETNA SPUR ROAD

STATION ACCESS ROAD

Train Station

N

Susitna River

Library

ACCOMMODATION

Fairview Inn	3
Swiss-Alaska Inn	1
Talkeetna Alaskan Lodge	5
Talkeetna Hostel	2
Talkeetna Roadhouse	4

0   400 yds

❺ (400 yds), Question Lake Cabin (7 miles) & George
Anchorage (112 miles) ▽▽ Parks Highway (14 miles)

stopped by Talkeetna on his way south. He died a few days later apparently from complications of the flu, but Talkeetna residents take a perverse pride in variously claiming that he was supplied with poisoned tobacco, was fed a dodgy stew at the *Fairview Inn*, or that the conviviality of the place induced him to indulge in one too many drinks. For the next few decades all Talkeetna had was this manufactured claim to infamy; the population steadily declined, a process only reversed by road access from 1964.

Arrival and information

The daily northbound **train** from Anchorage and a southbound one from Fairbanks and Denali stop at the station, half a mile south, where Talkeetna Taxi & Tours ($2 per ride; ☎733-8294) call on their frequent fixed schedule around the main points of interest in town.

Arriving by road you turn off at the Parks Hwy by the **visitor center** (daily: mid-May to mid-June 10am–5pm; mid-June to late Sept 8am–8pm; ☎733-2688 or 1-800/660-2688, *www.alaskan.com/talkeetnadenali*) at Talkeetna Junction then drive fourteen miles into town. Most shuttle buses shoot straight along the Parks Hwy and drop off at Talkeetna Junction, from where it is usually easy to hitch into Talkeetna. The only daily **direct bus** to Talkeetna in the summer is The Park Connection (daily from Anchorage; $39; ☎1-800/208-0200), though during the climbing season (mid-April to mid-June) you can ride with Talkeetna Shuttle Service (once or twice daily from Anchorage; $40; ☎733-1725 or 1-888/288-6008).

Northbound travelers who can't afford the full train fare from Anchorage to Fairbanks should catch a bus to Talkeetna then ride the train on to Denali from here – the most spectacular section of the journey.

A couple of gift shops in town provide information, but pretty much everything you need is right in front of your eyes. Mountaineers and those gripped by the climbing lore of the Alaska Range should drop by the **Talkeetna Ranger Station** (late April to early Sept daily 8am–6pm; early Sept to late April Mon–Fri 8am–4.30pm; ☎733-2231, *www.nps.gov/dena/mountaineering*), staffed by well-informed mountain enthusiasts, and a comfortable spot for browsing the mountaineering magazines and planning your days ahead in Denali.

Accommodation

Don't expect to be pampered in Talkeetna, it's not that kind of place, but there is plenty of reasonably priced and welcoming accommodation around; not least the two characterful old inns. **Camping** is either at *Talkeetna River Adventures* (☎733-2604; $12) a short walk from town through the woods, with RV and tent sites, showers, and laundry facilities; or at the *Talkeetna River Park*, at the western end of main street ($10 paid to the summertime host). Both are geared towards RVs so, though not officially sanctioned, most campers simply stroll a hundred yards further west from the latter and pitch on the river flats. During the season, **climbers** can often find space to doss down in the hangar of the people they're flying with: ask in advance. For a touch of adventure, it is also worth considering staying in one of the **lakeside cabins** a short flight from town.

Fairview Inn, Main St (☎733-2423, fax 733-1067). This old inn built in 1923 as an overnight resting point on the railroad, is perfectly halfway between Fairbanks and Seward. It has only been minimally modernized since then, with seven smallish rooms all with shared bathrooms. Nice as these are, be warned that the bar swings most nights until the early hours so it can get loud; but once it closes you don't have far to stagger. ②.

Question Lake Cabin (☎733-4678, *hezim@matnet.com*). Fully equipped, woodstove-heated, self-catering cabin located seven miles south of Talkeetna and a mile off the Talkeetna Spur

Rd. Question Lake is glimpsed through the trees and there's a canoe for getting out on the water. Excellent rates for stays of more than two nights. ③.

Swiss-Alaska Inn (☎733-2424, fax 733-2425). Large inn with modern and comfortable rooms handily sited close to town and with its own restaurant (see p.346). ⑤.

Talkeetna Alaskan Lodge, Mile 12.5 Talkeetna Spur Rd (☎733-9500 or 1-888/959-9590, fax 263-5559 *www.talkeetnalodge.com*). Brand new hotel built of raw logs and riverstones high on a ridge behind town with wonderful views of the Alaska Range. Even if you're not staying it is worth popping up for a drink or to sit beside the central fireplace. The attractive rooms are to international standards with satellite TV, dataports, and coffee makers, but you'll have to reserve well in advance to get one of the Denali-view rooms in the main lodge. ⑦.

Talkeetna Hostel International, I St (☎733-4678, fax 733-4679, *www.akhostel.com*). Welcoming house in the woods about ten-minutes' walk from downtown with clean, comfortable dorm bunks for $23, a private double room (②), and a small but well-equipped kitchen. Closed Oct–March. Rooms ②, bunks ①.

Talkeetna Roadhouse, Main St (☎733-1351, fax 733-1353, *rdhouse@alaska.net*). Talkeetna's other old inn dates back to 1917, with simple, but tidy rooms sharing baths. With no bar, it doesn't have the robust atmosphere of the *Fairview* but easily makes up for it with very hospitable staff and a cozy lounge which, in spring and early summer, is full of climbers planning their summit strategy. They also maintain a four-berth bunk room ($21 per person) with sheets and towels provided, single rooms (①), doubles (②), and a couple of larger, deluxe rooms (④) which share a bathroom with a clawfoot tub. Closed on weekdays from mid-Sept to mid-April and all of Jan. ①–④.

Trapper John's B&B (☎ & fax 733-2353 or ☎ 1-800/735-2354, *www.alaska.net/~trapper*). A wonderfully rustic log cabin with full kitchen, located within easy walking distance of downtown and alongside the Susitna River. It sleeps up to four (⑤) but can be taken by two. Sourdough pancakes are served in the host's cabin nearby. ④.

The town and activities

Poking around town or walking out to some of the local lakes during the day then returning for a good chinwag in the bar that night is a great way to get a feel for the area. But to get a real taste of what Talkeetna has to offer you're going to have to get out of town, either by boat or plane, and there is no shortage of people ready to advise you and provide the logistics.

The town

As you walk around town it's worth looking in at the **Talkeetna Historical Society Museum**, one block south of Main Street (May–Sept daily 10.30am–5.30pm and occasional winter weekends; $2.50), a cluster of four buildings including **Ole Dahl Cabin**, the oldest building in town. Inside you'll find the usual collection of pioneer artifacts, photos of Talkeetna old-timers, coverage of the antics of local bush pilots, and plenty on the construction of the railroad. The highlight is the topographically accurate twelve-foot-square scale **model of McKinley** based on years of detailed aerial photography done by **Bradford Washburn**, an authority on just about anything to do with the mountain (see box, p.349). Excellent examples of the work which earned him the title of the "Ansel Adams of the North" are arranged around the walls, and there are more up at the *Talkeetna Alaskan Lodge* (see "Accommodation", above). Look too for the biographies of Denali heroes, press clippings, and letters such as one from the widow of Frederick Cook (see box, p.348) asking for Ray Genet's opinion on her husband's summit claim. His reply is instructive. Throughout the summer the free ranger program features hour-long talks on the mountain's conquerors using the McKinley model as a prop.

Climbers die almost every season on the mountain – approaching a hundred in total – adding more and more names to the memorial in the **Talkeetna Cemetery**, a salutary reminder that despite the climbing traffic, the presence of two ranger stations on the West Buttress route, and specialist rescue helicopters permanently on call, the mountain always has the last say. The cemetery contains the grave of "the climber's pilot" Don Sheldon and is the spiritual resting place of rumbustious mountaineer and longtime Denali guide Ray Genet whose body remains on Mount Everest.

On the road into town, there's the **Museum of Northern Adventure** (May to mid-Sept daily 10am–6pm; $2), displaying two dozen waxwork dioramas depicting archetypal Alaskan lifestyles; note the letter to the Presley estate for permission (refused) to display a moose-dropping Elvis.

Flightseeing

On a clear day – perhaps one in three in summer, more in winter – don't miss the mile hike (or drive) along the approach road to the **viewpoint** from where the Alaska Range, even sixty miles away, looks simply magnificent. You might have to wait around for a couple of days until the weather plays ball, but an essential part of any visit to Talkeetna is a **flightseeing** trip to Mount McKinley. Don't delay until you get to Denali; you are closer to the mountain here, and the weather tends to offer better viewing from the south side of the range. The five air-taxi companies (see "Listings," p.347) all run similar 4–5 passenger bush planes and offer similar packages at competitive prices: shop around and see who will offer you the best deal. Planes book up rapidly in summer, can be hard to fill after mid-September, and in May are mostly reserved by climbers who fly to the mountain from here.

You've got a choice of three different circuits all flying over the confluence of the Susitna, Chulitna, and Talkeetna rivers then across the Peters and Dutch hills in the Denali State Park to the Alaska Range itself. The most **basic package** (1hr; $90–100) links the Tokositna and Ruth glaciers on the southeast side of the mountain, and flies up Great Gorge, a deep vertical-walled canyon filled with ice to a depth of 4000 feet. The **mid-priced flight** (1hr 15min; $120–135) includes all the above but loops around the back of the 14,573ft Mount Hunter to the 10,000ft base camp on the Kahiltna Glacier – the 50-mile-long tongue of ice that slices through the Alaska Range separating Mount McKinley from the second highest peak in the range, Mount Foraker. If you can afford it, go for the **grand tour** (1hr 30min; $140–150), which climbs higher up the Kahiltna then makes a complete mountain circuit with views of the 14,000ft Wickersham Wall, and the main body of Denali National Park on the north side of the range. When snow conditions permit, you can add a **glacier landing** (additional $30–40) either on the Kahiltna Glacier (typically April to early July) or at the Don Sheldon Amphitheater (April–July, and occasionally into Aug), a glacial cirque at the head of the Ruth Glacier.

Other activities

Beyond their bread-and-butter McKinley flights, the air-taxi companies will turn their hands to just about anything that involves flying. Talkeetna Air Taxi in particular specialize in tailored one- and two-day **glacier treks**, snowshoeing, and high-country skiing with all equipment provided. Backcountry trips can also be organized, flying you in to a base camp for a few days. Prices depend greatly on numbers, need for guides, and flying time, but $1000 for three days snowshoeing, trekking, and glacier skiing is typical.

To get out on the water, visit Talkeetna River Guides (☎733-2677 or 1-800/353-2677, *www.talkeetnariverguides.com*), who offer a couple of **rafting trips**, either on the gentle 2hr natural-history float trip (mid-May to mid-Sept daily 11am, 2pm & 5pm; $44), or a 4hr run on the Chulitna River ($84) which includes a little gold panning. Rafters after a little more adventure can try fly-in overnight trips such as three days on the Talkeetna River ($1025), taking in the Talkeetna Canyon, fourteen miles of Class III and IV water – claimed to be the longest such whitewater stretch in the world. Talkeetna Air Taxis runs a similar trip for $875.

The less adventurous might prefer trips run by Mahay's Riverboat Service (mid-May to Sept; ☎733-2223 or 1-800/736-2210, *www.mahaysriverboat.com*), who run a fifty-seat jet boat on some of the same shallow rivers almost scraping gravel bars hoping to catch sight of moose and bald eagles: trips are for two hours ($45), four hours ($95), or the full six hours ($175) into the Susitna River's wonderfully scenic Devil's Canyon. They'll also do backcountry dropoffs for hunters and fishers. Alaska River Excursions (☎733-7487 or 1-888/301-4142) offer somewhat more personal service in smaller jet boats either up into the lower Class III reaches of the Talkeetna Canyon (2.5hr; $75) or up the Susitna River (3.5hr; $95).

If you just want to go your own way but need to buy **camping and mountaineering supplies**, or pick up some USGS topo maps, visit Talkeetna Outdoor Center, at the far end of Main Street (☎733-2230, fax 733-1434, *journeys@alaska.net*).

Eating and drinking

There isn't a very broad selection of places to go in Talkeetna, and many spots close quite early, so the pickings are often slim. If you're stocking up on groceries, head for the Three Rivers or Nagley's Store, which also sells good **coffee**. As for evening entertainment, it tends to revolve around the **bars** at the *Fairview Inn* and the *West Rib*.

Fairview Inn (see "Accommodation", p.343). A classic, small-town Alaskan bar, with rough-wood floors and sepia-toned walls hung with beaver pelts, and very much the place to be. Portraits of former bar-proppers line the walls while a broad cross-section of tall-talking Talkeetna characters entertain visitors to the *Fairview*. Most weekends and some week-nights there's top-flight Alaskan live music, if not, there is always the bar piano and guitar.

Café Michele, Talkeetna Spur Rd (no phone). Downtown's finest dining in an airy room with a tempting menu of organic dishes. Lunches (gringo chili, $7) are modestly priced, though you'll pay more for dinner entrees ($17–20), which might be soy-ginger king salmon or roasted half-chicken.

Swiss-Alaska Inn (see "Accommodation", p.344). The *Inn*'s restaurant serves hearty breakfasts (their omelettes are particularly good), steak, and seafood dinners ($14–20) with specialties such as wiener schnitzel and German sausage.

Talkeetna Roadhouse (see "Accommodation", p.344). Talkeetna's best bakery and a great daytime café please guests with breakfasts until 1pm made up of sourdough hotcakes served with real maple syrup or eggs, bacon, homefried potatoes, and toast – the $7 half-plate is plenty for hearty eaters, the $10 full plate is for McKinley returnees. Build your own sandwiches for lunch or try the cheese pinto beans on a grilled corn muffin with salsa ($5.50). Dinner ($15–20) is only served on Friday and Saturday when there is a reservation-only family-style sitting; in other words, the menu is what the chef decides to make that night.

West Rib Pub & Grill, Main St (☎733-3354). Good pub grub with a pleasant deck for warm days, where an outdoor grill is put to use preparing burgers and sandwiches ($8). The bar inside has the town's finest selection of beers including Guinness on tap and top Alaskan microbrews.

Listings

Air-taxi companies Doug Geeting Aviation (☎733-2366 or 1-800/770-2366, fax 733-1000, *www.alaska.net/~airtours*); Hudson Air Service (☎733-2321 or 1-800/478-2321, fax 733-2333, *www.alaskan.com/hudsonair*); K2 Aviation (☎733-2291 or 1-800/764-2291, fax 733-1221, *www.flyk2.com*); McKinley Air Service (☎733-1765 or 1-800/564-1765, fax 733-1965, *www .alaska.net/~mckair*); Talkeetna Air Taxi (☎733-2218 or 1-800/533-2219, fax 733-1434, *www.talkeetnaair.com*).

Banks The nearest bank is in Wasilla, over an hour away, but there's an ATM at Three Rivers store on Main St.

Bike rental CGS Bicycles, Main St (May to mid-Oct; ☎733-1279), ATBs for $15 a half-day, $20 a day and $25 overnight.

Festivals Apart from the Moose Dropping Festival, Talkeetna plays host to the Wilderness Woman Competition (first weekend in Dec) in which competing "bachelorettes" struggle to complete a series of wintertime tasks – chopping wood, driving a snow machine through an obstacle course – to reach the kitchen where she prepares a sandwich and delivers it (along with a beer) to her bachelor sat watching football on TV. The event culminates in the Bachelor Ball and a Bachelor Auction. The four-day Talkeetna Bluegrass Festival (mid-Aug) has become too large for the town that bears its name and now takes place at Mile 102 on the Parks Hwy.

Gas Three Rivers store, Main St, has reasonably priced gas.

Laundry and showers Three Rivers store, Main St, has a coin-op laundry (daily 8am–9pm) and showers ($2).

Library The library (Tues noon–8pm, Wed & Fri 11am–6pm; ☎733-2359) is a mile south along the spur road and has free Internet access.

Post office open Mon–Fri 9am–5pm, Sat 10am–2pm: the **General Delivery Zip** code is 99676.

Taxes The town imposes a two percent sales tax and a five percent bed tax, already included in accommodation prices.

Denali State Park

From Talkeetna Junction the Parks Hwy continues north, and from Mile 132 to Mile 169 – still two-hours' drive short of the entrance to Denali National Park – you're in **Denali State Park**. It is a land of braided rivers, a thousand lakes, and tundra-capped hills rising above the spruce forests. There's none of the rigid organization of the National Park (which shares a similar name but remains a completely separate park), far fewer people, and yet sports many of the same attributes – great McKinley views and abundant moose, grizzlies, and black bears especially. There is little infrastructure here (and nowhere local to get information), so unless you come prepared for hiking and camping you may find it all a little too much trouble. With the National Park beckoning, you could easily pass through.

If you choose to stop, there are a few hikes worth leaving time for and a couple of campgrounds to use as bases; but stock up on groceries and any hiking maps and information you might need before you arrive. The key geographical feature for most park users is the 4500-foot Kesugi Ridge, which parallels the highway to the east and is followed by a sequence of hiking trails.

In the southern reaches of the park the highway passes *Mary's McKinley View Lodge*, Mile 134.5 (☎733-1555; ④), just half a mile short of **Denali Viewpoint South**, a huge turnout where boards point out the high points – Mount McKinley, Mount Hunter, and Moose's Tooth – and the glacial highlights – the Ruth,

TACKLING DENALI

Of the great mountains of the world, Denali (North America's highest peak at 20,320ft) is not particularly high: dozens of Andean peaks are higher, and if it were moved to the Himalayas Denali would barely rate a mention. Nonetheless, its subarctic location makes it one of the world's coldest mountains, the consequent extreme and unpredictable weather conditions raising its profile to the point where it is regarded as one of the world's most difficult mountains to climb. That very difficulty, and the sheer lonesome majesty that makes it one of the most sought-after peaks, has engendered a long and fascinating history of summit attempts and heroic conquests.

A HISTORY

No one, certainly no European, had ever stepped on the slopes of Denali until the twentieth century, but interest in conquering the mountain quickly reached fever pitch. In 1903, Alaska district judge and future congressman **James Wickersham** rounded up four local lads, equipped them with primitive climbing gear and led them up to 8000 feet on the north side where what is now known as the Wickersham Wall halted their progress. A couple of months later the explorer **Frederick Cook** led an exhausted party overland up to 11,300 feet. He later claimed to have reached the summit on his second expedition in 1906, however few believed him then or now. In 1906, he telegrammed to the world that he had successfully summited Denali, backing it up with a photo of himself on the summit and a detailed summit diary. The speed of his ascent immediately alerted the mountaineering community to possible deception, but he became the toast of American society, which was even more enthusiastic about his equally dubious claims to have beaten Robert Peary to the North Pole in 1909. Pertinent questions were soon being asked, and Cook's reputation was already in tatters when, in 1910, Belmore Brown settled the matter by replicating the "summit" photograph on an 8000-foot peak twenty miles from Denali.

As Brown took his photo he little realized that Denali's North Peak – 850 feet lower than the South Peak – had already been scaled by a group of Kantishna-based gold miners now known as the **Sourdough Expedition**. In what is still regarded as one of the most extraordinary mountaineering feats ever, four prospectors – led by an overweight fifty-year-old Welshman, **Tom Lloyd** – with no technical mountaineering experience and only the most rudimentary gear, succeeded in proving not only that Cook's claim was false, but that locals could outclimb anyone from "Outside." According to the *Fairbanks Daily News-Miner* they carried "less 'junk' with them than an Eastern US excursion party would take along for a one-day's outing in the hills"; certainly they wore only normal winter clothes and ate little but bacon, beans, and caribou meat. Nonetheless, they reached the North Peak without major incident and planted a fourteen-foot spruce trunk which they had hauled up to use as a flagpole. The Stars and Stripes they had hoped would be visible from Fairbanks wasn't, and in the light of the Cook farce their claim was widely disbelieved.

All speculation was laid to rest in 1913 when respected Episcopal missionary Archdeacon **Hudson Stuck** led a shoestring expedition that not only vouched for the Sourdoughs' success – the spruce pole was still upright three years on – but entered the record books as the first to reach the true summit. Doubters were satisfied and interest in the mountain waned to the point that it was nearly twenty years before anyone summited again, and almost forty before anyone thought of climbing it any other way than via the Muldrow Glacier route from the north, which had been used by all successful early expeditions.

In 1947, **Bradford Washburn** entered the scene and succeeded in climbing Denali along with his wife Barbara – the first woman to summit. But Washburn's real contribution was his detailed surveying work which identified the West Buttress Route, first climbed by a party led by Washburn in 1951. What made this route possible was the novel practice of glacier landings, allowing climbers and equipment to be deposited at 10,000 feet on the Kahiltna Glacier, on Denali's southwest side. Washburn's initial attempt was followed up by numerous other successes, and the West Buttress Route became firmly established as the preferred line of attack. The next twenty years perfected the approach and coincided with mountaineering's transformation into a mainstream sport: by the mid-1970s, every weather window from mid-April through to the end of July saw parties setting off for the mountain.

Since then new routes have been pioneered and increasingly contrived "firsts" have been attempted: the first winter expedition in 1967, the first solo ascent in 1970, the first hang-glider descent in 1976, and the first sled team ascent in 1979. Meanwhile, even people who would barely class themselves as mountaineers were attempting Denali by engaging **guides**. One of the first guides was **Ray 'the Pirate' Genet** – a veteran of the first winter ascent where he earned his nickname for the skull and crossbones he used to mark his clothing – who, together with **Don Sheldon**, bush pilot par excellence, helped scores of climbers reach the top. Genet died while guiding on Everest in 1979; his son, Taras, became the youngest climber to summit at the age of 12 in 1991 (the oldest climber summited when 71).

CLIMBING DENALI TODAY

Over the years the level of mortality, the high public profile of the mountain, and its administration by the Denali National Park have caused considerable controversy and it has taken the efforts of numerous working groups to finally settle on a system of administration which provides a tolerable level of safety without sacrificing the sense of adventure.

Today, all climbers must register their intentions at least sixty days in advance of their climb and pay $150: details are available in *Mountaineering: Denali National Park and Preserve*, a free booklet in eight languages available from the Talkeetna Ranger Station (see p.343). Almost all summit attempts now start with a flight – roughly $270 for the round-trip with gear – from Talkeetna to the Kahiltna Glacier at 10,000 feet where the Park Service maintains a Ranger Station throughout the climbing season. Radio contact with Talkeetna improves safety on the mountain and allows climbers to call for a flight out once they're finished. Of the twelve hundred or so climbers who make the attempt annually, around fifty percent are successful and over eighty percent of those use the West Buttress Route, typically making a series of gear shuttles to establish progressively higher camps over three weeks. The emphasis is very much on self-reliance, but emergency assistance is available at another Ranger Station at 14,200 feet, where staff actually spend much of their day picking up trash left by expeditions – typically over 1000 pounds a season. The presence of rangers on the mountain and scores of others scrabbling for position at regular campsites could lead to overconfidence, but as veteran climber Jonathan Waterman writes "The fact that the West Buttress Route is not technically difficult should not obscure the need to plan for extreme survival situations…the West Buttress route is a terribly underestimated climb."

If you fancy giving it a go, half a dozen authorized guiding services are listed on the Denali National Park Web site at *www.nps.gov/dena/mountaineering*, expect to pay $3500 for an attempt at the West Buttress Route.

Buckskin, and Eldridge glaciers. The *Lower Troublesome Creek* campground, Mile 137.2 ($5 per vehicle; pump water), marks the southern trailhead for the **Troublesome Creek Trail** (see box, below), which finishes at the large *Byers Lake* campground, Mile 147.1 ($10; pump water), the most organized around with a camp host in summer, a public-use cabin ($35) and excellent swimming and grayling and trout fishing. For the best McKinley views you need to get to the superb *Lakeshore* campground (free; lake water) accessible either by walking 1.8 miles along the **Byers Lake Loop Trail** (see box, below) or paddling across the lake.

Yet more mountain views reveal themselves from **Denali View North**, Mile 162.7, a large parking lot where you can overnight ($10 per vehicle) either in your RV or in a tent pitched at some nice walk-in sites. Before leaving the park you pass the Little Coal Creek trailhead, Mile 163.8, the northern terminus of the **Kesugi Ridge Trail**.

Cantwell and Broad Pass

The Parks Hwy has been gradually climbing ever since Wasilla, but five miles after leaving the Denali State Park it crosses **Hurricane Gulch**, Mile 174, on a single-span bridge 260ft above the stream then begins a more rapid ascent to **Broad Pass**, Mile 201, where both the train line and the highway squeeze through a rent in the Alaska Range. From here on everything flows north into the Yukon River then west to the Bering Sea, including the fledgling Nenana River which gently eases down into **CANTWELL**, Mile 210. Here, the **Denali Hwy** (see account starting on p.387) heads off 135 miles east to Paxson through remote country with limited services, so you may well want to fill your tank, and your

---

HIKES IN DENALI STATE PARK

Hikers hoping to tackle the park's longer trails must bring all camping gear (including a stove and fuel as no backcountry fires are allowed) and be competent with a map. Topo maps are available from the Alaska Public Lands Information office in Anchorage where you can also get the free, schematic *Denali State Park* leaflet. Note that the two longer hikes described below are both one-way hikes, though hitching back along the Parks Hwy is seldom a problem, or you could even organize for one of the buses to pick you up.

Byers Lake Loop Trail (4.8 miles; 2–3hr; negligible ascent). Gentle and scenic stroll around the lake starting and finishing at the *Byers Lake* campground.

Kesugi Ridge Trail (27.4 miles one-way; 2–3 days; 4000ft ascent). A magnificent trail starting at the *Byers Lake* campground and climbing rapidly above tree line, where you stay right until the descent to the Little Coal Creek trailhead. If all that isn't enough you can add 1000 feet of climbing to take in the summit of Indian Peak close to the northern end of the trail.

Troublesome Creek Trail (15.2 miles one-way; 7–9hr; 2000ft ascent). Black bears gorging on salmon in July and August earned the name for this creek which is followed from the *Troublesome Creek* campground before the moderate climb up onto open tundra pocked with small lakes. The views are spectacular though you'll need to keep your eyes down to follow the rock cairns which lead back into the forest and down to the *Byers Lake* campground. This can be combined with the Kesugi Ridge Trail to make a 36-mile expedition.

stomach at one of the two roadside diners. The Parks Hwy continues 27 miles north to the Denali National Park entrance, passing through a narrow defile which opens out onto long views of Mount Fellows with its ridgeline rocks said to look like a musher and her sled dogs. Thirteen miles before the park entrance you pass **Carlo Creek**, a distant but still feasible base for forays into the park and, six miles later, **McKinley Village**, a knot of accommodation covered in the following account.

Denali National Park

The six million acres of **DENALI NATIONAL PARK**, 240 miles north of Anchorage, holds a special, almost holy, place in the minds of Alaska's visitors – a vast wilderness carved out of the Alaskan heartland preserving an entire ecosystem. This is where everyone comes to see big game: bears browsing in the low brush, moose chomping on aquatic weed at Wonder Lake, a lone wolf loping along a river bar, or a herd of caribou disappearing into the infinity of the Teklanika Valley. It is scenes like this that bring home the sheer scale of the place; the park is about the same size as Massachusetts or half the size of Wales, and a round-trip along the road from the park entrance to Wonder Lake, right in the heart of the park, takes a full twelve hours.

For most, Denali's grail is the sight of the 20,320-foot **Mount McKinley**, equally known by its Athapascan name, **Denali**, "the great one." And great it is, rising a full 18,000 feet from tundra to tip, ranking as North America's highest mountain and boasting the greatest vertical rise of any mountain on the globe. It simply towers over its neighbors, most barely rising above 12,000 feet, and even its 17,400-foot neighbor, Mount Foraker, is dwarfed firmly in second place. These are the king and queen of the **Alaska Range**, a 600-mile crescent of jagged snow-capped peaks which arcs through the Alaskan Interior to form the backbone of Denali National Park; a mountain fastness still locked in the last ice age, spewing glaciers left and right. To the south the Ruth and Kahiltna glaciers have gouged out deep canyons on their fifty-mile passage out to the vegetated lowlands, while to the north the Muldrow crooks its arm around 7000ft foothills and melts away to become the McKinley River, one of the dominant features of the central wilderness area of the park.

Denali's scenic grandeur is made wonderfully accessible by the **Park Road**, ninety miles of gravel which winds from lowland **taiga** to alpine **tundra** on its passage through half a dozen river catchments and over as many high passes. Private vehicles are banned and visitors must board a system of shuttle buses which grind along offering a wonderful vantage for spotting, and photographing, wildlife almost undisturbed by human presence. The limited number of shuttle buses creates a bottleneck around the park entrance, but it is this that preserves the sanctity of the park and makes the wilderness so appealing once you get into it. For both human safety and animal protection, bus etiquette demands that you stay in the bus when animals are about but otherwise you can, and should, get off some time and explore away from the park road.

Mount McKinley so dominates its surroundings that it creates its own distinct **weather**, turning the moist drafts coming off the Gulf of Alaska into rain and, at higher elevations, snow. This affects the weather along the Park Road, but north of the Alaska Range precipitation is low – around fifteen inches a year – limiting

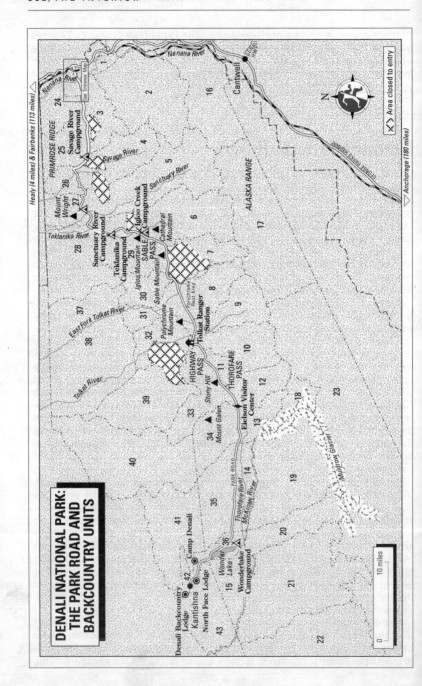

DENALI NATIONAL PARK:
THE PARK ROAD AND
BACKCOUNTRY UNITS

Healy (4 miles) & Fairbanks (113 miles)

Anchorage (180 miles)

Nenana River

Nenana River

See Entrance Map

PRIMROSE RIDGE

Savage River Campground

Savage River

Sanctuary River

Mount Wright

Igloo Creek Campground

Cathedral Mountain

SABLE PASS

Teklanika River

Sanctuary River Campground

Teklanika Campground

Igloo Mountain

Sable Mountain

East Fork Tolkat River

Polychrome Rest Area

Tolkat Ranger Station

Polychrome Mountain

Tolkat River

HIGHWAY PASS

Stony Hill

THOROFARE PASS

Eielson Visitor Center

Mount Galen

Thorofare River

PARK ROAD

McKinley River

Muldrow Glacier

ALASKA RANGE

Cantwell

N

Area closed to entry

Camp Denali

Denali Backcountry Lodge

Kantishna

North Face Lodge

Wonderlake Campground

Wonder Lake

10 miles

0

1
2
3
4
5
6
7
8
9
10
11
12
13
14
15
16
17
18
19
20
21
22
23
24
25
26
27
28
29
30
31
32
33
34
35
36
37
38
39
40
41
42
43

the amount of snowfall. Nonetheless, it can snow in any month of the year along the Park Road. June, July, and August are liable to have the best weather, but also the most bugs. May generally avoids the worst of the mosquito season and basks in long days, though snow cover may limit your movements. September is getting colder and darker but the fall colors and berry picking easily compensate.

Visiting Alaska without seeing Denali is unthinkable for most travelers, and therein lies the park's major problem. The place has become such an icon that few question what they expect and why they are going; and many come away disappointed after spending hours on a bumpy, dusty bus ride only to catch distant glimpses of caribou and moose. Many who come specifically to see Mount McKinley often don't realize that they've got a better chance of seeing it from Talkeetna or various roadside viewpoints south of the park: you can't even see the mountain from the park entrance where most people spend much of their time. Furthermore, during the summer months it is shrouded in cloud for two days out of every three. Spectacular as the scenery is, it is no more stunning than that along the Denali Hwy where the access is a lot simpler and the crowds incomparably thinner. Only a tiny fraction of visitors make use of the freedom to roam across trackless tundra, but if it is backcountry hiking you want then pretty much all of Alaska is out there waiting for you.

Some history

The caribou, Dall sheep, and moose so prized by photographers were once quarry to Athapascan Indians. Hunters followed the herds through the Alaska Range foothills in the summer months, picking berries and gathering plants along the way, then descended to the river valleys in the colder months. Towards the end of the nineteenth century, long before there were roads, railways, or even bush planes anywhere near Denali, gold prospectors entered the area. One Princeton-educated hopeful, William Dickey, spent time in the area reporting the existence of a huge mountain to the New York *Sun* (estimating it to be over 20,000 feet high) and naming it after, William McKinley, Republican nominee for the presidency. By 1905, prospectors found their El Dorado in Kantishna and a full-blown stampede ensued sprouting a tent city and then a boom town. Like so many gold towns it barely lasted out the winter, but the area did catch the attention of one **Charles Sheldon**, an East Coast naturalist intent on studying Dall sheep. Deploring the wreckage and unfettered hunting around Kantishna, as well as recognizing the unique nature of an almost intact ecosystem north of the Alaska Range, he lobbied Washington for the creation of a national park. In 1917, this central area between the ranges and stretching from Kantishna to the Nenana River was designated as McKinley National Park, the first in Alaska. Access was provided in 1923 by the railroad, and in 1957 by the Denali Hwy from Paxson, but it was the completion of the George Parks Hwy in 1973 that really sealed the park's future as Alaska's premier tourist destination.

In recognition of the mountain's Athapascan moniker the park was renamed Denali National Park, but despite petitions and thousands of newspaper column inches the mountain officially remains Mount McKinley.

The Park Road

Almost everyone who visits Denali National Park approaches using the shuttle buses which ply the **Park Road**, a ninety-mile dirt strip which winds its way into the heart of the park providing access to the backcountry. The road – asphalt to

DENALI'S CHANGING SEASONS

From early June to early September, Denali is at full tilt, then everything just shuts down for the rest of the year. Unless we've told you otherwise you can assume that all trips, tours, hotels, and restaurants mentioned in and around Denali are only guaranteed to be open through this summer season. The **shoulder seasons** (essentially the last two weeks of May and middle two weeks of Sept) are grayer; some things are operating and others not. As the winter snows melt in the early weeks of May the Park Road becomes accessible to cyclists and eventually the park service opens it to private vehicles as far as Teklanika (Mile 30). Hotels and restaurants start to open, then on about May 23 the season starts: the visitor center opens, shuttle buses start shuttling, private vehicles are limited to the first twelve miles of the Park Rd, and everything moves into top gear (though the Park Road won't open all the way to Wonder Lake until mid-June). Frenetic activity continues until around September 14 when shuttle buses stop and many hotels and restaurants close or reduce their menus. For the next four days the road is open to those who have won the **road lottery** (see "Listings," p.370). If the snow holds off after September 18 this can be a good time to visit as private vehicles are again allowed to drive as far as Teklanika and cyclists have the whole road, though they're not allowed to camp beyond Mile 30.

  In winter Denali is hard but beautiful; the moose are still about, the aurora is often on display, and both the mosquitoes and the bears are sleeping. The only way in though is by snow shoe, ski, or dog team; snow machines are not permitted and there are no services except for the *Riley Creek* campground. Before heading into the park in winter, make sure you call at the **Park Headquarters**, Mile 3.5 Park Road (daily 8am–4.30pm; ☎683-2294).

Mile 14; dirt thereafter – runs at right angles to the rivers, twisting and climbing from one watershed to another over six passes, each topping 3000 feet. That might sound a modest elevation, but even in July and August it is not unknown for these to be temporarily blocked by fresh snow.

The Park Road leaves the George Parks Hwy and climbs from the Nenana River passing the visitor center, train station, and a couple of campsites in the first two miles. Spruce forest gives way to willow around Mile 7 – good territory for spotting moose – and at Mile 9 you get a brief glimpse of Denali; the last you'll see until just before Eielson. Private vehicles can only go as far as the **Savage River checkpoint**, Mile 14, where there is a mile-long hiking trail along the river. Shuttle buses continue past the popular hiking territory of Primrose Ridge and descend to the Sanctuary River and campsite. Across a low pass you reach the Teklanika River, where there is a huge rest area used by all shuttles (Mile 30) and a campsite. Again this is good hiking territory. The small *Igloo Mountain* campground nestles between Igloo and Cathedral mountains, both impressive lumps of rock which make challenging destinations for those so inclined. Beyond the 3800ft **Sable Pass**, a long bridge crosses the East Fork of the Toklat River (Mile 44) and finishes at the Polychrome Rest Area, often used for hikes beginning at the river. The main channel of the Toklat River lies ahead over the 3500ft **Polychrome Pass**, aptly named when late sun catches the deep maroons, rust reds, and even faint blues of the rocks. The bed of the Toklat River provides more opportunities for lowland river-walking in country noted for its caribou, then the road climbs up to **Highway Pass** (Mile 58) the highest point on the road at 4100ft. A couple of miles further on you round **Stony Hill** to a superb view of Denali in its full glory, all 18,000 feet of it truly dominating the surrounding mountains. Just beyond **Thorofare Pass** you descend to **Eielson Visitor Center**, Mile 66 (June to mid-Sept daily 9am–7pm), where most day-visitors end their journey and head off on short hikes or join the easy ranger-led walk at 1.30pm daily. It lasts less than an hour and covers everything from flora and fauna to the history of mining in the area. The visitor center has a lovely deck with views of Denali, informative panels about the area, a small bookshop (but no food of any kind), and a standby list for those wanting to head back on the shuttle.

In a region full of spectacular scenery, the next few miles are some of the most scenic with the heart of the Alaska Range framing the vegetated face of the **Muldrow Glacier**, which comes within a mile of the road. You traverse rolling terrain dotted with beaver ponds favored by moose as you descend gradually beside the broad, gravel-bedded expanse of the McKinley River to **Wonder Lake** (Mile 86). Without some serious hiking, this is as close to the mountain as you can get and presents the ubiquitous postcard shot of the mountain reflecting alpenglow across the waters of the lake.

The road continues to **Kantishna** (Mile 91), an old gold mining inholding with a handful of backcountry lodges. The town is pitched well in brochures and sounds quite interesting but fails to live up to its promise. "No Trespassing" signs are everywhere, generators run much of the time, and though the lodges are undoubtedly luxurious, this may not be the Denali you were after.

Arrival, orientation, and information

Undoubtedly the finest way to arrive at Denali is by rail. **Trains** pull into Denali Park station and are met by a phalanx of courtesy buses run by individual hotels and hostels. If you're not being met by a bus to your accommodation, it can be a little bewildering. The *Morino* walk-in campsite is an easy stroll to the south but for everything else you'll need to unravel the complexities of the shuttle bus system (see box, p.358): the Riley Creek Loop bus stops at the rear of the train station parking lot. All **long-distance buses** pickup and dropoff at the visitor center, and most will let you down at any of the local hotels. If you alight at the visitor center you'll again have to master the shuttle buses to get any further.

If you are planning to travel beyond Mile 12 of the Park Road you should call at the visitor center to pay the park **entrance fee** of $5 per person ($10 per family; valid 7 days).

Orientation

Getting into Denali National Park involves spending at least some time on the eastern fringe, in and around the nameless huddle of buildings known variously as Denali Park, Nenana Canyon, or **Glitter Gulch**. The more staid businesses don't like the latter name, but it is less confusing than the other options. This is where you'll come to dine, visit offices of rafting and flightseeing operators, and perhaps stay.

About a mile south of Glitter Gulch (Mile 237.3) the Park Road cuts west and winds ninety miles right through the heart of the park to the former gold mines of Kantishna. Most of your time in the park will be spent close to this road, initially along the first two miles, an amorphous region known as the **entrance area**.

Here you'll find the visitor center, a couple of campgrounds, a post office, store and the train station.

The demand for accommodation close to the entrance of the park is so great in summer that a couple of other clusters of hotels have popped up along the George Parks Hwy: **McKinley Village**, seven miles south of the entrance area, and **Healy**, a still functional coal-mining town twelve miles north, which has some of the best accommodation options.

Information

Park formalities all revolve around the **visitor center** (late April to late May daily 10am–4pm; late May to Sept daily 7am–8pm; closed in winter; ☎683-2294, *www.nps.gov/dena*), where you'll need to go to book campsites and shuttle buses, and access the backcountry. Here you can also pick up free copies of the schematic *Denali Park Map* and the *Denali Alpenglow*, which has comprehensive coverage of park facilities and ranger programs and a guide to the various shuttle buses, campgrounds, and so forth. For more detailed maps you'll need to duck into the **bookshop** section of the visitor center, just next door to the **cinema**, which puts on a free orientation slide show every half-hour.

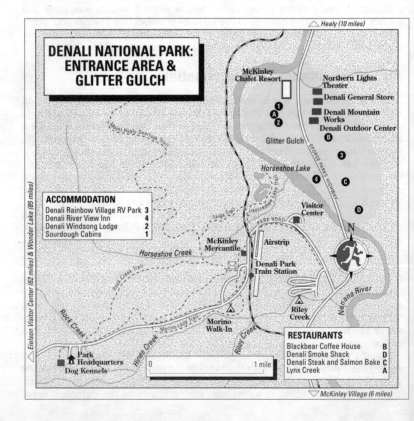

△ Healy (10 miles)

DENALI NATIONAL PARK: ENTRANCE AREA & GLITTER GULCH

McKinley Chalet Resort

Northern Lights Theater

Denali General Store

Denali Mountain Works

Denali Outdoor Center

Mount Healy Overlook Trail

Glitter Gulch

Horseshoe Lake

Horseshoe Lake Trail

GEORGE PARKS HIGHWAY

Taiga Trail

PARK ROAD

Visitor Center

N

ACCOMMODATION
Denali Rainbow Village RV Park 3
Denali River View Inn 4
Denali Windsong Lodge 2
Sourdough Cabins 1

McKinley Mercantile

Airstrip

Denali Park Train Station

Horseshoe Creek

Rock Creek Trail

Rock Creek

Eielson Visitor Center (62 miles) & Wonder Lake (85 miles)

Morino Loop Trail

Hines Creek

Morino Walk-In

Riley Creek

Riley Creek

Nenana River

Park Headquarters Dog Kennels

0   1 mile

RESTAURANTS
Blackbear Coffee House B
Denali Smoke Shack D
Denali Steak and Salmon Bake C
Lynx Creek A

▽ McKinley Village (6 miles)

RESERVING IN ADVANCE

By planning in advance and making reservations you can save a lot of time at the visitor center and unnecessary nights spent in the entrance area. Various tours, as well as **campgrounds** – *Riley Creek, Savage River, Teklanika*, and *Wonder Lake* – and the **shuttle buses** used to reach them, can all be reserved in advance.

By **phone**: bookings up to a day in advance of your arrival can be made by phone (in US ☎1-800/622-7275; international ☎272-7275) between 7am and 5pm (Alaska time) from the end of February to the middle of September. Pay by Visa, MasterCard, or Discover.

By **fax** and **mail**: any time after December 1 the previous year, but at least a month before your travel date (two days for fax on 264-4684) you can send your requests to Denali Park Resorts VTS, 241 W Ship Creek Ave, Anchorage, AK 99501. A form can be downloaded from the Denali NP Web site (see opposite) detailing the information required: number of adults and children, desired dates and alternatives, credit-card numbers and their expiry dates. The entrance fee ($5 for individuals, $10 for a family) should be included in any payments (check or money order).

Getting around

To relieve congestion and preserve the natural qualities of the park, the majority of the park is only open to official shuttle buses, bicycles, and foot traffic. **Car and RV drivers** can explore the first twelve paved miles of the Park Road, as far as Savage River, at their leisure (see p.365); but for further exploration, you'll have to abandon your vehicle in the *Riley Creek* campground overspill parking area (not the visitor center lot) and make use of the shuttle buses. If you aren't traveling by car but decide to stay around Healy for a day or two, you might find it handy to **rent a car** locally or just use **taxis** to get back and forth between the park and Healy (for both see "Listings", p.369).

Grappling with the various **shuttle buses** can be intimidating at first but with the aid of our box, overleaf, you should quickly grasp the basic points: the green buses are run by the parks service and are designed to link the campgrounds and visitor center and get you out into the backcountry; while the beige buses are operated by Denali Park Resorts, shuttling their hotel guests around, but are also open to the public. Unless you join one of the tours, you'll be using the beige buses to get from Glitter Gulch or McKinley Village to the visitor center, then the green buses to get into the park. One of the best ways of getting around is by **mountain bike**. You don't entirely avoid the tyranny of the visitor center as you'll still need to book campsites, but making your way along the Park Road at your own pace has obvious advantages. Certain rules restrict your movements – after all it is Denali – so you won't be allowed to stray off designated roadways and can only leave your machine in the bike racks at the *Sanctuary, Igloo,* and *Teklanika* campgrounds. On the plus side, you can hoist your bike onto a camper bus at no extra charge, get off where you want, then ride from there even using a sequence of buses and campsites to explore the whole road. During the spring and fall when there are no buses running and road closures are in effect, cyclists are still permitted to ride beyond closed gates though you must still use designated campgrounds.

DENALI'S SHUTTLES AND TOURS

Shuttle buses operate from the third week in May to the middle of September. The tour buses tend to operate for an extra week or two at either end of the season when they drop their rates slightly. Park Road shuttles are listed in order of importance to most readers.

ENTRANCE AREA

ARA Courtesy Shuttle (beige; free). These buses link the Denali Park Resorts hotels and are free to all. The circuit visits Glitter Gulch, the visitor center, and McKinley Village on a somewhat arcane timetable: copies are available from the visitor center and the relevant hotels. No reservations.

Riley Creek Loop (green; free). Makes a continuous run between the *Riley Creek* campground, the visitor center, Horseshoe Lake trailhead, and the train station. Schedules are posted at bus stops. No reservations.

Sled Dog Demonstration Shuttle (green; free). Runs two miles from *Riley Creek* campground and the visitor center to the Park Headquarters in time for the daily sled-dog demos at 10am, 2pm & 4pm. Note that there is no vehicle parking at the Park Headquarters. No reservations.

SHUTTLES ALONG THE PARK ROAD

Park Shuttle (green; Eielson $21 round-trip, Wonder Lake $27, Kantishna $31). Often known simply as "The Shuttle," this is the primary means of entering the backcountry, leaving the visitor center every half-hour for Eielson (3hr one-way) and every hour for Wonder Lake (5hr), with a few continuing to Kantishna (6hr). Schedules are well organized – even providing late train arrivees with a service to Polychrome Pass and back in the evening. To maximize your time in the park and your chance of seeing early-bird wildlife, try to get on one of the early buses (they start at 5am) and return on a late one (the last leaves Toklat at 6.30pm and arrives back at the visitor center at 9pm). **Reservations are essential** when outbound but coming back it is first-come, first-served: campers will sometimes be picked up if they're not full. Apart from the day-trip fees there are several passes, notably the

Accommodation

Accommodation around the Denali park entrance is highly polarized: you basically have to decide between camping (see box, p.362) or paying around $150 a double. The greatest concentration of **places to stay** is in **Glitter Gulch**, conveniently located among the restaurants and shops either side of the George Parks Hwy, a mile north of the park entrance, and easily accessible by frequent shuttle buses. These tend to be pricier options, and if you've got your own wheels you'll do better price-wise heading twelve miles north to the small town of **Healy**, where there's a number of competitively priced B&Bs and motels, all much better value than places closer to the park; as well as the region's only **budget hostel**. Consider too the small cluster of places near *McKinley Village Lodge*, seven miles **south of the park entrance**; shuttle buses are too irregular and infrequent to encourage much toing and froing but you can get by. We've listed a couple of places even further south along the George Parks Hwy, which are good value but lack shuttle service.

Three-for-Two Pass (Eielson $42, Wonder Lake $54, Kantishna $62), which allows three days travel as far as your chosen destination for the price of two.

Savage River Shuttle (green; $2 exact change only westbound, free on the return). A subspecies of the Park Shuttle leaving from the *Riley Creek* campground and the visitor center but only going as far as Savage River (Mile 15; 1hr). No reservations.

Camper Bus (green; $15.50). Buses with extra backpack and bike space designed to get both backcountry hikers and those using the campgrounds out into the park from Riley Creek, the visitor center, and *Morino* campground. These run five times a day, are only available to those with campground reservations or backcountry permits, and usually have a less comprehensive commentary than the shuttle buses. They won't usually pick up non-campers as they have an obligation to campers encountered along the way. Each camper bus can carry two bicycles at no extra cost and your fee is valid for any number of trips during your entire stay west of Savage River. A reservation is required for your first trip into the park; after that they'll pick you up if they have room.

TOURS

Alpenglow Tours (mini-van; $85; May to late Sept; ☎1-800/770-7275). By using a nimble minivan this tour manages to get to Kantishna and back in under eleven hours, with frequent wildlife viewing stops, continental breakfast, lunch at the McKinley Gold Camp, and a little gold panning along the way.

Kantishna Wilderness Trails (red and white; mid-June to early Sept; $109; ☎1-800/942-7420). A marathon day driving the entire 95 miles to Kantishna and back (13 hours in all) with lunch, gold panning, and dog-sled demo at the *Kantishna Roadhouse*. Sadly there is limited time for wildlife stops.

Natural History Tour (beige; $35; ☎1-800/276-7234). Three-hour guided bus ride as far as Primrose Ridge (Mile 17) with a natural-history angle. Park entrance fee included. Runs three times daily.

Tundra Wildlife Tour (beige; $64; ☎1-800/276-7234). Full-day (6–7hr) drive along the Park Road as far as Toklat (Mile 53) stopping frequently to observe wildlife. Box lunch and park entrance fee included. Runs twice daily.

Other than camping, the only accommodation inside the park is at **Kantishna**, ninety miles west of the park entrance at the end of the Park Road. It is not an especially attractive area by Denali standards but access to genuine wilderness is second to none. There are four resorts, all expensive and all offering comfortable accommodation, gourmet breakfast and dinner, a wide range of activities, and complimentary bus travel from the park entrance (fly-ins extra), which bypasses the visitor-center bottleneck. One-night visits are discouraged so you may need some flexibility to fit in with fixed schedules; and will probably need to book several weeks in advance.

The park service allows **RVs** into three of their Denali sites – *Riley Creek*, *Savage River*, and *Teklanika* (see box, p.362) – and you should really do everything you can to secure a place in one of these. Failing that, you're left with the commercial sites with line the George Parks Hwy, almost all of them little more than gravel parking lots with hookups but few concessions to aesthetics. The best are several miles south of the park, or twelve miles north in Healy.

Glitter Gulch

Denali Rainbow Village RV Park, Mile 238.6 (☎683-3362, fax 683-7275). Gravel parking lot right in the middle of Glitter Gulch. $17 dry, $23 with electricity. Showers are $3 extra.

Denali Riverview Inn, Mile 238.4 (☎683-2663, fax 683-7433, *www.alaskan.com /denaliriverview*). Plain modern rooms with two double beds, private bath, and satellite TV, all featuring a small deck with river views. There's a courtesy van on demand and rates drop forty percent in the first and last two weeks of the season. ⑥.

Denali Sourdough Cabins, Mile 238.8 (☎683-2773 or 1-800/354-6020, *www .denalisourdoughcabins.com*). Individual cabins with a queen bed well-separated by spruce trees and without TV or phone. ⑥.

Denali Windsong Lodge, Mile 238.6 (☎683-2282 or 1-800/208-0200 & fax 683-2545, *www .alaska-tour.com*). Large rooms with two double beds, river views, satellite TV, in-room coffee-maker, and courtesy transport to the visitor center. ⑦.

Healy and north of the park entrance

Alaskan Chateau B&B, Sulphide Rd (☎683-1377, fax 683-1380, *www.alaskanchateau.com*). Very comfortable and nicely decorated log cabins open year-round, all with private bathroom, fridge, microwave, coffee maker, and toaster, and some with full kitchen and a separate living area (⑥). The ones in the A-frame above a garage are especially appealing. The owner also operates Teresa's Car Rentals (see "Listings," p.369). Turn off the George Parks Hwy at Mile 248.8 into E Healy Spur Rd then right after 0.9 miles. ⑤.

Denali Dome Home B&B, 137 E Healy Spur Rd (☎683-1239, fax 683-2322, *denalidome @alaskaone.com*). Large geodesic dome with huge lounge areas and great views of the Alaska Range. The six rooms all have private bath (one has a sauna), and the breakfast is fantastic. Turn off the George Parks Hwy at Mile 248.8. Open year-round. ⑤.

Denali Hostel, Otto Lake Rd (☎683-1295, fax 683-2106, *www.denalihostel.com*). Compact and spotless self-catering hostel beautifully located 10 miles north of the park entrance with a complimentary shuttle service to the park in the morning, and back from the visitor center at 5pm (also meeting the train from Anchorage) and 9pm. The dorm rooms inside are single-sex and a little more spacious than the unisex bunkhouses; bring a sleeping bag or pay the single $3 linen charge. There is no camping, the hostel is closed during the day (10am–5pm) and check-in is from 5.30–10.30pm. Turn west off the George Parks Hwy at Mile 247 and go 1.3 miles. The hostel also runs a small year-round apartment in Healy (③). Open mid-May to late Sept and reservations are highly recommended. Apartment ③, bunks ①.

Denali RV Park, Mile 245.1 (☎1-800/478-1501 or 683-1500). Desolate RV park located six miles north of Glitter Gulch offering "dry" sites for $15 and full hookup for $26; rates drop by twenty percent after the first night. There is no provision for tents, but they do have pay showers, family units (⑤), and simple motel rooms with private bath ③.

McKinley RV and Campground, Mile 248.8 (☎1-800/478-2562 or 683-2379, fax 683-2281). The best RV park hereabouts and good for campers, too, though access to the park is difficult. Sites are all in the trees by a bend in the river and there is a coin-op laundry and showers. Tent sites $17.50, power and water $26.50.

Motel Nord Haven, Mile 249.5 (☎683-4500 or 1-800/683-4501 in Alaska, fax 683-4503, *www.ptialaska.net/~nordhavn*). New high-standard motel just north of Healy, with large rooms the match of any twelve miles further south. Each is equipped with queen bed, phone, dataport and TV, and there's free laundry, newspapers, and tea and coffee. Open year-round. ⑤.

Totem Inn, Mile 248.8 (☎683-2420, fax 683-2432). Roadside bar, diner, and inn right in the center of Healy with rooms remodeled from prefabricated workers' rooms with shower and TV (③), and some much larger, newer and plusher affairs (⑤).

South of the park entrance

Denali Cabins, Mile 229 (☎1-888/560-2489 or 683-2642, fax 683-2595, *www.alaskan.com /denalicabins*). Spacious cabins in a nice grassy area with a couple of hot tubs, just far enough away from the park to see the prices drop a little. Courtesy van available. Suite ⑦, full cabin ⑥, duplex cabin ④.

Denali Grizzly Bear Cabins & Campground, Mile 231.1 (☎683-2696, *www.alaskaone.com /dengrzly*). The most appealing commercial campground anywhere near Denali, set in the trees close to the Nenana River and with a range of attractive cabins all around. There are central cooking shelters (though no pans or crockery), coin-op showers, a store, and the ARA shuttle leaves from across the road at *McKinley Village Lodge*. Lowest rates are for campsites ($17 for up to four; water and electrical hookup $5 extra) then there are tent cabins ($24), and a range of more substantial walled cabins, some with cookstoves and showers, some of them quite luxurious. ①–⑤.

Denali River Cabins, Mile 231.1 (☎683-2500 or 1-800/230-7275, fax 683-2502, *www .denalirivercabins.com*). The best full-price rooms in the immediate area: all new cedar cabins with showers, linked by wooden walkways which drop down to the riverside deck and sauna. There's a hot tub and big lounge area too, but to eat there's only a choice between the restaurant at *McKinley Lodge* and the *Denali Roadhouse* restaurant and bar. Otherwise you'll need to catch the shuttle into Glitter Gulch. Rates drop thirty percent in May and September. Riverside ⑦, others ⑥.

McKinley Village Lodge, Mile 231.1 (☎683-8900 or 1-800/276-7234, *www.denaliparkresorts .com*). Cedarwood lodges in large blocks mostly fronting the Nenana River and containing large, if somewhat institutional rooms. Popular with tour groups. ⑧.

The Perch, Mile 224 (☎683-2523 or 1-888/322-2523, *www.alakone.com/perchrest*). Relatively low-cost cabins located thirteen miles south of the park entrance at Carlo Creek, made all the more appealing by their proximity to The Perch restaurant (see p.369). Cabins without bathroom (③) sleep four and come furnished with raw-log furniture and sofa with linen provided. Those with bathroom (④) are larger with an extra bed in a loft. ③/④.

Inside the park: Kantishna

Camp Denali (☎683-2290, fax 683-1568, *www.campdenali.com*). *Camp Denali* is undoubtedly the place to stay inside the park bounds and is the only place with views of McKinley. It was the first lodge here in 1951, founded by pioneering conservationists Celia Hunter and Ginny Hill Wood. The camp's ecological ethos extend to all aspects, with home-grown vegetables and naturalist tours often guided by visiting experts. *Camp Denali* comprises seventeen cabins strewn over a ridge each with separate outhouse and lovely communal lounge areas. Open early June to early September and with fixed departure dates which dictate minimum stays of three nights (Fri–Sun) or four (Mon–Thurs). $345 per person per night all inclusive. ⑨.

Denali Backcountry Lodge (☎1-800/841-0692, *www.denalilodge.com*). Without the fabulous views of *Camp Denali* but with similarly immediate access to wonderful surroundings. Accommodation is in cedar cabins with private facilities arranged around a spacious lodge, and there's a stack of self-guided walks and structured activities such as hikes, gold panning, naturalist presentations, and so on. Rates for double occupancy are $315 per person. ⑨.

North Face Lodge (☎683-2290, fax 683-1568, *www.campdenali.com*). Essentially part of *Camp Denali*, but more of a traditional hotel with a block of fully-plumbed rooms without Denali views. Open early June to early September and with fixed departure dates which dictate minimum stays of three nights (Fri–Sun) or four (Mon–Thurs). $345 per person per night all inclusive. ⑨.

Activities in and around the park entrance

With a vast proportion of Alaska's visitors making their way to Denali at some point it is hardly surprising that a considerable industry has built up to tap this rich vein. Except for the very organized who have everything booked in advance, in high season almost everyone spends half a day around the entrance area

CAMPGROUNDS IN DENALI

The difficulty with camping in Denali is getting a place in one of the campgrounds through a booking system (see box, p.357) that is as infuriating as it is effective at controlling access to the sites and the backcountry. All the sites at *Riley Creek*, *Savage River*, *Teklanika*, and *Wonder Lake* campgrounds can be reserved in advance, with the rest available from the visitor center up to two days in advance. Once you have booked your first night in any Denali campground you can then book up to fourteen consecutive nights at any of the sites where there is space. When you go into the visitor center you'll see a board with all the campgrounds listed along with the number of sites available for the next two nights (i.e. tonight and tomorrow night): chances are your preferred sites will not be available and you will have to spend your first night or two in a hotel or commercial campground. You then have two choices: either line up very early the next morning (it is common for there to be dozens of people waiting when the doors open), or resign yourself to staying in a less popular campground for a night or two. Once you're booked in for your first night you should find it pretty easy to reserve subsequent nights at any other campground, even the much sought after *Wonder Lake*, because you will have priority to do so. Hikers without vehicles often have an easier time than drivers since they can self-register at the *Morino* campground (that key first night) then trot down to the visitor center to reserve the remainder of their stay.

Whichever way you do it you'll have to pay the campsite **registration fee** ($4), which covers your entire stay at any one campground: changing sites means another $4 registration fee at each place. You are limited to a total stay of fourteen nights in campsites and in the backcountry.

Of the seven campgrounds, all except *Sanctuary River* and *Igloo Creek* have potable tap water and all are equipped with either flush or pit toilets. They are open from May to September though *Wonder Lake* only opens sometime in June (depending on snow cover) and *Riley Creek* is open all year. **Vehicles** are only permitted at *Riley Creek*, *Savage River*, and *Teklanika*. *Riley Creek*, *Teklanika*, and *Wonder Lake* have a free program of **ranger-led talks** which varies each night.

sorting out plans or simply waiting for a campsite or backcountry unit to become available. There are a few walks (see box, p.364) to keep you entertained but you'll soon find yourselves kicking your heels. Daytime relief comes in the form of **rafting** the Nenana River (see opposite), **flightseeing** around Mount McKinley (see p.365), or attending the forty-minute **sled-dog demonstration** (daily at 10am, 2pm & 4pm; free). The park service still maintains kennels and patrols the park in winter with dog teams, so hop on the free shuttle from the visitor center to see dogs put through their paces hauling a wheeled sled. It is a well-orchestrated show and you can't help but smile at the dogs' huge enthusiasm at the prospect of a run.

In the evening the **Alaska Cabin Nite**, at *McKinley Chalet* in Glitter Gulch (nightly 5.30pm & 8.30pm; $42), draws quite a crowd to its "dinner theater" which features a cabaret-style performance followed by the waitstaff in character dishing up heaps of ribs and salmon. Leave your critical faculties at home and it can be fun. If something scuppers your wildlife viewing plans in the park, there's some compensation in visiting the **Northern Lights Theater** (daily at 9am, 1pm,

The following campsites are listed in order of distance from the George Parks Hwy.

Riley Creek, Mile 0.5 (100 sites; $12). Large, vehicle-accessible family campground among the woods at the eastern extremity of the park that's often full of RVs. It is far superior to the commercial RV parks along the highway and comes equipped with a sewage dump station. Reserve in advance or pop by the nearby visitor center (p.356) and you'll be assigned a site. *Riley Creek* stays open all year, though there is no water in winter.

Morino, Mile 1.9 (60 sites; $6). Backpacker-oriented walk-in site close to the train station with small, grassy sites (two-person maximum) among the trees. Within walking distance of a grocery store and the visitor center. Sites are available on a first-come, first-served basis, with self-registration on arrival, but again it is usually packed.

Savage River, Mile 13 (33 sites; $12). Drive-in site accessible without going through the backcountry access system and offering distant views of Mount McKinley from its position high and dry above the river. Good hiking hereabouts up onto Primrose Ridge. Reserve at the visitor center.

Sanctuary River, Mile 23 (7 sites; $6). Primitive, wooded, tent-only site overlooking the river that makes a good hiking base. It is the first campground which requires use of the camper bus for access, only has river water (which needs treating) and open fires are not permitted.

Teklanika, Mile 29 (53 sites; $12). Large site open both to backpacking campers and to vehicle campers. The latter are given a pass to drive here but must then leave their vehicle here for a minimum of three nights before driving out. They can explore further using the Teklanika Pass ($21), which allows one reserved seat on either the camper bus or Park Shuttle, then unlimited use of those buses on a space-available basis.

Igloo Creek, Mile 34 (7 sites; $6). Small, secluded and quiet site requiring use of the camper bus for access. No piped water and no open fires.

Wonder Lake, Mile 85 (28 sites; $12). The jewel in Denali's crown. A beautiful campground with well-distributed campsites laid out across the sparse taiga almost all with sweeping views of the Alaska Range with McKinley's 14,000ft Wickersham Wall right in front of you. Arrive early in the day to avoid being relegated to the less fashionable sites without the grand view. Access by camper bus.

5pm, 6pm, 7pm & 8pm; $6.50), for a 35-minute showing of LeRoy Zimmerman's slides of the aurora and Denali wildlife projected onto a 34-foot screen and put to symphonic music.

Rafting

Half a dozen rafting companies (all but one based in Glitter Gulch) cover two stretches of the Nenana River several times a day. Upstream from Glitter Gulch, the seven-mile **"Wilderness"** section (Class I and II; 1.5–2 hours on the water) makes a pleasant drift on a sunny day, but is unlikely to reveal much remarkable wildlife. The lower **"Canyon"** section (Class III and IV), downstream from Glitter Gulch, is altogether more thrilling; definitely a whitewater run. Oared rafts and more maneuverable paddle-assisted rafts (see Basics, p.57) are used for the two-hour run through the Nenana Canyon to Healy. The river is always very cold – you will get wet – so there is a definite advantage to rafting with one of the companies that kits you out in a **dry suit**; in addition, bring thermal underwear and a fleece if you have them. The luxury of a dry suit might cost you a dollar or two

ENTRANCE AREA HIKES

There are essentially two types of hiking in Denali: arduous backcountry hiking (see p.366), and the relatively gentle strolls along smooth well-managed paths around the entrance area. The latter suffer to some degree from proximity to Glitter Gulch, but otherwise make for good hikes with a fair chance of seeing some wildlife. Some of these feature as part of free **ranger-led hikes** (consult the *Denali Alpenglow*). and all make good fillers while you are waiting to get access to the park proper.

Horseshoe Lake Trail (1.5 miles round-trip; 1hr; 250ft ascent). The most popular of the entrance-area walks is a jaunt through taiga forest to a placid beaver-dammed oxbow lake, best done in the early morning or late evening when wildlife takes over. Park just as you cross the train tracks, follow the line north for 100 yards then follow the signs on the right.

Morino Loop Trail (1.3-mile loop; 40min; 100ft ascent). A gentle wooded walk from near the train station past the *Morino* walk-in campground with views through the trees up Riley Creek.

Mount Healy Trail (5 miles round-trip; 2–4hr; 1700ft ascent). Although the most strenuous of the entrance-area hikes this one is easy at first as you gradually pull out of the trees to a scenic overlook. The second half follows unimproved trail getting progressively tougher to the finish just below a rocky bluff, from where it is possible to see the whole of the Riley Creek catchment, and McKinley on a clear day.

Roadside Trail (1.8 miles one-way; 1hr; 300ft ascent). A moderate trail linking the visitor center and train station with the Park Headquarters. Best tackled downhill after riding the free bus to the dog-sled demonstration at the Park Headquarters.

Rock Creek Trail (2.3 miles one-way; 1hr 30min; 400ft ascent). A slightly tougher but scenic and more rewarding alternative to the Roadside Trail best done either on your return from the Park Headquarters or combined with the Roadside Trail into a four-mile loop.

more but it's worth it, and you can sometimes offset that a little by opting for a 1pm or 2pm run, usually slightly cheaper since most train travelers have either just arrived or are preparing to leave.

Typically you can expect to pay $50–60 for the Wilderness run, a similar amount for the Canyon run and $75–80 for the four-hour combination. Most companies offer a paddle-raft option, adding $5–10 to reflect their increased insurance costs. Companies currently outfitting their customers with dry suits are Denali Outdoor Center (☎683-1925 or 1-888/303-1925, *www.denalioutdoorcenter.com*) and the slightly more expensive Healy-based Nenana Raft Adventures, Mile 248.5 George Parks Hwy (☎683-7238 or 1-800/789-7238, *www.raftdenali.com*). Most companies take anyone over five years of age on the Wilderness run, twelve for the Canyon.

In addition Denali Outdoor Center run a whitewater kayak school, rent kayaks, and operate **inflatable-kayak tours** (daily 8am & 1.30pm; $75) in self-bailing, blow-up boats on the Wilderness section. Having to control your own vessel is a much more challenging proposition than riding in a raft, but anyone with reasonable physical fitness can participate.

Flightseeing
The shortest and most competitively priced flights to Mount McKinley leave from Talkeetna, south of the Alaska Range, but several local companies fly from Glitter Gulch giving the Talkeetna set a good run for their money. The basic hour-long flight (around $170) largely follows the Park Road, overflying much of the same scenery, then turning up the Muldrow Glacier heading for the Wickersham Wall. To extend this right around Mount McKinley you'll be looking at an extra half-hour in the air and a cost of over $210. Two of the most professional set-ups are Peré Air (☎683-6033, *www.pereair.com*) and Denali Air (☎683-2261).

Day trips into the park

If time is tight, or you just want to supplement your other park escapades, then **drive to Savage River** twelve miles along the Park Road (there's no need for permits, tickets, or even park entrance fees). There are a number of pull-outs where you can park (but not overnight) and trudge off across the tundra. Note that on a clear day you can get a distant view of Mount McKinley near Mile 9. Even with this limited penetration you're still likely to see moose, especially in the late afternoon: bears, caribou, and Dall sheep tend to stay deeper in the park. Those without cars can achieve much the same by riding the **Savage River Shuttle** (see box, p.359), which goes as far as the *Savage River* campground.

It is definitely worth taking at least one bus ride along the Park Road if you've made it this far. The cheapest option is the **Park Shuttle** (for reservation information see p.358), which runs right out to Wonder Lake at the far end of the road. It is a wonderful trip but at eleven hours for the full there-and-back journey you may find that going as far as Eielson (7hr round-trip) is enough.

Leave early enough and you can engage in a little shuttle bus surfing, hopping off when something strikes your fancy, hiking up a ridge or across the tundra for a few hours, then leaping on the next one that has space available – although in the height of summer there isn't much space available and you may well find yourself stranded for a few hours. Strictly speaking you must pay for westbound travel and get eastbound bus rides free. Remember that there is nowhere to buy anything in the park (except for books at Eielson visitor center): take a good stock of food and drink for the day along with binoculars, camera with plenty of film, insect repellent, and sunglasses.

In addition to the Park Shuttle, there are a couple of other ways of spending your day in the park, either on one of the **bus tours** (see box, p.359) or a free **ranger-led walk**, the best being to Horseshoe Lake (daily; 2hr), and the more strenuous Discovery Hike (daily; 3–4hr), which requires sturdy hiking boots and the purchase of a bus ticket ($21) to get into the park.

Park campgrounds

Spending the day in the park riding the buses and going for the odd stroll is a wonderful experience, but you'll gain a much greater sense of the place if you're prepared to spend a few nights in one of the **campgrounds** (for reservation information see box, p.357). Not only does this give you the opportunity to get out on foot and do some serious hiking, but you'll also see animals in a more natural environment, away from the Park Road and not trying to get away from a busload of shutter-snapping visitors.

Drivers can use their own vehicles to get to *Riley Creek*, *Savage River*, and *Teklanika*, but for all other sites you'll need a place on the **camper bus**; usually less packed than the Park Shuttle. **Cyclists** can use their bikes, but for the more distant sites it might be better (or at least a lot easier) to use the camper buses as well. Those without gear can **rent equipment** from Denali Mountain Works (see "Listings," p.369).

There is no reason why you have to stick exclusively to campgrounds: one of the best ways to stay in the park is to **combine campgrounds with backcountry camping**. In fact spending a few days in the backcountry (see below) can be a very good way to bide your time while you wait for a particular campground to come free. The possession of a reservation for a backcountry unit gives you the freedom to then book a sequence of nights at both campgrounds and in backcountry units (up to a maximum of fourteen nights), though it does mean going back and forth between two different desks (and potentially long lines) in the visitor center.

Hiking and camping in the backcountry

The ease of access, availability of piped water, and the presence of rangers around make the campgrounds appealing, but the essence of Denali only truly reveals itself if you go **backcountry camping**. You'll have to show a fair bit of determination and flexibility, but it's worth the extra effort and there is no charge.

The original Mount McKinley National Park, which covered a thirty-mile-wide strip northwest of the central Alaska Range, is now designated as Denali National Park's **wilderness area**, and has been divided into 43 **backcountry units**, large chunks of land each with a daily quota of overnight stays. If you want to stay inside the park but outside the designated campgrounds you'll have to get yourself on this quota; something done at the visitor center.

There are **no advance reservations** for backcountry units, so everything must be done in person. Anyone intending to spend the night in the backcountry must first view the **backcountry simulator** video (25min) teaching you about dealing with bears, or, more to the point, how to avoid having to deal with them. Ideally the next step would be to decide where you want to go and book it, but in practice space is limited and you'll need to consult the Quota Board, which lists the number of free spaces in each backcountry unit. You can only make a reservation for your **first night** two days in advance (eg reserve Fri for Sun night), and even though there may be nights available three days hence, you can't book them unless you have already got a booking for the night after tomorrow. Once you've secured the first night you can go ahead and reserve up to fourteen continuous nights, so arrive at the visitor center early, accept what you can get for the first night or two, then home in on your desired area after that. **Smaller groups**, of course, have a better chance, and lone campers (a discouraged breed) can often get something at short notice. The backcountry desk at the visitor center has information on the backcountry units and topo maps, and we've given a few pointers below.

Once in the backcountry, you can keep returning to the road and using the camper buses to access the next unit you have booked, but too much chopping and changing can easily wreck the continuity of your wilderness experience and it is usually preferable to concentrate on one area, hiking well away from the Park

Road. It is probably asking too much, but it is better if you can arrive without too many preconceptions of where you want to hike, and just make the best of what you can get.

With your backcountry reservations made you'll be handed a free **bear-resistant food container** (see Basics, p.54) which is yours for the duration of your backcountry stay. Tuck it under your arm and amble over to the shuttle-bus desk to book onto a **camper bus** that will get you to within striking distance of your unit.

Backcountry units

Every **backcountry unit** has its own character, advantages, and limitations, all of which can take some time to work out, especially under pressure from others packed into the visitor center trying to do the same. What we've set out to do here is lay down a few general points to guide you in the right direction. For more detail, consult *The Backcountry Companion* (available for viewing in the visitor center), which has descriptions of each unit, and Trails Illustrated's 1:200,000 *Denali National Park and Preserve* map ($6), the best general map showing terrain and unit boundaries.

When planning your trip you should first make a note of regions which have been either permanently or temporarily closed to protect animal breeding habitats: maps at the backcountry desk in the visitor center make this clear. For your first night you will need to look at the 29 units (of the park's total of 43) that border the Park Road; the slow pace of travel in Denali and the sheer size of each unit dictates that your first and last backcountry night will be in one of these. For extended trips, carrying all your food can become a chore, one fortunately eased by provision of food caches at Toklat, Eielson, and Wonder Lake where you can stash extra supplies.

Note: The order of the following descriptions follows the road westbound.

Units 1, 2, 3, 24 & 25: the five units closest to the visitor center are just about accessible without using the camper bus but a little noisy with air traffic. This area was less recently glaciated and is therefore more richly vegetated than the rest of the units making the ridges and river valleys the best passage. Great fall berrying, and wonderful colors, possible sightings of black bears and moose.

Units 4 & 5: gradually narrowing river valleys with some thick brush and possible high crossings into neighboring units.

Units 26 & 27: plenty of good, dry, high-country hiking (Mount Wright and Primrose Ridge), good wildflowers and sheep plus walks along Savage River Canyon. Drinking water can be scarce in parts.

Units 6, 7, 8, 29, 30 & 31: mixed area of broad rivers, accessible high country (Igloo, Sable, and Cathedral mountains) and rolling hills of varying colors and textures that offer very rewarding hiking. Some dry tundra and great views of the Alaska and Outer ranges. Some large areas closed for habitat protection.

Units 9, 10 & 32: wide, braided valleys with spectacular glaciers at the headwaters but sometimes difficult river crossings. Steep slopes limit crossings between valleys.

Units 11 & 33: be prepared to get your feet wet in interesting little canyons or stick to the rolling and rugged hills with loose, exposed rock. Tough going but good views.

Units 12, 13 & 18: easy hiking close to Eielson visitor center and good views of nearby glaciers but quickly getting tougher, especially crossing the Muldrow Glacier or heading across the Thorofare River up into the steep mountains, glaciers, and scree of Unit 18.

Units 34, 35 & 36: plenty of rolling wet and dry tundra with some heavy brush and beaver pools making for hard going in the low country. Follow ridges and knolls or aim for the summit of Mount Galen. Wonderful views of the whole Alaska Range and Mount McKinley.

Units 14 & 15: swampy and mosquito ridden with heavy brush making hiking difficult but great views of the Alaska Range. Access to units 19, 20 & 21 across the river is difficult. No camping in the day-use area around Wonder Lake.

Units 19, 20, 21 & 22: these are all south of the McKinley River making access very difficult. You either need glacier-travel skills to cross the Muldrow Glacier or be prepared for a complex and often dangerous waist-deep crossing of the McKinley River. All are rugged with glaciers coming down to the lowlands and rigorous hiking. Unit 22 requires expedition logistics and consequently has no quota.

Units 40, 41, 42 & 43: lowland tundra with taiga high up and some thick brush to contend with, but great Alaska Range views if you're on the right side of the hills. Some difficult river crossings and some private property around old gold claims.

Units 37, 38 & 39: multiday hiking territory only accessible from neighboring units. A vast and little visited region of large rivers and spruce forests harboring black bears.

Unit 23: the backbone of the Alaska Range (including McKinley), all rock and ice and only for serious mountaineers.

Units 16 & 17: south of the Alaska Range and wetter than the rest of the units. Normally accessed from outside the park near Cantwell though Unit 16 but can be reached through Unit 2.

Practicalities

Chances are, hiking in Denali will be unlike anything you've experienced before. Forget the usual imprecations to stick to the trail and avoid cutting switchbacks: there are **no managed trails** in the main body of the park, so no switchbacks to cut. It is a guesstimation of which line is liable to afford the easiest passage then constant reappraisal while negotiating **tundra** – likened by some to hiking on foam-rubber basketballs on a waterbed. It is a continual process and (the physical difficulties aside) a much more tiring one than following a trail. Take heed: if twenty-mile treks across moors or along sierra trails are your norm, you'll need to revise your daily estimates down to five or six miles, at least until you learn the rhythm of the land.

This is a land where **following ridgelines** (also known just as ridges) often provides the easiest passage. But if you don't want to go up – and you can quite quickly reach the snow line even in the height of summer – then your best bet is to follow one of the many rivers; and that means **getting your feet wet**. With few exceptions it is hard going, but the rewards can be great: miles of barely touched wilderness deserted by man and with only the animals to keep you company; slopes drenched in wildflowers in the spring; or a larder of berries in fall.

A consequence of all this is that **we have intentionally avoided suggesting any routes to follow**. The rangers won't suggest any either; after all, the whole point of hiking in Denali – and its most inviting feature – is that you can make it up as you go along. This seems alien at first. You'll occasionally come across what are known as "social trails" where others have gone before you and worn a passage, and it takes a force of will not to follow them. You should find your own route (and this goes for each person in your party) to avoid creating "social trails," then, for the same reason, when it comes to camping, select an apparently unused spot and never stay for more than two nights.

Aside from all the usual considerations of bear safety and backcountry travel (for both, see Basics, p.54), it goes without saying that any party going into the backcountry needs at least one person who is a competent **map reader**. Backcountry rules dictate that you **must camp more than half a mile from the Park Road** and out of sight of it. Without some competence with topographical maps you may find a huge mountain or impassable river between you and your planned camping spot.

Eating and drinking

Eating is expensive in and around Denali but there is quite a range of options. Campers, and those taking long day-rides into the park on the shuttle buses will need **groceries**. If you're prepared to lug them from Anchorage or Fairbanks then you'll open up your culinary options considerably (particularly with fresh fruit and vegetables which are almost unheard of in Denali's shops) and save yourself a lot of money, but you can buy some food here. McKinley Mercantile, Mile 1.5 Park Rd (which has an espresso bar), and two stores in Glitter Gulch, all sell more or less the same limited range at similar prices.

If you are staying at McKinley Village, seven miles south, you may want to try the restaurant and bar at the hotel, and those staying in Healy can eat well enough at the diner-style *Totem Inn*, but all **the following restaurants are in Glitter Gulch**, within half a mile of each other either side of the George Parks Hwy.

Black Bear Coffee House (☎683-1656). A tiny log cabin with a sunny deck (and an attached cyber-lounge) serving good coffee and cakes plus soup, build-your-own sandwiches for $7, and usually one entree.

Denali/McKinley Steak and Salmon Bake (☎683-2733). A favorite on the tour-bus schedule so it fairly churns them through, but still provides a good salmon-bake dinner ($16), halibut dinner ($17), and salmon, halibut and ribs combo ($19) all including an all-you-can-eat salad bar.

Denali Smoke Shack (☎683-7665). A longstanding business recently relocated to spacious new premises. Tuck into teriyaki chicken ($15), king crab legs in garlic butter ($25), burgers and sandwiches, or one of several vegetarian dishes; tempeh fajitas go for $14. The bar area is often packed with tourists and river guides until the small hours.

Lynx Creek Pizza & Pub (☎683-2548). The best (pretty much the only) pizza for a hundred miles or more (from $13) competes for your attention with a gut-busting nachos grandissimo ($8 for vege, $10 for chicken) and Italian house specials like chicken Capri ($16). Wash it all down with draft microbrews or Italian plonk by the glass, then stick around for more until midnight. There's also a lunch buffet (11.30am–2pm) for $11.

The Perch, 13 miles south at Carlo Creek (☎683-2523). One of the finest restaurants in the district, perched on a bluff with views down to Carlo Creek from the picture windows and large deck. There's a full bakery on site, a deli that's great for lunches, and a full menu throughout the day: eggs Benedict for $9, pasta dishes from $16, steak and crab legs ($25–28), and they even do packed picnic lunches for park visitors ($9).

Listings

Banks There are no banks anywhere near Denali (Wasilla and Fairbanks are the closest); the nearest ATM is in Wally's Service Station in Healy, 11 miles north of the Park entrance.

Bike rental Denali Outdoor Center, Mile 238.9 George Parks Hwy (☎1-888/303-1925 or 683-1925) rent mountain bikes ($25 for half a day, $40 for a day, $37 a day multiday rentals).

Camping gear Denali Mountain Works, Mile 239 in Glitter Gulch (☎683-1542) sells camping gear at reasonable prices and rents two-person tents ($14 for first day then $7 a day, or $46 a week), sleeping bags ($10/$5/$33), binoculars ($7/$4/$26) and more. Bring a credit card for a deposit. McKinley Mercantile sells bulk white gas at just over $1 a pint; just take your bottle for a refill.

Car rental Teresa's Car Rentals (☎683-1377, fax 683-1380) rent late-model cars for $75 a day and they'll meet you at the train station.

Gas Healy and Cantwell both have gas all year round.

Internet access at the *Black Bear* Café (see overleaf).

Laundry *McKinley Campground* in Healy, 12 miles north of the park entrance has laundry facilities (8am–10pm).

Left luggage Lockers behind the visitor center cost only 50¢ for as long as you care to leave stuff, but at busy times you may have to wait a while for one to become free.

Long-distance buses Alaska Backpacker Shuttle (☎1-800/266-8625) and The Park Connection (☎1-800/208-0200) pick up at the visitor center, *Park Hotel* and train station; Alaskon Express (☎683-2406) and Parks Highway Express (☎1-888/600-6001) pick up at the visitor center and outside *Lynx Creek Pizza*.

Maps The visitor center stocks maps. Most quad maps ($4 each) cover three or four back-country sectors at one inch to the mile (1:63,360).

Medical assistance The Healy Clinic, E Healy Spur Rd (Mon–Fri 9am-5pm; ☎683-2211) is located in the Tri-Valley Community Center, 13 miles north of the park entrance.

Post office Close to the McKinley Mercantile in the entrance area. The **General Delivery** ZIP code is 99755.

Road lottery If you fancy attempting to win the right to drive the Park Rd on one of the fall lottery days (usually around Sept 15–18) then write (during July) to Road Lottery, Denali National Park, PO Box 9, Denali NP, AK 99755 enclosing a stamped self-addressed envelope along with your preferred dates. Out of around 12,000 applicants, 1600 are successful.

Showers McKinley Mercantile (daily 7.30am–8pm) offers $3 unlimited-time showers.

Taxes Denali and Healy both impose a seven percent bed tax which we've included in our price codes.

Taxis Healy has three taxi companies which run to the park entrance area for around $12 each way: Caribou Cabs ☎683-5000; Denali Taxi Service ☎683-2504; and Vantastic ☎683-7433.

North of Denali

From Denali it is 120 miles to Fairbanks, a journey which largely follows the course of the Nenana River to the town of the same name then cuts across the hills flanking the Tanana River. For the first few miles the Parks Hwy jostles for position with the railway as they squirm through the Nenana Gorge hugging the cliffs high above the rapids. The valley widens out at **HEALY**, a coal-mining town since 1918 and now home to the new Usibelli power station, powered by the product of open-cast mines artfully disguised behind a few rows of spruce. It is mainly of interest as a provider of accommodation to Denali visitors, so unless you plan to stay you might as well continue on through.

One point of passing interest, at Mile 251.1, is the start of the **Stampede Trail**, a rugged ninety-mile track with some notoriety as the refuge and final resting place of Chris McCandless, the subject of John Krakauer's biographical *Into the Wild* (see Contexts, p.504). It is mainly a winter trail to Kantishna in the heart of Denali National Park, but can be followed some of the distance in summer. You can hike from the parking lot about four miles in, but the unbridged Teklanika River is likely to stop further progress at Mile 10.

At Mile 276, the Parks Hwy crosses to the right bank of the Nenana River and, eight miles on, passes a side road to the ballistic-missile early-warning station at **Clear**, first established at the height of the Cold War in 1958 (there is no access to the site). On the last weekend in July or first in August you might want to continue to **Anderson**, six miles west of the Parks Hwy, for the **Anderson Bluegrass Festival**, a country and bluegrass extravaganza with regular acts from all over the state alongside Lower 48 headliners. You can stay at the spacious *Riverside Park RV & Camping* ($10 dry, $12 with electricity, dump station available), and eat and drink at the nearby *Dew Drop Inn*.

Nenana

Alaskan winters are long and break-up – the symbol of summer's imminent arrival, when ice-bound rivers finally thaw allowing vast sheets of jagged ice to crash and flip their way to the ocean – is the most anticipated event of spring. Nowhere celebrates this better than the small town of **NENANA**, at the confluence of the Nenana and Tanana rivers, 67 miles north of Denali National Park (Mile 305). Every year from the beginning of February to the first week in April local citizens begin compiling entries for the **Nenana Ice Classic**, a huge statewide lottery in which people chance $2 on their estimate of the time and date that the ice will break up. The festivities begin during the first week in March when a thirty-foot-high four-legged "tripod" is hauled 100 yards out onto the four-foot-thick ice of the Tanana River and firmly embedded there. A trip wire is then attached to a clock which stops the moment the ice breaks up. Back in 1917, railroad engineers wagered a total of $800 on the first such event: the pool now usually tops $600,000, half going to the organizers (for taxes, salaries, and promotion), and half split between those who guess the right time. The earliest the clock has stopped was April 20 in 1998, the latest was May 16 in 1945 and it almost

always happens between 9am and 9pm. Fish $2 out of your pocket and drop it in one of the red boxes found everywhere from early February to early April, or send it to Nenana Ice Classic, Box 272, Nenana, AK 99760. For more information visit their Web site at *www.ptialaska.net/~tripod*.

For most of the year, the **tripod** stands next to the **watchhouse** with its window theatrically set up with the clock frozen at the trip time of the last break-up and to the book of entries open at the winners' page. Standing beside what is the fastest navigable river in Alaska it is hard to imagine that these broad rolling waters would ever freeze up, but freeze they do, and the subsequent break-up proved to be the major obstacle to engineers trying to complete the Seward to Fairbanks railroad. Every year tumbling ice would wipe out the trestles of earlier bridges until they constructed the 700-foot Tanana River Bridge, then the longest single-span bridge in the country. In 1923 President Warren Harding came to drive in the **golden spike** on the north side of the river.

Being at the junction of two rivers, Nenana was important long before the railroad came through, and from 1866 through to the mid-1950s wooden steamboats used to ply the thousand miles of navigable waterways throughout the Interior. Nenana still serves as a goods entrepot with trains offloading onto barges which, through the 120 ice-free days of summer, supply remote villages. Recently the waterfront has been cleaned up and you can stroll along learning some of the history and looking across the water at **fishwheels** (see "Glossary," p.508) going about their automatic harvest. While you're in the vicinity it is worth briefly dropping in to the **Alfred Starr Nenana Cultural Center**, on the waterfront (Mon–Sat 11am–6pm, Sun noon–5pm; free), which concentrates on Athapascan lifestyle and artifacts with a little on historical Nenana and dog mushing for good measure. **St Mark's Episcopal Church**, just across the road, may well be locked (the visitor center has a key) but is also worth a few minutes of your time for the altar dressings made of bleached moosehide by local Athapascan women.

A block west, the baggage room of the former train station is now given over to the **Railway Museum** (mid-May to mid-Sept daily 8.30am–6pm; $1 donation expected), easy to dismiss as a miscellaneous collection of bear traps, telegraph insulators, and railway ephemera, but actually quite interesting for its material on the Ice Classic, including old entry books several inches thick.

Practicalities

Trains no longer stop in Nenana, though you can still get a brief look at the town's main sites via rail. As you wind through you go right past the Ice Classic watchhouse and tripod, get a good view of town as you cross the bridge then get a close-up of the plaque marking the spot where Harding drove in the golden spike, something you can't see from the road. Of course you only get the most fleeting glimpse, and for a more thorough investigation you'll need to drive, or arrive on one of the **shuttle buses** which run between Anchorage, Denali, and Fairbanks. The **visitor center** (mid-May to mid-Sept daily 8am–6pm; ☎832-9953) is located where the Parks Hwy meets A Street, the town's main drag, which runs the gauntlet of trinket shops to the former train station. Should you decide **to stay**, you'll find basic rooms at the *Nenana Inn*, corner of A and 2nd streets (☎832-5238; ③) where nonguests can get showers and do laundry; and more comfortable lodging at *Alaskan Retreat B&B*, corner of 4th and C streets (☎832-5431, fax 832-5566, *www.mtaonline.net/~gayle*; rooms ③, dorm ①), which has private rooms and a kind of dorm with beds for $25, including bedding, towels, a common area and use of a heated pool. **Campers** and RV drivers are well served at the central *Nenana Valley Campground*, corner of 4th and C streets (☎832-5230; full hookup $19, tents $13; closed Sept to late May).

The **best burgers** for miles around are served at *The Monderosa*, Mile 309 Parks Hwy, four miles north of town. In Nenana you'll find all you need along A Street: the *Two Choices Café* does good-value **meals** in the Alaskan tradition, and *Moochers Bar* has the town's ATM as well as an extensive liquor selection.

If none of this takes your fancy, press on twenty-odd miles towards Fairbanks (now only 53 miles to the north) to *Skinny Dick's Halfway Inn*, Mile 328, a bar and diner famed throughout the Interior for its extensive range of puerile T-shirts and souvenirs playing on the inn's name.

The Glenn Highway to Glenallen

The **Glenn Highway** – and its logical and geographical continuation, the **Tok Cutoff** – is the shortest road route from Anchorage to the Lower 48, meeting the Alaska Hwy at Tok, 328 miles to the northeast. The highway gets its name from Captain Edwin Glenn, who explored the area prior to World War II when an old system of tracks was upgraded to connect Anchorage to the Alaska Hwy, then under construction.

The entire road runs through sparsely populated country that, even on good asphalt, still has a very remote feel as you climb from one watershed to another over a series of low passes. Initially you climb up beside the Matanuska River, which drains west to Cook Inlet, but you eventually end up beside the Tazlina Valley, which spills down the Copper River into Prince William Sound. There's some very fine scenery, too, with the Talkeetna, Alaska, and Chugach ranges soaring up on either side and immense glaciers poking out of the mountains.

The presence of the highway seems to encourage people to drive straight through in a day, and while there are few specific attractions there is a fair bit to see, with some perseverance. Wildlife may be more elusive than in Denali but the animals are out there; the Dall sheep usually far up the roadside crags, bears in the woods, moose in and around the small lakes, and caribou roaming the glacial river bars.

Sutton, Chickaloon, and the Matanuska Glacier

Leaving Anchorage the Glenn Hwy runs past Eagle River and Eklutna (see p.327) and into Palmer in the Matanuska Valley (see p.330) before swinging east. Pulling out of Palmer (Mile 42) on the Glenn Hwy you first pass the junction with Fishhook–Willow Road (for Hatcher Pass and Independence Mine; Mile 49.5) and continue a dozen miles to **SUTTON** a small community which flourished in the 1920s around a rail siding from the days when this was coal country. The only reason to pause is the **Alpine Historical Park**, Mile 61.5 (mid-May to mid-Sept daily 10am–6pm; donation appreciated), a selection of relocated buildings on the former site of the Sutton Coal Washery, including the Chickaloon Bunkhouse and a coal museum in the old Sutton post office with material on the construction of the Glenn Hwy and the local Athapascans.

From Sutton the highway winds along the Matanuska Valley, gradually climbing as you penetrate deeper into the mountains that tower on both sides. After fifteen miles a wide spot in the road with a post office, small store and gas station constitutes **CHICKALOON** (Mile 76.5), home to Nova (☎1-800/746-5753, *www .novaalaska.com*), who run the most popular **rafting** trip in Alaska – the four-hour Class III–IV **Lion Head** (late May to early Sept 9am & 2pm; $75) along the upper reaches of the Matanuska River, for which there is a minimum age of twelve. Highly scenic and with a stop to explore the foot of the Matanuska Glacier, it is a wonderful trip made all the better by taking the evening run (mid-June to mid-July 7pm; $95) when the day's meltwater is at its peak – they even stop for a mid-trip burger. Downstream from Chickaloon township the river relents to Class II, run on the gentle family-oriented **Matanuska** trip (mid-May to mid-Sept; 3–4hr; $60, kids aged 5–11 $35). Across the road from the Nova office sits *King Mountain Lodge* (☎745-4280; rooms ②, cabins ①) which has been serving down-home Alaskan meals for over fifty years, has a bar full of wise-cracking signs, and a small stage for weekend bands, and rents miners' cabins and basic motel rooms. Ad hoc tent sites are free, though you may prefer the adjacent *King Mountain State Recreation Site* ($10; pump water) among the white spruce, some sites with river and King Mountain views.

The scenery just keeps getting better further up the valley, and is made more inviting by the presence of the diminutive *Lower Bonnie Lake Campground*, two miles off the highway at Mile 83.2 (free; lake water), which has good grayling fishing throughout the summer.

Around Mile 100 you catch your first glimpse of the **Matanuska Glacier**, a 27-mile-long tongue of ice poking out of the Chugach Mountains. During the last ice age it stretched as far as Palmer, and, though it has been chipped back considerably, is still some four miles wide at its terminus. Close contact can only be achieved by parting with $6.50 to drive to within 300 yards of the foot of the glacier through *Glacier Park Resort*, Mile 102.1 (mid-April to Sept; ☎745-2534). From the end of the road you can hike onto the glacier, and even dry camp nearby for $10 (which includes glacier access). Unless you are desperate to touch the ice, a better bet might be to get a longer, but still impressive, view from short hiking trails which thread along a bluff from *Matanuska Glacier State Recreation Site*, Mile 101.1 ($12 per vehicle; pump water), or from the magnificent picture windows while tucking into one of the excellent homemade meals at the hunting-lodge style *Long Rifle Lodge*, Mile 102.2 (☎745-5151, fax 745-5153; ③), which also has functional but pleasant rooms.

Tahetna Pass and Lake Louise

Excellent views of the Matanuska Glacier continue as you climb steadily east past Lion Head, a small mountain right in the middle of the valley named for its appearance from the east. Beyond Lion Head the valley opens out into country that's great for hiking or just sitting back with binoculars spotting wildlife. There are a couple of good **places to stay** in these parts with rooms to suit all budgets: the lovely *Tundra Rose B&B*, Mile 109.5 (☎745-5865 or 1-800/315-5865, fax 745-5854, *www.alaska.net/~tundrose*; suite ⑤, cabin ④), with its fabulous glacier views, is based around a log-built home with adjacent cabin and suite; while *Sheep Mountain Lodge*, Mile 113.5 (☎745-5121 or 1-877/645-5121, fax 745-5120, *www.alaska.net/~sheepmtl*; cabins ⑥, bunks $16, hookups $20), a dozen or so spacious, fully-fixtured cabins at the foot of a hill, is renowned for its population of Dall sheep. The lodge also has RV water and power hookups and acts as an HI

hostel with dorm beds, but no common room or kitchen. In compensation, there's a hot tub and sauna (free to guests, otherwise $5), and a modestly-priced **restaurant** that is a substantial cut above the average roadside diner, serving classy homemade meals and drinks from a well-stocked bar.

Glance back for a view of Lion Head, then press on past the **Squaw Creek** viewpoint and trailhead (Mile 118.4) to the 3000ft **Tahneta Pass** at Mile 121, the site of a couple of lodges and a gas station, and a good spot to look back at **Gunsight Mountain**, visible for miles approaching from the east, and distinguished by the missing-tooth serration on its summit ridgeline. The road passes the 1937 *Eureka Roadhouse*, the oldest on this highway, to the 3321ft Eureka Summit (Mile 129), the highest point on the Glenn Hwy. Views now expand south to the ice-capped Chugach Mountains and north across flatter country pocked by myriad small lakes and threaded by small creeks. The road stays high for a time, to the Little Nelchina River and the small, waterside *Little Nelchina River Campground*, Mile 137.7 (free; river water).

At Mile 159.8 a scenic gravel road spurs nineteen miles north to the shores of **LAKE LOUISE**, a popular spot with vacationing Alaskans, chiefly for swimming and lake trout fishing, the latter best done in spring and early summer. Campers can stay right by the lake at the *Lake Louise State Recreation Area*, Mile 17 ($12; pump water), the less hardy at *The Point Lodge*, Mile 17 (☎822-5566 or 1-800/808-2018, *www.alaskapointlodge.com*; ⑤).

Glenallen and around

The only people who will want to spend more than an hour in **GLENALLEN**, 145 miles east of Palmer (Glenn Hwy, Mile 187), are RV drivers eager for full hookups, and those without wheels needing transport into the Wrangell–St Elias National Park. Despite its setting at the nucleus of Alaska's central road system – where the Glenn and Richardson highways meet – it doesn't really amount to much, straggling along the highway for a mile or so with RV parks extending its domain further out.

Bus travelers will find Glenallen inconveniently spread out and will be dropped in one of two places: Alaskon Express and Alaska Direct buses stop in the center of town outside the *Caribou Café* (see overleaf); Parks Highway Express pull up at the Copper River Valley **visitor center** (summer daily 8am–7pm, mid-May 9am–6pm; ☎ & fax 822-5555, *www.traveltoalaska.com*) at **Glenallen Junction**, the meeting of the two highways, two miles to the east. If you get dropped here you'll have to walk, or thumb, into town.

For **buses into the Wrangell–St Elias National Park** along the McCarthy Road, contact the McCarthy Kennicott Shuttle (☎1-800/478-5292; for timetable and reservation details see p.380) who pick up in Glenallen and around the region. Alternatively you may be able to **rent a vehicle** in town (probably $60–70 a day with a $40 surcharge for driving the McCarthy road), though the last rental company recently closed: enquire through the visitor center.

Crack-of-dawn departures mean that those without their own vehicles will probably have to spend the night here **camping** either at the *Northern Nights Campground and RV Park*, Mile 188.7, close to the visitor center (☎ & fax 822-3199; tent $10, full hookup $17), or just dossing down in any quiet spot you can find. The *Dry Creek State Recreation Site*, Mile 118, three miles north of Glenallen Junction ($12 per vehicle; pump water), is better suited to drivers and comes with some quiet walk-in tent sites but lots of mosquitoes.

THE RICHARDSON HIGHWAY

The 368-mile **Richardson Highway**, from Valdez to Fairbanks, is the oldest road in the Interior, yet in its full 368 miles never passes through anything more than a small town. Its original construction was prompted by the abominable suffering of those who tried the Valdez Glacier route to the Yukon gold fields in the winter of 1898 (see p.492). The following year, Congress approved funds for the US Army to build a military road linking Fort Liscum in Valdez with Fort Egbert in Eagle and Captain Abercrombie began surveying the route on April 21. He soon had the Goat Trail cut through Keystone Canyon to bypass the Valdez Glacier using sleds, pack horses, and mules in trying conditions made worse by harsh weather and mosquitoes. In the few short months of summer, 93 miles of wagon road were forged and a further 114 miles were cleared and the streams bridged. The road was completed in 1900, but the gold-rush focus soon shifted to Fairbanks, and so did the main trail. The full journey from Valdez to Fairbanks could take up to two weeks, with travelers spending nights in roadhouses spaced a day's travel apart, this was particularly important during the winter when they had to journey in open carriages (the roads were so rough they induced motion sickness in closed carriages) with only wolf robes and a charcoal brazier for warmth. General Wilds Richardson had the road upgraded to a wagon road in 1907, the Alaska Roads Commission improved it for automobile use in the 1920s, and the road was finally paved in 1957.

For a roof over your head you've the choice of **cabins and rooms** at *Brown Bear Rhodehouse*, three miles east along Glenn Hwy at Mile 183.6 (☎822-3663; rooms ④, cabins ③), smarter rooms at the *Caribou Hotel*, Mile 187 (☎822-3302 or 1-800/478-3302 in Alaska, fax 822-3711; ⑥), or a B&B such as *Carol's*, Birch Road at Mile 186.8 (☎822-3594, fax 822-3800, *neeley@alaska.net*; ③) which has rooms inside and a trailer with kitchenette (④). **Meals** are no great shakes in Glenallen, but there's a summertime espresso stall beside the highway; you can fill your stomach adequately at the *Caribou Café*, part of the hotel complex, and the *Hitchin' Post*, Mile 187.8 (☎822-3338) is noted for its $3 breakfast specials, but is otherwise less good.

If you've got to get a few things sorted, you'll find everything you need along the highway: a **BLM office** (Mon–Fri 8am–4pm; ☎822-3217) at Mile 186.4; the **pharmacy** and 24-hr emergency clinic of Cross Road Medical Center (☎822-3203) at Mile 186.6; a **bank** (Mile 186.8); the **post office** (Mile 187.5); Park's Place Groceries (Mile 187.8); and a **laundry** (Mile 187.8).

The Wrangell–St Elias National Park

The **Wrangell–St Elias National Park** fills out the extreme southeast corner of the Alaskan Interior, on the point where four of the continent's great mountain ranges – the Wrangell, St Elias, Chugach, and Alaskan – cramp up against each other. It is bigger than the 22 largest parks in the Lower 48 put together; a place that defies superlatives. Even the usually unsensationalist US National Park Service literature breaks out in a rash of (justifiable) hyperbole by saying,

"Incredible. You have to see Wrangell–St Elias . . . to believe it – and even then you won't be so sure." Everything in Wrangell–St Elias is writ large: peak after peak (including twelve of the fifteen highest in the state: nine over 14,000 feet and fourteen over 10,000), glacier after enormous glacier (some the size of small states), canyon after dizzying canyon – all laced together by braided rivers, massive moraines and icy-cold lakes, with the volcanic 14,163-foot monster of Mount Wrangell still steaming on in the background.

As if all this weren't enough, it forms part of a contiguous cross-border wilderness with Canada's Kluane National Park Reserve and Tatshenshini-Alsek Park, and the Southeast's Glacier Bay National Park & Preserve, together forming the largest protected area on the planet that is recognized as a **World Heritage Site**.

Vegetation struggles to take hold in the higher reaches of the park, though tenaciously hangs on enough to support mountain goats and Dall sheep. Lower down the diversity goes wild, riparian fringes and wooded silty lowlands are home to bears, moose, and three sizeable herds of caribou.

The park was created in 1980, and remains – in terms of access and development – in its infancy, with private landowners still holding large chunks of its putative territory. It sees less than a tenth of the visitors Denali gets, and though bush-plane landing sites stud the territory, only two roads penetrate the park. The Nabesna Road (covered on p.388) cuts into the northern fringes, but most visitors approach the park along the **McCarthy Road**, a hundred-mile epic along the Copper and Chitina rivers to freewheeling **McCarthy** and the copper-mining ghost town of **Kennicott** with its thirty big, disused buildings now preserved as a National Historic Landmark. It is a fascinating place, dramatically sited and wonderfully photogenic, but the appeal of the area is as much in its access to stiff **hikes**, several easily accessible, but others requiring a bush plane.

Some history

In July 1900, two prospectors, "**Tarantula Jack**" Smith and **Clarence Warner** started poking around the tributaries of the Chitina River in search of gold. They found none but didn't go away empty handed. Legend has it that they spotted what looked to be a promising patch of grazing well above the snow line close to the crest of a sawtooth ridge. As experienced prospectors with little interest in sheep pasture it seems likely they knew full well that the green patch was something much more valuable than grass. Whatever the truth, they high tailed it up the slope and unearthed what became the **Bonanza Mine**, one of the continent's richest copper deposits, predominantly chalcocite, a phenomenally rich copper ore which sometimes assayed at almost eighty percent, and averaged thirteen percent at a time when commercial mines in Utah and Arizona were getting two percent.

Mining engineer, Stephen Birch, bought their claim (and others nearby), and with the backing of financier JP Morgan and the Guggenheim brothers, formed what was to become the Kennecott Copper Corporation. The mines were worthless without some means of getting the ore to smelters in the Lower 48 and the company set about the gargantuan task of building the Copper River & North Western railway (see box, p.380). Meanwhile, work began on what was to become the dedicated six-hundred-strong company town of **Kennicott**. Everything had to be hauled in – mostly on sleds during the winter when the rivers froze – so that processed ore would be ready to ship out to Cordova when the first train arrived in 1911. Overnight, the Kennecott mines became the richest in the world.

ACCOMMODATION
Kennicott Cottage	3
Kennicott Glacier Lodge	2
Kennicott River Lodge	4
Ma Johnson	6
Strelna Zephyr Bunkhouse	1
Willow Herb Depot	5

Meanwhile, five miles down the tracks, business-minded John Barrett had leased his homestead land to the CR&NW for turntable and switching operations. With the flood of prospectors making for Skolai Pass and **Chisana** (pronounced Shushanna), for what turned out to be Alaska's last gold rush in 1914, Barrett was able to sell off more land setting the stage for the development of **McCarthy**.

The Great Depression of the 1930s sent copper prices spiraling down and when the Chitina bridge washed out in 1932 the mines closed. They reopened in 1935, but thirty years of frantic production came to an end in 1938; the last train arrived in Kennicott on November 11 apparently with instructions for the station agent to collect his papers and belongings in ninety minutes and climb on board the return service.

Once the railroad bed became recycled as a road a few years later it became open season on looting anything not nailed down, and a fair bit that was. In the 1960s the Kennecott land was turned over to a faceless corporation who sold the managers' cabins to whatever hippies and recluses were interested. Since the formation of the National Park in 1980, and the Park Service's purchase of the whole

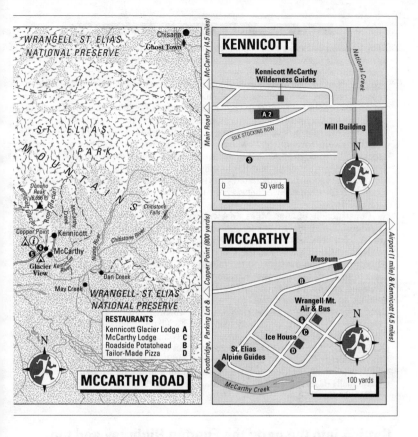

site (except for the private inholdings) in 1998, the steady decay has been arrested, meanwhile, visitors are beginning to come in serious numbers, some 50,000 a year (a tenfold increase over the past decade or so).

Information

Anyone planning to spend any time in the mountains to the east should call in at the **Wrangell–St Elias National Park Headquarters visitor center** (late May to early Sept daily 8am–6pm; early Sept to late May Mon–Fri 8am–5pm; ☎822-7261, fax 822-7216, *www.nps.gov/wrst*), in Copper Center at Mile 105.5 on the Richardson Hwy. Here, rangers will help you plan your hikes, sell books and topo maps, and generally offer advice on the area: the free *K'elt'aeni* newspaper is useful.

There's also a ranger station in Chitina (p.381), and an information kiosk at Copper Point (p.385). Before leaving Glenallen or Valdez, fill your tank and stock up with any groceries you may need; there's no gas or proper store in McCarthy. Campers wanting to stay at the free NPS campground should bring water with them. Neither McCarthy nor Kennicott have **banks** or a **post office**.

THE "CAN'T RUN & NEVER WILL" RAILWAY

The discovery of super-rich copper ore at the Bonanza mine offered the promise of great wealth but presented a seemingly insurmountable physical challenge. Only two years before, hundreds of prospectors had died trying to reach the Interior gold fields from the coast by crossing the Valdez Glacier, and the fledgling Valdez–Eagle Trail was inadequate and much too distant for transporting huge quantities of copper ore. In the spirit of the age it was decided to build a railroad. Master railroad builder Michael Heney (also responsible for Skagway's White Pass and Yukon Route, see p.164) was called in and plotted a 196-mile course up the Copper and Chitina rivers through narrow canyons and across deep gorges precariously spanned by wooden-lattice trestle bridges, some of which survive today. Icebergs, rapids, shifting sandbars and the howling Copper River wind all had to be taken into consideration, but undoubtedly the most challenging section was the 1550-foot span over the Copper River between the faces of two active glaciers – the Miles and the Childs.

Construction on the Miles Glacier Bridge – dubbed the "**Million Dollar Bridge**," though it actually cost appreciably more – began in earnest in the spring of 1908 but pessimists were not swayed and continued to refer to the Copper River & Northwestern Railway as the Can't Run & Never Will. Nonetheless, by March 1911 (in less than three years) the railway was completed all the way to Kennicott and remained the premier Alaskan construction feat until the Trans-Alaska Pipeline was built in the late 1970s. The entire line cost $23 million to build, and almost as much to maintain. Every year during spring break-up careening ice would wipe out many of the river bridges, which would then be rapidly rebuilt. During its 27-year life the railway hauled over $200 million in copper ore, but operation halted for good in 1938. In 1941 the company magnanimously gave the CR&NW right-of-way to the federal government who eventually transformed it into the McCarthy Road, but Cordova boosters' had long cherished ideas of putting in a highway along the Copper River to Chitina then to the Richardson Hwy. Hopes were finally dashed in 1964 when the Good Friday earthquake all but destroyed the Million Dollar Bridge.

Getting into the park: the Egerton Highway and the McCarthy Road

Getting into the Wrangell–St Elias National Park is only half the fun. It is a rugged backcountry drive which initially follows the smooth Egerton Hwy 33 miles to the village of Chitina, then the rough-dirt McCarthy Road to McCarthy and Kennicott. For nearly sixty bone-shaking miles it twists along the former trackbed of the Copper River & Northwestern Railway which still occasionally throws up old railway spikes as well as sharp rocks (beware of punctures and make sure your spare is functional). Conditions vary with the frequency of grading but at best it is slow, and can be an exacting drive.

Transport is a limiting factor. In general, rental agencies won't insure their vehicles for the journey, not that that seems to stop many people. Hitching can be a hit or miss affair, so you may need Backcountry Connections' McCarthy Kennicott Shuttle (mid-May to mid-Sept Mon–Sat; ☎822-5292 or 1-800/478-5292 in Alaska, fax 822-5292, *bakcntry@alaska.net*). They pick up in the morning from hotels and campgrounds around Glenallen and charge $99 for a same-day

The Wrangell-St Elias National Park can also be accessed along the Nabesna Road, about eighty miles further north. Our account is on p.388.

round-trip, $105 to spread it over several days: from Chitina the round-trip to McCarthy is $80 or $90. An excellent alternative is to **fly to McCarthy**, perhaps with a bit of aerial tour thrown in, obviating the need for a flightseeing trip once in McCarthy. In summer Wrangell Mountain Air (☎1-800/478-1160) run two daily flights into McCarthy from Chitina ($140 round-trip), and combine with the shuttle bus to offer a fly/drive round-trip (also $140). McCarthy Air (☎1-888/989-9891) will do charter flights for up to three people from Chitina ($200 one-way), Valdez ($450), Anchorage ($750) and elsewhere.

Copper Center

Trips into the park should start with a visit to **COPPER CENTER**, if only to call for info at the Park Headquarters visitor center (see p.379). This tiny Athapascan hamlet, sits on a bypass looping off the Richardson Hwy between Mile 100.2 and Mile 106.1, boomed in 1898 when three hundred stampeders who made it over the Valdez and Klutina glaciers stopped here at the ferry crossing over the Copper River. They came to recuperate, but there was little comfort through the harsh winter and many died, their headstones still evident in the **Stampeders Cemetery** in town. The heart of town beats around the *Copper Center Lodge*, Mile 101 (mid-May to mid-Sept; ☎822-3245, fax 822-5035, *www.alaska.net/~ccl*; rooms ④, with private facilities ⑤), an authentic descendant of the original roadhouse with smallish, fairly ordinary rooms let on a bed-and-breakfast basis, plus there's a good restaurant too. Two log bunkhouses formerly part of the *Lodge*, are now operated as the **George Ashby Memorial Museum** (June–Aug Mon–Sat 1–5pm; donations appreciated), packed to the rafters with memorabilia from the stampede and the copper years along with Russian icons and Athapascan basket-work.

The Egerton Highway to Chitina

The all-weather **Egerton Highway** cuts off the Richardson Hwy 36 miles south of Glenallen (Mile 82.6), and apart from the wonderful mountain scenery, there's little to distract you; though you may fancy the **Copper River Trail**, Mile 12.6 (7 miles round-trip; 3hr; mostly flat), which runs to the Copper River through excellent bird-watching territory. The small but beautifully formed *Liberty Falls State Recreation Site*, Mile 23.6 ($10; pump water), huddles by a cascading stream adjacent to the **Liberty Falls Creek Trail** (1 mile round-trip; 15–25min; 300ft ascent) which leads up through the spruce forest to a small ridge-end plateau with views of the cascading Liberty Creek and across the Copper River to the Wrangell Mountains.

The Copper and Chitina rivers join forces at **CHITINA** (pronounced CHIT-na), Mile 33, a hamlet locked in an aspen- and spruce-cloaked fold with an ancient, dilapidated appearance that belies its relatively recent genesis. It sprung to life in 1910 as a way station for the CR&NW railway and a transit point for rail passengers from Cordova taking the stage to Fairbanks and points inland. In the early 1940s, the rails were pulled up and buildings removed to the point that Chitina became virtually a ghost town, a point illustrated by one of the few local residents who painted phantoms on the walls of the remaining buildings. The red and king salmon runs on the silt-laden waters of the Copper River still drew dip netters every July and August, but it wasn't until the creation of the National Park in 1980 and the upsurge in tourism that Chitina started to revive. One short row of shopfronts has been tastefully preserved, notably Spirit Mountain Artworks which is worth a few minutes of your time for locally-produced paintings and photography, and quality Alaskan crafts. The essential stop here is the **Chitina Ranger Station** (late May to early Sept daily 10am–6pm; ☎823-2205), in the former home of a stagecoach-company manager, bedecked with fascinating photos of old-timers working the riverboats that carried supplies during the railroad construction. If you're hungry, you no longer have to make do with a burger from the *It'll Do Café*, Mile 33 (☎823-2234), since you can also eat pizza and espresso at *Raven Dance* (☎823-2254), half a mile back along the highway, and drink at *Uncle Tom's Tavern* (☎823-2253). Simple **cabins** are available at *Chitina Fishwheel Shop Cabin Rentals*, Mile 32 Egerton Hwy (no phone; ③) and *Chitina Guest Cabins*, Mile 32 Egerton Hwy (☎823-2266; ③). Hikers and bikers should consider detouring south along O'Brien Road (which is navigable for a few miles in dry conditions by ordinary vehicles) onto the **Copper River Trail** (see box, opposite) – not to be confused with the identically named one above – but for everyone else the McCarthy Road beckons.

The McCarthy Road

The **McCarthy Road** (typically open May to mid-Oct) has a speed limit of 35mph but if you've any respect for your rig you won't be troubling the state troopers. The sixty miles from Chitina to McCarthy is likely to take you at least two, maybe three, hours as you climb from 500ft to 1500ft through spruce, cottonwood, and aspen. The scenery is rugged mountains, but you occasionally come across incongruous patches of private property where a roadside airstrip provides access to a cluster of cabins, often with smooth lawns and brilliant flower beds. Soon after leaving Chitina the road crosses the Copper River, a concrete bridge replacing the railroad trestle which washed out every year at spring break-up and was rebuilt annually until 1939. Silt from glaciers on the southern flank of the Wrangell Mountains makes ordinary fishing impossible and this is one of only four Alaskan rivers where dip netting and fishwheels are permitted: you may well see them in the river if not obscured by dust storms which howl up the Copper River. On the east bank a free but often-windswept **campground** offers little temptation with the knowledge that you are now within the Wrangell–St Elias National Park and can informally camp beside the road (though not on any private property). There is slightly more formal accommodation at the commercial *Silver Lake* campground, Mile 10.9 (no phone; $10), which has tent sites and "dry" RV camping (both $10), does tire repair and rents canoes and rowboats for lake trout fishing ($4.50/hr); and *Strelna Zephyr Bunkhouse* two miles north up Nugget Creek Road at Mile 14.5 (☎240-3055; ③), a log cabin with just four bunks, a wood stove, and a sauna nearby: bring a sleeping bag. Nugget Creek Road also leads to the **trailhead** for the Dixie Pass and Nugget Creek trails (for both see box, opposite).

At Mile 17 the road teeters precariously over the **Kuskulana Bridge**, 238 feet above the Kuskulana River, which replaced earlier railroad trestles. An excellent example of these can be seen beside the road at Mile 29, where the tumbledown form of the **Gilahina Bridge** has tempted many a photographer: it is far from

HIKING AND BIKING OFF THE MCCARTHY ROAD

With McCarthy and Kennicott drawing you onward it is tempting to charge head-long to the end of the McCarthy Road. However, off-road cyclists should consider turning off at Chitina and following the Copper River Trail, while hikers should leave the road at Mile 14.5 and follow Nugget Creek Road to the **trailheads** for the challenging Dixie Pass Trail and the appreciably easier Nugget Creek Trail. Consult the staff at the Park Headquarters in Copper Center (p.379) for appropriate maps and more detailed trailhead information.

Copper River Trail (20 miles each way; 2–3 days; mainly flat). Deep river crossings prevent hikers from continuing to the coast at Cordova, but the first twenty miles of the old CR&NW trackbed, as far as the Uranatina River, are open to hikers and bikers (and even high-clearance vehicles). It flanks the surging gray water of the Copper River all the way and there are some spectacularly crumbling old trestle bridges – now bypassed by the road – as well as a couple of places where the narrowness of Wood Canyon forces the route into two short tunnels. Mostly it is too flat to be an exciting walk, but makes great cycling country with numerous places where you can throw down a tent for the night.

Dixie Pass Trail (22 miles round-trip; 2–3 days; 3300ft ascent). A fairly tough, but popular, there-and-back hike initially following a well-defined streamside track then requiring a bit more route finding to approach the 5100-foot Dixie Pass. The ascent of the pass is strenuous and some make it a day-hike from their camp at the base, but committed types are rewarded by the chance to camp high on the alpine tundra with stupendous vistas all around. You can either retrace your steps back to the trailhead, or make a long loop (45 miles in all; 5–7 days) by continuing north over Dixie Pass and down Rock Creek to join the **Kotsina Trail** which follows the Kotsina River as it loops around the western end of Hubbard Peak to the trailhead.

Nugget Creek Trail (29 miles round-trip; 2–3 days; 1700ft ascent). An easy-to-follow hike (or bike ride) gradually climbing through the forest along an old mining road up the Kuskulana valley, eventually offering great views of the Kuskulana Glacier. It isn't that hard, though at the wrong time of year the bugs can be awful and there are several boggy stream crossings. At the end is a poorly maintained NPS hut with bunks and a wood stove which can be used as a base for further explorations up the valley and around old mine buildings. Return the same way.

safe, so stay well clear. Between the two, at Mile 27, there's a pleasant, wooded camping spot (donations) with a couple of picnic tables and an outhouse. The only reason to stop before the end of the road is the crafty *Willow Herb Mountain Depot*, Mile 56.5 (☎554-4420, *wilherbmtn@aol.com*; ②), which sells USGS maps, fixes tires, and offers a cabin a short walk away in the woods with a wood stove, propane cooking, and a light breakfast; bring your sleeping bag. From here it is just a couple of miles to the road end by the Kennicott River, and the cluster of places to stay at **COPPER POINT**.

McCarthy, Kennicott, and around

In their heyday, Kennicott and McCarthy perfectly complemented each other. McCarthy was everything Kennicott wasn't and presented a licentious safety valve for the stiff-collared mining town. Both towns were officially "dry," but McCarthyites widely flaunted the rules enforced by the Kennecott Mining

Company up the hill. Kennicott had all the amenities – hospital with dental office, grade school, recreation hall, ball park, skating rink, and even a dairy – but McCarthy had the restaurants, pool halls, hotels, saloons, and brothels. The arrangement suited everyone: labor was short in the district and the company knew that few disgruntled workers quitting Kennicott would make it past McCarthy with their pockets full, and would soon return to work.

In some respects, the distinction remains; **MCCARTHY** is very much the social center of the district; the restaurants, and especially the bar, always seem packed with the residents of this scattered hamlet. All around, ancient log cabins, frame houses pieced together from whatever was available, and assorted rusting hulks give the town a kind of junkyard beauty. Cars can only get across the Kennicott River in the frozen depths of winter, so traffic is negligible and you can spend a couple of happy hours just ambling about, at some point directing yourself to the original CR&NW depot now transformed into the **McCarthy–Kennicott Historical Museum** (late May to early Sept daily 11am–6pm; free), with a model of boomtown McCarthy and material on life in the two towns, mining and the coming of the railroad.

Even if you are staying in McCarthy or Copper Point, almost everyone spends most of their time five miles up the main road at **KENNICOTT**, reached by shuttle bus along the road once traced by train tracks, or on foot along the parallel old Wagon Road. Kennicott's distinctive industrial buildings – all red with white trim – hug the mountainside on the moraine-strewn flanks of the Kennicott Glacier. Back in the 1920s the glacier was five hundred feet higher and completely obscured Fireweed Mountain across the valley, but the diminished hunk of ice now reveals magnificent mountain views as you hike up the tracks through town. The buildings are off-limits unless you take one of the excellent tours (see "Activities", opposite) but you can still wander the hillside paths looking for that photogenic angle of the fourteen-story ore mill, the power plant, workers' bunkhouses and numerous dilapidated cabins.

Arrival and getting around

At Mile 58.8, the McCarthy Road passes a **National Park information kiosk**, Mile 58.8 (June to early Sept daily 8.30am–12.30pm), and continues three-quarters of a mile until the road ends at a bleak and unsightly gravel parking lot ($5 a day). From there, visitors must cross the Kennicott River using a footbridge and proceed to McCarthy on foot: it is only half a mile to McCarthy, and a further four and a half miles to Kennicott. If you don't fancy the short walk into town, you may strike it lucky and find one of the shuttle **buses** – Wrangell Mountain Bus (☎554-4411) and Kennicott Shuttle (☎554-4440) – ready to transport you to either town. Normally they just ply the route between McCarthy and Kennicott, together providing one bus an hour throughout the day. They both charge $5 each way

---

KENNICOTT OR KENNECOTT

Explorer Robert Kennicott, part of the Abercrombie expedition in the 1860s, never came up this valley, but lent his name to the glacier which creaks off Mount Blackburn. The town which was later to grace its flanks goes by the same name, but a slip of the quill forever destined the mines and the mining company to the name Kennecott.

enabling you to ride up with one and down with the other. The most reliable bus stop is the museum (see opposite).

One of the best ways to make the most out of your time here is to **rent a bike**, most easily done at The Tramstation, right by the Kennicott River bridge ($15 half-day, $25 full day), or back down the road at the *Glacier View* campground (see below; $10 half-day, $20 full day).

Accommodation

Due to their remoteness, neither McCarthy nor Kennicott are cheap places to stay; following their roots, Kennicott goes for the more refined approach, while McCarthy offers something altogether more rustic (though not lacking in comfort). If you've got the cash and don't mind lugging your gear over the footbridge, you'll want to stay in McCarthy of Kennicott, but there is a growing cluster of **accommodation** at **COPPER POINT**, along the final mile of the McCarthy Road: all accommodation is marked on the map on p.378. Those on a tight budget will want to **camp**; best done three-quarters of a mile before the end of the road, where there's a stony National Park Service campground (free; no water). Alternatively, across the road there's *Glacier View Camping* (☎554-4490, *glacierview@gci.net*; $10) where anyone can get **showers** for $5, or continue to the road end where you can pitch a tent or park an RV at *Copper Point Camping* ($10, includes the $5 road-end parking fee). If you need a roof over your head, make for *Kennicott River Lodge and Hostel* (☎554-4441, winter ☎479-6822, *www.ptialaska.net/~grosswlr*, cabins ④, bunks ①), a newish log-built house with large common kitchen, a lounge with good mountain views, and a series of comfortable cabins, some fitted with four bunks and a sleeping loft for two, and charged at $25 per bed (plus $5 per shower); bring a sleeping bag (or rent for $2).

In **McCarthy**, the place to stay is *Ma Johnsons Hotel/McCarthy Lodge* (☎554-4402, fax 554-4404; ⑤), built in 1916 and evoking a suitable atmosphere with small but pleasant, shared-bath rooms, and a continental breakfast. B&Bs come and go but you can be sure that whatever is on offer will be well advertised around town.

Kennicott has a few more places to stay but no bar and only one restaurant (reserve for dinner), in the *Kennicott Glacier Lodge* (☎258-2350 or 1-800/582-5128, fax 248-7975, *www.kennicottlodge.com*; ⑦), which offers comfortable, modern shared-facility rooms, the best of them with balconies and glacier views. Rates include a transfer from McCarthy and a Kennicott tour. A couple of mill-managers' cottages on Silk Stocking Row have now been turned into self-catering accommodation. The best of these is *Kennicott Cottage*, at #16 (☎554-1616, *www.alaska.net/~kennicott/kcc.htm*; ⑥) where there's a full kitchen (breakfast goodies supplied), hot and cold running water, and an outhouse. You can either rent one room, or take over the whole place ($350) and fit in up to eight.

Activities

If you have the slightest interest in Alaska's industrial heritage, be sure to join one of the two-hour **Kennicott Tours** run by the two guiding companies listed overleaf (both late May to early Sept; $25), who jointly run four tours daily. This is the only way you can get into such buildings as the post office, the general store whose shelves lie empty but were still fully stocked until the 1970s, and the powerhouse which powered the mill and additionally provided underground steam heating to prevent the town's walkways from freezing up. A highlight of the tour

HIKES AROUND KENNICOTT AND INTO THE BACKCOUNTRY

Wonderful though it may be to simply wander around McCarthy and Kennicott, **hiking** is where the area truly comes to life. The views are breathtaking, especially if you choose, as many do, to take a short flight into the wilderness and begin hiking from there. As well, since there aren't any maintained trails, some mental preparation is required: read our comments in our Denali account (p.366). No backcountry permits are required but you should complete a backcountry itinerary at a park office and leave it with someone trustworthy. No one will come looking for you unless someone requests a search – discussing emergency contingencies with your pilot is essential. You'll almost certainly be camping in the wilderness, though the park service people at Copper Center will help you locate the eight free first-come, first-served fly-in **cabins** in the park. Below, we've listed a couple of local trails – one easy, one less so – along with one backcountry suggestion, though there are dozens of others. Again, ask your pilot for ideas.

Root Glacier Trail (6 miles round-trip; 2–3hr; 200ft ascent). From Kennicott the track leads north through the main mill buildings and out onto the lateral moraine giving excellent views of the surrounding mountains and the gleaming-white Kennicott Glacier which is accessible in places: don't stray far. There are some marginal **campgrounds** up here with an outhouse, bear-resistant food lockers and untreated water from Jumbo Stream.

Bonanza Mine (13 miles round-trip; 4–7hr; 3500ft ascent). A wonderful hike initially following a four-wheel-drive road and soon rising high above Kennicott as you approach the substantial ruins of Bonanza Mine. The road to the tree line is only passable by the fittest and most determined **mountain bikers**, but if you're motivated to ride up there it is a superb, and fast, ride down (though keep an eye out for ascending hikers). Start by following the Root Glacier Trail and turn uphill as you leave the last of the houses, then continue past the end of the road (roughly halfway) on a rough track past a fretwork of gantries and wooden pylons perched on rocky bluffs still carrying cables strung as they were when everyone left town. **Carry water** especially if you are planning to **camp out** up there.

Goat Trail (25 miles one-way; 3–8 days; 3000ft net descent). The Park's most popular fly-in multiday hike following the Chisana prospectors' route through the narrow Chitistone Canyon, twenty miles east of McCarthy, and past the four-hundred-foot Chitistone Falls, the highest continuously flowing falls in Alaska. It is a strenuous venture with several deep river crossings between the airstrips at each end. Expect to pay $200 for dropoff and pickup.

is catching all fourteen floors of the mill including the steps along the high-grade ore chute on which John Denver sang during a 1970s TV special – the stairs have been dubbed the "John Denver Memorial Staircase" by droll guides.

St Elias Alpine Guides, Motherlode Powerhouse in McCarthy (☎554-4445 or 1-888/933-5427, fax 345-9049, *www.ptialaska.net/~stelias*), is a highly professional mountain-guide service that runs unroped **glacier hikes** (half-day $55), mine hikes up to Bonanza, Jumbo, and Erie mines ($75 a day), **ice climbing** ($95 a day), and customized **backcountry expeditions** ($125 a day). Serious commitment is required for their longer adventures: eleven days hiking the Chitistone Canyon ($2200) with one guide to two customers, thirteen days rafting the

Colored fishing buoys, Chignik

Hurricane Gulch from the Alaska Railroad

Talkeetna Mountains

Picking blueberries by the roadside, Denali Highway

Gilahina Bridge, McCarthy Road

Creamers Field Migratory Wildfowl Refuge, Fairbanks

One tired pup

Disused wagons, Independence Mine

Denali and the Alaska Range, Denali N.P.

Abandoned bucket and dredge, Nome

Trans-Alaska pipeline near Delta Junction

Aurora borealis

Chitina and Copper rivers to the sea ($2300), or a fourteen-day attempt on an unclimbed peak in the Wrangell Mountains ($2600). In Kennicott, Kennicott-McCarthy Wilderness Guides (☎554-4444) offer a more limited range of trips from the half-day glacier trek ($50) to the full-day ice climbing ($100).

Several companies operate **flightseeing trips**; Wrangell Mountain Air (☎554-4411 or 1-800/478-1160, fax 554-4400, *www.wrangellmountainair.com*) quote very good prices starting with the underpowered "Glacier Tour" (35min; $50), and going up to the much more satisfying "Backcountry Tour" (70min; $95) and the mammoth "Grand Tour" (90min; $130) over the Bagley Icefield and right around the Wrangell Mountains. They will also drop you off for **hikes in the vast backcountry** (see box on p.386) and advise an itinerary to suit.

If the chilly glacial waters don't put you off, go **rafting** with Copper Oar, at the road-end parking lot (☎1-800/523-4453, in McCarthy 554-4453, *howmoz@aol .com*), who run the Nizina Canyon trip (daily; 5–8hr; $225), which includes five miles on a Class II–III stretch of the adjacent Kennicott River followed by the spectacular scenery of the Nizina Canyon and a return scenic flight. For more of a wilderness experience (with small portions of whitewater) you'll need to book ahead on trips like McCarthy to Chitina (3 days; $575) and McCarthy to Cordova (10 days; $2295).

Eating and drinking

If you are staying at Copper Point you need go no further than *Glacier View Camping*, Mile 59, where there's a small outdoor restaurant serving meals all day from bagels and muffins to barbecue pork and chicken ($8). For more choice, cross to McCarthy where the *McCarthy Lodge* serves up hearty meals in a dining room festooned with mining paraphernalia (pop in during the day to see what's cooking and to reserve a place), and has the district's only **bar**, the focal point for an evening's inactivity. Across the road *Tailor-Made Pizza* serve superb gourmet concoctions (starting around $15) on a mosquito-netted deck or around a wood-burning stove, and nearby, the *Roadside Potatohead* stand sells burgers, the popular Potatohead burrito and fresh-cut fries. In **Kennicott** the *Kennicott Glacier Lodge* (see p.385) has a restaurant (reserve for dinner), but no bar.

Paxson, Delta Junction, and the Denali Highway

The Glenn and Richardson highways spoke out from the Alaskan Interior's highway hub at Glenallen, both heading north towards the Alaska Hwy. A single road runs fourteen miles to Gakona Junction where the two highways separate. Turn right and you're on a section of the Glenn Hwy known as the **Tok Cutoff**, a road built in the early 1940s to connect the Alaska Hwy at Tok with Anchorage and Valdez. You can make it from Glenallen through to Tok in a little over two hours with only a couple of campgrounds and the **Nabesna Road** in the Wrangell–St Elias National Park to distract you. Keep straight on at Gakona Junction and you're on the **Richardson Highway**, with more to see including glaciers and distant buffalo. Perhaps best of all, though, is the access it gives to the wonderfully scenic **Denali Highway** at Paxson.

Northeast of Glenallen: the Tok Cutoff and the Nabesna Road

At Gakona Junction the Glenn Hwy bears northeast as the **Tok Cutoff**, which initially follows the Copper River then sneaks over a low pass in the Mentasta Mountains into the spruce forests around Tok, 125 miles away. Like all such Alaskan roads, it is thinly peopled with only the occasional roadhouse and gas station. The busiest section of the highway is the first five miles where you'll pass through **GAKONA**, centered on the *Gakona Lodge*, Tok Cutoff Mile 2, a 1929 roadhouse on the site of a 1905 ranch, and still fulfilling the role, now with a gas station, natural-food store, and restaurant overlooking the Gakona River. It is a mile on to River Wrangellers (☎822-3967 or 1-888/822-3967, *www.alaskariverwrangellers .com*) who operate **rafting trips**, pretty much to order, on at least half a dozen rivers in the Wrangell Mountains and Copper River Valley, the most popular being the three-hour scenic float ($55) along the Copper River. If you need to stay here, there's *Gakona RV Park*, Mile 4.2 (☎ & fax 822-3550) with tent sites for $12, full hookup for $20.

You'll barely notice the hamlet of **Chistochina** at Mile 33, though the roadhouse, which recently burned down, is being rebuilt at the time of writing and should be offering gas, food, and lodging when it's completed. The **Nabesna Road**, which cuts off at Mile 60 (see below), provides the only distraction on the road north, which passes a couple of **campgrounds**: the scenic streamside *Porcupine Creek State Recreation Site*, Mile 64.2 ($12; pump water); and *Eagle Trail State Recreation Site*, Mile 109.3 ($12; pump water). The latter has a mile-long nature trail, and a 2.5-mile hiking trail to an overview of the Tok Valley with evidence of the old Valdez–Eagle Trail and the telegraph line which followed it. There is even scope to hike up Clearwater Creek for around eight hours to get into Dall sheep country. From here it is sixteen miles to the crossroads town of Tok (see p.398).

The Nabesna Road

Despite the mind-boggling immensity of the Wrangell–St Elias National Park the only road access into the park aside from the **McCarthy Road** (see p.382) is the 42-mile-long **Nabesna Road**. This threads its way east between the Mentasta and Wrangell mountains into the northwestern corner of the park. Nabesna, a former gold mine which was worked from 1923 to 1942, is a much less-developed corner of the Wrangell–St Elias National Park than the area around McCarthy: the road is gravel all the way (with glacial stream crossings at miles 29.4, 31.2, and 35.5, often impassable in hot weather) and there are very few places offering a bed for the night. There are primitive **campgrounds** – *Twin Lakes* at Mile 28 and *Jack Creek* at Mile 36 – but come equipped and you can pitch pretty much anywhere you can find some flat ground.

The road continues through tiny **SLANA**, at Mile 1, which has a post office, then enters the Wrangell–St Elias National Park at Mile 4, the end of the asphalt. It is also where a four-mile side road leads to an area hacked out of the bush for the lovely, rustic *Huck Hobbit's Homestead Retreat & Campground* (☎822-3196; cabins $15 per person, camping $2.50 per person), comprising cozy log cabins with wood stoves, campsites each with picnic table and fire ring, canoes for rent ($35 a day), and bargain meals. The last mile to *Huck Hobbit's* can only be negotiated on foot or ATV so it's best to call ahead. Along the road there are wonderful views across the Copper River flats to the Wrangell Mountains and occasional turnouts where you can explore the lower hills, but no habitation until a couple of **hunting lodges** at Mile 25.5 and Mile 28.6 with rooms and basic food. If the road is in reasonable condition (or you've got good ground clearance) you can press on to the end of the road and the tiny mining community of Nabesna, though don't expect any visitor facilities. For the latest on road conditions, all manner of park-related information, and details for access to the lodges listed above, call at the **Slana Ranger Station**, Mile 0.2 (late May to early Sept daily 8am–5pm; winter by appointment; ☎822-5238).

North of Glenallen: along the Richardson Hwy

From **Gakona Junction** (Richardson Hwy, Mile 128.6), the Richardson Hwy runs 137 miles to Delta Junction, initially running across open, rolling country peppered with small lakes feeding tiny streams. **Campers** should consider stopping twenty miles north of Gakona Junction at the BLM's large *Sourdough Creek Campground*, Mile 147.5 (free; untreated river water only) right where the Trans-Alaska Pipeline crosses the Gulkana River, with sites dotted among the sparse black spruce. It comes equipped with a fishing deck, observation platform, and boat ramp where canoeists paddling the Gulkana (see box, p.397) pull out. If you are not kitted out for cooking you can still stop here and stroll a couple of hundred yards north to eat at the friendly *Sourdough Lodge and Roadhouse*.

The Richardson begins to climb into the foothills of the Alaska Range, imperceptibly at first, then more forthright as it rounds the 2641ft Hogan Hill and on the way to Meiers (3363ft) which overlooks the *Meier's Roadhouse*, Mile 170 (☎822-3151, fax 822-3151; ③), offering gas, groceries, a restaurant, cabins, and boat rental for use on the nearby lake. At Mile 175, a side road leads a mile and a half down to the extensive, partly-lakeshore *Paxson Lake* campground ($8; pump water) with a dump station, walk-in sites for $4, and a boat launch for the Gulkana River canoe trip to *Sourdough* campground (see box, p.397).

Ten miles on, **PAXSON**, Mile 185, marks the eastern terminus of the Denali Hwy (see p.394), but comprises little more than the gas, food, and lodging at the *Paxson Inn & Lodge* (☎ & fax 822-3330; ③) and *Paxson Alpine Tours & Cabins* (☎822-5972, *www.alaskan.com/paxsontours*; ⑤), with some superb new log cabins each with private bath, a small deck looking out towards Paxson Mountain and the sound of the Gulkana River right outside. They also run three-hour *Evening Wildlife Float Trips* ($45) in a raft through the Paxson Wildlife Reserve with the emphasis firmly on spotting nesting waterfowl and eagles, spawning sockeye salmon, moose, and whatever might turn up.

From midsummer well into September **red salmon** can be seen spawning right by the highway from a turnout at Mile 190. The road then skirts Summit Lake, reasonably appropriately named though with the mass of the Alaska Range stretching to the horizon in both directions you barely realize you are anywhere near a summit. In fact, the 3000-foot **Isabel Pass** lies just ahead with the **Gulkana Glacier** bearing down on it from the northeast. A 1.5-mile access road off Mile 200.4 of the Richardson runs to Fielding Lake where there's an appealing lakeside **campground** (free; lake water) with a boat ramp heavily used by fishers after lake trout, burbot, and grayling. The highway then follows the Delta River through a gap in the Alaska Range, where red and gray scree slopes cascade down the mountainsides, and continues to **Black Rapids Glacier**, Mile 225.4. It is now a retreating shadow of what it was in the winter of 1936–37 when this

"Galloping Glacier" surged three miles, almost overrunning the road: mounds of terminal moraine can be seen half a mile from the highway. A 500-yard hike on the east side of the road leads to Black Rapids Lake.

The Delta Valley now broadens out past another appealing campground, the *Donnelly Creek State Recreation Site*, Mile 238 ($8; pump water), and on to a couple of spectacular viewpoints. At Mile 241.3 where panels explain the genesis of the **Delta buffalo herd** (see below) which can often be seen in the distance across the river; and Mile 244 where there are stupendous views south to the dominant peaks of the Alaska Range – Deborah, Hess, and Hayes. Four miles on, a short gravel road leads to a trailhead for a well-worn but unmarked path leading up the north ridge of the 3910-foot **Donnelly Dome** (1900ft ascent), the alder and willow eventually thinning to reveal a great view of the Delta River, Tanana River, and the Alaska Range. Delta Junction is another eighteen miles on, beyond **Pump Station #9** (tours covered under Delta Junction, see p.392), and through the Fort Greely military base, once a way station for planes taking part in the wartime Lend-Lease program with Russia (see Contexts, p.489), and now in limbo. It was supposed to be closed down by 2001 and a prison built on the site, but the specter of a new national missile defense program has revived the base's hopes of survival.

Delta Junction and around

DELTA JUNCTION (Alaska Hwy, Mile 1422; Richardson Hwy, Mile 266), proclaims itself as being the end of the Alaska Hwy, which starts 1422 miles to the southeast in British Columbia. Technically this is accurate, as the remaining 98 miles of road to Fairbanks (the Richardson Hwy) already existed when the Alaska Hwy was completed in 1942. The Delta Junction CVB does a nice line in selling "I completed the Alaska Hwy" certificates, however, most people choose to celebrate their endeavors when they get to Fairbanks, a real city and a more fitting end to such an epic trip.

But you should still try to spend some time here, particularly if you've just driven the Alaska Hwy, since this makes a better spot to recuperate than Tok. Strung out along the Richardson and Alaska highways the town is attractive with farmland homesteads stretching all the way east to the Clearwater river system. To the south the Granite Mountains rise up majestically and if you are lucky in spring and fall, the skies can be filled with skeins of migrating geese.

Though close to the old Valdez–Fairbanks Trail, Delta Junction didn't really come into being until the 1920s when it was known as Buffalo Center, the site chosen for the government's **buffalo importation program**, designed to establish a sporting herd in Alaska five hundred years after the species had died out here. In 1928, 23 Minnesota plains bison were released and immediately developed a taste for the local barley crop. They still occasionally wander onto farmland around harvest time, but since its creation in 1979, they mostly confine themselves to the Bison Range, a 90,000-acre preserve some twenty miles to the south. Today, the herd is around five hundred strong, and can withstand a winter hunting season during which 15,000 hunters pay $10 just to apply for one of the 80–100 permits.

If you are in the vicinity around the last weekend of July, call ahead and check dates for the three-day **Deltana Fair**, a small-town agricultural fair with events such as the Cow Drop in which a ten-by-ten checkerboard of two-foot squares is laid out and folk lay bets on where a cow will place its mark. The star event though is Saturday's **Great Alaskan Outhouse Race**, where six-strong teams of locals construct stripped-down, lightweight, wheeled outhouses and strive to be the fastest to haul an occupied privy through a mile-and-a-half course.

The town and around

Delta Junction lines the three main roads that make up the town, spreading out from the central "Y," dominated by the visitor center (see overleaf). Behind it sits the **Sullivan Roadhouse** (late May to early Sept Mon–Sat 9am–5pm; free), which was built a few miles from Delta Junction in 1906 on what was then a

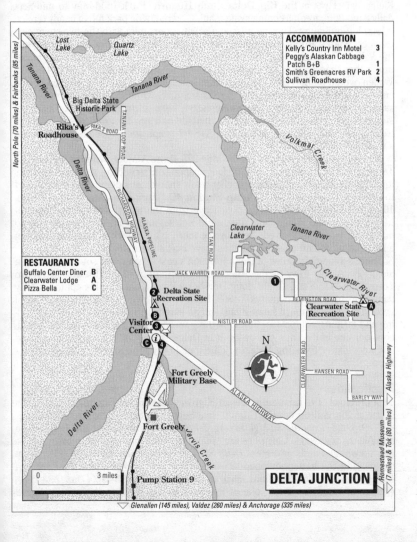

ACCOMMODATION
Kelly's Country Inn Motel   **3**
Peggy's Alaskan Cabbage
  Patch B+B   **1**
Smith's Greenacres RV Park   **2**
Sullivan Roadhouse   **4**

RESTAURANTS
Buffalo Center Diner   **B**
Clearwater Lodge   **A**
Pizza Bella   **C**

North Pole (70 miles) & Fairbanks (85 miles)

Lost Lake

Quartz Lake

Tanana River

Tanana River

Big Delta State Historic Park

Rika's Roadhouse

RIKA'S ROAD

TANANA LOOP ROAD

Delta River

RICHARDSON HIGHWAY

ALASKA PIPELINE

MILTAN ROAD

Volkmar Creek

Clearwater Lake

Tanana River

JACK WARREN ROAD

REMINGTON ROAD

Clearwater State Recreation Site

Clearwater River

Delta State Recreation Site

NISTLER ROAD

Visitor Center

CLEARWATER ROAD

HANSEN ROAD

Fort Greely Military Base

ALASKA HIGHWAY

BARLEY WAY

N

Fort Greely

Delta River

Jarvis Creek

Homestead Museum (7 miles) & Tok (80 miles)

Alaska Highway

0   3 miles

Pump Station 9

DELTA JUNCTION

Glenallen (145 miles), Valdez (260 miles) & Anchorage (335 miles)

winter-only shortcut off the Valdez–Fairbanks route. With the improvements made to the Richardson Hwy, the shortcut became little used and the roadhouse lay abandoned from 1922 until it was designated a historic landmark and moved to its current location in 1996. It has now been outfitted with period items, many of them originals – the double bed and stove in particular – donated by those who at some point lifted them in the first place (or their descendants). There's good material too on the roadhouse tradition, all brought to life with excerpts from the diary of early roadhouse worker, James Geoghegan, who also turned his hand to photography.

Roadhouses continue to be the main attraction nine miles north on the Richardson Hwy, at the **Big Delta State Historic Park** (mid-May to mid-Sept daily 8am–8pm; free), a compact and manicured riverside park full of neatly tended c.1900 log buildings. They've missed a great opportunity with the two-story centerpiece, **Rika's Roadhouse** (daily 9am–5pm), an original from the early days of the Valdez–Fairbanks Trail, which should at least have been turned into a museum, rather than a large gift shop. The Swede who ran the place until 1947, Rika Wallen, would be horrified, but it remains a fine log-built building, erected beside an important ferry crossing over the Tanana River. Outside, things improve with assorted outbuildings, such as a Swedish-style barn, a spring house used as a cool store in summer and a workshop now fitted out as a small **museum**, with artifacts from pioneer life. Here too is a WAMCATS telegraph station (see box, p.408) and a reasonable café/restaurant.

A couple of hundred yards north (Mile 275.4) the **Alaska pipeline spans the Tanana River** on a graceful 1200-foot suspension structure, the longest of its kind along the route. Pipeline propellerheads should consider calling a day ahead to get on a hour-long tour of **Pump Station #9** (tours June–Aug Mon–Sat 9am, 10am & 11am; $8; ☎869-3270); they leave from the pump station gatehouse at Mile 258.3 on the Richardson Hwy, eight miles south of Delta Junction, and no one under twelve is allowed. Actually the tour isn't that technical and apart from a lot of fat pipes and noisy jet engines there isn't a great deal to see.

There's a tangible sense of Delta Junction's past seven miles southeast of town along the Alaska Hwy at the **Alaska Homestead and Historical Museum Tour**, Mile 1415.5 and 1 mile along Dorshorst Road (June to mid-Sept tours daily 9am–7pm by appointment ☎895-4369; $10), which gives you a chance to stroll around an old sawmill, a homestead, and an extensive collection of old-time mining and farming equipment. For something more grounded in the natural world, consider one of the trips run by Do It In Delta! (☎895-4762), notably the relaxed and informative **Evening Safari** wildlife tour (early June to early Aug nightly 7–11pm; $25).

Practicalities

That precious "I've driven the Alaska Highway" certificate can be obtained for a dollar at the **visitor center** (May to late Sept daily 8am–8pm; ☎895-5068 or 1-877/895-5068, *www.alaska-highway.org/delta*) at the junction of the Richardson and Alaska highways. **Campers** are spoilt for choice here. Right in town you've got the wooded and convenient *Delta State Recreation Site*, Mile 267 ($10; pump water), and the better-equipped, RV-oriented *Smith's Green Acres RV Park and Campground*, Mile 268 (mid-April to Sept; ☎1-800/895-4369, fax 895-4110, *greenacresrvpark@knix.net*), one of the most highly rated in the state with full hookups for $21, and tent sites for $12 including showers. *Clearwater State Recreation Site*, eight miles north of Mile 1415 on the Alaska Hwy ($10; pump water), is even more appealing, beautifully tranquil, as well as on the spring and fall migration routes of sandhill cranes and geese. For **rooms** try the spacious and central *Kelly's Country Inn Motel*, in the center of town (☎895-4667; ④), or try *Peggy's Alaskan Cabbage Patch B&B*, off Jack Warren Road (☎895-4200 or 1-888/845-4200, fax 895-4468, *www.alaskaone.com/cabbage*; private bath ⑤, shared bath ③), which offers a couple of nice rooms with shared common area, and a hearty breakfast, or *Tanana B&B* (mobile ☎338-5500 or voicemail 474-8177; ⑤), a hand-built log cabin beside a clearwater creek seven miles down the Tanana River, and reached by the owner's boat. You can stay from 7pm to 11am on Monday and Tuesday, 11am–10am every other day of the week, and there's fishing from canoes and fresh eggs from the hens.

If all you need is **groceries** and an **ATM** then drop in at Delta Food Cache, on the Fairbanks road, which also has a decent bakery and espresso bar. More substantial fare is dished up across the street at *Buffalo Center Diner* (☎895-5989) and *Pizza Bella* (no phone) by the visitor center. Alternatively, join Deltoids – as some locals call themselves – for steaks and burgers on the deck overlooking the river at *Clearwater Lodge* (☎895-5152), right by the *Clearwater State Recreation Site*.

Other everyday needs are catered for with a **post office** on the Richardson Hwy a couple of hundred yards north of the visitor center, a branch of the National Bank of Alaska, a few hundred yards further north, a **laundry** a few steps north again and, opposite, a **library** (Tues–Thurs 9am–6pm, Sat 10am–6pm) with a **book swap**.

North of Delta Junction

The Richardson Hwy chugs out of Delta Junction along the Tanana Valley bound for Fairbanks almost a hundred miles north. It is sparsely populated country with only the odd roadhouse, a few simple campgrounds and a lot of forest. Nine miles north, you cross the Tanana River, right by Rika's Roadhouse (see opposite) and soon pass the turnoff to *Quartz Lake State Recreation Area*, three miles off the Richardson Hwy at Mile 277.8, a glassy lake stocked annually with rainbow trout, arctic char, and silver salmon, and supporting an ice-fishing shanty town in winter. There is lakeshore **camping** for $10.

With the exception of a few roadside viewpoints there is really nothing to stop for unless you want to break your journey camping at one of the state recreation areas along the way, the best being *Harding Lake*, Mile 321.5 ($10; pump water) with some quiet walk-in sites, lake swimming, barbecue pits, and firewood for sale ($5). Some thirty miles short of Fairbanks (Mile 334.7) you cross into the huge **Eielson Air Force Base**, and drive parallel to the main runway, which is often busy, especially at times when half the world hates the United States: they're very touchy about that pipeline.

The last patch of open country before the city is **Chena River Lakes Recreation Area**, Mile 346.7 (always open; fee charged late May to early Sept; $3 per vehicle, $1 per bike), a set of dams and channels designed to prevent a repeat of Fairbanks' devastating 1967 flooding. It isn't as unappealing as it may sound, with a lovely 2.5-mile Nature Trail, boating on Chena Lake (canoe $7 an hour, rowboat $8), biking along the levees, and wooded **camping** ($8; pump water).

The Denali Highway

The 135-mile-long **Denali Highway** (typically open mid-May to Sept), runs through some fine Alaska scenery along the south side of the Alaska Range. The land either side is managed by the Bureau of Lands Management (BLM), which allow a great deal more freedom than the National Park authorities giving easy access to great countryside with wonderful opportunities for wildlife viewing without the formal procedures. The road was originally built in 1957 (long before the Parks Hwy was even mooted) to provide road access into Denali National Park from the Richardson Hwy, but with the 1972 completion of the Parks Hwy the Denali Hwy was left mainly for recreational access. There are no towns along the way – just a handful of roadhouses – and all but 21 miles are gravel. This is a sizeable deterrent to RV drivers and those who obey their car-rental agency's demands to stick to hard-surfaced roads, leaving the road wonderfully free of traffic for everyone else, a godsend if you've recently been in Denali National Park and an incentive to **mountain bikers** as well.

The road is broad and firm but bumpy in places, though this doesn't seem to stop locals hurtling along at a fair lick. The full 135 miles can certainly be traversed in day, but it is rewarding to spend a night or two out here either in one of the roadhouses or one of the fine cheap campgrounds. You can even sleep beside the road, though all too often it is easy to tell where less considerate

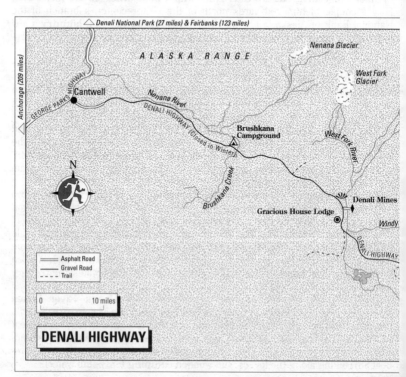

souls have done so before you: leave your spot cleaner than when you arrived. On the intervening days, stop a while to seek out trumpeter swans, moose, bald eagles, beavers, bears, and perhaps some of the 45,000-strong Nelchina caribou herd; or dip a line into one of the numerous lakes for grayling, char, and lake trout. **Hikers** mostly have to compete with ATVs on designated trails but for a wilderness experience you can just make it up as you go along: pick a direction and go.

The one season when the Denali Hwy is less than quiet is during the first three weeks of September when it becomes "boys-with-toys" territory. This is **hunting season** and everyone is out for moose or caribou: RVs lumber along towing trailers loaded mainly with four-wheeler ATVs, but also eight-wheeler amphibious vehicles, and even Everglades-style airboats, in fact just about anything to get to their quarry across this tough terrain. You'll see them parked up peering into their spotting scopes until something turns up, then they'll hop on their rig and hurtle off across the tundra hoping to beat the next guy to the kill. Presumably they get bored; the road signs here are more bullet-ridden than anywhere in the state – some achievement.

Remember that there is very little out here and you'll need to **come prepared**. Bring all the groceries you need and make sure your spare is good: expensive towing is available from Paxson, Gracious House, and Cantwell and there is tire repair at *Maclaren River Lodge*, but little else. **In winter**, the road is impassable

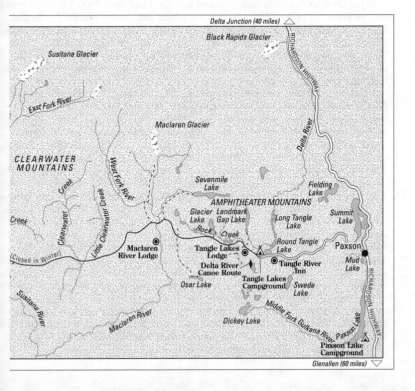

for ordinary traffic but becomes a popular route for snow-machiners, dog teams, and cross-country skiers.

Paxson to the Maclaren River

Paxson, at Mile 185 of the Richardson Hwy, marks the beginning of the Denali Hwy. The first 21 miles are deceivingly smooth asphalt, climbing out of the Gulkana River valley to reveal your first real glimpse of the Alaska Range stretching away to the west, and the small Gulkana and Gakona glaciers. The views to the south are no less impressive, the dominant peaks of the Wrangell Mountains – Sanford, Drum, and Wrangell – easily visible from the viewpoint at Mile 13.

Soon after, you enter the **Tangle Lakes Archeological District**, which flanks the highway for the next twenty miles (Miles 16–37). Here, the acidic soils of the subarctic tundra have preserved a dense cluster of 500 sites collectively recording ten thousand years of human occupation, much of it spent hunting bison. There are no sites to visit, and ATVs are also entitled to tear up the trails, but If you are still keen on hiking, try to get hold of the free *Trail Map and Guide* to the area from local visitor centers and inns, and look for trailheads at Mileposts 16, 24.7, and 37.

The first accommodation you'll come to is the *Tangle River Inn*, Mile 20 (mid-April to Sept; ☎822-3970, *www.tangleriverinn.com*; bunkhouse ①, cabins ①–③, rooms ③), with simple but comfy cabins, bunkhouse rooms with two single beds ($25 per person), showers ($5), gas, and reliable, tasty diner fare. They also rent canoes ($3/hr, $24 for 24hr), perfect for taking out on the beautiful subalpine **Tangle Lakes**, most easily accessed from *Tangle Lakes Campground*, Mile 21.5 (free; pump water), which sits in open country with wonderful mountain views. The campground and boat launch opposite are the starting points for running the Delta River and the Middle Fork of the Gulkana River **canoe routes** (see box, opposite).

Nearby, the large and modern *Tangle Lakes Lodge*, Mile 22 (☎688-9173, fax 688-9174, *www.alaskan.com/tanglelakes*; cabins ③), has nice lakeside cabins and one larger affair ($150) sleeping up to twelve, ideal for birding groups who flock here in June to spot arctic warbler, Smith's longspur, gyrfalcon, and long-tailed jeager. There are also rental canoes ($25 a day), an excellent restaurant serving comfort food cooked to perfection, and plenty of good short hikes nearby: ask locally. Half a mile on, a magnificent view north through **Landmark Gap** follows a glacial cut through the mountains along the migration route of the Nelchina caribou herd. From the high point of the **Maclaren Summit viewpoint** (Mile 37) the entire Maclaren River watershed is spread out before you, the Maclaren Glacier tucked into the mountains on the right disgorging its milky waters south and west through a broad landscape dotted with kettle lakes that could easily pass for a subarctic Wyoming. Where the Denali Hwy crosses the Maclaren River, *Maclaren River Lodge*, Mile 42 (open all year; ☎822-7105 or 1-888/880-4264, *www.akpub.com/akbbrv/macrl.html*; cabins ④, rooms ③, bunkhouse ①) offers decent food and a range of accommodation from bunks in an old miners' cabin sleeping six ($25) to basic rooms and much nicer cabins. They organize fly-in extreme skiing in winter, and in summer will airboat you thirteen miles up to the base of the Maclaren Glacier for a day-long **canoe float trip** along the Class I–II water past alpine tundra back to the lodge (June–Sept; $200 for as many as want to go) with good birding and fishing along the way.

The Maclaren River to Cantwell

For the next forty miles you follow moraine-formed hummocks and ridgelines with long views south, and the Clearwater Mountains now blocking your views of the Alaska Range to the north. Small hills are cut by narrow streams feeding kettle lakes where you might spy trumpeter swans drifting gracefully or moose grazing on aquatic weed. At Mile 79.5 the highway crosses the Susitna River, the largest in these parts, immediately preceded by a dirt road which winds its way six miles into the **gold-mining district of Denali**. There is plenty of day-hiking

CANOEING THE DELTA AND GULKANA RIVERS

Keen paddlers with a sense of adventure, an appreciation of the Alaskan wilderness and a boat of their own (rentals for river trips are almost impossible to come by and prohibitively expensive) should seriously consider tackling either the **Delta River** or one of the two main routes on the **Gulkana River** system. They run through outstanding scenery, the low rolling tundra framed by the peaks of the Alaska Range, and all require some knowledge of topographic maps, wilderness camping ability, and enough paddling skill to negotiate sweepers and Class II rapids. The remote nature of these trips and the difficulty of some of the rapids makes carrying some kind of patching kit essential, and somehow you've got to get back to your starting point without public transportation: a kindly non-paddling driver is really the only solution. The routes can usually be run from early June to mid-September, and there are free leaflets to the canoe routes published by the BLM and available through the Alaska Public Lands Information Centers in Anchorage and Fairbanks.

Delta River (29 miles; 2–3 days; Class I and II). The route starts at *Tangle Lakes Campground*, Denali Hwy Mile 21.5, and follows a series of small interconnected waterways through rolling tundra nine miles north to Lower Tangle Lake. Edging into the Amphitheater Mountains, a mile or so of Class II water is followed by a waterfall which must be portaged using a half-mile marked trail. A little more Class II and 12 miles of Class I follow until a tributary makes the river glacial and braided to the pull-out at Mile 212.5 on the Richardson Hwy. It is possible to continue to Black Rapids (an additional 17 miles; 1–2 days; Class III) but is only recommended for kayaks and rafts.

Gulkana River (50 miles; 4 days; Class I, II and III). From *Paxson Lake Campground*, Richardson Hwy Mile 175 (see p.389), cross three miles of the lake to enter demanding Class II and III rapids before joining the Middle Fork for several miles of easy floating. After 20 miles you hit the Class III–IV Canyon Rapids (easily portaged on a quarter-mile trail) which are followed by nine miles of shallow and potentially damaging Class II and III water, then seventeen miles of Class I to the finish at the *Sourdough Campground*, Richardson Mile 147.5.

Middle Fork Gulkana River (76 miles; 6–7 days; mostly Class I and II). The boat launch at Mile 22 on the Denali Hwy gives access to the southern sequence of Tangle Lakes, negotiated with three short, unmarked but easy to determine portages. A fourth (1.2 miles) brings you to Dickey Lake (possible float-plane access; subtract 1–2 days) and the start of the Middle Fork which descends through 3 miles of shallow water to a steep and rocky canyon (Class III–IV) requiring careful lining or a portage. After the canyon the river eases and joins the main stem of the Gulkana River (see above) down to the *Sourdough Campground* pull-out.

in here; make it up as you go along, but remember that existing gold claims are fiercely protected and Private Property signs shouldn't be treated idly. If you need a base for your explorations, it is only three miles along the Denali Hwy to *Gracious House Lodge*, Mile 82.5 (late May to mid-Sept; ☎333-3148 or 1-877/822-7307, fax 333-3148, *www.alaskaone.com/gracious*; ④, private bath ⑤), which has rooms with or without private bath, RV parking ($14), camping ($6), and showers ($5). You can eat a good **meal** here too, drink at the *Sluice Box* bar, buy gas, get tires fixed, and even go **flightseeing** for an hour ($240 for up to 3 people) over the Susitna Glacier and past Mount Deborah and Hess Mountain. Every few miles to the west of *Gracious House Lodge*, there is another good spot to roll out your sleeping bag in hopes of a crystalline dawn, but the next formal campground is the well-sited *Brushkana Campground*, Mile 104.5 ($8; pump water). From here it is only worth stopping at the **viewpoint** at Mile 124, from where Mount McKinley is visible on a clear day, before continuing to **Cantwell** (Mile 135).

Tok, the Fortymile, and the Taylor Highway

The **Fortymile gold district** butts up against Canada's Yukon Territory between the Yukon River (once the main access to the Klondike and the catalyst for development) and the Alaska Hwy (now the main road artery through the region). This was the grandfather of all Alaskan goldfields, experiencing its rush in 1886 when the town of Eagle became the supply hub connected to the Gulf of Alaska by the Valdez–Eagle Trail. As fortunes shifted elsewhere the trail fell into disrepair and the region languished until the completion of the Alaska Hwy in the early 1940s prompted the construction of the **Taylor Highway**, a new road into an old area, at least by Alaskan standards.

Mining still continues across the region scattered with the detritus of pioneering attempts to make a living from the earth: sagging old cabins, dilapidated sluices, even rusting hulks of dredges. Look, but don't get too close and stick to recognized highways; these people are fiercely protective of their claims (and have guns). This is also the territory of the **Fortymile caribou herd**, the focus of a five-year collaborative program (due to end in 2001) between the Alaska and Yukon authorities to boost numbers and expand the migration territory, partly by a controversial program of wolf sterilization and relocation. A half-million-strong herd once roamed north across the Steese Hwy and into the Central Yukon, but wholesale slaughter in the 1970s reduced the herd to around 6000. Data from 1999 indicates numbers are now up to 33,000 and growing. For the most part, it is sparsely populated with only a couple of places that deserve to be called towns: the likeable **Chicken**, with its welcoming bar and frontier spirit; and **Eagle**, one of Alaska's best preserved historic towns, neatly perched beside the roiling Yukon River.

If you're headed out this way you'll need to resupply In **Tok**, a dull crossroads town that will be the first real opportunity to fill up your belly and find a soft Alaskan bed if you've just driven up through Canada.

Tok and around

For most people, there is little reason to stop in **TOK**, Mile 1314 Alaska Hwy, a scattered collection of RV parks, gas stations, motels, and diners at the junction of

THE ALASKA HWY AND CANADIAN BORDER FORMALITIES

About the best way to earn a true appreciation of what Alaska is all about is to drive there through northern Canada along the epic **Alaska Hwy** – formerly the ALCAN and still often known by that name. It will only give you the vaguest sense of what early prospectors and trappers were up against, but you'll at least realize just how far Alaska is from everywhere else: once you hit the Yukon Territory you're still almost nine hundred miles from Fairbanks.

The 1422-mile Alaska Hwy (85 percent of it in Canada) was built in response to the United States' entry into World War II. A route was selected to link a series of pre-existing air bases through the Canadian north and construction began on March 9, 1942 with co-opted US soldiers working from both ends in atrocious conditions: mosquitoes, mountains, swamp, frigid rivers, and astonishingly bad weather even for these latitudes. Incredibly the two teams met less than seven months after starting, a magnificent effort costing $140 million. Travelers driving the Alaska Hwy right through British Columbia and the Yukon should obtain a copy of either the *Rough Guide to Canada*, or the *Rough Guide to the Pacific Northwest*, though we've given limited coverage in this book in Basics (see "Getting there from the US and Canada," p.7). Once **on Alaskan turf** it is 200 miles to the "official" end of the Alaska Hwy, at Delta Junction where it meets the Richardson Hwy for the final 98 miles to Fairbanks.

CROSSING THE CANADIAN BORDER
Alaska and the Canadian Yukon share two border crossings: the important **Alaska Hwy crossing** (open 24 hours a day, 365 days of the year), 92 miles east of Tok; and the minor **Top of the World Hwy crossing** (late-May to mid-Sept daily 8am–8pm Alaska time, 9am–9pm Yukon time), 122 miles northeast of Tok. The latter closes for the winter, but if the road is still passable, it is still possible to conduct the appropriate formalities with Canada Customs in Dawson City (☎867/993-5239), or before leaving Dawson call US Customs and Immigration in Tok (☎774-2242). And remember you'll have to **set your watch** back an hour heading to Alaska; forward an hour if Yukon-bound.

For those Canada-bound, a Yukon **road-condition** report can be heard at ☎867/456-7623 or 1-877/456-7623 or surfed at *www.gov.yk.ca/depts/cts/highways /report.html*.

two major highways. But for drivers arriving from Canada along the Alaska Hwy this is the first town of consequence and a thoroughly welcome opportunity to rest up, wash down the rig, fill up with Alaska-priced gas, and plan your next move. That said, there's certainly nothing to detain you more than one night, and you may fancy pressing straight on to Delta Junction (an easy two-hour drive to the west), or cutting south along the Tok Cutoff (see p.373) towards Glenallen and the Wrangell–St Elias Mountains.

The settlement began life as Tokyo Camp, which provided workers' accommodation during the construction of the Alaska and Glenn highways in the early 1940s, and shortened its name during World War II – pronounced now simply as the first syllable of Tokyo. Though maintained as a way station on the highways it got a boost in 1954 when the US Army built the now-defunct eight-inch fuel supply pipeline from Haines, through Tok to Fairbanks, and again in 1976 when the four prominent 700-foot masts were built as a long-range aid to navigation.

Tok now acts as a service town for numerous Athapascan villages scattered around the vicinity, but thrives on passing visitors lured in by offers of a free car wash with a tank of gas, and suchlike. Attractions don't rise much above the gift shops full of Alaska T-shirts, but Tok does make the claim to be Alaska's sled-dog capital (along with several other towns) and the Burnt Paw Gift Shop, Alaska Hwy near the junction, celebrates it by offering free, wheeled **sled-dog demos** (June–Aug Mon–Sat 7.30pm). Only if you've got kids will you want to trek three miles west along the Alaska Hwy to **Mukluk Land** (June–Aug daily 1–9pm; $5), a half-baked theme park with minigolf and a bouncy igloo.

Practicalities

Your first, perhaps only, stop should be for information. The **Tok visitor center**, Mile 1314 (May to mid-Sept; ☎883-5775, *www.akpub.com/akttt/tokcc*), is in what is reputed to be the largest log-built structure in the state (a cabin it isn't) simply packed with information on the whole state and a selection of displays – stuffed animals and material on the 1990 fire which nearly engulfed the town. Next door is the **Alaska Public Lands Information Center** (June–Aug daily 8am–7pm; Sept–May Mon–Fri 8am–4.30pm; ☎883-5667, *www.nps.gov/aplic/center*) stocked with specific material on wildlife and wilderness matters. Immediately across the road you can pick up details of the Tetlin National Wildlife Refuge from their **visitor center** (daily 8am–5pm; ☎883-5312).

If you just need food and cash then Frontier Foods, almost opposite the Tok visitor center, has a reasonable selection of **groceries**, a branch of the Denali State Bank (Mon–Fri 10am–6pm) and an **ATM**. The **post office** (Mon–Fri 8.30am–5pm, Sat 11am–4pm), just along the Alaska Hwy towards Fairbanks, has no sales window so you'll need to go to the grocery to get stamps. For **Internet access**, visit *Cyberhut*, Mile 1313.5 (daily 7am–10pm; ☎883-2665).

RV parks abound in Tok, all trying to outdo each other to lure trade, most charging $20–25 for full hookup: consistently reliable places include *Northstar RV Park*, Mile 1313.3 Alaska Hwy (☎883-4501) with **showers** for nonguests ($3.50) and a **laundry**; and the *Golden Bear Motel and RV Park*, Tok Cutoff (☎883-2561 or 1-888/252-2123, fax 883-5950, *www.akpub.com/akbbrv/golde.html*; ④), with $3 showers, tent spots for $15, modern motel rooms, and a good **espresso bar**. Dry

---

MOVING ON FROM TOK

Drivers headed west towards Fairbanks should continue with our account of Delta Junction (p.390); and those headed southwest to Glenallen, Anchorage, and the Wrangell–St Elias National Park should follow our account of the Tok Cutoff (p.388) in reverse order. The Alaska Hwy to the Canadian border, and the Taylor and Top of the World highways to Eagle and Dawson City are covered on the following pages.

Hitchhikers might expect that as an important junction, it would be easy to thumb a lift from Tok, but for some reason it isn't. People have been known to wait days, and those bound for Canada can be turned back at the border. This may be a good time to engage one of the **bus services** (for the lowdown on routes, see "Travel details," p.409). All stop close to the junction of the Alaska Hwy and Tok Cutoff: Alaskon Express pick up at the *Westmark Inn*; Alaska Direct stop by the Texaco station; and Parks Highway Express pull up by *Young's Café*.

campers can also **stay free** at the site behind the *Gateway Salmon Bake* (see below) in return for the purchase of a meal. **Campers** wanting a little more tranquility can head eighteen miles west to *Moon Lake State Recreation Site*, Mile 1332 ($10; pump water) with a boat launch, picnic area, good swimming, and even access for float planes which can often be seen tethered to the bank, or five miles east to the extensive *Tok River State Recreation Site*, Mile 1309.3 ($10; pump water) on the east bank of the Tok River.

If you aren't camping, the cheapest **place to stay** is the *HI-Tok International Hostel* (☎883-3745; PO Box 532; closed mid-Sept to mid-May; ①), a rustic place in an ex-army tent but with electricity, good hot showers (unless you're third in line) and two dorms (members $10, nonmembers $13); it is neither in town nor well signposted but is eight miles west along the Alaska Hwy (Mile 1322.5) then 0.7 miles down Pringle Drive. For something more convenient, try the *Snowshoe Motel*, Alaska Hwy towards Canada (☎1-800/478-4511, fax 883-4512; ③) where they throw in a continental breakfast, or the cozy Alaska-themed rooms at *Winter Cabin B&B*, Mile 1316.5 Alaska Hwy (☎883-5655; ③).

Good all-you-can-eat **meals** of salmon, halibut, and reindeer are served all day at the *Gateway Salmon Bake*, Mile 1313.1 Alaska Hwy, for around $18; the nearby *Fast Eddy's* serves a broad selection of diner fare along with gourmet pizzas ($18 is enough to two) and groaning plates of beef nachos ($10).

The Alaska Hwy to the Canadian border

Heading southeast from Tok, the Alaska Hwy runs towards the **Canadian border**, 92 miles away at Mile 1222. The initial arrow-straight twelve miles takes you past the *Tok River State Recreation Site*, Mile 1309.3 (see above) to **Tetlin Junction**, Mile 1301.7, where the Taylor Hwy heads north to Chicken, Eagle, and Dawson City in the Yukon.

Along most of the rest of the journey to the border, the Alaska Hwy forms the northern boundary of the **Tetlin National Wildlife Refuge** (*www.r7.fws.gov/nwr /tetlin/tetnwr*), broad marshy flatlands spotted with hundreds of miniature lakes. Here the glacial waters of the Nabesna and Chisana rivers, flowing south from the Alaska Range foothills, make up the headwaters of the Tanana River, one of Alaska's major fluvial arteries. These wetlands are right on the migration flight-path and provide a perfect habitat for one of the highest densities of waterfowl in the state – 143 nesting species and 47 migrants – as well as large numbers of black and grizzly bears, moose, caribou, wolves, and beavers. The Alaska Hwy provides access to the northern reaches, along with various pull-outs: interpretive panels at Mile 1227.9; Desper Creek (Mile 1225.6), with a canoe launch spot; and Highway Lake (Mile 1224.8), with its beaver lodge at the east end. You can **hike** and camp pretty much anywhere in the refuge, though some areas are managed by Native corporations and permission is required. A couple of the **best camping spots**, both on lakes and with great mountain views and wildlife viewing, are: *Lakeview* campground, Mile 1256.7 (free; untreated water only); and *Deadman Lake* campground, Mile 1249.3 (free; untreated water only) with its thousand-yard nature trail.

Eastbound travelers should call at the refuge's visitor center in Tok (see opposite): coming from the Canadian border, call at the Tetlin Wildlife Refuge **visitor center**, Mile 1229 (late May to early Sept daily 8am–5pm), where you'll find free copies of the *Tetlin Passage* newspaper, heaps of detailed hiking and camping information and a welter of interpretive talks, books, and displays.

The Taylor and Top of the World highways

As soon as you reach Tetlin Junction, twelve miles east of Tok, and turn off the Alaska Hwy onto the **Taylor Highway** (generally open mid-April to mid-Oct), it immediately feels more remote. There's no human habitation whatsoever until you reach the quirky settlement of **Chicken**, sixty miles down the line, then only the rusting hulks of gold dredges to remind you of what this area once meant to prospectors. Press on along increasingly narrow and lumpy roads and you can choose between the ordered former garrison town of **Eagle**, and the Top of the World Hwy into Canada and Dawson City.

From a practical point of view, most **rental cars are banned** on the Taylor and Top of the World highways and hitching can be a dispiriting experience (though not impossible), so you may have to rely on Alaska Direct or Parks Highway Express buses (see "Travel details," p.409), which both go through Chicken to Boundary and Dawson City, though neither go to Eagle.

The **Taylor Hwy** – detailed in a free BLM leaflet found locally – follows a tortuous course from one drainage to the next, climbing above 3500 feet three times – Mount Fairplay, Polly Summit, and American Summit – on its 160-mile journey to Eagle. The initial forty miles of blacktop reach **Mount Fairplay Summit** (Mile 33), giving long views over mixed forests and myriad tributaries of the Fortymile River before turning to a broad, smooth dirt road. Descending across tannin-rich rivers the color of strong tea you pass the only **camping** place before Chicken, the fairly pleasant *West Fork* campground ($8; pump water) at Mile 49.

Chicken

Having unearthed gold, early prospectors founded a tent city and decided to name it after the plump, poorly flighted, and tasty birds found in profusion hereabouts; but ptarmigan was too much for their collective lexicon and they settled on **CHICKEN**, now a tiny settlement 66 miles along the Taylor Hwy. There's not much to the place now with under twenty permanent residents, but it divides neatly into two sections. **Downtown Chicken** (*www.geocities.com/TheTropics /4097*), may just be the Alaska you're looking for, a classic piece of Alaskana comprising no more than a Western-style wooden sidewalk linking a gift shop, the *Chicken Creek Café*, and, best of all, the wonderfully battered old *Chicken Creek Saloon*, with a free pool table, a kick-it-to-make-it-go jukebox and a resident chicken. You never know who you might meet in the bar – gold panners, hunters, curious tourists, geologists – but somehow everyone gets on, oiled by beer and the congenial Susan, who runs the whole show.

There is nowhere formal **to stay** here, but you can stagger out to your RV parked overnight on the dirt lot, throw up a tent on the grassy verge, or just roll out your sleeping bag in a section of the café. Periodically make for the *Chicken Creek Café* for chicken soup, huge tooth-rotting cinnamon rolls, or the nightly salmon bake with homemade dill tartar sauce: they usually close around 8pm so come early. Apart from fairly pricey gas and a post office on the highway, that's about it for facilities; there isn't even a phone in town.

The now abandoned township of **Old Chicken** lies just across the highway from Downtown Chicken and is liberally festooned with Private Property signs. The track through it is actually public, but since all the interesting buildings are private you might as well troop a couple of hundred yards along the highway to

PADDLING THE FORTYMILE

Driving the Taylor Hwy through Chicken to Eagle only gives you a small taste of a prospector's lot in the time when all travel was done by river. Organized visitors can still sample something of this life by undertaking one of the multiday canoe journeys on the wild and scenic **Fortymile River**, a totally absorbing experience requiring considerable confidence in your abilities. You'll be spending at least one night (possibly a whole week) camping beside the river, seeing few people and having no one to help you if you swamp your boat or lose your supplies. It is important that you recognize which rapids should be portaged: misjudgments can have grave consequences, though the river's popularity in summer means that someone will eventually happen along.

First step is to obtain detailed route **information** from the BLM's Tok Field Office (☎883-5121): one free leaflet simply states the access points and float times, another adds more information on facilities and hazards along the way, and a list of the appropriate inch-to-the-mile maps. If you haven't got your own gear you'll need to look at renting a raft or canoe from Eagle Canoe Rentals, Box 4, Eagle, AK 99738 (mid-May to mid-Sept only; ☎547-2203) in Eagle, who charge $160 per two-berth canoe and $350 per six-berth raft, for four days.

The most commonly run section of the river is from the put-in point at South Fork Bridge (for access points see main text and the map on p.325) and paddle down **to Fortymile Bridge** (38 miles; 10–16 hours paddling) passing the few standing structures remaining from **Franklin**, a gold town which flourished in the late 1920s. A couple of miles above the pull-out you'll probably have to line your boats through the Falls, a Class II–III rapid portaged on the right. Keen boaters may wish to continue from **Fortymile Bridge to Eagle** (101 miles; typically 4–5 days) past the abandoned Steele Creek townsite, negotiating Deadman's Riffle and Canyon Rapids (both Class II–III), paddling into Canada then joining the Yukon River at the Fortymile townsite (deserted but being preserved) for the final fifty miles northwest to Eagle. Even more adventurous types can fly into the remote Joseph airstrip on the Middle Fork of the Fortymile River and paddle from there down to Fortymile Bridge (88 miles; 4–5 days) and then continue to the Yukon River and Eagle.

You should also be aware that if you are planning to paddle below the Fortymile Bridge take-out on down to the Yukon River and Eagle you'll be crossing into Canadian territory and will need to **contact US and Canadian customs** (see p.104).

the *Goldpanners*, a creekside gas station, gift shop, and RV park (dry parking $10) which runs the **Historical Town of Chicken Tour** (June–Aug daily 2pm; $5). It is a fascinating hour-long stroll around dilapidated buildings now being colonized by willow, made all the more poignant if you've read Robert Specht's *Tisha*, the true story of Anne Purdy (née Hobbs), who taught at the schoolhouse here in 1927. Like all the other buildings here, the **schoolhouse** was later put to an alternative use by the FE gold company who mined the area until the late 1960s. As the winter of 1967 set in they hauled out as usual, leaving all their gear ready for the next spring, but never returned. Everything remains in a state of partially arrested decay, scattered with enamel plates, incomplete record books, a *Glamour* magazine, and a wonderfully dated Sears catalog. The best-preserved building is the **hay barn**, later used as the dredge maintenance store and still sweetly smelling of hay and grease. Inside, copper gaskets hang on the wall, the repair schedule lies open on the bench, a working lathe sits in the corner, and all the pulleys still spin smoothly.

The Top of the World Highway and the road to Eagle

Beyond Chicken the highway starts to deteriorate noticeably, passing the BLM's **Chicken Field Station**, Mile 68 (mid-May to mid-Sept intermittently staffed), which marks the start of a trail to a lovely overlook of the **Cowden Dredge** in Mosquito Fork (2 miles round-trip; 1hr 30min). The highway continues wending its way from one Fortymile tributary to another, at Mile 75.3 reaching the **South Fork Bridge**, main access point for the Fortymile Canoe Route (see box, overleaf). You can **camp** seven miles up the road at *Walker Fork* campground, Mile 82 ($8; pump water), or continue past the rusting hulk of **Jack Wade Dredge**, Mile 86.

At Mile 95.7 you reach **Jack Wade Junction**, where the Taylor Hwy continues north to Eagle, and the **Top of the World Highway** spurs east towards Canada, appropriately running high along a broad subalpine ridge with expansive views down into the Fortymile mining district. **BOUNDARY** lies eight miles along and consists solely of *Boundary Lodge* (no phone; ①), a one-man operation with a cozy café and bar, gas that's expensive but usually a good deal cheaper than in Dawson, and a couple of simple cabins with beds and a wood stove sleeping three and as many as you can fit on the floor for $40. From there it is four miles to the hundred-and-forty-first meridian which defines the US–Canadian frontier (for border formalities see p.104) then 64 miles on to Dawson City.

Eagle

From Jack Wade Junction (see above), the **Taylor Highway** becomes increasingly narrow and winding, passing the Fortymile Canoe Route access point of **Fortymile Bridge**, Mile 112.6, on its 64-mile run to the Yukon River. **EAGLE**, 94 miles north of Chicken, spent the middle years of the twentieth century neglected on the south bank of the Yukon River but in the last twenty years has reinvented itself as the best-preserved town in the Interior. But this is no museum; though small and isolated it is very much alive, catering to prospectors and a few tourists in summer, and trappers in winter. Hugging an outside bend of the Yukon River only twelve miles downstream from the Canadian border, it is flanked by the pyramidal 1400-foot Eagle Bluff, where the birds which gave the town its name formerly nested.

Eagle's core is little changed since 1905. This is the result of sixty years of neglect, and thirty-odd years of preservation at the hands of the Eagle Historical Society, which was formed in the mid-1960s. They've done a wonderful job: all over town there are clapboard buildings restored and painted a fetching (but not original) white with green trim. They're all brought marvelously to life on the historical tours, which have undoubtedly contributed to the society's worldwide membership which, at three hundred members, is around twice the population of Eagle.

As the largest river town between Dawson and Fort Yukon, on the Arctic Circle, Eagle supports an extensive bush community sequestered in the forests beside tributaries of the Yukon. To learn more about their lives, read John McPhee's *Coming into the Country* (see "Books," in Contexts), or hang around until fall when you might see prospectors coming into town to redeem the summer's haul – some traders still have gold scales for this purpose.

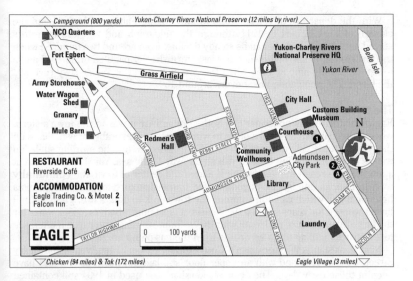

EAGLE

Campground (800 yards) — Yukon-Charley Rivers National Preserve (12 miles by river)
Chicken (94 miles) & Tok (172 miles) — Eagle Village (3 miles)

RESTAURANT
Riverside Café **A**

ACCOMMODATION
Eagle Trading Co. & Motel **2**
Falcon Inn **1**

0   100 yards

Some history

Eagle started life as a trading post on Belle Isle in the middle of the Yukon in 1880 and subsequently moved to the south bank when the townsite was surveyed in 1898. Unscrupulous land agents tried to talk up their price with exaggerated reports of gold-rich streams hereabouts, even trying in vain to flog off a corner lot to Jack London who called through in June 1898. Nonetheless, eager prospectors came in numbers and the town soon had a population of 1700. Lawlessness and a desire to control the Interior induced the US government to blaze the Valdez–Eagle Trail using soldiers stationed at Eagle's Fort Egbert.

From outside, Alaska was gradually seen in civilian rather than military terms and in 1900 Congress passed legislation for taxation, licensing, and the setting up of three judicial districts, one being in Eagle. From here James Wickersham presided as US District Judge over almost half of Alaska and a year later Eagle was incorporated as a city – the first in Interior Alaska. Anchorage wouldn't even be thought of for another 16 years, and Fairbanks was just a mudbank in the Chena River.

Eagle played another major role in the civilization of the north as a critical node in the **Washington–Alaska Military Cable and Telegraph System** (see box, p.408). Though geographically remote, it was no longer isolated. In fact in December 1905 this was the best-connected community in the Interior, a unique feature which lured explorer **Roald Amundsen** across four hundred miles of frozen rivers and mountain ranges by dog team. He came to announce to the world that, in the thirty months since he left his native Norway, he had successfully negotiated the Northwest Passage – the mariner's grail for much of the previous two centuries – and to beg his backers for more funds to continue the journey. It seems he liked Eagle (it had to be better than his sloop, locked in the polar ice of the Beaufort Sea for the nine-month winter) so he stayed a couple of months in a cabin off 1st Avenue on what is now Amundsen Street.

With the departure of Wickersham to burgeoning Fairbanks in 1904 and the closure of Fort Egbert in 1911 (though the telegraph and wireless operators stayed until 1925) Eagle began its steady decline: from around two hundred when the fort closed, to sixty-odd when the last sternwheeler paddled off in 1947 and a low point of only nine in 1953 when the completion of the Taylor Hwy reversed the trend. The population now hovers around 150.

The town

Eagle's waterfront is no longer the hotbed of activity it was in the town's stern-wheeler heyday, but it is still a place to which you are inexorably drawn. Stand on the rough promenade of Front Street and it feels as though the swirling silt-laden waters below are waiting to suck you all the way to the sea. You'll have to retreat a few steps to reach the geographical and social center of town, the **community well house**, an unmissable pagoda-roofed frame structure topped with a cupola housing a bell which can still summon the townsfolk to fight a fire. The windmill hasn't worked for years so, on a daily basis, it is a pump which provides water for the large proportion of residents who live without running water: you'll often see folk in trucks pulling up to fill drums from the gas-pump nozzle.

Next door stands **Wickersham's Courthouse**, corner of 1st Avenue and Berry Street, built in 1901 and with an upper floor still laid out much as it would have been in those early days. The desk Wickersham last used in 1904 still contained his papers in 1975 when the historical society began its restoration. Nowadays local guides from the society convene here for the absorbing three-hour

---

YUKON-CHARLEY RIVERS NATIONAL PRESERVE AND PADDLING THE YUKON

You'll need a fair degree of commitment to see anything of the **Yukon-Charley Rivers National Preserve**, a whopping chunk of unglaciated Alaskan Interior flanking the Yukon River – and its major tributary, the Charley River – for 130 river miles from just below Eagle, almost to Circle (see p.447). It is remote country almost devoid of human impact, though it was appreciably busier fifty to eighty years ago when sternwheelers forged their way up past Eagle to Dawson and prospectors worked the area for paydirt. A few of their spiritual descendants remain, hardy types (only 30 in the whole park year-round but more in summer) spinning out a subsistence lifestyle along the river or up the small tributaries. Most are reclusive enough that you won't see them, but you'll spot their nets, fish camps, and maybe a cabin or two, with the regular slap of Han Athapascan fishwheels as accompaniment.

In winter the river flows clear under six feet of ice, its surface used by snowmobiles and dog teams – the Yukon Quest dog-sled race comes right through here – but in summer the way to travel is by canoe. Paddling through the park, and along the Yukon River in general, is the only way to gain a sense of the region's interconnectedness; an appreciation of how much Dawson, Fortymile, Eagle and Circle were part of a riverine continuum that's impossible to achieve using the highways. The pleasure in traveling this country is the sheer sense of isolation, but you can fish while you drift, stop to hike up small streams, and pause to root around the few relics of the gold-rush era that remain: abandoned townsites, disused roadhouses, and the detritus of commercial gold dredging – one beached galleon still survives on Coal Creek in the heart of the park.

Historical Society Tour (June–Aug daily at 9am; $5; or by appointment ☎547-2325, *www.eagleak.org*), the only way you can get into the historic buildings. The tour continues downstairs in a small museum devoted to Wickersham's tenure, Amundsen's visit, and operations at Fort Egbert which, together with efforts to supply fuel for the riverboats, succeeded in completely denuding the surroundings. Eagle is still a border port but no longer has a permanent customs officer, obviating the need for the 1918 customs house, now turned into the **US Customs house museum** (visited on the tour), with period furniture arranged among beautifully hand-drawn pilots' charts of the Upper Yukon. The tour continues to **Fort Egbert**, a collection of wooden buildings dotted on the grass at the end of the airstrip. The **granary** contains a Model T Ford and a Model B dump truck still both used for the annual Forth of July parade through town, and the adjacent **mule barn** is much as it was left with four dozen stalls each marked with the name of its last occupant.

The tour varies a little depending on who is guiding that day, but might also include the plain, wooden **Hall of the Improved Order of Red Men**, an organization dedicated to "friendship, brotherly helpfulness, fraternal love, and good fellowship" though this didn't extend to the "red" men who lived in the district – it was strictly whites only.

If you want to get **out on the river**, consider a cruise on Gray Line's new *Yukon Queen II* (mid-May to early Sept; in Dawson ☎867/993-5599, fax 993-6408) which runs day-trips from Dawson to Eagle and back, leaving Dawson City at 9am (Yukon time) and departing Eagle at 2pm (Alaska time). Unfortunately, the trip is

---

PRACTICALITIES

There are no roads or maintained trails in the Yukon-Charley, nor even any publicly maintained airstrips, so unless you can get a bush pilot to fly you into the upper Charley River, your only access is by boat. The **Yukon-Charley Rivers National Preserve Headquarters**, 1st Ave, Eagle (mid-May to mid-Sept daily 8am–5pm; mid-Sept to mid-May Mon–Fri 8am–5pm; ☎547-2234, *www.nps.gov/yuch*) provide information and sell maps, and you'll need to **rent a canoe** from Eagle Canoe Rentals (mid-May to mid-Sept only; PO Box 4, Eagle, AK 99738, ☎ & fax 547-2203; also in Dawson at *Dawson City River Hostel* ☎867/993-6823) who hire two-person canoes in Dawson for the float down to Eagle (105 miles; 3–4 days; $110 rental per canoe), and in Eagle for the float down to Circle (165 miles; 5 days; $165 per canoe). Both trips can be undertaken at a steadier pace (canoes at an additional $20 a day) or you can undertake an epic combination from Dawson to Circle (270 miles; 9–10 days; $270). Canoes can be dropped in Circle but you'll need to fly back to your starting point: this is best arranged beforehand with Circle Air (☎520-5223) who charge $300 an hour for charters and also do fly-ins.

June to September is the time to travel, avoiding freeze-up (typically three weeks in mid-Oct) and break-up (usually another three weeks in mid-May) when huge chunks of tumbling ice make river travel extremely perilous or impossible. Once on the river self-sufficiency is paramount. Obviously you'll need to be competent paddlers – a midstream spill in such a broad, cold river can be lethal – and carry everything you need. You'll be **camping** on open beaches and river bars, where insects are kept at bay by the breeze, except for at four free public-use **cabins** (let on a first-come, first-served basis), including one at the two-story, log-built *Slavens Roadhouse*, long deserted but now converted for visitors' use. Remember to leave a float plan at the park headquarters in Eagle (and let them know you're safe at journey's end), take along your fishing tackle, and stay bear aware.

four hours each way, most spaces are filled by tours, and from this end the schedule only suits those who want to overnight in Dawson, but standby places (US$192 round-trip, US$117 one-way) may be available. Phone ahead to check space if are thinking of taking your bike on the boat from Eagle to Dawson. If you've got the time for a longer trip, but not the determination to tackle the Yukon by canoe (see box, overleaf), consider a few days on a riverboat with Upper Yukon Enterprises (run by the owners of the *Falcon Inn*; see below) who run to Dawson City and to Circle (both 3 days, 2 nights; $450), and offer custom trips.

Practicalities

Most of the town's commercial activity revolves around the *Eagle Trading Company*, Front St (☎547-2220; ③), a well-stocked grocery selling **gas** at inflated prices, operating a **motel** with comfortable spruce-paneled rooms, and letting functional **RV sites** by the river for $16, including showers. You'll need to book as far in advance as you can manage to stay at *Falcon Inn B&B*, Front Street (☎547-2254, fax 547-2255, *marlysho@aol.com*; ④), a modern log house with spectacular river views and tasteful decor that makes it one of the most appealing B&Bs in the Interior. The guests' lounge even has a wonderful turret and deck perfect for watching Eagle's daily routine or, with luck, the aurora. The town's peaceful **campground** ($8; untreated river water) lies half a mile northwest of Fort Egbert on the route of a water-supply line which once supplied Fort Egbert from American Creek. Ferret around in the trees and you'll come across the remains of structures where fires once heated the pipe to prevent it freezing. A couple of **cafés** open up during the height of the summer, but the town's staple is the *Riverside Café*, Front Street, a good diner that is ideal for just sitting watching the river roll by. Eagle is "damp," which means that there are **no alcohol sales** in town, but no one is going to stop you bringing a bottle or two in.

WAMCATS

As the Fortymile and Klondike gold rushes precipitated rapid population growth in the Alaskan bush, the need for improved communications increased. A post office had been established in Eagle in 1899 but a messenger from Valdez took two months, lost eleven horses, and cost the government $3000, to deliver just three letters. The initial solution involved a telegraph line to Dawson and Whitehorse in the Yukon from where messages were carried to Skagway and shipped to Seattle and the outside world. This was little better. Reluctant to rely on the Canadians, the government set about an "All-American" system, the **Washington–Alaska Military Cable and Telegraph System** (WAMCATS) in 1900. The Army Signal Corps, based in Eagle, was responsible for the construction and the job fell to 21-year-old Lieutenant **William Mitchell**, subsequently a vociferous advocate of airborne warfare, who masterminded the project. He instituted new ideas such as supplying the summer construction camps by sledding in supplies during the deathly cold winter, and banning thermometers. In essence the route followed the Eagle–Valdez Trail, still being completed at the time, which allowed better access for subsequent maintenance, using sheds spaced at forty-mile intervals. It was completed to Valdez in 1902 and on to Seattle in 1904. Meanwhile another team were working from Nome linking up with the Valdez–Eagle line to complete a 1500-mile web in 1903. WAMCATS remained in use until 1925 playing a critical role in the Serum Run (see box, p.468) in that year.

MCQUESTEN'S THERMOMETER

Trader Leroy Napoleon "Jack" McQuesten left a huge legacy in the North. He never found much gold, but when scouting around the Tron-diuck River in the Canadian Yukon he decided he'd seen enough color to justify widespread interest and sent word south that there was gold to be found, thereby kick-starting the gold rush in the "Klondike" (his bastardized version of Tron-diuck). He set up trading posts as a representative of the Alaska Commercial Company, including one at Fort Reliance on the Yukon where he once tried his hand at plowing his land with two young moose. Here he financed prospectors and, to aid newcomers in judging their outdoor plans, instituted **McQuesten's Thermometer**. It comprised a series of four vials – mercury (freezing point -40°F), coal oil (-50°F), Jamaica ginger (-60°F), and Perry Davis' painkiller (-75°F) – in a rack outside along with a note instructing people to shake each bottle in turn. If the mercury was frozen it was too cold to be out on the trail at night, and even the daytime was dangerous if the coal oil was solid. When the ginger froze folk should stay in their cabin, and when the painkiller wouldn't budge you shouldn't stray from your stove.

travel details

The most pleasurable way to get around the Interior is by **train**, though you are restricted to a single line which runs from Anchorage through Talkeetna and Denali to Fairbanks taking in the best of the scenery in comfort, at a price. **Buses** (listed along with route descriptions in Basics, p.38) are more frequent and broader in their coverage. Again the Anchorage–Denali–Fairbanks corridor is the busiest with a handful of companies doing a daily run in summer. Elsewhere there is a run from Anchorage through Glenallen and Tok into Canada with connections for Skagway; one from Fairbanks to Valdez; one from Anchorage through Glenallen to Valdez; one from Anchorage through Glenallen and Tok to Whitehorse, Yukon; and another from Fairbanks through Delta Junction, Tok, and Chicken to Dawson City, Yukon. There is just one bus from Glenallen to McCarthy.

With the exception of occasional trains (see Basics, p.36), nothing runs after the middle of September or before the middle of May.

TRAINS

Denali Park to: Anchorage (daily; 7hr 30min); Fairbanks (daily; 3hr 45min); Talkeetna (daily; 4hr 40min); Wasilla (daily; 6hr 20min).

Talkeetna to: Anchorage (daily; 3hr 30min); Denali Park (daily; 4hr 40min); Fairbanks (daily; 9hr); Wasilla (daily; 1hr 40min).

Wasilla to: Anchorage (daily; 2hr); Denali Park (daily; 4hr); Fairbanks (daily; 10hr 30min); Talkeetna (daily; 1hr 40min).

BUSES

Chicken to: Dawson City (3 weekly; 4–5hr); Fairbanks (3 weekly; 7hr); Tok (3 weekly; 1hr 30min).

Delta Junction to: Fairbanks (1–3 daily; 2hr); Glenallen (3 weekly; 3hr); Tok (1–3 daily; 3hr); Valdez (3 weekly; 5hr); Whitehorse, Yukon (3 weekly; 12hr).

Denali/Glitter Gulch to: Anchorage (4 daily; 5–6hr); Fairbanks (2 daily; 3–4hr); Talkeetna (1 daily; 4hr); Talkeetna Junction (2 daily; 3hr).

Glenallen to: Anchorage (1–2 daily; 4–5hr); Beaver Creek, Yukon (3 weekly; 5hr 15min); Chitina (daily; 1hr 30min); Delta Junction (3 weekly; 3hr); Fairbanks (3 weekly; 4hr 30min); McCarthy (daily; 4hr); Valdez (daily; 3hr 15min).

Palmer to: Anchorage (2 daily; 1hr); Beaver Creek, Yukon (3 weekly; 10hr); Glenallen (1 daily; 5hr); Valdez (1 daily; 9hr).

Talkeetna to: Anchorage (2–3 daily; 3hr); Denali/Glitter Gulch (1 daily; 4hr).

Talkeetna Junction to: Anchorage (2 daily; 3hr); Denali/Glitter Gulch (2 daily; 3hr); Fairbanks (2 daily; 7–9hr).

Tok to: Anchorage (6 weekly; 8–9hr); Beaver Creek, Yukon (3 weekly; 3hr 15min); Chicken (3 weekly; 1hr 30min); Dawson City (3 weekly; 6hr); Delta Junction (1–3 daily; 3hr); Fairbanks (1–3 daily; 5hr); Glenallen (3 weekly; 3–4hr); Skagway (3 weekly; overnight with a stop at Beaver Creek, Yukon); Whitehorse, Yukon (3 weekly; 7–8hr).

Wasilla to: Anchorage (2 daily; 1hr 15min); Denali/Glitter Gulch (2 daily; 4–5hr); Talkeetna Junction (1 daily; 1hr 15min).

CHAPTER SIX

FAIRBANKS AND THE ARCTIC NORTH

journey to Alaska seems incomplete without time spent in the **Far North**, a region comprising the Alaskan Arctic and Fairbanks, the state's second largest city and the hub of the north. It is stunningly dramatic here, with long winter nights lit by the shimmering strands of the **aurora borealis**, extreme temperatures that demand extraordinary measures just so that people can live here, and settlements which all seem to claim some superlative: lowest temperature, most isolated cabin, or furthest north something or other. The area is also where the legendary pipeline-building days of the mid-1970s were played out with construction crews earning big money then coming to town to squander fistfuls of cash nightly.

Today, the north is actually wilder than it was a century ago. Abandoned cabins remain where gold rushes once bustled with activity, and sternwheel steamers have been replaced by bush planes as the transportation mode of choice. The heart of the region is **Fairbanks**, a flat, sprawling place that does a good job of balancing urban life with the needs of cabin dwellers on its doorstep. If you've just spent some time in the Interior, city luxuries will be welcome, and it's easy to spend a few days here making forays out to assorted gold-rush relics, and soaking up the late evening sun as it glows off the Alaska Range. Before long you'll want to stray further, and the road system lends itself to easy trips to the resort at **Chena Hot Springs**, and increasingly more challenging journeys to the modest **Circle Hot Springs**, the near-primitive **Manley Hot Springs**, or even on to the daunting five-hundred-mile **Dalton Highway**, which runs along the route of the pipeline to **Deadhorse**, almost on the Arctic Ocean.

Fairbanks' roads will also take you to a few manageable hikes and easy canoe routes, but for the really challenging stuff – weeklong hikes and float trips – you'll need to get out to the **Gates of the Arctic National Park** or the **Arctic National**

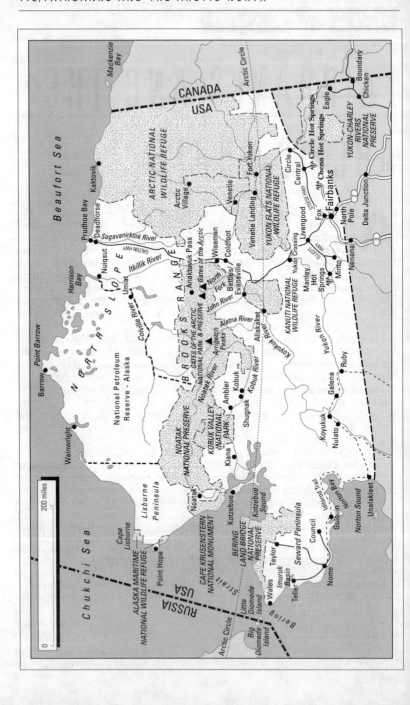

Wildlife Refuge, which jointly encompass much of the **Brooks Range**. Beyond the Brooks Range, the four-thousand-strong Iñupia city of **Barrow** clings to the edge of the land with only the ten-month-frozen sea between it and the North Pole. As a large Eskimo community, Barrow shares a lot in common with **Kotzebue**, a springboard for the inland **sand dunes** beside the Kobuk river. Kotzebue is often visited jointly with its near neighbor **Nome**, a former gold town where miners flocked to sift the precious metal from its sands, before eventually following the gold rush east to found Fairbanks.

FAIRBANKS

FAIRBANKS, 358 miles north of Anchorage, is the end of the road for most tourists, and marks the ultimate conclusion of the **Alaska Hwy** from Canada. If you've just driven the full fifteen hundred miles from Dawson Creek in British Columbia then some kind of celebration is in order. Catch it right and you can conduct your revelry under the ethereal glow of the **northern lights**, for this is aurora central, with sightings on some 240 nights a year.

Most visitors arrive in summer when nights aren't dark enough for aurora viewing, but residents play midnight baseball games in the 21 hours of natural light. At this time, it can be disconcerting stumbling out of a bar at 2am into bright sunshine, but it is better than the dead of winter when Fairbanks receives only three hours of direct sunlight daily and residents suffer from a high rate of depression.

Fairbanks lies just 188 miles south of the Arctic Circle and far from the moderating effects of the sea, a combination resulting in one of the most extreme temperature ranges found anywhere. The thermometer can rise to over 90°F in summer, but temperatures of minus 40°F are not uncommon in winter. Car (and truck) use in the winter is a problem, strategically placed electrical sockets enable engines to be plugged in and kept from freezing up, but some people leave their engines on when running errands resulting in exhaust fumes freezing into a disgusting photochemical smog known as **ice fog**, which blots out the weak winter light. This has forced Fairbanksans – as they call themselves – to relocate from the city center into the surrounding wilderness, producing one of the most thinly populated cities imaginable and encouraging car use: Fairbanks has even more vehicles per capita than LA and a network of four-lane freeways that could hardly be less friendly to pedestrians.

Fairbanks bills itself as Alaska's **"Golden Heart,"** a moniker reflecting its geographical position and the sense of community that has managed to outlast the rapid urbanization. Of course, it also alludes to the city's history as a gold town, a status that draws busloads to **Gold Dredge #8**, the state's only publicly accessible gold dredge, to **El Dorado Gold Camp**, and a couple of entertaining burlesque shows recalling those heady days. For more intellectual pursuits, the **University Museum** is among the best in the state wtih entertaining shows on the aurora borealis and Alaskan Native sports. To learn more about Alaskan sports, you can enjoy the traditional games to their fullest each July during the **World Inuit–Indian Olympics**.

Some history

Fairbanks was founded accidentally in 1901 by former Washington state miner, **ET Barnette**. After serving five years in a Washington prison for stealing his partner's gold, Barnette headed for Alaska and eventually found himself on the *LaVelle Young,* steaming up the Tanana River, bound for the Valdez–Eagle trail where he hoped to set up a trading post. The river level was low and Barnette talked the boat's captain into trying a "short cut" up the equally shallow Chena River. Grounded, the frustrated captain dumped 130 tons of mining equipment and supplies on the bank where 1st Avenue now meets Cushman Street, and left Barnette and his wife alone in the wilderness two hundred miles short of their destination.

Meanwhile, hapless Italian émigré, **Felix Pedro** – who had earlier discovered a wondrously rich stream then lost it – was stumbling around the Tanana Valley almost out of food when he spotted smoke from the *LaVelle Young* and headed towards it, eventually settling in with Barnette and company. Pedro continued his prospecting, and the following summer unearthed a small find. Barnette saw his chance and dispatched his cook to Dawson City to spread "the Great Lie" about a rich strike, managing to convince three hundred prospectors to make the journey. Fortuitously gold was eventually found and, in 1904, thousands joined the **gold rush**, flocking to the new city of Fairbanks, named for the Indiana senator Charles Fairbanks, who later became vice-president under Theodore Roosevelt.

Within five years Fairbanks was the largest and busiest city in Alaska, its 18,000 inhabitants enjoying electric lights, a sewerage system, fire and police departments, and a federal jail established in 1904. In this climate, Barnette was able to make a fortune, largely by embezzling a million dollars from the Washington-Alaska Bank, hastening his 1911 departure from the town he had originally founded.

The early surface gold strike turned out to be a freak occurrence. Most of the gold was deep below yards of frozen gravel; a mixed blessing since slow gold recovery sustained Fairbanks well beyond the typical two-year boom-and-bust cycle. By the 1920s, professional mining engineers came to exploit the deeper deposits using modern dredges that worked the rivers, scooping gold-bearing gravel with giant buckets, then spewing the spent "tailings" out the rear. Their heyday lasted only thirty years, but the evidence – vast piles of gravel and the occasional rusting hulk of a dredge – is hard to miss around neighboring Fox, Ester, and along the Chatanika River.

The region's fluctuating population was bolstered by World War II when huge **military bases** were built to thwart possible Japanese attacks and provide a stepping stone for American planes on their way from Montana to Russia and the European battlefields as part of the **Lend-Lease program**. Fairbanks then sputtered along until the city was chosen as the logistical headquarters for the construction of the **Trans-Alaska oil pipeline** (see box, p.454). For four years in the mid-1970s more than 20,000 oil workers were based here. Generous wage packages, sometimes topping $1500 a week (not much less than the price of a small sedan at the time), fueled rapid expansion and generated a freewheeling atmosphere. Fairbanks became a byword for excess, infamous for its riotous bars and well-patronized brothels. Then the pipeline was finished, and so it seemed was Fairbanks: unemployment hit twenty percent, property prices crashed, and the city's economy collapsed. Things have since stabilized, but the scars remain, especially downtown where empty parking lots have replaced blocks once solid with bars and bulging wallets.

Arrival, information, and city transport

The once daily Alaska Railroad **train** offers the most relaxing way to get here from Anchorage or Denali; creeping through the suburbs of Fairbanks and pulling up at the **train station** on Driveway Street (ticket office Mon–Fri 7am–3pm, Sat & Sun 7–11am), a mere five-minutes' walk north of downtown, at around 8pm each summer evening (no trains in winter). **Long-distance buses** (see "Listings," p.439 and "Travel details," p.485) mostly dropoff downtown outside the visitor center, some also calling at hostels and the main hotels.

You are most likely to use **Fairbanks International Airport**, four miles southwest of downtown, for bush- and float-plane flights into the Arctic; and if you're flying in via Anchorage. The MACS **bus** Yellow Line (Mon–Sat, not Sun; $1.50) only takes half an hour to get from the airport to downtown but the long wait between services makes it worth grabbing a **taxi** (around $12 downtown), or the Airlink Shuttle (☎452-3337; see overleaf) which charges $5 per person to your accommodation.

Information

Buses and trains arrive a few steps from the Fairbanks CVB **visitor center**, 550 1st Ave (June to early Sept daily 8am–8pm; early Sept to May Mon–Fri 8am–5pm; ☎456-5774 or 1-800/327-5774, fax 452-2867, *www.explorefairbanks.com*), which is well equipped to handle general inquiries about Fairbanks and points north. For anything outdoorsy it is better to head a couple of blocks to the **Alaska Public Lands Information Center** (APLIC), lower level, 250 Cushman St (June to early Sept daily 9am–6pm; early Sept–May Tues–Sat 10am–6pm; ☎456-0527, fax 456-0514, *www.nps.gov/aplic*), which covers everything to do with recreational use of public lands in the northern third of the state. Excellent displays and free videos detail wildlife, land use, survival techniques, river rescue, and canoe-trip planning, and the helpful staff are good at helping channel your hiking and canoeing ambitions. They've also got stacks of relevant books for sale and the most popular topographical **maps**: for all other maps, visit the UAF Geodata Center (see "Listings," p.439).

City transport and tours

Even if you've made it this far without a vehicle, when you reach Fairbanks you should think seriously about **renting a car** (for local agencies see "Listings," p.439). For a city of only 60,000 souls, Fairbanks is incredibly spread out and designed around the needs of the motorist. By using buses, the shuttle service outlined below and maybe renting a bike, it is possible to see most of Fairbanks, but services are painfully infrequent and two or three people traveling together will soon find a car a very good investment, particularly once you start straying outside the city limits. Most rental agencies won't insure their ordinary vehicles on gravel-surfaced roads (though your own insurance may cover you; check before leaving home), so if you are planning to visit Manley Hot Springs or drive the Steese Hwy to Circle Hot Springs then consider renting from Affordable Rentals, which has no problem with dirt roads except for the Dalton Hwy north of the Yukon.

If money is tight, or you're traveling alone, you may find yourself drawn to the MACS **bus** system, with its hub at the **transit center**, corner of N Cushman Street and 5th Avenue (Mon–Fri 6.30am–8pm, Sat 10am–6pm; transit hotline ☎459-1011). There are five routes, most running every hour or so from around 7am to 7pm on weekdays, with restricted services on Saturday and none at all on Sunday. The most useful lines are: Yellow, from downtown past Alaskaland and along Airport Way to the airport; Red, along College Road to the university campus; and Blue, past Alaskaland and several shopping centers to the university. **Fares** are only $1.50 per ride; $3 day-passes and $5 five-ride concessions are available from the driver.

You could always get around by **taxi** (for numbers see "Listings," p.438), but there are savings to be made by using **minibuses** run by Airlink Shuttle (☎452-3337, *airlink@burnitup.com*), who do door-to-door transfers based on a flat rate, shared-ride basis (assuming two passengers) – $3.50 in the city center, $5 to the airport and most of the city attractions, $15 to Fox, Ester, or North Pole. They also run city tours ($25): these visit the University of Alaska Museum (entry not included), and if you want to stay there longer they'll come back and pick you up later. For a romantic trip, there's Horse-Drawn Tours (mid-May to mid-Sept Tues–Sun 11am–7pm; $2.50 one-way, $4 round-trip; ☎452-8449), which runs a wheeled buggy behind two draft horses on a 45-minute run from the visitor center to Alaskaland.

A good alternative to the buses and shuttles is to **rent a bicycle** (see "Listings," p.438), though it is worth considering that even sights within the immediate vicinity of Fairbanks are widely scattered: Fox is eleven miles north, North Pole is fifteen miles southeast, and Ester is six miles northwest. Dedicated cycle trails are rare, but the invaluable *BikeWays* map (available free from the visitor center) details multiuse paths, quiet roads with broad shoulders, and the expressways where bikes are not permitted, along with the location of hills and bike repair shops. Bike-rental places will be able to point you in the direction of **mountainbike** trails, mostly in the cross-country ski area behind the university known as Skarland Trails (maps from the UAF Wood Center) and in Birch Hill Recreation Area just north of downtown (display near entrance).

Accommodation

Fairbanks' accommodation is broadly distributed over an already spread-out city. With a few exceptions, nondrivers will want to stay **downtown** (roughly within twenty-minutes' walk of the visitor center) where you'll have the best access to the bus system. **Hotels and motels** here are generally either pricey or drab, but fortunately there are a couple of good hostels and some excellent **B&Bs** at reasonable prices.

Possession of your own wheels opens up **suburban Fairbanks**, the domain of better-value motels, more good B&Bs, hostels, and some surprisingly sylvan campgrounds. Some of the best B&Bs and campgrounds lie beyond the city limits, often giving better access to the sights around Fairbanks without the hassle of the big city.

Reservations are pretty much essential from June to August when **prices** are correspondingly high, especially during the Golden Days festival in mid-July (see box, p.429). With the exception of the major festivals such as the Ice Art competition (see box, p.424), the city is free from visitors through much of the **winter** and hotel rates are about half that of summer.

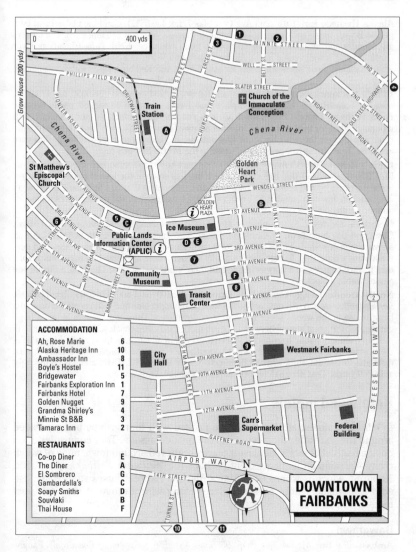

ACCOMMODATION

Ah, Rose Marie	6
Alaska Heritage Inn	10
Ambassador Inn	8
Boyle's Hostel	11
Bridgewater	5
Fairbanks Exploration Inn	1
Fairbanks Hotel	7
Golden Nugget	9
Grandma Shirley's	4
Minnie St B&B	3
Tamarac Inn	2

RESTAURANTS

Co-op Diner	E
The Diner	A
El Sombrero	G
Gambardella's	C
Soapy Smiths	D
Souvlaki	B
Thai House	F

DOWNTOWN FAIRBANKS

Hostels

In recent years, several hostels have sprung up around Fairbanks: none are right downtown but three are within a couple of miles. Because of the very short tourist season, all are "home hostels," with owners sharing varying portions of their home with guests, usually for very reasonable rates. Facilities, however, can be quite cramped and the owners aren't always on hand when you want them.

Alaska Heritage Inn, 1018 22nd Ave (☎451-6587, fax 456-6511). Combined hostel and budget B&B with single-sex dorms ($16), smallish rooms ($54), and $10 tent sites. The owners are friendly and available, not to mention a good resource: Keith runs Chandalar River Outfitters and is well versed in the Alaskan bush, and Velma is a St Lawrence Island Yup'ik who occasionally has sewn-skin items for sale. The MACS Red bus passes within two blocks. ①/②.

Billie's Backpackers Hostel, 2895 Mack Rd (☎479-2034 or 1-800/236-5350, fax 479-2034, *www.alaskahostel.com*). Handily sited place that always seems to be packed, partly because Parks Highway Express buses finish various runs here. Comfortable and relaxing, with mountain bikes for rent and cheap Internet access. Dorms ($20) each have their own bathroom and kitchen, there is a barbecue area outside, and laundry and bag-storage facilities are available. Tent spaces $10 per person. Close to the MACS Red bus route. ①.

Boyle's Hostel, 310 18th Ave (☎456-4944). Compact hostel on a suburban street (close to the MACS Red bus route) that lacks atmosphere but has some of the lowest prices in the area. Some dorms ($15) and rooms ($24) are in a half-basement so they're a little dark, but you get a full kitchen, low-cost laundry, TVs everywhere, a small garden, and rattling bikes rented for under $5 a day. ①.

Grandma Shirley's, 510 Dunbar St (☎451-9816, *www.mosquitonet.com/grandmashirleys*). Clean and tidy hostel run by Grandma Shirley who makes up the dorm beds ($17.80) on arrival (linen provided), keeps tea and coffee well stocked in the guest lounge area, and generally runs a tight ship. Guests use the family kitchen, there are basic bikes freely available, they'll store bags if you are away hiking and there's Internet access. The MACS Purple line passes within a block. ①.

North Woods Lodge, Chena Hills Drive (☎479-5300 or 1-800/478-5305, fax 479-6888, *northlodge@webtv.net*). An unusual hostel with adjoining cabins and B&B centered around a large house in the woods seven miles west of downtown. The common area is just a large garage, but the great atmosphere and hot tub more than compensates. Tom, the owner, will pick up from any public transport if you've reserved in advance, but you really need a vehicle to stay here. Follow Chena Pump Rd about a mile past the *Pumphouse* restaurant, turn right into Roland Rd, right where it intersects with E Chena Hills Drive and it is on the right after 300 yards. Tent sites $15 for two, dorm $15, cabins ②, B&B ③.

Hotels and motels

In summer, almost all the hotels are packed with tour groups being paraded around the state after their cruise up the Inside Passage. Tour companies often book a handful of large, lackluster places scattered around town, none of which really warrants a mention except perhaps the *Westmark Fairbanks Hotel*, 813 Noble St, which is where Gray Line's Alaskon Express buses stop. We've listed a few smaller, more personal places along with a range of the city's best motels.

Downtown

Ambassador Inn, 415 5th Ave (☎451-9555, fax 451-9556, *jenox@mosquitonet.com*). Family-run hotel with quite a few long-term residents and some fairly scruffy public areas, but the rooms, with cable TV, and a full kitchen, are central and pretty-good value. ④.

Bridgewater, 723 1st Ave (☎452-6661 or 1-800/528-4916, fax 452-6126, *www.fountainheadhotels .com*). Quality tourist hotel with comfortable rooms, a restaurant, and a nice lounge area. The larger corner rooms with river views are the best and are no more expensive, but in high demand. There is a complimentary pickup service from the train station and airport, and it is only open mid-May to mid-September. ⑥.

Fairbanks, 517 3rd Ave (☎456-6411 or 1-888/329-4685, fax 456-1792, *www.alaska.net /~fbxhotl*). Good-value downtown hotel done in ersatz Miami Beach Deco style, featuring small but cheerily decorated rooms each with cable TV, phone, and a washstand – some with private bath. Free airport and train station pickups. Shared bath ④, private bath ⑤.

Golden Nugget, 900 Noble at 10th (☎452-5141, fax 452-5458, *www.golden-nuggethotel.com*). Spartan but comfortable mid-range hotel with air-conditioned rooms, queen beds, and cable TV but not much of a view from any room. ⑤.

Suburban Fairbanks

College Inn, 700 Fairbanks St (☎474-3666 or 1-800/770-2177, fax 474-3668, *myoung@mosquitonet .com*). A number of long-term residents, and the ageing infrastructure make this a fairly dispiriting and characterless place to stay, but it is cheap, handy for the university, and on the MACS Blue and Red bus routes. Shared-bath rooms come with towels and HBO, and there is a kitchen, but no utensils, crockery, or cutlery. ②.

Golden North Motel, 4888 Old Airport Rd (☎479-6201 or 1-800/447-1910, fax 479-5766, *goldennorthmotel@alaska.com*). Friendly and spotlessly clean motel with neat rooms (some with separate lounge area) that come with cable TV and a complimentary continental breakfast. Located out towards the airport, they do courtesy train station and airport pickups, but you may find it inconvenient without your own wheels. Economy rooms ③, others ⑤.

River's Edge Resort Cottages, 4200 Boat St (☎474-3601 or 1-800/770-3343, fax 474-3665, *www.riversedge.ne*). A nice alternative to the usual options: boxy, modern, year-round cottages, right by the Chena River, with on-site restaurant and bar, and shuttles to all the major attractions. All cabins come with two queen-size beds and doors out onto a patio, and some have a riverfront setting. Standard ⑦, riverside ⑧.

B&Bs

The number of B&Bs in Fairbanks has boomed over the last decade or so, and there is now a wide selection from simple homestays to places approaching country-lodge standard. As ever, they provide an appealing alternative to motels and hotels, and few owners are prepared to jeopardize the reputation of Alaskan hospitality by skimping on the breakfasts. Places close to the city center are often just as good and no more expensive than more secluded places.

Downtown

Ah, Rose Marie, 302 Cowles St at 3rd Ave (☎456-2040, fax 456-6193, *www.akpub.com/akbbrv /ahrose.html*). Justly popular B&B that's a little cramped but imaginatively decorated and well-run by the charming host, John. A hearty breakfast is served on the glassed-in veranda. Single rooms start at ③, shared and private-bath room ④.

Fairbanks Exploration Inn, 505 Illinois St (☎451-1920 or 1-888/452-1920, fax 455-7317, *www.feinn.com*). A B&B made up of four guest bungalows which were built in 1927 as housing for the managers and dredgemasters of the FE Gold Company. Tastefully converted, they each have a lovely lounge area, and half a dozen comfortable rooms, most with queen beds. A large buffet breakfast is served in the central bungalow. Two-bedroom suites ⑧, rooms ⑥.

Minnie Street B&B Inn, 345 Minnie St (☎456-1802 or 1-888/456-1849, fax 451-1751, *www .minniestreetbandb.com*). Top-line B&B with every luxury taken to the nth degree: the beds are fully adjustable for firmness, there are in-room phones with modem links, and outside there's a spacious deck and a barbecue area. One room has a jacuzzi and some share a bathroom, but you always get bath robes, which some even wear down to the communally served full breakfast. There's also a business center with fax, copier, and Internet access. Room with jacuzzi ⑦, private bath ⑥, shared bath ⑤.

Suburban Fairbanks

7 Gables Inn, 4312 Birch Lane (☎479-0751, fax 479-2229, *gables7@alaska.net*). Popular and ever-expanding top-line B&B that is large enough to qualify as a small hotel; large rooms all with cable and VCR (most with spa bath) and flashy suites with a small kitchen. Shared facilities ⑤, private ⑥, suites ⑦.

Midge's Birch Lane, 4335 Birch Lane (☎388-8084 or 1-800/479-4895, *midge@alaska.net*). One of the best B&Bs in the city; neat, clean, and friendly, plus access to a large lounge with fireplace, a piano, and stacks of Alaska books and videos. All rooms are comfortable and one has a large queen bed, a walk-in wardrobe, private bath, and a deck that gets the afternoon sun (⑤). Breakfasts are excellent and may include blintzes or salmon quiche. It's about a twenty-minute walk from the university. Shared-bath rooms ④.

Out of town

Fox Creek B&B, Mile 1.1 Elliot Hwy, Fox (☎457-5494, fax 457-5464, *www.polarnet.com /~foxcreek*). Just two rooms in a secluded house twelve miles north of downtown and close to the *Howling Dog Saloon*. Quiet and comfortable, with big, cooked breakfasts. No credit cards. Private bath ⑤, shared ③.

A Taste of Alaska Lodge, 551 Eberhardt Rd, Mile 5.3 Chena Hot Springs Rd (☎488-7855, fax 488-3772, *www.atasteofalaska.com*). Somewhere in between a B&B and a small country lodge located on 280 acres on a ridge with wonderful views south over the city to the Alaska Range. Comfortable rooms have cable TV and all the expected appointments, and there's a hot tub for guests' use. They'll even take you dog mushing at any time of the year, and there's panning on their gold claim. Two-bedroom log house ⑧, suites ⑦, rooms ⑥.

Trailhead Cabins, Middle Fork (☎460-8907, *www.trailheadcabins.com*). A real Alaskan experience is waiting here in these cabins tucked just below the tree line on Haystack Mountain. They're a little inconvenient for Fairbanks (5 miles off the Elliott Hwy and 35-minutes' drive north of town), but make a great base for exploring the north. The single-room cabins ($40) sleep three and come with proper beds, cooking facilities, an outhouse, and supply of water, but no shower or running water. The Web site has a map to the cabins and a local trail map. ①.

Campgrounds and RV parks

Fairbanks is well served with places to park an RV, and many sites are pleasant places to pitch a tent, though none are entirely RV-free. Campgrounds within the city limits are right on bus routes, though drivers can save a few dollars by staying a short drive out of town.

Suburban Fairbanks

Alaskaland, Airport Way at Peger Rd (registration 8.30am–9pm; ☎459-1087). Park your RV in the Alaskaland parking lot and use their toilets, water, and dump station; no showers. $12 a night (four nights maximum). Mid-May to mid-Sept. Reached by the Alaskaland Tram and the MACS Blue and Yellow buses.

Chena River Recreation Site, University Ave at Airport Way (☎451-2695). A state parks campground by the Chena River that is surprisingly wooded and quiet for what is essentially a city campground. There are toilets, tables, a dump station, volleyball courts, and even a boat launch. Walk-in sites for $10, vehicle slots for $15. On the MACS Blue bus route.

Fred Meyer, 3755 Airport Way. No facilities are offered, but this store allows RVs to park overnight in its parking lot.

River's Edge RV Park, 4200 Boat St (☎474-3601 or 1-800/770-3343, fax 474-3665, *www.riversedge.net*). Fairbanks' largest RV park adjacent to the *River's Edge Resort Cottages* (see overleaf). Full hookup sites go for $26, tent sites are $16. Open mid-May to mid-Sept. The Yellow MACS bus passes outside.

Tanana Valley Campground, 1800 College Rd at Aurora Drive (☎456-7956). Peaceful, spruce-shrouded campground that's best for tenters, and RVers who only want electrical hookups. Sites all come with tables and fire pits (wood sold), showers are free ($3 for nonresidents), and there's a laundry. Best of all, it is located midway between downtown and the university area on the MACS Red bus line (hourly or better) and they have free bikes for guests' use. Electrical hookups $15, dry RV sites $12, tent sites $8. Open mid-May to mid-Sept.

Out-of-town campgrounds

Chena River Lakes Recreation Area, Mile 346 Richardson Hwy. Wooded camping and RV sites with no hookups located in an attractive recreation area (see p.441) seventeen miles southeast of Fairbanks. $8.

Ester Gold Camp, Old Nenana Hwy, Ester (☎1-800/676-6925, fax 474-1780). Basic RV park without hookups but with a dump station, showers, and a free coffee-and-muffin breakfast. Located at Ester (see p.432), six miles northwest of town and open late May to early September. $15.

Northern Exposures RV Park and Campground, Fox (☎474-8088 or 1-800/428-8303): A handy and peaceful base for exploring Fox, the Steese and Elliott highways, located eleven miles north of Fairbanks. Full hookup costs $18, tent spaces go for $12, and there are small cabins for $35.

The City and environs

Downtown Fairbanks shouldn't take up much of your time. Besides the CVB and Public Lands visitor centers and a couple of small museums there isn't much to divert your attention, despite the efforts of civic boosters. The double-whammy of mall mania and the absence of oil cash, which kept downtown buoyant in the 1970s, has turned once vibrant blocks into a depressing collection of neglected truck showrooms and parking lots with weeds pushing through the cracks. The only people found walking the streets are tourists abandoned at their package-tour hotels and residents without the financial wherewithal to buy their own cars. At the slightest provocation, it seems that the remaining downtown businesses might pack up and move out to the strip malls of Airport Way or the slightly more bohemian enclave of College Road. That said, there is hope for the area, with some of the old miners' cottages having been co-opted by small businesses – hairdressers, accountants, and graphic-arts businesses – and a recent flurry of new civic construction.

The most concentrated area of genuine interest for visitors is on the city's northern flank along College Road towards the university. Outside of the school's first-class museum, sights tend to revolve around animals and nature; you can visit a waterfowl refuge, walk around the pleasant confines of the **Georgeson Botanical Gardens** or drive north to view the musk oxen and caribou at the **Large Animal Research Station**.

There's an appreciably more kitschy approach at the forty-acre **Alaskaland** complex, which showcases early Fairbanks buildings and the restored SS *Nenana* sternwheeler along with assorted kids' entertainments; it can be quite fun and most of it is free. In contrast, rides along the Chena River on the replica sternwheeler, **Riverboat Discovery**, represent mass tourism in its most packaged form, and are far from cheap.

The sights in Fairbanks might only keep you entertained for a day or so, but the city makes the best base for attractions in the immediate vicinity. No one with kids will be able to keep them from visiting Santa at **North Pole**, fifteen miles to the southeast; fans of the gold-rush poet, Robert Service, will want to spend an evening in **Ester**, six miles west; and the district's mining heritage can be experienced at one of three extensive sites in **Fox**, eleven miles to the north.

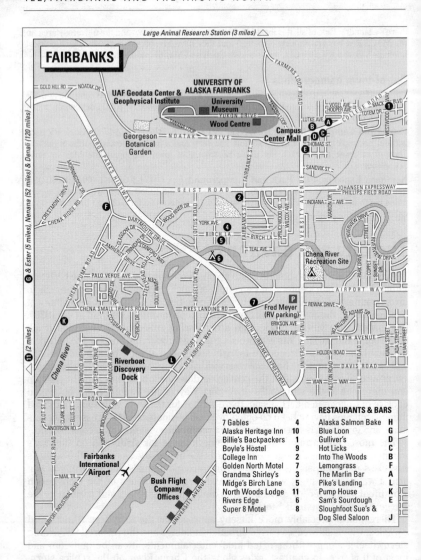

Large Animal Research Station (3 miles)

FAIRBANKS

GOLD HILL RD — NOATAK DR

UNIVERSITY OF
ALASKA FAIRBANKS

UAF Geodata Center &
Geophysical Institute

University
Museum

Wood Centre

YUKON DRIVE

FARMERS LOOP ROAD

TANANA LOOP DR

VOGEL AVE
HOOPER AVE

MACK
BLVD

COLLEGE ROAD

WESTWOOD WAY

TOTEM ST

LUTKE AVE — A

Georgeson
Botanical
Garden

NOATAK — DRIVE

TANANA LOOP DR

Campus
Center Mall

FAIRBANKS ST.

THOMAS ST.

B C

E

SANDVIK ST.

JOHANSEN EXPRESSWAY
PHILLIPS FIELD ROAD

GEIST ROAD

CRESTMONT DRIVE

CHENA RIDGE ROAD

GEORGE PARKS HIGHWAY

MOONWALKER DR

DARTMOUTH DRIVE

WOOD RIVER DR.

2

FAIRBANKS ST.

INDIANA AVE

MARTIN RD.

RIVERVIEW DRIVE

YORK AVE.

4

BIRCH LA.

5

LOFTUS ROAD

FAIRBANKS ST.

BIRCH LA.

APPLECROSS RD

WILLCOX AVE

TEAL AVE.

UNIVERSITY AVENUE

Chena River
Recreation Site

RIVERVIEW DRIVE

PARK DRIVE

COPPET DR.

SUNSET DR.

RIVERWOOD DR

GLASON DR.

CHENA PUMP ROAD

LAMHERST DRIVE

STANFORD WAY

TRINIDAD DR.

DRAKE RD.

ELDRIDGE AVE.

6

PALO VERDE AVE.

HOSELTON RD.

AIRPORT WAY

COSGRAVE DR.

PERCH RD.

CHENA SMALL TRACTS ROAD

PIKES LANDING RD.

REWAK DRIVE

WILSON ADAMS Dr.

P

Fred Meyer
(RV parking)

7

ERIKSON AVE
SWENSON AVE

SOUTH FAIRBANKS EXPRESSWAY

19TH AVENUE

NORDALE ROAD

KIANA STREET

ADA STREET

LILIAN STREET

K

Chena River

AIRPORT WAY

OLD AIRPORT WAY

HOLDEN ROAD

DAVIS ROAD

HILL RD.

ALSTON ROAD

VIAN — WAY

PILOT ST.

CLARK ST.

ELLIS ST.

DALE — ROAD

ANDERSON RD.

RAVENWOOD AVENUE

WESTERN AVENUE

BROADMOOR AVE.

L

Riverboat
Discovery
Dock

AIRPORT WAY

DALE ROAD

MAIL TR.

Fairbanks
International
Airport

AIRPORT INDUSTRIAL RD.

Bush Flight
Company
Offices

UNIVERSITY AVENUE

ACCOMMODATION		RESTAURANTS & BARS	
7 Gables	4	Alaska Salmon Bake	H
Alaska Heritage Inn	10	Blue Loon	G
Billie's Backpackers	1	Gulliver's	D
Boyle's Hostel	9	Hot Licks	C
College Inn	2	Into The Woods	B
Golden North Motel	7	Lemongrass	F
Grandma Shirley's	3	The Marlin Bar	A
Midge's Birch Lane	5	Pike's Landing	L
North Woods Lodge	11	Pump House	K
Rivers Edge	6	Sam's Sourdough	E
Super 8 Motel	8	Sloughfoot Sue's &	
		Dog Sled Saloon	J

G — & Ester (5 miles), Nenana (52 miles) & Denali (120 miles)

H (2 miles)

FARMERS LOOP ROAD

Downtown

Unless you've developed a deep interest in the machinations of Fairbanks' early civic leaders, skip the detailed self-guided downtown tour (free leaflet from the visitor center) and concentrate on a few key sights. The visitor center lies on the south bank of the languid Chena River where logs were once floated along for the construction of the town. It is now flanked by small patches of parkland, some long neglected, others overly tended. Foremost among the latter is **Golden Heart Plaza**, an open riverside area focusing on Malcolm Alexander's statue, *Unknown*

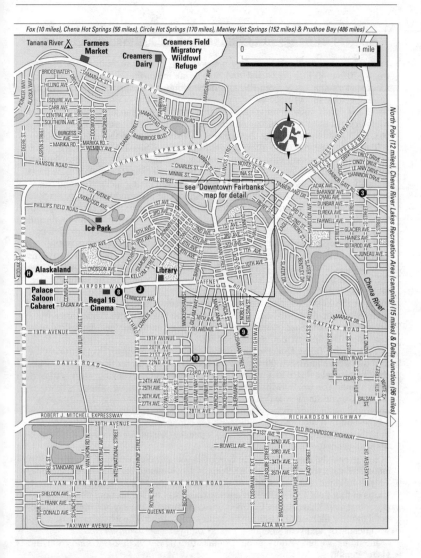

Map detail: Fox (10 miles), Chena Hot Springs (56 miles), Circle Hot Springs (170 miles), Manley Hot Springs (152 miles) & Prudhoe Bay (486 miles)

First Family, dedicated to the "indomitable spirit of the people of Alaska's Interior." Immediately west, a plaque marks the spot where Fairbanks' founder, ET Barnette, was left stranded with his supplies in 1901.

Cross the Chena River on the Cushman Street bridge to the prim **Church of the Immaculate Conception**, which wouldn't look out of place in New England, and contains an ornate pressed-tin ceiling and a beatific Madonna. The church was built south of the river in 1904 and moved to its current site during the winter of 1911. Back on the south bank, a walk west along 1st Avenue lets you view

WINTER IN FAIRBANKS – ICE ART AND THE YUKON QUEST

Fairbanks' winter temperatures stay below 0°F for months on end, metal-snapping freezes below -40°F are expected and -60°F is not unknown, so it is no surprise that most visitors stay away from the end of September (when the temperatures are already getting nippy) until the end of April, when the last of the snow melts away. Still a few hardy visitors do venture up this way, notably Japanese honeymooners who put great store in consummating their marriage under the **northern lights** (see box, p.426) and those making pilgrimages to Fairbanks' two major winter events.

The first of these is the **Yukon Quest** International Sled Dog Race (*www.yukonquest.com*), a thousand-mile classic between Fairbanks and Whitehorse, Yukon, over some of the wildest and most sparsely populated country anywhere. By most estimations it ranks second to the Iditarod in the sled-racing hierarchy (and is several hundred miles shorter), but many mushers cite its infrequent checkpoints to support their claim that it is the tougher of the two races. It is less a series of sprints between checkpoints than a grueling endurance test requiring heavier loads and more sleeping rough on the trail, rigorously testing the self-sufficiency, determination and dog-driving ability of the competitor. The race has been run in the second week of February (when river ice is at its thickest) since 1984 and alternates direction each year, starting in Fairbanks in odd-numbered years. It largely follows the route of the Steese Hwy from Fairbanks to Circle so, unlike the Iditarod, spectators can watch at various points. From Circle it then heads up the Yukon River through the Yukon-Charley National Preserve past Eagle to Dawson City where there is a compulsory 36-hour layover before the final run into Whitehorse. Most competitors use a team of fourteen dogs and take ten to fourteen days, hoping to take home the first prize of around $30,000.

Though the Yukon Quest is spectator-friendly, far more visitors come during the first two weeks in March for the **World Ice Art Championships** in the Ice Park on Phillips Field Road. It is virtually the Olympiad of ice carving, with sculptors from around the world (Morocco, Australia, and Brazil among others) striving to produce larger-than-life sculptures from blemish-free blocks of ice. The chunks are fashioned using saws, picks, chainsaws, chisels, sanders, angle grinders, even electric irons into sculptures up to 35 feet high. Along with prosaic natural subjects – polar bears, caribou, Natives ice-fishing – fantasy themes are popular, with images of medieval castles and jousting contests.

The event starts with the Single Block Classic, in which teams of two spend two and a half days shaping a single 8000-pound block measuring 5ft x 8ft by 3ft thick. This is followed (after a couple of days rest) by the Multi-Block Classic, where teams of four have five and a half days to transform twelve blocks (4ft x 4ft by 3ft) each weighing 3000 pounds. Competitors work through the day and night, with colorful lighting illuminating the works as they take shape. The whole process, along with details of next year's contest, can be found at *www.icealaska.com*.

Intending winter visitors should obtain the *Winter Activities Guide* from the visitor center.

---

some historic log cabins gone to seed – structures that would have been restored into residences or craft shops anywhere else in America.

It isn't often you see a stained-glass depiction of an Alaskan sled dog or an Iñupia on his way to church in the snow, but you can inside the 1947 **St Matthew's Episcopal Church**, 1029 1st Ave. It replaced the 1905 original built for Hudson Stuck, archdeacon of the Episcopal Church in Alaska from 1903 to

1920, noted primarily for his first ascent of Mount McKinley (see box, p.348). Another glass shows him leaving for the mountain complete with a huge cross around his neck which was later placed at the summit. A couple of blocks further on there's a classic example of a "**grow-house**," 1323 1st Ave, a basic log cabin that was extended out back with each new addition to the family, in this case five times.

There are also a couple of museums downtown, notably the enjoyable **Fairbanks Community Museum**, 450 Cushman St at 5th Avenue (June–Aug daily 10am–6pm; call for winter hours ☎452-7954; donation appreciated), that contains locally donated trapping, mining, and dog-sled-racing equipment along with a mock-up of a trapper's cabin, assorted prospecting implements, and a handmade Athapascan birch sled lined up next to its modern racing equivalent. Check out the nice little diorama of Barnette's Cache in the spring of 1902, the early photo of 1st Avenue with its waterfront bars and cafés, and movie posters of such forgotten classics as *Red Snow, Alaska Seas* and Abbott and Costello's *Lost in Alaska*. The museum also acts as the public face of the **Yukon Quest** dog-sled race (see box, opposite), selling related books, videos, and T-shirts.

A similar winter theme is pursued at the **Ice Museum**, 500 2nd Ave at Lacey Street (June to mid-Sept daily 10am–6pm; $8), a summertime chance to get a flavor of the annual Ice Art competition (see box, opposite). The impressive images screened in the half-hour slide show fall well short of the real thing, but you can see a few small sculptures by walking into two freezer rooms, one kept at the typical March daytime temperature of 20°F, the other maintained at the expected night time temperature of -15°F.

Along College Road and around the university

From the downtown area, College Road arcs out along the northern flank of the city (followed by Blue and Red MACS buses) and buildings become scarce after a mile or so to reveal the open fields of **Creamer's Field Migratory Waterfowl Refuge**, 1300 College Rd (unrestricted entry), on the site of Creamer's Dairy. It was established in 1903 with three cows brought from Nome by the brother-in-law of Charles Creamer, who operated it until 1965. Four years later, the state bought it and decided to continue the Dairy's rotation-planting program of oats, barley, and peas to further foster the attention of migratory wildfowl. The grasslands now provide a temporary resting place for several large species, including thousands of **sandhill cranes**, which leave their wintering grounds in Texas and New Mexico and pause here to recuperate in the spring, some sticking around through the summer, others flying on to Siberia. Many return in fall to fatten up for the return flight south. **Canada geese** make a slightly shorter passage from the Pacific Northwest – the first V-shaped skeins heralding the arrival of spring – and you might also expect to spot pintails, golden plovers and mallards. Visitors and locals park up beside College Road training binoculars and telephoto lenses at the fields, but you may as well head to the pleasant **trails** in the woods beside the original dairy buildings, which now house an instructive **visitor center** (June–Aug Tues–Fri 10am–5pm, Sat 10am–4pm; Sept Sat 10am–4pm). From there you can pick up one of two trails through the woods: the educational Boreal Forest Trail (2 miles) follows a packed-earth path and boardwalks through birch bog and out through grasslands regenerating after a fire; the seasonal Wetland Trail (1 mile) is best in early summer and leads to a bird observatory (mid-May to Aug daily). If you can time it right, try to join one of the two-hour **nature walks** led by volunteer naturalists (June–Aug Wed & Sat 9am, Tues & Thurs 7pm; free; for subject matter ☎459-7301).

Half a mile west is the site of the **Farmers Market** (May–Sept Wed 11am–6pm, Sat 9am–4pm, *www.tvfmarket.com*), a forum for local growers to sell their produce along with crafts, freshly baked sourdough bread, and more. As much as anything, it is a local meeting place, drawing a typically oddball cross-section of Alaskans: bush-dwellers, students, neo-hippies, and suburbanites.

A couple of miles further along College Road there is a small knot of restaurants, cafés, bars, and shops that constitutes the suburb of **College**, at the foot of the ridge from which the **University of Alaska Fairbanks** commands great views of the distant Alaska Range. This is the state's original campus and it still considers itself the most prestigious, though Anchorage now has a larger enrollment. The main reason to venture up here is to visit the University of Alaska Museum (see opposite), though during term time you might want to wander into the **Woods Center** and see what's happening around campus. You'll find a library (open to all), campus cafés and bars, and a handy rides board.

The **UAF Geophysical Institute**, Elvey Bldg, 903 Koyukuk Drive, presents a free educational program (June–Aug Thurs 2pm; ☎474-7558) with slide show, aurora video, and a visit to the Alaskan earthquake information center. Nearby, at the western end of the campus, a narrow track (see map, p.422) leads four

---

THE NORTHERN LIGHTS

"It is impossible to witness such a beautiful phenomenon without a sense of awe, and yet this sentiment is not inspired by its brilliancy but rather by its delicacy in light and colour, its transparency, and above all by its tremulous evanescence of form. There is no glittering splendour to dazzle the eye, as has been too often described; rather the appeal is to the imagination by the suggestion of something wholly spiritual..."

Robert Scott

Words never fully capture the dynamic majesty of the **aurora borealis**, but Scott comes close and, in *Arctic Dreams*, Barry Lopez perceptively writes of a "banner of pale light" appearing like "a ta'ai chi exercise: graceful, inward-turning, and protracted." Everyone has their own explanation: one Inuit legend suggests the lights represent spirits playing ball with a walrus skull; another asserts they are spirits carrying torches to guide nomads to the afterlife; and a third sees the souls of their ancestors in these undulating gossamer strands. Ever hopeful, early prospectors saw them either as reflections of the mother lode or vapors from rich deposits as yet unfound. Galileo was loath to offer an explanation, but named them Aurora, after the Roman goddess of the dawn.

As you gaze at these celestial pyrotechnics you feel no need or desire to explain them. It is enough just to marvel as silken curtains of light miraculously materialize, then just as soon curl up and disappear, or hang around for hours on end folding back on themselves, delicately changing hue from rose pink to pale green and on to white, fading with the early light of dawn. The curtain effect isn't illusory; the band of light may hang from an altitude of three hundred miles down to forty miles above the earth and stretch for hundreds of miles, and yet be only a hundred yards wide.

The University of Alaska Fairbanks is at the forefront of scientific research into the northern lights (and their southern hemisphere counterparts the aurora

hundred yards down through the fields to the **Georgeson Botanical Gardens**, West Tanana Drive (May–Sept daily 7am–8pm; $1; ☎474-1944). In spring and early summer, the gardens are filled with colorful flowers and lush leafy greens, and as the summer wears on, you'll see huge vegetables almost as large as those produced in the Mat-Su Valley. It is perfect for a sunny afternoon or evening, full of seats and shady bowers where you can breathe-in the fragrant air and gaze at the Alaska Range. There's a small visitor center (daily 10am–6pm), and free guided tours take place in summer (June–Aug Fri 2pm).

Unless you join one of the city tours, you'll need your own transport to get to the **Large Animal Research Station**, north of the university on Yankovich Road, off Farmers Loop Road. A roadside parking lot with viewing platforms gives you the chance to see herds of caribou and musk oxen; all part of the university's research program into their nutrition, physiology, and behavior. For a true sense of the ongoing work, hook up with one of the $5 guided tours (June–Aug Tues, Thurs & Sat 11am & 1.30pm; Sept Sat 1.30pm; ☎474-7207) that meet outside the main gate.

UNIVERSITY OF ALASKA MUSEUM

Most people agree that the **University of Alaska Museum**, 907 Yukon Drive (May & Sept daily 9am–5pm; June–Aug daily 9am–7pm; Oct–April Mon–Fri

---

australis). Both are caused by an interaction between the earth's magnetic field and the **solar wind**, an invisible stream of charged electrons and protons continually blown out into space by the innate violence of the sun. The earth deflects the solar wind like a rock in a stream, the magnetic field channeling the charged particles down towards the earth's magnetic poles. Here the protons and electrons release some of their energy as visible light – much like a neon sign – the common yellowish green produced by oxygen atoms, while the purples and rare deep reds are caused by nitrogen.

While their manifestations may seem gentle, the forces involved are immense, occasionally blocking out radio communications, and inducing magnetic fields in pipes, making them more susceptible to corrosion: even the oil pipeline is affected. The aurora's electrical charge can also cause power blackouts: on March 13, 1989; much of eastern Canada and northeastern USA was dark for six hours as a result of unusually powerful aurora activity.

The northern lights are a circumpolar phenomenon and it is only at times of extreme solar activity that they are seen at lower latitudes but in Fairbanks they are almost continual. In summer there is too much daylight to see them clearly, but as the nights grow longer your chances of a good showing increase. The **best viewing** is when the sky is clear and the air chilly, preferably at the vernal equinox around March 20. At this time the worst of the winter temperatures have passed and Fairbanks hotels do a roaring trade, some specializing in aurora packages aimed mostly at Japanese who have a particular passion for the lights, some believing that children conceived under the aurora will be successful in business.

For more information, consult the *Aurora Watcher's Handbook* by Neil Davis (University of Alaska Press) or UAF's aurora Web site (*www.pfrr.alaska.edu /~pfrr/aurora*), which has a weekly aurora forecast with map, and a stack of other material pertaining to the phenomenon.

9am–5pm, Sat & Sun noon–5pm; $5, combination package with the two shows $13.50; 24hr infoline ☎474-7505, *www.uaf.edu/museum*), is one of the finest in the state. Dramatic sculptures – including a couple of fine, modern totem poles – point the way to its eclectic displays, which are shoehorned into one large room, divided thematically. Stuffed examples of just about every Alaskan animal herald a section on extinct animals from dinosaur fossils and a huge-tusked mammoth skull to a reconstruction of **blue babe**, a steppe bison found in the permafrost in a local placer mine during the summer of 1979. It had died 36,000 years previously and, over time, the phosphorous in the tissue had reacted with the iron-rich soil to produce an all-over blueish tinge. Nevertheless, the bone, marrow, and skin were so well preserved that the cause of death – at the claws of the now extinct American lion – could be determined.

Sections are devoted to major geographic regions of the state, the Arctic partly represented by a replica of "the boulder patch," an undersea garden of soft corals and sponges found in the Beaufort sea which is frozen over for much of the year. The kelp manages to store photosynthesized energy in the summer then goes through its growing period while frozen over from November to April when the required nutrients are present. Elsewhere there's a two-ton lump of solid copper from the Wrangell Mountains; assorted ephemera of early Fairbanks life; engaging, if gruesome, footage of traditional whale and seal hunting alongside wooden snow goggles and a seal-gut parka with auklet feather detail; and the "Forced to Leave" video on the appalling conditions suffered by the Aleuts who were interned in the Alaskan Southeast during World War II: a powerful and moving indictment of US policy towards a section of its own people.

For those with a scientific bent, there is lengthy coverage of various strange aspects of permafrost (see box, p.459) along with a weighty discussion of the aurora and its provenance. If interested, check out **Dynamic Aurora** (June–Aug daily 10am & 3pm; $4), a slightly nerdy physics lecture that doesn't convey the poetry of the northern lights, but is enlivened by some excellent slides and the chance to wear prismatic glasses.

There is perhaps a broader appeal to the **Northern Inua Show** (June–Aug daily 11am & 2pm; $6.50 separately), a fast-paced 45-minute celebration of traditional Alaskan games. All major tribal groups are represented, though you are left without much of an impression of the distinction between the tribes. Many of the games are highly athletic, harking back to necessary honing of traditional hunting and survival skills: the stick pull is said to represent hauling hunted seals from the water and involves competitors sitting on the floor facing each other, the soles of their feet touching, with both holding onto a stick. The one who gets pulled up or lets go loses. These are included in the World Eskimo-Indian Olympics (see box, opposite), while others are simply for entertainment through the long winter nights, one for example is based on a competitor making faces while others have to refrain from laughing as long as possible.

Alaskaland and the riverboat Discovery

Somehow almost everyone winds up at half-baked **Alaskaland**, Airport Way at Peger Road (park grounds always open, shops open late May to early Sept daily 11am–9pm; free), a kind of low-key theme park reached using the Blue and Yellow MACS buses and the Horse-Drawn Tour (see p.416). The place seems unsure of what it wants to be, and can be dispiriting in the rain, though acquits itself well enough in fine weather, especially if you've got kids, who will undoubtedly enjoy the play areas, miniature golf, and toy train. Otherwise it is better to come in the late afternoon, take a quick tour of the buildings and stick around for the **Alaska Salmon Bake** (see p.436), and perhaps the nightly show at the *Palace Saloon* (see p.438).

Alaskaland was set up in 1967 as part of the state's centennial of the Alaska purchase and as a way to save some of Fairbanks's original log buildings. Some thirty historic structures have been preserved and lined up to form a pioneer street, though almost all the architectural and historical merit is camouflaged by the shelves of the trinket stores that now occupy the houses. It is still worth strolling along, pausing to duck into the period-furnished **Kitty Hensley House** (late May to early Sept daily 11am–9pm; free) and the **Wickersham House Museum** (late May to early Sept daily 11am–9pm; $1 donations appreciated), in the one-time residence of judge James Wickersham; the restored **Harding Car** that the President used when visiting Nenana in 1923 to drive the railroad's golden spike; and the **Pioneer Museum** (late May to early Sept daily 11am–9pm; free), with its material on early telegraph systems during the gold rush, a small collection of footwarmers used in open stages and sleighs, and a 1897 Rand McNally map showing trails to the Yukon and Klondike goldfields, including winter river routes. The adjacent forty-minute **Big Stampede Show** (6 times daily; $2) has the audience seated on a large turntable which revolves as fifteen scenes from the gold rush that have been painted on the walls are spotlighted in turn.

Though beached and in need of a lick of paint, the **SS Nenana** sternwheeler (late May to early Sept guided tours on demand daily 10am–8pm; $5, diorama only $2) lends the park a dramatic focus. It was launched in 1933, the last and one of the most luxurious of the great wooden-hulled sternwheeler steamers, coming

---

FAIRBANKS FESTIVALS

In early February the Yukon Quest sled-dog race (see box, p.424) is in town and the World Ice Art Championships take place over the first two weeks in March, immediately followed by the revelry of the Fairbanks Winter Carnival. Summer gets into full swing at the summer solstice (June 20 and 21) with the Midnight Sun Fun Run, a street fair, and the **Midnight Sun Baseball Game**, a longstanding tradition from the gold days (first played around 1905) in which Fairbanks' semi-pro team, the Goldpanners, play without artificial lights from dusk (around 10.30pm) until sunrise some two or three hours later. Around the middle of July the **World Eskimo-Indian Olympics** pits Native athletes against 25 grueling tests of skill, strength, and cunning such as the Ear Pull, in which a loop of string is passed around an ear of each contestant in a tug of war and the first to let the loop slip off or slacken loses; the Knuckle hop, a race in which competitors hop along on knuckles and toes; the one-foot high kick where the contestant hops, kicks a foot up to touch a seal-skin ball and lands on the same foot without falling over.

At much the same time (the week between the second and third weekends in July) the town comes alive for **Golden Days**, a festival with all manner of games, parades and events all ostensibly celebrating Felix Pedro's discovery of gold in the area. The last major event of the summer is the **Tanana Valley State Fair**, a traditional selection of rides, demonstrations and giant-produce competitions held on the State Fairgrounds on College Road during the second week of August. Up-to-date details of events can be found on the CVB's Web site *www.explorefairbanks.com*.

at the end of the era when the Interior waterways were the easiest (if not the only) way to get around in summer. But she was really a workhorse, carrying 300 tons of cargo and pushing up to six barges making the 770-mile run from Nenana to the mouth of the Yukon and back ten times in the five-month season. Until its conversion to oil in 1948, lumberjacks often worked with dog sleds through the winter to supply wood stockpiles. By 1955 air transport had rendered the steamers uneconomic and the *Nenana* languished until rescued in 1967 for Alaskaland. For a deeper insight into how the *Nenana* and her sisters influenced the development of the Interior, pop down to the cargo deck to the detailed 300-foot-long Tanana/Yukon Rivers Historical Diorama.

Unlike the *Nenana*, you and nine hundred others can actually ride on the **Riverboat Discovery**, Discovery Road, near the airport (mid-May to mid-Sept, 8.45am & 2pm and selected evenings at 6.30pm; $40; ☎479-6673), a replica sternwheeler that packs in the tour groups for its slick and not overly thrilling three-and-a-half-hour cruises. The Binkley family take pride in now having their fourth generation of riverboat captains at the helm for this narrated trip calling at a replica Athapascan fishing village, watching salmon being prepared for air-drying, being entertained by a bush pilot doing a short takeoff and landing beside the river, and having four times Iditarod winner Susan Butcher demonstrating dog sledding. If you can't be bothered getting out of your seat, you can watch it all on closed-circuit TV.

Fox

The only major route north of Fairbanks – and the access to most of the area's hot springs, canoe routes, and hiking trails – is the Steese Hwy. Following this a couple of miles north from downtown you reach the junction for **Birch Hill Recreation Area**, a cross-country skiing area in winter and the venue for summer Shakespeare plays (see p.437). Just beyond, the road to Chena Hot Springs diverts east. The Steese Hwy continues north to the **Hagelbarger Road viewpoint**, with views of the Alaska Range, and the **Trans-Alaska pipeline viewpoint**, Mile 8, where you can stand next to the pipeline, examine a section of the pipe and an old-style cleansing pig (see box, p.454) and glean information from the visitor center (late May to early Sept daily 8am–6pm).

FOX, eleven miles north of Fairbanks, appears to be an inconsequential road junction, with little of interest except for the *Northern Exposures RV Park*, the *Turtle Club* restaurant, and excellent *Howling Dog Saloon* (all listed in the appropriate sections). However, Fox has long been the center of the Fairbanks mining district – over the years the most lucrative of all of Alaska's gold fields – so far yielding some seven million ounces of the metal. All around, the stripped hillsides, mounds of tailings, and abandoned heavy machinery betray the decades spent unearthing gold, while the "Keep Out" signs underline the continued search. The new **Fort Knox** mine, some twenty miles north along the Elliott Hwy, continues the tradition and is now the largest mine in Alaska.

Felix Pedro first struck gold on what is now Pedro Creek, five miles northeast of Fox, setting in motion the establishment of Fairbanks and sparking the last of the major gold rushes. Loose flakes relatively easily teased from streambed gravels were soon gone and miners had to turn to increasingly more troublesome and labor intensive methods of extraction (see box, opposite). In some cases up to a hundred feet of frozen low-grade gravel had to be cleared away to reach ore-bearing layers. Several techniques were used, all requiring huge quantities of

GOLD FROM DIRT

The familiar image of the felt-hatted old-timer **panning** merrily beside a stream is only part of the story, but is a true enough depiction of the first few easy months after a gold strike. Initially all a miner needed was a pick and shovel, a pan, and preferably a special wooden box known as a "rocker" for washing the alluvial gravel. As the approach of winter gradually froze the landscape, the river levels dropped exposing fresh ground which had to be worked before the true onset of winter when gold extraction all but stopped.

When pickings got thinner, miners turned their attentions to the more tightly packed riverbanks. Hillside dams were constructed and water was piped under pressure to **sluicing** guns, or "giants," which blasted the auriferous gravel free, ready for processing either by traditional hand-panning or its mechanical equivalent, where "riffle plates" caught the fine gravel and carpet-like matting trapped the fine flakes of gold. Eventually the scale of these operations put individual miners out of business and many pressed on to fresh fields.

In **Fairbanks**, the efficacy of sluicing was limited by a thick layer of earth overlying the gold-rich permafrost gravel. The frozen silt-like "muck" had to be removed a few inches at a time by washing away the top layer and allowing the next few inches to thaw, a process known as **stripping**. It was only warm enough to work for five months of the year and it sometimes took three years to clear the overlay and expose the frozen gravel which then had to be **thawed**. This was achieved by drilling a grid of holes during the winter and pumping in cold water which gradually warmed the gravel as it percolated back to the surface, another highly time-consuming process finished off by steam-thawing the top layer which had refrozen over the winter. Obviously this could only be done by large companies, who subsequently brought in **gold dredges**, great clanking behemoths floating free in ponds of their own creation, but anchored to the banks. Buckets scooped out the newly thawed gravel, extracted the gold by passing it through five levels of separators and riffle plates, and spat the "tailings" out of the back. Gradually they moved forward opening the pond up in front, filling it in behind, and creating mile after mile of gravel mounds.

The flakes of "placer" gold found in rivers originally came from the "mother lode," gold-bearing quartz reefs deep underground. In Alaska this has mostly gone undetected or its extraction remains uneconomic, except for at the Independence Mine near Palmer. Here, **reef quartz mining** required a considerable investment in machinery and a whole town sprang up to tunnel, hack out the ore, and haul it to the stamper batteries. A series of steam-powered hammers would pulverize the rock which was then passed over copper plates smeared with mercury and onto gold-catching blankets before the remains were washed into the berdan – a special kind of cast-iron bowl. Gold was then separated from the mercury, a process subsequently made more efficient with the use of cyanide.

Reef mining has now ground to a halt, but rocker boxes and riffle plates are still used (though bulldozers have replaced shovels), and the hulking bucket dredges have been replaced by small-scale suction dredges which vacuum up the river and lake beds.

water which grubstake miners couldn't obtain. They were then supplanted by large mining companies which funded the construction of the **Davidson Ditch** which, from 1928 until 1959 brought water from the Chatanika River using 6 miles of pipe and 83 miles of ditch, parts of it still visible along the Steese Hwy.

Three local tours provide different perspectives on the eternal quest. The latest entry to the field is **Gold Rush Gold Camp**, Mile 8.5 Steese Hwy (mid-May to mid-Sept daily 8am–5pm; $18; ☎452-4653, *www.goldrushcamp.com*), a working mine that gives a diverting impression of the region's mining operations, without some of the more sanitized trappings of its competitors. Tours (every two hours 8am–4pm) visit the portal to a permafrost tunnel along with all manner of mining equipment and finish with the obligatory panning session.

Gold Dredge #8, Mile 9 Old Steese Hwy (mid-May to mid-Sept daily 9am–5pm; $17), is the only place in Alaska where you can safely walk around an authentic gold dredge, in this case a steel-hulled affair operated from 1928 to 1959, devouring cubic yard after cubic yard of gold-bearing gravel from Goldstream and Engineer creeks. Operations finally came to a halt after statehood when taxes increased and legal changes imposed by the federal government meant that workers could no longer be exploited to the same degree. The ensuing neglect also scuppered the dredge, which now rests on the bottom of its pond, but looks no less impressive. An hour-long tour around the dredge's workings – sieves, separation tables, and gold-collection riffles – comes sandwiched between a video on Alaska's dredging history and an opportunity to try your hand with a poke (small bag) of gold-bearing gravel ($4). Additional pokes are available, and you can stay all day panning poorer gravel from a nearby heap if you wish; just don't expect to make a fortune. The workers' mess has now been converted into a dining room, where a basic all-you-can-eat stew is served daily between 11am and 3pm ($8.50).

A more venerable method of obtaining gold from dirt is illustrated a couple of miles north at **El Dorado Gold Mine**, Mile 1.5 Elliott Hwy (mid-May to mid-Sept two-hour tours Tues–Fri & Sun 9.45am & 3pm, Mon & Sat 3pm; $28; ☎479-7613, *www.eldoradogoldmine.com*), reached by riding a replica of the Tanana Valley Railroad train that once ran through the main street of Fox. It now passes through a tunnel hewn from permafrost ground to reach the mining area where time-honored sluicing and separating techniques still used in small mines all over Alaska are demonstrated. It is all pretty light-hearted but quite informative, and there is, again, the opportunity to walk away with some gold at the end of the day. A free shuttle bus runs here from Fairbanks.

Ester

During the day there is no reason to drive the six miles west of Fairbanks to the former gold town of **ESTER**. All you'll find are a few houses scattered in the woods and the remains of large-scale mechanized mining equipment from the town's boom time from the late 1930s until the 1950s. In the evenings, tour buses arrive for shows centered around the **Ester Gold Camp**, Old Nenana Road (everything open late May to early Sept; ☎479-2500 or 1-800/676-6925, fax 474-1780, *www .alaskabest.com/ester*), a reconstruction of the original town that incorporates a couple of authentic early miners' cabins, but has had so many falsefronts and Western-style boardwalks added that everything you see is fake. The camp puts on "Service with a Smile" (nightly 9pm, additionally at 7pm on Wed–Sat in July; $14), a cheesy ninety-minute cabaret packed with gold-rush songs and poetry by Alaska's adoptive son, **Robert Service** (see box, p.177). The Bard of the North's best-known work is *The Shooting of Dan McGrew*, in which the action happens in the **Malemute Saloon**, a name revived for the rough-wood-and-sawdust bar where this nightly revue takes place. The saloon is actually quite modern, but incorporates part of the bar once installed in *Royal Alexandra Bar* in Dawson City on which Service reputedly jotted down some of his lines.

To make a night of it you could start off by dining at the *Bunkhouse Restaurant* which offers an all-you-can-eat **crab buffet** (daily 5–9pm; $26, $16 without crab) then amble over to the Aurorarama for the 45-minute "Crown of Light" **photo-symphony** (daily 6.45pm & 7.45pm; $8), LeRoy Zimmerman's medley of aurora and nature photos set to ponderous classical music; a poor substitute for the real thing.

If you feel liable to indulge in one too many Dan McGrew or Lady Lou cocktails then make use of the **complimentary bus** service (pickups from most major Fairbanks hotels in time for the Malemute shows; reservations required), or arrange to stay either in the on-site RV park (see, p.421), or the comfortable, if somewhat institutional, rooms at the *Gold Camp Hotel* ($70).

North Pole

For those who don't mind tourist-trap kitsch, **NORTH POLE**, just fifteen miles southeast of Fairbanks, is an essential stop. The town was incorporated and named in 1953 by local boosters who tried to entice toy manufacturers with the prospect of labeling their products "Made in the North Pole." The idea didn't quite work out as planned, but one trader moved here, opened up **Santa Claus House** – easily identified by the 22-foot Santa outside – and established the town as the self-appointed home of Santa Claus (summer 8am–7pm, winter 9am–5pm; ☎1-800/588-4078, 488-2200, *www.santaclaushouse.com*). If a child addresses a letter to "Santa Claus, North Pole," it ends up here, and the kids' letters pinned up on a wall inside the gift shop are the most charming thing about the place. Inquiries about the spirits of the elves, the health of the reindeer, and the temperature up at the North Pole are commonplace.

You can arrange for a North Pole franked letter from Santa to be sent in December for $5, and the smaller ones can sit on Santa's knee. To add to the entertainment value, they stuck to the theme when naming streets around here: to see Santa take the Santa Claus Lane exit from the Richardson Hwy into St Nicholas Avenue; or call for a free shuttle pickup at Fairbanks hotels and RV parks.

Outdoor activities

The pleasure of visiting Fairbanks is the unparalleled opportunity to get out into the wilderness; a number of activities are firmly associated with Fairbanks itself, but the proliferation of local bush-plane companies throws the **Arctic north** wide open to Fairbanks visitors. In general we have covered the remoter canoe and backpacking trips in the appropriate sections of the *GUIDE* – in particular see our accounts of the Gates of the Arctic National Park (p.460) and Arctic National Wildlife Refuge (ANWR) (p.463) – but to give a sense of the scope available, consult our "Exploring the North" box, overleaf.

Roaming along the banks of the Chena River or through Creamer's Field can be pleasant enough, but for more hearty **hiking** you'll need to get out of town, preferably along either the Chena Hot Springs Road for the Granite Tors Trail, Angel Rocks Trail, and Chena Dome Trail (for all see box, p.443), or, still further away, along the Steese Hwy for the Pinnell Mountain Trail (see box, p.446).

EXPLORING THE NORTH: TOUR AND BUSH-PLANE COMPANIES

We've discussed various trips throughout the text, but several companies operate a string of tours worth knowing about. We've listed the better ones below along with their most enticing trips.

Cape Smythe Air (☎852-8333 in Barrow; ☎442-3020 in Kotzebue; ☎443-2414 in Nome, *www.capesmythe.com*). Useful for Arctic adventurers with deep pockets keen to string a sequence of coastal town visits together. If you want to visit Prudhoe Bay, Barrow, and Kotzebue (and perhaps some smaller villages) you could travel to Prudhoe Bay by bus or Alaska Airlines then catch daily flights from there to Barrow ($219) or Point Lay ($172), to Point Hope ($166), and on to Kotzebue ($107), where you can pick up Alaska Airlines to travel on to Nome or Anchorage. It works out cheaper than separate trips based in Anchorage or Fairbanks.

Larry's Flying Service, 3822 University Ave, Fairbanks (☎474-9169, fax 474-8815, *www.larrysflying.com*). One of the major operators in the north serving tiny communities such as Anaktuvuk Pass, Fort Yukon, Galena, Ruby, Tanana, and Venetai. Their runs (daily at around 9am & 1pm; 3–5hr; $200–270) visit a selection of three or four of these towns setting down for around ten minutes at each and they also fly to Mount McKinley ($200).

Northern Alaska Tour Company, PO Box 82991, Fairbanks, AK 99708; ☎474-8600, fax 474-4767, *www.alaskasarctic.com*. Well-organized operation running a slew of flightseeing trips, some with remote landings, others using road transport for part of the journey. They do several trips to the Arctic Circle and Prudhoe Bay (covered in detail on p.452) as well as: Anaktuvuk Pass (8hr; $319), a round-trip flight into Anaktuvuk Pass with four hours in the village escorted by a Nunamiut Eskimo; Arctic Circle Air Adventure (4hr; $199), overflying the Arctic Circle and Gates of the Arctic National Park and spending a short time in Bettles; Barrow Adventure (8hr; $395), a round-trip flight to Barrow with a village tour; the Brooks Range Adventure ($319), with a late flight to Prospect Creek, drive to Wiseman where you stay in extremely rustic accommodation, then drive back to Fairbanks; and Prudhoe Bay Adventure (3 days; $619), driving the Dalton and taking a tour of the oil fields then flying back to Fairbanks. Extensions to take in Barrow, Nome, and Kotzebue are possible.

Trans Arctic Circle Treks (☎479-5451 or 1-800/479-8908, fax 479-8908, *www.alaskaone.com/transarctic*). This outfit runs several excursions north including a minivan tour to the Arctic Circle ($99; 12hr); an arduous two-day tour, called Arctic Blast ($899), which includes a one-day run up to Prudhoe, flight to Barrow, an overnight there, a tour to Point Barrow and flight back; and the three-day Prudhoe-and-back road trip with an oilfield tour and nights in Prudhoe and Coldfoot camping both nights in the Brooks Range ($579, with all meals and lodging). Barrow and bush-flight extensions are available.

Warbelow's Air Adventures, 3758 University Ave S, East Ramp, Fairbanks Airport (☎474-0518 or 1-800/478-0812, fax 479-5054, *www.akpub.com/fhwag /warbe.html*). Run bush-mail flights to Fort Yukon ($185), take the second one of the day (times vary), which also calls at Chalkyitsik at no extra cost. A Fort Yukon visit with escorted village tour goes for $218.

Canoeing offers a more leisurely pursuit in these parts. One of the most placid waterways is the Chena River, right in the heart of Fairbanks, where you can put-in at pretty much any of the city bridges and head off, upstream or down, for a few hours. A couple of companies (see Bicycle and canoe rental in "Listings," p.438) **rent gear** and will arrange transport if you'd rather try something more ambitious. The chief contenders here are the Chena River (see box, p.441), the Chatanika, and Birch Creek canoe routes (consult APLIC), and the Tanana River from the west end of Fairbanks to Nenana, a sixty-mile trip covered in one long stint or two more relaxed days with a night camped on the riverbank. If you'd rather be guided downstream, consider a day gently **paddle-rafting** the Chena River with Canoe Alaska ($99; ☎479-5183, fax 479-5383, *www.mosquitonet .com/canoeak*).

If all the talk of gold around Fairbanks has fired your imagination, you can try your hand at **gold panning** on the local streams with equipment and advice from Alaskan Prospectors and Geologists Supply (see "Listings," p.439). Other possibilities include learning something of **dog mushing** at Alaskan Tails of the Trails with Mary Shields ($25; ☎ & fax 457-1117, *www.maryshields.com*), and champagne **balloon flights** with Advanced Balloon Adventures (1hr in the air; $180; ☎455-7433, *advanced@alaska.net*).

Flightseeing

No matter how tight your budget, you really shouldn't miss out on a little **flightseeing**. If you feel you need to justify the expense, then visit one of the remote communities such as Bettles or Arctic Village, or take a whirlwind tour of a few of them on one of the **mail flights** ($160–190; see Larry's, and Warbelow's in the box, opposite) that makes a circuit of three or four settlements dropping off essential supplies and picking up the post. Another favorite approach is to take one of the **Arctic Circle overflights** (around $180; see Northern Alaska), usually tracing the silver thread of the pipeline and issuing a certificate to verify the fact you entered Arctic airspace. One of the best of these is Northern Alaska's "Arctic Circle Air Adventure" (4hr; $179), combining a crossing of the Arctic Circle, a weaving flight through the peaks of the Brooks Range, and half an hour in Bettles.

Almost all the flight companies are based next to each other on University Avenue S, on the southeast side of the main runway.

Eating

Fairbanks is one of the few places in northern Alaska where you can escape from the culinary tyranny of salmon, halibut, and burgers. As long as your tastes aren't too exotic and you are prepared to drive around you should be able to find pretty much anything you want here, and for no apparent reason, Thai seems to have become a Fairbanks specialty: there's even *Bahn Thai*, a Thai takeaway wagon on 2nd Avenue. Broadly, the cheaper places congregate around the western end of College Road towards the university, and the pricier places are further out, with the gaps being plugged by mid-range places and all the franchise joints you could ask for – especially along Airport Way. If you are thinking of bringing a jacket and tie, forget it. As long as your hiking boots are clean you'll not be turned away.

You'll find **grocery stores** in just about all the major malls: the closest to downtown is the 24-hour Carr's supermarket at 526 Gaffney Rd. For the freshest vegetables head to the Farmers Market (see p.426).

Downtown

Co-op Diner & Thai Taste, Co-op Plaza, 535 2nd Ave (☎451-9128). The best bet for all-day diner food downtown with the addition of three daily Thai specials.

The Diner, 244 Illinois St (☎451-0613). Reliable restaurant serving simple diner fare cooked to perfection and at the right price. A full breakfast ($6–9) will set you up for the day, and even the single giant pancake ($2) is enough for most appetites.

El Sombrero, 1420 Cushman (☎456-5269). A Mexican spot that wouldn't pass muster in Guadalajara, but it's cheap and cheerful.

Gambardella's, 706 2nd Ave (☎457-4992). Fairbanks' best Italian restaurant, and as one of the city's finest restaurants is surprisingly well priced. Weather permitting, diners spill out onto the terrace for notable lasagna, eggplant parmesan, and gourmet pizza, all helped down with good Italian and American wines. They also have an extensive takeout menu. Closed for Sun lunch.

Soapy Smith's, 543 2nd Ave (☎451-8380). Photos of the Klondike and an ancient kayak strung from the ceiling hardly make a convincing theme but the food is pretty decent: barbecue ribs come in under $8 and they do a delicious California burger with shrimp, avocado, and Swiss cheese ($8), also available in vegetarian form. Outside seating in summer.

Souvlaki, 310 1st Ave (☎452-5393). Bargain Greek and American dishes served in spartan surroundings. Stuffed grape leaves are only 50¢ each, Greek salad and *spanakopita* are both under $4 and crab quiche and souvlaki barely break $6. Closed Sun.

Thai House, 526 5th Ave (☎452-6123). A small but popular eatery serving the usual range of Thai dishes, all beautifully prepared and at modest prices around the $9 mark. The green and red curries with zucchini, peas, and peppers are especially good. Closed Sun.

Near the university

Gulliver's Books Café, 3525 College Rd (☎474-9574). Pleasant café, tucked above a cozy bookstore, serving chicken tarragon wraps, pesto turkey melts, bagels, biscotti, and coffee all at reasonable prices, plus free Internet access to boot. A rear deck catches the summer sun nicely.

Hot Licks, 3453 College Rd, near University (☎479-7813). A roadside shack with some outdoor seating selling milkshakes, espresso, and excellent ice cream made from local cream and natural flavors. Open May–Aug.

Sam's Sourdough, 3702 Cameron St at University Ave (☎479-0532). About the best greasy spoon in town with the usual diner menu as well as reindeer sausage and eggs ($8) and Sharon's Sourdough Omelet ($7.25) – complete with ham, mushrooms, onions, olives, and sour cream.

Suburban Fairbanks

Alaska Salmon Bake, at Alaskaland on Airport Way (☎452-7274 or 1-800/354-7274). Really hungry? Here's a stuff-in-as-much-salmon-ribs-and-halibut-as-you-can-for-$22 affair set on the flanks of Alaskaland out among relic mining machinery (and mosquitoes in high summer). It is open for dinner (mid-May to mid-Sept daily 5–9pm), and there are free shuttle buses from the bigger hotels.

Lemongrass, Chena Pump Plaza, cnr Parks Hwy and Chena Pump Rd (☎456-2200). Yet another low-cost quality Thai restaurant that challenges *Thai House*. Sparsely furnished with Thai musical instruments around the walls, and nicely prepared dishes for $7–10.

Pike's Landing, Mile 4.5 Airport Way (☎479-6500). A popular riverside complex with sports bar, Alaska's largest deck beside the Chena River, and some of Fairbanks' finest dining with the likes of jumbo black-tiger prawns ($24), crab-stuffed filet Bearnaise ($29), or chicken seared in Madeira ($20). Sunday brunch ($17) is a standout as well with a huge well-prepared spread and as many glasses of champagne as you could reasonably expect to drink at brunch.

The Pump House, Mile 1.3 Chena Pump Rd (☎479-8452). A local favorite and rightly so, this historic pumphouse by the Chena River comes stuffed with gold-mining paraphernalia and serves great food. The deck is the place to watch river life go by while tucking into burgers and halibut nuggets (both around $8), mostly charged at half price during happy hours (Sept–May 4–6pm & 10–11pm). The dining room is more formal, serving hearty portions of reindeer stew ($17), crab cakes ($19), or grilled salmon ($20); you may not have space for one of the wonderful desserts.

Sloughfoot Sue's, inside the *Captain Bartlett Inn*, 1411 Airport Way (☎452-1888). A good and reasonably priced spot for a breakfast of, say, eggs Benedict ($7) or a lunch of burgers and wraps, inside or out on the sunny deck.

Out of town restaurants

Turtle Club, Mile 10 Old Steese Hwy, Fox (reservations are recommended every night ☎457-3883). The *Turtle Club*'s reputation for the quality and quantity of its prime rib – $20 for the 16oz Turtle Cut, $27 for the 24oz Miners Cut – extends throughout the north, but they also do delicious jumbo prawns weighing in at five to the pound. Evenings only.

Two Rivers Lodge, Mile 16, Chena Hot Springs Rd (☎488-6815). Although it is a bit out of town, this lakeside lodge, with its stunning glassed-in dining area, promises to reward you for your trouble. Appetizers of Alaskan oysters Romano ($9) or spicy Louisiana alligator tail ($11) followed by Mediterranean linguini and shrimp ($17), halibut casserole au gratin ($23), some of the best steamed clams around, and a fabulous $28 bouillabaisse. There's also an extensive, mostly Californian, wine list. Open evenings, and for weekend lunches only.

Drinking and entertainment

You'll be disappointed if you arrive in Fairbanks expecting high fashion and up-to-the-minute music, but the city can provide a rollicking good time. Many visitors find themselves at one of the nightly cabaret revues at some stage but there is usually a band or two thrashing away in the corner of a dark room. Perhaps more than any other large town this is a place where Alaska's famed predominance of men is most apparent, and you'll never be short of a drinking partner in any of the numerous traditional Alaskan bars.

Check the Fairbanks *Daily News-Miner* for listings (especially on Thurs) and pick up the free biweekly *New Lemming*, a listings paper and forum for local writers, with controversial viewpoints its strong suit. Look out too for Fairbanks Shakespeare Theatre plays (*www.fairbanks-shakespeare.com*) held in the Birch Hill Recreation Area at 8pm from Thursday to Sunday on the last three weekends of July (tickets $18; CarrsTix ☎1-800/478-7328).

In Fairbanks

Dog Sled Saloon, inside the *Captain Bartlett Inn*, 1411 Airport Way. Straightforward peanut-shells-on-the-floor bar with a log-cabin interior and sports on big screens.

Into the Woods, 3560 College Road (☎479-7701). A combined bookshop and relaxed coffeehouse fashioned from an original pioneer cabin that hosts regular bluegrass performances, Celtic jams, and poetry evenings. It has also become a gathering place for left-leaning common-interest groups – environmental, human rights, and so on – reflected in the lively noticeboard.

The Marlin, 3412 College Rd (☎479-4646). Poky, wood-paneled cellar bar that supports the cutting edge of Fairbanks' music scene with live bands – blues, jazz, and rock – playing most evenings from around 9pm; small cover charge, if any.

The Palace Saloon, at Alaskaland on Airport Way (reservations ☎456-5960). Mock-up of a gold rush-era music hall that plays host to the entertaining, if slightly cheesy, cabaret-style Golden Heart Review (mid-May to mid-Sept nightly 8.15pm; $14). The show pokes fun at historic Alaskan life (specifically Fairbanks) through songs and stories including a dog-mushing interpretation of the old Abbott and Costello "Who's on first" routine. Though currently on hold, the Review has traditionally been followed by the considerably more risqué and topical Bush Show (typically mid-May to mid-Sept Fri & Sat 10pm); call to see if it has been revived.

Senator's Saloon at *The Pump House*, Mile 1.3 Chena Pump Rd (see p.437). The preferred watering hole for Fairbanks' smarter young set shooting pool or more likely hanging out on the deck with a cocktail or two.

Near Fairbanks

Blue Loon, Mile 353.5 Parks Hwy (☎457-5666, *www.theblueloon.com*). A cavernous late-closing hot spot five miles west of Fairbanks. Hosts local and touring bands (or maybe a DJ) several nights a week; $5 cover unless a top name is in town. They also screen cult and mainstream movies that don't make it to the local multiplex (typically Mon–Thurs 8pm, Fri & Sat 7pm, Sun 4pm; $5). Sporadically there is a weekend shuttle bus from outside *The Marlin* (see opposite): call to inquire. Closed Mon.

Fox Roadhouse, Mile 11 Old Steese Hwy (☎457-7461). The northernmost microbrewery in the US, built around the original *Fox Roadhouse*, and producer of Silver Gulch beer. There's also a restaurant serving sandwiches and burgers, some made with beer bread from the *Roadhouse*'s own brew.

Howling Dog Saloon, Mile 11 Old Steese Hwy, Fox (☎457-8780). The wildest watering hole in the district and a local legend promoted as the farthest north Rock & Roll bar in the World. The bands perform (every Fri & Sat, plus Wed & Thurs in midsummer; usually no cover) on what is fondly referred to as the "Pope and the Dope" carpet, the red pile on which John Paul II met Ronald Reagan in 1984 when they both happened to be making pit-stops on the tarmac in Fairbanks – the only time that an American President and the pope have met on American soil. If you're hungry they'll dish up fine pizzas, but most come to drink in a bar where knickers and bras hang from the moose rack. Open May–Oct.

Malemute Saloon, Ester Gold Camp, Old Nenana Rd, Ester. Nightly cabaret entertainment (see p.432) six miles west of Fairbanks, not far from the *Blue Loon*.

Refinery Lounge, Old Richardson Hwy, North Pole (☎488-0335). Typical dark bar with a large military clientele but very friendly and with an entertaining weekend band (Thurs–Sat) playing Top 40 tunes and "No Country." No cover.

Listings

Airlines Alaska (☎1-800/252-7522); Delta (☎1-800/221-1212); Northwest (☎1-800/225-2525); United (☎1-800/241-6522). See box on p.434 for a roundup of bush-plane services.

Banks and exchange Banks are located all over town (many of them drive-thru), all with ATMs which also crop up in supermarkets and convenience stores. Downtown there's a Key Bank branch at 100 Cushman. There is currently nowhere to exchange foreign bills in Fairbanks.

Bicycle and canoe rental If you are not staying at one of the hostels which have bikes to use or for rent, try 7 Bridges Boats and Bikes at the *7 Gables B&B*, 4312 Birch Lane (☎479-0751) who rent basic ten-speeds for $15 a day and mountain bikes for $20 as well as tandems ($25), two-person canoes for $30 a day ($100 a week). Beaver Sports, 3480 College Rd (Mon–Fri 10am–8pm, Sat 9am–7pm, Sun 1–5pm; ☎479-2494, fax 474-8012) rent higher-spec mountain bikes for $20 a day, Old Towne canoes at $24 a day ($85 a week), in-line skates ($13), and flat water kayaks ($8). Both places rent the necessary straps to carry the boats and 7 Bridges will transport canoes upriver for around $1.50 a mile.

Bookshop Gulliver's Books, 3525 College Rd (☎474-9574, *www.gullivers-books.com*) offer the city's best selection of new and used books. They're also at Shopper's Forum Mall, Airport Way (☎456-3657).

Camping equipment Beaver Sports, 3480 College Rd (☎479-2494), carries the best selection of camping and general outdoor gear along with various guidebooks and maps, and rent bikes and canoes.

Car rental International agencies all have desks at the airport; smaller local agencies frequently offer more competitive rates in return for slightly older vehicles and a poorer backup network. To get unlimited mileage and a courtesy pickup from your hotel expect to pay from $40 to $50 a day in July and Aug; phone around. Agencies include: Affordable, 249 Alta Way (☎452-7341 or 1-800/471-3101); Airport, 418 3rd Ave (☎456-2023, fax 452-1185, *www.alaskan.com/airportcarrental*); Arctic, at the airport (☎479-8044, fax 479-0190, *arctic@polarnet.com*); Aurora, cnr Danby Rd and Johansen Expressway (☎459-7033 or 1-800/849-7033, fax 459-7043); Avis, at the airport (☎474-0900, fax 474-2013); Budget, at the airport (☎1-800/474-0855 or 474-0855, fax 474-8383, *budget@ptialaska.net*); Dollar, at the airport (☎479-7368, fax 451-6435); National, 1246 Noble St (☎1-800/227-7368 or 451-7368); Rent-A-Wreck, 2105 S Cushman (☎452-1606, fax 452-1662); Payless, at the airport (☎474-0177, fax 479-0190, *www.paylessalaska.com*).

Cinema The multiscreen Regal 16, 1855 Airport Way (☎456-5113, *www.regalcinemas .com*), screens mainstream releases offering half-price tickets on shows starting before 6pm and all day Mon; the *Blue Loon* in Ester (see opposite) shows more alternative and cult movies.

Emergencies Police, Fire and Ambulance (☎911); Crisis Line (☎452-4357).

Gold prospecting Alaskan Prospectors, 504 College Rd at Blanch Ave (☎452-7398) cater to just about all gold-digging needs and have put together a starter kit ($20) that includes a pan, magnet, collection vial, a sample bag of gold-bearing gravel, and a textbook.

Hitchhiking As with any city it pays to get beyond the city limits before trying to thumb a ride: for the Richardson Hwy the Green bus will take you to North Pole, and the Blue bus works best for the Parks Hwy. A sensible alternative is to try to get a lift by consulting the rides board inside the Wood Center at the university.

Internet access Fast machines are available free at the Tanana Valley Campus, 2nd Floor, 510 2nd St (hours vary depending on classes, typically Mon–Fri 8.30am–8pm; ☎474-7400). There are also sluggardly machines available for the price of a coffee at *Café Latté*, 519 6th Ave (Mon–Fri 6.30am–6pm; ☎455-4898); *Gulliver's Books* (see p.436) offers 30min free use with a café purchase; the Noel Wien Library (see below) has free machines; and Kinko's stores (such as at 418 3rd St in Eagle Plaza Mall; ☎456-7348) have fast machines and all facilities (including down- and uploading to disk) at $10 an hour, charged by the minute.

Laundry and showers B&L, Eagle Plaza, 3rd St and Steese Hwy (daily 8am–11pm; ☎452-1355), and B&C, Campus Center Mall, University Ave (daily 8am–9.30pm; ☎479-2696) both have competitively priced washing machines and showers for $3; showers at Hamme Swimming Pool, 901 Airport Way (Mon–Fri 6am–9pm, Sat 9am–5pm; ☎459-1085) are a fraction cheaper.

Library The Noel Wien Library, cnr Cowles St and Airport Way (☎459-1020). The MACS Blue bus passes close by.

Long-distance buses All the following services operate roughly mid-May to mid-Sept, but call to check at the ends of the season which may run longer or be cut short. Alaska Backpacker Shuttle (☎1-800/266-8625) runs daily to Denali and Anchorage picking up at the visitor center; Alaska Direct (☎1-800/770-6652) runs to Delta Junction, Tok, and Whitehorse; Alaskon Express (☎451-6835) runs to Tok, Whitehorse, and Skagway picking up from the *Westmark Fairbanks* and *Westmark Inn* hotels; and Parks Highway Express (☎1-888/600-6001) makes one run to Denali and Anchorage, another to Valdez via Delta Junction, and a third to Tok, Chicken, and Dawson City, all picking up at the visitor center and *Billie's Backpackers*.

Maps The Alaska Public Lands Information Center (see p.415) handle most needs, and UAF Geodata Center and map office, Room 204, International Arctic Research Center, N Koyukuk

Drive on the university campus (Mon–Fri 8am–5pm; ☎474-6960, fax 474-2645, *maps @geewiz.gi.alaska.edu*) sells topographic maps ($4) for the whole state at 1:250,000 and 1:63,360 scales.

Medical assistance Fairbanks Memorial Hospital, 1650 Cowles St (☎458-5303).

Money transfer Western Union, 2105 S Cushman (☎452-1606, fax 452-1662).

Pharmacy inside Fred Myers supermarket, 3755 Airport Way (☎474-1433).

Photographic supplies Fairbanks Fast Foto, Shoppers Forum Mall, 1255 Airport Way (Mon–Fri 9am–8pm, Sat 9am–7pm, Sun 11am–6pm; ☎456-8896), is a good camera shop selling all the usual stuff as well as slide and pro film.

Post office, 315 Barnett St (Mon–Fri 9am–6pm). For **General Delivery** use the 99707 ZIP code.

Road conditions Interior roads ☎456-7623; State Highways ☎1-800/478-7675.

Taxes A hotel tax of eight percent is charged, and has already been incorporated into our price codes.

Taxis Alaska Cab (☎456-3355); Diamond (☎455-7777); Eagle Cab (☎455-5555); Fairbanks (☎452-3535).

Travel agency US Travel, 1211 Cushman St (☎456-7888), is open Mon–Fri 8am–6pm, Sat 10am–4pm.

AROUND FAIRBANKS

Fairbanks' importance stems less from the appeal of the city itself than from its location at the hub of the only four significant roads to penetrate the Alaskan north, three of which end at **hot springs**. One is smooth blacktop all the way; the rest are dirt roads twisting and bucking their way through the white- and black-spruce forests that cloak the surrounding rolling hills. Since public transportation is not an option, you'll need a car to get around, or be prepared for some slow hitching.

Beyond the immediate environs of Fairbanks there is very little sign of human activity. Small communities occasionally throw up a roadhouse, and river beds have obviously been turned over by gold dredges, but after a very short time both seem like blots on the pristine landscape. Predominantly, this is country to go **hiking, canoeing**, fishing, and, in winter, cross-country skiing and snow machining; all followed by a well-earned soak in a hot tub.

Easily the most accessible of these arterial spokes, and the only one you can explore in depth with the blessing of rental-car agencies (see our comments under "City transport and tours" on p.415), is **Chena Hot Springs Road**, which follows the Chena River – a gentle canoe and raft route – past trailheads for three excellent hikes, to the most developed of the region's hot springs.

The **Steese Hwy** is longer and feels appreciably more remote as it threads its way northeast to the Yukon River and to **Circle Hot Springs**, a reward for the arduous but immensely satisfying two-day Pinnell Mountain Trail. The only westbound road is the **Elliott Hwy** across 160 miles of ridgetop forest to the charming community of **Manley Hot Springs**, with its ancient roadhouse and primitive tanks filled by a naturally heated stream. The first few miles of the Elliott provide access to the start of the last of the north's four roads, the Dalton Hwy, which runs five hundred miles to Prudhoe Bay on the Arctic Ocean.

There are no visitor centers of any consequence out here, so find out all you need in Fairbanks at the **Alaska Public Lands Information Center**, which publishes a handy free leaflet detailing the points of interest along the Steese and

Elliott highways. Fairbanks is also the place to stock up on any supplies you might need, rent your outdoor gear and fill up with gas.

Chena Hot Springs and around

Of the spas around Fairbanks, **Chena Hot Springs**, sixty miles to the northeast, is the easiest to reach and the most developed. It is also the largest and is getting larger thanks to a major expansion program due to be completed in 2003. Weary miners and Fairbanksans have been coming out this way to ease their bones since 1905, when the Swan brothers discovered the rumored springs after a month-long slog up the Chena River. Travel wasn't much easier for early devotees who regularly took two weeks to get there, but the situation improved and by 1912 the route was even passable by bicycles, and is now tarmack. It is easy enough to zip there in an hour or so, but the **Chena River State Recreation Area**, with some attractive campgrounds, three excellent hikes (see box, p.443), and a gentle canoe trip (see box, below) make this an appealing area to spend a few days. And, of course, you can soak away your aches at the springs.

PADDLING THE CHENA RIVER

The clear and very cold waters of the **Chena River** flow west through gently rolling wooded country, eventually joining the Tanana River near Fairbanks. The narrower and more overhung upper sections are Class II (see Basics, p.58 for a description of whitewater classes) and require some skill, but below the *Rosehip* campground access point it is a gentle float trip for canoes, kayaks, and rafts ranging from a couple of hours up to several days. The rapids may not be too challenging, but trees frequently fall into the river creating dangerous "sweepers" and log-jams that you need to be aware of: ask locally. You'll also need to scout ahead when the river braids confusingly, but it is mostly pretty easy going and wonderfully relaxing; fishing and looking for moose, brown bears, beavers, and river otters while lazing in the sun. With frequent access points you can do as much or as little as you want, even staying on the river to **camp**, either in established campgrounds or on river bars where the breeze keeps bugs at bay (though keep an eye on water levels if it has been raining).

Unless you've got your own gear you'll want to **rent a canoe** in Fairbanks (see "Bicycle and canoe rental" on p.438) and either avail yourself of the agency's delivery service or (perhaps more cheaply) rent a car and be prepared to hitch back to your vehicle.

If you have some experience with Class II rivers and water levels are adequate (usually early to midsummer), use the highest access point at the **Angel Rocks Trailhead**, Mile 48.9, and be prepared to line your canoe around log jams and obstacles. Over the next 22 miles down to **Rosehip campground**, Mile 27 (8–13hr in all), there are five access points spaced thirty minutes to three hours apart. In general the river gets progressively easier as you go, but if you're in any doubt, put in at *Rosehip* for the easy float to Grange Hall Road, Mile 20.8 (2–4hr). It is even possible to paddle into Fairbanks (8 hours beyond Nordale Rd).

For more **information**, visit APLIC in Fairbanks, discuss your plans with the staff, and pick up the free leaflets put out by Alaska State Parks and the US Army Corps of Engineers, both detailing access points, levels of difficulty, and expected float times.

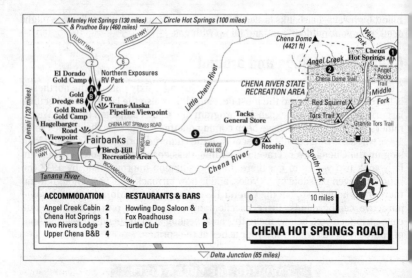

ACCOMMODATION
Angel Creek Cabin 2
Chena Hot Springs 1
Two Rivers Lodge 3
Upper Chena B&B 4

RESTAURANTS & BARS
Howling Dog Saloon &
Fox Roadhouse A
Turtle Club B

CHENA HOT SPRINGS ROAD

There are no regular buses to Chena Hot Springs, but the resort runs a **shuttle** for guests ($60 round-trip for one, $30 each for two or more), and hitching is feasible.

Along Chena Hot Springs Road

At Mile 23, **Tack's General Store** (daily 8am–8pm) constitutes one of the best pieces of Alaskana in these parts, a café, post office, and general store that also harbors a toy shop, hardware outlet, haberdashery, and video library. They also dish up overflowing plates of nachos and two dozen varieties of pie, notably the rhubarb and custard pie and some of the best blueberry pie around.

You enter the Chena River State Recreation Area at Mile 26 and soon find yourself repeatedly crossing bridges, the main access points for **paddling the Chena River**. Along here, hikers should keep their eyes open for trailheads for the **walks** listed in the box, opposite.

There is very little **accommodation** along the road, but the *Upper Chena B&B*, Mile 25.9 (☎488-6815, fax 488-9761; ⑨), is worth seeking out, a mile and a half off the road in a gorgeous spot right by the Chena River. It is made up of one spacious two-room cabin equipped with two double beds, a fully equipped kitchen, wood stove, TV, and a full bathroom and sauna (except in winter when there is no running water). There is also a road-accessible cabin, *North Fork*, Mile 47.7 (☎451-2695; ①). Otherwise you can **camp** either at the excellent *Rosehip* campground, Mile 27 ($10; pump water), the slightly less inviting *Tors Trail* campground, Mile 39.5 ($10; pump water), or the lakeside *Red Squirrel* campground, Mile 42.8 ($5; pump water); all spacious and equipped with picnic tables and fire rings.

Chena Hot Springs

If you've experienced the more rustic hot springs elsewhere in Alaska, then *The Resort at Chena Hot Springs*, Mile 56.5 (☎1-800/478-4681 or 452-7867, fax 356-3122, *www.chenahotsprings.com*; rooms ⑥, cabins ⑤), may come as something of a surprise. A major redevelopment in recent years has left the gently chlorinated pools (most of them indoors) all but surrounded by blocks of hotel rooms, an 18-hole golf course, and floodlit skiing. This is the getaway of choice from Fairbanks, since it's only an hour's drive, and a popular destination with visitors, fine for a sybaritic day or so in the solarium, a massage ($25 per half-hour), horseback riding ($60/hr), and of course a dip in the pool. In winter, dog-sled mushing, rides on a snow machine, and cross-country skiing take over, but the main draw is viewing the aurora borealis.

HIKES IN THE CHENA RIVER STATE RECREATION AREA

Chena River State Recreation Area flanks thirty miles of Chena Hot Springs Road encompassing the bald, spruce-flanked mountains on either side. Periodically you'll see **granite tors**, gnarled rock pinnacles poking up from the ridges providing the focus for a couple of lovely hikes. These were formed millions of years ago when molten rock forced its way through fissures, cooling into hard rock which has weathered better than the softer material that surrounded it.

APLIC in Fairbanks stocks free Alaska State Parks **information leaflets** on all these trails which are restricted to foot traffic except for Chena Dome Trail on which **mountain biking** is permitted (though it is very challenging). Hikes are listed in order of their distance from Fairbanks.

Granite Tors Trail (15-mile loop; 5–8hr, 2700ft ascent). An excellent hike of moderate difficulty starting along boardwalks over muskeg then climbing through thick woods and out onto alpine tundra past ancient granite outcrops rising up to sixty feet from the ground. You can do the hike in a day, camp out overnight, or sleep in the small free-use shelter at the midpoint; bring everything except a tent and expect to share it with others. It is a popular and highly scenic rock-climbing venue when dry; but if wet, misty weather brings out the best in the area, the ghostly tors are wreathed in swirling clouds of fog, exaggerating the already dramatic landscape. The trailhead is at Mile 39.5.

Angel Rocks Trail (3.5-mile loop; 2–3hr; 900ft ascent). The easiest of the local trails, it follows a beaver-dammed creek then climbs moderately to granite outcrops commanding a great view down the Chena River valley. It is especially striking in July when wildflowers are in full bloom. There are two alternative routes back to the trailhead (at Mile 48.9), and more ambitious hikers can continue from Angel Rocks to Chena Hot Springs (8.7 miles total; 3–4hr; 2000ft ascent total), a route which passes a free-use cabin.

Chena Dome Trail (29-mile loop; 2–4 days; 6000ft ascent). An arduous expedition (with a good viewpoint after one mile for the less committed) entirely encircling the Angel Creek drainage by means of a series of subalpine ridges separated by steep valleys and saddles. There are some wondrous views from the high points (Chena Dome reaches 4421ft), and there is always a chance of coming across a bear or wolverine, though July wildflowers and August blueberries are more likely. You can rent the *Angel Creek Cabin* by reserving in advance through the Division of Parks & Outdoor Recreation in Fairbanks (☎451-2695; $25 a night; sleeps five), but it is inconveniently sited in a valley 2000 feet below the trail near Mile 22.5, and it is far better to **camp**. Keep in mind that there is little (or no) **water** along the trail: carry as much as you can and be prepared to treat whatever you can find. The trailhead is at Mile 50.5 and you've got a 1.4-mile road walk back to the trailhead at the end of the hike.

The bar and restaurants are all open to the public, as are **the pools** (daily 9am–midnight; $8 for a day-pass) which are free to hotel guests. Rooms are comfortable and bland, but there are substantially more characterful, rustic cabins without plumbing, RV parking ($40), and **camping** by the river ($20). It is always worth asking for discounts in spring and fall, and small groups can often land a large room at a very reasonable rate.

Circle Hot Springs and around

Circle Hot Springs, 135 miles northeast of Fairbanks, manages to achieve an agreeable balance between the overdevelopment of Chena Hot Springs and the simple tank of hot water offered at Manley Hot Springs. Appealing though it is, you'll need to weigh your desire for a steamy soak against a 270-mile round-trip that will definitely make you earn your dip. Unless you've shopped around you may find that your rental car isn't insured off blacktop roads (see p.415) and, even if it is, the trip is probably only worthwhile when combined with other activities: hiking the Pinnell Mountain Trail, canoeing Birch Creek (consult APLIC in Fairbanks for details) or undertaking a little **gold panning** along the Chatanika River. If you are keen on gold panning, visit Alaska Prospectors in Fairbanks (see p.439) for details and equipment – a legacy of the times when the area was heavily mined. Around the turn of the twentieth century, sourdoughs on the Yukon headed to fresh prospecting grounds inland blazing the Circle–Fairbanks summer trail following a sequence of ridge tops south of the Chatanika River. Today a section of this is followed by the loosely defined 58-mile hiking and horse trail the Circle–Fairbanks Historic Trail. The winter trail, mostly using frozen watercourses, is now traced by the annual Yukon Quest International Sled Dog Race (see box, p.424).

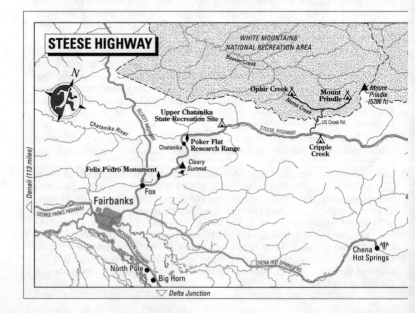

Along the Steese Hwy: Fox to Central

North from Fairbanks the Steese Hwy passes through **FOX**, from where it works its way northeast towards the Yukon River. At Mile 16.5, it passes the **Felix Pedro Historic Monument**, which marks the spot where, in July 1902, Felix Pedro discovered gold in the region. The creek across the road is open for recreational panning; there is a nostalgic quality to dipping your pan in here, even if it has been worked over so often that you'll never find anything worthwhile.

The highway then climbs steeply to **Cleary Summit**, Mile 20, a small-scale downhill ski area from where there are great views of the White Mountains to the north and Mount McKinley to the south. A steep descent drops you into a land only just beginning to recover from the ravages of intensive gold mining. Historically one of the most active centers of gold extraction was the township of **CHATANIKA**, Mile 28, once the terminus of the narrow-gauge Tanana Valley Railroad which supplied the region from Fairbanks. There's little left of Chatanika now, but something of the glory days can be found in the **Gold Dredge #3**, looming from behind a heap of tailings like some beached galleon. No one is going to worry if you follow one of the short trails for a quick look, but it is actually on private property opposite the *Chatanika Lodge*, Mile 28.6 (☎389-2164, fax 389-2166; ③) which serves decent food and has functional rooms.

A mile further on lies **Poker Flat Research Range**, the USAF's rocket-launch facility mainly used for aurora investigations; it can be visited on a two-hour **tour** (late May to late Aug roughly every second Fri 1.30pm; free; ☎474-7558, *fygipub@aurora.alaska.edu*) which starts at the gates.

In the thirty miles east of Chatanika there are two attractive **campgrounds**: the wooded, riverside *Upper Chatanika River State Recreation Site*, Mile 39 ($10; pump water) and *Cripple Creek* campground, Mile 60 ($8; pump water), again by

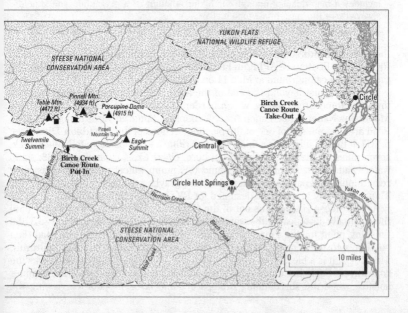

PINNELL MOUNTAIN TRAIL

As you thread your way along an exposed ridgeline between Pinnell Mountain and Porcupine Dome on the **Pinnell Mountain Trail** (27 miles one-way; 2–3 days; 3200ft ascent), the 5000-foot elevation combines with the proximity to the Arctic Circle – just seventy miles to the north – to make the midnight sun visible from June 18 to 24. Understandably, this is the busiest time to be up here – particularly the summer solstice on June 21 – but at any time from mid-June to mid-September you'll find great views of the Alaska and Brooks ranges. After an initial climb the trail follows a high, windswept and treeless ridge seldom dropping more than a few hundred feet before scaling the next low mountain. It can get a little monotonous, but long views and the occasional caribou maintain interest, and the threat of bear encounters adds zest. If this sounds too intense, just hike the first couple of miles from either of the two trailheads for great views and palpable solitude.

The hike is perhaps best done over two or three days spending the night in one or both of the emergency shelters (Ptarmigan Creek at 10.1 miles and North Fork at 17.8 miles), which are small but fully weatherproof (though not mosquito-proof) and can sleep six, in a pinch. Roof rainwater collected in a barrel outside can be used for cooking and is likely to be all you'll find along the way; come prepared. The large number of posts and cairns marking the route attest to the sometimes **atrocious weather** up here, so it is a good idea to **bring a tent**, also advisable at popular times when the shelters may be full.

Leave your vehicle near the finish at **Twelvemile Summit** (3190ft), Mile 85.5, and hitch back to the start at the higher of the two trailheads, **Eagle Summit** (3685ft), Mile 107.3. The hitch can be a long and dispiriting experience and is best not left until you are tired and hungry (and possibly wet and cold) at the end of your hike.

APLIC in Fairbanks stocks the excellent *Pinnell Mountain Trail* leaflet which includes a map detailed enough for hiking, though as a precaution you should always carry the appropriate topo maps.

the river and with some walk-in sites. Both are access points for the Chatanika River Canoe Route (see APLIC in Fairbanks for details), a Class I–II float down to the *Whitefish* campground at Mile 11 on the Elliott Hwy.

At Mile 57, just beyond the end of the asphalt, **US Creek Road** spurs north towards Nome Creek Valley, which borders the southern reaches of the White Mountains National Recreation Area. A couple of hundred yards along US Creek Road are the remains of one of the pipeline sections of the **Davidson Ditch** (see p.431), it then climbs over a thinly wooded ridge and drops down to Nome Creek, seven miles off the Steese Hwy. From here, *Ophir Creek* campground ($8; pump water) and *Mount Prindle* campground ($8; pump water) make good bases for recreational gold panning, catch-and-release grayling fishing, or just hanging out. They are mostly gravel plots designed for RVs but they're lovely spots.

As the Steese Hwy climbs out of the Chatanika Valley, trees thin visibly until they virtually disappear at the watershed of **Twelvemile Summit**, Mile 85.5, the finishing point for the Pinnell Mountain Trail (see box, above). The road then continues to the Pinnell Mountain Trail starting trailhead at **Eagle Summit**, Mile 107.3. It is a bleak spot where a long row of L-shaped snow poles marks the road ahead. Eagle Summit has even been known to receive snow on the summer solstice when the surrounding hilltops become favored spots for viewing the passage of the **midnight sun** as it brushes the horizon and begins its ascent for the new day.

From Eagle Summit the Steese descends for twenty miles to the small junction town of Central past Mammoth and Mastodon creeks, where wonderfully preserved examples of these ancient animals have been discovered embedded in the permafrost before being carted away to museums.

Rolling into **CENTRAL**, 127 miles northeast of Fairbanks, it is difficult to see just what it is central to, but back in the heady gold days this was the heart of the Circle Mining District from where prospectors would disperse up the gulches to stake their claims. The region revived on the back of rocketing gold prices in the late 1970s and has since maintained a solid following of summertime miners pursuing the dream. An insight into the power of gold over the prospectors' psyche comes through from the **Central District Museum** (late May to early Sept daily noon–5pm; $1), where staggering statistics of the quantity of gold pulled out of the surrounding hills are backed up by large nuggets and fascinating artifacts from the tough early years.

Only a few dozen souls permanently occupy Central, but this small town may nonetheless provide the creature comforts – simple cabins, straightforward diner food, and showers – you've been hankering after if you've just spent a couple of nights out on the Pinnell Mountain Trail. Choose between the *Central Motor Inn*, (☎520-5228, fax 520-5230; private bath ③, shared bath ②), where camping costs $10, and showers cost $3; and the adjacent *Crabb's Corner* (☎ & fax 520-5599; rooms ②; cabins ②), which has cabins with electricity (some with water) sleeping up to six, at a pinch, and free tent camping; showers are $3, laundry $2. Both have decent restaurants and sell gas, though it isn't cheap.

Circle Hot Springs

From Central, Circle Hot Springs Road spurs eight miles south to **CIRCLE HOT SPRINGS**, where vast quantities of hot spring water well out of the ground and fill a large open-air swimming pool (open 24hr; free to those with rooms and cabins, otherwise $5 all day), however it is chlorinated due to heavy use which makes it a bit like an outdoor swimming pool rather than a mineral bath, but it is still pretty good. The **Arctic Circle Hot Springs Resort** (☎520-5113, fax 520-5116; suites ⑤, rooms ⑤, cabins ④–⑤, hostel beds ①) is about all there is to Circle Hot Springs, and can arrange massage therapists ($35 for a 30min teaser, $60 for an hour tension reliever), but the tone shies away from "health spa" and leans more towards having fun in the warm waters and simply getting away from it all. The original 1930 building houses a good and reasonably priced restaurant, a bar open until 5am, and a range of **rooms** from jacuzzi-equipped honeymoon suites and comfortable shared-bath rooms to small "hostel" rooms where you can throw your sleeping bag down on the carpeted floor. Outside are cabins, some with cooking facilities and bathrooms, and an area for RVs ($10) and camping ($5). Tenters will find it quieter (and cheaper) two miles back down the road towards Central where there's a former BLM campground no longer sporting any facilities, but with river water and a lot of mosquitoes in midsummer.

Without your own vehicle, **access** is limited to $75 each-way flights from Fairbanks with Warbelow Air (Mon–Fri only; ☎1-800/478-0812).

Circle

Beyond Central, the progressively deteriorating Steese Hwy runs 35 miles to the Yukon River, sloping ever so gently along the way. In pre-Haul Road days this was the farthest north you could drive in the US, falling fifty miles short of the Arctic Circle; of course, that didn't stop geographically challenged miners from picking **CIRCLE** for the name of the first supply post to be built on the Yukon River, established here in 1893. Until the rise of Dawson City during the Klondike rush five years earlier, Circle was known as the largest log cabin city in the world, with a population of more than a thousand and a waterfront a mile and a half long. It even had its own opera house, prompting some to dub it the "Paris of the North," though the long winters and hard-scrabble mining life quickly made that a laughable characterization.

The exodus to the Klondike pretty much cleaned out Circle, but its location on the river and role as a stopping point for steamers kept it alive. Today it is a faintly dispiriting place of under a hundred people with none of the grace of its upstream neighbor, Eagle. Even the Yukon River – at this point some two-and-a-half miles wide – is stripped of its majesty when viewed from Circle, as you only see one relatively small branch. But the river remains the lure: float trips through the **Yukon-Charley National Preserve** (see box, p.406) usually end here, and Yukon River Tours (☎ & fax 773-8439) run **boat charters** (half-day $250, full day $500) for up to five people either upstream into the Yukon-Charley, or downstream to Fort Yukon on the **Arctic Circle** through the **Yukon Flats National Wildlife Refuge**. In this lake-filled country, the river braids out to over a sixty-mile breadth that's home to millions of geese, canvasbacks, swans, teal, scaup, and widgeon. The boat charters are run from the *Yukon Riverview Motel* (☎ & fax 773-8439; ③), which has basic motel rooms and public showers ($3.50). You can set up camp or park your RV nearby, beside the boat launch where there's an outhouse and tables, and then wander across to the Yukon Trading Post for expensive groceries, café food, and the bar.

Manley Hot Springs and around

Though recently straightened and improved, the **Elliott Highway** remains a fairly rough dirt road leading 160 miles north and west from Fairbanks through boreal forest into what seems like nowhere. The four-hour run ends at the Tanana River three miles beyond **Manley Hot Springs**, which is little more than a clearing in the woods with a classic roadhouse that claims to be Alaska's oldest continuously operated example for these archetypal hotel-cum-restaurant/bars. Nearby, a hot spring feeds tubs inside a greenhouse where grapes can be plucked off the vines trained above.

Along the Elliott Highway

The Steese Hwy runs eleven miles north from Fairbanks to Fox, from where the **Elliott Highway** (officially open all year, but difficult after snow; contact Fairbanks Department of Transportation ☎451-5204) winds its way north then southwest. Only the first 28 miles are paved, but the subsequent gravel is hard-packed and the road generally wide and fairly straight. If taken at a reasonable pace the road shouldn't provide any difficulty for ordinary cars, though services are almost nonexistent: stock up with crisp, **fresh water** at the Fox Spring, Mile 0.3, and with **gas** either in Fairbanks or at the Hilltop Truck Stop, Mile 5 – there is no more until you reach Manley Hot Springs almost 150 miles on. Remember too, that the first seventy miles form part of the truck route to Prudhoe Bay and you can expect to meet eighteen-wheelers barreling along: slow down and pull as far over as is safe.

For most of the journey there is little reason to stop other than to linger over the gorgeous wilderness you're driving through. Eleven miles north of Fox, the Lower Chatanika River State Recreation Area harbors the waterside *Olnes* campground ($10; pump water) and the appreciably more peaceful *Whitefish* campground ($5; pump water), both with drive-up sites just over a mile off the highway.

The highway then approaches the western end of the **White Mountains**, an eye-catching limestone range that stretches off to the northeast. Because much of the area is boggy, the majority of trails are only passable in winter. The one significant summer hiking trail is the arduous **Summit Trail** (44 miles round-trip; 4–5 days; 1000ft ascent, 2000ft descent), which starts at a trailhead at Mile 27.7 and initially crosses boardwalks and through dense forest before climbing up to tundra ridgetops. It ends at the lowland *Borealis–LeFevre* cabin (Fri & Sat $25, otherwise $20; reserve through the BLM ☎1-800/437-7021) but many prefer to turn back after camping in the high country making it a two- or three-day hike.

The highway continues north to the tiny homesteading community of **JOY**, which comprises little more than the *Wildwood General Store*, Mile 49.3, good for stocking up on a few essentials and a lot of souvenirs and T-shirts. At Mile 62.5 the rustic **Fred Blixt Cabin** (reservations up to 30 days in advance; call the BLM on ☎1-800/437-7021; Fri & Sat $25, otherwise $20), the only drive-in cabin in the area, sleeps five comfortably, has an outhouse nearby, and spring water which should be treated is readily available: bring a cooking stove, white gas, and firewood for heating.

Ten miles on (Mile 73) the Dalton Hwy continues north to Prudhoe Bay and the Elliott Hwy turns left to Manley Hot Springs passing the trailhead (Mile 92) for a fairly tough eleven-mile hiking trail leading south to **Tolovana Hot Spring**, where two wooden tubs huddle next to a gurgling stream. There are a couple of privately-owned rental cabins nearby (☎445-6706) with gas cooking stores and lights but nothing else: one sleeps four, while the other sleeps eight (Fri & Sat $150, otherwise $100).

Around Mile 95, there are impressive views over **Minto Flats**, a state game refuge which spreads south of the predominantly Athapascan village of Minto, reached by a side road at Mile 110.

Manley Hot Springs

MANLEY HOT SPRINGS, 160 miles northwest of Fairbanks, seems hacked out of the bush, consisting of an airstrip, a post office-cum-general store, gas station, and a few houses clustered beside the placid tree-hung Hot Springs Slough. When gold was discovered at the nearby Tofly and Eureka goldfields in the early 1900s, miners came to clean up in freely available hot water, and relished the fresh vegetables that could be grown in the warmer ground, a rare boon in Alaska. In 1902, JF "Daddy" Karshner set up a 320-acre market-gardening homestead around the springs – then known simply as **Hot Springs**. In 1906, he was bought out by a man going by the alias of **Frank Manley**, who turned up with several hundred thousand dollars and a shady reputation from his Texan past. He was later forcibly returned there, but was eventually acquitted of horse thievery. Manley established the first resort, a log-built four-story affair with electricity, a dance hall, billiard table, steam heating, and a "natatorium" for taking a dip at any time of year; it was an immediate hit with Fairbanks residents. The resort waned with Fairbanks' fortunes and finally burned down in 1913. Manley's name lived on however and in 1957 was tacked onto the name of the town; don't go calling the place Manley though or you'll raise the hackles of older residents. As river traffic came to a halt in the early 1950s, Manley Hot Springs' fate looked bleak, but the completion of a gravel road in 1959 has allowed for a trickle of tourist traffic.

The local population barely touches a hundred, and on a good Saturday night it seems they're all around the pool table and horseshoe bar inside the 1906 *Manley Roadhouse* (mid-May to Oct; ☎672-3161, fax 672-3221; room ②, with private bath ④; cabins ④), a wonderful chunk of Alaska's living heritage with good diner meals, beat-up chairs huddled around the oil-barrel stove and pianola, and rooms upstairs: the older rooms are small and share facilities but have more character; cabins sleep five. The patch of grass across the road makes a good **campground** ($5 per site; pay at the roadhouse), and for **rooms** you might also try *Gwen's Place* (☎672-3382; ④), a B&B along a dirt road just beyond the post office; the price charge includes breakfast, lunch, and dinner.

For the **hot springs**, head to The Bath House (open 24 hours, 365 days; $5 per person paid to the amiable owners, Chuck and Gladys, at the nearby house; ☎ & fax 672-3171), a verdant, heated greenhouse containing three simple concrete tubs supplied with cooled but untreated spring water. Grapes, Asian pears, cherries, and nectarines flourish here and you are welcome to sample whatever is ripe as you loll back for a few hours. Essentially once your group pays up the whole place is yours for as long as you wish, though at busy times you might want to welcome others in. To reach the bath house from the roadhouse, cross the bridge over the slough and continue three hundred yards towards Fairbanks.

ARCTIC ALASKA

Exactly what constitutes Arctic Alaska is hard to pin down but it does constitute some of **America's finest wilderness**, fierce and shockingly desolate and yet shot through by an intricate, fragile beauty. To geographers it is anywhere north of the **Arctic Circle**, an imaginary line at 66º 33' above which the sun fails to set at the summer solstice (June 21), nor rise on the winter solstice (December 21). For botanists the true Arctic begins at the tree line, where spruce give way to willows which creep along the ground, often for tens of yards, but never get off the ground; while ethnologists might argue that the Arctic is the preserve of the Iñupia and Yup'ik peoples.

Whichever way you define it, it covers pretty much everywhere north of Fairbanks. This is the land of the midnight sun, where summer days are endless as intense low-angled rays warm the air almost to 100ºF. For three brief months the thin covering of snow melts and the near-flat tundra thaws to a soggy, peaty landscape studded with myriad tiny lakes. Rainfall here is minimal, often less than some parts of the American Southwest deserts, but much of the north is underlain by **permafrost** (see box, p.459) which impedes drainage enough to sustain the lakes. Bears, caribou, moose, and Arctic foxes go through accelerated reproductive cycles in time for the arrival of the savage nine-month winter (spring and fall hardly exist), when snow blows across the tundra and the northern lights glow overhead.

The **Brooks Range** extends almost the width of Alaska, the tail end of the continental dividing range which starts at the southern tip of the Andes and stretches right up through the Mexican cordilleras and the US and Canadian Rockies. To the south the Alatna, Chandalar, John, Koyukuk, and Sheenjek rivers drain through the Interior forests into the Yukon and out to the Bering Sea; to the north the Anaktuvuk, Colville, and Sagavanirktok rivers flow across the barren treeless **North Slope** into the Beaufort Sea.

Despite the protection offered by a confusing patchwork of national parks, preserves, and wildlife refuges, much of the wilderness is under threat. Many of the more individualistic Alaskans object to the very idea of "tying up" land in this way, but the greatest danger is from the **oil lobbyists**. The face of the far north has already changed with the exploitation of the Prudhoe Bay field and its satellites, and the construction of the pipeline. As reserves dwindle, oil companies are campaigning for access to other areas. The National Petroleum Reserve – Alaska (NPR-A), west of Prudhoe Bay, was set aside for the Navy in 1923 and has already been explored, though in recent years, environmentalists have argued that it should remain free from development. They have a stronger hand in protecting the Arctic National Wildlife Refuge (ANWR) to the east, though with the high oil prices of recent times, there is considerable political pressure being applied to allow exploration in the northern coastal strip.

The only road access into the Alaskan Arctic is along the five-hundred-mile Dalton Hwy to **Prudhoe Bay** running parallel to the Trans-Alaska oil pipeline. It is a rugged trip in your own vehicle, so is best done as part of an organized tour taking in the Arctic Circle monument, a tour of the oil installation, the Arctic Ocean, and a lot of wonderful scenery. As it crosses the Brooks Range, the Dalton divides two of Alaska's largest and most remarkable protected areas, both conveniently visited directly by air from Fairbanks. To the west lies the **Gates of the Arctic National Park**, wonderful remote hiking and canoeing country accessed through the tiny village of **Bettles**. To the east is the still more remote **Arctic National Wildlife Refuge**, again good for hiking and floating.

Much of the north is thinly populated with only a few dozen tiny Native communities scattered across this vast area. The smaller hamlets are not really set up for visitors; the bigger stopoff points are decent but limited to three towns. There is an obvious draw to **Barrow**, the most northerly town on the continent, besides having the world's largest Eskimo population, it serves as the occasional stomping ground of polar bears. **Kotzebue** is smaller but a more predominantly Native town, well inside the Arctic Circle and the jumping-off point for trips out to the Kobuk Valley National Park. The one-time gold-rush town of **Nome** doesn't claim any superlatives but is perhaps the most immediately inviting of the three, with enough of a road system to encourage freelance exploration; it also serves as the end of the annual 1100-mile Iditarod sled-dog race from Anchorage.

The Dalton Highway to Prudhoe Bay

The Arctic location and remote nature of the **Dalton Hwy** exerts an almost irresistible pull; all five hundred lonely, desolate miles of it from Fairbanks to the Arctic Ocean, three hundred miles beyond the **Arctic Circle**. The journey is an adventure in itself, while the destination can be less rewarding. All you get is Prudhoe Bay, miles of pipes, and the service town of **Deadhorse**, which is nowhere near as exciting as it sounds. You can't even get to the Arctic Ocean except on a fairly perfunctory tour. For most of the year the Arctic pack-ice

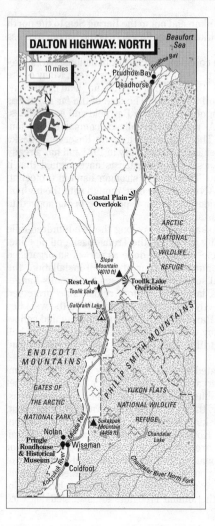

butts right up against the shore and it is not uncommon to have polar bears roaming through Deadhorse. Things are different in summer, when you are likely to be there, as both the bears and the ice floes are away over the northern horizon.

Those who like their wilderness pristine will be disappointed to learn that the **pipeline** runs above ground most of the way to Prudhoe Bay, though it quickly becomes a faithful companion pointing the way north. Both road and pipeline run through a ten-mile-wide corridor managed by the Bureau of Land Management (BLM), equipped with a few basic campgrounds. Along the way there are small lakes and streams which, after the rivers have cleared of snow-melt turbidity (July to mid-Sept) offer good fishing for grayling, Dolly Varden, lake trout, and northern pike. Hiking is more problematic, with neither formal trails nor waymarked trailheads, though if you are prepared to hike across tundra you can go wherever you want.

All around is federally managed wilderness: the **Yukon Flats** and **Arctic** national wildlife refuges to the east; the **Kanuti National Wildlife Refuge** and **Gates of the Arctic National Park** to the west. With all this controlled land about it is no surprise that there is plenty of **wildlife**. If you're lucky, the most impressive sight you'll see is the 18,000-strong Arctic caribou herd which migrates in late April and early May through Prudhoe Bay to the Kuparuk oil fields where the cows calve, then returns to the Brooks Range in August for the abundant lichen. Grizzlies, Dall sheep, moose and fox are also present, and musk oxen sometimes congregate near the pipeline – binoculars are a boon.

Flights and tours to the Arctic Circle and Prudhoe Bay

Alaska Airlines fly large jets into Prudhoe Bay/Deadhorse airport twice daily from Anchorage (though currently not from Fairbanks). Unless you are entitled to use the "Best of the West" airpass (see p.32) this will set you back about $570 if bought two weeks in advance; probably more than you want to pay to see an oil field. Frontier Flying Service fly direct from Fairbanks three days a week but again you'll pay over $500.

There seems a lot more purpose to the whole venture when combined with a road trip up the Dalton Hwy, and by joining a **bus/plane tour** you won't wreck your vehicle and will (generally) avoid doing the journey in both directions. Trips mostly involve driving up the Dalton in two days, taking the Prudhoe Bay tour then flying back either to Anchorage or to Fairbanks. Some do the same in reverse, but go for the former if you can; two days on the road certainly heightens the drama of arrival. Most companies only run trips every couple of weeks so it pays to enquire well in advance (for contact addresses see box on p.434). The cheapest of the all-inclusive packages – including road transport, flights and accommodation but not food – is with Northern Alaska's Prudhoe Bay Adventure (3 days; $619), which runs a minivan up the Dalton and offers an overnight extension taking in Barrow (additional $389). If you want to rough it, try Dalton Highway Express (☎ & fax 452-2031, *www.daltonhighwayexpress .com*), who make the run to Prudhoe Bay in a day (16hr) three days a week and charge $125 each way (bikes cost $60); or Trans Arctic Circle Treks, for an arduous three-day Prudhoe-and-back road trip with an oilfield tour and camping both nights in the Brooks Range ($579). Barrow and bush-flight extensions are available.

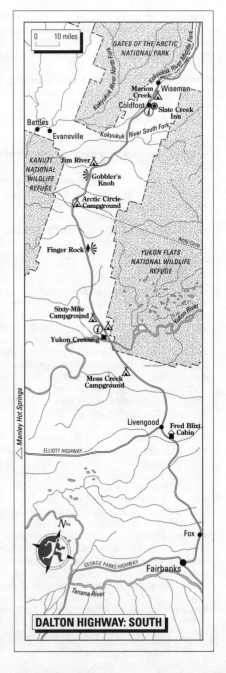

DALTON HIGHWAY: SOUTH

For those only wanting to visit the **Arctic Circle**, Northern Alaska offer a number of variations starting with the full-day Arctic Circle Drive Adventure (16hr; $119), driving up to the Arctic Circle and back. The Arctic Circle Fly Drive (11–12hr; $189) speeds the whole thing up by taking a flight to Prospect Creek, and Arctic Circle Native Culture (15hr; $319) also flies one-way and includes a couple of hours in the Brooks Range village of Anaktuvuk Pass. They're up against a number of other companies: All Points Alaska Tours do an Arctic Circle trip (2 days; $139) driving to the Arctic Circle, camping there (bring all your own gear) and driving back again; Dalton Highway Express do

ARCTIC OIL AND THE TRANS-ALASKA OIL PIPELINE

It is hard to overstate the importance of **oil** to the 49th state. Some jokingly contend that Alaska should break from the union and become an independent OPEC state; an idea that is not so far fetched when you consider that Alaska produces twenty percent of US oil, and ten percent of what the nation consumes. Alaskan taxes and royalties account for a third of the value of each barrel, an income that provides a whopping **eighty percent of the state budget**. It is no surprise then that Alaska is virtually controlled by oil interests, and it is easy to get the impression that state politicians are little more than puppets for the oil companies.

Oil rises naturally to the surface along the North Slope, historically providing lamp oil for Native Iñupia, and alerting hopeful white newcomers to the presence of deeper deposits. In February 1968, years of exploration paid off big-time when the Atlantic Richfield Company (now part of Phillips Petroleum) discovered a 23-billion-barrel reserve 9000 feet under **Prudhoe Bay**. This constituted one of the world's largest finds, but the Bay's location on the Arctic Ocean, where tankers could only penetrate the pack-ice for two months of the year, posed a thorny problem. The solution was to build a $900 million pipeline running 800 miles across the middle of the state to the northernmost ice-free port at Valdez. There was an immediate reaction from Alaskan Natives and environmentalists; the route of the planned pipeline would cross areas claimed by Native groups and not covered by any treaty. Consequently, the 1971 **Alaska Native Claims Settlement Act** (ANCSA) was rushed through offering land and cash in return for Natives relinquishing their claim on the remaining territory. Environmental concerns over damage to the tundra, disruption of animal migration routes, and the very idea of having a steel tube running hundreds of miles through untouched wilderness almost put a stop to the whole project, but the Arab oil embargo of 1973–74 finally forced the Federal Government's hand. One congressional vote swung the decision in favor of building the pipeline.

Over the years, oil production has declined, and in the late 1990s the rallying cry of "No decline in '99" rang around halls of the legislature in an effort to convince the state government to allow further exploration on the North Slope, particularly along the coast of the Arctic National Wildlife Refuge. At a time when oil prices were low, a report stated that there is "no economically recoverable amounts of oil" under ANWR if the price stays below $15 a barrel. On cue, the price of crude oil shot up towards $30 a barrel and the oil companies continue to apply pressure for more drilling, backed by many Alaskans as well as the Iñupia-owned Arctic Slope Regional Corporation which stands to profit from royalties on any oil extracted.

Even without new development, production will continue until at least 2030, and with current high demand for natural gas, there is even talk of a parallel pipeline to

a very basic one-day up and back road trip to the Arctic Circle ($79, bring your own lunch); and Trans Arctic Circle Treks take minivans on a one-day trip to the Arctic Circle (12hrs; $99).

Arctic enthusiasts can string together a sequence of coastal town visits with Cape Smythe Air (☎852-8333 in Barrow; ☎442-3020 in Kotzebue; ☎443-2414 in Nome), whose schedule allows you to catch a flight from Prudhoe Bay to Barrow ($219), on to Point Lay ($172), then to Point Hope ($166), and finally to Kotzebue ($107), from where Alaska Airlines fly on to Nome or to Anchorage. It works out cheaper than separate trips based in Anchorage or Fairbanks.

exploit North Slope natural gas. After all, Alyeska, the pipeline-operating company, has an obligation to restore the pipeline corridor to its original state once production ceases; something they want to put off as long as possible.

THE PIPELINE

The pipeline is 800 miles long, in places looking like some four-foot-wide silver anaconda draped across the land. Altogether only 380 miles are buried: where it encounters permafrost, the pipeline gracefully emerges from out of the ground, rising onto ten-foot-high support brackets then embarking on a zigzag passage across the skyline designed to accommodate earthquakes, and expansion and contraction in Alaska's extreme weather.

Pipeline construction began in November 1973 and employment peaked at over 21,000, with workers laboring away for wage packages of legendary proportions. With overtime and hardship bonuses, pipeline workers were pulling in up to $1500 a week (several times the national average at the time). Workers flocked up from the Lower 48 only to discover the work was long, hard, often lonely, and conducted in atrocious conditions, right through the Arctic winter.

The pipeline was finished in June 1977 at a cost of $8 billion, almost ten times the original budget, and the first oil was pumped from Prudhoe Bay on June 20, 1977. A Nenana Ice Classic-style lottery was conducted with $30,000 at stake for whoever could pick the exact time of the oil's arrival in Valdez – which turned out to be 38 days, 12 hours, and 56 minutes after it set off. Oil now makes the journey in about 6 days (averaging 5.5 mph), its passage through a complex series of pumping stations and valves managed from Valdez.

More than five hundred **animal crossings** had been incorporated into the pipeline; some just short runs of buried pipe, others achieved by raising sections of pipe more than usual above ground. The jury is still out on the success of these measures: caribou congregate around the pipe in spring when the grass tends to green up earlier, but pregnant cows tend to avoid the pipeline altogether.

Twelve **pump stations** were designed to move the oil along, each equipped with Rolls-Royce jet engines. As production has declined, four pump stations – #2, #6, #8 & #10 – have been mothballed. This leaves long sections without significant permanent staff, possibly compromising security. There have been small spills ever since the pipeline came on stream, but consequences of a major pipeline rupture were brought into sharp focus by the *Exxon Valdez* disaster (see box, p.234), and independent groups now monitor Alyeska's safety performance. They are continually highlighting weaknesses in the spill-response plan, leaking information on poor maintenance procedures and generally driving home the idea that the pipeline is now almost 25 years old and needs increased maintenance if a catastrophic environmental disaster is to be avoided.

Along the Dalton Highway

From Fairbanks, the route north follows the Steese and Elliott highways 73 miles north to Livengood, where you'll find the start of the 414-mile **Dalton Highway** (open year-round but chains needed Sept–May), named for James Dalton, an Arctic engineer who played a major role in the early oil discovery and development of the North Slope. Old hands know it by its original working title, the North Slope **Haul Road**, named in honor of its fast, stop-at-nothing trucks and built in an astonishing five months in the summer of 1974 in preparation for the construction of the pipeline alongside.

For years the road was limited to pipeline traffic, but regulations were gradually relaxed until the whole road was finally opened to the general public in 1994. Nonetheless, there remains a distinct work camp tenor along its length. There are no villages or rest stops, just slightly remodeled work camps mostly comprising prefabricated accommodation blocks. Don't expect much in the way of supplies either and remember that everything you buy will have an Arctic price tag.

Driving the Dalton Highway mustn't be undertaken lightly and you should seriously consider joining one of the bus tours. The problem isn't so much the driving (two hard days in each direction on gravel), it is the consequences if something goes wrong. There are only three places to buy gas on the Dalton – the Yukon River crossing, Coldfoot, and Deadhorse – and between Coldfoot and Deadhorse there is a 230-mile stretch with no services of any sort: towing fees can soon become astronomical. If you are determined, you'll either need your own vehicle or be prepared to shell out at least $100 a day for a **4x4 rental** from Arctic, Budget, National, or Payless in Fairbanks (see p.439). No insurance is offered with vehicles for driving the Dalton: Americans should check that their own vehicle insurance covers them, and foreigners should beef up their travel insurance to cover any eventualities. Rental companies don't generally allow their cars on gravel roads, and though you might choose to take the risk on the Steese or Elliott highways, this would be foolhardy on the Dalton. Travelers' folklore has it that the Dalton is always in one of two states, muddy or dusty; worse still, the forty-odd eighteen-wheelers that ply the road each day supplying Prudhoe Bay have a nasty habit of hefting large rocks through windshields. For high-clearance trucks serving the oil community the road is passable **in winter**, but the cold (down to minus fifty), darkness, and the general hostility of the environment pretty much rule it out for everyone else.

Whenever you go the rule is to **be prepared**. Allow for a couple of punctured tires (take two spares if you can) and a cracked windshield, drive with your lights on and expect to wait a while for help if you need it. Some even carry a CB radio tuned to Channel 19 to pick up the conversations between truckers and tour-bus drivers but, in summer at least, there is a reasonable amount of traffic and it is enough to carry emergency supplies – food, water, sleeping bag, and perhaps a cooking stove. For more info check the travel section of the Coldfoot visitor center's Web site at *www.aurora.ak.blm.gov/arcticinfo/travel-1.htm*.

If you are thinking of **hitching** to Deadhorse, then persistence and patience will eventually pay off, usually with hunters, miners, and road crews but seldom with Prudhoe-bound truckers. Remember to take everything you'll need to camp out for several days. The occasional **cyclist** with a spoke loose also makes the journey but it is tough, and mud and dust are a constant irritation. At least you can fix your own punctures.

The best source of **information** on the road (and the BLM-managed corridor that it largely runs through) is APLIC in Fairbanks (see p.415).

Mile 0 to Coldfoot (Mile 175)

From Mile 0 at Livengood, where the Dalton Hwy spurs off the Elliott Hwy, the Dalton crosses a rolling landscape dotted with white and black spruce, and strung with the gleaming pipeline. The first of several basic **campgrounds** is the wooded *Hess Creek*, Mile 24 (free; creek water); next to a stream noted for its whitefish and grayling fishing. At Mile 56, the Dalton crosses the broad, dirty swirl of the Yukon River on the sloping 2290-foot **EL Patton Bridge**, which has the pipeline strapped to its side. This is the only road crossing of the Yukon downstream of Whitehorse in Canada.

Just over the bridge the grandly titled **YUKON CROSSING** comprises a muddy (or dusty) expanse and the scruffy *Yukon Ventures* (☎655-9001; ⑤) with work-camp rooms (half-price for singles) and a café (7am–9pm) serving a buffet to tour-bus passengers, and burgers ($8) and steak or fish dinners ($13) to all comers. Adjacent, Yukon River Tours (☎452-7162, fax 452-5063, *dlacey@mosquitonet .com*) run hour-long boat trips (June–Aug 3 daily; $25) downstream past hand-built fishwheels, all with an environmental and culturally oriented narrative. The **BLM contact station** (June–Aug daily 9am–6pm; no phone) provides information on the countryside flanking the Dalton. Opposite, a patch of land beyond the pipeline acts as an undeveloped **campground** (free; no water). Four miles up the highway, the *Sixty-Mile* campground (free; water) sits on the site of an old pipeline-construction camp, right by the *Hotspot Café*, which provides some of the best eating on the Dalton.

North of the Yukon River the land begins to open out: trees become more sparse and the pipeline views get better. At Mile 98 the ancient forty-foot granite tor of **Finger Rock** pokes up from the bleak tundra, crooked as if warning of the perils of the road ahead. The adjacent viewpoint overlooks the shallow pools that form the headwaters of the Kanuti River, the main watershed encompassed by the **Kanuti National Wildlife Refuge** to the west.

The **Arctic Circle** is crossed at Mile 115 and marked by a series of explanatory panels, where everyone has their photo taken. There's a simple **campground** (free; water from Fish Creek a mile to the south) and picnic areas with barbecues among the aspen and black spruce. Unfortunately, the hills to the north preclude seeing the midnight sun from here, even on the solstice, so if this is what you've come for you'll need to press on to **Gobbler's Knob**, Mile 132, where there are panoramic views. The pipeline-constructors' **Prospect Camp**, at Mile 136, has the undeveloped *Jim River* **campground** half a mile off the road and holds the record for the lowest temperature recorded in Alaska: -80ºF (-62ºC) on Jan 23, 1971.

As the miles roll by, the open arctic tundra gives way to the foothills of the Brooks Range, blunt, conical hills skirted with white birch rising above broad willow-studded glacial valleys. Gradually the valleys deepen into the Middle Fork of the Koyukuk River and you hit the former workcamp of **COLDFOOT**, Mile 175. It bills itself as "the world's northernmost truck stop" and is indeed your last chance for accommodation, food, and gas before Deadhorse 239 miles on. None are cheap, but unless you are camping, there isn't much choice. Most tours spend the night here too. Coldfoot supposedly gets its name from prospectors searching north for more golden pastures and getting metaphorical cold feet around this point, but a literal interpretation suits equally: in 1989 the mercury stayed below

-60ºF for seventeen days in a row. But it also gets hot here in summer: 1988 recorded a high of 97ºF. Workers' **accommodation** has been transformed to create the *Slate Creek Inn* (☎678-5224, fax 678-5202; ⑤), with reasonably comfortable twin rooms (singles $110), a truckers café (open year round, 24hr), and a parking lot where you can camp ($10) and hook up an RV ($30 including dump station): showers are $5 extra and there's $3 laundry. There are also very limited groceries, a post office (Mon, Wed & Fri 1.30–6pm), phones, and an interagency **visitor center** (June to early Sept daily 10am–10pm; ☎ & fax 678-5209, *www.aurora.ak.blm.gov/arcticinfo*), which presents a changing program of half-hour slide shows (nightly 8pm; free) and supplies information on all the preserves and parks in this area. This is the place to come for directions to the scanty remains of the original townsite of Coldfoot, and advice if you're thinking of hiking into the Gates of the Arctic National Park (see p.460) from the highway.

Campers are better off five miles north at *Marion Creek* campground ($8; pump water and free firewood), where there are tables, fire pits, a summertime campground host, and great views of the Brooks Range.

Wiseman to Mile 414

Miners prospecting in 1908 who weren't put off by the low temperatures of Coldfoot chose to settle thirteen miles north at **WISEMAN**, at the head of the Middle Fork of the Koyukuk River – the "willow river." It is now a small, thriving cluster of log cabins hacked out of the spruce, supporting a couple of dozen people year-round and a few dozen more who arrive for summer hunting, fishing, and gold extraction. Several original buildings have survived, one of which houses the **Pringel Roadhouse & Historical Museum** (June–Aug daily 9am–1pm & 2–5pm; free), full of evocative old photos and assorted mining equipment. You can stay here at the rustic log-cabin *Arctic Getaway B&B* (☎678-4566; ④), or at the simpler *Boreal Lodging* (☎678-4566; ③). Wiseman also makes for a good jumping-off point for hiking into the eastern fringes of the **Gates of the Arctic National Park**, the only way to experience the park without a costly flight. Consult APLIC in Fairbanks or the Coldfoot visitor center for details.

At Mile 203.5 the great marble face of the 4459-foot **Sukakpak Mountain** rises up on your right, and is traditionally thought of as the border marker between Iñupia and Athapascan territory. Trees in these parts look like sporadic frayed matchsticks, and they finally disappear altogether around Mile 235, the point where you start to climb the Brooks Range past lightly vegetated talus slopes cascading from snow-capped 7000-foot peaks. This is undoubtedly the scenic highlight of the journey as you breach the North American continental divide cresting at the scenic **Atigun Pass**, Mile 245, which at 4800 feet is the highest road in Alaska. It is also the highest point for the pipeline which, in recent years, has been considerably rerouted in places prone to landslips.

The steep initial descent soon mellows as you enter a broad glacial landscape followed by gently shelving river valleys. Pump Station 4 heralds an excellent place to break the last leg of your journey, the undeveloped *Galbraith Lake* **campground**, Mile 275 (free; lake water), which is the last recognized site in the north. People do park overnight at wayside viewpoints further on, but this isn't strictly legal and there is nowhere to camp at Deadhorse.

From now on the **pipeline** is almost always above ground, gleaming across the landscape in the low arctic sun; especially around **Toolik Lake**, Mile 284 (rest area), where USAF operate an arctic biology research camp. **Dall sheep** are

PINGOS, POLYGONS, AND PERMAFROST

One of the defining features of the Alaskan north goes almost entirely unseen, though it's effects can be very evident, particularly on the North Slope. Year-round temperatures are so low that most of the ground remains frozen as **permafrost**, stretching from a foot or so below the surface to a depth of up to two thousand feet. Nothing would be able to grow, except that the weak summer sun manages to warm enough of the surface to form an **active layer** in which plants can take root and burrowing insects can go about their business.

The permafrost shrinks slightly during the cold winter, forming small vertical cracks. In spring these fill with melt water and refreeze, a cyclic process that, over the years, forms an **ice wedge**, broad near the surface and tapering to a point several feet underground. There's often a hump on the ground above an ice wedge, and when several form next to one another they create a surface pattern made up of **polygons**, typically ten to seventy feet across. If the top of the ice wedge becomes exposed it may melt to form a **thermokarst lake**, or just a very wet active layer. As the active layer begins to freeze it pushes up the ground to form a **pingo**, a rounded hummock on the surface which can grow, over several hundred years, to over two hundred feet high. Eventually it will break through the insulating active layer and the ice will begin to melt, gradually destroying all trace of the pingo.

often in evidence on the flanks of **Slope Mountain**, Mile 301, which marks the point where the Dalton joins the Sagavanirktok River on its journey to the Arctic Ocean at Prudhoe Bay. You know you are onto the final straight when you hit the **Coastal Plain Overlook**, Mile 356, a low hilltop from where you can see the sixty miles of the North Slope fading away to the ocean while steadily losing six hundred feet of elevation. The sky seems endless, and the land begins to exhibit truly arctic phenomena – **pingos, polygons**, and **thaw lakes** (see box, above) – all caused by arcane facets of the annual thaw over hundreds of feet of permafrost. Most visible of these are the pingos, conical mounds rising up to over two hundred feet above the plain.

Deadhorse and Prudhoe Bay

The end of the road comes at **DEADHORSE**, 640 miles north of Anchorage. You're still a dozen miles short of the Arctic Ocean and another 1200 miles from the North Pole: Alaska's southernmost town, Ketchikan, is closer. Deadhorse is a weird place; not really a town at all but an industrial area where venturing outdoors (and there is little reason to do this) risks stumbling onto restricted territory or getting bowled over by a fifty-ton truck. Nonetheless, the shallow lakes and flat tundra all around can be attractive enough on a warm evening – the median summertime temperature is only 40°F, but it feels warmer in the constant sun. Tucked in among the power plants, workshops, and aircraft hangars is a set of workers' rooms which have been converted into a surprisingly comfortable hotel.

The fence and checkpoint which mark the ultimate end of the Dalton Hwy separate Deadhorse from **PRUDHOE BAY**, the production facility where North Slope oil begins its six-day journey south to Valdez. There are no refinery-style flare stacks or sci-fi fractionation columns here, just a dendritic web of pipelines. But it's not just wasteland, in between lie acres of marshy grasslands and lakes seemingly undamaged by the industry all around. Quite likely it will appear as though nothing is happening: most of the activity is in the winter when ice roads, built to protect the tundra, make transport easier than it would be across boggy permafrost.

Practicalities

Unless you are already on one of the North Slope bus tours, the only way you can see anything of Prudhoe Bay is to take one of the near-identical **tours** offered by two hotels (see below) in town. The most basic is the hour-long Arctic Ocean Shuttle ($25), visiting a less than idyllic breakwater on Prudhoe Bay where you can dip your toe in the **Arctic Ocean**: full immersion is not encouraged, and may only be possible from late July until early September when the pack ice melts away from the shore. The pricier option is the three-hour Oilfield Tour ($50), which also visits the ocean and drives along the gravel roads between the production units, finishing at a series of explanatory panels at Mile 0 of the pipeline. There you can step out to feel the temperature of the un-insulated pipeline hot with oil fresh from the primeval depths.

Morning tour departures pretty much dictate that you spend the night in Deadhorse. **Accommodation** is either at the *Prudhoe Bay Hotel* (☎659-2449; private bath ⑦; shared bath ⑥), which includes three meals in its rates (otherwise $13 for breakfast, $16 for lunch, and $22 for dinner); or the *Arctic Caribou Inn* (☎659-2368 or 1-877/659-2368, fax 659-2692, *www.arcticcaribouinn.com*; room with private bath ⑤, shared bath ④); both pretty classy by Haul Road standards. RVs can park up beside the *Arctic Caribou Inn* ($15 with electricity, showers $10), but there is **no designated campground**. Both Deadhorse and Prudhoe Bay are "damp" areas, so there are no liquor sales, though you can bring your own.

The lone **general store** (10.30am–9pm in summer) contains the **post office** (1–3.30pm & 6.30–9pm), and stocks the *Anchorage Daily News*, a very modest supply of groceries, hardware, and the North Slope's finest selection of arctic workwear.

Gates of the Arctic National Park

In the great American tradition of naming vast tracts of wilderness after a single geographic feature the **Gates of the Arctic National Park** (no entry fee), two hundred miles northwest of Fairbanks, gets its name from Frigid Crags and Boreal Mountain, a pair of mountains in the far eastern reaches of the park. As he was forging his way up the North Fork of the Koyukuk River in the 1930s, wilderness advocate **Robert Marshall** encountered "a precipitous pair of mountains, one on each side," and was immediately struck by how these sentinels framed the way north, the veritable "Gates of the Arctic." He later put his considerable influence behind the campaign to have the area designated a national park, which it eventually became after the 1980 passage of the ANILCA.

These "Gates of the Arctic" now form part of the nation's second-largest national park (after the Wrangell–St Elias), occupying an area four times the size of Yellowstone, the largest park in the Lower 48. The park straddles the central Brooks Range, a labyrinth of rugged mountains rising in waves up to 8000 feet, deeply incised by plunging U-shaped valleys which give the whole place an uncanny openness. It all comes cloaked in boreal forest, alder thickets, and a thin mantle of energy-sapping arctic muskeg, a result of the permafrost that underlies the whole of the park. Such conditions don't support a great variety of animals, though on a longish trip you might reasonably expect to see brown bears, wolves, moose, Dall sheep, caribou, and wolverines.

Kobuk Eskimos and Koyukon and Kutchin Athapascans have lived in harmony with the land for centuries, as they continue to do in the Native villages of Allakaket, Anaktuvuk Pass, Evansville, Shungnak, and Kobuk, using the land for subsistence hunting, fishing, trapping, and gathering. Their ancestors, back in 1885 and 1886, guided early white explorers and prospectors, who eventually turned up payable quantities of gold on the Koyukuk, sparking the rush of 1898. All of a sudden there were small paddlesteamers and riverboats churning upstream from the Yukon River bound for trading posts at Bettles, Coldfoot, and Wiseman. For the next three decades miners scoured the southern flanks of the central Brooks Range with varying degrees of success, followed by the geological, geographic, and mineral-survey teams which brought Robert Marshall to the area.

Much of the land here was only surveyed while planning the park – the last place in the US to be fully mapped – and few landmarks are named, even on the largest scale topo maps. It remains **wholly remote**. There is only one Native village – Anaktuvuk Pass – within the bounds of the park, and eight others dotted around the perimeter, none claiming over four hundred souls. Within the park itself there are no facilities and no roads, not even tracks apart from those left by Dall sheep, the migrations of the western arctic caribou herd, and those made by subsistence hunters in pursuit.

To travel here you need to be completely self-sufficient, and since the scale and logistics are so mind-boggling, those who come tend to stay for a while. Only around four thousand recreational visitors make it into the park each year (about what Denali gets in a day) and they stay an average of eleven days. For those prepared to make the commitment of time, energy, and money it is a hugely rewarding place to be. Most people come either to **hike** or take a multiday **float trip** on one of six designated **Wild Rivers** – the Alatna, John, Kobuk, Noatak, North Fork Koyukuk, and Tinayguk – all possible under your own steam, but a good deal easier with guided or guide-assisted trips, mostly operated from Bettles. These trips concentrate on only a few spots, so much of the rest of the park remains entirely untouched – one research biologist apparently spent five months each summer season here for eleven years and saw only six people the whole time.

Even more than most places in Alaska, your experience will be dictated by **the weather**. Most visitors arrive after mid-June when frozen rivers have completed their thaw, and move on by early September. Mosquitoes can be so bad in July and early August that headnets are de rigueur, thus making mid- to late August and September particularly appealing, provided you're prepared for cooler temperatures. On average it snows eight or nine months of the year and some years only July is snow-free. Throughout summer you'll seldom experience a completely dark night, and the park receives continuous sunlight for thirty days in June and July. Consequently, July basks in a relatively balmy average daily maximum of **seventy degrees** (average daily minimum 46°F). Over the whole park, rainfall is low, but most falls in summer so you'll need to be protected from the cold, and the rain.

Access in summer is almost exclusively by float plane from Bettles (reached by scheduled bush flights from Fairbanks). Before entering the park you'll be required to work through a "backcountry simulator" program in Bettles or Anaktuvuk Pass, to ensure you are fully competent in outdoor skills. **Leave no trace** is the ethic: such is the delicacy of the arctic environment that even minimal impact takes a long time to recover, so special care is needed in the more heavily visited areas. Two of the most popular **float trips** are: on the headwaters of the **Noatak River** (5–9 days; Class I–II) among wonderful angular peaks; and the **North Fork of the Koyukuk** (5 days; Class I–III) with the entry point in the shadow of the Gates themselves followed by a float down to Bettles. You are unlikely to be totally alone on these rivers, but adventure operators and bush pilots in Bettles can advise on more solitary rivers. **Hiking areas** are more widely distributed. Essentially you can arrange to be flown in pretty much anywhere there is water or a gravel river bar to land on, then either use that as a base, or hike to some prearranged pickup point. Again there are more popular areas, but it is probably best to ask about places less frequented, if only to reduce impact on busier areas.

Keen hikers and rock climbers should head a hundred miles northwest of Bettles to **Arrigetch Peaks**, granite spires rising 3000 feet from the surrounding land, that grace numerous Gates of the Arctic publicity brochures. The name – loosely "fingers of an extended hand" – comes from a Nunamuit Eskimo legend of the Creator who placed his glove on the land as a reminder of his presence.

Getting there

Frontier Flying Service (☎474-0014 or 1-800/478-6779, fax 474-0774, *info @frontierflying.com, www.frontierflying.com*) run regular daily flights from Fairbanks to Bettles (see opposite) charging around $260 round-trip. Northern Alaska (see box, p.434) run their excellent-value **Arctic Circle Air Adventure** (4hr; $199), giving you a flight north from Fairbanks along the route of the pipeline, then among the southern peaks of the park, and low through the John River valley to Bettles, then back to Fairbanks. *Bettles Lodge* (see opposite) extend the experience on their **Arctic Circle Tour** ($365) by including lunch at the lodge and their Koyukuk River Tour; and even encourage you to stay overnight ($425 in total, based on double occupancy).

The biggest **wilderness operator** in the Gates of the Arctic is Bettles-based Sourdough Outfitters, PO Box 26066, Bettles, AK 99726 (☎692-5252, fax 692-5557, *www.sourdough.com*) who offer a staggering array of guided, guide-assisted, and unguided trips for all seasons – hiking, paddling in inflatable canoes, rafting, wildlife viewing, and dog sledding. Prices are dependent on group size in the case of unguided trips and inclusive of flights from Fairbanks for the guided trips. Select from: unguided backpacking to the Arrigetch Peaks (7 days; $400 per person assuming four passengers); unguided canoeing on the headwaters of the Noatak (7 days; $750); guided backpacking around the Arrigetch Peaks (7 days; $1650); and guided rafting on the North Fork of the Koyukuk (6 days; $1650). They also **rent gear** by the day with every fifth day free: rigid canoes ($25), small rafts ($35), canvas wall tents ($15), sleeping bags ($4), and so on. Even if you are planning your own excursion, you might consider taking along a guide ($175–250 a day plus the guide's transport cost). Apart from providing peace of mind, the guide is usually bursting with information about the area's cultural significance, good fishing spots or ways up apparently inaccessible peaks and saddles. Note that float trips are best in June and July when the water levels are high.

The folks at the *Bettles Lodge* (see opposite) also organize a smaller, but competitively priced, range of planned but unguided trips.

Bettles

BETTLES, 185 miles northwest of Fairbanks and 35 miles above the Arctic Circle, is an object lesson in how planes have changed life in bush Alaska. When gold was being sifted from the Koyukuk River around the turn of the twentieth century, Bettles stood on its bank as the highest point accessible to sternwheelers. Here supplies bound for Wiseman and Coldfoot were transferred to flat-bottomed scows which could negotiate the riffles upstream. During World War II, planes were being ferried to Russia on the lend-lease scheme and the military needed an airstrip midway between Fairbanks and Barrow. Bettles was the spot, but the best land lay on a gravel bar five miles upstream. An airstrip was built and over the years the whole town relocated leaving **Old Bettles** moldering on its cutbank, the willows, cottonwoods, and alders taking over the sagging remains of the cabins.

The population of Bettles and its contiguous Native twin, **Evansville**, only amounts to fifty-odd, and the airstrip is the center of town. There are no roads to the outside so everyone comes in or out by plane. Unless you arrive with immediate plans to fly off to the park you can suddenly feel stranded. A way out is to join *Bettles Lodge* for their two-hour **Koyukuk River Tour** ($75) which checks out former gold-prospecting sites and Old Bettles.

Summer is the busiest time in Bettles for those bound for the Gates of the Arctic, but in March, **northern-lights viewing** from Bettles is the attraction and Japanese becomes the town's lingua franca.

Information, accommodation, and food

Before heading into the park you'll need to pop along to the **Bettles Ranger Station and visitor center** (June to mid-Sept daily 8am–5pm; mid-Sept to mid-May Mon–Fri 8am–5pm; ☎692-5494) where you are required to participate in the backcountry orientation program, and can also discuss your trip plans and obtain a bear-resistant food canister.

On the way to the visitor center you pass the 50-year-old *Bettles Lodge* (☎692-5111 or 1-800/770-5111, fax 692-5655, *www.alaska.net/~bttlodg*; jacuzzi rooms ⑦, lodge ⑥, bunks ①); which has a nice mosquito-proof veranda for knocking back a beer or two during the long evenings. **Accommodation** is either in the rustic lodge where rooms share a central bathroom, in less characterful modern rooms some with jacuzzi, in a very basic bunkhouse ($16), or free camping outside (showers $4, with towel and soap $5). The only other accommodation in town is *Holly Hollow Cabins* (contact Sourdough Outfitters; ④), modern self-catering cabins sleeping up to four.

You'll almost certainly be **eating** at *Bettles Lodge*; decent meals (book for dinner; $15–20) and burgers come at tolerable prices; and there are a couple of espresso vendors in the peak season.

Arctic National Wildlife Refuge

The **Arctic National Wildlife Refuge** (ANWR) is something special, a profound wilderness where human impact is so slight that you will inevitably find yourself slowing to the pace of the land. It is the largest and northernmost of all America's wildlife refuges, encompassing the entire northeastern corner of Alaska. It's enormous size enables it to present the full sweep of arctic and subarctic ecosystems. Heavily wooded, serpentine river valleys dominate the south, notably the Sheenjek, Ivishak, and Wind river, all three now designated "Wild and Scenic." North of the Brooks Range (which bisects the refuge) lies the treeless expanse of the North Slope, threaded by braided river system and innumerable lakes laden with arctic char and winding across open tundra through caribou-calving areas.

It is one of the last true wildernesses, so thick with wildlife that it has been dubbed an arctic Serengeti, with not a single introduced species. It is a critical calving area for the 180,000-strong **Porcupine caribou herd**, the most important polar-bear denning habitat in the US, and 140 bird species have been spotted, with ducks, loons, geese, and swans in astounding numbers. It was the protection of the Porcupine herd that drew the attention of some of Alaska's earliest and most effective conservationists, **Celia Hunter** and **Ginny Wood**, who along with other like-minded souls met in Fairbanks in 1960 to establish the statewide Alaska Conservation Society. Ecologists Olaus and Margaret Murie lent weight to the campaign – Margaret later writing of their northern travels in *Two in the Far North* (see p.505) – and within months they had helped establish ANWR. Unfortunately, such refuges have always had limited protection, and oil interests are now keen to offset declining reserves by surveying within the northern sectors of ANWR. Public pressure has so far limited exploration.

If oil production ever goes ahead, it will be the first time the hand of man has ever fallen heavily on this land. The Native Gwich'in have traditionally relied upon the caribou migrations for their survival, and trappers and hunters have built the odd riverside shack over the decades, but there is really nothing but wilderness: no roads nor visitor facilities of any kind. If you do set aside the time and the considerable chunk of money needed to get into the reserve you'll be on your own, except for some of the thickest and most voracious mosquitoes in Alaska.

Many of the companies operating trips into ANWR do so through the small Gwich'in village of **FORT YUKON**, 140 miles northeast of Fairbanks and eight miles north of the Arctic Circle. It lies at the confluence of the Porcupine and Yukon rivers right on the southern edge of ANWR, and was one of the first interior villages to find its way onto white-men's maps when, in 1847, it was transformed into a Hudson's Bay Company trading post.

Getting there

Getting into ANWR is neither easy nor particularly cheap, and staying there means being totally self-sufficient. For these reasons, most people who come here do so on a guided trip either traveling on horseback with Chandalar River Outfitters, or flying in for an extended float trip with one of several companies listed in the same section.

If you are heading into ANWR independently, you've got a choice of bush-plane companies (see box on p.434) which make regular flights to Fort Yukon for around $180 round-trip, and will advise on pilots for onward travel. If you just want a taster, join one of the trips run by Warbelow's: a regular bush-mail flight (4hr; $185) which briefly calls here and continues to other small villages; the Native Village Tour (3–4hr; $218) which starts with the bush-mail flight then includes a 45-minute tour of the village. Larry's Flying Service also run a bush-mail flight and an equivalent to the Native Village Tour for about the same prices.

Nome and around

Of all the towns in the Alaskan North, the former gold town of **NOME**, over five hundred miles northwest of Anchorage and a similar distance west of Fairbanks, has the greatest all-around appeal. The town itself may be unprepossessing, but it is a fascinating place with a diverting history and a slew of fun events throughout the year, not least the **Iditarod** Sled Dog Race, which finishes here in March. Though not connected to the Interior highways, Nome also lies at the hub of an extensive road system which fans out across the **Seward Peninsula** giving access to miles of bird-rich coastline, untold acres of undulating tundra periodically dotted with the detritus of gold mining, some secluded hot springs, and a couple of small towns including the Iñupia Eskimo village of Teller.

Locals say "There's no place like Nome" and that is true enough. Once the greatest and most exuberant of Alaska's gold-rush towns, it is now down to around four thousand people – about half white, half Eskimo – but retains a kind of subarctic Wild West feel, particularly along the main Front Street, its seaward side lined with what seems like an endless row of initially intimidating dark bars. The streets are dusty, the restaurants scruffy, and drab buildings which may not be old look like they've seen many a hard winter. Houses sit on stubby poles to prevent them sinking into the mire of thawed permafrost and come surrounded by gardens where grass has been replaced by the odd dredge bucket, parts of a dismembered snow machine and maybe an old freight container. Still, it is attractively set on **Norton Sound**, which remains frozen from around mid-November through to late May, but thaws to reveal Nome's golden beach – famed not for the quality of its sand but for the **gold** amongst it which drew thousands at the end of the nineteenth century.

People still work the beach, and with no claims to stake, visitors are welcome to try their hand, though most of the twenty thousand annual visitors are content to watch the professionals and explore the surroundings, relishing the 24hr light that comes from being just a hundred miles shy of the Arctic Circle. Many hope to see animals, but despite the seasonally icy seas, you are very unlikely to see **polar bears** around Nome, though they sometimes make an appearance around the northern Seward Peninsula when the pack ice is firm. A much better bet are the **reindeer** which have been grazed across the peninsula since they were introduced over a hundred years back as a meat source. **Musk oxen** too were reintroduced here in the 1970s from a growing herd near Delta Junction and now number around 1800. The Seward Peninsula is considered prime **birding** territory with 180 species either resident or paying a flying visit from late May to July when Asiatic transients can be found. As the sea ice melts, the birds congregate along shore margins and in newly opened ponds making shorebird and waterfowl spotting particularly good from the road system.

Some history

Long before the town of Nome existed, British navigators plotted the coastline, almost arbitrarily giving headlands and inlets the names of their patrons or home towns. On a particularly uninspired day in the 1850s, one officer spied the eminence on the northern shore of Norton Sound and merely marked "? Name" on his chart. Back home, cartographers mistook his scribble for C. Nome, and Cape Nome it became.

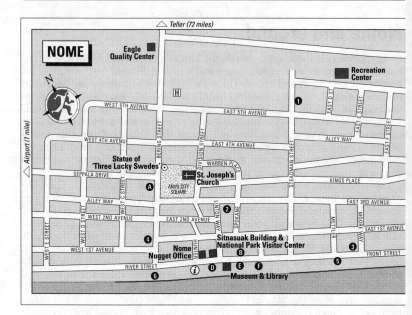

At the time there were only a few Iñupia encampments along the coast, and it looked likely to stay that way after the Reverend Hudson Stuck visited in the 1890s and declared "A savage forbidding country, this...Seward Peninsula, uninhabited and unfit for habitation; a country of naked rock and bare hillside and desolate, barren valley, without amenities of any kind and coursed with a perpetual icy blast." It remained almost uninhabited until 1898 when the "**Three Lucky Swedes**" – actually two Swedes and a Norwegian – found gold below a mountain with a tall rock in the shape of an anvil. They called it Anvil Creek and the waterside settlement which formed four miles to the south became Anvil City. This was easily confused with the nearby village of Anvik, so the US post office forced a change and **Nome** took the name of the nearby cape.

Initially the rush to Nome was no different to the dozens of others across Alaska over the last few decades of the nineteenth century. There were only 250 people here when, in July 1899, John Hummel, a prospector from Idaho who was too sick to go to the rich creeks, realized that the ruby-colored sand at his feet was laced with gold. This beach made of gold soon became known as the "Poor Man's Paradise" since prospectors needed none of the usual miners' trappings; a bucket, a shovel and a primitive rocker would suffice. There were no stakes to claim since the beach was open to all and if another prospector left his diggings you could move in. Better still, there was no desperate overland struggle of the Klondike, no icy passes to cross and no frozen ground to thaw, just golden sands ready for sifting as soon as you stepped off the steamer. The pickings weren't especially rich, but three thousand prospectors arrived before winter ice halted the steamers, and many more arrived overland by any means possible, even cycling.

By 1900, the beach was overrun with tents, some 25 miles of them with their owners standing shoulder to shoulder extracting paydirt – over $2 million worth

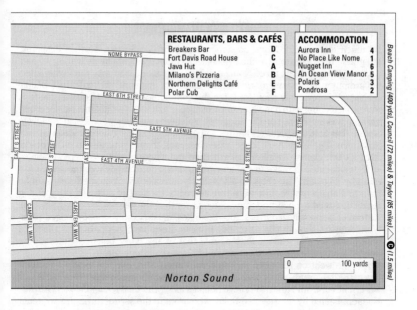

RESTAURANTS, BARS & CAFÉS

Breakers Bar	D
Fort Davis Road House	C
Java Hut	A
Milano's Pizzeria	B
Northern Delights Café	E
Polar Cub	F

ACCOMMODATION

Aurora Inn	4
No Place Like Nome	1
Nugget Inn	6
An Ocean View Manor	5
Polaris	3
Pondrosa	2

Beach Camping (400 yds), Council (72 miles) & Taylor (85 miles) ▷
● (1.5 miles)

NOME BYPASS

EAST 6TH STREET

EAST 5TH AVENUE

EAST 4TH AVENUE

EAST S STREET

EAST H STREET

EAST J STREET

EAST K STREET

EAST L STREET

EAST M STREET

EAST N STREET

CAMPBELL WAY

CARSTENS WAY

Norton Sound

0   100 yards

in total. As you'd imagine, claim jumping was rife, some of the best of the stories retold by Rex Beach in *The Spoilers* (see Contexts, p.505). The US census in 1900 recorded that one-third of all non-Natives in Alaska were in Nome – a total of 12,488 people, though estimates put the real figure closer to 20,000. So much for the thoughts of Hudson Stuck, though he returned fifteen years after the founding of Nome and his opinions hadn't changed. He wrote "Nothing in the world could have caused the building of a city where Nome is built except the thing that caused it: the finding of gold...It has no harbor or roadstead, no shelter or protection of any kind; it is in as bleak and as exposed a position as a man would find if he should set out to hunt the earth over for ineligible sites."

Nome had the typical gold-town plethora of churches, bars, and brothels (not necessarily in that order) plus a French lingerie store, and four piano removers, but by the end of 1900 the population was already beginning to decline. Still, it remained an important service town to mining communities around the Seward Peninsula and as the terminus for the **Iditarod Trail**, a winter route across the Alaskan Interior from Seward through the short-lived gold town of Iditarod. Life in Nome ticked by, beleaguered by storms and fires which destroyed the downtown area, until it hit the headlines again in 1925 with the diphtheria epidemic that nearly killed hundreds but for the heroic exploits of those who took part in the **serum run** (see box, overleaf).

Arrival, getting around, and information

To get to Nome you have to fly, and with the high cost of tickets many choose to come on one of the Anchorage-based **package tours** jointly run by Alaska Airline Vacations (late May to early Sept; ☎1-800/468-2248) and Northern

THE SERUM RUN

As much as for gold, Nome is remembered for the **Serum Run**, a desperate attempt in the 1920s to save the lives of sick Nome residents by delivering an anti-toxin. In January 1925, three Nome children were diagnosed with the highly infectious diphtheria, and memories of the influenza epidemic that killed 91 people seven years previously soon panicked the community. Immediate quarantine laws were enacted, but with a meager stock of ageing half-spent antitoxin a call for external help was tapped out on the telegraph. Adequate supplies were dispatched from Seattle, but that was over a month's sail away; fortunately a decent stock of antitoxin turned up in an Anchorage warehouse, and thoughts turned to using one of Alaska's two planes. Aviation was primitive and winter conditions were atrocious, so it was decided to make use of an existing mail route and deliver the serum 674 miles by dog sled. The glass phials (suitably insulated) were immediately sent by train to Nenana where they were transferred to the first of a special relay of dog teams designed to cover the route much faster than the normal thirty-day passage. Instead of being relieved every 100–125 miles, mushers were mostly staged twenty miles apart, though champion dog musher, **Leonhard Seppala**, was allotted a ninety-mile section – more than double that of any other musher. Naturally he needed his best team and rejected one of his weaker dogs, **Balto**.

As time went on the need for the serum intensified, but bad weather brought down the telegraph wires and made communication impossible. Several teams were sent out from Nome to relieve Seppala along the final leg and it was **Gunnar Kaasen**, hauled by the rejected Balto, who brought the serum through a whiteout into Nome just five days and seven and a half hours after it left Nenana. The phials were frozen but still useable, the epidemic was stemmed, and the nation rejoiced.

All the mushers involved were rewarded with cash payouts and presented with a medal by President Coolidge but, as the team that actually delivered the serum, it was Kaasen and Balto who were feted with the greatest praise. This rankled Seppala, especially when Kaasen and Balto were taken on national lecture tours and offered film roles, Kaasen was given $1000 by the manufacturers of the serum, and Balto even had his statue erected in New York's Central Park, where it remains today.

In recent years, Seppala's name has become the better known. Every year during the Iditarod – a race founded on the spirit of the Serum Run but following a quite different route – the Leonhard Seppala Humanitarian Award is awarded to the musher who exhibits the most concern for his animals.

Alaska Tour Company (see the "Exploring the North" box, p.434). The two-day trips ($496 based on double occupancy) visit both Nome and Kotzebue and spend the night in a hotel in the town of your choice, and there is a three-day variation ($547).

Flights with Alaska Airlines to Nome cost around $360 round-trip if bought 21 days in advance ($480, 7-day advance), though there are often Web specials for as little as $300, and it is worth considering an Anchorage–Kotzebue–Nome–Anchorage loop which will cost around $470 if booked two weeks in advance.

You'll arrive at the **airport**, a mile and a half west of town, from where you can walk, or call a **cab** (try Checker Cab ☎443-5211 or Nome Cab ☎443-3030), which will cost about $5. Once in town you can walk pretty much anywhere, though if you are planning to explore the road system you'll need to **rent a car** (see

"Listings," p.471). The airline tours (open to everyone) include a **guided town tour**: try Nome Discovery Tours (☎443-2814, *www.nome.net/~discover*), who do half-day tours ($45) visiting the town, an arctic gold mine, and the tundra; and full-day tours ($80) that see more of the road system.

The **visitor center**, 96 Front St (mid-May to mid-Sept daily 9am–9pm; mid-Sept to mid-May Mon–Fri 9am–6pm; ☎443-6624, fax 443-5832, *www.nomealaska.org*) has everything you need to know about Nome and its environs, plus a selection of videos on the region, and a stuffed musk ox. Anyone thinking of exploring the Bering Land Bridge National Preserve, or any of the national parks, preserves, and monuments around Kotzebue, should call in at the **National Park Information Center**, 179 Front St (mid-May to mid-Sept Mon–Fri 8am–6pm, Sat 1–6pm; mid-Sept to mid-May Mon–Fri 9am–5pm; ☎443-2522 or 1-800/471-2352, *www.nps.gov/bela*).

Accommodation

For what is essentially a frontier town, Nome has some pretty decent accommodation with new **hotels** opening every couple of years. Of course you pay for high standards, but there are modestly priced **B&Bs** and smaller hotels right in town and easily accessible. Unfortunately there's nowhere really cheap: those on a budget will have to **camp on the beach**, an accepted practice, around a mile east of the visitor center. It is free but the only facilities are a couple of outhouses: water can be obtained from a hose outside the visitor center and there are **public showers** ($4) at the recreation center (see "Listings," p.472).

The main busy season is from late May to mid-September, but if you are thinking of coming to see the end of the Iditarod, you'll want to plan your accommodation up to a year in advance. Places fill up fast and you definitely don't want to arrive with nothing arranged. The eight percent bed tax is included in our price codes.

An Ocean View Manor, Front St (☎443-2133, *mamaw@nome.net*). Attractive B&B right beside the Bering Sea with a lovely communal lounge built around a stone fireplace. Shared- and private-bath rooms. ④.

Aurora Inn and Suites, Front St (☎443-3838 or 1-800/354-4606, fax 443-6380, *aurora@nome .net*). Currently Nome's top-line hotel, opened in 1999 and featuring a sauna, and large rooms with kitchenettes, some with sea views. Executive suite ⑦, room with kitchenette ⑥, standard room ⑤.

No Place Like Nome, cnr Steadman St and 5th Ave (☎443-2451). About the cheapest B&B in town but pleasant and with five rooms. ④.

Nugget Inn, 2 Front St (☎443-4189 or 1-877/443-2323, fax 443-5966, *www.nome.net /~nuggetin*). Longstanding hotel, right by the Burl Arch (see overleaf), that's patronized by tour groups despite the fairly basic, poky rooms with small private bathroom. They do however come with phone and cable TV, some have sea views, and improvements are promised by the new owners. ⑤.

Polaris, 1st and Bering sts (☎443-2000, fax 443-2217). Fairly scruffy and sometimes noisy hotel that is only recommended for lone travelers not geared for camping. You can get a single room here for around $45, and they have separate "igloos" that are quite decent, though you may have to ask specifically. ④.

Ponderosa Inn, 291 Spokane St at 3rd (☎443-5737, fax 443-4149). Some of the nicest rooms in town, with fairly simple but tasteful decor, cable TV, and the option of a full kitchen. Suites ⑥, rooms ⑤.

The town

To get your bearings, follow the *Historical Walking Tour* brochure obtained free from the visitor center on Front Street. The tour starts outside by the finish line of the Iditarod, where the **Burl Arch** is constructed each year to mark the end of the final sprint down Front Street.

Following Front Street and keeping the huge boulders of Nome's protective sea wall on your right you pass the offices of the **Nome Nugget** (*www.nomenugget .com*), the town's newspaper which claims to be the oldest in the state, though the *Wrangell Sentinel* challenges the claim. It is always a good read and comes out each Thursday at a cost of 50¢ – the same as it was when it was founded in 1900 when the gold-rush economy inflated prices enormously. Diagonally opposite, below the library, sits the **Carrie M McLain Memorial Museum**, 200 Front St (June–Sept daily noon–8pm; Oct–May Tues–Sat noon–6pm; $1 donation appreciated; ☎443-6630), a small-town museum that packs in the history of the Serum Run, stacks of photos and artifacts from the gold rush, a large ivory collection and assorted changing exhibits.

Continuing in the same direction, you can **pan for gold** anywhere along the beach between the end of the sea wall and the *Fort Davis Roadhouse*. Rent a pan from Nome Outfitters, 235 1st Ave at Spokane Avenue (☎443-2880), and don't expect to get rich; this area has been well panned already though you'll probably get a few flakes. A measure of how little gold is left lies further on (about a mile from the visitor center) where the rusting **Swansberg Dredge** has lain idle beside the road since the 1950s.

Back in town, the distinctive focal point is the inappropriately tall spire of **St Josephs Church**, which thrusts upwards as if mocking the overoptimism of 1901, when there were perhaps twenty thousand souls to minister to. Blindingly white in the low subarctic sun it casts its shadow over **Anvil City Square**, a wide expanse of grass with one corner graced by statues of the **Three Lucky Swedes**, none looking especially delighted with their good fortune.

Eating and drinking

Eating in Nome is more a function than a pleasure, though as the largest town for hundreds of miles there is a reasonable choice of places to dine, at a price. Those on a tight budget may prefer to patronize the AC Value Center, about a mile north of downtown on Bering St, with its deli, bakery, *Burger King*, and **groceries**, all costing around forty percent more than in Anchorage.

The approach to **drinking** is equally pragmatic, with locals from Nome and the surrounding "dry" villages bringing the Front Street bars enthusiastic patronage.

Breakers Bar, Front Street (☎443-2531). Ever-popular drinker's bar that vies with the *Anchor Bar*, just down the street, for top conviviality honors.

Fort Davis Roadhouse, 2 miles east along Front St (☎443-2660). The closest thing in Nome to fine dining, but especially noted for its Friday and Saturday steak-and-seafood buffet. Expect to pay around $25 for entrees.

Gold Dust Saloon, in the *Nugget Inn*. Lively bar that's a little more sophisticated than the frontier-style places along the street.

Milano Pizzeria, 250 Front St (☎443-2924). Probably the better of the town's two pizzerias, though nothing special. Also pasta dishes and daily Japanese specials.

Northern Delights, Front St (no phone). New nonsmoking café successfully carving a niche for itself with its gourmet coffee and bagel sandwiches.

Polar Cub Restaurant, 225 Front St (☎443-5191). The best value of the downtown restaurants and with great sea views. It is good for all-day breakfast with four-egg omelettes ($8) and five-stack pancakes ($6), as well as burgers ($8) and dinners such as liver and onions ($9) or a plate of halibut, prawns, and potatoes ($18).

VFW Hall & Bar, Steadman Ave. Just $15 for a big steak and fries makes this the best weekend dinner deal in town, and the beer's cheap too in this veterans hall (just sign the book on the way in) with large windows.

Listings

Airlines Alaska Airlines (☎443-2288); Bering Air (☎443-5464); Cape Smythe Air Service (☎443-2414 or 1-800/478-5125, fax 443-2548).

Banks National Bank of Alaska, 250 Front St (Mon–Thurs 10am–5pm, Fri 10am–6pm) has an ATM in the foyer.

Books Arctic Trading Post, 67 Front St, has the town's best selection of books on the region, the Iditarod, and more.

Canoe rental Nome Outfitters, 235 1st Ave at Spokane (☎443-2880) rents canoes and gold pans.

Car rental Stampede Vehicle Rentals, Bering Straits Native Corporation Building, 157 Seppala Drive (☎443-3838 or 1-800/354-4606, fax 443-2980), rents two-wheel-drive pickups from $75 a day with unlimited mileage, and a slew of more expensive rigs, all with airport pickup and dropoff. Alaska Cab Garage (☎443-2939, fax 443-2739) also charge $75 for a two-wheel-drive truck, $85 for a 4x4 or suburban and $110 for large vans.

Festivals The Nome calendar abounds in festivals, kicking off with a bunch of events designed to coincide with the Iditarod Sled Dog Race around the second and third weeks in March, notably the Miners & Mushers Ball and the Bering Sea Ice Golf Classic (third Sat), a six-hole charity tournament with Astroturf greens, orange balls, huskies dressed up as caddies, arcane rules, and warming tots of vodka. In May you might fancy the Polar Bear Swim (Memorial Day, if the retreating sea ice permits) in 35ºF water with a certificate for full immersion. At summer solstice there's a Midnight Sun street festival which usually coincides with the Nome River Raft Race, using home-built rigs. And in September (Labor Day) there's a Bathtub Race along Front St with water, bubbles, and a bather, soap, and a bath mat in each tub.

Internet access see Library, below.

Laundry Currently no public laundry service, but someone is bound to open one soon; ask around.

Library The Kegoayah Kozga Library, 200 Front St (Mon–Thurs noon–8pm, Fri & Sat noon–6pm; ☎443-5133) has a free paperback swap and free **Internet access** booked by the half-hour.

Medical assistance Nome Medical Clinic, 3rd floor, Sitnasuak Building, 179 Front St (☎443-7767) is open office hours and for emergencies.

Post Office 320 E Front St. The **General Delivery** ZIP code is 99762.

Shopping Nome is a good place to buy Iñupia and Yup'ik crafts with a good range at fair prices, and the person selling may know (or be) the person who did the work. Local crafts can be bought at Sitnasuak Heritage Gallery, 179 Front St (☎443-2632), where whale vertebrae, walrus tusks, baleen, and the like have been imaginatively turned into fine pieces including especially beautiful spirit masks. Cheaper and generally lower-quality pieces can be found at the Arctic Trading Post (see Books above). Also visit Chukotka–Alaska Inc, 185 W 1st at D St (☎443-4128), a fabulous treasure trove of books, Russian watches, dolls, and T-shirts, and Lomonosov porcelain with superb local Eskimo crafts.

Showers Recreation Center, 425 6th Ave (Mon–Fri 6am–10pm, Sat closed, Sun 1–10pm; ☎443-5543), where your $4 entry fee gets you all-day use of racquetball courts, gym, weight room, sauna, and bowling alley.

Swimming In the sea if you dare, or at the high-school pool three miles northwest of town (☎443-5717).

Taxes Nome imposes a four percent sales tax plus a four percent bed tax.

Travel agency Arctic Travel, 50 Front St (☎443-7777 or 1-800/443-7776, fax 443-2277).

Around Nome

Though Nome is interesting itself, the real pleasure in visiting the Seward Peninsula is getting out on the three equally fascinating roads in the vicinity – all three hundred miles of them – which is something you can't really do from any of Alaska's other bush communities. Along the way you'll see stacks of mining castoffs, abandoned buildings from dozens of old mining claims, rusting hulks of earth movers, unidentified ironmongery, and ditches dug across the hills to divert essential sluicing water to the claims. It is even claimed that there are 44 dilapidated **gold dredges** visible from the road system, though it will take eagle eyes to spot them all. There is also plenty of wildlife viewing with musk oxen often close to the road, a good chance of seeing some of the 25,000 semi-nomadic **reindeer** that roam the Peninsula, bears, and rare birds blown over from Asia, including bristle-thighed curlew, bluethroat, and white and yellow wagtails.

Generally the **roads are open early to mid-June** depending on the thaw, and close once the snows arrive around the end of September. With the exception of a restaurant and a B&B in Teller and a couple of roadhouses, there are no services or gas stations anywhere outside Nome. Of course there is no public transport, so you'll need to either **bring your own bicycle** or **rent a car** from Nome (see "Listings," overleaf).

To explore beyond the road system, you'll have to take to the air, either into the **Bering Land Bridge National Preserve**, or across the Bering Strait to the **Russian Far East** and the garrison town of Provideniya.

The road to Council

At the turn of the twentieth century there were small gold towns all around Nome, but most died away as quickly as they formed. **COUNCIL**, 72 miles northeast of Nome, is one of the few survivors, ticking by with a few dozen summer residents, and just a handful of hardy year-rounders. It is reached along the imaginatively named **Nome–Council Road** (usually snow-free June–Sept), which heads east from Nome along the coastline littered with beach shacks where miners work the sands and fishers dry their catch on driftwood frames. This continues past the expansive viewpoint of **Cape Nome** at Mile 13, the prime **birding wetlands** of **Safety Sound** at Mile 20, and the nearby *Safety Roadhouse*, good for a refreshment stop. At Mile 30 the road turns inland four miles to the ghost town of **Solomon**, heralded by the roadside "**Last Train to Nowhere**," a rusting steam locomotive which originally pulled the elevated railway in New York; was brought here in 1903 but abandoned in 1907 with the collapse of the Council City and Solomon Railroad. Standing lonely on the open tundra it is a salutary reminder of just how sudden the boom could turn to bust. Beyond the scattered remains of Solomon's buildings the road continues to Council, unique in these parts for its stand of spruce trees: half of Nome comes out here before the road closes in the

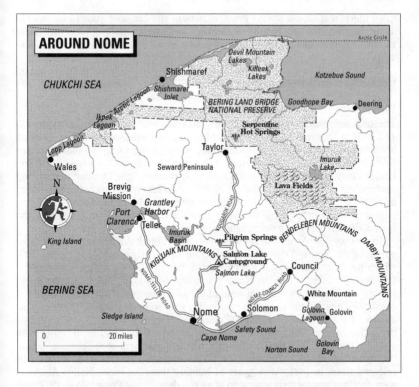

fall to snag their Christmas trees. Crossing the shallow river into Council – where there are no facilities for visitors – can usually be done in ordinary vehicles, though knowledge of the river bottom is needed; ask locally, or leave your vehicle and hitch across.

Kougarok Road to Taylor

The most extensive and scenic of the area's roads is the **Kougarok Road** (or Nome–Taylor Rd) to Taylor, a private mine some 85 miles to the north. Along the way, you'll view snowy mountain scenery, hot springs, and more of the detritus of mining life than you'll find anywhere else.

Following the Council Road out of Nome, turn left just past the Fort Davis Roadhouse and continue to *Dexter Roadhouse*, Mile 8.5, a bar rumored to have once been owned by **Wyatt Earp**, who also built the *Dexter Saloon*, downtown Nome's first two-story structure, and managed to get fined $50 for assaulting a policeman on Front Street.

There's no formal accommodation anywhere along the road, but there's wonderful free **camping** at the beautiful, lakeside *Salmon Lake*, Mile 40, with picnic tables, grills, and outhouses. At Mile 53, a side road branches seven rough and gravelly miles left to a small cluster of buildings amid the cottonwoods at the undeveloped **Pilgrim Hot Springs** (call Louie Green ☎443-5583 for permission to go there; it is almost always granted), where you can soak your cares away in an outdoor wooden tub. Nearby is a locked clapboard Catholic church with a tiny steeple, the principal legacy of an orphanage which operated here from 1919 to 1940.

The road ends at the Kougarok bridge, from where it is possible to set out on foot for Serpentine Hot Springs (see opposite), two to three days walk away.

Teller

The only substantial Native community accessible on the local road system is **TELLER**, a 150-strong Iñupia reindeer-herding and subsistence village 73 miles northwest of Nome. It is picturesquely set, strung along a thin spit that separates Norton Sound from Grantley Harbor, but there really isn't a whole lot there. Unlike many Native communities it is of fairly recent origin, founded as a trading center during the gold years around 1900. It was a barely viable community when, in 1926, bad weather forced Norwegian explorer **Roald Amundsen** to make an impromptu visit in his dirigible *Norge* after the first transpolar flight, a seventy-hour 3500-mile journey from Spitzbergen.

There may not be much to see once you arrive, but it is a lovely two-hour drive out along the **Nome–Teller Road** (generally open early or mid-May to mid-Oct), which heads out past Nome's high school, where there is a sign marking the "Discovery Claim," close to Nome's original 1898 gold find in Anvil Creek. Beyond the marker you contour around the hills a couple of miles back from the coast, then head inland to open high country with spiky mountains. There is a fair chance of seeing some of the 25,000 **reindeer**, a species brought here to replace the native caribou which died out towards the end of the nineteenth century. As a way of trying to help the local Iñupiat regain some form of self-determination, the Reverend Sheldon Jackson (see p.121) imported several from Russia and released them in 1891. After years of hunting them for meat, Native Alaskans were finally given formal ownership of all reindeer on the Peninsula in 1937, and since then have developed husbandry techniques to exploit the velvet for the Asian "medicinal" market.

Around Mile 35 you drop down again to the coastal strip then pass an old wooden dredge (Mile 54) artfully decaying on the far bank of the adjacent river, before the final run into Teller. To get beyond Teller you'll have to engage the services of **Grantley Harbor Tours** (☎642-3682 or 1-800/478-3682) who run guided tours ($99) including wildlife viewing, a sample of Eskimo culture, and a trip to the spot where Amundsen put down. For something a good deal more ambitious, contact Iditarod veteran **Joe Garney** (☎642-2139), identifiable by the raucous kennel outside his house, who will teach you to run sled dogs while sharing the modern Iñupiat lifestyle of his home. Ideally you'll want to devote ten days (at around $200 a day) so that you can learn the ropes for a few days in town before heading out to his cabin and sweatlodge sixty miles upriver, catching food for you and the dogs as you go. From mid-April to mid-May there's enough snow and 24-hour light, but you'll need to fly into Teller as the road won't be open.

For something to **eat** in Teller, head along to the two-story Teller Commercial Building, where you can also enquire about **lodging** at *Bloggett B&B* (☎642-3333, fax 642-3451; ⑤), with a common area, full kitchen, and comfortable if simple rooms with breakfast ingredients supplied.

Ever since the first Bering Air flights broke through the "ice curtain" in 1988 it has been possible to **visit Russia from Alaska**. The nearest town of any size is **Provideniya**, a military port that has gradually been wound down during the 1990s, though it is still considered a "closed" area and retains a Cold War mentality. Unless you've got some special reason to visit, there are plenty of equally (if not better) ways to spend your money and planning energy within Alaska, but if you are curious there are a couple of possibilities. The easiest way to go is to join one of the Nome-based trips run by Circumpolar Expeditions (☎272-9299 or 1-888/567-7165, fax 278-6092, *www.alaska.net/~wallack*) who, along with escorted tours to Kamchatka (6 days $1549; 9 days $2595), run a 3-day tour ($1149) to Provideniya and its environs, including Eskimo villages. Prices include travel, lodging, meals, and some entertainment, but not Russian visa ($150).

You can do things a good deal cheaper by buying a seat fare with Bering Air ($250 each way; ☎443-5464, *www.beringair.com*), but you'll need to reserve several weeks in advance, and will need to organize an invitation to visit Russia before applying for a visa. Bering Air can often help to organize the "invitation" and facilitate the issue of a visa, though there will be a charge. They may also be able to arrange accommodation, usually in furnished apartments.

Bering Land Bridge National Preserve

During the ice-bound Pleistocene era around 13,000 years ago, the sea level dropped so much that the 55 miles of sea between the Seward Peninsula and Russia was dry land and Asiatic peoples migrated into the unpeopled Americas. Evidence from Alaska's oldest known archeological site, the nine caves of Trail Creek (not open to the public), indicates that some of the first people to set foot on the North American continent strode across the low tundra that now forms the **Bering Land Bridge National Preserve** (*www.nps.gov/bela*), seventy miles northeast of Nome.

There are **no roads**, **no facilities** of any kind, and hardly any people in this gently rolling and largely treeless landscape, so you'll need to come fully prepared. Access is by float plane, easiest after mid-June when most of the larger lakes have thawed. The most obvious destination for **hikers** is the otherworldly **lava fields** in the southern quarter of the park, reached by flying into Imuruk Lake; currently the only charter flights are with Cape Smythe and Bering Air out of Kotzebue, though it is always worth asking around in Nome. There are no trails, so you can just make it up as you go along, though the staff at the visitor centers in Nome and Kotzebue will advise on possible itineraries.

Another possibility is a visit to **Serpentine Hot Springs**, a hundred miles north of Nome, and thirty miles beyond the end of the Kougarok Road. Here in the vast open country, water at 140–170ºF wells up inside a bathhouse which is maintained by the park service along with the adjacent bunkhouse-style **cabin** (first-come, first-served; free), which sleeps at least fifteen and has a wood stove for heating and a propane stove for cooking; bring a sleeping bag and food. You can walk here from the end of the Kougarok Road (2–3 days each way) following an old ridgeline track now illegally used by four-wheelers, ride a mountain bike if conditions are reasonably dry, or fly, though the rough airstrip puts many pilots off and prices are $500–700 for a planeload. Remember that there are bears up here and no trees for food storage, so you'll need to bring bear-resistant food canisters.

Kotzebue and around

The Iñupia Eskimo town of **KOTZEBUE** perches on the outer edge of the Baldwin Peninsula some six hundred miles northwest of Anchorage. It is just 26 miles north of the Arctic Circle, but for that reason alone it has become a fairly popular destination for tourists lured by 24 hours of daylight (from mid-May to the end of July), and some 37 days around the solstice when the sun never goes down at all.

Kotzebue is second only to Barrow as the world's largest Eskimo community and is a predominantly Iñupia town that exists on the cusp of mainstream Alaskan society. The comforts that people expect of town life are here, but there's also the tenor of a Native "village" that shares more in common with Barrow than it does with its (relatively) near neighbor Nome. Some eighty percent of the 3500 residents are Iñupia, and it is they who run the town, primarily through the Northwest Arctic

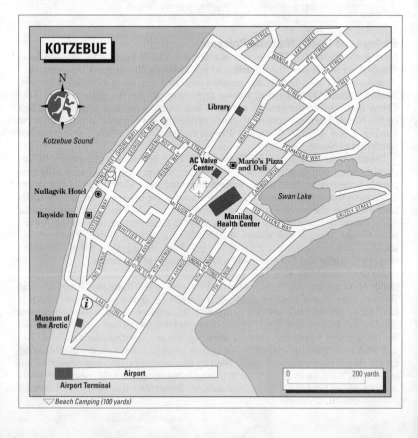

Native Association (NANA), the regional corporation which represents the town and ten villages spread over much of northwest Alaska. NANA, under the banner Tour Arctic, is also the public face of tourism here, operating package tours, the museum, and the main hotel. For this reason, **independent travelers** are poorly served: unless you are bound for the **wilderness rivers** to the northeast, or have friends here, you'll soon find yourself with little to do and the prospect of an expensive night in a hotel. Without a boat or a plane there is no way out of town, and even walking the streets you might find that people are not as interested in you as you may be in them. That said, NANA does a good job of presenting the local culture through the museum, and "culture camp," and if you are prepared to take your time, contact with locals can be very rewarding.

Though the seascape is attractive, Kotzebue isn't a pretty town, and gives the impression of being temporary. The streets are unpaved, telephone wires hang loosely, and the whole town can look like a graveyard for shipping containers with every second home having one as a storage shed. It can all seem very different, though, as you stroll along the beach in the golden light watching the **midnight sun** appear to roll along the tops of the hills across Kotzebue Sound.

For the record, Kotzebue was long known as Qikiqtagruk, but takes its current name from Russian navigator, Otto von Kotzebue, who charted the area while searching for the Northwest Passage in 1816.

The town

Visitors not taking the comprehensive local bus tour that comes as part of the Tour Arctic packages are left with little to do but wander the streets aiming for Shore Avenue (aka Front St), where much of the town's activity takes place, and where, during the ice-free months of mid-June to mid-September, you can see supply barges being unloaded. These tend to be laden with fuel oil and construction materials since everything else (including cars) comes in by plane.

The showcase for the region's Iñupia way of life, and a little of its history, is the **Museum of the Arctic**, corner of 2nd and 3rd avenues (mid-May to mid-Sept daily 10am–10pm), which does have some static displays – notably its room full of stuffed specimens of just about every Arctic animal – but focuses on its hour-long culture **demonstrations** (at 3pm & 6pm). These include a slide show, traditional dancing, storytelling, and a **blanket toss**, in which several people gather round a walrus-hide blanket and use it to toss one of their number into the air repeatedly, gaining height each time, supposedly once used as an aid to spotting a potential meal. The museum and demonstration are run by NANA who charge $25, but offer a joint $35 ticket which includes a visit to the adjacent **culture camp** (by itself $20). The aim of this forty-minute session is to show outdoor summer life as it is still practiced by the local Iñupia. Driftwood racks are set up for drying salmon, smoky fires are started to keep the bugs off, ropes are made from walrus skin, and sewing and tanning procedures are demonstrated using alder bark for dye, and seal skins to make waterproof pants.

Head along 3rd Avenue to the junction of Mission Street where a block is devoted to the town **cemetery**, complete with a few **spirit houses**. The large building nearby is the **Maniilaq Health Center**, an impressive new hospital with a lobby (Mon–Fri 9am–5pm) that is worth some attention for its excellent display of Native craftwork: a beautiful seal-gut parka, a soapstone and ivory Madonna, an ulu knife with a handle of mastodon ivory, an exquisite box made of Dall sheep horn and baleen, and much more.

Getting there and information

Like Nome, the only way to get to Kotzebue is to fly, and most people arrive on **packages** that are fairly inflexible but keep costs manageable. Reservations are handled by Alaska Airlines Vacations (☎1-800/468-2248) and Northern Alaska Tour Company (see box, p.434), who both run their tours jointly with NANA (*www.tour-arctic.com*). The cheapest trip is the Anchorage-based one-day tour ($366) which includes a village bus tour, a brief walk on the tundra, a visit to the museum and the culture camp. A choice of two-day trips ($496 based on double occupancy) combine Kotzebue with Nome, one spending the night at the *Nullagvik Hotel*, the other overnighting in Nome; and there's a three-dayer ($547) with nights in both towns. An extra night can be added (sleeping in Kotzebue; $350 extra) allowing a day to fly to the Eskimo village of Kiana to the north, then back along the Kobuk River, past the Great Kobuk Sand Dunes, and over the Selawik National Wildlife Refuge (see both opposite).

Alaska Airlines **flights** from Anchorage to Kotzebue cost around $360 round-trip if bought 21 days in advance, though Web specials sometimes drop as low as $300, and there's an Anchorage–Kotzebue–Nome–Anchorage loop which will cost around $470. Committed Arctic tourists could also get here directly from Barrow with Cape Smythe Air (☎442-3020); for details see box on p.434.

An alternative is to organize your travels though Arctic Circle Educational Adventures, 200 W 34th Ave, Suite 903, Anchorage, AK 99503 (☎276-0976, fax 274-3738, *www.fishcamp.org*) who, from mid-June to August, run *LaVonne's Fish Camp* (☎442-6013) on the coast about five miles from Kotzebue. It is a peaceful spot frequently visited by locals out hunting or gathering, and great for birding or just lazing around in the 24hr light. Accommodation is in cozy cabins, family-style meals are served, and rates (typically $250–350 a day) depend on what you do since all trips are customized.

The only source of tourist assistance in town is the **Public Lands Information Center**, 1542 2nd Ave (June–Aug daily 8am–6pm; Sept–May occasionally 3–5pm; ☎442-3760, fax 442-3816, *www.nps.gov/kova*) which manages Cape Krusenstern National Monument, Kobuk Valley National Park, and Noatak National Preserve but will help with local queries.

You'll probably walk wherever you want to go, but you can always call Polar Cab ☎442-2233.

Accommodation and eating

Accommodation is very limited, with most packages using the *Nullagvik Hotel*, 308 Shore Ave (☎442-3331, fax 442-3340; ⑥), which is comfortable enough though not great value for what you pay. Almost next door you'll find the marginally cheaper though inferior *Bayside Inn*, Shore Avenue (☎442-3600, fax 442-3604; ⑤). There is no campground and free **camping** isn't particularly encouraged, nor is it a very appealing option with the best spot being a narrow strip above the steeply shelving beach just south of the airport. If it is windy, tethering your tent can be a problem.

Eating options are as limited as accommodation and equally high priced. The *Nullagvik Hotel* has an **espresso bar** in its craft shop, and the *Niggivik Restaurant* (literally "a place to eat"; summer only) which has large picture windows overlooking the sea and serves good meals from a standard Alaskan menu. The *Bayside* also has a restaurant and you can eat in or take away at the spartan *Mario's Pizza & Deli*, 606 Bison St (442-2666), which also does burgers and Japanese and Chinese dishes. **Groceries** are available from the AC Value Center, there's free **Internet access** at the Chukchi **library** on 3rd Avenue (Mon–Fri noon–8pm, Sat noon–6pm), a National Bank of Alaska with ATM resides at the corner of 2nd Avenue and Lagoon Street, the **post office** is near the corner of Shore Avenue and Mission Street, and it is worth remembering that Kotzebue has a six percent **sales tax**, plus another six percent hotel tax, though these have both been included within our accommodation price codes. Kotzebue is a **damp community** with no alcohol sales, though you can bring a bottle or two with you.

Around Kotzebue

Kotzebue may be a fairly limited destination in itself, but it does offer relatively easy access to some of the finest wilderness in the Alaskan Arctic. Set aside $200 to see something of the **seabird oasis** of the Selawik National Wildlife Refuge, the Noatak National Preserve with its **superb rafting rivers**, and the massive **sand dunes** stranded over a hundred miles from the sea in the Kobuk Valley National Park. It is also possible to fly from here to the Bering Land Bridge National Preserve (see p.475); and for committed paddlers to go **sea kayaking** along the bird- and sea mammal-rich barrier islands of **Cape Krusenstern National Monument**.

The single most alluring sight around these parts is the **Great Kobuk Sand Dunes** in the southern reaches of the **Kobuk Valley National Park** – Alaska's smallest and one of the country's least-known national parks. Located over a hundred miles inland and fifty miles north of the Arctic Circle the dunes are an unlikely sight spread over 25 square miles and rising up to 250 feet above the surrounding boreal forest. Formed from glacier-ground sand, they are thought to be the remains of a once much larger dune-field created when ancient retreating glaciers left land free of stabilizing vegetation. The northernmost dunes lie only a mile or so from the Kobuk River the easiest access point, especially for rafters (see below).

If you are on one of the Tour Arctic packages you can fly over the dunes by adding a day ($350), which is partly spent in the village of Kiana. Those going it alone will probably not want to spend time in the villages – Kiana, Ambler, Kobuk, and others – which are tiny and fairly insular communities where you are going to feel very out of place unless you know someone there. Perhaps the best way to see the area is by going **flightseeing** on a scheduled flight, which may briefly stop at several villages. Bering Air (☎442-3187) and Cape Smythe Air (see box, p.434) both operate flights to Kivalina and over the Cape Krusenstern National Monument ($120 round-trip), and to Kobuk via Ambler and Shugnak (about $200 round-trip). People with a taste for adventure and time on their hands should seriously consider a float trip on one of the remote and scenic rivers in these parts.

Rafting the Noatak and Kobuk rivers

Some of Alaska's most satisfying **float trips** run through the Noatak National Preserve and the Kobuk Valley National Park. None are short and all require considerable logistical commitment, though you could always join one of the very few commercial trips; try Nichols Expeditions, 497 N Main St, Moab, Utah 84532 (☎1-800/648-8488, fax 435/259-2312, *www.nicholsexpeditions.com*) who run just one nine-day Fairbanks-based trip each summer for around $2500. Canoes, rafts, and folding kayaks are all acceptable means of transport on the rivers: either bring your own or get the latest on rentals in Kotzebue through the Public Lands Information Center. Note that the flight prices below is the passenger fare; rafts, canoes, and gear will put you well over your personal luggage limit and it may work out cheaper to negotiate a charter flight. In all cases you'll need to be entirely self-sufficient on the river. There are no facilities except in the villages and you are unlikely to see many people, except during the fall hunting season when hunters drive noisy boats upstream to access prime caribou areas.

Access to the dunes is from the lower section of the **Kobuk River** (navigable June to late Sept; Class I) from Ambler to Kiana, a run of 85 miles usually taking 5–6 days. Flights into Ambler and out of Kiana with Bering Air cost a total of $200. To extend the trip by three or four days, start by flying into Kobuk, 45 miles higher upstream. The truly committed can run the whole 260 navigable miles from Walker Lake, in the Gates of the Arctic National Preserve (and accessed from Bettles) down to Kiana in 15–20 days, though there are a few short upper sections where you'll need to portage or line your boats. The **Salmon River**, a tributary of the Kobuk with its confluence downstream of the dunes, is another popular float.

Like the Kobuk, there are several ways to approach the **Noatak River** (navigable June–Sept; Class I–II) with plenty of landing spots for float planes allowing you to do as much or as little as you please. Again Bettles is a good starting point for flying into the headwaters from where you could take 16–18 days to float down to Noatak, and another couple of days to the mouth, which is just 15 miles across Kotzebue Sound from Kotzebue. Kayaks and canoes (but not rafts which are too susceptible to high winds) could then pick a calm morning and paddle across to Kotzebue. For more details on these and other rivers, consult Karen Jettmar's *The Alaska River Guide* (see "Books," p.507).

Barrow

Many people visit **BARROW**, 500 miles north of Fairbanks, simply because it is the northernmost settlement on the American continent, and just eleven miles from Point Barrow, the very tip of the United States. Though 330 miles north of the Arctic Circle, there is still eight hundred miles of ocean to the North Pole and for ten months of the year it is ice all the way. This far north the sun doesn't rise for two months in the middle of winter, but after the middle of May the sun doesn't set until the end of July – midnight sun for 82 days – and the ice gradually breaks up and melts away just over the horizon.

But the appeal isn't just geographic. This is the largest Eskimo community in Alaska with almost all the four thousand residents claiming Iñupia heritage – you'll hear Iñupiaq spoken as much as English. It is also the administrative capital of **North Slope Borough**, a vast region of Arctic Alaska with another 4500 people distributed through eight widely-scattered villages. It also encompasses the North Slope oil fields and the royalties from oil sales make this the richest Native region, and yet Barrow can look depressingly utilitarian, little more than a shanty town. They've got warm homes, well-stocked supermarkets, and a frequent jet service to Fairbanks and Anchorage, and yet no amount of money can combat the isolation, fierce weather, permafrost, and the ever-present threat of polar bears on the prowl.

BARROW

ARCTIC OCEAN

BROWERVILLE

RESTAURANTS
Arctic Pizza	D
Brower Café	A
Ken's Restaurant	E
Pepe's	B
Sam & Lee's	C

ACCOMMODATION
Airport Inn	2
King Eider Inn	3
Top of the World Hotel	1

Point Barrow (12 miles)

Whalebone Arch

Supermarket

Iñupiat Heritage Center

Library

Tasigarook Lagoon

CHUKCHI SEA

Isatkoak Lagoon

N

Bank

Mound Sites

Bus Transfer Station

Will Rogers Monument

Cape Smythe Air

Airport

Terminal Buildings

Arctic Grocery

0   400 yards

Freshwater Lake (1 mile) & Wiley Post Crash Site (16 miles)

Despite the wealth and modernity, **whaling** fundamentally defines the community, and whatever you may think about whaling elsewhere it is hard not to begrudge a people going about their life much as they have for thousands of years. During the spring or fall whale hunt, it is hard not to be swept along by the buzz that goes around town when word comes in from the ice of a successful kill. There are no factory whaling ships here, just small skin boats and men with hand-held harpoons twenty or thirty miles out across the ice trying to spear a thirty-foot bowhead as it passes along one of the narrow "leads" (breaks in the sea ice): northbound in spring, southbound in the fall. Successful kills – and by no means are all hunts successful – are then hauled onto the ice by up to fifty people applying themselves to one end of a pulley system. Each village gets an annual quota based on the known population – Barrow is usually allotted about a dozen – but each strike is counted whether the whale is killed or not, so a poor season can be over pretty quickly.

Barrow is only slowly gearing itself towards tourism and much of the people's daily life that makes the town special will be inaccessible to the casual visitor. A partial solution is to join one of the hotel-and-cultural-package **tours**, though this is still a somewhat mainstream experience. Fly here independently and your moves are limited and fairly expensive, though there is an excellent museum, tours to Point Barrow with the hope of seeing polar bears, and plenty of good **birding** on the surrounding tundra.

The **timing** of your visit is all important. In May, when the rest of the state is gearing up for summer, Barrow is still in the grip of winter: the sea ice doesn't usually break up and melt away until mid-July. May and early June is the spring whaling season and it is white to the northern horizon. Mid- to late June heralds the end of whaling and **Nalukataq**, a celebration of a successful hunt including a genuine blanket toss. Through May, June, and July birders flock to Barrow too for easy spotting on the treeless tundra where birds nest on tufted mounds: eiders, snowy owls, jaegers, swans, and arctic terns are some of the feathery attractions. Winter begins to set in by the end of September, ice starts to form at the shore and spreads out to create an ice pack about ten feet thick. For most people winter is off-limits, though the fall whale hunt makes October a good time to visit if you want to see polar bears.

Arrival, getting around, and information

Most visitors arrive in Barrow on **package tours** jointly run by Tundra Tours, Northern Alaska Tour Company (see box, p.434) and Alaska Airlines Vacations (mid-May to mid-Sept daily; ☎1-800/468-2248, *www.alaskaair.com*). These are hardly cheap but almost always work out to be the lowest-cost option, and include a town tour plus a "culture program" at the museum with storytelling, dances, and a blanket toss. Their two-day tour ($440) gives you two full days in town, a night at the *Top of the World Hotel*, and the town tour; the one-day tour ($395) gives you most of a day in Barrow and also includes the tour. These are all ex Fairbanks, but you can add one or more Anchorage legs for $85 each; a saving if you need to get back to Anchorage. There's also a Fairbanks-based winter variation (overnight $554, one-day $497) with a tour to Point Barrow.

For more flexibility, take one of several **flights** a day with Alaska Airlines which cost upwards of $366 round-trip from Fairbanks, and at least $425 from Anchorage.

Getting around is easy. The airport borders the south side of town and you can walk anywhere you need to go in about ten or fifteen minutes. If you've got heavy bags, then pick up one of the Yellow Line **buses** (7am–10pm; $1 exact fare) which run every twenty minutes around the center from the transfer station on Ahkovak Street, a hundred yards to the left when you step out of the airport terminal. There's also a Red Line which runs to **Browerville**, Barrow's eastern suburb about a mile away across Isatkoak Lagoon (aka Middle Lagoon), and the Blue Line that runs four miles out towards Point Barrow ($2). Alternatively engage the services of one of the half-dozen **taxi** companies which all charge $5 anywhere within Barrow and Browerville: Barrow Taxi (☎852-2222) is as good as any. There are very few roads around here, but **rental cars** are available from UIC Construction Vehicle Rental (☎852-2700) just opposite the bus transfer station on Ahkovak Street for around $85 a day.

Pick up the handy *Visitor's Guide* from the major hotels and from the Iñupiat Heritage Center. There's free Internet access (though email is discouraged) at the Tuzzy Consortium Library (Mon–Thurs noon–9pm, Fri & Sat noon–5pm), right by the Iñupiat Heritage Center at the corner of Ahkovak Street and C Avenue. **Banking** needs are satisfied by the National Bank of Alaska, 1780 Kiogak St (Mon–Thurs 10am–5pm, Fri 10am–6pm), and while there is an ATM, it can only be used during banking hours.

Accommodation

The town's biggest **hotel**, and the one where all the package tours stay is the *Top of the World*, 1200 Agvik St (☎852-3900 or 1-800/882-8478, fax 852-6752, *www .topoftheworldhotel.com*; ⑦), which has newish deluxe, and noticeably ageing standard rooms (at opposite ends of the price code) with all the expected amenities. Cheaper and very pleasant rooms can be found at the *Barrow Airport Inn*, 1815 Momegana St (☎852-2525, fax 852-2528; ⑤), which mainly caters to people up here on business and has some rooms with kitchenettes as well as cable TV and continental breakfast with fresh-baked bread. Barrow's newest hotel, the *King Eider Inn*, by the airport at 1752 Ahkovak St (☎852-4700 or 1-888/303-4337, fax 852-2025, *www.kingeider.net*; ⑦), has the nicest rooms in town (some with kitchenettes), a guest sauna, and free coffee and muffins.

There is **no budget accommodation** in Barrow and beach **camping** is discouraged, not least because, for much of the year, there are polar bears about. They seldom come into town, and when the sea ice has melted there are unlikely to be any around, but you can never be sure.

The town

Barrow's airport goes by the grandiose title of the **Wiley Post/Will Rogers Memorial Airport**, in honor of pioneer aviator Wiley Post and entertainer, homespun philosopher, and all-round spokesman for rural America Will Rogers who, in 1935, died when their plane went down sixteen miles south of Barrow while they were searching for a new air route to Siberia. A concrete **monument** stands at the corner of Ahkovak and Momegana streets just across from the terminal building.

Continue west along Ahkovak Street towards the sea and, overlooking the beach, you'll find a series of low **mounds**, that are nothing much to look at but represent an important archeological site with the remains of sod houses. Follow the beach to the northeast through what constitutes the center of town, and you'll eventually come to Barrow's original **whaling station**, now a restaurant, and beside it a **whalebone arch** that seems to feature on most postcards of Barrow.

To learn something of European and Eskimo whaling hereabouts visit the new **Iñupiat Heritage Center**, 5421 North Star St (Mon–Fri 8.30am–5pm; $5), a modern and well laid-out museum which provides a wonderful evocation of the Iñupia spirit, celebrating traditional and modern life in the eight villages of North Slope Borough. Here you are greeted by a couple of skin kayaks suspended from the rafters – one 1912 model is long and thin for ocean travel, the other (from 1920) wider and more stable for river crossings. There's excellent material on the early arctic environment of Beringia, the ice-age land bridge that provided passage for proto-Eskimos from east Asia. Best of all though is the material on subsistence living, particularly the annual bowhead hunts with some superb photos of whale recovery and chopping up the muktuk. Artifacts haven't been neglected, and there's a beautiful toboggan made from whale baleen, exquisite gut parkas and the ivory needles used to sew them, and animism and religion nicely juxtaposed with spirit masks presented next to angels carved from ivory.

Activities and tours

The perfect complement to any trip to Barrow is the **Polar Bear Swim**, not a single event, but a summer-long chance (roughly mid-July and after mid-Sept) to experience full Arctic submersion and receive membership of the Polar Bear Club

($10), a certificate, a patch, and the opportunity to buy a members-only T-shirt. See Fran Tate or any of the staff at *Pepe's*.

Alternatively, **hike** out of town across the tundra, but go prepared to combat cold, wind, hunger, and mosquitoes, and ask locally about recent polar bear movements. Leaving word of your plans with your hotel before making for destinations such as Point Barrow (see below); Barrow's water supply known as Freshwater Lake, a mile south of town, and the site where Wiley Post and Will Rogers crashed sixteen miles southwest of town. This last hike passes "Hollywood" the site of the filming of the early 1970s Disney movie *Track of the Giant Snow Bear*.

Out of town the prime destination is **Point Barrow**, eleven miles to the northeast and beyond the end of the road. To get there you really need to go on foot or on a tour. For some the attraction is just being at the **northernmost point in the US**, but when the sea ice is in, especially after a successful whale hunt when the waste is dumped there, this becomes prime **polar bear** territory.

This wouldn't be a good time to walk, but John Tidwell of Alaskan Arctic Adventures (☎852-3800) leads customized tours out here, and elsewhere, in a caterpillar-tracked van or off-road vehicle with the emphasis on viewing wildlife; perhaps arctic foxes, whales, seals, walruses, and loads of birds. The two-hour

---

DRY ALASKA

Most Native authorities recognize that excessive alcohol consumption is a major problem among their people, not just for its antisocial effects but as a serious health risk. Some estimate that approaching fifty percent of adult Natives have some form of alcohol problem, a state of affairs undoubtedly exacerbated by the erosion of traditional values.

After the American purchase in 1867, the sale of alcohol to Natives – who already had a reputation for drunkenness – was banned, a selective prohibition which continued until 1953 when federal laws overruled such discrimination. Drunkenness again became rampant, and in 1980 village councils were given the power to restrict sales within their own communities in an effort to contain the destructive behavior. Many communities decided that the route to redemption was through outlawing alcohol in the village altogether and they became **dry**. Others chose to manage sales through stores owned or controlled in some way by the community, but remained **wet**. Some felt that problems could be dealt with more openly if they were **damp**, with drink sales proscribed, but importation of supplies allowed. Barrow and other villages chose to be **soggy**, periodically voting on their status. Whatever the moral benefits, dry towns appear to have lower instances of assault, homicide, and suicide.

Of course, any form of prohibition is of only minimal use. Alcohol does get in (or is made), and obtaining supplies can become more of an obsession than drinking the stuff ever was. Bootleggers can make huge profits on bottles of whisky which can change hands for ten times the retail price. There is also an effect on "wet" airline hub communities, particularly Fairbanks, which sell huge quantities of alcohol to those on a binge during infrequent town visits. The sight of the terminally drunk around the downtown bar quarter is a sad one and it can only be hoped that as Native communities regain their self-respect and revive the culture which supports it, the drive for binge drinking will subside and the necessity of managing alcohol availability will cease to exist.

tour (Mon–Sat only) costs $130 for two people; get more together and costs go down.

From September to June, John's son, John, runs Arctic Mushing Tours ($85 for one, $150 for two; ☎852-6874) where you get a full two hours learning to run a **dog sled** and can even head off across the tundra viewing wildlife.

Eating and not drinking

Those on a tight budget should head for the AC Value Center, corner of Ahkovak Street and C Avenue in Browerville (daily 9am–10pm), the retail heart of Barrow with everything from snow machines, furniture, and clothing down to expensive **groceries** and even fresh flowers flown in daily from Anchorage. There's a **food court** too with a deli, pizzas, Mexican, subs, and cinnamon rolls. Groceries are also available more centrally from Arctic Grocery, corner of Pisokak and Apayauk streets in Barrow.

There's a pretty decent selection of restaurants, all as pricey as you'd expect for such a remote location, and all serving burgers, sandwiches, and breakfasts as well as their specialty. *Pepe's North of the Border*, 1204 Agvik St (☎852-8200), serves genuine Mexican dishes under a ceiling strung with piñatas, with tacos starting from $3, a burrito plate for $17, Ortega burgers for $10, and steaks from $25 to $30. The best pizza is at *Arctic Pizza*, 125 Apayauq St (☎852-4222) which also has a huge range of salads, Mexican dishes, pasta dishes, even Jambalaya, all served in an upstairs dining room with good sea views. *Sam & Lee's*, 1052 Kiogak St (☎852-5555), is good for Chinese, as is *Ken's Restaurant* on Ahkovak St (☎852-8888) which also has the best-value breakfasts in town ($8–12). If you find yourself over in Browerville, pop into *Brower Café* on Stevenson Street (☎852-3663) in what was the original whaling station.

Barrow is currently a damp community (see box, opposite), so there are **no alcohol** sales, but you can bring in a liter of spirits, a gallon of beer, or two liters of wine without a permit.

travel details

As the only large town covered by this chapter, **Fairbanks** is understandably the hub of all transportation networks. Its only **train** line has daily service in summer (roughly mid-May to mid-Sept) running south to Denali National Park and Anchorage; **buses** (again only mid-May to mid-Sept) run mostly parallel to the train line to Denali and Anchorage but also run east towards the Canadian border, and southeast to Valdez; and **planes** fan out to just about every tiny bush community imaginable, the most important of which we've listed below.

TRAINS

Fairbanks to: Anchorage (daily; 12hr); Denali National Park (daily; 3hr 45min); Talkeetna (daily; 8hr 30min).

BUSES

Fairbanks to: Anchorage (2 daily; 9–10hr); Beaver Creek, Yukon (4 weekly; 12hr); Dawson City (3 weekly; 10hr); Delta Junction (1–3 daily; 2hr); Denali/Glitter Gulch (2 daily; 3–4hr); Glenallen (3 weekly; 4hr 30min); Nenana (2 daily; 2hr); North Pole (8 daily, not Sun; 40min); Talkeetna Junction (2 daily; 7–9hr); Tok (1–3 daily; 5hr); Valdez (3 weekly; 7–8hr); Whitehorse, Yukon (3 weekly; 14hr).

FLIGHTS

Barrow to: Anchorage (2–3 daily; 3hr); Fairbanks (2 daily; 1hr 20min).

Bettles to: Fairbanks (2–3 daily; 1hr 20min).

Fairbanks to: Anaktuvuk Pass (1–4 daily; 1hr 30min); Anchorage (10–12 daily; 1hr); Arctic Village (1–3 daily; 1hr 30min); Barrow (2 daily; 1hr 20min); Bettles (2–3 daily; 1hr 20min); Prudhoe Bay/Deadhorse (1 daily; 1hr); Seattle (6–9 daily; 3hr 30min–5hr).

Kotzebue to: Anchorage (2–3 daily; 1hr 30min); Nome (2 daily; 45min).

Nome to: Anchorage (2–3 daily; 1hr 30min–3hr).

Prudhoe Bay/Deadhorse to: Anchorage (1 daily; 1hr 40min); Barrow (2 daily; 1hr 30min); Fairbanks (1 daily; 1hr).

A BRIEF HISTORY

Alaska's recorded history is both brief and frenetic; a tale of repeated exploitation to the point of exhaustion followed by stagnation until the next big boom. But there is a parallel Alaska populated by four main groups of Native people with a much longer oral history.

THE FIRST PEOPLE

Alaska has been inhabited longer than anywhere else in the Americas. The recent discovery of skeletons exhibiting Caucasoid features points to early colonization of the "New World" from Europe, perhaps over a frozen North Atlantic. This conjecture is highly controversial, but it is much more certain that Asiatic people arrived sometime after 15,000 years ago. One commentator on early Native American migrations describes the body of archeological evidence as "a confusing morass of conflicting data and opinions," but it is known that during the most recent ice age, from 25,000 to 12,000 years ago, the sea level dropped enough to occasionally reveal the arctic continent of **Beringia** under what is now the northern half of the Bering Sea and the southern limit of the Chukchi Sea. This "**land bridge**" was in fact a flat, dry, intensely cold, windy, and generally inhospitable steppe-tundra several hundred miles wide. It existed for a geological blink of the eye, but long enough for many generations of proto-Aleuts and Eskimos to make it their home as they followed herds of large herbivores such as bison and mammoths eastward. The romantic image of noble hunters crossing the land bridge and following deer through a sylvan corridor overhung with vast glaciers is almost certainly just that. The oldest confirmed archeological site discovered so far – at Healy Lake near Fairbanks – dates back only around 11,000 years, so it seems that Eastern Beringia (modern-day Alaska) probably wasn't populated until the land began to flood at the end of the last ice age forcing the people to higher levels. For millennia, that is where they stayed, their passage south to more temperate lands blocked by the great North American ice sheets.Some contend that there was just one major migration from which all Native Americans are descended, but linguistic and cultural evidence points to at least two separate and distinct groups arriving a significant period apart. From the earliest migration developed the forest-hunting culture that spreads throughout the Americas and gave us the Na-Dene language group which includes the **Tlingit** of the Alaskan Southeast, the **Athapascans** of the Alaskan Interior, and their close kin the Navajo and Apache of the American Southwest. A later migration – but still before the flooding of the land bridge – brought the Aleut-Eskimo groups, genetically the most Asiatic of all Native Americans, who pursued a culture based on sea mammals across the Arctic to Greenland. From this second migration evolved the **Aleuts** and Alaska's two main Eskimo groups the **Yup'ik** and **Iñupiaq**. These groups occupied geographically and climatically distinct regions forcing them to develop their own ways of shaping the land to their needs.

EUROPEAN EXPLORATION AND OCCUPATION – 1640 TO 1867

For the best part of 12,000 years, Native Alaskans forged their own destiny without interference from outside, though the Yearbooks of the Sung dynasty record that, in 458 AD, five Buddhist monks led by **Hwui Shan** sailed up the coast of the Kamchatka Peninsula, then east through the Aleutian Islands to mainland Alaska.

Significant impact on their affairs didn't come until late in the European "Age of Discovery," the high latitudes and short summers deterring all but the hardiest of explorers.

Spaniard **Bartholeme de Fonte** made the first claim of discovery having battled his way up from Spanish Mexico into the waters of the Inside Passage in 1640. He reported nothing of interest and almost a century passed before Russian Czar Peter the Great sent a party led by Danish explorer **Vitus Bering** to search for whatever lay to the east. On his first trip in 1728 he confirmed the suspicion that Siberia and the Americas were separate, and gave his name to the sea which divides the two landmasses, but fog prevented him spotting North America. It wasn't until his third journey, in 1741, that he finally set foot on the Alaskan mainland near what is now Cordova. Bering died of scurvy soon after, but his lieutenant, Alexis Chirikof, continued, making it as far as Sitka before returning to Russia with news of huge quantities of **sea otters**, their pelts then highly prized for fur hats. Over the next sixty years the Aleutian Islands were alive with Russian *promyshleniki* (traders and hunters) who found that the Aleuts were far more efficient at killing otters than themselves. They enslaved the Aleuts, forcing them to slaughter the otters to the brink of extinction. A revolt in 1743 was put down with similar ferocity and the Aleuts resigned themselves to economic domination by the *promyshleniki* and cultural suffocation at the hands of the Russian Orthodox missionaries. Over the years they adopted the faith wholeheartedly and the Aleutian Chain remains an Orthodox stronghold, but they paid with their culture, their stories, and their way of life. It is only in the last few decades that the Aleuts have begun to revive their traditions.

Soon the British, Spanish, and Americans were all after this sea-otter bounty, the Spanish (a waning but still major sea power) sending expeditions up the coast from their Mexican base at San Blas. But apart from adding a few Spanish names to the sea charts around Prince of Wales Island and carting off a few boatloads of furs they failed to consolidate their claim to hegemony over the entire west coast of the Americas.

While the carnage continued, further exploration was driven by the search for the **Northwest Passage**, a long-sought trade route from the North Pacific into the North Atlantic. In 1778, **James Cook** sailed north from Vancouver Island charting and naming features all the way to Turnagain Arm in Cook Inlet,

near present-day Anchorage. He then continued west along the Aleutian Chain and up the coast to Icy Cape in the Arctic Ocean, 250 miles north of the Arctic Circle, where the pack ice drove him back. Cooks' lieutenant, George Vancouver, returned in the 1790s claiming the coast for Britain and, with meticulous precision, mapping the Inside Passage leaving behind charts which were still in use at the turn of the twentieth century.

Despite Bering's earlier forays into Alaskan waters, it wasn't until 1784 that **Grigorii Shelikov** established the first non-Native settlement in Alaska at Three Saints Bay on Kodiak Island, and eight years later Catherine II granted him a monopoly on furs in Alaska as head of the **Russian-American Company**. In stepped the company's manager **Alexander Baranov**, the self-styled "Lord of Alaska," to oversee the expansion of Russian interests. He moved the original Russian settlement up the coast to Kodiak in 1790 and within a decade his political guile and uncompromising business acumen extended Russian influence throughout southern Alaska; even as far as Fort Ross in northern California. As seal and otter populations plummeted he moved his operations to Southeast Alaska, establishing a fort in 1799. Three years later it was destroyed by aggrieved Tlingits armed by the British and Americans, but he returned in 1804, backed by a Russian Navy warship, and re-established the Russian presence on the site naming it New Archangel, later **Sitka**. Through savvy trading and pragmatic treaties with the Spanish, British, and Americans they were able to develop a considerable mini-empire, and fashioned Sitka as "an American Paris."

Russian influence spread quickly, even to areas where no Russians were seen. **Tlingit** traders adapted their existing trade patterns to obtain pelts from communities far from any foreign outpost; the *promyshleniki* then stayed in Alaska just long enough to load up the pelts and refresh their supplies. The more entrepreneurial Tlingit families turned good profits and raised the stakes at traditional **potlatches** (see p.509) holding them more frequently and giving away goods with impunity.

From the 1820s to the 1850s the sea otter and fur trade declined dramatically and Russian energies were diverted to their troubles at home. This was still a largely unexplored land, only given some shape on world maps after an 1824 treaty between Russia, Britain, and the United States defined the boundaries of Alaska more or less along the current international frontier. It had become such a drain on resources that the Russian Navy had to take control of the declining Russian-American Company. Mining engineer P.P. Doroshin subsequently uncovered a few flakes of gold in the Kenai River Valley, but this wasn't enough to revive interest especially since Russia was now dogged by poor relations with Britain in the aftermath of the Crimean War of the 1850s. Meanwhile, expansionary pressure from Britain through their Canadian territories, and from the United States through the newly-opened Pacific Northwest, made it increasingly obvious that Russia was liable to lose its Alaskan territory. They started looking around for a buyer.

SEWARD'S FOLLY – AMERICAN ALASKA FROM 1867 TO 1896

Russia had first tried to interest the United States in Alaska as early as 1859, but Congress' reluctance and the intervention of the American Civil War left the matter unresolved. Meanwhile, Russia's hold on its territory was being eroded by its own inability to finance armed forces so far from home, and by the British Hudson's Bay Company, which had established trading posts in the Alaskan Interior. The Americans saw an opportunity, and on March 30, 1867, Andrew Johnson's Secretary of State, **William Seward**, signed the **Treaty of Purchase** in Washington DC. On October 18, at a ceremony in the Russian Alaskan capital of Sitka, the Russian government formally signed over Alaska for a sum of $7.2 million, a paltry 2¢ an acre. Of course the Russians didn't actually own the Alaska they were selling: no treaties had been entered into with the Natives, and none would be until ANCSA in 1971.

The Russian withdrawal was complete. After 120 years of contact they left Alaska virtually unchanged except for a decimated sea-mammal population, a smattering of triple-bar crosses, a few picturesque Russian Orthodox churches and the Aleut race almost wholly converted to the faith. The purchase price was undoubtedly low, but many Americans felt it was a waste of money and dubbed America's new land **"Seward's Folly"** or "Seward's Icebox." After all, the territory was largely uncharted, fur seals

were all but wiped out, there was only the vaguest hint of the territory's gold wealth, and oil would have been considered of little value even if its presence had been known. The Federal Government now owned one of its territories outright, a unique state of affairs that has informed much of what has happened since. Alaskans might like to think they are masters of their own domain but every significant stage of Alaskan development has been done with the approval of the Federal Government.

That is not to say that the Feds had immediate control over Alaska. Initially there was very little to control; the Natives managed their own affairs, and no one else had much reason to go there. The United States took almost no notice of its new possession, keeping a lose rein and allowing the frontier ethic to prevail. Before they left, the Russians had managed to stabilize the fur-seal population on the Pribilof Islands in the Bering Sea, but in 1870 the American Commercial Company was given the monopoly in the region and resumed the slaughter. The company soon controlled much of Alaska's meager trade, and still operates in bush Alaska today.

Meanwhile, naturalist **John Muir** visited the Southeast in 1879 and 1880 fired with enthusiasm for Alaska's glaciers, whose role in shaping the mountain landscape had only recently been unraveled. His *Travels in Alaska* catalogs his mainly fair dealings with the Natives but he was less complimentary about the role of the American missionaries he often traveled with. By 1885 one of these missionaries, **Sheldon Jackson**, had whipped up the proselytizing zeal of as many denominations as possible and they had agreed to divide up Alaska into a number of ecclesiastical monopolies (see p.121). Each denomination got some easily accessible spots and some remote tracts and committed themselves to converting the Natives without treading on each other's patch.

The US Army was responsibile for keeping the peace in Alaska and, fearing an Indian uprising, felt compelled to map as much of the territory as it could. Three **exploratory expeditions** were sent between 1883 and 1885: one up the Yukon River, one up the Copper River, and a third overland from the Copper River across the mountains to the Tanana River. The largely peaceful nature of the Indians they encountered allayed the government's fears and did little to encourage further investigation. Meanwhile, in 1884, the Federal Government passed the **Organic Act** effectively providing local government for Alaska. Until this was extended in 1900, Alaska made do with just a judge, an attorney, and a marshal, all stationed in Sitka and with virtually no influence anywhere else. It wasn't a favored posting and those that ended up there were often incompetent if not wantonly unjust and self-serving. Alaska languished until the discovery of gold.

AN ALASKAN ELDORADO

Alaska traces its modern development only as far back as the gold rushes that swept across the northwest of the continent mostly from 1880 to the early 1900s. They completely transformed the physical and social makeup, driving Alaska from neglected territory towards eventual statehood.

The first big Alaskan rush came in 1880 when **Joe Juneau** and **Richard Harris** discovered gold on the site of present-day Juneau. Hundreds flocked here and the town grew rapidly, taking over from Sitka as the capital of Alaska in 1900. Meanwhile, intrepid Interior prospectors had uncovered gold in the **Fortymile** around Eagle, and together these sparked widespread interest in Alaska and the North. But everything up until now had just been a curtain-raiser for the big show that was about to unfold in the Canadian Yukon. In 1896, "Skookum" Jim Mason, "Dawson" Charlie and George Washington Carmack found gold on a tributary of the **Klondike** River and started a massive stampede to get to the fields through Alaska. In the twelve months from spring 1897 over 60,000 hopefuls set off from Seattle and other Pacific ports, many struggling along the treacherous Chilkoot Trail over the Chilkoot Pass from Skagway, while others tried the All-American Route from Valdez, and the better-off rode sternwheelers up the Yukon River.

Initial gold strikes were wildly exaggerated, and few fortunes were made, but most gleaned more modest sums often returning to the Lower 48 after a season or two penniless having blown their earnings in the bars and brothels that sprung up in the towns alongside the diggings. Typically the initial tent city grew into a shambolic wooden town over the first year but lay almost abandoned by the second winter when the easiest pickings had been taken. But

the Klondike gold rush opened up the Interior as never before. Few people had previously spent much time away from the coasts, but now there were sternwheelers plying the Yukon and smaller rivers, the White Pass & Yukon Route railway was built from Skagway, telegraph lines were established, and all-weather roads eventually replaced the winter dog-sled routes.

Alaska had its own minor gold rush in 1896 when gold was discovered around **Turnagain Arm**, close to present-day Anchorage. Hope, Girdwood and Sunrise City sprung up, but by 1898 interest had been siphoned off north to the Seward Peninsula where the beaches of **Nome** produced as much gold as the Klondike, and then **Fairbanks**, the last of the major rushes, in 1902. Mining has continued on a steadier scale ever since, occasionally buoyed by the hikes in the price of gold, primarily in 1934 and again in the early 1970s. Wherever you go in rural Alaska you'll find claims fiercely protected, and meet eternally optimistic prospectors happy to tell you how much they're going to make next year.

To put all this in perspective, the Californian gold fields of the 1840s and 1850s gave up five times as much as all the Alaskan gold fields together, and South Africa produces more gold in a year than Alaska has in a hundred.

The **effect on the Interior Natives** was profound. The newcomers failed to respect their "ownership" of the land, duped their hosts, and treated them inhumanely. They brought alcohol, destroyed the environment, and carried diseases that weren't cured by Native medicines but responded impressively to the white doctors' potions, thereby increasing dependence. And yet those with an entrepreneurial bent made the best of their circumstances; a case in point being the Chilkoot Indians who were aggressive businessmen and refused to let prospectors along their trail inland. Eventually they opened it up, but monopolized the packing services along the trail charging very respectable rates. Nonetheless, the events of the gold-rush years hastened the breakdown in Native society.

The Federal Government couldn't ignore Alaska any longer. Even if the rumors of lawlessness on the frontier were only half true there had to be some form of local government. In response, a Civil Code was enacted in 1900 allowing for taxation, licensing and the division of Alaska into three judicial districts, with judges at Sitka, Eagle, and St. Michael. Communication between these three centers was so poor that Congress set the army to work building a network of telegraph cables known as the Washington–Alaska Military Cable and Telegraphs System (WAMCATS; see box, p.408). Less then forty years after the purchase, Alaska was becoming well and truly American.

AFTER THE GOLD RUSHES

The changes initiated by the gold rushes were consolidated in the years immediately afterwards. By 1906 Alaska had a nonvoting delegate in Congress, it attained territorial status in 1912, the first territorial legislature the following year gave women the vote (long before the federal government extended such a basic right), and in 1916 Judge James Wickersham introduced the first Statehood Bill. Alaska was getting aspirations. The infrastructure was improving too: WAMCATS was linked directly to Seattle by 1904, the first car drove the Richardson Hwy between Valdez and Fairbanks in 1913, and in 1914 the Federal Government put its weight behind a new railroad between Seward and Fairbanks, in the process creating **Anchorage**.

While almost everyone's head was being turned by the gold, folk with a longer vision had begun to establish **salmon canneries**, the birth of an industry, which was to become the mainstay of the Alaskan economy. The first cannery was built in 1878 at Klawock on Prince of Wales Island, and by 1900 there were fifty canneries operating between Ketchikan in the Southeast and Bristol Bay on the Bering Sea.

With the easy pickings stripped from the gold fields most people left, but others started to look around for a more settled life **homesteading**. The 1861 Homestead Act that paved the way for opening the American West was not applied to Alaska until 1898, and even when it was many found it impossible to make a living from their allocated 160 acres in Alaska's short growing season and had to supplement their income by hunting and trapping. It was a lonely life, as communities were reliant on slow river travel in the summer, hazardous sled-dog routes in the winter and, for four to six weeks each spring (break-up) and fall (freeze-up), were pretty much stuck. The situation began to change in the late 1920s with the advent of **bush planes**,

which had more of an impact in Alaska than anywhere else in the US, and remain an essential link in large sections of the state. All of a sudden a village a week's travel from Fairbanks could be reached in an hour, dog teams contracted to deliver the US mail started disappearing, and commercial sternwheeler services were reduced, though they didn't completely stop until the late 1950s.

For the next few decades, Alaska seldom featured in the national consciousness except for the **conquest of Mount McKinley** in 1913, and the Serum Run of 1925 (see box, p.468) when Nome was saved from an epidemic by a heroic delivery of antidote by a series of dog teams. Native Alaskans in particular had been ignored and denied voting rights, though a 1922 court case paved the way for Alaskan Natives (along with all other US Natives) to be granted citizenship. Despite this legal status, Alaska's first peoples remained marginalized with a crumbling social structure, weak leadership, and increasing problems with alcoholism. Franklin Roosevelt took some notice in 1935, when as part of his New Deal, the **Matanuska Valley Colony** was established on some of Alaska's most fertile land around Palmer, just north of Anchorage. This was the only real attempt at organized settlement in Alaska, and though not wholly successful, Alaska could at last begin to partly feed itself. Until this point there was no large-scale agriculture, and everything that couldn't be obtained locally was imported from Seattle.

WORLD WAR II AND ITS AFTERMATH

The United States' entry into World War II, after the Japanese bombing of Hawaii's Pearl Harbor in 1941, provided Alaska's next great leap forward. By 1940 war looked likely and Alaska's strategic importance and vulnerability were brought into sharp focus. The military machine swung into action – the first non-extractive industry to have an effect on the Alaskan economy – establishing military bases in Anchorage, Delta Junction, Dutch Harbor, Fairbanks, Kodiak, Nome, Sitka, and Whittier. The only way to get substantial quantities of materials and machinery up to Alaska was by sea, and the military wanted something safer and more easily protected. The answer was the **Alaska Highway** (aka the ALCAN), a 1500-mile road punched through the wilds of northern British Columbia and the Yukon Territory to Fairbanks in Alaska. It was an immense and logistically difficult project, and yet it was completed (in a primitive but useable condition) in seven short months in 1942. It is now much improved and remains the only road link to the Lower 48. Military buildup now continued apace, fueling a booming economy as the United States spent a total of a billion dollars to support up to 150,000 troops.

The tip of the Aleutian Islands is only around a thousand miles from northern Japan and the US had no way of providing logistical support when, in 1943, the Japanese bombed Dutch Harbor and occupied the two remote Aleutian Islands of Attu and Kiska – the only successful invasion of US soil in the war (see "The Aleuts" box, p.316). Apart from a brief postwar recession, the boom continued with increased military spending and construction during the Cold War. This, along with the civilian benefits of the Alaska Hwy, brought tremendous population growth and economic expansion: the timber industry got under way, and both mining and fishing became more formalized. Alaska's carefree youth was coming to an end.

STATEHOOD AND THE TRANS-ALASKA PIPELINE

Alaska became a territory in 1912 (the same year as New Mexico and Arizona became the 47th and 48th states), but this had little appreciable effect on the land and its people. Renewed calls for statehood came in the early 1950s when the impotence of local representation in Congress started to rankle and proponents claimed they needed statehood as protection from outside interests, particularly overfishing in the salmon industry. Counterclaims that Alaska would be a financial burden on federal resources won out for a time, but then in 1957 economically viable quantities of oil were discovered along the Swanson River on the Kenai Peninsula. All of a sudden Alaska looked more appealing and, in 1958, Congress approved the **Alaska Statehood Act**. Dwight Eisenhower declared Alaska as the 49th state on January 3, 1959 (beating Hawaii to the title by eight months), and Alaskans could finally rid themselves of their perceived status as second-class citizens.

Until now, Alaskans had felt that a combination of limited funds and a small and thinly-spread population had prevented them from truly taming this great land. Rural poverty was still the norm and though there was now a railway linking the two biggest cities, the road system was still rudimentary and planes were beyond the means of most residents. Looking around the four-lane highways and shopping malls of Anchorage and Fairbanks today it is hard to imagine just how different this was at the turn of the 1960s. Statehood brought a spirit of optimism manifest in accelerated population and economic growth. This took a body blow five years later with the 1964 **Good Friday earthquake** (see box, p.195), which left a scar on the psyche of the Alaskan people but came with the silver lining of reconstruction.

Until statehood, the federal government had owned something like 99 percent of all the land in Alaska, the remaining one percent was made up by land given up for homesteading. As part of the Statehood Act, and to help Alaska become self-sufficient, the US government promised to transfer control of over a quarter of the land, and the state of Alaska was given 25 years to make their choices. One of the earliest selections was large tracts of the North Slope, flanking the Arctic Ocean where, in 1968, the Atlantic Richfield company discovered **huge oil deposits beneath Prudhoe Bay**, thereby altering Alaska's financial destiny. The trouble was, the only feasible way to get the oil to market was by constructing an 800-mile pipeline right across the heart of the state. Environmentalists were immediately up in arms, but what worried the consortium of oil companies most was land ownership. The oil companies needed permission to cross land which was almost exclusively federally-owned, but some of this was contested by newly resurgent Native groups who were demanding recognition of their first-people rights, a topic pointedly ignored at Statehood. In the spirit of the late 1960s and early 1970s Natives found a sympathetic ear in the federal courts and among the wider public. The government couldn't really approve pipeline construction until these Native claims were settled. There was also a desire to at least partially right the wrongs meted out on Native Alaskan's over two centuries of white intervention, and with all that oil waiting to be tapped, whites were keen to settle. Understandably, Native leaders played it for all they could get. In 1971, Nixon signed the **Alaska Native Claims Settlement Act** (ANCSA) which extinguished Native land titles in return for almost $1 billion and 44 million acres – roughly a tenth of Alaska – spread between 60,000 people. At the time the settlement was widely regarded as the most generous and fair of any deal with aboriginal people; every man, woman, and child getting $17,000. In hindsight, some believe the Natives were duped, their naive representatives sucked in by the machinations of international commerce and politics. Since ANCSA, oil companies have taken over $100 billion worth of oil off the North Slope and the Alaska state government has received a third of that in taxes and royalties.

ANCSA drastically changed economic status of Natives. The $1 billion was paid over a decade into twelve (later thirteen) regional corporations and over 200 villages with the responsibility to invest half and distribute the rest to individuals and village corporations. Instead of being communal owners of the land, the people now became shareholders in their corporations, so the act effectively forced Native Alaskans into a capitalist world they neither wanted nor were prepared for. As John McPhee writes in *Coming into the Country*, "the bluntest requirement of the Alaska Native Claims Settlement Act was that the natives turn white." This came at a time when the Native way of life was under threat. Snow machines were replacing sled dogs, homes were getting modern conveniences, and the men working on the pipeline could send back weekly remittances large enough to supply the whole village with booze for a month. Without the social context others grew up with, binge drinking became the huge problem it still is.

The regional corporations found themselves rich, and immediately started buying up real estate, canneries, and businesses all over Alaska and beyond; a case in point is the Cook Inlet region's CIRI who now own sightseeing cruise companies in Prince William Sound and Kenai Fjords National Park, and hotels throughout Southcentral Alaska.

With Native opposition to the pipeline largely defused, the environmental challenge lost steam and eventually collapsed, and when oil prices went stratospheric as a consequence of the 1973 Arab oil crisis, Congress gave the go-ahead. Construction of the **Trans-Alaska pipeline** began in 1974, and as thousands of workers, and hundreds of millions of dollars started flowing into the state, Alaskan aspirations went through the roof. Everyone was riding the oil wave, not least the workers with their huge pay packets: Fairbanks was the base for much of the construction and sprouted bars and brothels to cope with hordes of suddenly wealthy men; Anchorage boomed as the Alaskan headquarters of most of the oil companies; and Valdez tripled in size for the construction of the deep-water oil terminal.

This period also marked a shift in the sociopolitical makeup of the state. The heritage of gold prospecting, hunting, trapping, and commercial fishing left a strongly **Libertarian** streak through the state manifest in an almost paranoid mistrust of any form of authority and government. But this had always been softened by a broadly liberal outlook: Alaskans even voted to legalize marijuana for home use in the 1970s (though this was later rescinded). With the discovery of oil and the construction of the pipeline many of the newcomers were Southerners – from Texas, Oklahoma, and the Bible belt – and Alaska shifted from being a mostly Democratic state to repeatedly returning Republican congressmen and senators.

REAPING THE OILY REWARDS

The pipeline was completed in 1977 at a cost of $8 billion, making it the largest private construction job in history. The crews went home (though many individuals stayed) and the state settled back to reap the proceeds of the oil. But there was unfinished business. The 1971 ANCSA agreement had established the size of the Native settlement but not the details of how the lands would be divided up, something left for the 1980 **Alaska National Interest Lands Conservation Act** (ANILCA). In this, Congress set aside almost a third of the state in new or expanded parks. In a sense it marked the start of the Americanization of Alaska: the old freedoms (however illusory) were perceived as being eroded as the land was "tied up." All of a sudden there were rules about where you could go, where you could hunt and how much fish and game you could take. As the Feds were perceived to be taking away, the State garnered popularity by abolishing all individual state taxes in 1980, and two years later paying the first **Permanent Fund Dividend** (see "Money for Nothing" box, p.183), in which over $1000 has been paid annually to every resident.

Oil fueled massive growth in the mid-1980s with Alaskans enjoying the highest income of any state. The State's coffers were bulging and money was lavished on all manner of civic institutions such as the museum and performing arts center in Anchorage. As a consequence of the 1976 **Molly Hooch Decree**, the state was obliged to provide secondary schooling in any community that had an elementary school, and though no other state would have had the money to comply, the timing was right and Alaska went ahead with the program. Now even tiny settlements have swanky new schools, often the finest building in the district and usually put to multiple use – community hall, sports hall, movie theater, and so on.

Despite widespread belief to the contrary, it couldn't last and the bubble burst in 1986 when oil prices plummeted. Banks collapsed, thousands left the state, and property prices crashed. But recovery wasn't far behind, riding on the back of the 1989 **Exxon Valdez disaster** (see box, p.234). When eleven million gallons of crude oil spilled from the *Exxon Valdez* tanker, a massive clean-up kicked in, many involved in the clean-up operation made a stack of cash, and became locally known as the "spillionaires."

A MATURING ECONOMY AND THE FUTURE

Through the 1990s and into the new century, Alaska's traditional economic mainstays have been under threat. Oil remains the source of Alaskan wealth, new fields are being tapped every couple of years, but these are small and as production declines from large fields like Prudhoe Bay, the net profits are waning. Oil companies are clamoring for new areas to be opened up for exploration, the most contentious being the coastal strip of the Arctic National Wildlife Refuge which is thought to contain rich deposits currently inaccessible because of reserve status and public pressure: Jimmy Carter even tried unsuccessfully to get Bill Clinton to declare ANWR a National Monument, thereby putting it beyond oil-company reach. Oil still brings in 85 percent of Alaska's revenue, but the recent rise in world oil prices only serves to delay the inevitable need to diversify.

For the last few decades **forestry** has been a big earner, with activities concentrated in the nation's two largest national forests, the Tongass, which encompasses almost the entire Southeast, and the Chugach, covering much of Southcentral and the southern Interior. Falling world prices for spruce pulp and timber have hit the industry hard and pulp and saw mills have closed all over Southeast. Many lay the blame firmly at the feet of the Federal Government, who own the forests and have cut [sic] back on the sale of timber-cutting rights. During the Clinton years, the government were seen as bowing to pressure from environmental groups seeking the preservation of some of the world's largest tracts of untouched temperate rainforest.

Alaska's fishery is the other big earner, particularly the super-rich **salmon fishing** industry, though this is subject to wild swings which fisheries experts are continually trying to explain. Overfishing often gets the blame for low returns, but poor years are often followed by bumper harvests. Still, supplies seem to be in ever greater demand, and the issue of international fish quotas came to a head in the summer of 1997 when Canadian fishers sought to stop Alaskans "poaching" what they perceived to be Canadian fish. Fishing boats surrounded the tourist-laden Alaskan ferry *Malaspina* in the Canadian port of Prince Rupert, and held it hostage for three days, eventually releasing them when the matter was resolved in an out-of-court settlement.

Over the years, other fish species, along with king crab and tanner crab have been all but wiped out by overfishing and the industry now has a system of quotas aimed to prevent the recurrence of this cycle.

Ever since World War II, the **military** has been a big spender in the state, but with the end of the Cold War and progressive rounds of military belt-tightening things look bleak. So far Alaska has escaped the worst of the cuts, but no one is looking forward to a bright future.

Alaska has thrived on these boom-and-bust economies, but all currently look to be on a downward cycle. No one knows what the next boom will be, or if there will be one, so over the last decade or so Alaska has attempted – with limited success – to stabilize its economy. As elsewhere, the great hope is **tourism**, which has been expanding steadily over the last couple of decades and looks set to continue. Yet with such a short tourist season, and the prevalence of cruise-ship packages that see a lot of the profits leave the state, it seems unlikely that tourism can fill the void left by the decline of its extractive industries.

How this affects the state remains to be seen, but Alaska finds itself in a strange position. Speak to Alaskans and you'll hear a lot of Libertarian rhetoric that borders on the survivalist. Anything that smacks of government interference is immediately jumped on hard, and yet Alaska has the highest per capita state spending in the country, pays an annual dividend of almost $2000 to every resident, runs the railroad and state ferry system, and owns almost a third of the state's entire surface area. Against these (whisper it) socialist tendencies there is the cherished lack of state income tax, though as oil revenues decline and no one seems to have the political will to dip into the Permanent Fund, it seems only a matter of time until some form of taxation will have to be imposed. It'll be a big fight.

CHRONOLOGY

11,000 years ago earliest record of human presence in Alaska.

1725 Peter the Great sends Vitus Bering to explore the North Pacific.

1728 Vitus Bering sails through the Bering Strait naming St Lawrence Island.

1733 Georg Wilhelm Stellar becomes the first naturalist to visit Alaska on Bering's second expedition.

1741 Bering's third expedition sights the Alaskan mainland on July 15; Bering dies on the way home.

1745 Russian fur hunters overwinter in the Aleutian Islands; first European habitation.

1774 Spaniard Juan Perez sights southern end of Prince of Wales Island.

1778 English Captain James Cook charts Alaska coast and reaches Unalaska.

1784 Grigorii Shelikov establishes first white settlement at Three Saints Bay, Kodiak.

1792 Catherine II grants Alaskan fur monopoly to Grigorii Shelikov.

1795 The first Russian Orthodox Church established in Kodiak.

1804 Russians establish settlement at modern-day Sitka.

1847 Hudson's Bay Company establishes Fort Yukon at the confluence of the Porcupine and Yukon rivers; Russian hegemony in Alaska challenged.

1849 Russian mining engineer discovers gold and coal on the Kenai Peninsula.

1857 Coal mining begins at Coal Harbor on the Kenai Peninsula.

1865 Extensive exploration of Alaska as Western Union Telegraph Company prepares to put telegraph line across Alaska and Siberia.

1867 US purchases Alaska from Russia.

1871 Gold discovered at Indian River near Sitka.

1880 Tlingit Kowee leads Richard Harris and Joseph Juneau to gold near Juneau; Juneau established.

1881 Presbyterians under Sheldon Jackson begin mission schools.

1884 Congress passes Organic Act providing a civil government for Alaska.

1890 Large corporate salmon canneries begin to appear.

1897–1900 Klondike gold rush.

1898 Gold discovered in Nome.

1900 Civil Code for Alaska enacted; Capital moved from Sitka to Juneau.

1902 Felix Pedro discovers gold near Fairbanks.

1910 The Sourdoughs make first ascent of North Peak of McKinley.

1911 Sea otters given complete protection after international agreement between US, Great Britain, Canada, Russia, and Japan.

1912 Alaska given territorial status.

1913 Anchorage established as a construction camp for the Alaska Railroad.

1923 President Warren G Harding comes to Alaska to drive the last spike in Alaska Railroad.

1935 Matanuska Valley Project brings New Dealers to Alaska.

1940 Beginning of military expansion.

1942 Japan bombs Dutch Harbor; invades Aleutians. ALCAN Hwy built.

1959 Alaska becomes 49th state.

1964 Good Friday earthquake strikes Southcentral and parts of Southwest Alaska.

1968 Oil discovered at Prudhoe Bay.

1971 Alaska Native Claims Settlement Act signed into law.

1976 Molly Hooch Decree requires secondary schooling throughout the state.

1977 Trans-Alaska Pipeline completed from Prudhoe Bay to Valdez.

1980 Congress passes Alaska National Interests Lands Conservation Act.

1982 First Permanent Fund Dividend paid out.

1986 Oil price drops below $10 a barrel, initiating economic slump.

1989 The *Exxon Valdez* oil tanker spills 11 millon gallons of crude into Prince William Sound.

1994 Federal trial awards $5 billion in restitution for the *Exxon Valdez* disaster. Canadian fishermen detain Alaskan ferry over fishing rights.

1999 SeaLife Center opens in Seward, partly funded by restitution from the *Exxon Valdez* disaster.

2000 The state supports Republican nominee George W Bush in the presidential election.

ALASKAN LANDSCAPES: TERRAIN, FLORA, AND FAUNA

A visit to any Alaskan bookstore will reveal racks of books on the state's impressive geology, flora, and fauna and indeed there is much to be covered: mountain ranges, deep fjords, lakes and wetlands, and all sorts of species occupying those environments. What follows is just a general overview of animals, plants, and landscape you can expect to find along the way.

GLACIERS, VOLCANOES, AND EARTHQUAKES

The popular cliches of Alaska's appearance spring from the realities of Southeast, where ancient **glaciers** carved out deep **fjords** since filled in by the sea to create the narrow channels of the Inside Passage. Most islands shelve steeply into deep water and beaches are rare. In several places glaciers calve off icebergs directly into the fjords, but many glaciers have receded to the point where they no longer reach the water. The most rapidly receding glaciers are those in Glacier Bay; once land has been ice-free for around 200 years it achieves the mix of

mature spruce and hemlock found all over Southeast.

Large sections of Southcentral around Prince William Sound, and the Kenai Peninsula have a similar topography, though without a narrow network of channels. Here several tidewater glaciers are often fed by large **icefields** high in the Wrangell – St Elias, Kenai, and Chugach mountains, where enormous quantities of snow accumulate.

Further north, the Interior is sliced through by the **Alaska Range**, a jagged chain of icy peaks topped by **Denali**, the highest mountain in North America. Glaciers exist here, too, but precipitation is much lower than on the coast and with less weight driving them downhill they tend to move much slower. Around the coast, glaciers tend to be clean and white; by the time they reach their terminus (possibly hundreds of years later) most Interior glaciers have accumulated so much surface debris they appear an unappealing brown.

By the time winds reach northern Alaska most of their moisture has been lost as snow over the coastal mountains and the Alaska Range leaving nothing left for the **Brooks Range**, the ultimate northern extension of the Rockies. Though glacially sculpted, there is no longer the snowfall to support large glaciers, and most of the tops remain bare.

Most Alaskan mountain ranges are the result of the folding of the earth's crust, but in places this process is given a helping hand by **volcanoes**, around fifty of which form an orderly line from the highest, the 14,000 foot Mount Wrangell in the east, out along the Alaska Peninsula and right out to the western end of the Aleutian Islands. They add a certain grace to the skyline, particularly from the western shore of the Kenai Peninsula and from the ferry trip along the Alaska Peninsula to Dutch Harbor.

The volcanoes form part of the **Pacific Ring of Fire** where the North American and Pacific tectonic plates meet. It is the interaction of these two plates that is at the root of all Alaska's **earthquake** activity. It is said that in the twentieth century, a quarter of all the energy released worldwide by earthquakes was released in Alaska. Little wonder then that an earthquake of over seven on the Richter Scale is expected on average every fifteen months, and three of the ten largest earthquakes ever recorded occurred in Alaska, the 1964 Good

Friday quake (see box, p.195) coming in second.

FORESTS, TAIGA, AND TUNDRA

Alaska has four main vegetation zones: temperate forest, boreal forest, taiga, and tundra. Most of the southern coastal regions come cloaked in deep-green temperate **rainforests**, mainly comprising the huge **Sitka spruce** – the state tree – and **western hemlock**, with a little yellow and red cedar mixed in. With spruce commonly measuring up to eight feet in diameter it is not surprising that the loggers have been hard at work. Some areas have been clear cut, most noticeably on Prince of Wales Island, but for long stretches in the Southeast rainforest covers every square inch of land up to the tree line. Closer inspection reveals an understory of low scrub made almost impenetrable by abundant **devil's club**, with its broad green leaves and five-foot stems covered in spines. Above the tree line, thickets of **alder** and **willow** predominate before giving way to alpine tundra (see below).

Southcentral Alaska also has its share of rainforest, though cedar don't make it this far north, and only spruce makes it as far as Kodiak, the western limit of the rainforest. North of Anchorage, dense woods continue only to the Matanuska Valley, where **boreal forest** takes over. Characterized by scattered stands of white spruce, cottonwood, lodgepole pine, and paper birch, it lacks the grandeur of the rainforest, but makes up for it with spectacular seasonal changes, the buds of the deciduous trees producing fully opened leaves in what seems like hours, then turning to shades of gold in fall, which also goes by in a flash.

Further north, particularly beyond the Alaska Range, you're into **taiga**, a Russian word meaning "little land of sticks." It is an appropriate description for a sparse landscape only periodically dotted with short white and black spruce, the latter taking decades to grow by an inch in diameter. The trees are usually interspersed with dwarf willow and **muskeg**, a kind of swampy peat bog which in wetter areas develops into a network of ponds linked by small slow-moving streams.

Trees finally disappear altogether up in the Brooks Range, where **moist tundra**, then takes over – all the way to the Arctic Ocean. Many of the taiga species are still in evidence, but usually more stunted: nothing grows above knee height. As everywhere in the north, there are species of willow, which here might only be an inch high, but spread for up to a hundred yards along the ground. On very flat ground it forms soggy **wet tundra**, the limited rainfall unable to penetrate the underlying **permafrost**, and collecting on the surface forming numerous lakes.

Anywhere in the state with hills high enough will allow you to climb out of the forest and into **alpine tundra**. Again the vegetation is very low to the ground, with heather and an abundance of wildflowers, including the state flower, the beautiful blue **forget-me-not**.

WILDLIFE

One of the most enticing things about a visit to Alaska is the opportunity to see the sort of **wildlife** rarely on view elsewhere. The highlights among the land dwellers – bears, moose, caribou, and wolves – can usually be seen with a little patience anywhere that's not built-up, though chances are best in Denali where the shuttle buses give direct access to wild country. Below we've gone into detail about those animals in which you are probably most interested, although during the course of your travels you will most likely come across a range of species.

BEARS

With the exception of the city centers, the mountain tops, and a few islands, Alaska is **bear** country.

Most of the bear-viewing sites around the state focus on the **brown bear**, which goes by three names – **brown, grizzly, and Kodiak** – but is essentially the same species, and is easily identified by its shoulder hump and broad stubby face. Whatever the name, they've become something of an icon of all places wild. There are only around 300 left in the Lower 48, but up here there are almost 40,000 of them.

In inland areas they're known as **grizzlies**, generally solitary animals each roaming over fifty square miles of territory to satisfy its mixed diet of berries, roots, willow shoots, ground squirrels, and occasionally something bigger like a moose calf or caribou. Except during the mating season around July, you'll usually see solo males or mothers still being followed by cubs, which stay with them for two summers before being forced out on their own.

Large grizzly males can stand up to seven feet tall and weigh 600 pounds, though this is small in comparison with their coastal kin, the **brown bears**. The presence of salmon-rich salmon streams means that all a brown bear has to do is wait for the salmon run, stand by the stream and pluck out fish until sated. Later in the season it is even easier as the salmon die and float downstream where the bears scavenge. Brown bears put on a huge amount of weight at this time attaining something close to 800 pounds. The ready food also reduces the amount of territory needed for each bear, and so at places such as Brooks Camp in Katmai National Park, and Pack Creek near Juneau you'll see several brought together by the rich pickings. The biggest of all brown bears are **Kodiak brown bears**, on Kodiak Island, which are the world's largest land carnivore, occasionally reaching eleven feet and 1400 pounds.

Alaska also has **black bears**, mostly around the coast where you'll see them foraging along the shore, but also inland where they prefer denser undergrowth, seldom venturing out onto open ground. They're usually much smaller than grizzlies but can't always be distinguished by their color, which can vary from black through cinnamon brown to a rare blue-gray known as a **glacier bear**. The lack of a shoulder hump and a much narrower pointy face than the grizzly makes them easy to identify.

Anyone with a little patience will see black and brown bears while they're in Alaska, but **polar bears** are a different matter. They only inhabit the arctic rim, roaming the pack ice for most of the year hunting seals and only heading south when the pack ice forms in winter, returning to polar regions in spring. At up to eleven feet and reaching 1400 pounds they are an impressive sight, and people go to great expense to see them. The best bets are northern coastal settlements such as Barrow and Kaktovik during their spring and fall whaling seasons in May and September. The whale's entrails are usually left at a dump site where the bears come scavenging.

MOOSE

Lugubrious-looking **moose** are a much more visible part of the Alaskan landscape than bears, and are found everywhere except most islands in Southeast, Kodiak, and the Aleutians. You'll see them (usually alone or with a calf) grazing in city parks in suburban Anchorage or standing belly-deep in roadside ponds chomping on aquatic vegetation and willow shoots. Alaskan moose are the largest of all moose, itself the largest member of the deer family, and a bull (male) will weigh in at over 1200 pounds and stand five feet high at the shoulder. Size usually distinguishes bulls from cows (females), but a bull also grows an impressive set of antlers, usually known as a "rack" – up to 75 inches across, though 45 is more normal – which is shed annually and regrown through the summer. To see the bull moose in full-racked glory you need to be here in fall, which is also hunting season. Throughout most of the year cows have one or two calves in tow, only chasing them away in spring when they are about to give birth again.

CARIBOU AND REINDEER

Caribou are also members of the deer family but are less than half the size of moose and live socially in huge herds that are constantly on the move. They graze on open ground for a while then, at the slightest hint of danger, flit off across the landscape at great speed. This is their first line of defense against their main predator, wolves. Alaska's million or so caribou are found in over a dozen main herds, mostly occupying areas far away from human habitation, especially north of the Brooks Range, though you've a fair chance of spotting them in Denali National Park and along the Denali Hwy. In late fall there are also viewing possibilities in the Interior along the Taylor, Richardson, and Glenn highways. They migrate throughout the year, in winter searching out areas with little snow cover so that they can use their broad hooves to scrape away for the limited grazing below – caribou means "scraping hooves" in the Maine Algonquin dialect. Uniquely within the deer family, the females also grow antlers, both sexes shedding them every year.

Caribou are very closely related to **reindeer**, a northern European and Asian subspecies that has been domesticated. A number of animals were imported from Siberia late in the nineteenth century and their ancestors are still found on the Seward Peninsula near Nome, though some have apparently escaped and joined caribou herds.

WOLVES

For centuries the **wolf** has been feared, despised, and hunted to extinction in many parts of the world, but extensive research over the last few decades – much of it in Alaska – is beginning to balance the prejudice with some respect for this complex animal. Wolves are found throughout Alaska, however their natural shyness and sensitivity to human development makes them hard to spot. Shaded from black to almost white, they tend to live in packs of six to twelve, and sometimes up to thirty, usually sticking to a home territory but ranging widely in search of caribou. It is this behavior which puts them in danger, since wolves are not protected in Alaska. Even those that normally live in protected areas, such as the wilderness areas of Denali National Park, often stray into unprotected areas and are shot. Of Alaska's roughly 8000-strong wolf population, around 1500 are shot or trapped each year, partly to manage caribou numbers, but also for sport.

DALL SHEEP

Dall sheep are the world's only wild white sheep, something which undoubtedly provides suitable camouflage in winter, but looks like a poor evolutionary move in summer when you can spot them high in the hills from miles away. Their agility on steep terrain and a tendency to stick to high ground gives them some protection. As does the rams' distinctive curled horns which grow a little bit fiercer each year. Along the Seward Hwy south of Anchorage, around the Copper River Delta near Cordova, and in Denali you'll see visitors training their binoculars on distant hills watching Dall sheep graze oblivious to the spectators.

MARINE LIFE

Alaska is surrounded by a rugged shoreline that offers sanctuary to enormous numbers of marine mammals. **Whales** pass through northbound in spring to their summer feeding grounds in the Arctic Ocean, then return in fall to their subtropical breeding territory. Most of the rest stay year-round feeding on the abundant fish and crustaceans. And herein lies the conflict that is threatening-sea mammal populations. Commercial fishing fleets are getting ever more efficient at emptying the sea of their target species making it increasingly difficult for

sea mammals to feed themselves. Quota systems attempt to strike a balance, but economic interests often prevail, especially in small communities where fishing is the sole livelihood.

A lot of Alaska's visitors spend a huge portion of their time standing beside rivers casting a line hoping to hook a prize salmon (see opposite), but this isn't all the rivers have to offer. **Trout** are also prevalent in several varieties, probably the largest and most sought after being the **steelhead**, which normally weighs around ten pounds, fights hard once on a line, and tastes good. Others go for the smaller **cutthroat**, **rainbow**, **brook**, and **lake trout**, or the oddly named Dolly Varden, which gets its name from its pink spots, said to resemble a dress work by the Dickens character of the same name, from *Barnaby Rudge*.

Rivers in the far north are often devoid of salmon and trout, but are full of arctic grayling, a small fish mostly weighing under a pound and distinguished by its sail-like dorsal fin.

SEA MAMMALS

Kings of the sea are the whales, which can usually be seen on whale watching trips throughout Southeast and Southcentral Alaska. **California gray whales** make their migration route in April, while **humpback whales** are more accommodating, usually passing through in May and September with some hanging around for most of the summer. You may be lucky enough to see one **breaching**, rising completely out of the water before crashing back into the sea.

Probably the most common sightings are of **orca**, previously known as killer whales, though they are in fact the largest in the dolphin family. Usually around twenty feet long, they have a distinctive black-and-white patterning and a very pronounced dorsal fin. There are pure-white **belukha whales** (aka beluga) in Cook Inlet, though numbers are in decline and sightings less frequent.

Another marine mammal in decline is the **Stellar sea lion**, named by William Stellar, a naturalist aboard Bering's second voyage in 1742. It is a huge beast with bulls weighing over a ton, something achieved by eating a lot of pollock. This bottom-dwelling fish has been caught in huge quantities in the last few decades (primarily for use as imitation crab), roughly corresponding to the drop in Stellar sea lion numbers. Those that are left favor rookeries on remote islands, and sightings are rare unless you make a specific journey.

The **Northern fur seal** is a slightly smaller member of the same family, and it spends much of its time out at sea before returning each summer to the cramped beaches of the Pribilof Islands where up to a million fur seals breed. Hunting of fur seals has been banned by international treaty since 1911, when the same protection was afforded the **sea otter**. Because of its supremely soft and immensely valuable fur, the sea otter was hunted very close to extinction, but a few survived in remote spots and since 1911 numbers have increased dramatically. They can be seen all around the southern Alaskan coast, their almost human faces peering back at you inquisitively as they float on their back cracking open a mussel using a stone they've picked up from the bottom.

SALMON

If there is one creature that is discussed more than any other in Alaska it is **salmon**, a fish that supports huge commercial operations and is the subject of the state's main pastime. There are five species of Pacific salmon, all prevalent in Alaska, and all go by two names (deciphered below) which are used interchangeably. Wherever you go in Alaska there is an enormous quantity of information about the different types, their characteristics, and the **unusual life cycle**, which sees them spending a few years at sea then returning to the stream they were born in to breed and then die. Here, we've just provided the most basic information to get you started.

The largest of the species is the **king salmon** (or **chinook**), a deep-bodied fish which can grow up to 97 pounds, though 11–40 pounds is more common except in the Kenai River which has a reputation for huge fish. They typically run fairly early in the season from mid-May to mid-July. **Silver salmon** (or **coho**) have a similar full-bodied shape but are smaller, averaging 6–12 pounds, and run late, mostly in September right through to mid-November. **Red salmon** (**sockeye**) are widely considered to be the best tasting and have brilliant-red flesh. As they swim up the rivers in June and July their skin turns from a greenish-blue to a green head and deep-red body. They average around ten pounds. The most abundant of the five species are **pink salmon** (or **humpback**), which grow to around 4–6 pounds and have a pronounced hump on their back. They

run from mid-August to mid-September though many get caught before they ever make it into the rivers and are canned. Lastly, there's **chum salmon** (or **dog**), the most lowly of the breed and the species traditionally caught for feeding to sled dogs. They weigh 10–20 pounds and typically run from mid-August to mid-September.

BIRDS

Alaska has exemplary birdlife. There have been some 440 species recorded here, and some come in countless quantities, completely covering vast areas of wetlands.

The one bird most (at least most Americans) want to see is the **bald eagle**, a national symbol that remains relatively rare in the Lower 48 but is so abundant in Alaska that after a while you'll almost cease to notice them. The white-feather hood that gives them their bald appearance certainly lends a noble countenance, something enhanced by their unruffled posture as they sit in the trees, but they often eschew the noble art of hunting in favor of some opportunistic scavenging. **Golden eagles** are also in evidence, mostly in the Interior where they hunt for small mammals on the tundra.

Waterfowl and shorebirds make up a large portion of Alaska's summer bird population, and the numbers are staggering: over twenty million pass through the Copper River Delta each spring including the world's entire population of **western sandpiper**; and some 24 million nest and feed on the delta of the Yukon and Kuskokwim rivers between May and September, including sandhill cranes, black brant, the entire North American populations of emperor geese and spectacled eider, and assorted loon and ducks. Worth special mention are the world's largest waterfowl, the **trumpeter swans**, with wingspans up to seven feet. They were once thought to be on the brink of extinction, until a large flock was discovered in the Copper River Delta, still the best place to see them.

Alaska's state bird is the **willow ptarmigan**, a poorly flighted game bird similar to a large quail. They live throughout inland Alaska, mostly in high country where they burrow into snow drifts to protect themselves from the cold, and from hungry wolves. They're even blessed with feathers on their legs and feet to protect them, but otherwise their survival instinct is poor: early pioneers found them to be easy to catch and good eating.

BOOKS

Many of the following books are widely distributed in Alaska but have only limited availability outside the state. If you are keen to buy before you travel the easiest solution is to check booksellers on the Web such as *www.powells.com*, *www.amazon.com*, *www.amazon.co.uk*, *www.barnesandnoble.com* and others. Another line of enquiry is to approach the Alaska Natural History Association, 750 W 2nd Ave, Suite 110, Anchorage, AK 99501 (☎907/274-8440, fax 274-8343, *www.alaskanha.org*) who have a strong line in maps, guides of all kinds, coffee-table glossies, kids books, and videos.

Where two publishers are given, these refer to US and UK publishers respectively; wherever we've cited a single publisher, it's the same publisher in both countries.

TRAVEL AND IMPRESSIONS

Jon Krakauer, *Into the Wild* (Anchor/Pan). In 1992, in an abandoned bus just north of Denali National Park, idealistic young Chris McCandless died after repeatedly ingesting mildly-toxic plant matter while pursuing high-minded but poorly thought-out dreams of self-sufficiency and aesthetic purity. Climber, author, and *Outdoors* magazine contributor, Jon Krakauer, reconstructs the peregrinations of Chris's last couple of years and weaves them in with tales of like-minded adventurers and his own youth. A fascinating and unashamedly self-indulgent tale.

Mark Lawson, *The Battle for Room Service: Journeys to all the Safe Places* (Pan Books, o/p/Picador). Denali, Fairbanks, and Barrow make for an entertaining chapter on Lawson's world tour of "activity challenged" and "differently interesting" places. Astute observations of both the state and those drawn to it.

Barry Lopez, *Arctic Dreams* (Bantam/Panther). Lopez takes you forever deeper into the interstices of Arctic life and landscapes weaving together philosophy, science, ethics, polar history, and ecology into a magisterial volume that is in turns poetic, pragmatic, and lyrical. It's essential reading for anyone visiting the Arctic north of Alaska or with even the faintest interest in Arctic ecosystems.

John McPhee, *Coming into the Country* (Noonday). The single most accurately observed and sharply written volume on modern Alaska, even if it is approaching a quarter of a century since McPhee traveled in the Brooks Range, along the Yukon River and through the Interior. His evocation of Alaska and the Alaskan character is both matchless and timeless.

Joe McGinniss, *Going to Extremes* (Plume/New American Library). McGinniss ranks alongside John McPhee as a spot-on commentator on the turbulent mid-1970s oil-boom years but with a different slant. Whereas McPhee writes about what he likes, McGinniss writes about what he doesn't; some cheap shots perhaps, but funny and often just as true today as when it was written.

John Muir, *Travels in Alaska* (Houghton Mifflin/Mariner). A powerful collection of reflections on his trips to the Alaskan Southeast between 1879 and 1890; a time when very few Americans had been there, and most of them were missionaries. There are tediously long descriptions of forests and glaciers (their land-sculpting actions barely understood at this time) which are offset by his tremendous enthusiasm for the landscape and indomitable spirit of exploration.

Gary Paulsen, *Winterdance: The Fine Madness of Alaskan Dog Racing* (Harcourt Brace/Indigo). Entertaining and harrowing autobiographical account of Paulsen's seventeen-day ordeal as an ignorant novice undertaking the Iditarod sled-dog race.

Alastair Scott, *Tracks across Alaska: A Dog Sled Journey* (Atlantic Monthly). Wilder-the-better travel writing which transcends the genre. Scott arrived in Alaska with almost no knowledge of dog sledding, but ended the winter making a month-long sled journey from Manley Hot Springs to Nome which he uses as the thread that links deep insights into the Bush. Well worth seeking out.

HISTORY, SOCIETY, AND POLITICS

Ernest S. Burch and Werner Forman, *The Eskimos* (University of Oklahoma/Macdonald Orbis). Informative and well-written treatise on the traditional Eskimo way of life that is pan-Arctic in scope but with frequent reference to the Alaskan experience. Beautifully photographed, with an emphasis on some exquisite Eskimo crafts.

Brian M. Fagan, *The Great Journey* (Thames & Hudson). Probably the best lay-reader's explanation of current anthropological and archeological theories about the origins of Native Americans. More information than most people need to know but a good read nonetheless.

Jay Hammond, *Tales of Alaska's Bush Rat Governor* (Epicenter). Enjoyable and thoroughly readable autobiography of Alaska's Republican (but very independently minded) governor from 1974 to 1982 – the state's most formative oil industry years. Outspoken, self-effacing, and seldom pulling punches, Hammond charts his life as bush pilot, trapper, and fishing guide on remote Bristol Bay to the chains of high office and the Governor's mansion in Juneau.

Nick Jans, *The Last Light Breaking: Living Among Alaska's Inupiat Indians* (Alaska Northwest Books). A rare Alaskan voice amid all the impressions of outsiders, beautifully written and with insightful discussion of the Alaskan bush and Iñupiaq Eskimos.

Claus M. Naskee and Herman E. Slotnik, *Alaska: A History of the 49th State* (University of Oklahoma Press). Probably the best all-around history of Alaska.

Don O'Neill, *The Firecracker Boys* (St Martin's Press). Indictment of government action and arrogance over Project Chariot, a real-life plan to carve a new harbor out of the Alaskan Coast, just north of Kotzebue, with six thermonuclear bombs.

Harry Ritter, *Alaska's History* (Alaska Northwest Books). A handy pocket history of the state with plenty of photos and anecdotes, though a little superficial for history buffs.

John Strohmeyer, *Extreme Conditions: Big Oil and the Transformation of Alaska* (Cascade Press). A damning study of how oil-inspired greed has altered the face of Alaska and still threatens its downfall. Earnest at times but entertaining and a real eye-opener.

MEMOIRS

Rex Beach, *The Spoilers* (Reprint Services Corp). Firsthand tales of the Nome gold rush written in 1919 and currently only available in expensive hardback reprints, though second-hand copies can be found.

Art Davidson, *Minus 148°* (The Mountaineers). Huddled in a tiny snow cave at Denali Pass with temperatures at -50° and wind speeds reaching 150mph the team making the first successful ascent of Mount McKinley in winter (in 1967) experienced a wind chill off the bottom of the scale, below -148° degrees. Drawing on the diaries and reminiscences of the others involved, Davidson has woven an Alaskan mountaineering classic, free of unnecessary jargon and with human frailty playing as important a part as selfless heroism.

Ray Hudson, *Moments Rightly Placed: An Aleutian Memoir* (Epicenter Press). A kind of "Zen and the Art of Basket Weaving" title in which Washington State native Ray Hudson tells of his years in Unalaska during which he shocked the locals by taking up basket weaving – traditionally a woman's task. A sensitive and moving story of the assimilation from stranger to friend.

Beth Johnson, *Yukon Wild* (Berkshire Traveller Press). The adventures of four Texas women who paddled 2000 miles through America's last frontier down the Yukon River. Sometimes wordy but always interesting.

Lael Morgan, *Good Time Girls of the Alaska–Yukon Gold Rush* (Epicenter Press). Life and high times on the Alaskan goldfield as seen by the other kind of gold digger. An empathetically told series of true stories with a heap of fascinating detail and a good deal of humor.

Margaret Murie, *Two in the Far North* (Alaska Northwest). A very readable memoir by one of Alaska's earliest conservationists that gives a real sense of how Alaska has changed over the decades, from her youth in Fairbanks in the 1910s, through trips into the Arctic in the 1920s and 1950s, to her involvement in the creation of national parks and wildlife refuges (especially ANWR) in the mid-1970s.

Jonathan Raban, *Passage to Juneau* (Vintage/Picador). Raban continues his later-life maritime peregrinations up the Inside Passage from Seattle haunted by the ghost of British explorer George Vancouver and the spirit of two temperamental underwater Native American gods. It is a fascinating journey through history, literature, art criticism, and his own rites of passage, even if only part of it is actually in Alaska.

Kim Rich, *Johnny's Girl* (Alaska Northwest Books). Intriguing and well-written tale of growing up in 1960s and 1970s Anchorage as the daughter of one of the major players in the fledgling city's small-town gambling and prostitution gangland. An interesting insight into the underworld machinations and its impact on modern Anchorage.

Jonathan Waterman, *In the Shadow of Denali* (Lyons Press). Well-written personal odyssey touching on all aspects of Denali as a mountaineer's quarry and lifelong focal point. Subject matter jumps around – brief life stories, tales of mountain guiding, and work as a park ranger – but the whole still manages to convey a vivid impression of what the mountain means to its devotees. A good read for anyone already drawn by Denali.

LITERATURE

Susan B. Andrews & John Creed (eds), *Authentic Alaska: Voices of its Native Writers* (University of Nebraska). A rare chance to read Native Alaskan literature unfiltered by white eyes. Forthright stories of life as it is lived today in rural Alaska from fifty writers covering a wide range of topics.

Sue Henry, *Murder on the Iditarod Trail* (Avon Mystery). The first and perhaps best-known novel by this popular Alaskan murder mystery writer. An easy and pretty-entertaining tale of intrigue on Alaska's 1100-mile dog race with much of the background material factually correct. *Termination Dust* and *Sleeping Lady* are also worth checking out.

Jack London, *The Call of the Wild*; *White Fang* (Pocket Books/Penguin). Two classic tales

describing London's view of the human condition portrayed through the life of a domestic dog progressively turning wild in the former, and pretty much the reverse process in the latter. Though mostly set in the Yukon during the Klondike rush, the scenes of hardship, camaraderie, and arduous dog sledding translate into the Alaskan experience at the same time.

Wayne Mergler (ed) *The Last New Land: Stories of Alaska Past and Present* (Alaska Northwest Books). Modern anthology with excerpts of everything from Native legends and early exploration to the oil years and climbing Denali. A great starting point.

James A. Michener, *Alaska* (Crest/Mandarin). A lumbering brick of a book that's about what you'd expect from the master of rambling historic novels, partially redeemed by a guide to where fiction parts company from fact. Forget it and read John McPhee instead.

Robert Service, *The Best of Robert Service* (Perigee/A & C Black). The best value for your money of all the Service poetry anthologies including favorites such as *The Shooting of Dan McGrew* and *The Cremation of Sam McGee*.

Robert Specht, *Tisha* (Bantam). One of Alaska's most popular reads, written as a romantic novel, but in fact a largely true story of Anne Hobbs, a nineteen-year-old white school teacher who, in 1927, lived in Chicken and courageously insisted on treating everyone as equals, in the process falling in love with a half-Athapascan.

John Straley, *The Woman Who Married a Bear* (Signet/Orion). The best of Alaskan crime fiction by Sitka-based Straley, telling tales of ineffectual private investigator, Cecil Younger, who has a habit of being in the right spot as convoluted stories solve themselves. *The Curious Eat Themselves*, *The Music of What Happens*, and *Death and the Language of Happiness* are also worth reading.

Barbara Vine, *No Night is Too Long* (Onyx/Penguin). Ruth Rendell takes on a *nom de plume* for this engaging psychological thriller mostly set in the Alaskan Southeast and the Pacific Northwest. The denouement is as convoluted and unguessable as you'd expect from Rendell at her best.

Velma Wallace, *Two Old Women: An Alaskan Legend of Betrayal, Courage and Survival*; *Bird*

Girl and the Man Who Followed the Sun: An Athabaskan Legend from Alaska (Harper Perennial). Modern retelling of traditional Alaskan folk tales, simply told, but immediately engaging.

REFERENCE AND SPECIALIST GUIDES

Editors of Alaska Magazine, *The Alaska Almanac* (Alaska Northwest Books). Definitive, annually-updated Alaska fact-book chock-full of everything from air services to the Yukon Quest Sled Dog Race, and with irreverent quips from Anchorage oddball comic Mr Whitekeys (see p.210).

Editors of Vernon Press, *The Milepost* (Vernon). Alaska's biggest-selling travel book which details just about every stream crossing, pull-out, and gas station on the entire Alaskan road system mile-by-mile.

WILDLIFE

Robert H. Armstrong, *Guide to the Birds of Alaska* (Alaska Northwest books). The pick of the general bird books to Alaska with a section on identification, clear photos, and detailed material on habitat.

Rita M. O'Clair, Robert H. Armstrong and Richard Carstensen, *The Nature of Southeast Alaska* (Alaska Northwest Books). Lively field guide to the plants, animals, and habitats of Southeast Alaska that eschews dry lists in favor of weaving together and interpreting the ecosystem. Highly readable and full of entertaining insights for the nonspecialist.

Tom Walker, *Alaska's Wildlife* (Graphic Arts Center Publishing Co). Beautifully presented coffee-table book with superb shots of the best of the state's fauna taken by Alaska's premier wildlife photographer. The text includes discussion of how the shots were taken.

HIKING, MOUNTAINEERING, AND BACKCOUNTRY TRAVEL

Dean Littlepage, *Hiking in Alaska* (Falcon). A comprehensive guide to hiking throughout the whole state with a hundred hikes spanning a range of abilities, each laid out with maps and elevation plans.

Jon Nierenberg, *Backcountry Companion: Denali National Park and Preserve* (Alaska Natural History Association). A fairly brief but clear and understandable introduction to Denali's backcountry units, their flora, terrain, and wildlife. Helpful for planning your backcountry travels and rightly avoids suggesting hikes.

R.J. Secor, *Denali Climbing Guide* (Stackpole Books). Accurate and detailed guide to most of the routes up Denali. Well researched and perfect for the summit aspirant, but intriguing for those who just dream.

Kristian Sieling, *The Scar: Southcentral Alaska Rock Climbing* (Global Motion). Definitive guide to the region's rock climbing, mostly covering Anchorage's after-work rock playground and the crags along the Seward Hwy south of the city.

CANOEING, KAYAKING, AND RAFTING

Andrew Embick, *Fast & Cold: A Guide to Alaska Whitewater* (Skyhouse). The serious kayaker's guide to Alaska with all the big stuff – the Turnback Canyon of the Alsek, Devil's Canyon on the Talkeetna – included in detail and plenty of inspirational boating history and river-running accounts.

Karen Jettmar, *The Alaska River Guide: Canoeing, Kayaking and Rafting in the Last Frontier* (Alaska Northwest Books). A general guide for river runners with little in the way of inspiration, but plenty of relevant information – simple diagrams, pointers to more detailed maps, access to put-ins and take-outs, craft suitability – and a few black-and-white photos.

Jim and Nancy Lethcoe, *Cruising Guide to Prince William Sound* (Prince William Sound Books). Detailed coverage of sea kayaking in Prince William Sound divided into two volumes covering the eastern and western areas.

GLOSSARY OF ALASKAN TERMS

ALASKA DAY Commemorates the formal transfer of Alaska from Russia to the US in Sitka on Oct 18, 1867.

ALEUT (AL-ee-oot) Native of the Aleutian Islands.

ALPENGLOW Rich pink hues around the mountains particularly in the low winter light.

ALUTIIQ (a-LOO-tick) Academic but increasingly general term for Alaskan Natives living between the west end of the Alaskan Peninsula and Prince William Sound, including Kodiak Island.

ANCSA Alaska Native Claims Settlement Act (see p.495).

ANILCA Alaska National Interest Lands Conservation Act (see p.495).

ATHAPASCAN (also Athabascan) Native of the Alaskan Interior.

BALEEN Long, black, fibrous strips from the mouth of a baleen whale, used by Eskimos to make fine baskets and souvenirs.

BELUKHA (also beluga) Species of small, white whale.

BIDAR, BIDARKA Russian terms for Eskimo skin vessels. A bidar is a large, open boat (see "Umiak"); the bidarka is a kayak with one, two, or three hatches.

BLANKET TOSS Eskimo game using a walrus hide to toss an individual into the air. Originally used for spotting whales and other quarry over the horizon.

BORE TIDE A broken wave of foaming whitewater up to six feet high. A rare phenomenon that only occurs in perhaps sixty places around the world, two of them in Alaska.

BREAK-UP Two-week period in April or May when warmer temperatures, longer days, and melting snows build up pressure below the ice then burst through causing the resulting ice floes to thunder down the flooded Interior rivers. Signals the end of winter.

BUNNY BOOTS Thermal footwear made of double-skinned white rubber with an air layer in

between, developed by the US Army in the Korean War and said to keep active feet warm down to –60ºF.

BUSH Rural Alaska away from the rail and highway systems.

CABIN FEVER Irritable and depressed state brought on by extended periods indoors during the long, dark Alaskan winter.

CACHE A tiny food-storage cabin raised high above the ground by stilts out of reach of bears and other animals. By extension, any food store.

CHEECHAKO Pejorative jargon for a newcomer or first-time visitor who has not wintered in Alaska or mastered Alaskan ways.

DENA'INA (DEHna Eena) Name of the Athapascan language and people of Southcentral Alaska around Cook Inlet.

DEW LINE Array of Distant Early Warning sensors built across the North Slope in the mid-1950s to detect Soviet missiles.

DIAMOND DUST Tiny ice crystals suspended in the winter air.

DOLLY VARDEN Possibly the only fish named for a fictional character, in this case Dolly Varden from Dickens' *Barnaby Rudge*, who wore a pink-spotted dress which the markings on this trout are said to resemble.

ESKIMO General term for northern people; in Alaska this includes the Yup'ik and Iñupiaq peoples, and in Canada the Inuvialuit and Inuit. Though the word is said to derive from an Algonquin word for "eater of raw flesh" it is not considered disparaging or offensive in Alaska.

ESKIMO ICE CREAM (aka *akutuq* in Iñupiaq and *akutak* in Yup'ik) Traditional desert made from whipped seal oil, berries, and snow.

FISHWHEEL Mechanical fish harvester used in murky glacial rivers. Can catch up to a thousand salmon a day on a good run.

FLUME Artificial channel for water, used in gold mining.

FREEZE-UP The opposite of break-up, usually in late October.

FROST HEAVES Undulations in the road surface or house foundations built on permafrost, caused by repeated annual freezing and thawing.

GRUBSTAKE MINING Process whereby a banker or trader would supply a prospector with the means – food, tools, etc – to pursue his prospecting on the understanding that the advance would be repaid many fold when he struck paydirt.

HAIDA Coastal Natives of the Southeast.

HOMESTEADING Now largely defunct practice of giving settlers land in return for building a house and making the land "useful" within a certain period.

HONEY BUCKET Outhouse slops receptacle in places where it is not possible to dig a pit.

IGLOO Iñupiaq Eskimo word for house or dwelling. In Alaska, traditional houses were often made of driftwood and sod, not the ice houses used by Canadian Eskimos when out hunting.

INUIT See "Eskimo", opposite.

IÑUPIAQ, IÑUPIAT Language of Alaskan Eskimos in northwest Alaska as far south as Unalakleet. Distinct from Yup'ik.

KAYAK Yup'ik and Iñupiaq word for the familiar one-person, skin-covered boat.

LOWER 48 The contiguous United States, a term often used disparagingly.

MUKLUKS Knee-length boots, made of sealskin or moose hide and bound with thongs; lightweight, warm, and perfect for cold snow.

MUKTUK Whale blubber and the associated skin layer (usually from bowhead or belukha whales) eaten as an Eskimo delicacy either raw, pickled, frozen, or boiled and fermented.

MUSKEG Mossy peat bogs which cloak much of Interior Alaska, often covered with short plants such as blueberries or crowberries.

NATIVE ALASKAN Refers to anyone born in the state, except when the "N" is capitalized when it refers only to those with indigenous heritage.

NORTH SLOPE Gently shelving Arctic flatlands north of the Brooks Range.

OUTHOUSE Outside toilet comprising a hole in the ground surrounded by anything from a poorly-built hut to a sturdier more modern structure. The outhouse has been both raised to an art form (bookshops stock several outhouse picture books) and a sport with several summer festivals featuring outhouse carrying races.

OUTSIDE Everywhere that's not Alaska, see "Lower 48".

OUTSIDER Not an Alaskan.

PANHANDLE Nickname for Southeast Alaska, derived from the shape of the state.

PERMAFROST Soil that remains frozen throughout the year.

PERMANENT FUND Large stash of oil money.

POKE A small bag containing gold dust, or sometimes just gold-bearing gravel.

POTLATCH A massive feast thrown by Southeast coastal Natives.

QIVIUT (pronounced KIH-vee-yoot) Soft underhair of the musk ox which is knitted or woven into scarves and other garments.

RACK Set of antlers, generally used to refer to a "moose rack."

RV Recreational vehicle or motorhome.

SKIJORING Cross-country skiing while being helped along by a dog in traces out front.

SKOOKUM Native word for strong, used favorably as a nickname particularly during the early gold rushes.

SLED DOG Any dog used to pull a sled. Most sled dogs in Alaska are not huskies.

SLOUGH (pronounced "sloo") Slow-moving backwater which loops off the main river.

SMOLT Juvenile salmon large enough to enter and survive in saltwater.

SOURDOUGH Long-time Alaskan and what a cheechako becomes after about thirty years. Derived from the long-lasting yeasty mixture carried by pioneers to lighten breads and hotcakes.

SUBSISTENCE Living off the land (and sea). Controversially, all Alaskans (not just Natives) have rights to undertake subsistence hunting and fishing.

TAIGA Marginal subarctic landscape sparsely populated by spruce and birch.

TERMINATION DUST The first snow that covers the top of the mountain in the fall. So called because this is a sign of the termination of summer in Alaska.

TLINGIT Major coastal Native peoples of Southeast Alaska.

TRACES Reins used to attach a team of sled dogs to the sled.

TSIMSHIAN Southeast Alaskan Natives originally from British Columbia.

TSUNAMI A seismic wave often misnamed a tidal wave.

TUNDRA A treeless expanse covered with low-lying plants.

ULU, ULUAQ The Iñupiaq and Yup'ik words for the broad semicircular shaped knife, often also called a woman's knife.

UMIAK Open seal-skin boat about thirty feet long and fitted with a sail, often used as a support boat while men in kayaks hunted.

WILLIWAWS Sudden gusts of wind caused by air building up on one side of a mountain then bursting through into an otherwise sheltered area.

YUP'IK Eskimo people of central western Alaska.

INDEX

A

Abercrombie State Park 297
accommodation 44–48
Akutan 312
Alaska Center for the
    Performing Arts 195
Alaska Cultural Center 235–236
Alaska Highway 399
Alaska Native Heritage
    Center 203
Alaska Peninsula 309–320
Alaska Peninsula ferries 310
Alaska pipeline (see Trans-
    Alaska oil pipeline)
Alaska Railroad 36
Alaska Raptor Center 122
Alaskaland 428
Alaskan Experience Center 195
Aleutian Islands 309–320
Alpine Historical Park 373
Alutiiq Museum 297
Alyeska Resort 220
Anan Wildlife Observatory 103
ANCHORAGE 181–215
    accommodation 188–193
    Anchorage Museum of History
        and Art 196
    arrival 184–186
    city transport 187–188
    cycling 188
    downtown 194–198
    drinking and entertainment 208–210
    Eagle River 204–205
    eating 205–208
    hiking 200–201
    information 186
    listings 212–214
    midtown and the coastal trail
        198–202
    North Anchorage 203–205
    shopping 210–212
    South Anchorage 202–203
    winter activities 204
Angoon 127
ARCTIC ALASKA 450–485
Arctic Circle 454, 457
Arctic National Wildlife
    Refuge 463–465

aurora borealis 426–427

B

backcountry dangers 54–55
Baranov Museum 296
Barlett Cove 151
Barrow 480–485
bear viewing 147–148, 291,
    300–301, 307, 309
bears 500
Begich, Boggs Visitor Center
    223
Bering Land Bridge National
    Preserve 475–476
Bettles 463
bird-watching 224, 247, 319
birds 503
Black Rapids Glacier 389
books 504–507
Brooks Camp 306–307
buses 38–39
Byron Glacier 224

C

Caines Head State Recreation
    Area 257
Canadian border 399
canoeing 57, 90, 307, 397, 403,
    441
Cantewell 397
Cantwell 350–351
Captain Cook State Recreation
    Area 269
car rental 39
Chena Hot Springs 441–444
Chena River State Recreation
    Area 441, 443
Chicken 402
Chief Shakes Hot Springs 104
Chief Shakes Island 101
Chignik 311
Childs Glacier Recreation Area
    248
Chilikadrotna River 302
Chilkat Bald Eagle Preserve
    159
Chilkoot Trail 174–175
Chiswell Islands Wildlife
    Refuge 259
chronology, historical 498
Circle 447–448

Circle Hot Springs 444, 447
Clam Gulch 270
clamming beaches 269
Coffman Cove 95
Cold Bay 311
Cooper Landing 264
Copper River Delta 247
Copper River Highway 247
Cordova 241–248
costs 23
Council 472–473
Craig 94
credit cards 24
customs 15
cycling 43–44, 173, 308, 319,
    383

D

Dalton Highway 451, 456
Deadhorse 459
Delta Junction 390–393
Denali, climbing and history of
    348–349
Denali Highway 394–398
Denali National Park
    351–370
    accommodation 358–361
    campgrounds 362–363, 365
    camping 366–368
    day-trips 365
    eating and drinking 369
    entrance-area hikes 364
    flightseeing 365
    getting around 357
    hiking 366
    information 356
    listings 369–370
    orientation 355–356
    Park Road 353–355
    practicalities 368
    rafting 363
    reservations 357
    shuttles and tours 358–359
Denali State Park 347–351
Dig Afognak 301
directory for overseas travelers
    62–63
Dorothy G Page Museum
    334–335
Douglas 141
driving 39–42
Dutch Harbor 313–320
Dyea 173

E

Eagle 404–409
Eagle River 204–205
Eklutna 327–330
El Capitan Cave 95
El Dorado Gold Mine 432
Eldred Passage 283
Elliott Highway 448–449
email 26
Erskine House 296
Ester 432
Evansville 463
exchange rates 23
Exit Glacier 257
Exxon Valdez oil spill 234–235

F

FAIRBANKS 413–440
  accommodation 421
  around Fairbanks 440–450
  arrival 415
  aurora borealis viewing 426–427
  city transportation 415–416
  Creamer's Field Migratory
    Waterfowl Refuge 425
  downtown 421–425
  drinking and entertainment
    437–438
  eating 435–437
  Fairbanks Community Museum
    425
  festivals 429
  information 415
  listings 438–440
  outdoor activities 433–435
  tours 416
  University of Alaska Museum
    427–428
  World Ice Art Championships 424
False Pass 312
ferries 33–36
festivals 61
fishing 59, 89, 237, 282, 266,
  288, 297
flights
  from Australia and New Zealand 12
  from Britain 3
  from Ireland 6
  from North America 7
  within Alaska 31–33
flightseeing 142, 173, 237,
  300, 345, 387, 398
flora and fauna 499–503
food and drink 48–52
Fort Knox Gold Mine 430

Fox 430
Fox Island 259

G

Garnet Ledge 103
**Gates of the Arctic National
  Park** 460–463
George Parks Highway 339–341
getting around 31
Girdwood 220–223
Glacier Bay National Park
  148–153
glaciers 71, 499
Glenallen 375–376
Glenn Highway 373–375
glossary 508–510
Goddard Hot Springs 124
gold panning 444
Gold Rush Cemetery 173
Good Friday earthquake 195,
  231
Gulkana Glacier 389
Gustavus 151–153

H

Haines 154–162
Halibut Cove 282–283
Halibut Derby 282
halibut fishing 237, 282, 319
health 21
hiking
  Anchorage 200–201
  Denali 348–350, 354
  Gates of the Arctic National Park
    461
  Haines 160
  Homer 277
  Juneau 140–141
  Kachemak Bay State Park 279
  Ketchikan 83
  Kodiak 299
  Lake Clark National Park 302
  McCarthy Road 383
  Palmer 333
  Petersburg 109
  practicalities 53–57
  Prince of Wales Island 90
  Seward 258
  Sitka 123
  Skagway 171
  Turnagain Arm 221
  Unalaska/Dutch Harbor 318–319
  Valdez 236
  Valley of 10,000 Smokes 308

Whittier 227
Wrangell 101
history 489–497
hitching 43
holidays and festivals 60–61
Homer 271–279
Homer Spit 276, 278
Hoonah 127
Hope 250
Hydaberg 91
Hyder 96

I

Iditarod 335, 336–337, 465, 467
Imaginarium Science Discovery
  Center 195
Independence Mine 338
insurance 19–20
INTERIOR, THE 323–410
Izembek National Wildlife
  Refuge 312

J

Juneau 128–145
  accommodation 132–134
  Alaska Brewing Company 139
  around Juneau 145
  arrival 129
  Douglas 141
  downtown 134–137
  drinking and entertainment 144
  eating 142–144
  flightseeing 142
  hiking 140–141
  information 131
  listings 144–145
  Mendenhall Glacier 139
  outdoor activities 142
  State Capitol 136

K

Kachemak Bay State Park 281
Kake 126
Kasaan 94
Kasilof 270
Katmai National Park 303
Kenai 267–269
Kenai Fjords National Park 251
Kenai National Wildlife Refuge
  262, 265
Kenai Peninsula 248–288
Kennicott 384–386
Ketchikan 69–86

King Cove 311
King Salmon 305
Klawock 91
Knife Creek Glaciers 308
Knik 335
Kodiak 292–299
Kodiak Island 291–300
Kodiak National Wildlife
    Refuge 300
Kotzebue 476–479

L

Lake Clark National Park
    301–303
Lake Louise 375
LeConte Glacier 112
Lowell Point 257

M

Maclaren River 396, 397
mail 26
Manley Hot Springs 448–449
maps 28–30
marine life 502
Matanuska Glacier 374
Mat-Su Valley 326–327
McCarthy 383–384
McCarthy Road 382
McClaren River 396
McNeil River State Game
    Sanctuary 309
McQuesten's Thermometer 409
media 30
Mendenhall Glacier 139
Metlakatla 87–89
Million Dollar Bridge 248, 380
Misty Fiords National
    Monument 86–87
Moose Dropping Festival 341
Mount Eyak ski area 244–246
Mount Marathon 258
Mount McKinley 349, 351
Mount Versatovia 122, 123
Mulchatna River 302
Museum of the Aleutians 318
Museum of the Arctic 477

N

Naknek 306
Nancy Lake State Recreation
    Area 339–340

Near Island 297
Nenana 371–373
nightlife 61
Nikiski 269
Ninilchik 270
Nome 465–472
North, Arctic (see "Arctic
    Alaska")
North Pole 433
Northeastern Kenai Peninsula
    249–251
northern lights 426–427

O

outdoor activities 52–60

P

Palmer 330
paragliding 221
Pasagshak Road 300
Paxson 396
Pelican 128
permafrost 459
Permanent Fund Dividend 183
Petersburg 105
Petroglyph Beach 100
Pilgrim Hot Springs 473
Port Alsworth 302
Portage Glacier 223
Pribilof Islands 320–321
Prince of Wales Island
    89–96
Prince William Sound
    224–248
Prudhoe Bay 459

R

rafting 142, 245, 302, 374,
    387, 461, 479
Resurrection Bay 259
Resurrection Bay Historical
    Society Museum 256
Richardson Highway 240–241,
    376
roadhouses 44
Russian Bishop's House 119
Russian Orthodox Cathedral of
    the Holy Ascension 317

S

Sadie Cove 283
salmon 503

salmon fishing 266
Sand Point 311
Sandy Beach 107
Savonoski Loop 307
Saxman 80
sea kayaking 58, 124, 245, 260,
    479
Seldovia 284–288
Serum Run 468
Service, Robert 177
Seward 251–262
Seward Highway 219–220
Seward's Folly 491
Sheldon Jackson Museum 119
Shugyak Island 301
Sitka 113–126
Sitka National Historic Park 122
Six-Mile Creek 249
Skagway 162–179
Smith, Jefferson "Soapy" 165,
    168
Soldotna 266–267
SOUTHCENTRAL ALASKA
    216–288
SOUTHEAST ALASKA
    67–180
SOUTHWEST ALASKA
    289–322
Stikine River 104
Sutton 373–374

T

Talkeetna 341–347
Talkeetna Historical Society
    Museum 344
Talkeetna Junction 341
Taylor Highway 402
telephones 25
Teller 474
Tenakee Springs 127
Tetlin National Wildlife Refuge
    401
Thorne Bay 95
Tlikakila River
Tok 398
Top of the World Highway 404
Totem Heritage Center 78–79
totem poles 67, 76–77
Tracy Arm Fjord 145–147
trains 36–38
Trans-Alaska oil pipeline 430,
    454, 495

travelers' checks 24
Turka Bay 283
Turnagain Pass 249

U
Unalaska 313
US embassies and consulates
16

V
Valdez 229–240
Valdez Arm 233

Valdez Museum 233
Valley of 10,000 Smokes 308
visas 15

W
WAMCATS 408
Wasilla 333–338
Web sites 29–30
Western Kenai Peninsula 262
whale watching 112, 128, 268
White Pass and Yukon Railroad
170–172

Whittier 225–229
wilderness lodges 48
wildlife 53, 500
Willow 340
working in Alaska 17–19
Wrangell 96–102
**Wrangell–St Elias National
Park** 376–387

Y
Yukon–Charley Rivers National
Preserve 406–407

Stay in touch with us!

ROUGHNEWS is Rough Guides' free newsletter. In three issues a year we give you news, travel issues, music reviews, readers' letters and the latest dispatches from authors on the road.

ROUGH GUIDES: Travel

Alaska
Amsterdam
Andalucia
Argentina
Australia
Austria

Bali & Lombok
Barcelona
Belgium &
   Luxembourg
Belize
Berlin
Brazil
Britain
Brittany &
   Normandy
Bulgaria
California
Canada
Central America
Chile
China
Corsica
Costa Rica
Crete
Croatia
Cuba
Cyprus
Czech & Slovak
   Republics

Dodecanese &
   the East Aegean
Devon &
   Cornwall
Dominican
   Republic
Dordogne & the
   Lot
Ecuador
Egypt
England
Europe
Florida
France
French Hotels &
   Restaurants
   1999
Germany
Goa
Greece
Greek Islands
Guatemala
Hawaii
Holland
Hong Kong &
   Macau
Hungary

Iceland
India
Indonesia
Ionian Islands
Ireland

Israel & the
   Palestinian
   Territories
Italy
Jamaica
Japan
Jordan
Kenya
Lake District
Languedoc &
   Roussillon
Laos
London
Los Angeles
Malaysia,
   Singapore &
   Brunei
Mallorca &
   Menorca
Maya World
Mexico
Morocco
Moscow
Nepal
New England
New York
New Zealand
Norway
Pacific
   Northwest
Paris
Peru
Poland
Portugal
Prague
Provence & the
   Côte d'Azur
The Pyrenees
Romania
St Petersburg
San Francisco

Sardinia
Scandinavia
Scotland
Scottish
   highlands and
   Islands
Sicily
Singapore
South Africa
South India
Southeast Asia
Southwest USA
Spain
Sweden
Switzerland
Syria

Thailand
Trinidad &
   Tobago
Tunisia
Turkey
Tuscany &
   Umbria
USA
Venice
Vienna
Vietnam
Wales
Washington DC
West Africa
Zimbabwe &
   Botswana

AVAILABLE AT ALL GOOD BOOKSHOPS

ROUGH GUIDES: Mini Guides, Travel Specials and Phrasebooks

MINI GUIDES

Antigua
Bangkok
Barbados
Beijing
Big Island of Hawaii
Boston
Brussels
Budapest
Cape Town
Copenhagen
Dublin
Edinburgh

Florence
Honolulu
Ibiza & Formentera
Jerusalem
Las Vegas
Lisbon
London Restaurants
Madeira
Madrid
Malta & Gozo
Maui
Melbourne
Menorca

Montreal
New Orleans

Paris
Rome
Seattle
St Lucia
Sydney
Tenerife
Tokyo
Toronto
Vancouver

TRAVEL SPECIALS

First-Time Asia
First-Time Europe
Women Travel

PHRASEBOOKS

Czech
Dutch
Egyptian Arabic
European
French
German
Greek

Hindi & Urdu
Hungarian
Indonesian
Italian
Japanese
Mandarin
  Chinese
Mexican
  Spanish
Polish
Portuguese
Russian
Spanish
Swahili
Thai
Turkish
Vietnamese

AVAILABLE AT ALL GOOD BOOKSHOPS

ROUGH GUIDES:
Reference and Music CDs

REFERENCE

Blues:
  100 Essential CDs
Classical Music
Classical:
  100 Essential CDs
Country Music
Country:
  100 Essential CDs
Drum'n'bass
House Music
Hip Hop
Irish Music
Jazz

Music USA
Opera
Opera:
  100 Essential CDs
Reggae
Reggae:
  100 Essential CDs
Rock
Rock:
  100 Essential CDs

Soul:
  100 Essential CDs
Techno
World Music

World Music:
  100 Essential CDs
English Football
European Football
Internet
Money Online
Shopping Online
Travel Health

ROUGH GUIDE MUSIC CDs

Music of the Andes
Australian Aboriginal
Bluegrass
Brazilian Music
Cajun & Zydeco
Music of Cape Verde
Classic Jazz
Music of
  Colombia
Cuban Music
Eastern Europe

Music of Egypt
English Roots Music
Flamenco
Music of Greece
Hip Hop
India & Pakistan
Irish Music
Music of Jamaica
Music of Japan
Kenya & Tanzania
Marrabenta
  Mozambique
Native American
North African
Music of Portugal
Reggae
Salsa
Samba
Scottish Music
South African Music
Music of Spain
Sufi Music
Tango

Tex-Mex
West African Music
World Music
World Music Vol 2
Music of Zimbabwe

Will you have enough stories to tell your grandchildren?

©2000 Yahoo! Inc.

Yahoo! Travel

Do You YAHOO!?